Java™ RMI

Related titles from O'Reilly

Java™ RMI

William Grosso

O'REILLY®

Beijing · Cambridge · Farnham · Köln · Paris · Sebastopol · Taipei · Tokyo

Java™ RMI
by William Grosso

Copyright © 2002 O'Reilly & Associates, Inc. All rights reserved.
Printed in the United States of America.

Published by O'Reilly & Associates, Inc., 1005 Gravenstein Highway North,
Sebastopol, CA 95472.

O'Reilly & Associates books may be purchased for educational, business, or sales promotional
use. Online editions are also available for most titles (*safari.oreilly.com*). For more information
contact our corporate/institutional sales department: (800) 998-9938 or *corporate@oreilly.com*.

Editors:	Robert Eckstein and Mike Loukides
Production Editor:	Matt Hutchinson
Cover Designer:	Emma Colby
Interior Designer:	Melanie Wang

Printing History:

January 2002:	First Edition.

ISBN: 1-56592-452-5
[M]

[10/02]

This book is dedicated to John Stallings, who taught me how to think.

Table of Contents

Preface

This book is intended for Java developers who want to build distributed applications. By a distributed application, I mean a set of programs running in different processes (and quite possibly on different machines) which form, from the point of view of the end user, a single application.* The latest version of the Java platform, Java 2 (and the associated standard extension libraries), includes extensive support for building distributed applications.

In this book, I will focus on Java's Remote Method Invocation (RMI) framework. RMI is a robust and effective way to build distributed applications in which all the participating programs are written in Java. Because the designers of RMI assumed that all the participating programs would be written in Java, RMI is a surprisingly simple and easy framework to use. Not only is RMI useful for building distributed applications, it is an ideal environment for Java programmers learning how to build a distributed application.

I don't assume you know anything about distributed programs or computer networking. We'll start from the ground up and cover all the concepts, classes, and ideas underlying RMI. I will also cover some of the more advanced aspects of Java programming; it would be irresponsible to write a book on RMI without devoting some space to topics such as sockets and threading.

In order to get the most out of this book, you will need a certain amount of experience with the Java programming language. You should be comfortable programming in Java; you should have a system with which you can experiment with the code examples (like many things, distributed programming is best learned by doing); you should be fairly comfortable with the basics of the JDK 1.1 event model (in particular, many of the code examples are action listeners that have been added to a button); and you should be willing to make mistakes along the way.

---

* In this book, *program* will always refer to Java code executing inside a single Java virtual machine (JVM). *Application*, on the other hand, refers to one or more programs executing inside one or more JVMs that, to the end user, appear to be a single program.

About This Book

This book covers an enormous amount of ground, starting with streams and sockets and working its way through the basics of building scalable client-server architectures using RMI.

While the order of chapters is a reasonable one, and one that has served me well in introducing RMI to my students at U.C. Berkeley Extension, it is nonetheless the case that skipping around can sometimes be beneficial. For example, Chapter 10, which discusses object serialization, really relies only on streams (from Chapter 1) and can profitably be read immediately after Chapter 4 (where the first RMI application is introduced).

The book is divided into three sections. Part I, *Designing and Building: The Basics of RMI Applications*, starts with an introduction to some of the essential background material for RMI. After presenting the basics of Java's stream and socket libraries, we build a simple socket-based distributed application and then rebuild this application using RMI. At this point, we've actually covered most of the basics of building a simple RMI application.

The rest of Part I (Chapters 5 through 9) presents a fairly detailed analysis of how introducing a network changes the various aspects of application design. These chapters culminate in a set of principles for partitioning an application into clients and servers and for designing client-server interaction. Additionally, they introduce an example from banking which is referred to repeatedly in the remainder of the book. After finishing the first section, you will be able to design and build simple RMI applications that, while not particularly scalable or robust, can be used in a variety of situations.

Part II, *Drilling Down: Scalability*, builds on the first by drilling down on the underlying technologies and discussing the implementation decisions that must be made in order to build scalable and secure distributed applications. That is, the first section focuses on the design issues associated with the client-server boundary, and the second section discusses how to make the server scale. As such, this section is less about RMI, or the network interface, and more about how to use the underlying Java technologies (e.g., how to use threads). These chapters can be tough sledding—this is the technical heart of the book.

Part III, *Advanced Topics*, consists of a set of independent chapters discussing various advanced features of RMI. The distinction between the second and third sections is that everything covered in the second section is essential material for building a sophisticated RMI application (and hence should be at least partially understood by any programmer involved in the design or implementation of an RMI application). The topics covered in Part III are useful and important for many applications but are not essential knowledge.

What follows is a more detailed description of each chapter in this book.

Part I, Designing and Building: The Basics of RMI Applications

Chapter 1, *Streams*

Streams are a fairly simple data structure; they are best thought of as linear sequences of bytes. They are commonly used to send information to devices (such as a hard drive) or over a network. This chapter is a background chapter that covers Java's support for streams. It is not RMI-specific at all.

Chapter 2, *Sockets*

Sockets are a fairly common abstraction for establishing and maintaining a network connection between two programs. Socket libraries exist in most programming languages and across most operating systems. This chapter is a background chapter which covers Java's socket classes. It is not RMI-specific at all.

Chapter 3, *A Socket-Based Printer Server*

This chapter is an exercise in applying the contents of the first two chapters. It uses sockets (and streams) to build a distributed application. Consequently, many of the fundamental concepts and problems of distributed programming are introduced. Because this chapter relies only on the contents of the first two chapters, these concepts and problems are stated with minimal terminology.

Chapter 4, *The Same Server, Written Using RMI*

This chapter contains a translation of the socket-based printer server into an RMI application. Consequently, it introduces the basic features of RMI and discusses the necessary steps when building a simple RMI application. This is the first chapter in the book that actually uses RMI.

Chapter 5, *Introducing the Bank Example*

The bank example is one of the oldest and hoariest examples in client-server computing. Along with the printer example, it serves as a running example throughout the book.

Chapter 6, *Deciding on the Remote Server*

The first step in designing and building a typical distributed application is figuring out what the servers are. That is, finding which functionality is in the servers, and deciding how to partition this functionality across servers. This chapter contains a series of guidelines and questions that will help you make these decisions.

Chapter 7, *Designing the Remote Interface*

Once you've partitioned an application, by placing some functionality in various servers and some functionality in a client, you then need to specify how these components will talk to each other. In other words, you need to design a set of interfaces. This chapter contains a series of guidelines and questions that will help you design and evaluate the interfaces on your servers.

Chapter 8, *Implementing the Bank Server*

After the heady abstractions and difficult concepts of the previous two chapters, this chapter is a welcome dive into concrete programming tasks. In it, we give the first (of many!) implementations of the bank example, reinforcing the lessons of Chapter 4 and discussing some of the basic implementation decisions that need to be made on the server side.

Chapter 9, *The Rest of the Application*

The final chapter in the first section rounds out the implementation of the bank example. In it, we build a simple client application and the launch code (the code that starts the servers running and makes sure the clients can connect to the servers).

Part II, Drilling Down: Scalability

Chapter 10, *Serialization*

Serialization is the algorithm that RMI uses to encode information sent over the wire. It's easy to use serialization, but using it efficiently and effectively takes a little more work. This chapter explains the serialization mechanism in gory detail.

Chapter 11, *Threads*

This is the first of two chapters about threading. It covers the basics of threading: what threads are and how to perform basic thread operations in Java. As such, it is not RMI-specific at all.

Chapter 12, *Implementing Threading*

In this chapter, we take the terminology and operations from Chapter 11 and apply them to the banking example. We do this by discussing a set of guidelines for making applications multithreaded and then apply each guideline to the banking example. After this, we'll discuss pools, which are a common idiom for reusing scarce resources.

Chapter 13, *Testing a Distributed Application*

This chapter covers the tenets of testing a distributed application. While these tenets are applied to the example applications from this book, they are not inherently RMI-specific. This chapter is simply about ensuring a reasonable level of performance in a distributed application.

Chapter 14, *The RMI Registry*

The RMI registry is a simple naming service that ships with the JDK. This chapter explores the RMI registry in detail and uses the discussion as a springboard to a more general discussion of how to use a naming service.

Chapter 15, *Naming Services*

This chapter builds on the previous chapter and offers a general discussion of naming services. At the heart of the chapter is an implementation of a much more scalable, flexible, and federated naming service. The implementation of this new naming service is combined with discussions of general naming-service principles and also serves as another example of how to write code with multiple threads in mind. This chapter is by far the most difficult in the book and can safely be skipped on a first reading.

Chapter 16, *The RMI Runtime*

There's an awful lot of code that handles the interactions between the client and the server. There doesn't seem to be a generally approved name for this code, but I call it the "RMI Runtime." The RMI Runtime handles the details of maintaining connections and implements distributed garbage collection. In this chapter, we'll discuss the RMI Runtime and conclude with an examination of many of the basic system parameters that can be used to configure the RMI Runtime.

Chapter 17, *Factories and the Activation Framework*

The final chapter in Part II deals with a common design pattern called "The Factory Pattern" (or, more typically, "Factories"). After discussing this pattern, we'll dive into the Activation Framework. The Activation Framework greatly simplifies the implementation of The Factory Pattern in RMI.

Part III, Advanced Topics

Chapter 18, *Using Custom Sockets*

RMI is a framework for distributing the objects in an application. It relies, quite heavily, on the socket classes discussed in Chapter 2. However, precisely which type of socket used by an RMI application is configurable. This chapter covers how to switch socket types in an RMI application.

Chapter 19, *Dynamic Classloading*

Dynamic class loading allows you to automatically update an application by downloading .*class* files as they are needed. It's one of the most innovative features in RMI and a frequent source of confusion.

Chapter 20, *Security Policies*

One of the biggest changes in Java 2 was the addition of a full-fledged (and rather baroque) set of security classes and APIs. Security policies are a generalization of the applet "sandbox" and provide a way to grant pieces of code permission to perform certain operations (such as writing to a file).

Chapter 21, *Multithreaded Clients*

Up until this chapter, all the complexity has been on the server side of the application. There's a good reason for this—the complexity on the client side often involves the details of Swing programming and not RMI. But sometimes, you need to build a more sophisticated client. This chapter discusses when it is appropriate to do so, and covers the basic implementation strategies.

Chapter 22, *HTTP Tunneling*

Firewalls are a reality in today's corporate environment. And sometimes, you have to tunnel through them. This chapter, which is the most "cookbooky" chapter in the book, tells you how to do so.

Chapter 23, *RMI, CORBA, and RMI/IIOP*

This chapter concerns interoperability with CORBA. CORBA is another framework for building distributed applications; it is very similar to RMI but has two major differences: it is not Java-specific, and the CORBA specification is controlled by an independent standards group (not by Sun Microsystems, Inc.). These two facts make CORBA very popular. After briefly discussing CORBA, this chapter covers RMI/IIOP, which is a way to build RMI applications that "speak CORBA."

About the Example Code

This book comes with a lot of example code. The examples were written in Java 2, using JDK1.3. While the fundamentals of RMI have not changed drastically from earlier versions of Java, there have been some changes. As a result, you will probably experience some problems if you try and use the example code with earlier versions of Java (e.g., JDK1.1.*).

In addition, you should be aware that the name RMI is often used to refer to two different things. It refers to a set of interfaces and APIs that define a framework for distributed programming. But it also refers to the implementation of those interfaces and APIs written by Javasoft and bundled as part of the JDK. The intended meaning is usually clear from the context. But you should be aware that there are other implementations of the RMI interfaces (most notably from BEA/Weblogic), and that some of the more advanced examples in this book may not work with implementations other than Javasoft's.

Please don't use the code examples in this book in production applications. The code provided is example code; it is intended to communicate concepts and explain ideas. In particular, the example code is not particularly robust code. Exceptions are often caught silently and `finally` clauses are rare. Including industrial strength example code would have made the book much longer and the examples more difficult to understand.

Conventions Used in This Book

Italic is used for:

- Pathnames, filenames, directories, and program names
- New terms where they are defined
- Internet addresses, such as domain names and URLs

`Constant Width` is used for:

- Anything that appears literally in a Java program, including keywords, datatypes, constants, method names, variables, classnames, and interface names
- Command lines and options that should be typed verbatim on the screen
- All JSP and Java code listings
- HTML documents, tags, and attributes

Constant Width Italic is used for:

- General placeholders that indicate that an item should be replaced by some actual value in your own program

Constant width bold is used for:

- Text that is typed in code examples by the user

 This icon designates a note, which is an important aside to the nearby text.

 This icon designates a warning relating to the nearby text.

Coding Conventions

For the most part, the examples are written in a fairly generic coding style. I follow standard Java conventions with respect to capitalization. Instance variables are preceded by an underscore (_), while locally scoped variables simply begin with a lowercase letter.

Variable and method names are longer, and more descriptive, than is customary.* References to methods within the body of a paragraph almost always omit arguments—instead of `readFromStream(InputStream inputStream)`, we usually write `readFromStream( )`.

Occasionally, an ellipsis will show up in the source code listings. Lines such as:

```
catch (PrinterException printerException){
    ....
}
```

simply indicate that some uninteresting or irrelevant code has been omitted from the listings in the book.

The class definitions all belong to subpackages of `com.ora.rmibook`. Each chapter of this book has its own package—the examples for Chapter 1 are contained in subpackages of `com.ora.rmibook.chapter1`; the examples for Chapter 2 are contained in subpackages of `com.ora.rmibook.chapter2`, and so on. I have tried to make the code for each chapter complete in and of itself. That is, the code for Chapter 4 does not reference the code for Chapter 3. This makes it a little easier to browse the source

---

* We will occasionally discuss automatically generated code such as that produced by the RMI compiler. This code is harder to read and often contains variables with names like `$param_DocumentDescription_1`.

code and to try out the individual projects. But, as a result of this, there is a large amount of duplication in the example code (many of the classes appear in more than one chapter).

I have also avoided the use of anonymous or local inner classes (while useful, they tend to make code more difficult to read). In short, if you can easily read, and understand, the following snippet:

```
private void buildGUI( ) {
    JPanel mainPanel = new JPanel(new BorderLayout( ));
    _messageBox = new JTextArea( );
    mainPanel.add(new JScrollPane(_messageBox), BorderLayout.CENTER);
    createButtons( );
}
```

you should have no problem following along with the example code for this book.

Applications

The source code for this book is organized as a set of example applications. In order to make it easier to browse the code base, I've tried to follow a consistent naming convention for classes that contain a main( ) method. If a class Foo contains a main( ) method, then there will be a companion class FooFrame in the same package as Foo. Thus, for example, the ViewFile application from Chapter 1 has a companion class ViewFileFrame. In fact, ViewFile consists entirely of the following code:

```
package com.ora.rmibook.section1.chapter1;

public class ViewFile {
    public static void main(String[] arguments) {
        (new ViewFileFrame()).show( );
    }
}
```

Having top-level GUI classes end in Frame makes it a little easier to browse the code in an IDE. For example, Figure P-1 shows a screenshot of JBuilder 3.0, displaying the source files related to Chapter 2.

Compiling and Building

The example code in the book compiles and runs on a wide variety of systems. However, while the code is generic, the batch files for the example applications are not. Instead of attempting to create generic scripts, I opted for very simple and easily edited batch files located in chapter-specific directories. Here, for example, is the *NamingService.bat* batch file from Chapter 15:

```
start java -cp d:\classes -Djava.security.policy=c:\java.policy com.ora.rmibook.
chapter15.basicapps.NamingService.
```

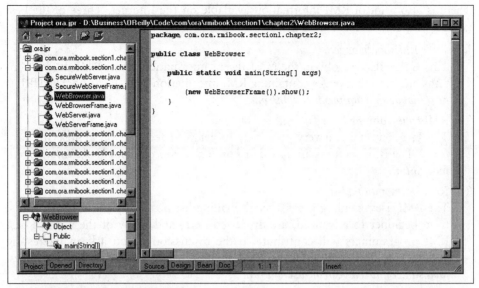

Figure P-1. Screenshot of JBuilder 3.0

This makes a number of assumptions, all of which are typical to the batch files included with the example code (and all of which may change depending on how your system is configured):

- *start* is used as a system command to launch a background process. This works on Windows NT and Windows 2000. Other operating systems launch background processes in different ways.
- The *d:\classes* directory exists and contains the *.class* files.
- There is a valid security policy named javapolicy located in the *c:* directory.

In addition, the source code often assumes the *c:\temp* directory exists when writing temporary files.

Downloading the Source Examples

The source files for the examples in this book can be downloaded from the O'Reilly web site at:

> *http://www.oreilly.com/catalog/javarmi*

For Further Information

Where appropriate, I've included references to other books. For the most part, these references are to advanced books that cover a specific area in much greater detail than is appropriate for this book. For example, in Chapter 12 I've listed a few of my favorite references on concurrent programming.

There is also a lot of RMI information available on the Internet. Three of the best general-purpose RMI resources are:

Javasoft's RMI home page
This is the place to obtain the most recent information about RMI. It also contains links to other pages containing RMI information from Javasoft. The URL is *http://java.sun.com/products/jdk/rmi/.*

The RMI trail from the Java Tutorial
The Java Tutorial is a very good way to get your feet wet on almost any Java topic. The RMI sections are based at *http://java.sun.com/docs/books/tutorial/rmi/index.html.*

The RMI Users mailing list
The RMI users mailing list is a small mailing list hosted by Javasoft. All levels, from beginner to advanced, are discussed here, and many of the world's best RMI programmers will contribute to the discussion if you ask an interesting enough question. The archives of the mailing list are stored at *http://archives.java.sun.com/archives/rmi-users.html.*

How to Contact Us

We have tested and verified the information in this book to the best of our ability, but you may find that features have changed (or even that we have made mistakes!). Please let us know about any errors you find, as well as your suggestions for future editions, by writing to:

O'Reilly and Associates, Inc.
1005 Gravenstein Highway North
Sebastopol, CA 95472
(800) 998-9938 (in the U.S. or Canada)
(707) 829-0515 (international or local)
(707) 829-1014 (fax)

We have a web page for this book, where we list errata, examples, and any additional information. You can access this page at:

http://www.oreilly.com/catalog/javarmi

To ask technical questions or comment on the book, send email to:

bookquestions@oreilly.com

For more information about our books, conferences, software, Resource Centers, and the O'Reilly Network,, see our web site at:

http://www.oreilly.com/

Acknowledgments

This book has been a long time coming. In the original contract, my first editor and I estimated that it would take nine months. As I write these words, we're closing in on two years. My editors at O'Reilly (Jonathan Knudsen, Mike Loukides, and Robert Eckstein) have been patient and understanding people. They deserve a long and sustained round of applause.

Other debts are owed to the people at the Software Development Forum's Java SIG, who listened patiently whenever I felt like explaining something. And to U.C. Berkeley Extension, for giving me a class to teach and thereby forcing me to think through all of this in a coherent way—if I hadn't taught there, I wouldn't have known that this book needed to be written (or what to write). And, most of all, to my friends who patiently read the draft manuscript and caught most of the embarrassing errors. (Rich Liebling and Tom Hill stand out from the crowd here. All I can say is, if you're planning on writing a book, you should make friends with them first.)

I'd also like to thank my employer, Hipbone, Inc. Without the support and understanding of everyone I work with, this book would never have been completed.

PART I

Designing and Building: The Basics of RMI Applications

CHAPTER 1

Streams

This chapter discusses Java's stream classes, which are defined in the `java.io.*` package. While streams are not really part of RMI, a working knowledge of the stream classes is an important part of an RMI programmer's skillset. In particular, this chapter provides essential background information for understanding two related areas: sockets and object serialization.

The Core Classes

A *stream* is an ordered sequence of bytes. However, it's helpful to also think of a stream as a data structure that allows client code to either store or retrieve information. Storage and retrieval are done sequentially—typically, you write data to a stream one byte at a time or read information from the stream one byte at a time. However, in most stream classes, you cannot "go back"—once you've read a piece of data, you must move on. Likewise, once you've written a piece of data, it's written.

You may think that a stream sounds like an impoverished data structure. Certainly, for most programming tasks, a `HashMap` or an `ArrayList` storing objects is preferable to a read-once sequence of bytes. However, streams have one nice feature: they are a simple and correct model for almost any external device connected to a computer. Why *correct*? Well, when you think about it, the code-level mechanics of writing data to a printer are not all that different from sending data over a modem; the information is sent sequentially, and, once it's sent, it can not be retrieved or "un-sent."* Hence, streams are an abstraction that allow client code to access an external resource without worrying too much about the specific resource.

Using the streams library is a two-step process. First, device-specific code that creates the stream objects is executed; this is often called "opening" the stream. Then, information is either read from or written to the stream. This second step is

---

* Print orders can be cancelled by sending another message: a cancellation message. But the original message was still sent.

device-independent; it relies only on the stream interfaces. Let's start by looking at the stream classes offered with Java: InputStream and OutputStream.

InputStream

InputStream is an abstract class that represents a data source. Once opened, it provides information to the client that created it. The InputStream class consists of the following methods:

```
public int available( ) throws IOException
public void close( ) throws IOException
public void mark(int numberOfBytes) throws IOException
public  boolean markSupported( ) throws IOException
public abstract int read( ) throws IOException
public int read(byte[] buffer) throws IOException
public int read(byte[] buffer, int startingOffset, int numberOfBytes) throws
    IOException
public void reset( ) throws IOException
public long skip(long numberOfBytes) throws IOException
```

These methods serve three different roles: *reading data, stream navigation,* and *resource management.*

Reading data

The most important methods are those that actually retrieve data from the stream. InputStream defines three basic methods for reading data:

```
public int read( ) throws IOException
public int read(byte[] buffer) throws IOException
public int read(byte[] buffer, int startingOffset, int numberOfBytes) throws
    IOException
```

The first of these methods, read( ), simply returns the next available byte in the stream. This byte is returned as an integer in order to allow the InputStream to return nondata values. For example, read( ) returns −1 if there is no data available, and no more data will be available to this stream. This can happen, for example, if you reach the end of a file. On the other hand, if there is currently no data, but some may become available in the future, the read( ) method blocks. Your code then waits until a byte becomes available before continuing.

 A piece of code is said to *block* if it must wait for a resource to finish its job. For example, using the read( ) method to retrieve data from a file can force the method to halt execution until the target hard drive becomes available. Blocking can sometimes lead to undesirable results. If your code is waiting for a byte that will never come, the program has effectively crashed.

The other two methods for retrieving data are more advanced versions of read( ), added to the InputStream class for efficiency. For example, consider what would happen if you

---

created a tight loop to fetch 65,000 bytes one at a time from an external device. This would be extraordinarily inefficient. If you know you'll be fetching large amounts of data, it's better to make a single request:

```
byte buffer = new byte[1000];
read(buffer);
```

The read(byte[] buffer) method is a request to read enough bytes to fill the buffer (in this case, buffer.length number of bytes). The integer return value is the number of bytes that were actually read, or −1 if no bytes were read.

Finally, read(byte[] buffer, int startingOffset, int numberOfBytes) is a request to read the exact numberOfBytes from the stream and place them in the buffer starting at position startingOffset. For example:

```
read(buffer, 2, 7);
```

This is a request to read 7 bytes and place them in the locations buffer[2], buffer[3], and so on up to buffer[8]. Like the previous read( ), this method returns an integer indicating the amount of bytes that it was able to read, or −1 if no bytes were read at all.

Stream navigation

Stream navigation methods are methods that enable you to move around in the stream without necessarily reading in data. There are five stream navigation methods:

```
public int available( ) throws IOException
public long skip(long numberOfBytes) throws IOException
public void mark(int numberOfBytes) throws IOException
public  boolean markSupported( ) throws IOException
public void reset( ) throws IOException
```

available( ) is used to discover how many bytes are guaranteed to be immediately available. To avoid blocking, you can call available( ) before each read( ), as in the following code fragment:

```
while (stream.available( ) >0 )) {
    processNextByte(stream.read( ));
}
```

There are two caveats when using available( ) in this way. First, you should make sure that the stream from which you are reading actually implements available( ) in a meaningful way. For example, the default implementation, defined in InputStream, simply returns 0. This behavior, while technically correct, is really misleading. (The preceding code fragment will not work if the stream always returns 0.) The second caveat is that you should make sure to use buffering. See "Layering Streams" later in this chapter for more details on how to buffer streams.

The skip( ) method simply moves you forward numberOfBytes in the stream. For many streams, skipping is equivalent to reading in the data and then discarding it.

 In fact, most implementations of skip( ) do exactly that: repeatedly read and discard the data. Hence, if numberOfBytes worth of data aren't available yet, these implementations of skip( ) will block.

Many input streams are unidirectional: they only allow you to move forward. Input streams that support repeated access to their data do so by implementing *marking*. The intuition behind marking is that code that reads data from the stream can mark a point to which it might want to return later. Input streams that support marking return true when markSupported( ) is called. You can use the mark( ) method to mark the current location in the stream. The method's sole parameter, numberOfBytes, is used for expiration—the stream will retire the mark if the reader reads more than numberOfBytes past it. Calling reset( ) returns the stream to the point where the mark was made.

 InputStream methods support only a single mark. Consequently, only one point in an InputStream can be marked at any given time.

Resource management

Because streams are often associated with external devices such as files or network connections, using a stream often requires the operating system to allocate resources beyond memory. For example, most operating systems limit the number of files or network connections that a program can have open at the same time. The resource management methods of the InputStream class involve communication with native code to manage operating system-level resources.

The only resource management method defined for InputStream is close( ). When you're done with a stream, you should always explicitly call close( ). This will free the associated system resources (e.g., the associated file descriptor for files).

At first glance, this seems a little strange. After all, one of the big advantages of Java is that it has garbage collection built into the language specification. Why not just have the object free the operating-system resources when the object is garbage collected?

The reason is that garbage collection is unreliable. The Java language specification does not explicitly guarantee that an object that is no longer referenced will be garbage collected (or even that the garbage collector will ever run). In practice, you can safely assume that, if your program runs short on memory, some objects will be garbage collected, and some memory will be reclaimed. But this assumption isn't enough for effective management of scarce operating-system resources such as file descriptors. In particular, there are three main problems:

- You have no control over how much time will elapse between when an object is eligible to be garbage collected and when it is actually garbage collected.
- You have very little control over which objects get garbage collected.[*]
- There isn't necessarily a relationship between the number of file handles still available and the amount of memory available. You may run out of file handles long before you run out of memory. In which case, the garbage collector may never become active.

Put succinctly, the garbage collector is an unreliable way to manage anything other than memory allocation. Whenever your program is using scarce operating-system resources, you should explicitly release them. This is especially true for streams; a program should always close streams when it's finished using them.

IOException

All of the methods defined for InputStream can throw an IOException. IOException is a checked exception. This means that stream manipulation code always occurs inside a try/catch block, as in the following code fragment:

```
try{
    while( -1 != (nextByte = bufferedStream.read( ))) {
        char nextChar = (char) nextByte;
        ...
    }
}
catch (IOException e) {
    ...
}
```

The idea behind IOException is this: streams are mostly used to exchanging data with devices that are outside the JVM. If something goes wrong with the device, the device needs a universal way to indicate an error to the client code.

Consider, for example, a printer that refuses to print a document because it is out of paper. The printer needs to signal an exception, and the exception should be relayed to the user; the program making the print request has no way of refilling the paper tray without human intervention. Moreover, this exception should be relayed to the user immediately.

Most stream exceptions are similar to this example. That is, they often require some sort of user action (or at least user notification), and are often best handled immediately.

---

[*] You can use SoftReference (defined in java.lang.ref) to get a minimal level of control over the order in which objects are garbage collected.

Therefore, the designers of the streams library decided to make IOException a checked exception, thereby forcing programs to explicitly handle the possibility of failure.

 Some foreshadowing: RMI follows a similar design philosophy. Remote methods must be declared to throw RemoteException (and client code must catch RemoteException). RemoteException means "something has gone wrong, somewhere outside the JVM."

OutputStream

OutputStream is an abstract class that represents a data sink. Once it is created, client code can write information to it. OutputStream consists of the following methods:

```
public void close( ) throws IOException
public void flush( ) throws IOException
public void write(byte[] buffer) throws IOException
public void write(byte[] buffer, int startingOffset, int numberOfBytes) throws
    IOException
public void write(int value) throws IOException
```

The OutputStream class is a little simpler than InputStream; it doesn't support navigation. After all, you probably don't want to go back and write information a second time. OutputStream methods serve two purposes: *writing data* and *resource management*.

Writing data

OutputStream defines three basic methods for writing data:

```
public void write(byte[] buffer) throws IOException
public void write(byte[] buffer, int startingOffset, int numberOfBytes) throws
    IOException
public void write(int value) throws IOException
```

These methods are analogous to the read( ) methods defined for InputStream. Just as there was one basic method for reading a single byte of data, there is one basic method, write(int value), for writing a single byte of data. The argument to this write( ) method should be an integer between 0 and 255. If not, it is reduced to modulo 256 before being written.

Just as there were two array-based variants of read( ), there are two methods for writing arrays of bytes. write(byte[] buffer) causes all the bytes in the array to be written out to the stream. write(byte[] buffer, int startingOffset, int numberOfBytes) causes numberOfBytes bytes to be written, starting with the value at buffer[startingOffset].

The fact that the argument to the basic write( ) method is an integer is somewhat peculiar. Recall that read( ) returned an integer, rather than a byte, in order to allow instances of InputStream to signal exceptional conditions. write( ) takes an integer, rather than a byte, so that the read and write method declarations are parallel. In other words, if you've read a value in from a stream, and it's not −1, you should be able to write it out to another stream *without* casting it.

Resource management

OutputStream defines two resource management methods:

```
public void close( )
public void flush( )
```

close( ) serves exactly the same role for OutputStream as it did for InputStream—it should be called when the client code is done using the stream and wishes to free up all the associated operating-system resources.

The flush( ) method is necessary because output streams frequently use a buffer to store data that is being written. This is especially true when data is being written to either a file or a socket. Passing data to the operating system a single byte at a time can be expensive. A much more practical strategy is to buffer the data at the JVM level and occasionally call flush( ) to send the data en masse.

Viewing a File

To make this discussion more concrete, we will now discuss a simple application that allows the user to display the contents of a file in a JTextArea. The application is called ViewFile and is shown in Example 1-1. Note that the application's main( ) method is defined in the com.ora.rmibook.chapter1.ViewFile class.* The resulting screenshot is shown in Figure 1-1.

---

* This example uses classes from the Java Swing libraries. If you would like more information on Swing, see *Java Swing* (O'Reilly) or *Java Foundation Classes in a Nutshell* (O'Reilly).

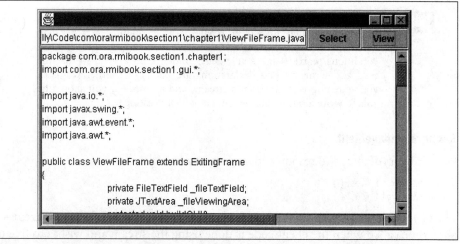

Figure 1-1. The ViewFile application

Example 1-1. ViewFile.java

```java
public class ViewfileFrame extends ExitingFrame{
// lots of code to set up the user interface.
// The View button's action listener is an inner class

    private void copyStreamToViewingArea(InputStream fileInputStream)
        throws IOException {
        BufferedInputStream bufferedStream = new BufferedInputStream(fileInputStream);
        int nextByte;
        _fileViewingArea.setText("");
        StringBuffer localBuffer = new StringBuffer();
        while( -1 != (nextByte = bufferedStream.read()))   {
            char nextChar = (char) nextByte;
            localBuffer.append(nextChar);
        }
        _fileViewingArea.append(localBuffer.toString());
    }

    private class ViewFileAction extends AbstractAction {
        public ViewFileAction() {
            putValue(Action.NAME, "View");
            putValue(Action.SHORT_DESCRIPTION, "View file contents in main text area.");
    }

        public void actionPerformed(ActionEvent event) {
            FileInputStream fileInputStream = _fileTextField.getFileInputStream();
            if (null==fileInputStream) {
                _fileViewingArea.setText("Invalid file name");
            }
            else {
                try {
                    copyStreamToViewingArea(fileInputStream);
                     fileInputStream.close();
```

Example 1-1. ViewFile.java (continued)

```
            }
            catch (java.io.IOException ioException)  {
                _fileViewingArea.setText("\n Error occured while reading file");
            }
        }
    }
```

The important part of the code is the View button's action listener and the copyStreamToViewingArea( ) method. copyStreamToViewingArea( ) takes an instance of InputStream and copies the contents of the stream to the central JTextArea. What happens when a user clicks on the View button? Assuming all goes well, and that no exceptions are thrown, the following three lines of code from the buttons's action listener are executed:

```
FileInputStream fileInputStream = _fileTextField.getFileInputStream( );
copyStreamToViewingArea(fileInputStream);
fileInputStream.close( );
```

The first line is a call to the getFileInputStream( ) method on _fileTextField. That is, the program reads the name of the file from a text field and tries to open a FileInputStream. FileInputStream is defined in the java.io* package. It is a subclass of InputStream used to read the contents of a file.

Once this stream is opened, copyStreamToViewingArea( ) is called. copyStream-ToViewingArea( ) takes the input stream, wraps it in a buffer, and then reads it one byte at a time. There are two things to note here:

- We explicitly check that nextByte is not equal to −1 (e.g., that we're not at the end of the file). If we don't do this, the loop will never terminate, and we will we will continue to append (char) -1 to the end of our text until the program crashes or throws an exception.

- We use BufferedInputStream instead of using FileInputStream directly. Internally, a BufferedInputStream maintains a buffer so it can read and store many values at one time. Maintaining this buffer allows instances of Buffered-InputStream to optimize expensive read operations. In particular, rather than reading each byte individually, bufferedStream converts individual calls to its read( ) method into a single call to FileInputStream's read(byte[] buffer) method. Note that buffering also provides another benefit. BufferedInputStream supports stream navigation through the use of marking.

 Of course, the operating system is probably already buffering file reads and writes. But, as we noted above, even the act of passing data to the operating system (which uses native methods) is expensive and ought to be buffered.

Layering Streams

The use of `BufferedInputStream` illustrates a central idea in the design of the streams library: streams can be wrapped in other streams to provide incremental functionality. That is, there are really two types of streams:

Primitive streams

> These are the streams that have native methods and talk to external devices. All they do is transmit data exactly as it is presented. `FileInputStream` and `File-OuputStream` are examples of primitive streams.

Intermediate streams

> These streams are not direct representatives of a device. Instead, they function as a wrapper around an already existing stream, which we will call the *underlying stream*. The underlying stream is usually passed as an argument to the intermediate stream's constructor. The intermediate stream has logic in its `read()` or `write()` methods that either buffers the data or transforms it before forwarding it to the underlying stream. Intermediate streams are also responsible for propagating `flush()` and `close()` calls to the underlying stream. `BufferedInputStream` and `BufferedOutputStream` are examples of intermediate streams.

> `close()` and `flush()` propagate to sockets as well. That is, if you close a stream that is associated with a socket, you will close the socket. This behavior, while logical and consistent, can come as a surprise.

Compressing a File

To further illustrate the idea of layering, I will demonstrate the use of `GZIPOutputStream`, defined in the package `java.util.zip`, with the `CompressFile` application. This application is shown in Example 1-2.

`CompressFile` is an application that lets the user choose a file and then makes a compressed copy of it. The application works by layering three output streams together. Specifically, it opens an instance of `FileOutputStream`, which it then uses as an argument to the constructor of a `BufferedOutputStream`, which in turn is used as an argument to `GZIPOutputStream`'s constructor. All data is then written using `GZIPOutputStream`. Again, the `main()` method for this application is defined in the `com.ora.rmibook.chapter1.CompressFile` class.

The important part of the source code is the `copy()` method, which copies an `InputStream` to an `OutputStream`, and `ActionListener`, which is added to the Compress button. A screenshot of the application is shown in Figure 1-2.

Streams, Reusability, and Testing

InputStream and OutputStream are abstract classes. FileInputStream and File-OutputStream are concrete subclasses. One of the issues that provokes endless discussions in software design circles centers around method signatures. For example, consider the following four method signatures:

```
parseObjectsFromFile(String filename)
parseObjectsFromFile(File file)
parseObjectsFromFile(FileInputStream fileInputStream)
parseObjectsFromStream(InputStream inputStream)
```

The first three signatures are better documentation; they tell the person reading the code that the data is coming from a file. And, because they're strongly typed, they can make more assumptions about the incoming data (for example, FileInputStream's skip() method doesn't block for extended periods of time, and is thus a fairly safe method to call).

On the other hand, many people prefer the fourth signature because it embodies fewer assumptions, and is thus easier to reuse. For example, when you discover that you need to parse a different type of stream, you don't need to touch the parsing code.

Usually, however, the discussions overlook another benefit of the fourth signature: it is much easier to test. This is because of memory-based stream classes such as: ByteArrayInputStream. You can easily write a simple test for the fourth method as follows:

```
public boolean testParsing( ) {
        String testString = "A string whose parse results are easily checked for"
            + "correctness."
        ByteArrayInputStream testStream = new ByteArrayInputStream(testString
            getBytes( ));
        parseObjectsFromStream(testStream);
        // code that checks the results of parsing
}
```

Small-scale tests, like the previous code, are often called *unit tests*. Writing unit tests and running them regularly leads to a number of benefits. Among the most important are:

- They're excellent documentation for what a method is supposed to do.
- They enable you to change the implementation of a method with confidence—if you make a mistake while doing so and change the method's functionality in an important way, the unit tests will catch it.

To learn more about unit testing and frameworks for adding unit testing to your code, see *Extreme Programming Explained: Embrace Change* by Kent Beck (Addison Wesley).

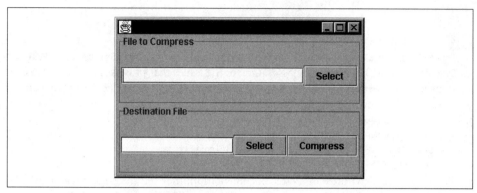

Figure 1-2. The CompressFile application

Example 1-2. CompressFile.java

```
private int copy(InputStream source, OutputStream destination) throws IOException {
        int nextByte;
        int numberOfBytesCopied = 0;
        while(-1!= (nextByte = source.read())) {
            destination.write(nextByte);
            numberOfBytesCopied++;
        }
        destination.flush( );
        return numberOfBytesCopied;
    }

private class CompressFileAction extends AbstractAction {
    //  setup code omitted

    public void actionPerformed(ActionEvent event) {
        InputStream source = _startingFileTextField.getFileInputStream( );
        OutputStream destination = _destinationFileTextField.getFileOutputStream( );
        if ((null!=source) && (null!=destination)) {
            try {
                BufferedInputStream bufferedSource = new BufferedInputStream(source);
                BufferedOutputStream bufferedDestination = new
                    BufferedOutputStream(destination);
                GZIPOutputStream zippedDestination = new
                    GZIPOutputStream(bufferedDestination);
                copy(bufferedSource, zippedDestination);
                bufferedSource.close( );
                zippedDestination.close( );
            }
            catch (IOException e){}
        }
    }
```

How this works

When the user clicks on the Compress button, two input streams and three output streams are created. The input streams are similar to those used in the ViewFile application—they allow us to use buffering as we read in the file. The output streams, however, are new. First, we create an instance of FileOutputStream. We then wrap an instance of BufferedOutputStream around the instance of FileOutputStream. And finally, we wrap GZIPOutputStream around BufferedOutputStream. To see what this accomplishes, consider what happens when we start feeding data to GZIPOutputStream (the outermost OutputStream).

1. write(nextByte) is repeatedly called on zippedDestination.

2. zippedDestination does not immediately forward the data to buffered-Destination. Instead, it compresses the data and sends the compressed version of the data to bufferedDestination using write(int value).

3. bufferedDestination does not immediately forward the data it received to destination. Instead, it puts the data in a buffer and waits until it gets a large amount of data before calling destination's write(byte[] buffer) method.

Eventually, when all the data has been read in, zippedDestination's close() method is called. This flushes bufferedDestination, which flushes destination, causing all the data to be written out to the physical file. After that, zippedDestination is closed, which causes bufferedDestination to be closed, which then causes destination to be closed, thus freeing up scarce system resources.

Some Useful Intermediate Streams

I will close our discussion of streams by briefly mentioning a few of the most useful intermediate streams in the Javasoft libraries. In addition to buffering and compressing, the two most commonly used intermediate stream types are DataInputStream/DataOutputStream and ObjectInputStream/ObjectOutputStream. We will discuss ObjectInputStream and ObjectOutputStream extensively in Chapter 10.

DataInputStream and DataOutputStream don't actually transform data that is given to them in the form of bytes. However, DataInputStream implements the DataInput interface, and DataOutputStream implements the DataOutput interface. This allows other datatypes to be read from, and written to, streams. For example, DataOutput defines the writeFloat(float value) method, which can be used to write an IEEE 754 floating-point value out to a stream. This method takes the floating point argument, converts it to a sequence of four bytes, and then writes the bytes to the underlying stream.

If DataOutputStream is used to convert data for storage into an underlying stream, the data should always be read in with a DataInputStream object. This brings up an important principle: *intermediate input and output streams which transform data must be used in pairs*. That is, if you zip, you must unzip. If you encrypt, you must decrypt. And, if you use DataOuputStream, you must use DataInputStream.

Compressing Streams

`DeflaterOutputStream` is an abstract class intended to be the superclass of all output streams that compress data. `GZIPOutputStream` is the default compression class that is supplied with the JDK. Similarly, `DeflaterInputStream` is an abstract class which is intended to be the superclass of all input streams that read in and decompress data. Again, `GZIPInputStream` is the default decompression class that is supplied with the JDK.

By and large, you can treat these streams like any other type of stream. There is one exception, however. `DeflaterOutputStream` has a nonintuitive implementation of `flush()`. In most stream classes, `flush()` takes all locally buffered data and commits it either to a device or to an underlying stream. Once `flush()` is called, you are guaranteed that all data has been processed as much as possible.

This is not the case with `DeflaterOutputStream`. `DeflaterOutputStream`'s `flush()` method simply calls flush() on the underlying stream. Here's the actual code:

```java
public void flush() throws IOException {
    out.flush();
}
```

This means that any data that is locally buffered is not flushed. Thus, for example, if the string "Roy Rogers" compresses to 51 bits of data, the most information that could have been sent to the underlying stream is 48 bits (6 bytes). Hence, calling `flush()` does not commit all the information; there are at least three uncommitted bits left after `flush()` returns.

To deal with this problem, `DeflaterOutputStream` defines a new method called `finish()`, which commits all information to the underlying stream, but also introduces a slight inefficiency into the compression process.

 We've only covered the basics of using streams. That's all we need in order to understand RMI. To find out more about streams, and how to use them, either play around with the JDK—always the recommended approach—or see *Java I/O* by Elliotte Rusty Harold (O'Reilly).

Readers and Writers

The last topics I will touch on in this chapter are the `Reader` and `Writer` abstract classes. Readers and writers are like input streams and output streams. The primary difference lies in the fundamental datatype that is read or written; streams are byte-oriented, whereas readers and writers use characters and strings.

The reason for this is internationalization. Readers and writers were designed to allow programs to use a localized character set and still have a stream-like model for communicating with external devices. As you might expect, the method definitions are quite similar to those for InputStream and OutputStream. Here are the basic methods defined in Reader:

```
public void close()
public void mark(int readAheadLimit)
public boolean markSupported()
public int read()
public int read(char[] cbuf)
public int read(char[] cbuf, int off, int len)
public boolean ready()
public void reset()
public long skip(long n)
```

These are analogous to the read() methods defined for InputStream. For example, read() still returns an integer. The difference is that, instead of data values being in the range of 0–255 (i.e., single bytes), the return value is in the range of 0–65535 (appropriate for characters, which are 2 bytes wide). However, a return value of –1 is still used to signal that there is no more data.

The only other major change is that InputStream's available() method has been replaced with a boolean method, ready(), which returns true if the next call to read() doesn't block. Calling ready() on a class that extends Reader is analogous to checking (available() > 0) on InputStream.

There aren't nearly so many subclasses of Reader or Writer as there are types of streams. Instead, readers and writers can be used as a layer on top of streams—most readers have a constructor that takes an InputStream as an argument, and most writers have a constructor that takes an OutputStream as an argument. Thus, in order to use both localization and compression when writing to a file, open the file and implement compression by layering streams, and then wrap your final stream in a writer to add localization support, as in the following snippet of code:

```
FileOutputStream destination = new FileOutputStream(fileName);
BufferedOutputStream bufferedDestination = new BufferedOutputStream(destination);
GZIPOutputStream zippedDestination = new GZIPOutputStream(bufferedDestination);
OutputStreamWriter destinationWriter = new OutputStreamWriter(zippedDestination);
```

Revisiting the ViewFile Application

There is one very common Reader/Writer pair: BufferedReader and BufferedWriter. Unlike the stream buffering classes, which don't add any new functionality, BufferedReader and BufferedWriter add additional methods for handling strings. In particular, BufferedReader adds the readLine() method (which reads a line of text), and BufferedWriter adds the newLine() method, which appends a line separator to the output.

These classes are very handy when reading or writing complex data. For example, a newline character is often a useful way to signal "end of current record." To illustrate their use, here is the action listener from ViewFileFrame, rewritten to use BufferedReader:

```
private class ViewFileAction extends AbstractAction {
public void actionPerformed(ActionEvent event) {
        FileReader fileReader = _fileTextField.getFileReader();
        if (null==fileReader) {
            _fileViewingArea.setText("Invalid file name");
        }
        else {
            try {
                copyReaderToViewingArea(fileReader);
                fileReader.close();
            }
            catch (java.io.IOException ioException) {
                _fileViewingArea.setText("\n Error occured while reading file");
            }
        }
    }

    private void copyReaderToViewingArea(Reader reader) throws IOException {
        BufferedReader bufferedReader = new BufferedReader(reader);
        String nextLine;
        _fileViewingArea.setText("");
        while( null != (nextLine = bufferedReader.readLine())) {
            _fileViewingArea.append(nextLine + "\n");
        }
    }
```

CHAPTER 2

Sockets

In this chapter, we review Java's socket classes. Sockets are an abstraction that allow two programs, usually on different machines, to communicate by sending data through streams. Strictly speaking, the socket classes (which are defined in the java.net package) are not part of RMI. However, RMI uses Java's socket classes to handle communication between distinct processes. Thus, a basic knowledge of how sockets work is fundamental to understanding RMI. This chapter's coverage, though far from complete, constitutes the core of what an RMI programmer needs to know.

Internet Definitions

The Internet is built out of computers that are connected by wires.* Each wire serves as a way to exchange information between the two computers it connects. Information is transferred in small, discrete chunks of data called *datagrams*.

Each datagram has a header and a data area. The *header* describes the datagram: where the datagram originated, what machines have handled the datagram, the type and length of the data being sent, and the intended destination of the the the datagram. The *data area* consists of the actual information that is being sent. In almost all networking protocols, the data area is of limited size. For example, the Internet Protocol (frequently referred to as IP) restricts datagrams to 64 KB.

The Internet Protocol is also an example of what is frequently called a *connectionless protocol*—each datagram is sent independently, and there is no guarantee that any of the datagrams will actually make it to their destination. In addition, the sender is not notified if a datagram does not make it to the destination. Different datagrams sent to the same destination machine may arrive out of order and may actually travel along different paths to the destination machine.

Connectionless protocols have some very nice features. Conceptually, they're a lot like the postal service. You submit an envelope into the system, couriers move it

---

* Or, in the case of wireless networks, things that behave like wires.

around, and, if all goes well, it eventually arrives at the destination. However, there are some problems. First, you have no control over which couriers handle the envelope. In addition, the arrival time of the envelope isn't particularly well-specified. This lack of control over arrival times means that connectionless protocols, though fast and very scalable, aren't particularly well suited for distributed applications.

Distributed applications often require three features that are not provided by a connectionless protocol: programs that send data require *confirmation* that information has arrived; programs that receive data require the ability to *validate* (and request retransmission) of a datagram; and finally, programs that receive data require the communication mechanism to *preserve the order* in which information is sent.

To see why, consider what happens if you were to send a document to a printer using IP. The document is probably bigger than 64 KB, so it's going to be broken down into multiple datagrams before being sent to the printer. After the printer receives the datagrams, it has to reconstruct the document. To do this, the printer has to know the order in which the datagrams were sent, that it received all the datagrams that were sent, and that line noise didn't corrupt the data along the way.

> Just because distributed applications "often require" these additional features doesn't mean that connectionless protocols aren't useful. In fact, many applications can be built using connectionless protocols. For example, a live audio feed is very different from printing in that, if the datagrams arrive jumbled, there's really no repair strategy (it's a live feed). In such cases, or in cases when information is constantly being updated anyway (for example, a stock ticker), the superior speed and scalability of a connectionless protocol is hard to beat.

To help out, we use the Transmission Control Protocol (TCP). TCP is a communications layer, defined on top of IP, which provides reliable communication. That is, TCP/IP ensures that all data that is sent also arrives, and in the correct order. In effect, it simulates a direct connection between the two machines. The underlying conceptual model is a direct conversation, rather than a courier service. When two people are engaged in a face-to-face conversation, information that is sent is received, and received in the correct sequence.

TCP works by extending IP in three ways:

- TCP adds extra header information to IP datagrams. This information allows recipients to tell the order in which datagrams were sent and do some fairly robust error-checking on the data.

- TCP extends IP by providing a way to acknowledge datagram receipt. That is, when data is received, it must be acknowledged. Otherwise, the sender must resend it. This also provides a way for recipients to tell senders that the data was received incorrectly.

- TCP defines buffering strategies. The computer receiving data over the network often has a fixed amount of space (its buffer) to hold data. If the sender sends information too quickly, the recipient may not be able to correctly handle all the information—there might not be enough room in its buffer. The solution to this problem is simple: when using TCP, the sender must wait until the recipient tells the sender how much buffer space is available. Once it does, the sender may transmit only enough information to fill the buffer. It then must wait for the recipient to indicate that more buffer room is available.

TCP/IP networking is almost always implemented as part of the operating system. Programming languages use libraries to access the operating system's TCP/IP functionality; they do not implement it themselves.

Sockets

Sockets are an abstraction for network connections that first appeared on Unix systems in the mid-1970s. In the intervening 25 years, the socket interface has become a cornerstone of distributed programming. Java supports sockets with the classes and interfaces defined in the java.net package.

Specifically, java.net contains two classes that are the core Java classes used when reliable communication between two different processes is necessary: Socket and ServerSocket. They have the following roles:

Socket
    Enables a single connection between two known, established processes. In order to exchange information, both programs must have created instances of Socket.

ServerSocket
    Manages initial connections between a client and a server. That is, when a client connects to a server using an instance of Socket, it first communicates with ServerSocket. ServerSocket immediately creates a delegate (ordinary) socket and assigns this new socket to the client. This process, by which a socket-to-socket connection is established, is often called *handshaking*.[*]

Another way to think of this: sockets are analogous to phone lines; ServerSockets are analogous to operators who manually create connections between two phones.

Creating a Socket

In order to create a socket connection to a remote process, you must know two pieces of information: the *address* of the remote machine and the *port* the socket uses.

---

[*] More precisely, handshaking refers to any negotiation that helps to establish some sort of protocol or connection. Socket-based communication is simply one example of a system with a handshaking phase.

Addresses are absolute—they specify a single computer somewhere on your network or the Internet—and can be specified in many ways. Two of the most common are:

A human-readable name
> For example, *www.oreilly.com* is an address.

A 32-bit number
> This number is usually written as four distinct 8-bit numbers, separated by three dots. For example, 204.148.40.9 is the IP address of a computer somewhere on the Internet.

Ports, on the other hand, are relative addresses. A port is an integer that specifies a particular socket, *once a machine is known*. The operating system uses ports to route incoming information to the correct application or process.

The basic procedure for a Java client program using a socket involves three steps:

1. Create the socket. To do this, you need to know the address and port associated with a server.

2. Get the associated input and output streams from the socket. A socket has two associated streams: an InputStream, which is used for receiving information, and an OutputStream, which is used to send information.

3. Close the socket when you're done with it. Just as we closed streams, we need to close sockets. In fact, closing a stream associated with a socket will automatically close the socket as well.

This last step may not seem crucial for a client application; while a socket does use a port (a scarce operating-system resource), a typical client machine usually has plenty of spare ports. However, while a socket connection is open between a client and a server, the server is also allocating resources. It's always a good idea to let the server know when you're done so it can free up resources as soon as possible.

A simple client application

The steps we've just seen are illustrated in the WebBrowser application, as shown in Example 2-1. WebBrowser is an application that attempts to fetch the main web page from a designated machine. WebBrowser's main( ) method is defined in the com.ora. rmibook.chapter2.WebBrowser class.

Example 2-1. The WebBrowser application

```
public class WebBrowserFrame extends ExitingFrame {
//   ....
    private void askForPage(Socket webServer) throws IOException {
        BufferedWriter request;
        request = new BufferedWriter(new OutputStreamWriter(webServer.
            getOutputStream( )));
        request.write("GET / HTTP/1.0\n\n");
        request.flush( );
    }
```

Example 2-1. The WebBrowser application (continued)

```
    private void receivePage(Socket webServer) throws IOException {
        BufferedReader webPage=null;
        webPage = new BufferedReader(new InputStreamReader(webServer.getInputStream( )));
        String nextLine;
        while (null!=(nextLine=webPage.readLine( ))) {
            _displayArea.append(nextLine + "\n");// inefficient string handling
        }
        webPage.close( );
        return;
    }

    private class FetchURL extends AbstractAction {
        public FetchURL( ) {
            putValue(Action.NAME, "Fetch");
            putValue(Action.SHORT_DESCRIPTION, "Retrieve the indicated URL");
        }

        public void actionPerformed(ActionEvent e) {
            String url = _url.getText( );
            Socket webServer;
            try {
                webServer = new Socket(url, 80);
            }
            catch (Exception invalidURL) {
                _displayArea.setText("URL " + url + " is not valid.");
                return;
            }
            try {
                askForPage(webServer);
                receivePage(webServer);
                webServer.close( );
            }
            catch (IOException whoReallyCares) {
                _displayArea.append("\n Error in talking to the web server.");
            }
        }
    }
}
```

Visually, WebBrowser is quite simple; it displays a JTextArea, a JTextField, and a JButton. The user enters an address in the text field and clicks on the button. The application then attempts to connect to port 80[*] of the specified machine and retrieve the default web page. A screen shot of the application before the button is pressed is shown in Figure 2-1.

The WebBrowser application is implemented as a single subclass of JFrame. The socket-related code is contained in the Fetch button's ActionListener and in the two

---

[*] Port 80 is an example of a well-known port. It is usually reserved for web servers (and most web sites use it).

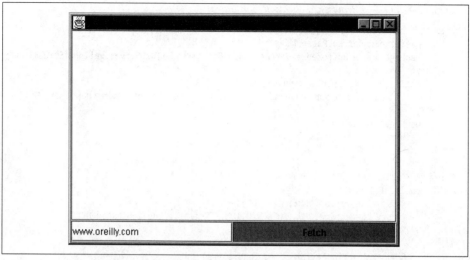

www.oreilly.com | Fetch

Figure 2-1. The WebBrowser application before fetching a web page

private methods askForPage( ) and receivePage( ). If all goes well, and no exceptions are thrown, the following code is executed when the button is clicked:

```
String url = _url.getText( );
Socket webServer = new Socket(url, 80);
askForPage(webServer);
receivePage(webServer);
```

That is, the program assumes that the text field contains a valid address of a computer on which a web server runs. The program also assumes that the web server is listening for connections on port 80. Using this information, the program opens a socket to the web server, asks for a page, and receives a response. After displaying the response, the program closes the socket and waits for more input.

Where did the number 80 come from? Recall that in order to create a socket connection, you need to have a machine address and a port. This leads to a boot-strapping problem—in order to establish a socket connection to a server, you need the precise address. But you really want to avoid hardwiring server locations into a client application. One solution is to require the server machine to be specified at run-time and use a *well-known port*. There are a variety of common services that vend themselves on well-known ports. Web servers usually use port 80; SMTP (the Internet mail protocol) uses port 25; the RMI registry, which we will discuss later, uses port 1099. Another solution, which RMI uses, is to have clients "ask" a dedicated server which machine and port they can use to communicate with a particular server. This dedicated server is often known as a *naming service*.

The code for asking and receiving pages is straightforward as well. In order to make a request, the following code is executed:

```
private void askForPage(Socket webServer) throws IOException {
    BufferedWriter request;
    request = new BufferedWriter(new
        OutputStreamWriter(webServer.getOutputStream( )));
    request.write("GET / HTTP/1.0\n\n");
    request.flush( );
}
```

This acquires the socket's associated OutputStream, wraps a formatting object (an instance of BufferedWriter) around it, and sends a request. Similarly, receivePage( ) gets the associated InputStream, and reads data from it:

```
private void receivePage(Socket webServer) throws IOException {
    BufferedReader webPage=null;
    webPage = new BufferedReader(new InputStreamReader(webServer.getInputStream( )));
    String nextLine;
    while (null!=(nextLine=webPage.readLine( ))) {
        _displayArea.append(nextLine + "\n");// inefficient string handling
    }
    return;
}
```

Protocols and Metadata

It's worth describing the steps the WebBrowser application takes in order to retrieve a page:

1. It connects to the server. In order to do this, it must know the location of the server.

2. It sends a request. In order to do this, both the client and the server must have a shared understanding of what the connection can be used for, and what constitutes a valid request.

3. It receives a response. In order for this to be meaningful (e.g., if the client is doing something other than simply displaying the response), the client and server must again have some sort of shared understanding about what the valid range of responses is.

The last two steps involve an application-level protocol and application-level metadata.

Protocols

A protocol is simply a shared understanding of what the next step in communicating should be. If two programs are part of a distributed application, and one program tries to send data to the other program, the second program should be expecting the data (or at least be aware that data may be sent). And, more importantly, the data should be in a format that the second program understands. Similarly, if the second program sends back a response, the first program should be able to receive the response and interpret it correctly.

HTTP is a simple protocol. The client sends a request as a formatted stream of ASCII text containing one of the eight possible HTTP messages.* The server receives the request and returns a response, also as a formatted stream of ASCII text. Both the request and the response are formatted according to an Internet standard.†

HTTP is an example of a *stateless* protocol. After the response is received, the communication between the client and the server is over—the server is not required to maintain any client-specific state, and any future communication between the two should not rely on prior HTTP requests or responses. Stateless protocols are like IP datagrams—they are easy to design, easy to implement in a robust way, and very scalable. On the other hand, they often require more bandwidth than other protocols because every request and every response must be complete in and of itself.

Metadata

An interesting thing happens when you click on the Fetch button: you get back a lot more than the web page that would be visible in a web browser such as Netscape Navigator or Internet Explorer. Figure 2-2 shows screenshot of the user interface after the button is clicked.

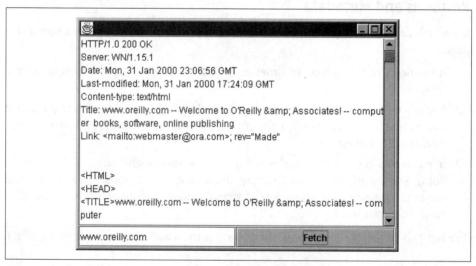

Figure 2-2. The WebBrowser application after fetching a web page

This is the response associated to the main O'Reilly web page. Notice that it starts with a great deal of text that isn't normally displayed in a web browser. Before the

---

* One of CONNECT, DELETE, PUT, GET, HEAD, OPTIONS, POST, or TRACE.
† Internet RFC 822. Available from *www.ietf.org*.

page contents, or the formatting information for the page contents are sent, the web server first tells the client about the information it is sending. In this case, the server first informs the client that the response is being sent using the HTTP 1.0 protocol, that the client requested succeeded without any problems (this is what "200 OK" means), that the page being sent hasn't changed in a few hours, and that the page is composed of HTML text. This type of information, which consists entirely of a description of the rest of the response, is usually called *metadata*.

 We've already encountered the metadata/data distinction before in our discussion of datagrams. Each datagram contains a *header* (the metadata) and *data* (the data). One of the things that TCP added to IP was extra metadata to headers that allowed datagram recipients to correctly reassemble the data in several datagrams into one coherent unit.

Metadata is ubiquitous in distributed applications. Servers and clients have independent lifecycles, both as applications and as codebases. Enabling robust communication between a client and a server means that you can't simply send a message. You have to say what type of message you're sending, what it is composed of, what version of the protocol and specifications are being used to format the message, and so on.

We'll do this manually in the next chapter, when we build a socket application. RMI, on the other hand, automatically generates descriptions of Java classes. These descriptions, stored in `static longs` named `serialVersionUID` (one integer for each class), will be more fully discussed in Chapter 10.

ServerSockets

So far, we've focused on how to write a client program using sockets. Our example code assumed that a server application was already running, and the server was accepting connections on a well-known port. The next logical step in our discussion of sockets is to write an application that will accept connections. Fortunately, this isn't much more complicated than creating a client application. The steps are:

1. Create an instance of `ServerSocket`. As part of doing so, you will supply a port on which `ServerSocket` listens for connections.
2. Call the `accept()` method of `ServerSocket`. Once you do this, the server program simply waits for client connections.

The accept() method

The key to using `ServerSocket` is the `accept()` method. It has the following signature:

```
public Socket accept() throws IOException
```

There are two important facts to note about accept(). The first is that accept() is a blocking method. If a client never attempts to connect to the server, the server will sit and wait inside the accept( ) method. This means that the code that follows the call to the accept( ) method will never execute.

The second important fact is that accept( ) creates and returns an instance of Socket. The socket that accept( ) returns is created inside the body of the accept( ) method for a single client; it encapsulates a connection between the client and the server.

Therefore, any server written in Java executes the following sequence of steps:

1. The server is initialized. Eventually, an instance of ServerSocket is created and accept( ) is called.

2. Once the server code calls accept( ), ServerSocket blocks, waiting for a client to attempt to connect.

3. When a client does connect, ServerSocket immediately creates a new instance of Socket, which will be used to communicate with the client. Remember that an instance of Socket that is returned from accept( ) encapsulates a connection to a single client.[*] ServerSocket then returns the new Socket to the code that originally called accept( ).

A Simple Web Server

To illustrate how to use ServerSocket, we'll write a simple web server. It's not a very impressive web server; it doesn't scale very well, it doesn't support secure sockets, and it always sends back the same page. On the other hand, the fact that it works at all and can be written in so few lines of code is a testament to the power of sockets. The main( ) method for our web server is contained in the com.ora.rmibook. chapter2.WebServer class.

The heart of our web server is the startListening( ) method:

```
public void startListening() {
    ServerSocket serverSocket;
    try {
        serverSocket = new ServerSocket(80);
    }
    catch (IOException e) {return;}
    while(true) {
        try {
            Socket client = serverSocket.accept(); // wait here
            processClientRequest(client);
            // bad design—should handle requests in separate threads
            // and immediately resume listening for connections
            client.close();
        }
```

---

[*] Setting up this socket involves some communication with the client; this communication (which is completely hidden inside the socket libraries) is again called *handshaking*.

```
        catch (IOException e){}
    }
}
```

This application works exactly as described in the preceding comments: an instance of ServerSocket is created, and then accept( ) is called. When clients connect, the call to accept( ) returns an instance of Socket, which is used to communicate with the client.

The code that communicates with the client does so by using the socket's input and output streams. It reads the request from the socket's input stream and displays the request in a JTextArea. The code that reads the request explicitly assumes that the client is following the HTTP protocol and sending a valid HTTP request.*

After the request is read, a "Hello World" page is sent back to the client:

```
private void processClientRequest(Socket client) throws IOException {
    _displayArea.append("Client connected from port " +
    client.getPort() + " on machine " + client.getInetAddress() +"\n");
    _displayArea.append("Request is: \n");
    readRequest(client);
    sendResponse(client);
}

private void readRequest(Socket client) throws IOException {
    BufferedReader request=null;
    request = new BufferedReader(new InputStreamReader(client.getInputStream( )));
    String nextLine;
    while (null!=(nextLine=request.readLine( ))) {
        // Ideally, we'd look at what the client said.
        // But this is a very simple web server.
        if (nextLine.equals("")) {
            break;
        }
        else {
            _displayArea.append("\t" + nextLine + "\n");
        }
    }
    _displayArea.append("-------------------------------------\n");
    return;
}

private void sendResponse(Socket client) throws IOException {
    BufferedWriter response;
    response = new BufferedWriter(new OutputStreamWriter(client.getOutputStream( )));
    response.write(_mainPage);
    response.flush( );
}
```

---

* Among other things, the readRequest( ) method assumes that the presence of a blank line signals the end of the request.

Figure 2-3 is a screenshot of our web server in action, handling a request made using Netscape Navigator 6.

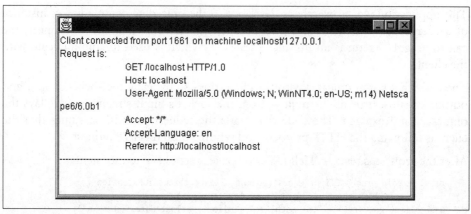

Figure 2-3. The WebServer application

Note the use of metadata here. When a web browser asks a web server for a page, it sends information in addition to what page it wants—a description of how the page should be sent and what the page should contain. In the previous example, the web browser stated what protocol is being used (HTTP 1.0), what type of web browser it is (Netscape 6), what sort of response is desired (indicated by the two "Accept" lines), and the site that referred to the page being requested (i.e., if you clicked on a link to request the page, the page you were on is passed to the web server as well).

Customizing Socket Behavior

In addition to the basic methods for creating connections and sending data, the Socket class defines a number of methods that enable you to set some fairly standard socket parameters. Setting these standard socket parameters won't change how the rest your code interacts with the socket. However, it will change the socket's network behavior. The methods, paired along get( )/set( ) lines, are:

```
public boolean getKeepAlive( )
public void setKeepAlive(boolean on)

public int getReceiveBufferSize( )
public void setReceiveBufferSize(int size)
public int getSendBufferSize( )
public void setSendBufferSize(int size)

public int getSoLinger( )
public void setSoLinger(boolean on, int linger)

public int getSoTimeout( )
public void setSoTimeout(int timeout)
```

```
public boolean getTcpNoDelay( )
public void setTcpNoDelay(boolean on)
```

In the rest of this section, we discuss these parameters in more detail:

```
public boolean getKeepAlive( )
public void setKeepAlive(boolean on)
```

> One problem with distributed applications is that if no data arrives over a long period of time, you need to wonder why. On one hand, it could be that the other program just hasn't had any information to send recently. On the other hand, the other program could have crashed. TCP handles this problem by allowing you to send an "Are you still alive?" message every so often to quiet connections. The way to do this is to call setKeepAlive( ) with a value of true. Note that you don't need to worry about one side of the connection dying when you use RMI. The distributed garbage collector and the leasing mechanism (which we'll discuss in Chapter 16) handle this problem automatically.

```
public int getReceiveBufferSize( )
public void setReceiveBufferSize(int size)
public int getSendBufferSize( )
public void setSendBufferSize(int size)
```

> The setReceiveBufferSize( ) and setSendBufferSize( ) methods attempt to set the size of the buffers used by the underlying protocol. They're not guaranteed to work; instead they are officially documented as methods that give "hints" to the operating system. However, the operating system is free to ignore these hints if it wants to.

> The basic trade-off is this: assuming the TcpNoDelay property is set to false, then using larger buffers mean larger chunks of data are sent. This results in a more efficient use of network bandwidth, as fewer headers get sent and fewer headers have to be parsed along the way. On the other hand, using larger buffers often means that there is a longer wait before data is sent, which may cause overall application performance to lag.

```
public int getSoLinger( )
public void setSoLinger(boolean on, int linger)
```

> setSoLinger( ) and getSoLinger( ) refer to how long the system will try to send information after a socket has been closed. Recall that under TCP/IP's buffering stategy, information is often held at the sender's side of the wire until the recipient is ready to handle it. Suppose that an application opened a socket, wrote some data to the socket, and immediately closed the socket. By default, the close( ) method will return immediately, and the operating system will still attempt to send the data on its own. If the setSoLinger( ) method is passed in a boolean of false, it will continue to behave this way.

> If the method is passed in a boolean of true, the close( ) method of the socket will block the specifed number of seconds (an integer), waiting for the operating system to transmit the data. If the time expires, the method returns, and the

operating system does not transmit the data. The maximum linger time is 65,535 seconds, even though you can pass in a much larger integer; a value of –1 means the operating system will keep trying forever. The platform default is generally the best option.

```
public int getSoTimeout( )
public void setSoTimeout(int timeout)
```
When you try to read data from a socket's input stream, the read methods all block while they wait for data. The timeout simply states how long they should wait before throwing an exception. A value of 0 means the socket will wait forever; this is the default behavior.

```
public boolean getTcpNoDelay( )
public void setTcpNoDelay(boolean on)
```
Recall that one of the things TCP adds to IP is buffer management. The program that receives data has a fixed-length buffer in which to receive information and must tell the sender when buffer space becomes available. If buffer space becomes available at a very slow rate (e.g., if data is being removed from the buffer very slowly), then it's possible that the recipient will send messages such as, "Send me three more bytes of data. I've got the buffer space for it now." This behavior, which results in a horrible waste of bandwidth, is called the *silly-window problem*.

TCP usually avoids the silly window problem by grouping information before sending it. That is, rather than sending small amounts of information repeatedly, TCP usually waits until a large amount of information is available and sends it together. The setTCPNoDelay( ) method enables you to turn this behavior off. An argument of true will force the sockets layer to send information as soon as it becomes available.

Special-Purpose Sockets

Socket and ServerSocket are object-oriented wrappers that encapsulate the TCP/IP communication protocol. They are designed to simply pass data along the wire, without transforming the data or changing it in any way. This can be either an advantage or a drawback, depending on the particular application.

Because data is simply passed along the network, the default implementation of Socket is fast and efficient. Moreover, sockets are easy to use and highly compatible with existing applications. For example, consider the WebBrowser application discussed earlier in the chapter. We wrote a Java program that accepted connections from an *already existing* application (in our case, Netscape Navigator) that was written in C++.

There are, however, two important potential downsides to simply passing along the data:

- The data isn't very secure.
- Communications may use excessive bandwidth.

Security is an issue because many applications run over large-scale networks, such as the Internet. If data is not encrypted before being sent, it can easily be intercepted by third parties who are not supposed to have access to the information.

Bandwidth is also an issue because data being sent is often highly redundant. Consider, for example, a typical web page. My web browser has 145 HTML files stored in its cache. The CompressFile application from Chapter 1, on average, compresses these files to less than half their original size. If HMTL pages are compressed before being sent, they can be sent much faster.

> Of course, HTML is a notoriously verbose data format, and this measurement is therefore somewhat tainted. But, even so, it's fairly impressive. Simply using compression can cut bandwidth costs in half, even though it adds additional processing time on both the client and server. Moreover, many data formats are as verbose as HTML. Two examples are XML-based communication and protocols such as RMI's JRMP, which rely on object serialization (we'll discuss serialization in detail in Chapter 10).

Direct Stream Manipulation

As with most problems, security and bandwidth issues have a simple, and almost correct, solution. Namely:

> If your application doesn't have security or bandwidth issues, or must use ordinary sockets to connect with pre-existing code, use ordinary sockets. Otherwise, use ordinary sockets, but layer additional streams to encrypt or compress the data.

This solution is nice for a number of reasons. First and foremost, it's a straightforward use of the Java streams library that does exactly what the streams library was intended to do. Consider the following code from the CompressFile application:

```
OutputStream destination = _destinationFileTextField.getFileOutputStream();
BufferedOutputStream bufferedDestination = new BufferedOutputStream(destination);
GZIPOutputStream zippedDestination = new GZIPOutputStream(bufferedDestination);
```

Rewriting the first line yields the exact code needed to implement compression over a socket:

```
OutputStream destination = _socket.getOutputStream();
BufferedOutputStream bufferedDestination = new BufferedOutputStream(destination);
GZIPOutputStream zippedDestination = new GZIPOutputStream(bufferedDestination);
```

Subclassing Socket Is a Better Solution

There is, however, a related solution that has identical performance characteristics and yields much more reliable code: create a subclass of Socket that implements the layering internally and returns the specialized stream.

This is a better approach for three reasons:

- It lowers the chances of socket incompatibilities. Consider the previous example—any part of the application that opens a socket must also implement the correct stream layering. If an application opens sockets in multiple locations in the code, there's a good chance that it will be done differently in different places (e.g., during an update a developer will forget to update one of the places in the code where a socket is opened).* This is especially true if the application has a long lifecycle.

- This sort of error is particularly bad because it isn't caught by the compiler. Instead, incorrectly encoded data will be sent over the wire, and the recipient will either then throw an exception (the good case) or perform computations with incorrect data (the bad case).

- It isolates code that is likely to change. If most of the application simply creates instances of a subclass of Socket or, better yet, calls a method named something like getSocket( ) on a factory object, and uses only the basic methods defined in Socket, then the application can quickly and easily be modified to use a different subclass of Socket. This not only allows an application to seamlessly add things such as an encryption layer, but it can be very useful when trying to debug or monitor a distributed application (see the LoggingSocket class from the sample code provided with this book as an example of this).

- Custom sockets can be used with RMI. RMI is an object-oriented layer for distributed programming, built on top of the sockets library. Though it doesn't give application programmers direct access to the socket input and output streams, it does allow programmers to specify what type of sockets to use when making a connection between a client and a server (via the RMIClientSocketFactory and RMIServerSocketFactory interfaces; see Chapter 18 for more details).

A Special-Purpose Socket

Creating custom socket classes is only little bit more complicated than you might expect from the previous discussion. Example 2-2 shows the complete implementation of CompressingSocket, a socket that uses the compressing streams to save bandwidth:

---

* This is a particular instance of a more general principle known as *Once and Only Once*. Namely: if information is written down two ways, one of the versions will soon be out of date. See *http://www.c2.com/cgi/wiki?OnceAndOnlyOnce* for a detailed discussion of this idea.

Example 2-2. CompressingSocket.java

```java
public class CompressingSocket extends Socket {
    private InputStream _compressingInputStream;
    private OutputStream _compressingOutputStream;

    public CompressingSocket() throws IOException {
    }

    public CompressingSocket(String host, int port) throws IOException {
        super(host, port);
    }

    public InputStream getInputStream() throws IOException {
        if (null==_compressingInputStream) {
            InputStream originalInputStream = super.getInputStream();
            _compressingInputStream = new CompressingInputStream(originalInputStream);
        }
        return _compressingInputStream;
    }

    public OutputStream getOutputStream() throws IOException{
        if (null==_compressingOutputStream) {
            OutputStream originalOutputStream = super.getOutputStream();
            _compressingOutputStream= new CompressingOutputStream(originalOutputStream);
        }
        return _compressingOutputStream;
    }

    public synchronized void close() throws IOException {
        if(null!=_compressingOutputStream) {
            _compressingOutputStream.flush();
            _compressingOutputStream.close();
        }
        if(null!=_compressingInputStream) {
            _compressingInputStream.close();
        }
    }
}
```

All that we did to write CompressingSocket was move the stream's customization code inside the Socket class definition. Note that in order to do this, however, we also had to override the close( ) method to close the special-purpose stream we created. There's one other subtlety here: we didn't use GZIPInputStream and GZIPOutputStream directly. Instead, we defined custom stream classes that wrapped around GZIPInputStream and GZIPOutputStream. Here is our implementation of CompressingOutputStream:

```java
public class CompressingOutputStream extends OutputStream {
    private OutputStream _actualOutputStream;
    private GZIPOutputStream _delegate;
```

```
        public CompressingOutputStream(OutputStream actualOutputStream) {
            _actualOutputStream = actualOutputStream;
        }

        public void write(int arg) throws IOException {
            if (null==_delegate) {
                _delegate = new  GZIPOutputStream(_actualOutputStream);
            }
            _delegate.write(arg);
            return;
        }

        public void close() throws IOException  {
            if (null!=_delegate) {
                _delegate.close();
            }
            else {
                _actualOutputStream.close();
            }
        }

        public void flush() throws IOException  {
            if (null!=_delegate) {
                _delegate.finish();
            }
        }
    }
}
```

We needed to use this extra layer of indirection because of the way that GZIPOutputStream handles flush(). Recall that subclasses of DeflaterOutputStream don't actually commit all data to the underlying stream when flush() is called. This means we're faced with the following problems:

- Because we're subclassing Socket, clients will call getInputStream() and getOutputStream().

- When they're done sending data, clients will call flush() to make sure all the data has been sent.

- Some of the data won't be sent when the client calls flush().

To handle these problems, we implement flush() so it calls finish(). Remember, though, that clients and servers must use the same type of socket (if the client compresses, the server must uncompress). In practice, this simply means that we also need to create a subclass of ServerSocket and override the accept() method to return a CompressingSocket. Example 2-3 shows the complete code for CompressingServerSocket.

Example 2-3. CompressingServerSocket.java

```
public class CompressingServerSocket extends ServerSocket {
    public CompressingServerSocket(int port) throws IOException { super(port); }
```

Example 2-3. CompressingServerSocket.java (continued)

```
public Socket accept( ) throws IOException {
    Socket returnValue = new CompressingSocket( );
    implAccept(returnValue);
    return returnValue;
}
}
```

This works by creating an instance of CompressingSocket and passing it as an argument to implAccept( ). implAccept( ) is a protected method that actually listens for connections and blocks. When a connection is made, implAccept( ) configures the CompressingSocket it has been passed and then returns.

Logging and Tracing

Frequently, the portions of code that perform data translation are also the ideal points to insert logging, tracing, and debugging code. For example, in the com.ora.rmibook. chapter2.sockets package, there are three classes that together illustrate the general idea: LoggingInputStream, LoggingOutputStream, and Recorder. LoggingInputStream and LoggingOutputStream don't perform any data manipulation at all, but they do have a reference to an instance of Recorder. And they tell the recorder whenever data flows through them, as in the following code snippet from LoggingInputStream:

```
public int read(byte[] b) throws IOException {
    int numberOfBytes = super.read(b);
    _recorder.incrementCounter(numberOfBytes);
    return numberOfBytes;
}
```

While this implementation is very primitive (the recorder is told the number of bytes received, but does not, for example, know where they came from), the idea is clear. Subclassing Socket, and using the custom subclass in your application, can provide a powerful hook for analyzing network performance.

Factories

Recall that from the list of three reasons to subclass Socket, we said:

> It isolates code that is likely to change. If most of the application simply creates instances of a subclass of Socket or, better yet, calls a method named something like getSocket( ) on a factory object, and uses only the basic methods defined in Socket, then the application can quickly and easily be modified to use a different subclass of Socket.

The idea behind a factory is simple: a factory is an object that knows how to build instances of some other class or interface. That is, it is a generalization of the traditional way of creating an instance of some class. At the risk of belaboring the point, calling a constructor can be broken down into three steps:

1. Find the class object. The class object is referred to by name (the programmer knows the class explicitly).
2. Call the constructor. Again, the programmer has explicit knowledge. Usually this step, and the prior one, are simply a line of the form `Classname.constructor( )`.
3. Use the returned object. The returned object is an instance of the named class.

Factories generalize each of these steps:

1. Find the factory. In a single process, this is usually done by having the programmer know the factory classname and having the factory be a singleton instance.
2. Call the creation method. The programmer has explicit knowledge of what methods are available.
3. Use the returned object. The returned object is an instance of some class that has the right type (e.g., implements the interface the factory is defined to return).

We'll revisit the idea of factories several times over the course of this book. Using factories is one of the most important idioms in designing and building scalable distributed systems. For now, it suffices to note that each of these changes adds important flexibility to a program.

Socket Factories

Factories are often used when there is an identifiable part of a program, easily encapsulated in one (or a few) objects, which is likely to change repeatedly over time and which may require special expertise to implement. Replacing sockets is a perfect example of this; instead of calling the constructor on a specific type of socket, code that needs to use a socket can get one by calling a factory.

This allows the sockets in an application to be changed by simply changing the code in one place—the factory—rather than changing the calls to the constructor everywhere in the program.

Because this is such a common usage, Javasoft, as part of the Java Secure Sockets Extension (JSSE), defined the `javax.net` package, includes two abstract classes: `SocketFactory` and `ServerSocketFactory`. Here are the method definitions for `SocketFactory`:

```
public abstract java.net.Socket createSocket(java.net.InetAddress host, int port)
public abstract java.net.Socket createSocket(java.net.InetAddress address,  int port,
    java.net.InetAddress clientAddress, int clientPort)
public abstract java.net.Socket createSocket(java.lang.String host, int port)
public abstract java.net.Socket createSocket(java.lang.String host, int port,
    java.net.InetAddress clientHost, int clientPort)
public static SocketFactory getDefault( )
```

With the exception of `getDefault( )`, these look exactly like constructors for a subclass of Socket. `getDefault( )` is a hook for a singleton—the idea is that code can get the system's default SocketFactory (which is set as part of an application's initialization phase) and then create a Socket using it, without ever knowing the classnames of either the default SocketFactory or the particular subclass of Socket it returns. The resulting code, which looks a lot like the following, is truly generic and rarely needs to be rewritten:

```
SocketFactory socketFactory = SocketFactory.getDefault( );
// gets default factory
// connects to server
Socket connectionToServer = socketFactory.createSocket(hostMachine, portNumber);
```

Of course, anyone who writes a custom socket needs to do a little more work and implement the factories. In particular, a vendor shipping a special-purpose socket should actually ship at least four classes: a subclass of Socket, a subclass of ServerSocket, a subclass of SocketFactory, and a subclass of ServerSocketFactory.

 The java.rmi.server package defines a similar, though simpler, pair of interfaces: RMIClientSocketFactory and RMIServerSocketFactor. These enable you to customize the sockets used by the RMI framework (ordinary sockets are used by default). We will discuss these further in Chapter 18.

Security

Compressing data, while possibly improving performance, does not make an application more secure. And code that allows you to monitor network use is only tangentially related to security. You could, for example, notice that an awful lot of data is being requested by an application running on an unauthorized site.

There's a good reason for this: there are subclasses of Socket that you can use to provide more secure communications. But, without a fair amount of training and knowledge of security, you shouldn't even think about writing one yourself—security is hard, and it's much too easy to make a mistake. What's worse, mistakes are hard to detect until someone has taken advantage of them. This is not to say that you shouldn't use custom sockets to implement security. It's just that you should use one of the standard and thoroughly tested solutions, rather than trying to implement your own.

Whenever information is transferred from one person (or application) to another, there are three potential security risks that arise:

Data confidentiality
    This issue arises because the transfer medium may be insecure. For example, if you're using the Internet to send information, you can't possibly guarantee the security of all the computers and cables the information passes through en route. While the information is being transferred, it might also be received and read by an unintended third party. The usual solution for this problem is to encrypt the information so that only authorized recipients can read it.

Data integrity

This issue also arises because the transfer medium may be insecure. Basically, this means that the information may be altered en route. The usual solution for this problem is to attach a secure checksum to the information being transferred. The recipient can compute the checksum of the received information and compare it to the attached checksum. This is commonly referred to as a *digital signature*.

Authorization and validation

Being able to securely send information to a third party isn't particularly helpful if we have no way of validating who the third party is. Authorization and validation refers to the process by which participants in an exchange have their identities verified. The usual solution for this is to rely on a third party that validates both participants. This third party can be either an internal application, such as a Kerberous ticket server, or a commercial entity that validates entities, such as Verisign.

 There are many different ways to authenticate a participant in an exchange. And you can often tighten up security via some form of partial authentication even if it's hard to establish the exact identity of a participant. For example, the RMI registry restricts certain operations based on IP addresses; the software that attempts to perform the operation must be running on the same machine as the registry. This is a very simple, and easily implemented, scheme. But, if the local machine is reasonably secure, then it is a fairly effective form of authentication.

Your goal as an application developer is to think about and add in the appropriate type of security to your program. Note that I say *appropriate*; not all users need to be authenticated, and not all data needs to be encrypted.

As a practical matter, the first step in building a secure system is realizing the attempt is futile. That is, there is no such thing as a perfectly secure system. Instead, your goal in implementing a security infrastructure should be *practical security*. A good working definition of this concept is provided by Bruce Schneier's *Applied Cryptography, 2nd Edition* (John Wiley & Sons):

> Different algorithms offer different degrees of security; it depends on how hard they are to break. If the cost required to break an algorithm is greater than the value of the encrypted data, then you're probably safe. If the time required to break an algorithm is longer than the time the encrypted data must remain secret, then you're probably safe. If the amount of data encrypted with a single key is less than the amount of data necessary to break the algorithm, then you're probably safe.

Using SSL

The Secure Sockets Layer (SSL) is a standard protocol for both authenticating users and encrypting data that is then sent over ordinary sockets. That is, implementations of SSL are conceptually similar to CompressingSocket—they take data and transform it before sending it over the wire. The only difference is that CompressingSocket *compresses*, while SSL sockets first *authenticate* (at the beginning of a session) and then *encrypt*.

SSL has three helpful features:

- It's a publicly defined protocol. SSL was first defined and implemented by Netscape. But the specification is publicly available[*] and has been subject to intense public scrutiny.

- It's commonly used. Almost every language that can use sockets has at least one SSL library package already implemented for it. And it is easy to define a secure version of a protocol by simply specifying that the secure version is a layer on top of SSL instead of simply being defined over cleartext sockets. This, for example, is the way HTTPS (the secure version of HTTP) is defined. Thus, in almost any situation where sockets can be used, SSL can be used with minimal extra programmer overhead and very few code changes.[†]

- It's good enough. While not absolutely secure, SSL meets the criteria for practical security in a wide variety of situations.

 SSL has been around, in one form or another, since 1995. Currently, there are three versions in active use: SSL2, SSL3, and Transport Layer Security (TLS). SSL2 is the oldest version of the spec and is very widely used. SSL3 is newer, and TLS is a successor to SSL3 (the main change from SSL3 is that the Internet Engineering Task Force has taken over stewardship of the standard). Neither SSL3 nor TLS seems to be widely adopted at this point.

The SSL Handshake

SSL is defined and implemented as a communication protocol layered on top of an ordinary socket connection. That is, in order to establish an SSL connection, a socket connection is first established. This socket connection is used by the client and server to negotiate a way to exchange information securely. After this negotiation process, often called the *SSL handshake*, the socket is used to transmit the encrypted information.

The SSL handshake is necessary for two main reasons. The first is that the SSL specification is still evolving. It's not enough for the participants to use SSL; the client and server must agree on a version of SSL to use. The second reason is that SSL supports a variety of encryption algorithms (commonly referred to as *ciphersuites*). Once a version of SSL is agreed upon, the ciphersuite and the values of the keys used for encryption still need to be arranged.

---

[*] For example, from *http://home.netscape.com/eng/ssl3/*.

[†] There will, of course, be *computational* overhead. After all, encrypting and decrypting data takes time.

Ciphersuites

JSSE 1.02, which can be downloaded for free from Javasoft, contains implementations of 15 distinct ciphersuites:

```
SSL_DH_anon_WITH_DES_CBC_SHA
SSL_DH_anon_WITH_3DES_EDE_CBC_SHA
SSL_DHE_DSS_WITH_DES_CBC_SHA
SSL_DHE_DSS_WITH_3DES_EDE_CBC_SHA
SSL_DH_anon_EXPORT_WITH_DES40_CBC_SHA
SSL_DHE_DSS_EXPORT_WITH_DES40_CBC_SHA
SSL_RSA_WITH_RC4_128_MD5
SSL_RSA_WITH_RC4_128_SHA
SSL_RSA_WITH_DES_CBC_SHA
SSL_RSA_WITH_3DES_EDE_CBC_SHA
SSL_DH_anon_WITH_RC4_128_MD5
SSL_RSA_EXPORT_WITH_RC4_40_MD5
SSL_RSA_WITH_NULL_MD5
SSL_RSA_WITH_NULL_SHA
SSL_DH_anon_EXPORT_WITH_RC4_40_MD5
```

Explaining exactly what these names imply is well beyond the scope of this book. But there are two important points to note:

- Five of the ciphersuites are anonymous (i.e., they contain the string "anon" in their name). Anonymous cipher suites don't require client or server authentication.
- A wide variety of different strength encryption algorithms are supported. Generally speaking, algorithms based on DES (i.e., containing the string DES) or those exportable from the United States (i.e., containing the word "EXPORT") are weaker and computationally much less expensive. Thus, the reference implementations run the gamut from fairly weak (SSL_DH_anon_EXPORT_WITH_DES40_CBC_SHA) to impressively secure (SSL_RSA_WITH_RC4_128_MD5).

The SSL handshake proceeds in four basic stages:

1. The client says hello. The first thing that happens is the client sends a message to the server that contains information about the client. In particular, this message contains information about which versions of SSL the client supports, which ciphersuites the client supports, and which compression algorithms the client supports.

2. The server says hello back to the client. The server responds to the client by sending a message that tells the client which ciphersuite and compression algorithms will be used for the encrypted communication. The server is free to choose any cryptographic algorithm that the client and server both support; in practice, the server usually chooses the strongest cryptographic algorithm supported by both the client and server.

3. The participants are authenticated. Ciphersuites can be anonymous or involve authenticating the participants. If the chosen ciphersuite involves authentication, it happens at this point.

4. Ciphersuite details are negotiated. In particular, the client and server exchange keys that will be used to encrypt further data exchanges.

Using SSL with JSSE

As part of JSSE, Javasoft ships an implementation of SSL. More precisely, JSSE contains the `javax.net.ssl` package, which contains two socket factories:

SSLSocketFactory
> This implements the SocketFactory interface.

SSLServerSocketFactory
> This implements the ServerSocketFactory interface.

Obtaining and Using JSSE

If you want to use JSSE with either JDK1.2 or JDK1.3, you will need to download it from Javasoft. JSSE is available for download from *http://java.sun.com/products/jsse/*. You can obtain a set of jar files (currently jcert.jar, jnet.jar and jsse.jar) and some additional documentation from there.

JSSE will also be included in JDK1.4 by default.

In order to use JSSE, you must make the JSSE jar files available to the JVM. The best way to do this is to include them as standard extensions by placing them in your extensions directory (the extensions directory is a subdirectory of the lib directory which is installed with the JVM. On the author's machine, the extensions directory is located at *c:\jdk1.3\jre\lib\ext*).

Alternatively, you can include the JSSE files on your classpath.

Using a nonauthenticating SSL socket then involves four code-level steps:

1. Providers must be registered with the Security class in the java.security package. Providers implement ciphersuites, which then become available to the SSL factories. This must be done on both the client and server sides.

2. Create and configure a server socket. As part of doing so, you select from the available ciphersuites and set authentication levels.

3. Create and configure a client socket. As part of doing so, you select from the available ciphersuites and set authentication levels.

4. Attempt to send data. When you first attempt to send data, in either direction, the SSL handshake occurs. There's an important detail here: because the handshake is delayed as long as possible, you get to create the sockets on either side,

and call methods on them to define ciphersuites, before the SSL handshake occurs.

 Using authenticating sockets involves more work. In order to authenticate a participant, a trusted third party has to vouch for the participant. That is, you need to install SSL Certificates obtained from a Certificate authority. While this involves extra work, the basics of using an SSL socket remain the same. For this reason, in this book, our examples use nonauthenticating (but encrypting) SSL sockets.

We will now examine each of these steps in more detail.

Registering providers

Security in Java 2 is managed by the java.security package. In particular, java.security contains two important class definitions: Security and Provider. Here's what the Javadoc has to say about each:

Security:

This class centralizes all security properties and common security methods. One of its primary uses is to manage providers.

Provider:

This class represents a "provider" for the Java Security API, where a provider implements some or all parts of Java Security, including:

- Algorithms (such as DSA, RSA, MD5 or SHA-1).

- Key generation, conversion, and management facilities (such as for algorithm-specific keys).

Each provider has a name and a version number and is configured in each runtime in which it is installed.

That is, Security is basically a set of static methods, such as addProvider(), which allow Java code to easily access various cryptographic algorithms, each of which is encapsulated within an instance of Provider. Given these classes, the way the SSL factories work is simple: they coordinate the SSL handshake and use the ciphersuites that have been installed with Security.

Therefore, in order to use SSL, you must install at least one instance of Provider. Fortunately, JSSE comes with a subclass of Provider, com.sun.net.ssl.internal.SSLProvider, which implements a wide selection of cryptographic algorithms. The following code installs the provider by creating an instance of com.sun.net.ssl.internal.SSLProvider and calling java.security.Security's addProvider() method. It then lists the supported ciphersuites.

```
java.security.Security.addProvider(new com.sun.net.ssl.internal.ssl.Provider());
SSLServerSocketFactory socketFactory = (SSLServerSocketFactory)
    SSLServerSocketFactory.getDefault();
String[] suites = socketFactory.getSupportedCipherSuites();
System.out.println("Supported cipher suites:");
```

```
    for (int counter = 0; counter < suites.length; counter ++) {
        System.out.println("\t" + suites[counter]);
    }
```

 The Javasoft implementation of SSL is what Sun Microsystems, Inc. calls a "reference implementation." That is, the Javasoft implementation of SSL is intended to define correct behavior for the interfaces and classes associated with SSL implementations, and is explicitly not intended for production use. In particular, the implementations of cryptographic algorithms are rather slow. In a production environment, you'd probably want to purchase faster providers.

Configuring SSLServerSocket

Once you've installed a provider on the server side, the next step is to create and configure an instance of SSLServerSocket. In addition to being a subclass of ServerSocket, SSLServerSocket defines the following nine methods:

```
public String[] getSupportedCipherSuites()
public String[] getEnabledCipherSuites()
public void setEnabledCipherSuites(String[] suites)
public void setEnableSessionCreation(boolean flag)
public boolean getEnableSessionCreation()
public void setNeedClientAuth(boolean flag)
public boolean getNeedClientAuth()
public void setUseClientMode(boolean flag)
public boolean getUseClientMode()
```

While the precise details of these methods are beyond the scope of this book, there are three that are particularly useful:

setEnabledCipherSuites()
> This method allows you to choose which ciphersuites the instance of SSLServerSocket will support.

setEnableSessionCreation()
> The enableSessionCreation property defaults to true. If enableSessionCreation is set to false, new sessions (e.g., new SSL connections) cannot be created.

setNeedClientAuth()
> Using this method with an argument of false explicitly disables client authentication, even for cryptographic algorithms that usually require client authentication.

To create and configure an instance of SSLServerSocket, you first obtain an instance of SSLServerSocketFactory. Next, create an instance of SSLServerSocket, and then call the appropriate methods. The following code creates an instance of SSLServerSocket, which uses a single, anonymous ciphersuite:

```
public static String ANON_CIPHER = "SSL_DH_anon_WITH_RC4_128_MD5";
public static String[] CIPHERS = {ANON_CIPHER};
public SSLServerSocket createServerSocket(int port) {
    try {
```

```
java.security.Security.addProvider(new com.sun.net.ssl.internal.ssl.
    Provider( ));
SSLServerSocketFactory socketFactory = (SSLServerSocketFactory)
    SSLServerSocketFactory.getDefault( );
SSLServerSocket returnValue = (SSLServerSocket) socketFactory.
    createServerSocket(port);
returnValue.setEnabledCipherSuites(CIPHERS);
returnValue.setEnableSessionCreation(true);
return returnValue;
    }
    .....
}
```

After this code executes, the instance of SSLServerSocket returned by createServer( ) is ready to be used just like any other instance of ServerSocket. That is, the accept( ) method can be called, and when an instance of SSLSocket successfully completes the SSL handshake with it, accept( ) will return an instance of SSLSocket, which can be used for secure two-way communication.

Configuring SSLSocket

Once you've installed a provider on the client side, the next step is to create and configure an instance of SSLSocket. This process is analogous to how an instance of SSLServerSocket is created on the server side. In particular, the following code gets the default SSLSocketFactory and proceeds to create an instance of SSLSocket:

```
public static String ANON_CIPHER = "SSL_DH_anon_WITH_RC4_128_MD5";
public static String[] CIPHERS = {ANON_CIPHER};
public Socket createSocket(String host, int port) {
    try {
        java.security.Security.addProvider(new com.sun.net.ssl.internal.ssl.
            Provider( ));
        SSLSocketFactory socketFactory = (SSLSocketFactory) SSLSocketFactory.
            getDefault( );
        SSLSocket returnValue = (SSLSocket) socketFactory.createSocket(host, port);
        returnValue.setEnabledCipherSuites(CIPHERS);
        return returnValue;
    }
    ..
}
```

Sending data

It's important to note that at this point, we've created and configured two sockets: an SSLServerSocket on the server side and an ordinary SSLSocket on the client side. There has not, however, been any communication between them. The SSL handshake has not yet occurred, and no information, of any type, has been sent over the wire. This is because we need time, once we've created the sockets, to configure them.

The SSL handshake occurs the first time we attempt to send or receive data on the client side. That is, the first time code such as the following is executed, the SSL sockets will attempt to complete a handshake:

```
InputStream inputStream = sslsocket.getInputStream( );
inputStream.read( );
```

Revisiting Our Web Browser

With the discussion of SSL under our belt, we can almost reimplement our web server as a secure web server. In our original web server, we created an instance of ServerSocket in the startListening( ) method:

```
public void startListening( ) {
    ServerSocket serverSocket;
    try {
        serverSocket = new ServerSocket(80);
    }
    ....
}
```

We can replace this with the following code:

```
public void startListening( )  {
        ServerSocket serverSocket;
        try {
            serverSocket = getSSLServerSocket(443);
        }
        ....
    }

    private static String ANON_CIPHER_1 = "SSL_DH_anon_WITH_DES_CBC_SHA";
    private static String ANON_CIPHER_2 = "SSL_DH_anon_WITH_3DES_EDE_CBC_SHA";
    private static String ANON_CIPHER_3 = "SSL_DH_anon_EXPORT_WITH_DES40_CBC_SHA";
    private static String ANON_CIPHER_4 = "SSL_DH_anon_WITH_RC4_128_MD5";
    private static String ANON_CIPHER_5 = "SSL_DH_anon_EXPORT_WITH_RC4_40_MD5";
    private static String[] CIPHERS = {ANON_CIPHER_1, ANON_CIPHER_2, ANON_CIPHER_3,
        ANON_CIPHER_4, ANON_CIPHER_5};
    static {
        java.security.Security.addProvider(new com.sun.net.ssl.internal.ssl.
            Provider( ));
    }
    private ServerSocket getSSLServerSocket(int port) throws IOException  {
        SSLServerSocketFactory socketFactory = (SSLServerSocketFactory)
            SSLServerSocketFactory.getDefault( );
        SSLServerSocket returnValue = (SSLServerSocket) socketFactory.
            createServerSocket(port);
        returnValue.setEnabledCipherSuites(CIPHERS);
        returnValue.setNeedClientAuth(false);
        returnValue.setEnableSessionCreation(true);
        return returnValue;
    }
```

This code creates an instance of SSLServerSocket that will work with five different anonymous ciphersuites and listen on port 443, which is the default port for https:// requests. And this almost works. Sadly, if you attempt to connect to a running instance of SSLWebServer using Netscape Navigator 4.6, you'll get the error dialog shown in Figure 2-4.

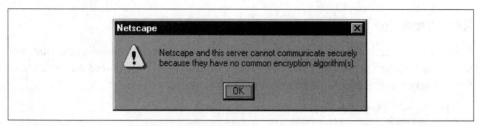

Figure 2-4. SSL error dialog for Netscape Navigator 4.6

Actually, this is pretty impressive; a legacy application written in C and released in 1998 communicated with our SSL server, engaged in an SSL handshake, and realized that there was no way to establish a common ciphersuite (web browsers require servers to authenticate themselves). This cross-language compatibility is one of the strongest reasons to adopt SSL as an encryption and authentication layer.

CHAPTER 3

A Socket-Based Printer Server

In the previous two chapters, we covered the basics of using streams and sockets. In this chapter, we'll use what we have learned to build a simple server application. Along the way, we'll confront many of the problems that distributed applications face. And our solutions will help to introduce and explain most of the basic RMI infrastructure.

A Network-Based Printer

The application we're going to build is a very simple one; it takes a local printer and makes it available over the network via a socket-based API. Our intended architecture looks like the diagram shown in Figure 3-1.

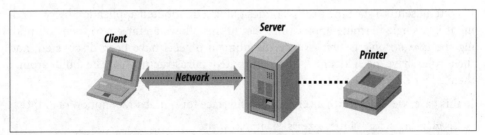

Figure 3-1. A network printer using a socket-based API

This figure illustrates three main components:

The client application

This is a program running on a separate machine somewhere on the network. There is nothing special about the machine this program runs on (in fact, many different machines can run this program). It is responsible for presenting a user interface to the user, getting print requests, and sending those requests to the server application. The client application is written entirely in Java and is therefore easy to install on any machine with a JVM.

The server application

This is a program that resides on a single, designated machine on the network. The machine it runs on is connected locally to a printer. The server application's roles are to receive print requests over the network from the client program, perform whatever intermediate tasks are necessary, and then forward the request to the printer.

The printer

In this example, we're assuming that the printer exists and is activated, and that the code for interfacing a Java program to a local printer has been written. Printer manufacturers are fairly good at providing printer drivers. However, if we implement this part of the application, it could require the use of the Java Native Interface to communicate advanced commands to a printer driver written in C or C++. One consequence of this is that the server application may not entirely be a Java program and, therefore, installing the server might involve significant modifications to the underlying operating system.*

 Figure 3-1 is a very vague diagram. It's more of a requirements diagram than an architectural diagram for a networked application. In particular, it doesn't actually say anything about the class structure of our program. We'll redraw it later, filling in many more details. Drawing diagrams like this one can be very useful, however, as a means of understanding just what it is that we need to build.

The Basic Objects

It's often useful to start the process of designing a distributed application by pretending it is a single-machine application. Doing this allows architects to focus on finding the *domain objects* first.† Once the domain objects have been discovered, and their roles have been defined, the distributed infrastructure can be built around them.

In this case, we'll start with a very simple interface for our abstract notion of `Printer`:

```java
public interface Printer extends PrinterConstants {
    public boolean printerAvailable();
    public boolean printDocument(DocumentDescription document) throws
        PrinterException;
}
```

---

* For example, installing a printer driver on Windows NT might involve upgrading a system DLL.

† "Domain objects" is a very loose and nebulous term. Roughly speaking, domain objects are classes that represent end-user ideas and abstractions. For example, a class named `AccountEntry` is probably a domain object, whereas a class named `NetworkFlowControlBuffer` probably isn't.

Our goal is to take a concrete implementation of the `Printer` interface[*] and make it available over the network.

This definition of `Printer` relies on two additional classes: `DocumentDescription` and `PrinterException`. These are both fairly simple classes, designed more to encapsulate related pieces of information than to implement complex behavior. The definition of `DocumentDescription` begins with five state variables that encapsulate the print request:

```
public class DocumentDescription {
    public static final int FAST_PRINTING = 0;
    public static final int HIGH_QUALITY_PRINTING = 1;

    public static final int POSTSCRIPT = 0;
    public static final int PDF = 1;

    private DataInputStream _actualDocument;
    private int _documentType;
    private boolean _printTwoSided;
    private int _printQuality;
    private int _length;
```

The only interesting aspect of this is the decision to use `Stream` to represent the actual document, rather than storing just a filename. Doing this makes the implementation of the printer server much simpler for two reasons:

- There is no guarantee that the machine the server is running on has access to the same files as the machine running the client program.

- If we just use the filename, and the file is edited before the actual printout occurs, we won't accurately reflect the user's request.

Using streams in the interface also makes it possible for us to print things other than files. For example, we can print the contents of a JTextArea by calling getText( ) on the JTextArea, wrapping the resulting instance of String in a StringBufferInputStream, and passing that to the printer.

`PrinterException` is a similar class. It's a custom exception that holds two pieces of information: how many pages were actually printed and a description of what went wrong with the printer:

```
public class PrinterException extends Exception {
    private int _numberOfPagesPrinted;
    private String _humanReadableErrorDescription;
}
```

---

[*] We won't actually connect to a printer. While it's a fun weekend project to wrap an existing printer driver (such as the limited one presented in the java.awt.print package), doing so is beyond the scope of this book. Instead, we'll just use a very simple implementation called NullPrinter.

The Protocol

Now that the basic objects are in place, we have a better idea of what will happen inside our application: the client will send a DocumentDescription to the server, and the server will respond to whether the print request succeeded. In the event that it didn't, the server will send a PrinterException to the client containing more information.

In order to make this concrete, we need to address two fundamental issues. The first involves how the client will find the server. The client somehow needs to know the machine address and port number of the server process. The traditional way of solving this problem is to define it either as constants in a class or via a well-known text file accessible by both the client and the server. For this implementation, we'll use the former and define some constants in an abstract class:

```
public abstract class NetworkBaseClass {
    public static final String DEFAULT_SERVER_NAME = "localhost";
    public static final int DEFAULT_SERVER_PORT = 2100;
    public static final int DEFAULT_SERVER_BACKLOG = 10;
    ....
}
```

As long as this class is available to both the client and the server, we've solved the location problem.

The next issue is to define and implement an application protocol. In other words, we must address the question of how the client and server communicate once they have connected. In our case, the information flow follows these two steps:

1. The client sends an instance of DocumentDescription to the server.

2. The server sends back a response indicating whether the document was successfully printed.

After the client receives the server's response, the connection is closed, and there is no shared state between the client and the server. This means that these two steps completely define our protocol.

 The process in which a client takes a request, including arguments and data, and puts it into a format suitable for sending over a socket connection is often referred to as *marshalling* the request (sometimes the client is said to be *marshalling* the data). The server is then said to *demarshall* the request or data. In older references, marshalling is sometimes referred to as *pickling*, and demarshalling is then called *unpickling*. No one really seems to know why (or why the names changed).

Encapsulation and Sending Objects

The first step in solving this problem is figuring out how to send our objects, DocumentDescription and PrinterException, over the wire. There are two basic design options for doing this:

The internal approach
> In this approach, the objects know how to push their state into, and read their state out of, a stream. That is, if you want to send an instance of DocumentDescription over a stream, call a method named something similar to writeToStream( ), and the instance writes itself out.

The external approach
> In this approach, there is a third, external object that knows about both the object you want to send over the socket and the stream classes. This third object knows how to encode the object and put the relevant information into the stream.

These approaches both have their good points. With the internal approach, data can be totally encapsulated within an object and still have the knowledge to send itself over the wire. Letting the object do the encoding and decoding makes the internal approach a more object-oriented way of doing things. In addition, the internal approach simplifies maintenance; colocating the marshalling code with the object to be marshalled makes it easier to keep the two synchronized or to tell when they're out of synchronization (someone who's changing the object can easily change the marshalling code at the same time).

On the other hand, the external approach allows you to have more than one marshalling routine for a given object and to gracefully choose which protocol to use based on circumstances. The external approach also allows you to put all the marshalling code in one place, which makes the actual protocol easier to understand and improve upon.

Note that the difference between these two approaches is not so much the code that's written—in either approach you still need to marshall the object—but where the marshalling code is placed within the application. In our case, we've chosen to use the internal approach.

DocumentDescription

Example 3-1 shows the source for DocumentDescription, including the marshalling code.

Example 3-1. DocumentDescription.java

```
public class DocumentDescription {
    public static final int FAST_PRINTING = 0;
    public static final int HIGH_QUALITY_PRINTING = 1;
```

Example 3-1. DocumentDescription.java (continued)

```java
    public static final int POSTSCRIPT = 0;
    public static final int PDF = 1;

    private DataInputStream _actualDocument;
    private int _documentType;
    private boolean _printTwoSided;
    private int _printQuality;
    private int _length;

    public DocumentDescription(InputStream source) throws IOException {
        readFromStream(source);
    }

    public DocumentDescription(InputStream actualDocument, int documentType, boolean
        printTwoSided, int printQuality) throws IOException {
        _documentType = documentType;
        _printTwoSided = printTwoSided;
        _printQuality = printQuality;
        BufferedInputStream buffer = new BufferedInputStream(actualDocument);
        DataInputStream dataInputStream = new DataInputStream(buffer);
        ByteArrayOutputStream temporaryBuffer = new ByteArrayOutputStream( );
        _length = copy(dataInputStream, new DataOutputStream(temporaryBuffer));
        _actualDocument = new DataInputStream(new ByteArrayInputStream(temporaryBuffer
            toByteArray( )));
    }

    public DocumentDescription(InputStream actualDocument, int documentType, boolean
        printTwoSided,
        int printQuality, int length) {
        _actualDocument = new DataInputStream(actualDocument);
        _documentType = documentType;
        _printTwoSided = printTwoSided;
        _printQuality = printQuality;
        _length = length;
    }

    public int getLength( ) {
        return _length;
    }

    public int getDocumentType( ) {
        return _documentType;
    }

    public boolean isPrintTwoSided( ) {
        return _printTwoSided;
    }

    public int getPrintQuality( ) {
        return _printQuality;
    }
```

Example 3-1. DocumentDescription.java (continued)

```java
public void writeToStream(OutputStream outputStream) throws IOException {
    BufferedOutputStream buffer = new BufferedOutputStream(outputStream);
    DataOutputStream dataOutputStream = new DataOutputStream(buffer);
    writeMetadataToStream(dataOutputStream);
    copy(_actualDocument, dataOutputStream, _length);
}

public void readFromStream(InputStream inputStream) throws IOException {
    BufferedInputStream buffer = new BufferedInputStream(inputStream);
    DataInputStream dataInputStream = new DataInputStream(buffer);
    readMetadataFromStream(dataInputStream);
    ByteArrayOutputStream temporaryBuffer = new ByteArrayOutputStream( );
    copy(dataInputStream, new DataOutputStream(temporaryBuffer), _length);
    _actualDocument = new DataInputStream(new ByteArrayInputStream(temporaryBuffer
        toByteArray( )));
}

private void writeMetadataToStream(DataOutputStream dataOutputStream) throws
    IOException {
    dataOutputStream.writeInt(_documentType);
    dataOutputStream.writeBoolean(_printTwoSided);
    dataOutputStream.writeInt(_printQuality);
    dataOutputStream.writeInt(_length);
}

private void readMetadataFromStream(DataInputStream dataInputStream) throws
    IOException {
    _documentType = dataInputStream.readInt( );
    _printTwoSided = dataInputStream.readBoolean( );
    _printQuality = dataInputStream.readInt( );
    _length = dataInputStream.readInt( );
}

private void copy(InputStream source, OutputStream destination, int length) throws
    IOException {
    int counter;
    int nextByte;
    for (counter = 0; counter <length; counter++) {
        nextByte = source.read( );
        destination.write(nextByte);
    }
    destination.flush( );
}

private int copy(InputStream source, OutputStream destination) throws IOException {
    int nextByte;
    int numberOfBytesCopied = 0;
    while(-1!= (nextByte = source.read( ))) {
        destination.write(nextByte);
        numberOfBytesCopied++;
    }
    destination.flush( );
```

Example 3-1. DocumentDescription.java (continued)

```
        return numberOfBytesCopied;
    }
}
```

The careful eye will note that metadata has once again crept into the picture. Namely, when DocumentDescription's writeToStream( ) method is called, five pieces of information are sent:

- The document type
- Whether the print request is for a two-sided printout
- What quality printing is desired
- The length of the document
- The actual document

Sending the document's length along with the document is redundant. After all, if you have a copy of the document, you can compute the length of the document. However, sending the length helps out in demarshalling. For instance, the demarshalling code in the readFromStream( ) method assumes that the stream contains:

1. An integer
2. A boolean
3. An integer
4. An integer
5. A number of bytes totaling the third integer.

Put succinctlly, the demarshalling code relies on the metadata to help it know when it should stop reading from the stream.

> Of course, the overwhelming lesson of actually implementing (or even just reading) marshalling code is that it is boilerplate code. Once you have sockets and streams, marshalling is a snap.

PrinterException is implemented in much the same way as DocumentDescription.

Network-Aware Wrapper Objects

Implementing the rest of our protocol requires a pair of objects to manage the communication, one on the client side and one on the server side. The client-side object is responsible for initiating the communication and sending an instance of DocumentDescription to the server. The server-side object listens for client connections, receives instances of DocumentDescription once the client has connected, and sends responses to the client.

Spooling

Note that the client program here uses an extravagant amount of memory. In order to compute the length of the document, we make an in-memory copy of the entire document before we send it through the socket. If the document is 38 MB (rather typical for a Powerpoint presentation these days), we make a 38 MB buffer and create an in-memory copy of the entire file there.

A much better way to do this is to send the document in smaller pieces, each of which is preceded by an integer indicating the length of the following piece. That is, instead of sending the length of the document followed by the document, we can send the length of the first chunk followed by the first chunk, then the length of the second chunk followed by the second chunk. Conceptually, this is a lot like breaking the document into a linked list of "content nodes."

For example, suppose the document is 18,012 bytes, and we decide to send 1000-byte pieces. The information sent to the stream might be:

> 1000, followed by the first set of a thousand bytes
> 1000, followed by the second set of a thousand bytes
> ....
> 1000, followed by the eighteenth set of a thousand bytes
> 12, followed by the last twelve bytes

Doing things this way uses slightly more bandwidth, but it also allows us to send arbitrarily large documents without exhausting the memory available on the client machine. This works because at any given time, we need to have only a small percentage of the file in memory.

The downside to doing things this way is that we might run into an unexpected disk failure in the middle of our print request. The current implementation reads the entire file and then sends the request. The spooling implementation interweaves these two tasks. If the file suddenly becomes unavailable (for example, if the file server gets rebooted), our application is going to have a problem.

In practice, this means our printing protocol needs to be a little bit more complicated. After each chunk of content, we need to also include a status code:

> 1000, followed by the first set of thousand bytes, followed by STATUS_OKAY
> 1000, followed by the second set of thousand bytes, followed by STATUS_OKAY
> ....
> 1000, followed by the eighteenth set of a thousand bytes, followed by STATUS_OKAY
> 12, followed by the last twelve bytes, followed by STATUS_DONE

Both of these objects inherit from a convenience class named NetworkBaseClass, which defines a few constants and has convenience methods for closing sockets and streams:

```
public abstract class NetworkBaseClass {
    public static final String DEFAULT_SERVER_NAME = "localhost";
```

```
    public static final int DEFAULT_SERVER_PORT = 2100;
    public static final int DEFAULT_SERVER_BACKLOG = 10;

    public void closeSocket(Socket socket) {
        if (null!=socket) {
            try {
                socket.close( );
            }
            catch (IOException exception){ }
        }
    }

    public void closeStream(InputStream stream) {
        //  omitted (similar to close socket)
    }

    public void closeStream(OutputStream stream) {
        // omitted (similar to close socket)
    }
}
```

ClientNetworkWrapper

ClientNetworkWrapper is the client side object which encapsulates the protocol. The core of this encapsulation is the sendDocumentToPrinter( ) method:

```
private String _serverMachine;
private int _serverPort;

// almost all the set-up and initialization of object code omitted....

public void sendDocumentToPrinter(DocumentDescription documentDescription) throws
    ConnectionException, PrinterException {
    Socket connection = null;
    try {
        connection = new Socket(_serverMachine, _serverPort);
        documentDescription.writeToStream(connection.getOutputStream( ));
        readStatusFromSocket(connection);
    }
    catch (IOException e) {
        e.printStackTrace( );
        throw new ConnectionException( );
    }
    finally {
        closeSocket(connection);
    }
}

private void readStatusFromSocket(Socket connection) throws PrinterException,
    IOException {
    InputStream inputStream = connection.getInputStream( );
    DataInputStream dataInputStream= new DataInputStream(inputStream);
    BufferedReader reader = new BufferedReader(new InputStreamReader(inputStream));
    boolean response = dataInputStream.readBoolean( );
      if (response) {
```

```
        return;
    }
    throw new PrinterException(inputStream);
}
```

The points to note about this method are:

- It is a straightforward procedural wrapper around the protocol; a connection is made, an instance of DocumentDescription is sent, a return value is read from the socket's input stream, and a PrinterException may be thrown based on the return value. Once you've defined the protocol, writing ClientNetworkWrapper is straightforward.

- Once again, the information that has already been read is used to help interpret the remainder of the stream. Since the communication is entirely via a stream of bytes, the server can't simply throw an exception and expect it to be propagated to the client application (you can't throw an exception through a socket connection). But the server can send a boolean that the client interprets as a signal that there is more information available. The client knows that if there is more information sent, it is a marshalled instance of PrinterException and behaves accordingly.

We're cheating a bit on exceptions. In particular, what if there were more than one type of exception that could be thrown? Instead of just passing a boolean back from the server, we'd need to pass more metadata. For example, we could pass back a boolean indicating that an exception has been thrown, followed by a string containing the name of the exception class, followed by the actual instance data. The client would receive the boolean and create an instance of the class by getting the class object with Class.forName( ) and then using the reflection API to find the appropriate constructor.

ServerNetworkWrapper

We need to implement a companion object on the server side. This class, Server-NetworkWrapper, has to listen for connections using an instance of ServerSocket and then implement the mirror image of the client-side protocol. In other words, when the client side is sending information, the server should be listening. And when the client side is listening, the server should be sending.

The details of managing the connection are contained in the accept( ) method:

```
public void accept( ) {
    while (true) {
        Socket clientSocket = null;
        try {
            clientSocket = _serverSocket.accept( );// blocking call
            processPrintRequest(clientSocket);
        }
        catch (IOException e) {e.printStackTrace( );}
        closeSocket(clientSocket);
    }
}
```

The protocol itself is implemented in the processPrintRequest( ) method. As on the client side, this method is a straightforward implementation of the protocol—it reads an instance of DocumentDescription from the stream, tries to print the document, and encodes the printer's response:

```
private void processPrintRequest(Socket clientSocket) {
    InputStream clientRequestStream;
    OutputStream clientResponseStream;
    DataOutputStream dataOutputStream;
    DocumentDescription documentToPrint;
    try {
        clientRequestStream = clientSocket.getInputStream( );
        clientResponseStream = clientSocket.getOutputStream( );
        dataOutputStream = new DataOutputStream(clientResponseStream);
        documentToPrint = new DocumentDescription(clientRequestStream);
    }
    catch (IOException e) {
        e.printStackTrace( );
        return;
    }
    try {
        try {
            _printer.printDocument(documentToPrint);
            dataOutputStream.writeBoolean(true);
        }
        catch (PrinterException printerError) {
            dataOutputStream.writeBoolean(false);
            printerError.writeToStream(dataOutputStream);
        }
    }
    catch (IOException ee) {ee.printStackTrace( );}
}
```

The Application Itself

Once we've written the data objects and the objects that encapsulate the network protocol, writing the rest of the application is easy. The server doesn't even need a user interface; it consists of the main( ) function, which instantiates a printer, creates an instance of ServerNetworkWrapper, and then calls accept( ) on the instance of ServerNetworkWrapper:

```
public static void main(String args[]) {
    try {
        File logfile = new File("C:\\temp\\serverLogfile");
        OutputStream outputStream = new FileOutputStream(logfile);
        Printer printer = new NullPrinter(outputStream);
        ServerNetworkWrapper serverNetworkWrapper = new
            ServerNetworkWrapper(printer);
        serverNetworkWrapper.accept( );
    }
    catch (Exception e) {
```

```
            e.printStackTrace( );
        }
    }
```

Writing the Client

Apart from the user interface, the client application is equally straightforward. Our user interface is shown in Figure 3-2.

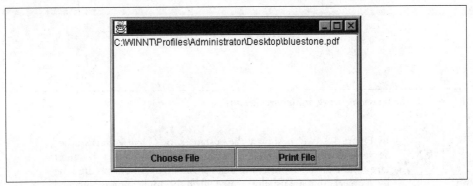

Figure 3-2. The user interface for the printer client

The Choose File button uses a JFileChooser to let the user select a file (whose name is displayed in the text area). All the network communication is done using ActionListener, which has been added to the Print File button. And all ActionListener does is instantiate ClientNetworkWrapper and call sendDocumenttoPrinter( ):

```
private class PrintFile implements ActionListener {
    public void actionPerformed(ActionEvent event) {
        try {
            ClientNetworkWrapper clientNetworkWrapper = new ClientNetworkWrapper( );
            FileInputStream document = new FileInputStream(_fileChooser
                getSelectedFile( ));
            clientNetworkWrapper.sendDocumentToPrinter(document);
        }
        catch (Exception exception) {
            _messageBox.setText("Exception attempting to print " +
                (_fileChooser.getSelectedFile( )).getAbsolutePath( ) +
                "\n\t Error was: " + exception.toString( ));
        }
    }
}
```

Redrawing the Architecture Diagram

We are now in a position to redraw our earlier architecture diagram, including more details about the application structure. The resulting diagram is shown in Figure 3-3.

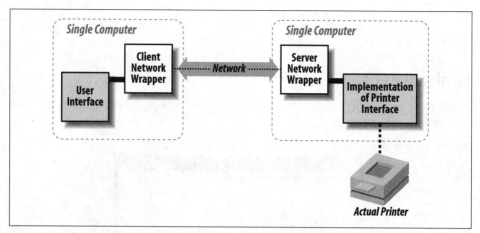

Figure 3-3. The revised network printer architecture

In Figure 3-3, we've shown the instances of `ClientNetworkWrapper`, `ServerNetworkWrapper`, and the implementation of the `Printer` interface. These are all *architectural objects*. Architectural objects are long-lived objects that are usually created when the application is launched. In addition, they are usually unique, and most of the application thinks of them as part of the computing environment. When drawing a simple diagram of a networked application, it is often convenient to omit the data objects entirely, and simply sketch the key architectural objects.

Evolving the Application

At this point, we're done with the first version of the application. We've successfully used sockets to implement the networking portion of a simple, distributed printing application. But the words "first version" are very important. There's a long list of features we haven't implemented—some because we were lazy, others because they probably wouldn't be requested in the first version of an application. For example:

- Users will want more than one printer to be available.

- Users will want to have a print queue. Important documents should be moved to the top of a print queue; less urgent jobs should wait until the printer isn't busy.

- If we're going to have a print queue, it would be nice to be able to explicitly access the queue, both to see the entire queue, and to make queries about our job. It should also be possible to cancel a print request that is in the queue but hasn't already been sent to the printer.

- As we scale to more users, application responsiveness will become important. This is especially true on a LAN, as it is almost certainly faster to send a document than it is to print it. Hence, we should decouple printing a document from receiving it over the wire. In particular, the current implementation of `ServerNetworkWrapper`'s accept( ) method, shown here, will force the client applications to wait until an existing print job is finished before they can send a document:

```
public void accept( ) {
    while (true) {
        Socket clientSocket = null;
        try {
            clientSocket = _serverSocket.accept( );// blocking call
            processPrintRequest(clientSocket);
        }
    }
}
```

- Managers will want to track resource consumption. This will involve logging print requests and, quite possibly, building a set of queries that can be run against the printer's log.

None of these features are particularly hard to implement.[*] Consider, for example, the first item in the list: *Users will want more than one printer to be available.* Implementing this requires two things:

- A way for the client application to find out which printers are available and present a choice to the user.
- A way for the client application to tell the server how to route the document to a particular printer.

This leads, almost immediately, to the beginnings of an object-oriented decomposition. Namely, there are two different types of servers, a dispatcher and a printer:

- The dispatcher knows which printers are available and which are currently busy. Clients ask it questions before submitting print requests. There is only one dispatcher (at least, at first).
- The printer is an object that encapsulates the information about a specific printer. Namely, it accepts requests, handles queries about a specific print job, and manages the print queue. There can be many different instances of this type of server.

And when the client application sends a request to the server application, it needs to send the following information:

The server it is talking to
Whether to the dispatcher or to a printer. If to a printer, which printer?

The method it is calling
Unlike our implementation, which did only one thing, each of these server objects is capable of performing multiple tasks. Therefore, the client must specify which task it wants the server to perform.

---

[*] They do, however, involve understanding and correctly using threads. It's not particularly difficult code, but threading bugs can be subtle. Chapters 11 and 12 contain more information on threads.

The arguments for the method

Most methods require arguments. For example, canceling a print job requires telling the printer which print job is being cancelled.

What These Changes Entail

What we're seeing is a fundamental fact of life in distributed applications. As a socket-based distributed application grows more complex, the socket-level protocol it uses tends to evolve into something that looks more like the method-dispatch mechanism of an object-oriented programming language.

Moreover, as the application evolves, a significant percentage of the additional code deals with protocol changes: marshalling and demarshalling objects, specifying additional methods that can be invoked, and so on. This additional code has three bad properties: there's a lot of it, it's tedious to write, and it needs to be maintained.

Versioning issues can also arise. It can be inconvenient to reinstall the client application everywhere whenever a new feature is added. But since new features translate almost directly into protocol changes, this means that a robust application has to account for the possibility that the client and server were compiled at different times, from different versions of the code base and, therefore, use different protocols. This is usually handled by sending additional metadata specifying the protocol version along with every request.

CHAPTER 4

The Same Server, Written Using RMI

In this chapter, we continue our discussion by reimplementing the printer server using RMI as a distribution mechanism instead of sockets. As part of doing so, I will introduce the core infrastructure of RMI in a familiar setting. In fact, the application itself will look remarkably similar to the socket-based version. By the end of this chapter, you will have received a glimpse at how an RMI application is structured and the basic sequence of steps required to build one.

The Basic Structure of RMI

In the previous chapter, we covered the basics of implementing a socket-based distributed application. In doing so, we reinforced the lessons of the previous two chapters on streams and sockets. In addition, we discovered that the code necessary for writing a socket-based distributed application falls into five basic categories:

- Code that actually does something useful. This code is commonly referred to as *business logic*.[*] An example is an implementation of the Printer interface.

- User interface code for the client application.

- Code that deals with marshalling and demarshalling of data and the mechanics of invoking a method in another process. This is tedious code, but it is straightforward to write and is usually a significant percentage of the application.

- Code that launches and configures the application. We used a number of hardwired constants (in NetworkBaseClass) to enable the client to initially connect with the server. And we wrote two main( ) methods—one to launch the client and one to launch the server.

- Code whose sole purpose is to make a distributed application more robust and scalable. This usually involves one or more of the following: *client-side caching* (so the server does less work); increasing the number of available servers in a

---

[*] "Business logic" is actually a generic term that refers to the code that justifies the application's existence (e.g., the code that actually implements the desired functionality).

way that's as transparent as possible to the client; using *naming services* and *load balancing*; making it possible for a server to handle multiple requests simultaneously (*threading*); or automatically starting and shutting down servers, which allows the *server lifecycle* to conserve resources.

In any distributed application, programmers need to write the first and second types of code; if they did not need to write the business logic, the application wouldn't be necessary. Similarly, the user interface, which enables users to access the business logic, needs to be written for any application. And the fifth type, code that enables the application to scale, can be the most difficult and application-specific code to write.

The third and fourth types of code, however, are different. Most of this code can be automatically generated without much programmer thought or effort.[*] It may seem difficult to write marshalling code if you've never done so before. However, by the second time, it's easy. By the third time, most programmers are flat-out bored by the task.

We will see in this chapter that RMI either already contains—or will automatically generate—most of the code in the third and fourth categories. Indeed, this alone is a compelling reason to use RMI.[†]

Methods Across the Wire

Though convenient, automatically generating marshalling and demarshalling code is mostly a side effect produced in the service of a much more important goal. In a nutshell:

> RMI is designed to make communication between two Java programs, running in separate JVMs, as much like making a method call inside a single process as possible.

This is an ambitious goal. How does RMI achieve it?

Recall that in order to communicate with the printer server, we wrote an object, `ClientNetworkWrapper`, which did three things:

- It opened a socket.
- It told an instance of `DocumentDescription` to write itself to the stream.
- It read and interpreted information from the input stream associated with the socket.

In addition, we wrote a companion object, `ServerNetworkWrapper`, which played an analogous role on the server side.

---

[*] As a corollary, it ought to be generated automatically. Code that bores the programmer is code that is likely to contain errors.

[†] Or a similar object-distribution framework such as CORBA.

RMI relies on two similar types of objects that are automatically generated by the RMI Compiler from an implementation of the server: stubs and skeletons. A *stub* is a client-side object that represents a single server object inside the client's JVM. It implements the same methods as the server object, maintains a socket connection to the server object's JVM automatically and is responsible for marshalling and demarshalling data on the client side. A *skeleton* is a server-side object responsible for maintaining network connections and marshalling and demarshalling data on the server side.

 The word *stub* is actually used to mean two different things. Depending on context, it might refer to a stub class that is automatically generated from a server class object. Alternatively, it might refer to an instance of a particular stub class (that is, to a reference to a specific instance of the server class). Because stubs have such a well-defined role in a distributed architecture, the meaning is usually clear from context. Similarly, *skeleton* can either refer to the skeleton class or to an instance of the skeleton class.

The basic procedure a client uses to communicate with a server is as follows:

1. The client obtains an instance of the stub class. The stub class is automatically pregenerated from the target server class and implements all the methods that the server class implements.

2. The client calls a method on the stub. The method call is actually the same method call the client would make on the server object if both objects resided in the same JVM.

3. Internally, the stub either creates a socket connection to the skeleton on the server or reuses a pre-existing connection. It marshalls all the information associated to the method call, including the name of the method and the arguments, and sends this information over the socket connection to the skeleton.

4. The skeleton demarshalls the data and makes the method call on the actual server object. It gets a return value back from the actual server object, marshalls the return value, and sends it over the wire to the stub.

5. The stub demarshalls the return value and returns it to the client code.

Stubs and skeletons are shown in Figure 4-1.

If this approach seems familiar, it's because the stub and the skeleton are really automatically generated, object-oriented versions of the objects we created for our socket-based printer server.

Let's take a close look at this. Here is part of the stub generated for our NullPrinter class:

```
public final class NullPrinter_Stub extends java.rmi.server.RemoteStub implements
    com.ora.rmibook.chapter4..Printer, java.rmi.Remote {
```

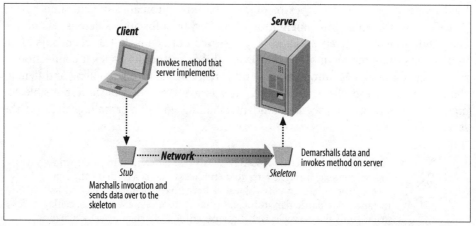

Figure 4-1. A basic RMI call with a stub and skeleton

---

rmic: The RMI Compiler

Stubs and skeletons are generated from server class files by a command-line application called rmic. This application ships with Sun's version of the Java Development Kit (JDK). The simplest invocation of rmic uses the following format:

```
rmic [full class name including packages]
```

For example:

```
rmic com.ora.rmibook.chapter4.printers.NullPrinter
```

Assuming the class is on your classpath, this will generate two additional class files in the same directory as the original class file. The names of the generated classes will be the original class name, appended with _Skel and _Stub. Thus, our example will generate the following two classes:

```
com.ora.rmibook.chapter4.NullPrinter_Skel
com.ora.rmibook.chapter4.NullPrinter_Stub
```

The most commonly used flag with rmic is -keep, it automatically generates the Java source code used for the stub and skeleton classes, which we'll see later.

```
    ...
    // methods from remote interfaces

    // implementation of printDocument(DocumentDescription)
    public boolean printDocument(com.ora.rmibook.chapter4.DocumentDescription $param
        DocumentDescription_1) throws om.ora.rmibook.chapter4.PrinterException,
        java.rmi.RemoteException {
        try {
            ...
            java.rmi.server.RemoteCall call = ref.newCall((java.rmi.server.
                RemoteObject) this, operations, 0, interfaceHash);
            try {
```

```
            java.io.ObjectOutput out = call.getOutputStream( );
            out.writeObject($param_DocumentDescription_1);
    }
    catch (java.io.IOException e) {
        throw new java.rmi.MarshalException("error marshalling
            arguments", e);
    }
    ref.invoke(call);
    boolean $result;
    try {
        'java.io.ObjectInput in = call.getInputStream( );
        result = in.readBoolean( );
    }
     catch (java.io.IOException e) {
        throw new java.rmi.UnmarshalException("error unmarshalling
            return", e);
    }
    finally {
        ref.done(call);
    }
    return $result;
```

While this may seem a bit more complex than the code we wrote for the socket-based printer server (and the fact that we're showing only part of the code indicates that stubs are actually quite a bit more complicated than the ClientNetworkWrapper class might have led us to expect), the fact remains: the stub implements the Printer interface, and the implementation of each method in the Printer interface simply pushes data onto a stream, and then reads data from a stream.

Strictly speaking, skeletons aren't really necessary. They can be replaced by a more generic framework that uses Java's reflection API to invoke methods on the server side. We'll cover this in more detail in Chapter 8. In this book, however, our code uses skeletons.

Passing by Value Versus Passing by Reference

In the first section of this chapter, we stated that RMI automatically generates most of the marshalling and demarshalling code required to build a distributed application. It's easy to see how RMI could automatically do this for primitive argument types. After all, an int is simply four consecutive bytes. Automatically marshalling and demarshalling objects, on the other hand, is a more difficult task. And, in order to do so correctly, RMI requires us to distinguish between two main types of objects: those that implement the Remote marker interface and those that implement the Serializable marker interface.

A *marker interface* doesn't define any methods; it simply provides information (available by reflection) about other code. In this case, RMI checks to see whether a given object implements either Remote or Serializable and behaves differently in either case.

Remote objects are servers. That is, they have a fixed location and run in a specific JVM on a particular computer somewhere in the network; they are the objects that receive remote method invocations. In RMI, remote objects are passed by reference. That way, if two instances of some remote object type exist, they are logically distinct. For example, in the current application, each Printer is a remote object, and any two instances of Printer are not equal.

Serializable objects, on the other hand, are objects whose location is not important to their notion of identity. That is, while they do have a location, the location is not particularly relevant to their state. Instead, serializable objects encapsulate data and are mobile—they can be passed from one JVM to another. Hence, serializable objects are very much like the primitive datatypes, such as float and int, which are also always passed by value.

Note that if an argument is a remote object (e.g., a server), the skeleton doesn't send a serialized copy of the server. Instead, it creates a stub that serves as a reference to that object and sends a serialized copy of the stub over the wire. What about arguments that are neither serializable nor remote? Well, if it's a primitive datatype, it is passed by value as well. But if it's an object and is neither serializable nor remote, an exception is thrown.

The Architecture Diagram Revisited

While the printer application is simple enough so that the RMI-based application is similar to the socket-based application, RMI does add one more conceptual wrinkle. Recall that in the socket-based version, we used a set of constants to help the client find the server:

```
public abstract class NetworkBaseClass {
    public static final String DEFAULT_SERVER_NAME = "localhost";
    public static final int DEFAULT_SERVER_PORT = 2100;
    public static final int DEFAULT_SERVER_BACKLOG = 10;
    ....
}
```

That's a bad design strategy. If the server is moved to another computer, or if you want to use the same client to talk to multiple servers, you need to deploy a new version of the client application.

A much better strategy is to have a centralized *naming service*. A naming service is an application that runs on a central server and functions like a phone book. In order for a client to connect to a server, it must do two things:

1. It must connect to the naming service and find out where the server is running.

2. It must then connect to the server.

At first glance, a naming service appears to suffer from the same design flaw as NetworkBaseClass. Instead of hardwiring the location of the server into our client code, we're hardwiring the location of the naming service. There are, however, a

Serialization

Serialization is a general purpose mechanism for taking an object and encoding it as a stream of bytes. The underlying design rationale is fairly simple.

The Java Language Specification defines encodings for primitive types such as integer or float. If an object's instance variables are all primitive types, then by adopting a few conventions (such as, "The first thing encoded will be the a string containing the name of the class"), we can automatically define a way to encode an object. We call such objects *easily serialized* objects. If an object's instance variables point to either primitive types or to easily serialized objects, then it is easy to see how to automatically generate an encoding for this object as well. The general idea is this: if a class definition has references only to primitive types or to classes that are themselves serializable, then the class is, itself, serializable. We call such classes *obviously serializable*.

If a class isn't obviously serializable, and it needs to be passed by value anyway, then the programmer needs to write code that defines how to serialize the class. For example, if the generic framework can't figure out how to marshall and demarshall the object, the programmer needs to provide code that does so.

And that's all that serialization is: a flexible implementation of the code that "automatically encodes" serializable objects so they can be passed by value over the wire. I'll cover the exact details of the serialization algorithm (and their consequences for the design of an RMI application) in much greater detail in Chapter 10. For now, three simple rules will suffice:

- Classes that are intended to be serialized must declare that they implement the Serializable marker interface. This declaration can either be direct or inherited (e.g., our implementation of PrinterException implements Serializable because Exception is defined to implement Serializable).

- Any nonserializable superclass of a serializable class must have a zero-argument constructor. They can have other constructors, but the zero-argument constructor is the one that the serialization mechanism will use if it creates a copy of the object.

- Any class that is declared to be serialized must either be obviously serializable or must contain code that allows the serialization mechanism to proceed anyway. The most common way of accomplishing this second task is to declare some variables to be *transient* and then implement a pair of private methods, readObject() and writeObject(), which the serialization mechanism will call instead of using the automatic encoding for the object.

number of differences that combine to make this a more palatable solution. Among the most significant are:

- Naming services are fairly simple applications that place limited demands on a computer. This means that the server running a naming service doesn't need to be upgraded often.

- Naming services are stable applications with simple APIs. They are not updated or revised often.

- The application may actually have several servers. Rather than hardwiring all their locations into the client application, we need only one predetermined location.

The first two are especially important. Some common reasons for moving a server application to a new machine include scaling the application or providing for changes in application functionality. In the case of a naming service, however, the hardware will likely be sufficient to handle the load for quite a long period of time. Moreover, because the naming service is a simple and well-understood application that rarely changes, chances are that the implementation is a reliable piece of code. In other words, a computer running a naming service can often be set up and left alone.

In RMI, the default naming service that ships with Sun Microsystem's version of the JDK is called the RMI registry.* Messages are sent to the registry via static methods that are defined in the java.rmi.Naming class. Including the RMI registry in our printer application architecture leads to the diagram in Figure 4-2.

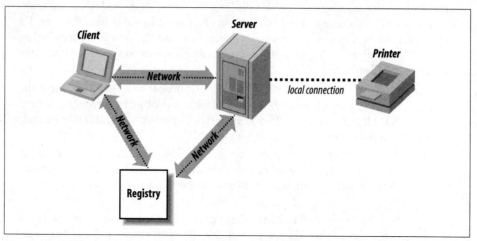

Figure 4-2. Adding an RMI registry to the architecture diagram

While we've introduced only one new server into our application, we've added two new types of messages to those that are flowing across the network:

The registry must be told about the printer server. This must happen before any other types of messages can be sent. Note that the printer server is a remote object, so what really gets passed to the registry is a stub (recall that stubs are serializable and can therefore be passed by value). This stub knows on which

---

* More often referred to as simply "the registry."

computer the printer server runs, and on which port the skeleton receives messages. Thus, the stub can relay method calls to the printer server's skeleton.

The client must communicate with the registry to find out how to connect with the printer server. The client must do this before the client can actually request that a document be printed. As a result of this, the client will obtain a copy of the stub that the server originally sent to the registry.

And, of course:

The client must send print requests to the printer server. All of the communication in the socket-based version of the printer server is of this type.

 In order to provide distributed garbage collection, RMI also sends other types of messages dealing with *renewing leases*. We will cover these messages (which are sent automatically and don't require any work by application developers) in Chapter 16.

A Note on Application Topology

As we mentioned earlier, the RMI registry is the naming service that comes with RMI. It's a small application with a minimal interface and some very curious restrictions. Among the most severe of those restrictions is this: launch code (the code that binds servers into the registry) has to be running on the same computer as the RMI registry.

This restriction was implemented for security reasons. If there are no restrictions on what can be bound into the registry, then it becomes very easy for malicious code to subvert a registry. For example, a malicious application could use this weakness to replace the real servers with counterfeit ones. However, this causes fairly significant difficulties—getting servers bound into the registry becomes somewhat convoluted.

In most cases, we'll want to replace the registry with a more flexible naming service (we'll talk about this in much greater detail in Chapters 14 and 15). Until we do so, however, I'll present these examples with little thought to these restrictions.

Implementing the Basic Objects

Now let's start implementing the RMI-based printer server. As in the socket-based version, we have three basic objects: the `Printer` interface, the `DocumentDescription` object, and the `PrinterException` object. Conceptually, these objects are the same as their counterparts in Chapter 3. However, as might be expected, using RMI will force us to change a few details.

The Printer Interface

There are two basic changes to the Printer interface: it now extends the Remote interface, and every method is defined to throw RemoteException, a subclass of Exception defined in the package java.rmi. This class is shown in Example 4-1.

Example 4-1. Printer.java

```
public interface Printer extends PrinterConstants, Remote {
    public boolean printerAvailable( ) throws RemoteException;
    public boolean printDocument(DocumentDescription document) throws RemoteException,
        PrinterException;
}
```

That Printer extends Remote shouldn't be a surprise—the whole point of the application is to turn a local printer into a server that can receive calls from clients' applications running on other computers.

The other change involves adding RemoteException to each method signature. RemoteException is an exception thrown by RMI to signal that something unforeseen has happened at the network level. That is, it's a way for the RMI infrastructure to tell a client application that "something went wrong in the RMI infrastructure." For example, if the server crashes while handling a client's request, RMI will automatically throw a RemoteException on the client side.

Adding RemoteException to every method has one important consequence. Recall that rmic is used to automatically generate a stub class for each implementation of Printer. This stub implements the Printer interface and, therefore, every method implemented by the stub is declared to throw RemoteException. However, because RemoteException is a checked exception, any client-side code trying to invoke a method on the server must do so inside a try/catch block and explicitly catch RemoteException.

Making RemoteException a checked exception is one of the most controversial design decisions in the entire RMI framework. On one hand, it forces programmers writing client-side code to think about how to gracefully handle network failures. On the other hand, it is often the case that the catch block for a RemoteException doesn't do anything interesting. Moroever, forcing programmers to catch RemoteException in their client code merely winds up making the code much harder to read and understand.

Notice that the printDocument( ) method is still defined as throwing PrinterException. If the implementation of Printer throws a PrinterException, the RMI skeleton will automatically marshall the PrinterException object and send it across the wire to the stub. The stub will demarshall the instance of PrinterException and throw it again. At this point, the exception will be caught by the catch( ) block. What's happening here is simple: since RMI, via the stub and skeleton, controls the communication between the client and server, it can also automatically propagate exceptions across the network and rethrow them on the client side. Contrast this to the socket-based version, where Printer returned a status argument that the client was free to ignore.

Implementing a Printer

In order to implement a printer, we need to do two things: write and compile the actual server code and generate the stub and skeleton using rmic. The code for NullPrinter itself is almost identical to the code used in the socket-based version. The only difference is that the NullPrinter class extends java.rmi.server. UnicastRemoteObject., as shown in Example 4-2.

Example 4-2. NullPrinter.java

```
public class NullPrinter extends UnicastRemoteObject implements Printer {
    private PrintWriter _log;
    public NullPrinter(OutputStream log) hrows RemoteException  {
        _log = new PrintWriter(log);
    }
```

UnicastRemoteObject is a convenient base class for RMI servers. It handles most of the tasks associated with creating a server. For example, the constructors of UnicastRemoteObject cause a server socket to be created automatically and start listening for client method invocations. Restating this slightly: when we instantiate NullPrinter, it immediately starts listening on a port for client requests. The RMI infrastucture handles all the details of opening a socket and listening for client requests.

After compiling the server, we need to generate stubs and skeletons. The stubs and skeleton classes are in the same package as the server class (in this case, com.ora. rmibook.chapter4.printers). In this case, we simply use:

```
rmic -keep -d d:\classes com.ora.rmibook.chapter4.printers.NullPrinter
```

Examining the skeleton

Just as we briefly examined the generated stub, it's also worth looking for a moment at the skeleton that's generated. The generated skeleton has one major method, named dispatch( ). dispatch( ) is the method that actually forwards requests to the server. Here's a snippet of code from the dispatch( ) method of our skeleton:

```
public void dispatch(java.rmi.Remote obj, java.rmi.server.RemoteCall call,
    int opnum, long hash) throws java.lang.Exception {
  ... // validation and error-checking code omitted
  com.ora.rmibook.chapter4.printers.NullPrinter server =
      (com.ora.rmibook.chapter4.printers.NullPrinter) obj;
  switch (opnum)  {
      case 0: // printDocument(DocumentDescription) {
          com.ora.rmibook.chapter4.DocumentDescription
              $param_DocumentDescription_1;
        try  {
            java.io.ObjectInput in = call.getInputStream( );
            $param_DocumentDescription_1 =
                (com.ora.rmibook.chapter4.DocumentDescription)
                    in.readObject( );
        }
        catch (java.io.IOException e)  {
            throw new java.rmi.UnmarshalException(
                "error unmarshalling arguments", e);
        }
        catch (java.lang.ClassNotFoundException e)  {
            throw new java.rmi.UnmarshalException(
                "error unmarshalling arguments", e);
        }
        finally  {
            call.releaseInputStream( );
        }
        boolean $result = server.printDocument($param_DocumentDescription_1);
        try  {
            java.io.ObjectOutput out = call.getResultStream(true);
            out.writeBoolean($result);
        }
        catch (java.io.IOException e)  {
            throw new java.rmi.MarshalException(
                "error marshalling return", e);
        }
         break;
      }
  }
}
```

Let's look at the arguments of this method first. The method takes an instance of Remote, a RemoteCall, an int, and a long. These arguments have the following meanings:

- The instance of Remote is actually an instance of NullPrinter.
- RemoteCall is an object that encapsulates a socket connection. The instance of RemoteCall being passed is a connection to a particular client.

- The integer is mapped to a particular method on the server. That is, when rmic compiles the stub and the skeleton, it numbers all the methods. Afterwards, instead of passing the method name, it passes the associated integer. This saves bandwidth and also makes the skeleton more efficient by allowing it to perform method dispatch based on integer comparisons, rather than using string comparisons.
- The long is an integrity check. Each method defined in NullPrinter has a unique long associated with it. This long is a hash of the method name and all the arguments. Sending this hash, along with the method number, helps to prevent versioning problems.

So what does this method do? It essentially contains marshalling and demarshalling code, similar to the code written by hand for the socket-based version of the printer server.

The Data Objects

We still have two further objects to implement: DocumentDescription and PrinterException. Let's start with PrinterException. Example 4-3 shows the source code for PrinterException.

Example 4-3. PrinterException.java

```java
public class PrinterException extends Exception {
    private int _numberOfPagesPrinted;
    private String _humanReadableErrorDescription;

    public PrinterException() {
        // zero arg constructor needed for serialization
    }

    public PrinterException(int numberOfPagesPrinted, String
        humanReadableErrorDescription) {
        _numberOfPagesPrinted = numberOfPagesPrinted;
        _humanReadableErrorDescription = humanReadableErrorDescription;
    }

    public int getNumberOfPagesPrinted() {
        return _numberOfPagesPrinted;
    }

    public String getHumanReadableErrorDescription() {
        return _humanReadableErrorDescription;
    }
}
```

This is exactly what a generic exception* should be; it has enough state for the catch block to print out or display a meaningful error message. You can easily imagine a client popping up a dialog box to tell the user what went wrong, as in the following code snippet:

```
catch (PrinterException printerException) {
    String errorMessage =  "Print failed after " + printerException
        getNumberOfPagesPrinted( ) + " pages.";
    JOptionPane.showMessageDialog(SimpleClientFrame.this, errorMessage,
        "Error in printing" , JOptionPane.INFORMATION_MESSAGE);
    _messageBox.setText("Exception attempting to print " + (_fileChooser
        getSelectedFile( )).getAbsolutePath( ) + "\n\t Error was: " +
        printerException getHumanReadableErrorDescription( ));
}
```

Even more impressively, `PrinterException` has no "extra" networking code. For example, it does not contain any code that either reads or writes from a stream. This is possible because RMI automatically uses serialization to send objects over the wire.

DocumentDescription

The other object we pass by value is an instance of `DocumentDescription`. However, we have a problem here: `DocumentDescription` stores the document as an instance of `InputStream`, and `InputStream` doesn't implement the `Serializable` interface. This means that the generic serialization mechanism won't work with `DocumentDescription`. We're going to have to write custom marshalling and demarshalling code ourselves. The code is shown in Example 4-4.

Example 4-4. DocumentDescription.java

```
public class DocumentDescription implements Serializable, PrinterConstants {
    private transient InputStream _actualDocument;
    private int _length;
    private int _documentType;
    private boolean _printTwoSided;
    private int _printQuality;

    public DocumentDescription( ) {
    // zero arg constructor needed for serialization
    }
....
    private void writeObject(java.io.ObjectOutputStream out) throws IOException {
        out.defaultWriteObject( );
        copy(_actualDocument, out);
    }
}
```

---

* This is a generic exception because it covers wide range of devices. Since it's impossible to define all the different types of exceptions a printer can generate (and create subclasses of `PrinterException` for each one), we simply rely on the user to interpret the exception. `java.sql.SQLException` follows a similar design strategy.

Example 4-4. DocumentDescription.java (continued)

```
    private void readObject(java.io.ObjectInputStream in) throws IOException,
        ClassNotFoundException {
        in.defaultReadObject();
        ByteArrayOutputStream temporaryBuffer = new ByteArrayOutputStream();
        copy(in, temporaryBuffer, _length);
        _actualDocument = new DataInputStream(new ByteArrayInputStream(temporaryBuffer
            toByteArray()));
    }
```

We start by declaring _actualDocument to be transient. transient is a Java keyword that tells the serialization mechanism not to serialize the variable's value out. We then implement writeObject(), which does two things:

- Calls out.defaultWriteObject(). This invokes the generic serialization mechanism (which is the default) to write out all nontransient objects. That is, when out.defaultWriteObject() is called, everything but _actualDocument has been encoded in the stream.

- Copies _actualDocument to the stream, exactly as we did for the socket-based version of the program.

Similarly, in readObject(), we first call defaultReadObject(), which retrieves all the nontransient values, including _length, from the stream. We then read _actualDocument from the stream.

> Why doesn't InputStream implement the Serializable interface? The answer is that InputStream is an abstract base class whose concrete subclasses often have machine-specific state. For example, FileInputStream explicitly refers to a file on a hard drive and probably has a file descriptor as part of its state. Making objects such as FileInputStream serializable makes very little sense, since you can't guarantee that either the file or the file descriptor will be available (or meaningful) when the information is deserialized. Similarly, classes such as Frame or Thread, which encapsulate operating-system resources, are not serializable.

The Rest of the Server

To finish building our server, we need to write launch code. Launch code is code that is application-specific, but not business-domain specific, and handles the details of registering a server with a naming service such as the RMI registry. In our case, this boils down to two pieces of code: a Java program that runs PrinterServer and a batch file that starts the RMI registry and then runs our program. The former is shown in Example 4-5.

Example 4-5. SimpleServer.java

```
public class SimpleServer implements NetworkConstants {
    public static void main(String args[]) {
```

Example 4-5. SimpleServer.java (continued)

```
    try {
        File logfile = new File("C:\\temp\\serverLogfile");
        OutputStream outputStream = new FileOutputStream(logfile);
        Printer printer = new NullPrinter(outputStream);
        Naming.rebind(DEFAULT_PRINTER_NAME, printer);
    }
    catch (Exception e) {
        e.printStackTrace();
    }
    }
}
```

This creates an instance of `NullPrinter` and then binds it into the registry under the name `DEFAULT_PRINTER_NAME`. The only surprising detail is this: if everything is successful, our program will exit `main()`. Don't worry; this is normal. The fact that the RMI registry has a reference (e.g., a stub) for the server keeps the application alive even though we've exited. I'll explain why, and how this works, in Chapter 16.

 Note that we used `rebind()` instead of `bind()` in our launch code. The reason is that `bind()` fails if the name we're binding the server to is already in use. `rebind()`, on the other hand, is guaranteed to succeed. If another server is bound into the registry using the name we want to use, that server will be unbound from the name. In reality, `bind()` is rarely used in launch code, but is often used in code that attempts to repair or update a registry.

The format of names that are bound into the registry is fairly simple: they follow the pattern *//host-name:port-number/human-readable-name*. *host-name* and *port-number* are used to find the registry.

The batch file, *rmiprinterserver.bat*, consists of the following two commands:

```
start rmiregistry
start java com.ora.rmibook.chapter4.rmiprinter.applications.SimpleServer
```

start is a Windows command that executes the rest of the line in a separate process. It is equivalent to putting an ampersand (&) after a command in a Unix shell. Thus, invoking *rmiprinterserver.bat* from the DOS shell launches the RMI registry in another process, launches `SimpleServer` in a third process, and then returns to the command prompt to wait for further instructions.

The Client Application

Once the changes to the data objects have been made and the skeletons and stubs have been generated from the server, the networking part of the client application is a remarkably straightforward piece of code. Recall that our client application had the GUI shown in Figure 4-3.

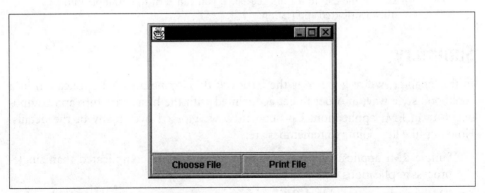

Figure 4-3. Printer/client application GUI

The only part of this that's changed is the `ActionListener` attached to the Print File button. And it's much simpler:

```java
private class PrintFile implements ActionListener {
    public void actionPerformed(ActionEvent event) {
        try {
            FileInputStream documentStream = new FileInputStream(_fileChooser
                getSelectedFile());
            DocumentDescription documentDescription = new
            DocumentDescription(documentStream);

/*

            New network code follows

*/
```

```
                Printer printer = (Printer) Naming.lookup(DEFAULT_PRINTER_NAME);
                printer.printDocument(documentDescription);
            }
        catch (PrinterException printerException){
            ....
            }
        }
        ...
    }
```

All this does is use a predetermined name, which must be the same name as the server used to bind, to locate an object inside the RMI registry. It then casts the object to the correct type (the RMI registry interface, like many Java interfaces, returns instances of Object) and invokes the printDocument( ) method on the server. And that's it! We've finished reimplementing the socket-based printer server as an RMI application.

 In this code example, as in many of the examples in this book, the client and server must be located on the same machine. This is because the call to Naming.lookup( ) simply used DEFAULT_PRINTER_NAME (with no hostname or port number specified). By changing the arguments used in the call to Naming.lookup( ), you can turn the example into a truly distributed application.

Summary

In this chapter, we've gone over the basics of developing an RMI application in a cookbook-style way, in order to get acquainted with the basic structure and components of an RMI application. Consequently, we glossed over many of the details. However, the key points to remember are:

- Simple RMI applications are, in fact, not much more complicated than single-process applications.

- RMI includes reasonable default solutions for the common problems in building distributed applications (serialization handles marshalling and demarshalling, the registry helps clients find servers, and so on).

- Even when problems arise (e.g., DocumentDescription), the code is remarkably similar to, and simpler than, the analogous socket code.

- The conceptual cost to using RMI isn't all that high. In most cases, using RMI amounts to adding an extra layer of indirection to your code.

- The application evolution problems mentioned in Chapter 3 aren't nearly so forbidding when using RMI. The default mechanisms, and the automatically generated stubs and skeletons, handle many application evolution problems nicely.

CHAPTER 5

Introducing the Bank Example

Now that we've seen two versions of the same application, one written using sockets and one written using RMI, it's time to take a step back and look at the whole process of designing a distributed application. In order to do this, this chapter and the following five chapters all concentrate on a single shared example: a distributed banking system. In this chapter, we'll get things underway by talking about the system requirements of a distributed banking system, sketching a rough architecture for the application and discussing the problems that arise in networked applications. By the end of this chapter, you'll have a better idea of the design decisions and choices that must be made to build a distributed system, as well as how to begin.

The Bank Example

> When traveling, take advantage of more than 13,000 Bank of America ATMs coast to coast. We're in 30 states and the District of Columbia. As a Bank of America Check Card or ATM cardholder, there's no ATM fee when you use an ATM displaying a Bank of America sign...
>
> —Bank of America Advertisement

A simple banking application implementing an automatic teller machine is, in many ways, the ideal first application for someone learning to design and build distributed programs. Why? The most obvious benefit is that the application is easy to understand; most readers of this book know exactly what an ATM is supposed to do. Moreover, there isn't a great deal of "business logic" involved, and the business logic that does exist is straightforward. Finally, there's very little GUI interface code to deal with. This means that most of our discussion deals with the distributed parts of the application, rather than the details of exactly how to process a transaction or which buttons need to be disabled when.

Another important fact is that a banking application is inherently a distributed application with a centralized server (or cluster of servers). In other words, it adheres to a traditional model of a client-server application, in which the two roles are strongly differentiated:

Server

> The server is centralized on a small set of carefully maintained machines that few people can access. It is long-running and has important data, which it is responsible for maintaining over the course of the application's lifetime. All the business logic runs inside the server.

Client

> The client is a relatively short-lived program. Any persistent state the client stores, other than user-interface configuration information, should be stored in the server. The client's role in the application is to provide the user with a way to interact with the server. The client application makes very few demands on the client machine and can be run on a wide range of computers.

Moreover, a banking application involves two very important aspects of distributed programming: security and scalability. *Security* involves two different things: authenticating users (such as when an ATM user enters his or her PIN) and guarding sensitive data. When information is sent across a computer network, there is the possibility of a third party eavesdropping to discover sensitive information. This is especially true over the Internet and is an important reason for the widespread adoption of encryption standards such as the Secure Sockets Layer (SSL).

Scalability allows the server to handle many clients at the same time. The bank application has a centralized server that not only stores the bank account information in a very small number of places, but is responsible for authenticating clients. This means that all 13,000 of the Bank of America ATMs mentioned at the beginning of this section are probably being served by a very small number of machines, which have to handle a lot of simultaneous clients.

Sketching a Rough Architecture

The first thing to do when building a distributed application is sketch a rough architecture. The key words here are *sketch* and *rough*. We're talking about a preliminary design at the level of the architectural diagrams used in the previous chapters. And even though doing this can be difficult, there are several facts that help you out:

- There are really only four or five different distributed application architectures. Most distributed applications look fairly similar to each other.

- You're using Java and RMI. This narrows down some design choices for you and helps you make design decisions.

- You don't actually have to get it right. Rough architectures are not cast in stone; they help you focus and narrow the rest of the design, turning vast and open-ended questions into things that are easier to think about. In particular, they let you place pieces of functionality at various points on the network, and help you design the remote interfaces. This effectively turns the task of designing a distributed application into the task of designing single-process components.

Five Steps to a Sketch

Once you've sketched a rough architecture a few times, the process becomes ingrained. However, the following sequence of steps can be helpful the first few times:

1. Figure out what you're going to build. This might sound obvious, but it's important. You need some set of requirements for the application, not just what it does for any given single user, but also information about how many users it supports, how many users it needs to support concurrently, and requires what sort of networking environment. Most of the time, this information will be imprecise. That's perfectly fine. Estimates are fine; flying blind is dangerous.

2. Find a basic use case that will motivate the rough architecture. This amounts to narrowing down the information in step 1. A set of requirements usually lists all the things that the application must do. Your task in this step is to imagine a typical user and figure out what she does with the application—a use case. This approach helps prioritize the requirements and provides an incremental path for design and development. Your goal will be to design an application that supports the basic use case and adapt that application to support other use cases and requirements.

3. Figure out what you can safely ignore for now. A typical rough sketch ignores scalability and security. Both of these are important, and both have the potential to be enormous headaches, but both are also issues that can usually be dealt with later in the development process. At the start, it's usually safe to assume that there are only a few clients and that they operate inside a trusted environment.

4. Figure out what design decisions are imposed on the application by the deployment environment. Distributed applications are rarely off-the-shelf, shrink-wrapped applications purchased as a commodity item; they're designed for a specific environment. As such, there's little point in designing them without taking the client's environment into account. There are usually four main issues involved: using a pre-existing persistent store (e.g., a relational database), interoperating with a legacy application or applications, network speed, and security.

5. Narrow down the servers to a few canonical choices. Once you've gone through steps 1 through 4 and isolated the basic use case, you'll notice that you're already talking in terms of specific servers. This step involves taking those servers and thinking about what their exact role in the system is.

And that's it. If you follow these five steps, you'll be able to produce a rough sketch of the architecture. To help make this concrete, the next section will do this for the bank example.

The Basic Use Case

We've already discussed the bank example a little bit and understand what it is that the application is supposed to do (step 1). The next step is to create a basic use case. In subsequent sections, we will assume that the following sequence of actions is typical for an ATM user:

1. The user walks up to the ATM and inserts an identification card.

2. The user enters a password.

3. If the password is correct, the user is given permission to perform transactions. This permission lasts until the identitication card is removed.

4. The user is given a menu of choices. The typical choices are: display an account balance, withdraw money, or deposit money. That is, the first menu consists of a generic list of actions that are valid with any account.

5. After choosing an action, the user is given a list of valid accounts from which to choose (e.g., "Checking" or "Savings"). The user chooses an account and then the transaction proceeds.

6. After performing between one and five transactions, the user leaves, taking his or her identitification card.

Additional Design Decisions

The third and fourth steps in sketching out an architecture involve figuring out which design decisions can be safely postponed and which restrictions the deployment environment will place upon our application. Since this is an RMI book, however, we'll make the following assumption:

> There will be a server, or servers, written in Java and registered with a naming service. The client, also written in Java, will connect to the naming service, retrieve a stub for the server, and use the stub to communicate with the server.

Design Postponements

As mentioned previously, we will postpone consideration of two key issues: security and scalability.

Security

Writing a security layer is difficult for two reasons. The first is that doing so often requires a good understanding of some rather complicated mathematics. The second is that it's pretty hard to test. Consider, for example, the functionality involved in depositing money to a bank account. It's easy to imagine a sequence of automated tests that will give you confidence that the code is correct. It's much harder to imagine a series of tests that will ensure that no one can intercept and decode privileged information or that the passwords used for authentication are secure. For these reasons, most applications that need security wind up using a thoroughly tested library or package that provides it.

For the bank example, we need to do two things: authenticate the user via password mechanism (i.e., make sure the user has the authority to perform operations on a given account) and guarantee that the information sent between the client and the server is secure from eavesdropping. Since this second task is easily accomplished via SSL—and doesn't impact our design at all—postponing security issues amounts to assuming that the user authentication task is easily solved and doesn't significantly impact the rest of the design.

 RMI allows you, via the definition custom socket factories, to use any type of socket as the basic network communication layer. By default, RMI uses the socket classes found in the java.net package. The relationship between SSL and RMI is discussed in Chapter 18.

Scalability

Our basic use case implies two very nice properties of our application. The first is that there isn't a great deal of state associated with a client. The second is that there isn't a lot of interaction between distinct clients.

The first property implies that state management is fairly simple. When a client executes the basic use case, the server needs to authenticate the client and get the client's bank account data from a persistent storage mechanism. It's plausible for us to assume that authentication is a once-per-client-session cost, and that the associated bank account information is not a large amount of information nor hard to retrieve from the server.

The second property amounts to the following two assumptions:

- Two clients don't usually access the same bank account at the same time.

- Requests that one client makes (e.g., a deposit or withdrawal) won't affect other clients.

 Note the presence of the word "usually"—we will, in later chapters, insert safeguards to guarantee data integrity in the case that multiple clients attempt to access the same account at the same time. Those safeguards won't affect our scalability assumptions, however.

We can restate these assumptions in a more general form:

- Two clients don't usually access the same changeable information at the same time.

- The changeable information is relatively isolated. Changes one client makes rarely affect other clients and do so in a known way.

These generalized assumptions, and the assumption that the state associated to a client is small, imply that once the single-client application is written, it will be fairly easy to make the application scale. Hence, we can safely postpone worrying about scalability until we understand the single-client scenario. This is because of the following three implications:

- The changeable information, which is small and well-defined, can be cached in server memory.

- Processing can be isolated. Therefore, you can use multiple servers on multiple machines without worrying about server communication.

- Because clients rarely access the same information simultaneously, caching the changeable information is still a valid strategy even with multiple servers.

These generalized assumptions hold for a surprisingly large number of applications (the *what-I-put-in-my-shopping-cart-doesn't-affect-your-shopping-cart-at-all* principle). And often, the key to making an application scale is figuring out how the generalized assumptions fail and limiting the resulting problems. For example, both of the generalized assumptions fail in a scheduling application. That is:

- People trying to schedule meetings often access the same information simultaneously, such as the schedules of other people and the list of available rooms and locations.
- A scheduling decision made by one user can definitely affect the other users.

The trick is to realize that you still have some sort of isolation going on. There are actually two types of isolation in the scheduling scenario: the people who need to be at a meeting and the geographic location of the meeting. If I need to meet with Bob and Sandy in Colorado, and you need to meet with Alex and Pat in Oregon, then our requests are completely independent, and that fact should be reflected in the code.

 A little confused? It's okay. Read this section again later. The key thing to remember is that if you can isolate the clients from each other, or control how the clients affect each other, then the application can be made to scale without too many problems.

Implications of the Environment

In a banking environment, one further design decision has already been made. Most banking applications, and indeed most applications that have a real need for reliable, long-term, centralized storage of information, use some sort of database to store and retrieve data.

Thus, we will also assume that our server (or servers) will rely on some sort of third-party persistence mechanism to provide long-term storage and retrieval of information. We won't need to implement this functionality, or make any decisions about how it is implemented. Our sole responsibility will be to build a communications layer between our application and the already existing database.

A Distributed Architecture for the Bank Example

The assumptions we just made are very plausible and apply to a wide variety of situations. But when we combine these assumptions with what we learned from the printer example, we have enough information to sketch out our architecture.

Even without having more information about the bank's computing environment and systems, and without having much of a requirements document beyond our single use case, we can still get a good feel for the architecture of our banking application. A simple architectural diagram might look something like what's shown in Figure 5-1.

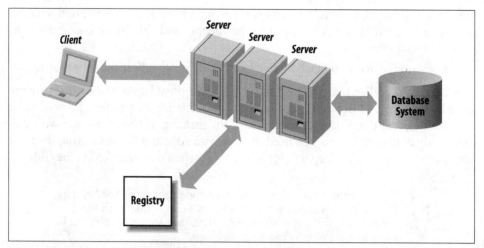

Figure 5-1. Simple architecture diagram for the bank example

Here, each component's task is described:

Client
> Responsible for managing interaction with a user, usually via a GUI. It obtains a stub to a server from the registry and then invokes methods on the server.

Stub (not pictured)
> Implicitly, and without client knowledge, handles details of SSL connection.

Registry
> Maintains a mapping of human-readable names to server stubs and responds to queries by returning serialized copies of stubs.

Skeleton and launch code (also not pictured)
> We'll discuss these in detail later.

Servers
> Handle what is usually called "business logic." That is, they respond to client requests, manipulate data, and occasionally store that data out to a database. In particular, servers respond to requests from a client and make requests of the database.

Database system
> Responsible for long-term persistence and integrity of important data. This already exists; our main task with respect to it will be figuring out how to manage the communication between our servers and it.

Given this, the main architectural questions that need to be resolved are: how many servers are there and what are they? There are two obvious choices: a single instance of Bank or many instances of Account.

In the first case, there is a single server whose interface contains methods such as the following:

```
public Money getBalance(Account account) throws RemoteException;
public void makeDeposit(Account account, Money amount) throws RemoteException,
    NegativeAmountException;
public void makeWithdrawal(Account account, Money amount) throws RemoteException,
    OverdraftException, NegativeAmountException;
```

Note that each method is passed an account description parameter (presumably, though not necessarily, as a value object). This immediately suggests the second alternative: make each account a separate server. The corresponding methods look similar; they simply have one fewer argument:

```
public Money getBalance() throws RemoteException;
public void makeDeposit( Money amount) throws RemoteException,
    NegativeAmountException;
public void makeWithdrawal( Money amount) throws RemoteException,
    OverdraftException, NegativeAmountException;
```

In this scenario, there are many instances of a class that implements Account. These instances, however, are not running in distinct JVMs. Instead, many small server objects are all residing inside a few JVMs. Hence, they are implicitly either sharing, or contending, for resources.

In later chapters, I refer to these two options as *the bank option* and *the accounts option*, respectively.

Problems That Arise in Distributed Applications

Now that we've got a preliminary description of how the application will be structured, a question arises: what is the role of the network in all of this? Or stated more precisely, this important question is:

> What problems does making the application distributed cause?

The answer is that there are two main new problems associated to building a distributed application: the possibility of partial failures and the latency of the network. Let's look at both in more detail.

Partial Failures

A partial failure occurs when one of the programs becomes inaccessible to the other programs that are running. This can happen because the program has crashed or because the network is experiencing problems. In either case, the possibility of partial failure can cause problems for the application designer.

Consider, for example, our typical use case. Step 5 stated:

> After choosing an action, the user is given a list of valid accounts from which to choose (e.g., "Checking" or "Savings"). The user chooses an account and then the transaction proceeds.

This translates, in the account option, into:

> The client program gets a stub for the appropriate account object from a server somewhere. It then proceeds to make method calls on the account server until the transaction is completed.

And the stub, as with RMI applications, plays a role very similar to that of an object reference. That is, it exposes methods that the client application calls.

And this is where partial failure is particularly insidious and unexpected. Suppose the server crashes, or becomes otherwise unavailable, in the middle of a transaction. How does an application gracefully recover? The client application cannot know what the server did before becoming inaccessible, and the server (when it becomes accessible again) doesn't know if it received all the messages that the client sent.

In a single-process program, the analogous scenario is this:

> An object gets a reference to another object and calls a method on it. But, even though the reference is valid, the object referred to isn't there, and an exception is thrown.

This is a very strange thing. It can happen in languages such as C++, where programmers are explicitly responsible for memory management. But this should never happen in a garbage-collected language.

 I said this *should* never happen. In point of fact, you can run into situations where you have a reference to an object that doesn't exist because of the way threads are defined in the Java Language Specification. We'll discuss this in more detail in Chapter 11.

Network Latency

The other major problem I mentioned is network latency. Put succinctly, invoking a method or transferring data over a network is slow. People designing distributed systems usually estimate that the overhead of a distributed method call on a fast local area network is on the order of a few milliseconds. However, on a congested LAN, or when calls have to go across the Internet, method calls can be much slower. And if data needs to be sent or returned, the remote call takes even longer.

Remote method calls have two main effects: sending data over the wire slows an application down and doing so slows down other distributed applications due to increased network congestion.

This last point is very important. Designers of distributed applications can't assume that their program is the only one on the network. During peak business hours, lots of data will be flowing across the network. This means that 1) there is less bandwidth available to any given application, and 2) using lots of bandwidth impacts the performance of all the distributed programs on the network, not just the one using lots of bandwidth.

To demonstrate this, try the following experiment:

1. Clear your web browser's cache and go to a static web site with a lot of images.
2. Click your browser's Reload button.

The difference in speed between the first and second viewings of the web page is mostly due to the difference between having the images cached on your local hard drive versus downloading them across the network. (You still may have to download the text in the page. But most of the images should be cached by your web browser.) In other words, the difference is mostly due to network latency.

Clearly, if communicating between two programs across a network is expensive, then a well-designed application needs to somehow account for this, minimizing the number of calls made across the network, the amount of data sent across the network, and the time the user has to wait because of network latency.

Minimizing the number of calls, the amount of data sent, and the time the user must wait because of network latency are actually three different, and sometimes conflicting, goals. For example, using compression may reduce the amount of data sent over the network but may result in the user waiting longer (because of the time it takes to uncompress the data).

CHAPTER 6

Deciding on the Remote Server

In Chapter 5, we briefly discussed the architecture of the bank example. In addition, we discussed the fundamental problems that arise when building distributed applications. In this chapter, I build on that discussion by introducing a set of basic evaluation criteria that will help you refine designs and choose between various design options.

A Little Bit of Bias

> Good code invariably has small methods and small objects...no one thing I do to systems provides as much help as breaking it into more pieces
>
> —Kent Beck, Smalltalk Best Practice Patterns

The experienced distributed systems programmer will notice a certain bias in this chapter[*] towards what I call *small-scale, semi-independent servers*. The "small-scale" part of this is easy to explain. By and large, I build servers with very limited functionality (as little as is reasonable, given the restrictions imposed by the fact that we're building a distributed system). Then, I tend to give them large interfaces, exposing the same functionality in multiple ways.

As far as I know, there's no knockdown argument in favor of this style of designing and building programs. Many programmers who have built object-oriented systems tend to agree with Kent Beck.[†] In my experience, his quote almost holds for distributed systems as well—building small servers leads to flexible designs that evolve gracefully over time. However, there is a slight difference, due to network latency, for distributed systems. In a single-process system, it costs almost nothing to make five method calls to an object. If you need to get five related pieces of information, it's perfectly fine to make five method calls (in fact, it's better for code simplicity and maintenance not to have redundant methods). In distributed systems, you need to

---

[*] To be honest, the bias permeates the rest of the book, too. If I didn't have opinions, I wouldn't be an author.

[†] And his implied style of programming.

consider how often those five method calls are made and the impact of network latency on application performance. We'll return to this discussion in Chapter 7 when we talk about interface design.

"Semi-independent" is a harder idea to explain. The point is this: if your distributed design requires several instances of a specific server class running in parallel, the instances should be able to run on separate machines (or at least in separate JVMs) without significantly impacting performance. In other words, these instances should be able to run independently. If instances of a server class need to frequently communicate with each other or share state in some significant way, then they're not really separate objects, and the design might be flawed.

Of course, *complete* independence is very hard to achieve. For one thing, if the servers all use the same database server, there will always be the possibility that they could interfere with each other. That's why it's called *semi*-independent.

Important Questions When Thinking About Servers

In Chapter 5, we introduced two major problems that arise in the design of distributed applications: network latency and the possibility of partial failure. Clearly, when designing a server (or choosing between design alternatives), you should take these problems into account. In particular, your goal should be to minimize the impact of network latency and to avoid the problems caused by partial failures.

The problem is translating the desire to avoid these problems into specific design criteria. What follows is a list of questions you should ask yourself when making design decisions or evaluating designs. This list isn't intended to be complete; as you get more experienced at designing distributed systems, you will undoubtedly come up with more questions, and your own ways of thinking about these problems. It is, however, a good start.

Each of these questions has an associated discussion, followed by a subsection entitled, "Applying this to Bank versus Accounts." The goal is to take what is, admittedly, a rather abstract list of questions and make them more concrete. We do this for each one by exploring whether we should pursue the Bank option or the Account option in implementing the bank example. Unfortunately, the discussion is somewhat inconclusive. As is often the case, there really isn't a decisive reason for choosing one over the other. Put succinctly, neither Bank nor Account is "correct," although one is more useful than the other.

 In order to simplify the discussion, we will assume that each server is individually entered in the registry. That is, that the client finds the server (either Bank or an instance of Account) by first making a lookup call to the RMI registry.

Client-Side Caching

There is an ugly truth lurking in the attempts to minimize problems caused by either network latency or the possibility of partial failures. Often, the attempt to mitigate these problems will cause other, equally vexing, problems to arise. Consider, for example, the problem of network latency. One solution to this problem is to implement a *client-side cache*.

The idea is simple: in a data-intensive application (say, for example, an application that allows users to view information from a database), the client should fetch only a given piece of data once. Though this seems reasonable, there are two substantial problems with it: indexing the client-side cache and maintaining the client-side cache.

Let's talk about indexing the client-side cache. This becomes a problem because identical queries are rarely issued to a server. If the client makes the same method call with the same arguments to the same server, it can simply use the cache and avoid all of the overhead associated with calling the server. But a more sophisticated use of the cache, such as realizing that the answers to a particular database query are a subset of the ones from a previous query, involves replicating some amount of server functionality on the client side. This can be difficult to do.

The second problem is maintaining the cache. Over the course of a client session, two things can happen. The first is that the cache can grow to be excessively large, which forces the client to develop a strategy for discarding cached information, and the second is that the cached information can become invalid.

To solve this second problem, the client usually adopts one of three solutions. It automatically expires information after a certain time period (which also helps keep the cache small), it occasionally asks the server whether information in the cache is still valid, or it relies on the server to let it know when the data becomes invalid via an event model. These last two alternatives require substantial programmer effort and may actually result in the program's performance suffering.

The end result? If a client-side cache is implemented, it's usually implemented as a data structure indexed by exact arguments, uses a fixed length FIFO queue to limit cache size, and automatically expires information that gets too old. In fact, this is what a web browser does, although it also validates its cache. In other words, before displaying a cached web page, a web browser asks the web server if the page has been changed since it was last retrieved.

You'd like to think that the extra control and knowledge you have when building a customized application would lead to a better solution than the one used by a generic client such as a web browser. Sadly, this often isn't the case.

Does Each Instance of the Server Require a Shared/Scarce Resource?

Suppose you find yourself designing a system that requires many instances of a particular type of server. For example, in our current dilemma, there can be literally millions of Account servers located inside a much smaller number of JVMs. One sure tip-off that the design has gone bad is the realization that there's a scarce resource to which all your servers require exclusive access.

Sometimes this is obvious. For example, consider our printer server. It makes little or no sense to create multiple printer servers connected to the same printer—it's not even clear what a second printer server would do! Other times, this is more subtle and requires a fair amount of thought.

Memory, in general, is not an issue here

As long as the instances of servers can comfortably reside within a single JVM, memory is not an issue. The amount of memory required by a server can be divided into two pieces: client-specific state and general-purpose state. For example, in an e-business application, the client's current order is clearly client-specific; the general catalog of items available for sale is general-purpose.

Generally speaking, the amount of memory required by a set of servers is a constant (the general-purpose state) plus an amount proportional to the number of currently active clients. However, the latter value is often proportional to the number of currently open socket connections. This is one example of why memory is not going to be the bottleneck. You'll swamp other scarce resources long before memory becomes a problem that can't be solved by popping more memory modules in the machine.

 This might seem false in the case of our accounts. If there are 25 million accounts, then the amount of memory required for 25 million server objects would seem to be substantial, independent of the number of clients currently connected. The factory pattern, which we discuss in Chapter 17, is designed to explicitly handle this problem.

Sockets in RMI aren't a limitation either

It used to be that socket allocation was a major resource limitation. This was caused by the combination of two factors:

- Processes on most major operating systems were only allowed to have a limited number of sockets open.[*] In fact, the actual limit is usually the number of *file descriptors* a process can have open; file descriptors are used for both files and sockets.

- Each server required an instance of ServerSocket to listen for connections.

The combination of these two factors is deadly. It means that a very small number of servers can be running inside a single process. And since launching a process in Java requires launching a JVM, which consumes a significant amount of memory and operating-system resources, this can quickly become a major issue.

---

[*] The limit is built into the operating system and is usually less than or equal to 1024.

RMI* solves this problem by reusing sockets. In other words, if a client JVM sets up a socket connection to a server JVM, then the connection is actually kept alive for a short period of time by the RMI infrastructure. If, after the client request has been handled, a second request is made from the same client JVM, that request will reuse the same socket connection. This means that the number of socket connections required by an RMI server is approximately: 1 + number of simultaneous requests.

 This is only an approximation because there may be temporary open, unused socket connections that correspond to completed requests. In practice, this can be significant. If you find that unused sockets are being retained for long periods of time and constitute a significant resource limitation, then you can either set parameter values to config- ure how long the RMI runtime keeps unused sockets open (we'll dis- cuss this, and other settings, in Chapter 16) or use a custom socket factory to achieve a similar effect (we'll discuss custom socket facto- ries in Chapter 18).

Note that this number is entirely dependent on the number of clients and how busy they are. It does not depend at all on the number of servers.

Socket reuse is actually a fairly significant benefit to using RMI. It's not all that hard to implement, but doing it right requires a fair amount of code and some forethought.

The RMI Runtime

Now that we've discussed sockets, it's time to admit that our architectural diagrams are hiding a bit of the complexity of RMI. Neither stubs nor skeletons use sockets directly.

Instead, stubs use an object called a RemoteRef, which handles the actual details of com- municating with a remote process. This extra layer of indirection allows the RMI infra- structure to manage network communications and conserve scarce resources. From the networking point of view, it makes both socket sharing and distributed garbage collection possible. It also enables RMI to effectively share a thread pool across multi- ple servers. We'll explore this much more fully in Part II. The networking details are covered in Chapter 16, and thread pools are discussed in Chapters 11 and 12.

We'll ignore the RMI runtime for the rest of this chapter and for the rest of Part 1. However, it's not a bad idea to keep the fact that sockets are shared in the back of your mind. It's also good to remember that when we draw a stub and a skeleton in a picture, we really mean something like that shown in Figure 6-1.

---

* That is, the Sun Microsystems, Inc. implementation of RMI. Socket sharing isn't actually required by the RMI specification.

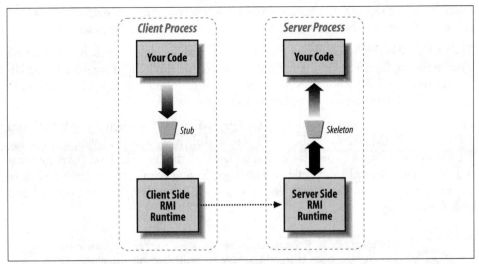

Figure 6-1. Stubs and skeletons interact with the RMI runtime and not directly with the network

An example of a resource limitation

Suppose you're in a situation where you want to log information about requests that are made. For example, you might want to use a log file for one or more of the following activities:

- Debugging servers during initial deployment and testing
- Recording information about actual server failures in long-standing systems
- Providing detailed data for analyzing network traffic patterns
- Providing tracking information in case a transaction is later disputed
- Providing a local persistent store to help servers recover from crashes

The first two of these are important but don't really concern us. But the last three can be quite important and useful.[*] If you have a large number of server objects residing inside a single JVM, and each of them wants to use a log file, you can wind up running out of file descriptors very quickly.[†]

Moving things to a singleton resource object handles this problem

Of course, now that we've discussed log files in detail, you've probably guessed what the real issue is. It's not the *log* aspect, it's the *file* aspect that causes problems. If each of the servers, for example, needed to open different files based on client

---

[*] Indeed, a quick search on the Internet reveals the existence of at least 12 companies selling products that analyze web-server logs to help web-site owners spot traffic patterns and fix problems.

[†] Another example of this would be a mail server which stores each person's mail in a separate file and has multiple servers which implement the Mailbox interface.

requests, then changing our design to use a single server wouldn't help us. We would still need to open all those files, and that would still use up our file descriptors.

The real issue is that we could have gotten away with a single log file, but instead we used many log files. Hence, there is a solution to this problem: if we need to log client requests, and we want to have several small-scale, semi-independent servers in the same JVM, then we can do one of two things.

First, each server can attempt to open a single, shared log file when it needs to record information. If the attempt fails, it will wait and then try again. Having a single log file solves the resource issue—we no longer use a plethora of file descriptors for what is a secondary piece of functionality. However, having each account open and close the same file is incredibly inefficient. The same file winds up getting opened and closed repeatedly.

 Moreover, since accounts can now block each other (i.e., when one has the file open, the others have to wait), we run headlong into threading and timing issues. We'll deal with threading in Chapters 11 and 12.

Instead of having each server open and close the same file, it makes more sense to implement a singleton object, a logger, residing in the JVM. Rather than attempting to open the file directly, the servers simply call methods on the logger, which handles the details of the filesystem interaction, as shown in Figure 6-2.

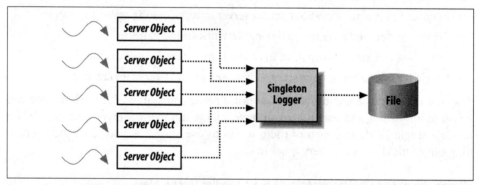

Figure 6-2. A singleton logger can often minimize consumption of scarce resources

The heuristic that comes from this discussion is that if our design starts relying too heavily on shared resources, then we're implicitly creating dependencies and resource contention among our servers. This means we should encapsulate those resources inside code that manages access to them.

"Shared singleton resource" is a design pattern that applies in many cases. The most common case is *database connection pools*. Recall that database connection objects are incredibly expensive to create. You can usually have only a small number of them; otherwise, you'll run out of database cursors. To solve this problem, most programmers create a *connection pool*: a set of database connection objects that are repeatedly used. A server grabs a connection from the pool, uses it, and then returns it to the pool so other servers can use it.

Applying this to Bank versus Accounts

Let's start by making some assumptions. It's quite possible that logging will be required for the account objects. It's also very likely that our persistent store, almost certainly a relational database, has a table that records transactions with some degree of detail. For example, the database stores the type of transaction (at the very least, whether it's a deposit or a withdrawal), the amount of the transaction, and the time of the transaction. If we're lucky, the database might also store the balance of the account before and after the transaction.

However, the database probably already has a fixed schema, which we're not allowed to alter. Yet, as our bank moves into the age of the Internet, we could easily want to record more information. For example, we may want to record more detailed information about where from, exactly, the request came. Was this a withdrawal of extra cash from a supermarket cashier? Was a casino involved? Was some other bank's ATM involved? Was the transaction generated by an Internet-based service that provides automatic bill paying by mimicing an ATM? And so on.

Because our primary information is stored in a shared resource (the original database) for both the Bank and Accounts options, and because to access this information we need to store it in a second database,* the answer to this question doesn't favor either the Bank option or the Account option.

Advantage: neither

How Well Does the Given Server Replicate/Scale to Multiple Machines?

This is only important if you anticipate the application scaling to handle demands beyond the capacity of a single JVM on a single machine. For example, it seems unlikely that our printer server will ever really need this sort of scalability.

In order to answer this question, consider the following scenario: a single JVM, containing all our servers, is created. Clients find the servers using the registry and proceed

---

* In order to make ad-hoc queries across accounts.

to make calls on them. However, this system doesn't scale very well, and users are upset by how badly the system performs. Then, an order comes down from on high: two JVM's, each containing "half" of the server, should be created. In addition, a new third server, which knows how to redirect clients to a "correct server," should be built. Clients will make a simple query to the third server to find out which server should handle their requests, and then conduct all their business with the designated server.

In other words, we will distribute the processing and then implement a simple form of *load balancing*. This new architecture looks something like Figure 6-3.

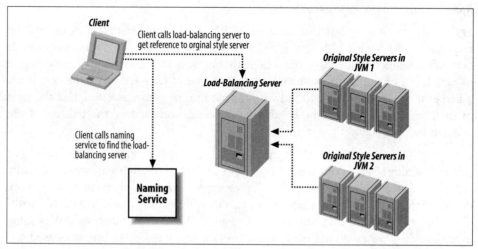

Figure 6-3. Load-balancing architecture

Now the question becomes: how hard is it to implement this scenario? If we need to, can we easily migrate from the single JVM scenario to the multiple JVM scenario?

Applying this to Bank versus Accounts

Accounts easily scale to multiple machines. Since they register as small-grained servers in the naming service, they are location-independent. That is, in order to distribute the servers on two machines, they are simply launched in separate JVMs and registered from there. Consider the following code, which launches a set of Account servers given names and balances:

```
public static void main(String[] args) {
    Collection nameBalancePairs = getNameBalancePairs(args);
    Iterator i = nameBalancePairs.iterator();
    while(i.hasNext()) {
        NameBalancePair nextNameBalancePair = (NameBalancePair) i.next();
        launchServer(nextNameBalancePair);
    }
}

private static void launchServer(NameBalancePair serverDescription) {
    try {
```

```
    Account_Impl2 newAccount = new Account_Impl2(serverDescription.balance);
    RemoteStub stub = UnicastRemoteObject.exportObject(newAccount);
    Naming.rebind(serverDescription.name, stub);
    System.out.println("Account " + serverDescription.name + " successfully
        launched.");
}
    catch(Exception e){}
}
```

This can easily be run on more than one machine, launching different sets of accounts. All that is required is that the function getNameBalancePairs( ) return different accounts when the code is run on different machines. When the client asks the naming service for Account, it automatically gets a stub for the correct server regardless of on which computer the server runs.

Bank, on the other hand, doesn't easily spread to multiple machines. After all, the whole idea behind Bank is that all the accounts can be manipulated using a single server. We run into problems when two clients, communicating with two different Bank servers, try to manipulate the same account information. That is, suppose each client calls:

```
public void makeWithdrawal(Account account, Money amount) throws RemoteException,
    OverdraftException, NegativeAmountException;
```

In addition, suppose that each of these calls attempt to withdraw all the money in the account. If both clients are calling the same instance of Bank, we can easily imagine that the code is clever enough to spot the problem.* However, if the clients are talking to two instances of Bank, running as separate servers on distinct computers, the only way to spot the problem is to have the servers communicate with each other.

One solution to this problem is to use the persistent store as a shared resource. That is, before attempting to make a deposit or a withdrawal, Bank can always check to see whether the operation is possible. But this solution can be difficult to implement and makes the interaction with the database more complex. What's more, all this really does is take messages that should be sent directly from one Bank to another and route them through a third-party server. This may cause performance problems.

An alternative solution, which might seem rather clever, is to register the Banks with the naming service. However, instead of registering them under Bank names, register them under the names of the accounts. That is, each instance of Bank would be registered many times, once for each account it supports. Clients would look up an account and be directed to an instance of Bank. By partitioning the accounts ("Bank 1 handles those accounts, Bank 2 handles these accounts..."), we avoid the problem when two servers manipulate the same account information.

---

* Exactly how to write this sort of code will be covered in Chapters 11 and 12.

This solution still requires some changes in the implementation of Bank. The problem, however, is that if we don't change the implementation of Bank, then once a client has a reference to Bank, it can call any method on any account. This explicitly breaks the partitioning we've set up. More importantly, it violates the single most important rule of client-server programming: servers should never trust clients to "do the right thing," especially when sensitive data is involved.

 This is worth repeating: servers should *never* trust clients to do the right thing, especially when sensitive data is involved. Why? Clients tend to get rewritten more often than servers. Hence, their code evolves more rapidly and is tested less thoroughly.[*] Since one client-side error can result in a corrupted server, it's just good sense for the server to validate all incoming data. Paranoia is not just the best policy, it's the only reasonable policy.

Of course, once we've added the additional layer of code to make sure that clients are invoke only transactions on permissible accounts, we no longer deal with our original implementation of Bank anymore. We've created an intermediate abstraction and transformed Banks into Branches.

Advantage: Accounts (slightly)

Can a Single Server Handle a Typical Client Interaction?

Suppose the system architecture has many servers, each of which implements a specific piece of functionality (in the current case, each Account server implements services for a specific account). Then we need to wonder about three things:

- How many of the servers does the client need to know about during the course of a typical conceptual operation?

- How many of the servers does the client need to know about during the course of a typical user's work session?

- How many of the servers does a client need to know about at any given time?

These are all slightly different questions. The first one is the most important, because it touches on both network latency and the problem of partial failure. The second and the third are mostly about avoiding problems due to partial failures. We'll discuss the first question in detail and omit the second and third questions. While you need to think about these questions, the associated analysis is similar to that required for the first question.

---

[*] Not to mention the possibility of malicious clients...

How many of the servers does the client need to know about during the course of a typical conceptual operation?

Suppose that the client, in order to do what the user thinks of as a single task, must send messages to three distinct servers. That is, suppose we have the following client-side sequence:

1. The client sends a message to the first server and gets a response.
2. The client sends a message to the second server and gets a response.
3. The client sends a message to the third server and gets a response.

This is often a bad design decision. Servers are usually closer and more reliably connected to each other than to the client. That is, the typical distributed architecture really looks something like Figure 6-4.

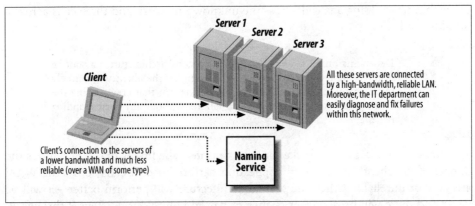

Figure 6-4. Typical distributed architecture with servers linked together via a fast LAN

However, consider the alternative architecture shown in Figure 6-5.

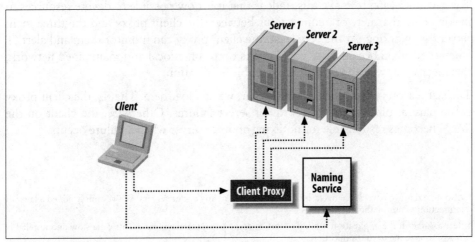

Figure 6-5. Adding a client proxy

Note the addition of the *client proxy*. The role of the client proxy is to implement the single conceptual operation on behalf of the client. That is, we've split the client into two pieces: the actual client that the user interacts with and the client proxy that runs inside the high-speed LAN near the server.*

In this architecture, the sequence of operations is:

1. The client sends a message to the client proxy.
2. The client proxy sends a message to the first server and gets a response.
3. The client proxy sends a message to the second server and gets a response.
4. The client proxy sends a message to the third server and gets a response.
5. The client proxy returns the appropriate response back to the client.

The net effect? We've traded three calls across an unknown, potentially slow, and unreliable network for one call across the unknown network and three calls across a well-known LAN.

 Depending on the client's location, the second architecture may not be faster or more reliable. Suppose, for example, the client was actually on the same high-speed LAN as the proxies. In that case, adding the client proxy adds another point of failure, without any corresponding benefit.

This trade is a good trade to make for three reasons. The first is that it minimizes the impact of the client's location on application performance. If calls across the WAN are slow or unreliable,† then the second architecture will perform better—it will be faster and there will be a smaller chance of partial failure during steps 2 through 4. And, even if the client is on the LAN, we've still reduced the variance in application response time.

The second reason to make this trade is that it is now possible to devote resources to making sure that network connections between the client proxy and the three main servers are working. At the very least, the client proxy can monitor them and alert IT when they fail. Since all these connections occur on a local and maintained network, this means that we can build a more reliable application.

The last reason is that when failures occur, we can log them. That is, the client proxy is the natural place to store records of server failures. Otherwise, the client on the WAN becomes responsible for notifying another server when a failure occurs.

---

* Also note that we haven't changed the implementation of any of our servers. We've simply added a layer of indirection to our method invocations.

† Rest assured, if the application is at all useful, at some point there will be clients on a slow and unreliable WAN connecting to the application.

This sort of reasoning is also important when you're actually designing the server interfaces. Just as you don't want the client to send messages to multiple servers as part of a single conceptual operation, you also don't want the client to send multiple messages to the same server as part of a single conceptual operation.

Applying this to Bank versus Accounts

Whether a single instance of Bank or Account can handle a typical client interaction depends on our use case. There are two potential sources of difficulty:

- Clients accessing multiple accounts serially. That is, they first access one account. After they're done with that account, they access a second account, and so on.
- Clients performing more complex financial operations. For example, a client transfers money from her savings account to her checking account.

The first of these isn't an issue. Because RMI shares sockets, the cost in terms of establishing socket connections to the server is identical in either case. And since clients are accessing only one account at a time, the overall cost is similar. The second, however, is a much more significant issue. Here's what I typically do at an ATM:

1. I give it my ATM card and enter my PIN.
2. I check the balance on my checking account.
3. I withdraw money from my checking account.
4. While the ATM is processing my request, it shows me an advertisement for a home mortgage.
5. I get the money.
6. I log off, getting a printed receipt.*

If my interaction is typical, then a single instance of Account or Bank can easily handle a typical customer interaction. However, suppose I was a more demanding customer. For example, I might check my savings account balance at the same time and then decide to transfer money from my savings account to my checking account. That is, suppose we had to support operations that crossed account boundaries. We can easily imagine adding the following method to our implementation of Bank:

```
transferMoney(Account source, Account destination, Money amount)
```

This means that transferring money is accomplished by single remote call to a single server. If we add the stipulation that all of a client's accounts are in a single instance of Branch, we also handle the cases when Bank is split apart into multiple Branches. And, since a single server is handling all the communication to the database, this operation can be handled in a single database transaction.

---

* Note the resemblance to our typical use case.

Why is using a single database transaction important? Databases provide *all-or-none* semantics for sequences of related operations, grouped as a *transaction*. The key point is that you don't want the deposit to succeed if the withdrawal fails (or vice-versa). The bank can just use a single database connection to manage this.

Accounts, on the other hand, don't work so well in this case. They are inherently too fine-grained to support transferring money cleanly. Even if we add the following method to our Accounts:

```
transferMoney(Account destination, Money amount)
```

it's hard to see how to support this functionality cleanly—two instances of our Account server will have to participate in a single database transaction.

In general, if the clients will frequently perform operations that require more than one participating account, Bank will be a much simpler and more robust piece of code.

Advantage: Bank (slight to significant, depending on use cases)

How Easy Is It to Make a Server Handle Multiple Simultaneous Clients?

We really have no way of answering this right now; handling multiple clients requires some knowledge of threading, which we will cover in Chapters 11 and 12. There are two general rules of thumb, though:

- The smaller and simpler a server is, the easier it is to make it safely handle multiple clients. In particular, if a server is likely to handle requests from a single client or about a single resource, then it is easier to make it handle multiple clients at one time.

- If you notice that your problem is getting really difficult, or that the solution is inefficient, then you've chosen the wrong design.

Applying this to Bank versus Accounts

The account option wins easily here.

How Easy Is It to Tell Whether the Code Is Correct?

The general heuristic is this: the smaller the server, the easier it is to tell whether it is correct. And the easier it is to thoroughly test its functionality.

One complicating factor is the possibility that more than one server may be involved in handling a client request. If the choice is between three small servers interacting with each other to handle a request or one large and more complex server that doesn't need to interact with any other servers, this question may be harder to answer.

Applying this to Bank versus Accounts

Assuming that a single server can adequately support the typical client, there's no argument here. Accounts are simpler. The interface is simpler, the code is easier to write, and there are fewer lines of code.

 In fact, when you look at either Account or Bank, the striking thing is just how much behavior is delegated to other (presumably bullet-proof) components. Connection management is delegated to the RMI Runtime, and most data persistence and integrity issues are handled by a database server.

Advantage: Accounts (tentative)

How Fatal Is a Server Failure?

There are two types of failures relevant to this question: failures associated with an individual server and failures associated with an entire JVM. For example:

- The server has a NullPointerException. That might take the server out of service, but probably won't hurt the rest of the system.
- The JVM runs out of memory. All servers in the JVM are effectively dead.

Given this, there are two distinct questions that need to be considered. The first is: how many clients does a particular failure affect? And the second is: how hard is it to recover from a failure?

 One rule of thumb: when thinking about how fatal a server failure might be, simply ask yourself, "How much client-specific state does the server have and from how many clients?"

Applying this to Bank versus Accounts

At the level of "single server failed," if an instance of Account fails, one particular bank account is inaccessible and the data associated with it may be corrupted, which could cause problems in recovery. However, the recovery process is three straightforward steps: check the data, relaunch the server, and use rebind( ) to reclaim the name in the registry.

If an instance of Bank, or even of Branch, fails, a much larger amount of data could be corrupted. In addition, when an instance of Bank fails, everyone is affected (i.e., all the clients are hit, not just one or two). It's hard to imagine Account failing; it's a fairly simple object. Failures are more likely to be of an entire JVM or an entire machine, rather than of a single instance of Account.

Advantage: Accounts

How Easy Is It to Gracefully Extend the Software and Add New Functionality?

There are two basic facts of life that must be accounted for:

Requirements are constantly changing. If your application is to be successful, it will need to evolve. This is especially true immediately after the first version is deployed—users will use the application and immediately spot all of the things they should have mentioned (but didn't think of) during requirements analysis.

Smaller servers are easier to modify and extend. Simple objects are much easier to modify or replace. This is especially true when the distributed architecture involves a layer of indirection. This is the case, for example, when a factory is used. We'll discuss factories in Chapter 17.

Applying this to Bank versus Accounts

In this case, because they're both simple servers, it's pretty much a wash.

Advantage: neither

Should We Implement Bank or Account?

As is often the case, either will work. The actual code used to implement the server is similar in either case. And, ultimately, the decision is often simply a matter of taste. In this case, we'll go with many small servers and many instances of Account. This will give us many small advantages and buy us one big headache: the problems associated with resource allocation. We'll deal with these problems in the next chapter and again in Chapter 17. But for now, it's Account.

CHAPTER 7

Designing the Remote Interface

In the previous chapter, we discussed the architecture of the bank example in detail and concluded that implementing many small Account servers seems like a good design decision. In this chapter, we'll tackle the design of Account's remote interface. As part of this, we will also discuss the issues involved in building data objects, objects designed to be passed by value over the wire. By the end of this chapter, you will have a list of basic design criteria that will help you design your own remote interfaces.

Important Questions When Designing Remote Interfaces

> Every program has (at least) two purposes: the one for which it was written, and another for which it wasn't.
>
> —Alan Perlis

Now that we've decided to have many little Account servers, the next step is to design the Account server interface. Just as the choice of server architectures was substantially influenced by the problems that arise in the design of distributed applications, the design of the server interface is also affected by both network latency and the possibility of partial failure.

But interfaces also need to be designed with the application's (or at least the server's) lifecycle in mind. As the quote at the beginning of this section suggests, the simple truth is that nobody ever really knows how an application, or even a server, will be used once it is deployed. Over time, how an application is used and what functionality it needs to support will change. A needlessly brittle interface, one that embodies too many assumptions about the exact use of the application, will make it harder to evolve the codebase.

As in the previous chapter, I've attempted to capture a series of design points in the form of questions. Again, the list isn't intended to be complete; as you get more experienced at designing distributed systems, you will come up with more questions and your own ways of thinking about these problems.

Unlike the decision between various server architectures, we have only one candidate interface here. Hence, we will take a slightly different approach by starting with a potential interface and then discuss it in light of the design questions.

Here's the interface we'll implement:

```java
public interface Account extends Remote {
    public Money getBalance( ) throws RemoteException;
    public void makeDeposit(Money amount) throws RemoteException,
        NegativeAmountException;
    public void makeWithdrawal(Money amount) throws RemoteException,
        OverdraftException, NegativeAmountException;
}
```

 Remember that every method in a remote interface (e.g., an interface that extends Remote and is intended to be used as the public interface to a server) must be declared as throwing RemoteException.

The following questions ought to be asked about any proposed remote interface.

Should We Pass Method Objects?

A method object contains at least part of the information about which operation is performed by the server. For example, you could imagine that, instead of the makeDeposit( ) and makeWithdrawal( ) methods, we used a single postTransaction( ) method. The Account interface may then look like the following, in which Transaction is an abstract class that implements the Serializable interface and has at least two concrete subclasses, Deposit and Withdrawal:

```java
public interface Account extends Remote {
    public Money getBalance( ) throws RemoteException;
    public void postTransaction(Transaction transaction) throws RemoteException,
        TransactionException,;
}
```

We'll call the former style of interface *method-oriented* and this style of interface *passing a method object.*

Interfaces that involve passing a method object tend to be very stable; the method signatures don't change, but the class hierarchy for arguments becomes more elaborate. For example, implementing a way to transfer money between accounts involves creating a new subclass of Transaction. If we use dynamic class loading (which we'll talk about in Chapter 19), we can then add new features and functionality to our server without ever having to shut it down.

Of course, in real life you would never load code from a client without thoroughly thinking through the security implications. Without a well-thought-out security policy, this approach can be summarized as, "Allow the client to load a virus into the mission-critical part of the application." We'll cover security more thoroughly in Chapter 20. For the moment, however, we will bypass this consideration.

Method-oriented interfaces, on the other hand, tend to evolve over time; new functionality is directly reflected in new methods. Consider, for example, our earlier example of transferring money between accounts. In a method-oriented interface, this involves adding a new method to the interface:

```
public void transferMoneyTo(Account destinationAccount, Money amount) throws
    RemoteException, OverdraftException, NegativeAmountException;
```

This style of interface design has three main advantages. The first is that the compiler can catch many more errors. Using many methods and making the signatures of each method as restrictive as possible prevents coding errors. The second is that the code is easier to read. The difference between:

```
account1.transferMoneyTo(account2, amount)
```

and:

```
TransferMoney transferMoney = new TransferMoney(account2, amount);
account1.postTransaction(transferMoney);
```

might not seem all that significant. But the first one is slightly more readable, and slight improvements in code readability have an enormous cumulative impact. The final reason is that new methods allow us to introduce new, focused exception types, enabling the server to throw more meaningful exceptions. In addition, it easily enables client-side developers to know which validation steps they can perform before sending a request to the server.

Given the advantages that method-oriented interfaces have, the best time to use method objects in an interface definition is when the interface must be absolutely stable. This usually happens when the server itself is providing a generic and reusable service, or when the application design involves polymorphic layers implementing the same interface.

Applying this to the Account interface

Since the main reason to use method objects doesn't apply, we've relied instead on the following rule of thumb:

If it isn't an object on the client side, it shouldn't be an object in the interface.

What this means is simple: our envisioned client is a simple, ATM-style application. It displays a form as shown in Figure 7-1, gets information from the user, and sends it over the wire to the server.

A Generic and Reusable Service

We've already run across one example of a generic and reusable service: the RMI registry. The RMI registry provides a generic lookup service that can be used by almost every RMI program. As such, the interface must be both generic (i.e., it cannot reflect any application-specific functionality) and unchanging (changing the registry interface would affect far too many programs). This leads to interface methods such as the static methods in `java.rmi.Naming`—a server then implements methods such as:

```
public static Remote lookup(String name) throws NotBoundException,
    MalformedURLException, RemoteException
```

which are easily reused in many applications. The price is that client code, which receives instances of `Remote`, must immediately cast the return value before it can do anything. Client applications almost always use `lookup`, as in the following line of code:

```
Factory factory = (Factory)Naming.lookup(ACCOUNT_FACTORY_NAME);
```

This lack of strong typing skills can lead to runtime errors if programmers are not careful.

Another example of a generic and reusable service is a channel-based event server.[a] As with a naming service, the idea is to take a design pattern that many distributed applications use, and build a reusable and generic piece of infrastructure that supports it well. There are four main types of objects involved:

Events

> These are instances of the `Event` class; `Event` is an abstract class that implements `Serializable` and which has four fields that identify an event and provide basic time-stamp information. Developers create subclasses of `Event` in order to define application-specific events.

Event sources

> This is a server that creates instances of `Event` and sends them to the Event Channel. There are no interfaces associated with event sources (since, from the point of view of the event system, these never receive any method calls).

The Event Channel

> This is the main server. The Event Channel receives instances of `Event` from event sources and forwards them to any clients that may have subscribed. As such, it implements the `EventChannel` interface. Because all the events flow through it, this must be a highly scalable and robust piece of code with fairly complex features such as logging, event prioritization, and the ability to store events in the case of network or client failure.

Event clients

> These are passive recipients in the event infrastructure. They are RMI servers that implement the `EventListener` interface so the Event Channel can send them events. They never reply to the Event Channel.

---

a. This event service is loosely based on a simplified version of the CORBA model. You can build arbitrarily complex event services. But most of the time these interfaces, and the implied functionality, are more than sufficient.

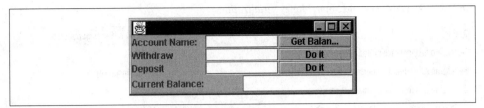

Figure 7-1. A simple GUI for the banking application

A client this simple doesn't need a Transaction object. But if it has one, it does something like the following:

1. Displays the form to get data from the user
2. Uses the entered data to build a Transaction object
3. Sends the Transaction object to the server
4. Immediately clears the reference to the Transaction object

In cases like this, putting the arguments inside method objects is often pointless. It makes the client a little more complicated, uses a little more bandwidth due to the overhead of sending the method object, and makes the interface harder to debug.

Should We Pass Objects as Arguments or Use Primitive Values?

A similar but less abstract question is this: to what extent should arguments to remote methods be bundled together in objects? For example, in our interface, we have:

```
public void makeDeposit(Money amount) throws RemoteException,
    NegativeAmountException;
```

In order to use this, we need to take the floating point number that the textfield contains and turn it into a Money object before sending it over the wire.

The reason to pass primitive arguments is simple: bandwidth. Objects are bigger than primitive values and more expensive to send.* Sending objects instead of primitive values can increase the bandwidth by an enormous percentage. As an example, consider a generic Money class. We don't need to provide an entire definition of the class to illustrate our point. For now, it suffices to know that Money is basically a wrapper class that contains a single integer.

Now let's show some serialization statistics generated using instances of two classes: NaiveMoney and SmartMoney. NaiveMoney is a straightforward implementation of the IntegerWrapper class. SmartMoney is an implementation designed to be more efficient with serialization. The differences in output between the two are shown in Table 7-1.

---

* Objects are also more expensive to marshall and demarshall. But that's not usually a significant issue.

Table 7-1. NaiveMoney and SmartMoney serialization

Action	Amount of bytes generated
Serializing first instance of NaiveMoney	235
Serializing subsequent instances of NaiveMoney	40 (per instance)
Serializing first instance of SmartMoney	162
Serializing subsequent instances of SmartMoney	15 (per instance)

Note that, in either case, using objects to encapsulate data is expensive—an integer in only four bytes long. Even when we use SmartMoney, we send 11 "extra" bytes. You can see that, in a high-volume application, inefficiencies due to serialization have the potential to be a significant difference.

On the other hand, turning a set of primitive arguments into a set of objects and passing the objects over the wire can make revising code much simpler. If we need to add another property to an object, only the code that actually uses that new property needs to change. That is:

- The entire code base should be recompiled and tested.
- The only code that needs to change is the code affected by the new feature.

This avoids a fair amount of drudge work, speeds up development, and avoids several of the errors that occur simply because programmers are easily bored. Our previous rule of thumb was:

> If it isn't an object on the client side, it shouldn't be an object in the interface.

This should be modified to:

> If it isn't an object on the client side, it shouldn't be an object in the interface unless the object is a natural collection of a set of related values that is likely to change in the future.

 Another closely related, and much wittier, heuristic is attributed to Alan Perlis: *if you have a procedure with 10 parameters, you probably missed some.* The practical meaning of this is that if you have a remote call with a large number of arguments, you should group the arguments into objects. In practice, a remote call with more than four arguments deserves to be thought out more.

Applying this to the Account interface

It's not clear if Money should be an object on the client side. On the one hand, there is a single textfield for inputting the amount of the transaction, and it is clear that we shouldn't pass a floating-point number for precision. (It's a bad idea to introduce unnecessary floating-point error into a financial application.) On the other hand, what the client winds up doing is parsing the textfield, creating an integer cents value, and then creating an instance of Money to pass over the wire.

A Generic and Reusable Service II

In terms of code, Event is simply a wrapper around four fields:

```
public abstract class Event implements Serializable {
    public int uniqueID;
    public String name;
    public Date occurredOn;
    public Date expirationDate;
}
```

And EventListener is a very simple interface as well:

```
public interface EventListener extends Remote {
    public void remoteEventOccured(Event event) throws RemoteException;
}
```

But EventChannel is more complex—it needs to manage the registration of EventListeners, which may care about only specific types of events. It must allow events to be broadcast at different priorities and export some type of management API:

```
public interface EventChannel extends Remote {
    public static final int MAX_PRIORITY = 100;
    public static final int LEAST_PRIORITY = 0;

    public void addListener(EventListener listener) throws RemoteException;
    public void removeListener(EventListener listener) throws RemoteException;

    public void addListenerForEventType(EventListener eventListener,
        Class EventType) throws RemoteException;
    public void removeListenerForEventType(EventListener eventListener,
        Class EventType) throws RemoteException;

    public void setDefaultPriorityForEventType(Class EventType,
        int defaultPriority) throws RemoteException;
    public void announceEvent(Event event, int priority) throws
        RemoteException;
    public void announceEvent(Event event) throws RemoteException;

    public void enableLogging(boolean logEvents) throws RemoteException;
    public void automaticallyExpireEvents(boolean
        checkExpirationsBeforeSending) throws RemoteException;

    public void stopAcceptingEvents() throws RemoteException;
    public void resumeAcceptingEvents() throws RemoteException;
    public void clearEventQueue() throws RemoteException;

    public void stopBroadcastingEvents() throws RemoteException;
    public void resumeBroadcastingEvents() throws RemoteException;
}
```

The deciding factor is the "unless" we added to the rule of thumb. Using a Money object allows us to eventually deal with different types of money. Our current implementation implicitly assumes that the return value is in United States currency.* It's much more reasonable to allow a whole variety of Money classes, which explicitly state their currency type, rather than assume that the value is a single integer.

Should We Receive Objects as Return Values or Receive Primitive Values?

The previous question addressed packaging data to send to the server. This question concerns sending a return value to the client. In addition to the reasons for passing objects as arguments, there is one compelling reason to always return objects: you only get to return one thing.

This is actually a very important distinction. Passing two arguments is often cheaper in terms of bandwidth than passing one combined argument.† Returning two distinct values is incredibly expensive; the client has to make a second call to retrieve the second return value, which means that the rule of thumb for return values is:

> You only get to return one thing, so make it an object. Doing so makes it much easier to add additional information later on and greatly simplifies maintaining and enhancing your application.

This is especially applicable when there is a candidate return class already defined in your system—for example, if the type of one of the arguments would make a reasonable return value. It's usually a sign of good design when the client and the server are both passing around the same types of objects. (On that note, if you find yourself using the same abstractions in many places, then you're either very lazy or you've found a good set of abstractions for the problem at hand.)

The major exceptions to this rule of thumb are boolean-valued success flags. Suppose you need only a return value indicating whether an operation succeeded. For example, you could imagine a method such as:

```
public boolean performOperation( )
```

Sometimes this is a reasonable thing to do; sometimes all the client wants to know is whether an operation succeeded. But before defining a method that returns a boolean-valued success flag, there are two things to consider:

- Is there an expected return value? Or does it almost always return true? If so, you should consider using a void signature and throwing an exception to indicate failure. The combination of a void signature and an exception leads to much more readable code because it effectively documents the intent and expected

---

* More precisely, it assumes that the currency is in terms of dollars and cents. We could be implementing a Canadian, or even an Australian, bank.

† Because when you create the class that contains the two arguments, you are creating an extra piece of information that will be sent over the wire.

behavior of the method and allows client code to be structured much more clearly.

- If the return value isn't what you expected, do you want to get an explanation from the server? It's really quite rare for a client application to care whether an operation failed or succeeded and not care why an operation failed. Perhaps the client application wants to report the problem. This also argues for an object return value or an exception in the case of failure. However, since the exception class can have extra attributes, it's easy to return the reason for the failure as part of the exception.

Applying this to the Account interface

getBalance( ) returns an object, which is an instance of Money. This decision was made especially easy by the fact that we already had a Money class floating around. For makeDeposit( ) and makeWithdrawal( ), we went with void return values and exceptions that tell the client more about the failure on the server side.

Do Individual Method Calls Waste Bandwidth?

There are two different problems that usually arise here. The first comes about because serialization creates *deep copies*. Deep copies are complete and recursive copies of objects. For example, if object A contains a reference to object B, then a deep copy of A contains a reference to a deep copy of B instead of a reference to B.

To see why deep copies can cause problems, suppose that one of the arguments being passed is an instance that contained a reference to another instance. Serialization makes a copy of the first instance. And, as part of the process, the serialization mechanism makes a copy of the second instance as well. All of the data associated with both instances is sent over the wire, and two instances are created on the receiving side. Of course, two instances aren't usually a problem. The problem arises when there is a complex and tangled web of several interrelated objects. If one is sent over the wire, the serialization mechanism may send all of them over the wire, as illustrated in Figure 7-2.

This problem, however, isn't really about the interface. It's about how to properly take advantage of the serialization mechanism. We'll discuss this in more detail in Chapter 10.

The second bandwidth-related problem that can arise results from method calls that return multiple values. For example, we could imagine a MortgageSalesHelper server with an interface that contains methods such as:

```
public interface MortgageSalesHelper extends Remote {
    public ArrayList getAllAccountsWithBalanceOver(Money amount) throws
        RemoteException;
    // ...
}
```

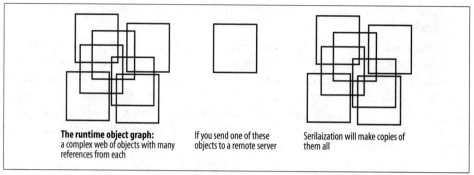

The runtime object graph: a complex web of objects with many references from each

If you send one of these objects to a remote server

Serilaization will make copies of them all

Figure 7-2. Serialization makes deep copies

This is a fairly typical remote method—it asks for all of the accounts with a certain minimum balance. But there is no upper bound on the number of accounts that can be returned. If 50,000 accounts have a balance greater than amount, 50,000 accounts will be returned. Methods that can return an arbitrarily large number of distinct return values (all of which are equally valid), are usually bad design for a number of reasons:

They degrade perceived client performance. The user clicks a button and waits. The server gets all the answers, packages them up, and sends the result to the client. If there are a lot of return values, not only will the server have to serialize more objects, the client will have to deserialize many more objects before it can display any information to the user.

They increase performance variance. The previous reason holds even if we assume the network is infinitely fast (since the client still has to demarshall the return value). This reason is more about the effect of the network—returning a large amount of data in a single network operation makes application performance vulnerable to network congestion. If the network is slow, and a large amount of data is being sent, then application performance will suffer.

They involve a large, all-at-once network hit. The first two reasons are from the point of view of a single application. This takes the larger picture into account. An application that decides to fling enormous amounts of data around in large chunks is being a bad network citizen. Moreover, in the brave new world of the Internet, many applications are being hosted at third-party locations, called hosting facilities. Hosting facilities generally charge based on bandwidth consumed, both overall bandwidth and burst rates.

They involve a larger single-client commitment on the part of the server. Generally speaking, clients should avoid requests that are atomic (e.g., single-method calls) and that either lock a large amount of information (e.g., prevent the server from performing other tasks involving data) or require the server to provide significant processing power. Serializing a large data set locks the data set and involves significant processing overhead.

They penalize client mistakes. What if the query was badly formulated? If a query involves a large number of return values, we'd much rather present partial results to the user as soon as possible and give them a chance to realize that the query was badly formulated. For example, suppose the user inputs $100 instead of $1,000 to getAllAccountsWithBalanceOver( ). Using iterators makes it much easier to incorporate this sort of functionality into the client.

The solution to these problems is to use an iterator, which returns data in chunks. That is, use a pair of interfaces such as the following:

```
public interface SalesHelper extends Remote {
    public AccountIterator getAllAccountsWithBalanceOver(Money amount) throws
        RemoteException;
    .....
public interface AccountIterator extends Remote {
    public int getNumberOfRemainingAccounts( ) throws RemoteException;
    public AccountList getNext(int numberToFetch) throws RemoteException;
}
```

This way, the client program can make a request, and then fetch the results as needed.

 Another reason for preferring iterators, which we'll discuss in Chapter 21, is the idea of background downloading. Briefly, you download the first segment of the return values, and then, while the user is looking at those, download the rest using the iterator in much the same way that an email client downloads the rest of your email while you read the first message.

Applying this to the Account interface

Our return types are Money, void, and void. We're probably doing fine at this point.

Is Each Conceptual Operation a Single Method Call?

> Writing a distributed application in this model proceeds in three phases. The first phase is to write the application without worrying where the objects are located and how their communication is implemented. The developer will simply strive for the natural and correct interface between objects.
>
> —Waldo et al.

One of the biggest issues involved in building a distributed object-oriented program is that there is a certain amount of tension between the "object-oriented" part and the "distributed" part. To understand this, let's consider our distributed printer again.

The second release of our printer application will almost certainly need some status and maintenance functionality. That is, users will want to ask the printer about its state and possibly alter the queue (either to remove print requests or move a high-priority print request up in the queue). An object-oriented interface for this might be:

```
public interface Printer extends Remote {
    public int getNumberOfSheetsInPaperFeeder( ) throws RemoteException;
    public int getTonerLevel( ) throws RemoteException;
    public int getEstimatedNumberOfMinutesUntilPaperRunsOut( ) throws
        RemoteException;
    public int getNumberOfJobsInQueue( ) throws RemoteException;
    public int getNumberOfPagesLeftInCurrentJob( ) throws RemoteException;
    public int getNumberOfPagesForJob(int jobNumber) throws RemoteException;
    // ...
}
```

There are three things to note here:

- Many of these methods are frequently used as part of a higher-level attempt to determine printer status, such as displaying it in a monitoring application or printer-status web page.

- If the printer was in the same process space as the object calling these methods, this method decomposition is close to correct.* Inside a single process, calling each method when necessary is fairly cheap. And the benefits of object-oriented design (the information about printer state can be obtained from the printer by querying the printer) are clear.

- This is an awful interface for a distributed printer.

Indeed, the third point follows directly from the first. Distributed method calls are expensive and very slow compared to standard method calls. If we know in advance that a client will often make the same sequence of method calls to get information about the printer's status, we should design a new object that contains the return value of all the methods and then add a special getStatus( ) method to the Printer interface:

```
public class PrinterStatus extends Serializable {
    public int nunmberOfSheetInPaperFeeder;
    public int tonerLevel;
    public int estimatedNumberOfMinutesUntilPaperRunsOut;
// ...
}
public interface Printer extends Remote{
    public PrinterStatus getStatus( ) throws RemoteException
//  ....
}
```

This new interface lets us make a single call to the printer server and get all the status information in one object. From a performance point of view, any interface

---

* Long years of painful experience have taught the author never to claim a design is correct. But "close to correct" is usually a defensible claim.

change that reduces the number of distributed method invocations by a linear factor[*] is a great idea. Note also that we're now returning an object instead of integers. Changing the interface in this way means that our earlier design heuristic, *return objects rather than primitive values*, is also satisfied.

On the other hand, the idea of having a separate status object clearly violates information encapsulation. Which is to say, it violates the single most important precept of object-oriented design. Compounding the offense is that the status object is purely data—it has no associated behavior and, in fact, looks suspiciously like a struct from the C programming language.

Some system architects may consider this a bad thing. Pay them no heed. It is reasonable, and even a good idea, to first design server interfaces as if they were same-process objects. But performance considerations demand that you then add a set of methods that group together frequently performed sequences of commands.

Iterators, again

One final point needs to be made. You might have noticed that the use of iterators violates this rule. With iterators, we make a remote call, get a reference to an iterator, and then need to make a second remote call to the iterator before we actually get any return values. The solution is to wrap the return value from the first remote call in a data object that also contains the first set of return values. Returning to the bank example, this would look like:

```
public interface SalesHelper extends Remote {
    public AccountSet getAllAccountsWithBalanceOver(Money amount) throws
        RemoteException;
    .....

public class AccountSet implements Serializable {
    public ArrayList firstSetOfAccounts;
    public AccountIterator theRestOfTheAccounts

public interface AccountIterator extends Remote {
    public int getNumberOfRemainingAccounts() throws RemoteException;
    public ArrayList getNext(int numberToFetch() throws RemoteException;
}
```

Doing things this way seems a bit complicated. But it does something quite nice—it lets us define a *threshold value* for when an AccountIterator is necessary. For example, we might set the threshold to 50 accounts. Here's what then happens when we call getAllAccountsWithBalanceOver( ):

- If there are 50 or fewer Accounts to return, we return an AccountSet with the answers and theRestOfTheAccounts set to null.

---

[*] For example, we're not getting rid of 3 method invocations we're reducing them by a factor of 4.

- If there are more than 50 Accounts to return, we return the first 50 as part of an AccountSet, along with a reference to an iterator from which the rest can be obtained.

This is a nice compromise. This interface is a little more complicated than the previous versions. However, it lets us handle small numbers of return values gracefully, and simultaneously allows us to handle large numbers of return values.

Applying this to the Account interface

In our basic use case, each conceptual operation is accounted for by a single method call. If it turns out that customers really want to transfer money, then this design point argues that we will need to add a transferMoney( ) method, rather than implement the transfer on the client side by having it perform a makeWithdrawal( ) followed by a makeDeposit( ).

Does the Interface Expose the Right Amount of Metadata?

The methods in a server's interface can be broken into two distinct categories:

The functional methods
These are called when the server is supposed to do something. That is, they expose the server's inherent functionality.

The descriptive methods
These are called when the client wants more information about the server. That is, they describe the server, rather than request an operation.

The sort of information returned by descriptive methods, information that describes a server, is often called the server's metadata. Exposing a server's metadata via descriptive methods is often useful for the following purposes:

Validation
The client has a stub to a server. But before requesting an operation, the client needs to make sure that the server can handle the operation.

Choosing between different servers
There are many servers implementing the same interface, and the client needs to make a choice between them.

To understand these uses, let's consider our printer server again. We could add the following metadata to our printer server:[*]

- Types and sizes of paper the printer can use
- Whether the printer can handle foils
- Whether the printer can print in color

---

[*] And, just to drive the point home, imagine adding this to the socket-based version of the printer server. *Ouch.*

- How many pages per minute the printer prints
- The printer's location
- The current queue information and printer status
- Types of files supported by the printer

None of this information actually exposes any printer functionality; it simply exposes the printer's capabilities. But we can imagine it making the application much friendlier to the end user. For example:

Validation
> The client application knows about the document to be printed, and it knows about the user's default printer. It checks to see whether the user's default printer can handle the document. If validation fails, the printer client finds all the printers on the local network and figures out which ones are capable of printing the document.

Choosing between different servers
> Since validation failed, the user looks at the list of potential printers and uses secondary characteristics such as printer location, printer speed, and the current state of printer queues in order to decide where to send the document.

Applying this to the Account interface

There is metadata associated to each account. Information such as the following is metadata:

- The account's owner
- The account number
- The type of account

However, this metadata is also already handled in our design. We're planning on registering individual accounts in a naming service. That is, in order to actually get a reference to a server, the client must already know the server's metadata. Because of this, we don't need to expose any metadata in the Account interface.

Have We Identified a Reasonable Set of Distributed Exceptions?

Earlier, I talked about why you should think about returning objects, rather than primitive values. The same reasoning applies to exceptions. You want to return, in a single object, all the information the client needs in order to proceed with error handling. For example, suppose the user tries to withdraw money. There are at least five different types of errors that can occur:

- The registry doesn't know about the account the client is trying to access.
- The registry returns a stub, but the account server has crashed.

- The account server tries to access the database but cannot (and so refuses to permit the withdrawal).
- The user has tried to withdraw more money than she has in the account.
- The user has tried to withdraw a negative amount of money.

The first of these doesn't need a distributed exception—the call to `Naming.lookup()` will simply return `null`; the error handling is entirely on the client side.

The second involves a transmission failure; the client tried to invoke a remote method, but RMI was unable to communicate with the server. This results in the stub throwing a `RemoteException`.

The third isn't a `RemoteException` at all—the remote method call worked perfectly, but the database was inaccessible. This should result in a message to the user, suggesting that she try again later. Alternatively, the client could intercept this message and automatically try again.

The last two cases are both cases of "bad data." But they are nonetheless very different. In the first case, the user submitted a request that could conceivably have been valid. For example, the user tried to withdraw $280 when she only had $75 in her account. There is simply no way for the client application to know that this is an invalid request without sending a message to the server. Throwing an instance of `OverdraftException` seems like a perfectly reasonable way to tell the client what went wrong.

The fifth case, on the other hand, might seem a bit contrived. After all, the client application should have been able to detect that the user was attempting to withdraw a negative amount of money without even talking to the server. And, therefore, the request to the server should never even have been sent.

The key word here in both of the previous sentences is *should*. The simple fact is that client programs, especially ones that are undergoing revision as part of the application lifecycle, sometimes inadvertently omit data validation steps that they *should* have performed. Your goal in building a server is to prevent a minor coding error on the client side from cascading into a major data corruption problem on the server side. The following two rules of thumb will help you do so:

- Always explicitly validate data on the server side to make sure a badly written (or hostile) client application doesn't corrupt important information.
- Any time you validate data on the server side, you should make the validation step a *checked exception.*[*] This helps the programmers writing the clients know what sorts of validation are necessary and gives them a good idea of the types of validation they should perform on the client side.

---

[*] A checked exception is an exception that must be caught.

Of course, in addition, the client should validate information whenever possible. Consider the following two situations:

- The user types a negative amount into a textfield and clicks on Deposit. The client application calls the server, the server throws an exception, and the client displays an error dialog to the user. Total elapsed time: 11 seconds.

- The user types a negative amount into a textfield and clicks on Deposit. The client attempts to validate the data and immediately displays an error dialog. Total elapsed time: 0.2 seconds.

These two applications are functionally equivalent. But the first one relies on the server to do things that ought to be done by the client. As a result, it can feel slow and unresponsive.

In general, how much validation should be done by the client is an open question. But there are certain minimal standards. For example, if it is possible for the client application to tell that a piece of data is wrong without using any other information, then the client application ought to do so. Simple client-side checks such as, "Is the value a positive number?" can noticeably improve an application's responsiveness.

Applying this to the Account interface

Given that the arguments will be instances of Money, what could possibly go wrong? There are two main cases:

- The user tries to withdraw more money than she has in the account.
- A negative amount of money is either deposited or withdrawn.

We've handled both of these cases explicitly. The first leads to an OverdraftException, and the second causes a NegativeAmountException.

Since exceptions are simply subclasses of Exception, they can have extra instance variables. Usually, this additional state is just used to give a complete description of the failure. But, in the case of OverdraftException, we also use it to say whether the withdrawal succeeded:

```
public class OverdraftException extends Exception
{
    public boolean _withdrawalSucceeded;
    public OverdraftException(boolean withdrawalSucceeded)
    {
        _withdrawalSucceeded = withdrawalSucceeded;
    }

    public boolean didWithdrawalSucceed()
    {
        return _withdrawalSucceeded;
    }
}
```

There are two slightly more marginal cases we didn't handle:

- No instance of money is passed in (a `null` argument is passed to the server).
- An instance of money worth precisely 0 dollars and 0 cents is either deposited or withdrawn.

Whether these really merit their own exception types is a matter of ongoing debate in the programming community. In general, there comes a point at which programmers say that the benefits from the extra precision and information provided by lots of exception types is outweighed by the sheer annoyance of trying to read an interface in which each method can throw four or five different exceptions.

My opinion is that these really do merit their own exception types.[*] In fact, the best course of action is probably to use five exceptions. The four we've explicitly outlined, as well as an abstract superclass of all of them called `BadMoneyArgumentException`, which has a descriptive string associated with it.

The interface should then be defined using all the exceptions, with as much precision as is reasonable. The server should throw the most precise exception it can and log the requests and exceptions in an error file. Clients, on the other hand, will probably just catch `BadMoneyArgumentException`; most clients don't really use the finer-grained distinctions that the server makes.

This compromise preserves most of the benefits of the fine-grained exception hierarchy and allows room for clients to change and take advantage of the extra information the server provides without forcing them to catch four unrelated exceptions.

Building the Data Objects

The classic slogan-level definition of an object is usually written in the form of an equation:

Object = Data + Behavior

A data object is an object in which the behavior is de-emphasized, and the object's identity isn't important. Two distinct data objects are equal if the data they encapsulate is equal. They're used to group related pieces of information together in order to pass them over the wire more easily and in a more comprehensible form.

Data Objects Don't Usually Have Functional Methods

Data objects don't usually have many functional methods (descriptive methods are fine; they're how you get the data after all). Every functional method on a data

---

[*] The decision not to include lots of different exception types in the book's example code is mainly motivated by pedagogical considerations—it prompts this discussion and also includes an example of an exception that contains a success flag. Plus, of course, too many exceptions does make example code harder to read.

object, every behavior you add, introduces dependencies between the client code and the server code. Suppose, for example, the server needs a new behavior on the data object. Then you need to do one of two things:

- Use two different versions of the data object. That is, use the new one in the server and the old one in the client. Be careful with serialization and make sure that the two different versions of the data object have compatible serializations.

- Recompile, retest, and redeploy the client application when you change the data object.

In practice, you wind up doing the first. Redeployment is a lot of work, and old versions of client applications tend to persist in strange places anyway.* But a careful look at the first option reveals something interesting: the data is versioning independently of the behavior. If you're explicitly managing data independently of behavior, there are two distinct objects involved.

For this reason, most complex distributed applications tend to have a translation layer. That is, they get data objects off the wire and then translate the data objects into other types of objects, which are more useful in the current application. While this level of indirection can seem excessive when you're first building an application, it turns out to be incredibly convenient as soon as the clients and servers start having distinct lifecycles.

The general principle is:

> In a distributed system, you want the things that involve the network to be as stable as possible. Interfaces shouldn't change quickly and should add only new methods. Data objects shouldn't change at all.

Interfaces Give You the Data Objects

The end result of designing the server interfaces is that we also know what the data objects are. That is, while we don't yet know the internal structure of the data objects, we do know their names and the roles they play within the application.

Most of the time, the interface design process also makes it pretty easy to guess what the fields should be, and therefore, which methods the data objects need to support. Here, for example, is the complete implementation of Money:

```
package com.ora.rmibook.chapter7.valueobjects;
import java.io.*;

public class Money extends ValueObject {
    private int _cents;
```

---

* The author still has a copy of Netscape Navigator 2 (Gold).

```
    public Money(Integer cents) {
        this(cents.intValue( ));
    }

    public Money(int cents) {
        super(dollars + " dollars " + cents + " cents.");
        _cents = cents;
    }

    public int getCents( ) {
        return _cents;
    }

    public void add(Money otherMoney) {
        _cents += otherMoney.getCents( );
    }

    public void subtract(Money otherMoney) {
        _cents -= otherMoney.getCents( );
    }

    public boolean greaterThan(Money otherMoney) {
        if (_cents > otherMoney.getCents( )) {
            return true;
        }
        return false;
    }

    public boolean equals(Object object) {
        if(object instanceof Money) {
            return (_cents == otherMoney.getCents( ));
        }
        return false;
    }
}
```

 Even though we think we're dealing with United States currency, we're using only cents, rather than storing both dollars and cents. This is an old trick from financial applications—it makes the object simpler to write without losing any information.

Accounting for Partial Failure

I said earlier that data objects are objects in which the behavior isn't quite so important. There is one very important exception to this: a data object must implement equals( ) and hashCode( ), and these methods must be implemented based on the underlying values of the object's data. The default methods, inherited from java. lang.Object are based on the location of the instances in memory.

In the case of Money, equals( ) is implemented directly, and hashcode( ) is inherited from ValueObject:

```
public abstract class ValueObject implements Serializable {
    private String _stringifiedRepresentation;
    private boolean _alreadyHashed;
    private int _hashCode;

    public ValueObject(String stringifiedRepresentation) {
        _stringifiedRepresentation = stringifiedRepresentation;
        _alreadyHashed = false;
    }

    public String toString() {
        return _stringifiedRepresentation;
    }

    public int hashCode() {
        if (false == _alreadyHashed) {
            _hashCode = _stringifiedRepresentation.hashCode();
            _alreadyHashed = true;
        }
        return _hashCode;
    }
}
```

 Unlike equals( ), with which you simply need to compare data fields, implementing hashCode( ) can be difficult—you have to come up with a good hashing algorithm for your objects. The way ValueObject does this is a fairly common trick—you generate a unique string for the values of your object and then use String's hashing algorithm. It's not foolproof, and it can be expensive if you don't cache the hashcode, but it's simple and works fairly well.

To see why it's so important to correctly implement equals( ) and hashCode( ), consider the following sequence of events:

1. Sue tries to withdraw money from her account.

2. The client application sends the request to the server, which then starts to process the request.

3. While the server is processing the request, Larry the rodent bites through the network cable.

4. After a while, the client application times out.

5. Later, when the network comes back up, Sue tries to withdraw money again.

What happens? Well, the message arrived at the server, and the account was debited. However, Sue never got confirmation, nor did she get her money from the ATM. And later on, she resubmitted the "same" request.

We need a way for our banking application to gracefully handle this problem. One possibility is this: the client application, when it realizes that the network is back up, calls a method to cancel the previous transaction. But there's a problem—the server cannot simply trust the client and reverse the transaction (i.e., deposit the money) because of the following scenario:

1. Sue tries to withdraw money from her account.
2. The client application sends the request to the server.
3. Before the request gets to the server, Larry the rodent bites through the server power cord, thus shutting down the server.
4. After a while, the client application times out.
5. Later, when the network comes back up, Sue tries to withdraw money again.

The client application has no way of differentiating between these two scenarios—all it knows is that, after it sent the request, the server became unreachable.

But from the server's point of view, these are very different scenarios. In the first case, Sue's account has to be credited. In the second case, the server should not credit Sue's account. This means that, when the server receives a request from a client (for a transaction to be cancelled), the server must double check to make sure the transaction actually occurred.

Thus, it is very important for data objects to correctly implement equals( ) and hashCode( ). A given server may store objects in a container that relies on equals( ) to test for membership (for example, an ArrayList). Or it may use a container such as HashMap, which relies on hashCode( ).

Another aspect of this is that the server should also check incoming requests to make sure the same request hasn't been issued twice. Because of this, it's fairly common to explicitly use an identity field inside a data object. For example, two print requests may have identical data fields simply because the user wanted to print two copies of a document before a big meeting. It would be really annoying if the printer arbitrarily rejected such requests. So, DocumentDescription can be modified to add a request_identity field, which contains a unique integer. This is extra information that has nothing to do with the actual printing functionality but lets the printer server tell whether it is receiving the same request, or a new request that just happens to result in the same document being printed again.

CHAPTER 8

Implementing the Bank Server

In the previous chapter, we discussed the interfaces and data objects for the bank example. In this chapter, we'll continue with the development cycle by building the servers and discussing the various design options that are available. This chapter is much shorter than the previous two because most of the intellectual heavyweight lifting has already been done. Nonetheless, by the end of this chapter, we will have fully implemented the servers for the bank example.

The Structure of a Server

The server objects you write in RMI are just the tip of the iceberg. When you add the automatically generated code and the pre-existing libraries and runtime, every RMI server has the layered structure at runtime shown in Figure 8-1.

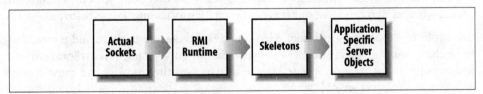

Figure 8-1. Runtime structure for RMI servers

These components have the following roles:

Actual sockets

> These are just instances of Socket and ServerSocket, exactly as discussed in Chapter 1. The number of sockets is explicitly controlled by the RMI runtime and is usually proportional to the number of RMI clients connected to a JVM.

RMI runtime

> This listens and receives any data coming in over the socket. Because it knows the wire protocol that RMI uses, the RMI runtime can take the data that comes in from the socket and break it apart into distinct method calls (encapsulated as

instances of java.rmi.server.RemoteCall). It looks at each of these distinct method calls and forwards them to the appropriate skeleton's dispatch() method. There is only one RMI runtime per JVM.

Skeletons

The skeleton is a piece of automatically generated code responsible for implementing dispatch(). As part of the implementation of dispatch(), the skeleton demarshalls the invocation arguments and performs validation checks related to class versions. It then calls the correct method on the server object. There is a single skeleton per server instance.

> Using different skeletons for different classes is not, strictly speaking, necessary. We'll talk about why you want to get rid of them, and how to do so, later in this chapter.

Application-specific server objects

This is the code that you write. It implements the remote interface for the server and usually has no other behavior. There are as many instances of these as are required by the application.

Note that the first three layers can all throw instances of RemoteException. Generally speaking, this means that something went wrong in the RMI infrastructure shown earlier. So your server code should never throw a RemoteException.

Implementing the Server

We need to make one RMI-related decision when building our server. We have to decide whether to implement our server objects by subclassing UnicastRemoteObject.

UnicastRemoteObject is a class defined in the java.rmi.server package and is intended to be the generic superclass for RMI servers. Simply subclassing UnicastRemoteObject and implementing the appropriate remote interfaces is the simplest and most convenient way of building an RMI server.

A Server That Extends UnicastRemoteObject

Example 8-1 shows an implementation of Account that subclasses UnicastRemoteObject. One particularly important point is that none of the code, with the possible exception of the class declaration, has anything to do with the network. To an astonishing extent, this is ordinary Java code.

> It is traditional in client-server circles to give interfaces descriptive names and then tack on an _Impl for the implementation. Thus, we have an interface called Account and an implementation called Account_Impl. This isn't a particularly pleasant naming convention, but it is traditional.

Example 8-1. Account_Impl.java

```java
public class Account_Impl extends UnicastRemoteObject implements Account {
    private Money _balance;
    public Account_Impl(Money startingBalance) throws RemoteException {
        _balance = startingBalance;
    }

    public Money getBalance() throws RemoteException {
        return _balance;
    }

    public void makeDeposit(Money amount) throws RemoteException,
        NegativeAmountException {
        checkForNegativeAmount(amount);
        _balance.add(amount);
        return;
    }

    public void makeWithdrawal(Money amount) throws RemoteException, OverdraftException,
        NegativeAmountException {
        checkForNegativeAmount(amount);
        checkForOverdraft(amount);
        _balance.subtract(amount);
        return;
    }

    private void checkForNegativeAmount(Money amount) throws NegativeAmountException {
        int cents = amount.getCents();
        if (0 > cents) {
            throw new NegativeAmountException();
        }
    }

    private void checkForOverdraft(Money amount) throws OverdraftException {
        if (amount.greaterThan(_balance)) {
            throw new OverdraftException(false);
        }
        return;
    }
}
```

A Server That Does Not Extend UnicastRemoteObject

The alternative implementation of Account, which doesn't extend Unicast-RemoteObject, is substantially the same code. In fact, the code shown in Example 8-2 has only two differences:

- Account_Impl2 doesn't declare that it extends UnicastRemoteObject.
- Account_Impl2 implements equals() and hashCode() directly.

These are important points. However you choose to implement your server, whether you choose to extend UnicastRemoteObject or not, the code for the methods defined in the Account interface is almost identical. The difference is in the code that ties your server to the RMI runtime, not in the code that implements your business logic. In other words, the decision to extend UnicastRemoteObject has no impact on that code.

Example 8-2. java

```java
public class Account_Impl2  implements Account {
    private Money _balance;
    public Account_Impl2(Money startingBalance) throws RemoteException {
        _balance = startingBalance;
    }

    public Money getBalance() throws RemoteException {
        return _balance;
    }

    public void makeDeposit(Money amount) throws RemoteException,
        NegativeAmountException {
        checkForNegativeAmount(amount);
        _balance.add(amount);
        return;
    }

    public void makeWithdrawal(Money amount) throws RemoteException, OverdraftException,
        NegativeAmountException {
        checkForNegativeAmount(amount);
        checkForOverdraft(amount);
        _balance.subtract(amount);
        return;
    }

    private void checkForNegativeAmount(Money amount) throws NegativeAmountException {
        int cents = amount.getCents();
        if (0 > cents) {
            throw new NegativeAmountException();
        }
    }

    private void checkForOverdraft(Money amount) throws OverdraftException {
        if (amount.greaterThan(_balance)) {
            throw new OverdraftException(false);
        }
        return;
    }

    public boolean equals(Object object) {
        //  Three cases. Either it's us, or it's our stub, or it's not equal.
        //  "our stub" can arise, for example, if one of our methods took an instance of
        //  Account.
        //  A client could then pass in, as an argument, our stub.

        if (object instanceof Account_Impl2) {
```

Example 8-2. java (continued)

```
            return (object == this);
        }
        if (object instanceof RemoteStub) {
            try {
                RemoteStub ourStub = (RemoteStub)RemoteObject.toStub(this);
                return ourStub.equals(object);
            }
            catch(NoSuchObjectException e){
            // we're not listening on a port, therefore it's not our
            // stub
            }
        }
        return false;
    }

    public int hashCode( ) {
        try {
            Remote ourStub = RemoteObject.toStub(this);
             return ourStub.hashCode( );
        }
        catch(NoSuchObjectException e){}
        return super.hashCode( );
    }
}
```

Extending UnicastRemoteObject

We now have two candidate server objects that are almost identical. The only difference is that Account_Impl extends UnicastRemoteObject, and Account_Impl2 doesn't. In order to choose between these options, we need to examine exactly what extending UnicastRemoteObject does.

There are two main benefits to UnicastRemoteObject: it automatically connects to the RMI runtime and it knows how to check for equality with other remote objects. However, extending UnicastRemoteObject can sometimes cause minor problems for two reasons: it prevents server classes from subclassing other classes (because Java is a single inheritance language), and it can sometimes prematurely expose an object to remote method calls.

The benefits of UnicastRemoteObject

UnicastRemoteObject has three constructors. They are:

```
protected UnicastRemoteObject( )
protected UnicastRemoteObject(int port)
protected UnicastRemoteObject(int port, RMIClientSocketFactory csf,
    RMIServerSocketFactory ssf)
```

RMI is built as a layer on top of sockets. By default, RMI uses the standard sockets defined in the java.net package. But you can choose to use different types of sockets by creating a socket factory. We'll talk about socket factories in more detail in Chapter 18. For now, the third constructor can be ignored.

The first method is documented as, "Create and export a new UnicastRemoteObject object using an anonymous port." This means that the RMI runtime will choose which port to use. In the latter two constructors, you must specify a port. In either case, the port is the port number on which a ServerSocket associated with the server listens.

If you specify a port, you're ensuring that the server will listen for connections on that specific port. This is because the constructor for UnicastRemoteObject automatically hooks the instance of UnicastRemoteObject into the RMI runtime—as soon as the constructor for UnicastRemoteObject returns, the object is actually listening for remote method calls.

If you don't specify a port, then RMI can reuse the same server socket for multiple servers. We'll discuss the ins and outs of socket reuse more thoroughly in Chapter 16. For now, it's enough to know that, unless you need to specify the port, letting RMI do so can help conserve system resources.

While nothing in the code for Account_Impl actually did anything related to RMI, the implicit call to UnicastRemoteObject's constructor did. This means that the launch code associated with the bank example needs to do only two things: create the servers, and register them with the naming service. The launch code for Account_Impl is, essentially, a loop around the following two lines of code:

```
Account_Impl newAccount = new Account_Impl(serverDescription.balance);
Naming.rebind(serverDescription.name, newAccount);
```

If, on the other hand, we don't subclass UnicastRemoteObject, we'll need to explicitly register our listeners with the RMI runtime as well as with the naming services. The launch code for Account_Impl2 is, essentially, a loop around the following three lines of code:

```
Account_Impl2 newAccount = new Account_Impl2(serverDescription.balance);
RemoteStub stub = UnicastRemoteObject.exportObject(newAccount);
Naming.rebind(serverDescription.name, stub);
```

exportObject( ) is a static method defined on UnicastRemoteObject that starts the RMI runtime listening for messages to an instance of a server class. There are actually three such methods, which are parallel to UnicastRemoteObject's constructors:

```
static RemoteStub exportObject(Remote obj)
static Remote exportObject(Remote obj, int port)
```

```
static Remote exportObject(Remote obj, int port, RMIClientSocketFactory csf,
    RMIServerSocketFactory ssf)
```

In spite of the declared return types of the two final methods, these methods all return instances of RemoteStub.

The other benefit of extending UnicastRemoteObject is that UnicastRemoteObject implements equals( ) correctly. If you look at the documentation for UnicastRemoteObject, it contains the following, rather cryptic, assertion:

> Objects that require remote behavior should extend RemoteObject, typically via UnicastRemoteObject. If UnicastRemoteObject is not extended, the implementation class must then assume the responsibility for the correct semantics of the hashCode, equals, and toString methods inherited from the Object class, so that they behave appropriately for remote objects.

This comment is mostly a reference to the problems associated with passing around stubs for remote servers. What happens when you need to tell whether a stub is equal to a server? For example, in Chapter 7 we speculated about the possible need for a transferMoney( ) method call with the following signature:

```
public void transferMoney(Account destinationAccount, Money amount) throws
    RemoteException, OverdraftException, NegativeAmountException;
```

It's quite conceivable that problems will arise if destinationAccount is the server that receives the transferMoney( ) call. This means we should do two things:

- Create a new exception type, DuplicateAccountException, and declare the method as throwing it as well:

  ```
  public void transferMoney(Account destinationAccount, Money amount) throws
      RemoteException, OverdraftException, NegativeAmountException,
      DuplicateAccountException
  ```

- Add checking code to our implementation of transferMoney( ) along the lines of, "If the destination account is the same as the source account, throw a DuplicateAccountException."

This second step should be simple and should boil down to the following code:

```
if (equals(destinationAccount)) {
// throw exception
}
```

If our implementation of Account extends UnicastRemoteObject, this will work because UnicastRemoteObject's equals( ) method handles stubs correctly. If our implementation of Account does not extend UnicastRemoteObject, then we'll need to override equals( ) to handle the case of stubs ourselves. UnicastRemoteObject handles hashCode( ) in a similar manner: the hash of a server is equal to the hash of its stub.

Overriding equals( ) and hashCode( ) doesn't require a lot of code, but it is rather tricky. You need to worry about three distinct things: the computer on which the server runs, the identity of the JVM in which the server runs,* and the identity of the server object inside the JVM. The best course of action is to rely on stubs to get it right. That's why in the `Account_Impl2` code, the implementations of `equals()` and `hashCode()` worked by obtaining a stub and relied on the fact that the people at Sun Microsystems, Inc., who implemented RMI, know how to find out these three pieces of information.

 Since the RMI runtime maintains hashtables of servers and stubs, you actually do need to override `equals()` and `hashCode()` if there is a chance that a server could be compared to a stub.

The costs of UnicastRemoteObject

There are really only three situations when you wouldn't extend `UnicastRemoteObject`. The first is, obviously, if you need your server to subclass another object. Java is a single-inheritance language for implementations. If you want a server class to inherit from a particular class, then your server class cannot also inherit from `UnicastRemoteObject`.

One solution in such cases is to use what the CORBA specifications call "ties." A tie is a class that implements a remote interface but delegates all the behavior to the "real server." That is, the server you implement actually consists of two objects:

The tie server
> This extends `UnicastRemoteObject` and implements the remote interface. The implementation, however, simply forwards all method calls to the real server.

The real server
> This is a subclass of another class. However, it also implements the remote interface and receives method calls from the tie server.

If the remote interface is large, however, this can be rather cumbersome.

The second problem is that subclasses of `UnicastRemoteObject` immediately begin listening for remote method invocations. Suppose the subclass constructor is particularly time-consuming, as in the following code snippet:

```
public class PrinterManager_Impl extends UnicastRemoteObject implements
    PrinterManager {
    public PrinterManager_Impl() {
        super(5150);// The well-known port of the printer manager :-)

        // go out to the registry and find all the printers.
        // establish links to each of them and get information on their queues so that
        // users can simply query us to find out about all the printers
        }
}
```

---

* Since more than one JVM can be running on a single computer, you need to worry about which JVM contains a specific object.

As part of UnicastRemoteObject's constructor, the printer manager will immediately be available to remote method invocations. That is, it will listen for remote method invocations even before PrinterManager_Impl's constructor has finished.

Usually, this is not a problem. In fact, most of the time, servers can't be found by clients until the server is registered with a naming service. Recall that our launch code for Account_Impl, which is fairly typical launch code, did this only after the constructor finished:

```
Account_Impl newAccount = new Account_Impl(serverDescription.balance);
Naming.rebind(serverDescription.name, newAccount);
```

However, if you're not using a naming service and providing another way for clients to connect with the server, you may need to be careful when extending UnicastRemoteObject.

> Practically speaking, the only time you need to worry about this is if you use a "well-known port" to connect to a server. That is, instead of using UnicastRemoteObject's zero-argument constructor, you pass in a port number. This can be convenient because it enables a client to bypass a naming service. On the other hand, you need to be careful because the client could attempt to connect after the server has been vended (e.g., after UnicastRemoteObject's constructor returns), but before the constructor has completed.

The third reason for not extending UnicastRemoteObject is that you might want to extend either Activatable or PortableRemoteObject. Activatable and PortableRemoteObject are classes provided by Javasoft that play a role similar to the one played by UnicastRemoteObject. That is, UnicastRemoteObject provides the standard mechanisms for exporting an ordinary server. Activatable provides the standard mechanisms for exporting servers that take advantage of the activation framework, and PortableRemoteObject provides the standard mechanisms for exporting servers that use RMI/IIOP. We'll cover the Activation Framework in Chapter 17 and RMI/IIOP in Chapter 23.

Generating Stubs and Skeletons

Now that we've written and compiled the servers, we need to generate stubs and skeletons. This is easy; we simply need to invoke the RMI compiler, rmic. Here, for example, is the invocation of rmic we use to generate stubs and skeletons for the bank server:

```
rmic -keep -d d:\classes com.ora.rmibook.chapter8.Account_Impl com.ora.rmibook
    chapter8.Account_Impl2
```

rmic works by generating Java source code for the stubs and skeletons and then compiling those Java files. The -keep flag simply tells rmic to save the source code to *.java* files.

rmic takes a *.class* file and creates a pair of companion files, a stub and a skeleton, in the same package as the *.class* file. Thus, the above invocation of rmic actually generates four Java class files:

com.ora.rmibook.chapter8.Account_Impl_Skel
com.ora.rmibook.chapter8.Account_Impl_Stub
com.ora.rmibook.chapter8.Account_Impl2_Skel
com.ora.rmibook.chapter8.Account_Impl2_Stub

There's an interesting subtlety here. rmic requires the actual implementation's class files. It seems, at first glance, that the compiled interface files might suffice. However, the designers of RMI decided that the stubs and skeletons should satisfy the following two requirements:

1. There should be a unique stub/skeleton pair per server, so we can do things such as register the server in the naming service.

2. The stubs and skeletons should implement all the remote interfaces that the server does, so that casting when you retrieve objects from the naming service is a local operation.

Because servers can implement more than one remote interface, these two requirements force rmic to work from the implementation files instead of the interfaces.

Getting Rid of the Skeletons

Earlier in this chapter, I noted that:

> Using different skeletons for different classes is not, strictly speaking, necessary. We'll talk about why you want to get rid of them, and how to do so, later in this chapter.

The reason many different types of skeletons aren't necessary is plain: as part of a method call, RMI must already send over enough information to describe the method that needs to be called and the server object on which it should be called. A well-written generic dispatch method could then take this information and use Java's Reflection API to call the method directly without the intervention of a skeleton class.

Early versions of RMI required skeletons. In Java 2, the skeletons were made optional. In order to build a system that doesn't use skeletons, you simply need to tell rmic that you are using the "1.2" protocol, as in the following example:

```
rmic -keep -v1.2 -d d:\classes com.ora.rmibook.chapter8.Account_Impl com.ora.rmibook.
    chapter8.Account_Impl2
```

This will generate stub classes for `Account_Impl` and `Account_Impl2`. However, it will not generate skeletons.

The major reason for getting rid of skeletons is that doing so can simplify deploying and updating an application. The major reason to keep skeletons is that class-specific skeletons are slightly faster than generic ones, which must use the reflection API. In practice, there's not much difference either way, and I prefer to use skeletons simply because as a programmer who cut his teeth on CORBA, I feel that a distributed program without skeletons isn't quite proper.

CHAPTER 9

The Rest of the Application

In previous chapters, we discussed how to design and build servers. In this chapter, we'll finish the application off by building the launch code and assembling a simple client. In addition, we'll motivate much of the second section of this book by talking about the server lifecycle. By the end of this chapter, you will have seen all the steps involved in designing and building a distributed application using RMI and will be ready to start thinking about how to make your application scale.

There is an apparent paradox here. The server code, while difficult to think through and frequently tricky to implement, is often less than half of the total application. The client code, which I relegate to the section "Build the Client Application," is a large and complex part of the application.

There are two reasons for this apparently confusing situation. The first is that we have, to some extent, already discussed client-side issues when we discussed how to choose servers and design interfaces. A large percentage of that discussion was motivated by client-side concerns: what people will do with the application and how to design servers that support the intended uses.

The second reason is quite simply that most of the client code doesn't involve the distributed parts of the application. While getting an instance of JTable to refresh properly is a difficult task, and people who write a good user interface are more than worthy of respect, this book is long enough without adding a guide to writing a client-server GUI.

The Need for Launch Code

One feature of our discussion of distributed applications is that we have explicitly separated the code that launches the servers from the code that actually is the server. In other words, a server right now consists of two logically distinct pieces:

- The code that executes client commands
- The code that starts the servers running in the first place (i.e., the code that launches the code that executes the client commands)

I've been referring to the second type of code as *launch code*. This might seem a little confusing. The two tasks *are* logically distinct—at least when the distinction is phrased as in the preceding points. But it may seem as if we're being overly precise; it's not obvious that launch code needs to be broken into separate classes.

Moreover, as we saw in Chapter 8, when discussing whether to extend Unicast-RemoteObject, there's a blurry line here. Deciding to extend UnicastRemoteObject involves making the server immediately available for remote messages. This appears, at first glance, to be an aspect of launching the server rather than being part of "executing the client commands."

But the distinction between server code and launch code is an important one that will only grow in importance over the course of this book. The first aspect of separating out the launch code is simply that it makes it easier to postpone and revisit deployment decisions. Recall, for example, the discussion in Chapter 6 that centered around the question, "How well does the given server replicate/scale to multiple machines?" We had the following hypothetical scenario:

> A single JVM, containing all our servers, is created. Clients find the servers using the registry and proceed to make calls on them. However, this system doesn't scale very well, and users are upset by how badly the system performs. Then, an order comes down from on high: two JVM's, each containing "half" of the server, should be created. In addition, a new third server, which knows how to redirect clients to a "correct server" should be built. Clients will make a simple query to the third server to find out which server should handle their requests, and then conduct all their business with the designated server.

What is happening here is that, as the application evolves, the launch code is rewritten independently of the server code. Moreover, the rate of revision and the reasons for revising the launch code are entirely different from the rate of revision and the reasons for revising the server code.

The Idea of a Server Lifecycle

Launch code is just the tip of the iceberg. Launching a server is very important. There are also other equally important and related tasks that aren't handled by either of our two previous points. For example, we have completely ignored the question of how to manage scarce resources. If many servers co-exist in the same JVM, then there is always a possibility they will compete for scarce resources.

A related problem is persistence. Servers have state. Since servers crash, this state needs to be stored using a persistent storage mechanism, which is usually based on a file system. But if all the servers are constantly accessing the persistent storage mechanism, usually a relational database, they will compete with each other and swamp the persistence mechanism.

All of this helps to motivate the idea that the next level of thinking about your distributed application should center on *managing the server lifecycle*. That is, the next level of distributed application design centers on the following three questions:

- When should servers be launched?
- When should servers be shut down?
- When should servers save their state to a persistent store?

These are especially pertinent questions in the bank example. We potentially have millions of server objects, but only a small percentage of the accounts are active at any given time. And, once an account has been active, it is unlikely to be active again for quite some time. After all, very few people directly access their bank account more than once per day.

With this discussion behind us, it should be clear that launch code (which is the first step towards managing the server lifecycle) does not belong inside the server objects.

Our Actual Launch Code

Launch code typically consists of two things: a set of batch files* that are run from a command line and start one or more Java applications running, and Java code. In our case, these are very simple. There are two batch files: one to launch the servers and one to run the client application. The server batch file consists of the following code:†

```
start rmiregistry
start java com.ora.rmibook.chapter9.applications.ImplLauncher Bob 100 0 Alex 12 23
```

That is, it starts the RMI registry running and then runs a piece of Java code that launches the server objects. The ImplLauncher application, shown in Example 9-1, is only slightly more complicated.

Example 9-1. ImplLauncher.java

```
package com.ora.rmibook.chapter9.applications;

import com.ora.rmibook.chapter9.*;
import com.ora.rmibook.chapter9.valueobjects.*;
import java.util.*;
import java.rmi.*;

public class ImplLauncher {
    public static void main(String[] args) {
        Collection nameBalancePairs = getNameBalancePairs(args);
        Iterator i = nameBalancePairs.iterator();
```

---

* In Unix terminology, shell scripts.

† This is a windows-specific batch file. Depending on which platform you actually use, the batch file may look different.

Example 9-1. ImplLauncher.java (continued)

```
        while(i.hasNext()) {
            NameBalancePair nextNameBalancePair = (NameBalancePair) i.next();
            launchServer(nextNameBalancePair);
        }
    }

    private static void launchServer(NameBalancePair serverDescription) {
        try {
            Account_Impl newAccount = new Account_Impl(serverDescription.balance);
            Naming.rebind(serverDescription.name, newAccount);
            System.out.println("Account " + serverDescription.name + " successfully
                launched.");
        }
        catch(Exception e){}
    }

    private static Collection getNameBalancePairs(String[] args) {
        int i;
        ArrayList returnValue = new ArrayList();
        for (i=0; i< args.length; i+=3) {
            NameBalancePair nextNameBalancePair = new NameBalancePair();
            nextNameBalancePair.name = args[i];
            Integer cents = new Integer(args[i+1]);
            nextNameBalancePair.balance = new Money(cents);
            returnValue.add(nextNameBalancePair);
        }
        return returnValue;
    }

    private static class NameBalancePair {
        String name;
        Money balance;
    }
}
```

All this does is parse the command-line arguments, create instances of `AccountImpl` corresponding to them, and then register those instances with the RMI registry. So, after running our batch file, we have two instances of `Account` registered with the registry. One corresponds to Bob, who has exactly $100 in his account, and one corresponds to Alex, who has $12.23 in her account.

Of course, this is an unrealistic piece of launch code. In a real bank, the customer account information wouldn't be stored as command-line arguments to a batch file. But, as a pedagogical device, it's pretty nifty.

Build Test Applications

We all know that code needs to be tested. Thoroughly. So the following sad story shouldn't be necessary. But I'm going to tell it anyway.

Once upon a time, I worked for a consulting company, building a distributed application for a client. The application was written in Objective-C* for computers running the NeXTSTEP† operating system. And it utilized NeXT's Portable Distributed Objects (PDO) framework.

We wrote the application. Each object worked correctly. The networking worked fine. And we even tested the application with all 10 developers running it at once. The server worked beautifully, the application ran quickly, and everything was wonderful.

The customer was skeptical. So the application was rolled out to a limited number of users for testing. Everything worked fine, and the customer was enthused. We delivered an application that worked well, and we actually came in ahead of schedule. We were beaming with pride as they rolled out the application to the entire organization.

At which point, of course, the application no longer worked. It turned out that the server wasn't quite as robust as we'd thought. It couldn't handle large numbers of simultaneous clients. And our testing, which was actually quite thorough, failed to uncover this fact.

Let's examine why. We tested:

- The underlying server logic that handled each client request
- The connection logic (so clients could find the servers easily)
- The ability of the application to handle a dozen or so users

But we assumed that this would be sufficent ("If it can do this stuff, it's working fine"). This was a very bad mistake. Simulate the client's environment as much as you can. If you're planning to deploy 500 clients, you need to actually test with 500 clients. Actually, test with more clients than you plan to have. Successful applications frequently see heavier use than expected.

Testing our banking application isn't really very feasible right now. For one thing, stress testing is usually done with applications that simulate dozens of clients simultaneously. For another, our implementation of `AccountImpl` won't actually work correctly if more than one client connects with it simultaneously (it isn't threadsafe). But testing is an important part of the development process, and thus deserves to be mentioned in our overall sketch of the RMI development cycle.

Build the Client Application

The client application is normally built simultaneously with the server application. Once the server interfaces are defined, server-side development can proceed

---

* Never heard of it? Think "Smalltalk with a C syntax."
† An obscure Unix variant.

in isolation. Client developers usually use "fake servers," which implement the remote interface in trivial ways and run in the client process when developing the client application. This allows server developers a little more freedom to design and develop their part of the application; it avoids forcing them to commit to a total architecture early in the development cycle.

 Another reason why clients and servers are often built simultaneously is that the skills required to build them are fairly distinct. Developers building the client application have to know how to build a good user interface (e.g., have mastered a substantial portion of the Swing toolkit) and don't really need to read anything in this book past this chapter. People building servers can make do with far less knowledge of the user interface components, but should definitely read the entire book.

In order for this to work, however, client-side developers must take care to heed one simple rule of thumb:

Consume as few server resources as possible, for as short a time as is reasonable.

This rule of thumb has two main consequences: don't hold connections to a server you're not using, and validate arguments on the client-side whenever reasonable.

Don't Hold Connections to a Server You're Not Using

The client has to connect to the server. Recall that, in a typical application, this is done in two steps:

1. The client connects to the naming service.
2. The client gets a connection to the server it wants by making a call to the naming service.

When using the RMI registry, this is often accomplished in a single line of code. For example, our bank client connects to a particular account in the following line of code:

```
_account = (Account)Naming.lookup(_accountNameField.getText());
```

The essence of this rule of thumb is this: as soon as is reasonable, set the stub variable to null. In the account client, we actually have a pair of methods for handling our connections. One establishes the connection and one releases it.

```
private void getAccount() {
    try {
        _account = (Account)Naming.lookup(_accountNameField.getText());
    }
    catch (Exception e) {
        System.out.println("Couldn't find account. Error was \n " + e);
        e.printStackTrace();
    }
    return;
}
```

```
private void releaseAccount( ) {
    _account = null;
}
```

Next, whenever we need to make a method call, we call both of these. For example, here is the code that gets the account balance (all of our operations are implemented as subclasses of ActionListener):

```
private class GetBalanceAction implements ActionListener {
    public void actionPerformed(ActionEvent event) {
        try {
            getAccount( );
            resetBalanceField( );
            releaseAccount( );
        }
        catch (Exception exception) {
            System.out.println("Couldn't talk to account. Error was \n " +
                exception);
            exception.printStackTrace( );
        }
    }
}
```

This establishes a connection, makes the query, and then releases the connection. Doing this enables the RMI runtime to perform distributed garbage collection and thus allows the server to perform cleanup actions (e.g., releasing resources, persisting state) at fairly appropriate times. However, in order for this to work, clients have to be good distributed citizens and relinquish their connections when they are done.

 It's possible to take this too far. If the client is going to make more method calls on the same server in a short period of time, it's perfectly reasonable to keep a reference to the stub. If the client doesn't keep a reference to the active stub, the client will just have to contact the naming service again, and re-establish the same connection to the server.

Validate Arguments on the Client Side Whenever Reasonable

When we discussed how to design a remote interface in Chapter 7, one of the key questions was, "Have we identified a reasonable set of distributed exceptions?" There were two reasons for this. One was so that the client could behave correctly when the server experienced a failure. And the second was so that the client could validate method arguments as much as possible.

It makes little sense for the client to invoke a remote method when it knows beforehand that such an invocation is already invalid. In our example, one major exception that the server could throw is `NegativeArgumentException`. However, the client is just as capable of checking this on its own without invoking a remote method. For example, when the client calls:

```
public void makeWithdrawal(Money amount) throws RemoteException, OverdraftException,
    NegativeAmountException;
```

on an instance of `AccountImpl`, the client has no way of knowing whether the amount requested is an overdraft. However, it can certainly check to make sure the amount being withdrawn isn't a negative amount of money. In our implementation, we've defined a new subclass of `Money`, `PositiveMoney`, to handle this issue.

`PositiveMoney`'s constructor validates the cents values to make sure they are positive. And, since `PositiveMoney` extends `Money`, `PositiveMoney` will be a perfectly acceptable argument to the methods in our `Account` interface. Here is the constructor for `PositiveMoney`:

```
public PositiveMoney(int cents) throws Exception {
    super(cents,);
    if ((_cents < 0)) {
        throw new Exception("Bad Value for Money");
    }
    return;
}
```

This isn't a very impressive code change, and it might seem like I'm belaboring an obvious point. But the difference between the following two scenarios is enormous:

- The user accidentally enters $–120.00 as her withdrawal amount. She presses a button, waits 15 seconds and is told, "You can't withdraw a negative amount."

- The user accidentally enters $–120.00 as her withdrawal amount. As soon as she presses a button, she is told, "You can't withdraw a negative amount."

The first application is perceived as slow and, consequently, not well designed; the second one is much faster. You can greatly improve perceived application performance by defining a rich set of exceptions and checking as many of them as possible on the client side.

The Actual Client Application

The actual client application is a very simple GUI shown in Figure 9-1. The implementation of this application consists of two objects. The first is simply a wrapper class that implements `main( )`, shown in Example 9-2.

Do ATMs Really Do This?

The example of checking to see whether a withdrawal amount is negative probably seems a little contrived. But look at your ATM machine the next time you make a withdrawal. There isn't even a minus key there. You are physically prevented from entering an incorrect amount.

Moreover, if your bank is anything like mine, it has rules governing the amount you can withdraw. My bank has the following two rules:

- The amount of money being withdrawn must be a multiple of $20.
- No more than $300 can be withdrawn in any given day.

These are enforced by two local checks and then three checks at the server. The local checks are:

- The amount of money being withdrawn must be a multiple of $20.
- The amount being withdrawn cannot be more than $300.

The checks at the server are:

- The amount of money being withdrawn must be a multiple of $20.
- The amount being withdrawn cannot be more than $300.
- The total withdrawn for the day cannot be more than $300.

The first two checks are performed on the client side, for the reasons we've been discussing in the this chapter. They're also repeated on the server side, to prevent a badly written (or malicious) client from causing data integrity problems.

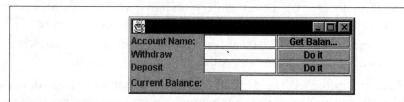

Figure 9-1. The banking application GUI

Example 9-2. BankClient.java

```
package com.ora.rmibook.chapter9.applications;

import java.rmi.*;
import java.rmi.server.*;

public class BankClient
{
    public static void main(String[] args) {
        (new BankClientFrame()).show( );
    }
}
```

Most of the client application is in a second object that creates the user interface and has a set of `ActionListeners` attached to buttons. This object is shown in Example 9-3.

Example 9-3. BankClientFrame.java

```java
public class BankClientFrame {
    private JTextField _accountNameField;
    private JTextField _balanceTextField;
    private JTextField _withdrawalTextField;
    private JTextField _depositTextField;
    private Account _account;

    protected void buildGUI() {
        JPanel contentPane = new JPanel(new BorderLayout());
        contentPane.add(buildActionPanel(), BorderLayout.CENTER);
        contentPane.add(buildBalancePanel(), BorderLayout.SOUTH);
        setContentPane(contentPane);
        setSize(250, 100);
    }

    private void resetBalanceField() {
        try {
            Money balance = _account.getBalance();
            _balanceTextField.setText("Balance: " + balance.toString());
        }
        catch(Exception e) {
            System.out.println("Error occurred while getting account balance\n" + e);
        }
    }

    private JPanel buildActionPanel() {
        JPanel actionPanel = new JPanel(new GridLayout(3,3));
        actionPanel.add(new JLabel("Account Name:"));
        _accountNameField = new JTextField();
        actionPanel.add(_accountNameField);
        JButton getBalanceButton = new JButton("Get Balance");
        getBalanceButton.addActionListener(new GetBalanceAction());
        actionPanel.add(getBalanceButton);
        actionPanel.add(new JLabel("Withdraw"));
        _withdrawalTextField = new JTextField();
        actionPanel.add(_withdrawalTextField);
        JButton withdrawalButton = new JButton("Do it");
        withdrawalButton.addActionListener(new WithdrawAction());
        actionPanel.add(withdrawalButton);
        actionPanel.add(new JLabel("Deposit"));
        _depositTextField = new JTextField();
        actionPanel.add(_depositTextField);
        JButton depositButton = new JButton("Do it");
        depositButton.addActionListener(new DepositAction());
        actionPanel.add(depositButton);
        return actionPanel;
    }
}
```

Example 9-3. BankClientFrame.java (continued)

```java
    private JPanel buildBalancePanel( ) {
        JPanel balancePanel = new JPanel(new GridLayout(1,2));
        balancePanel.add(new JLabel("Current Balance:"));
        _balanceTextField = new JTextField( );
        _balanceTextField.setEnabled(false);
        balancePanel.add(_balanceTextField);
        return balancePanel;
    }

    private void getAccount( ) {
        try {
            _account = (Account)Naming.lookup(_accountNameField.getText( ));
        }
         catch (Exception e) {
            System.out.println("Couldn't find account. Error was \n " + e);
            e.printStackTrace( );
        }
        return;
    }

    private void releaseAccount{
        _account = null;
    }

    private Money readTextField(JTextField moneyField){
        try {
            Float floatValue = new Float(moneyField.getText( ));
            float actualValue = floatValue.floatValue( );
            int cents = (int) (actualValue * 100);
            return new PositiveMoney(cents);
        }
        catch (Exception e) {
            System.out.println("Field doesn't contain a valid value");
        }
        return null;
    }

    private class GetBalanceAction implements ActionListener {
        public void actionPerformed(ActionEvent event) {
            try {
                getAccount( );
                resetBalanceField( );
                releaseAccount( );
            }
            catch (Exception exception){
                System.out.println("Couldn't talk to account. Error was \n " +
                    exception);
                exception.printStackTrace( );
            }
        }
    }
```

Example 9-3. BankClientFrame.java (continued)

```
private class WithdrawAction implements ActionListener {
    public void actionPerformed(ActionEvent event) {
        try{
            getAccount( );
            Money withdrawalAmount = readTextField(_withdrawalTextField);
            _account.makeWithdrawal(withdrawalAmount);
            _withdrawalTextField.setText("");
            resetBalanceField( );
            releaseAccount( );
        }
        catch (Exception exception){
            System.out.println("Couldn't talk to account. Error was \n " +
                exception);
            exception.printStackTrace( );
        }
    }
}

private class DepositAction implements ActionListener {
    public void actionPerformed(ActionEvent event) {
        try {
            getAccount( );
            Money depositAmount = readTextField(_depositTextField);
            _account.makeDeposit(depositAmount);
            _depositTextField.setText("");
            resetBalanceField( );
            releaseAccount( );
        }
        catch (Exception exception) {
            System.out.println("Couldn't talk to account. Error was \n " +
                exception);
            exception.printStackTrace( );
        }
    }
}
}
```

Deploying the Application

The final step in implementing a distributed application is deployment. Deploying an application can be a difficult and tedious task. RMI applications are no different than ordinary applications in this regard. They do, however, add one new wrinkle: you need to deploy stubs along with your client.

Recall that when you finish writing the code, you need to generate stubs and skeletons. The stubs, even though they're generated from the server classes, are part of the client application. This can become an issue because, if you modify the server, you may need to redistribute the stubs. Even though "the client code" hasn't changed, if either the server classes (AccountImpl in the current case) or the data objects have changed, RMI will throw an exception if you use an older version of the stub classes in the client application.

You also need to make sure that the naming service has the stubs on its classpath. This usually catches first-time users of RMI by surprise, but it's necessary because the registry has a stub for every server that gets registered. The registry doesn't simply hold on to the serialized bytes; it actually instantiates the stub and stores the stub in a hashtable. In order to do this, the registry needs to have access to the stub classes.

We'll discuss why the registry does this in Chapter 14. For now, just remember: the stubs need to be deployed with the client application and with the registry.

Drilling Down: Scalability

Serialization

Serialization is the process of converting a set of object instances that contain references to each other into a linear stream of bytes, which can then be sent through a socket, stored to a file, or simply manipulated as a stream of data. Serialization is the mechanism used by RMI to pass objects between JVMs, either as arguments in a method invocation from a client to a server or as return values from a method invocation. In the first section of this book, I referred to this process several times but delayed a detailed discussion until now. In this chapter, we drill down on the serialization mechanism; by the end of it, you will understand exactly how serialization works and how to use it efficiently within your applications.

The Need for Serialization

Envision the banking application while a client is executing a withdrawal. The part of the application we're looking at has the runtime structure shown in Figure 10-1.

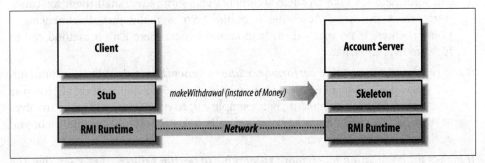

Figure 10-1. Runtime structure when making a withdrawal

What does it mean for the client to pass an instance of Money to the server? At a minimum, it means that the server is able to call public methods on the instance of Money.

One way to do this would be to implicitly make Money into a server as well.[*] For example, imagine that the client sends the following two pieces of information whenever it passes an instance as an argument:

- The type of the instance; in this case, Money.
- A unique identifier for the object (i.e., a logical reference). For example, the address of the instance in memory.

The RMI runtime layer in the server can use this information to construct a stub for the instance of Money, so that whenever the Account server calls a method on what it thinks of as the instance of Money, the method call is relayed over the wire, as shown in Figure 10-2.

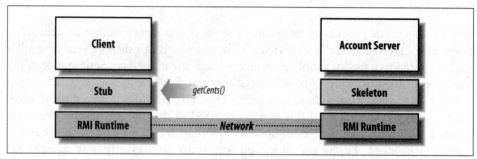

Figure 10-2. Relaying a Money method call from the server

Attempting to do things this way has three significant drawbacks:

You can't access fields on the objects that have been passed as arguments.
Stubs work by implementing an interface. They implement the methods in the interface by simply relaying the method invocation across the network. That is, the stub methods take all their arguments and simply marshall them for transport across the wire. Accessing a public field is really just dereferencing a pointer—there is no method invocation and hence, there isn't a method call to forward over the wire.

It can result in unacceptable performance due to network latency. Even in our simple case, the instance of Account is going to need to call getCents() on the instance of Money. This means that a simple call to makeDeposit() really involves at least two distinct networked method calls: makeDeposit() from the client and getCents() from the server.

It makes the application much more vulnerable to partial failure. Let's say that the server is busy and doesn't get around to handling the request for 30 seconds. If the client crashes in the interim, or if the network goes down, the server cannot

---

[*] Just to be clear: doing things this way would be a bad idea (and this is not the way RMI passes instances over the wire).

process the request at all. Until all data has been requested and sent, the application is particularly vulnerable to partial failures.

This last point is an interesting one. Any time you have an application that requires a long-lasting and durable connection between client and server, you build in a point of failure. The longer the connection needs to last, or the higher the communication bandwidth the connection requires, the more likely the application is to occasionally break down.

 The original design of the Web, with its stateless connections, serves as a good example of a distributed application that can tolerate almost any transient network failure.

These three reasons imply that what is really needed is a way to copy objects and send them over the wire. That is, instead of turning arguments into implicit servers, arguments need to be completely copied so that no further network calls are needed to complete the remote method invocation. Put another way, we want the result of makeWithdrawal( ) to involve creating a copy of the instance of Money on the server side. The runtime structure should resemble Figure 10-3.

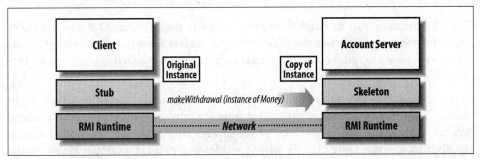

Figure 10-3. Making a remote method call can create deep copies of the arguments and return values

The desire to avoid unnecessary network dependencies has two significant consequences:

Once an object is duplicated, the two objects are completely independent of each other. Any attempt to keep the copy and the original in sync would involve propagating changes over the network, entirely defeating the reason for making the copy in the first place.

The copying mechanism must create deep copies. If the instance of Money references another instance, then copies must be made of both instances. Otherwise, when a method is called on the second object, the call must be relayed across the wire. Moreover, all the copies must be made immediately—we can't wait until the second object is accessed to make the copy because the original might change in the meantime.

These two consequences have a very important third consequence:

***If an object is sent twice, in separate method calls, two copies of the object will be
created.*** In addition to arguments to method calls, this holds for objects that are
referenced by the arguments. If you pass object A, which has a reference to
object C, and in another call you pass object B, which also has a reference to C,
you will end up with two distinct copies of C on the receiving side.

Drilling Down on Object Creation

To see why this last point holds, consider a client that executes a withdrawal and
then tries to cancel the transaction by making a deposit for the same amount of
money. That is, the following lines of code are executed:

```
server.makeWithdrawal(amount);
....
server.makeDeposit(amount);
```

The client has no way of knowing whether the server still has a copy of amount. After
all, the server may have used it and then thrown the copy away once it was done.
This means that the client has to marshall amount and send it over the wire to the
server.

The RMI runtime can demarshall amount, which is the instance of Money the client
sent. However, even if it has the previous object, it has no way (unless equals( ) has
been overridden) to tell whether the instance it just demarshalled is equal to the previous object.

More generally, if the object being copied isn't immutable, then the server might
change it. In this case, even if the two objects are currently equal, the RMI runtime
has no way to tell if the two copies will always be equal and can potentially be
replaced by a single copy. To see why, consider our Printer example again. At the
end of Chapter 3, we considered a list of possible feature requests that could be
made. One of them was the following:

> Managers will want to track resource consumption. This will involve logging print
> requests and, quite possibly, building a set of queries that can be run against the
> printer's log.

This can be implemented by adding a few more fields to DocumentDescription and
having the server store an indexed log of all the DocumentDescription objects it has
received. For example, we may add the following fields to DocumentDescription:

```
public Time whenPrinted;
public Person sender;
public boolean printSucceeded;
```

Now consider what happens when the user actually wants to print two copies of the
same document. The client application could call:

```
server.printDocument(document);
```

twice with the "same" instance of DocumentDescription. And it would be an error for the RMI runtime to create only one instance of DocumentDescription on the server side. Even though the "same" object is passed into the server twice, it is passed as parts of distinct requests and therefore as different objects.

> This is true even if the runtime can tell that the two instances of DocumentDescription are equal when it finishes demarshalling. An implementation of a printer may well have a notion of a job queue that holds instances of DocumentDescription. So our client makes the first call, and the copy of document is placed in the queue (say, at number 5), but not edited because the document hasn't been printed yet. Then our client makes the second call. At this point, the two copies of document are equal. However, we don't want to place the same object in the printer queue twice. We want to place distinct copies in the printer queue.

Thus, we come to the following conclusion: network latency, and the desire to avoid vulnerability to partial failures, force us to have a deep copy mechanism for most arguments to a remote method invocation. This copying mechanism has to make deep copies, and it cannot perform any validation to eliminate "extra" copies across methods.

> While this discussion provides examples of implementation decisions that force two copies to occur, it's important to note that, even without such examples, clients should be written as if the servers make independent copies. That is, clients are written to use interfaces. They should not, and cannot, make assumptions about server-side implementations of the interfaces.

Using Serialization

Serialization is a mechanism built into the core Java libraries for writing a graph of objects into a stream of data. This stream of data can then be programmatically manipulated, and a deep copy of the objects can be made by reversing the process. This reversal is often called *deserialization*.

In particular, there are three main uses of serialization:

As a persistence mechanism
If the stream being used is FileOutputStream, then the data will automatically be written to a file.

As a copy mechanism
If the stream being used is ByteArrayOutputStream, then the data will be written to a byte array in memory. This byte array can then be used to create duplicates of the original objects.

As a communication mechanism

If the stream being used comes from a socket, then the data will automatically be sent over the wire to the receiving socket, at which point another program will decide what to do.

The important thing to note is that the use of serialization is independent of the serialization algorithm itself. If we have a serializable class, we can save it to a file or make a copy of it simply by changing the way we use the output of the serialization mechanism.

As you might expect, serialization is implemented using a pair of streams. Even though the code that underlies serialization is quite complex, the way you invoke it is designed to make serialization as transparent as possible to Java developers. To serialize an object, create an instance of ObjectOutputStream and call the writeObject( ) method; to read in a serialized object, create an instance of ObjectInputStream and call the readObject( ) object.

ObjectOutputStream

ObjectOutputStream, defined in the java.io package, is a stream that implements the "writing-out" part of the serialization algorithm.* The methods implemented by ObjectOutputStream can be grouped into three categories: methods that write information to the stream, methods used to control the stream's behavior, and methods used to customize the serialization algorithm.

The "write" methods

The first, and most intuitive, category consists of the "write" methods:

```
public void write(byte[] b);
public void write(byte[] b, int off, int len);
public void write(int data);
public void writeBoolean(boolean data);
public void writeByte(int data);
public void writeBytes(String data);
public void writeChar(int data);
public void writeChars(String data);
public void writeDouble(double data);
public void writeFields( );
public void writeFloat(float data);
public void writeInt(int data);
public void writeLong(long data);
public void writeObject(Object obj);
public void writeShort(int data);
public void writeUTF(String s);
public void defaultWriteObject( );
```

---

* RMI actually uses a subclass of ObjectOutputStream to customize its behavior.

For the most part, these methods should seem familiar. `writeFloat()`, for example, works exactly as you would expect after reading Chapter 1—it takes a floating-point number and encodes the number as four bytes. There are, however, two new methods here: `writeObject()` and `defaultWriteObject()`.

`writeObject()` serializes an object. In fact, `writeObject()` is often the instrument of the serialization mechanism itself. In the simplest and most common case, serializing an object involves doing two things: creating an `ObjectOutputStream` and calling `writeObject()` with a single "top-level" instance. The following code snippet shows the entire process, storing an object—and all the objects to which it refers—into a file:

```
FileOutputStream underlyingStream = new FileOutputStream("C:\\temp\\test");
ObjectOutputStream serializer = new ObjectOutputStream(underlyingStream);
serializer.writeObject(serializableObject);
```

Of course, this works seamlessly with the other methods for writing data. That is, if you wanted to write two floats, a String, and an object to a file, you could do so with the following code snippet:

```
FileOutputStream underlyingStream = new FileOutputStream("C:\\temp\\test");
ObjectOutputStream serializer = new ObjectOutputStream(underlyingStream);
serializer.writeFloat(firstFloat);
serializer.writeFloat(secongFloat);
serializer.writeUTF(aString);
serializer.writeObject(serializableObject);
```

 `ObjectOutputStream`'s constructor takes an `OutputStream` as an argument. This is analagous to many of the streams we looked at in Chapter 1. `ObjectOutputStream` and `ObjectInputStream` are simply encoding and transformation layers. This enables RMI to send objects over the wire by opening a socket connection, associating the `OutputStream` with the socket connection, creating an `ObjectOutputStream` on top of the socket's `OutputStream`, and then calling `writeObject()`.

The other new "write" method is `defaultWriteObject()`. `defaultWriteObject()` makes it much easier to customize how instances of a single class are serialized. However, `defaultWriteObject()` has some strange restrictions placed on when it can be called. Here's what the documentation says about `defaultWriteObject()`:

> Write the nonstatic and nontransient fields of the current class to this stream. This may only be called from the `writeObject` method of the class being serialized. It will throw the `NotActiveException` if it is called otherwise.

That is, `defaultWriteObject()` is a method that works only when it is called from another specific method at a particular time. Since `defaultWriteObject()` is useful only when you are customizing the information stored for a particular class, this turns out to be a reasonable restriction. We'll talk more about `defaultWriteObject()` later in the chapter, when we discuss how to make a class serializable.

The stream manipulation methods

ObjectOutputStream also implements four methods that deal with the basic mechanics of manipulating the stream:

```
public void reset();
public void close();
public void flush();
public void useProtocolVersion(int version);
```

With the exception of useProtocolVersion(), these methods should be familiar. In fact, reset(), close(), and flush() are standard stream methods. useProtocolVersion(), on the other hand, changes the version of the serialization mechanism that is used. This is necessary because the serialization format and algorithm may need to change in a way that's not backwards-compatible. If another application needs to read in your serialized data, and the applications will be versioning independently (or running in different versions of the JVM), you may want to standardize on a protocol version.

 There are two versions of the serialization protocol currently defined: PROTOCOL_VERSION_1 and PROTOCOL_VERSION_2. If you send serialized data to a 1.1 (or earlier) JVM, you should probably use PROTOCOL_VERSION_1. The most common case of this involves applets. Most applets run in browsers over which the developer has no control. This means, in particular, that the JVM running the applet could be anything, from Java 1.0.2 through the latest JVM. Most servers, on the other hand, are written using JDK1.2.2 or later.[*] If you pass serialized objects between an applet and a server, you should specify the serialization protocol.

Methods that customize the serialization mechanism

The last group of methods consists mostly of protected methods that provide hooks that allow the serialization mechanism itself, rather than the data associated to a particular class, to be customized. These methods are:

```
public ObjectOutputStream.PutField putFields();
protected void annotateClass(Class cl);
protected void annotateProxyClass(Class cl);
protected boolean enableReplaceObject(boolean enable);
protected Object replaceObject(Object obj);
protected void drain();
protected void writeObjectOverride(Object obj);
protected void writeClassDescriptor(ObjectStreamClass classdesc);
protected void writeStreamHeader();
```

These methods are more important to people who tailor the serialization algorithm to a particular use or develop their own implementation of serialization. As such, they require a deeper understanding of the serialization algorithm. We'll discuss

---

[*] The main exception is EJB containers that require earlier versions of Java. At this writing, for example, Oracle 8*i*'s EJB container uses JDK 1.1.6.

these methods in more detail later, after we've gone over the actual algorithm used by the serialization mechanism.

ObjectInputStream

ObjectInputStream, defined in the java.io package, implements the "reading-in" part of the serialization algorithm. It is the companion to ObjectOutputStream—objects serialized using ObjectOutputStream can be deserialized using ObjectInputStream. Like ObjectOutputStream, the methods implemented by ObjectInputStream can be grouped into three categories: methods that read information from the stream, methods that are used to control the stream's behavior, and methods that are used to customize the serialization algorithm.

The "read" methods

The first, and most intuitive, category consists of the "read" methods:

```
public int read( );
public int read(byte[] b, int off, int len);
public boolean readBoolean( );
public byte readByte( );
public char readChar( );
public double readDouble( );
public float readFloat( );
public intreadInt( );
public long readLong( );
public Object readObject( );
public short readShort( );
public byte readUnsignedByte( );
public short readUnsignedShort( );
public String readUTF( );
void defaultReadObject( );
```

Just as with ObjectOutputStream's write( ) methods, these methods should be familiar. readFloat( ), for example, works exactly as you would expect after reading Chapter 1: it reads four bytes from the stream and converts them into a single floating-point number, which is returned by the method call. And, again as with ObjectOutputStream, there are two new methods here: readObject( ) and defaultReadObject( ).

Just as writeObject( ) serializes an object, readObject( ) deserializes it. Deserializing an object involves doing two things: creating an ObjectInputStream and then calling readObject( ). The following code snippet shows the entire process, creating a copy of an object (and all the objects to which it refers) from a file:

```
FileInputStream underlyingStream = new FileInputStream("C:\\temp\\test");
ObjectInputStream deserializer = new ObjectInputStream(underlyingStream);
Object deserializedObject = deserializer.readObject( );
```

This code is exactly inverse to the code we used for serializing the object in the first place. If we wanted to make a deep copy of a serializable object, we could first serialize the object and then deserialize it, as in the following code example:

```
ByteArrayOutputStream memoryOutputStream = new ByteArrayOutputStream( );
ObjectOutputStream serializer = new ObjectOutputStream(memoryOutputStream);
serializer.writeObject(serializableObject);
serializer.flush( );

ByteArrayInputStream memoryInputStream = new ByteArrayInputStream(memoryOutputStream.
    toByteArray( ));
ObjectInputStream deserializer = new ObjectInputStream(memoryInputStream);
Object deepCopyOfOriginalObject = deserializer.readObject( );
```

This code simply places an output stream into memory, serializes the object to the memory stream, creates an input stream based on the same piece of memory, and runs the deserializer on the input stream. The end result is a deep copy of the object with which we started.

The stream manipulation methods

There are five basic stream manipulation methods defined for `ObjectInputStream`:

```
public boolean available( );
public void close( );
public void readFully(byte[] data);
public void readFully(byte[] data, int offset, int size);
public int skipBytes(int len);
```

Of these, `available( )` and `skip( )` are methods first defined on `InputStream`. `available( )` returns a boolean flag indicating whether data is immediately available, and `close( )` closes the stream.

The three new methods are also straightforward. `skipBytes( )` skips the indicated number of bytes in the stream, blocking until all the information has been read. And the two `readFully( )` methods perform a batch read into a byte array, also blocking until all the data has been read in.

Methods that customize the serialization mechanism

The last group of methods consists mostly of protected methods that provide hooks, which allow the serialization mechanism itself, rather than the data associated to a particular class, to be customized. These methods are:

```
protected boolean enableResolveObject(boolean enable);
protected Class resolveClass(ObjectStreamClass v);
protected Object resolveObject(Object obj);
protected class resolveProxyClass(String[] interfaces);
protected ObjectStreamClass readClassDescriptor( );
protected Object readObjectOverride( );
```

```
protected void readStreamHeader();
public void registerValidation(ObjectInputValidation obj, int priority);
public GetFields readFields();
```

These methods are more important to people who tailor the serialization algorithm to a particular use or develop their own implementation of serialization. Like before, they also require a deeper understanding of the serialization algorithm, so I'll hold off on discussing them right now.

How to Make a Class Serializable

So far, we've focused on the mechanics of serializing an object. We've assumed we have a serializable object and discussed, from the point of view of client code, how to serialize it. The next step is discussing how to make a class serializable.

There are four basic things you must do when you are making a class serializable. They are:

1. Implement the Serializable interface.

2. Make sure that instance-level, locally defined state is serialized properly.

3. Make sure that superclass state is serialized properly.

4. Override equals( ) and hashCode( ).

Let's look at each of these steps in more detail.

Implement the Serializable Interface

This is by far the easiest of the steps. The Serializable interface is an empty interface; it declares no methods at all. So implementing it amounts to adding "implements Serializable" to your class declaration.

Reasonable people may wonder about the utility of an empty interface. Rather than define an empty interface, and require class definitions to implement it, why not just simply make every object serializable? The main reason not to do this is that there are some classes that don't have an obvious serialization. Consider, for example, an instance of File. An instance of File represents a file. Suppose, for example, it was created using the following line of code:

```
File file = new File("c:\\temp\\foo");
```

It's not at all clear what should be written out when this is serialized. The problem is that the file itself has a different lifecyle than the serialized data. The file might be edited, or deleted entirely, while the serialized information remains unchanged. Or the serialized information might be used to restart the application on another machine, where "C:\\temp\\foo" is the name of an entirely different file.

Another example is provided by the Thread[*] class. A thread represents a flow of execution within a particular JVM. You would not only have to store the stack, and all the local variables, but also all the related locks and threads, and restart all the threads properly when the instance is deserialized.

 Things get worse when you consider platform dependencies. In general, any class that involves native code is not really a good candidate for serialization.

Make Sure That Instance-Level, Locally Defined State Is Serialized Properly

Class definitions contain variable declarations. The instance-level, locally defined variables (e.g., the nonstatic variables) are the ones that contain the state of a particular instance. For example, in our Money class, we declared one such field:

```
public class Money extends ValueObject {
    private int _cents;
    ....
}
```

The serialization mechanism has a nice default behavior—if all the instance-level, locally defined variables have values that are either serializable objects or primitive datatypes, then the serialization mechanism will work without any further effort on our part. For example, our implementations of Account, such as Account_Impl, would present no problems for the default serialization mechanism:

```
public class Account_Impl extends UnicastRemoteObject implements Account {
    private Money _balance;
    ...
}
```

While _balance doesn't have a primitive type, it does refer to an instance of Money, which is a serializable class.

If, however, some of the fields don't have primitive types, and don't refer to serializable classes, more work may be necessary. Consider, for example, the implementation of ArrayList from the java.util package. An ArrayList really has only two pieces of state:

```
public class ArrayList extends AbstractList implements List, Cloneable, java.io.
    Serializable {
    private Object elementData[];
    private int size;
...
}
```

---

[*] If you don't know much about threads, just wait a few chapters and then revisit this example. It will make more sense then.

But hidden in here is a huge problem: ArrayList is a generic container class whose state is stored as an array of objects. While arrays are first-class objects in Java, they aren't serializable objects. This means that ArrayList can't just implement the Serializable interface. It has to provide extra information to help the serialization mechanism handle its nonserializable fields. There are three basic solutions to this problem:

- Fields can be declared to be transient.
- The writeObject( )/readObject( ) methods can be implemented.
- serialPersistentFields can be declared.

Declaring transient fields

The first, and easiest, thing you can do is simply mark some fields using the transient keyword. In ArrayList, for example, elementData is really declared to be a transient field:

```
public class ArrayList extends AbstractList implements List, Cloneable, java.io.
    Serializable {
    private transient Object elementData[];
    private int size;
...
}
```

This tells the default serialization mechanism to ignore the variable. In other words, the serialization mechanism simply skips over the transient variables. In the case of ArrayList, the default serialization mechanism would attempt to write out size, but ignore elementData entirely.

This can be useful in two, usually distinct, situations:

The variable isn't serializable
If the variable isn't serializable, then the serialization mechanism will throw an exception when it tries to serialize the variable. To avoid this, you can declare the variable to be transient.

The variable is redundant
Suppose that the instance caches the result of a computation. Locally, we might want to store the result of the computation, in order to save some processor time. But when we send the object over the wire, we might worry more about consuming bandwidth and thus discard the cached computation since we can always regenerate it later on.

Implementing writeObject() and readObject( )

Suppose that the first case applies. A field takes values that aren't serializable. If the field is still an important part of the state of our instance, such as elementData in the case of an ArrayList, simply declaring the variable to be transient isn't good enough. We need to save and restore the state stored in the variable. This is done by implementing a pair of methods with the following signatures:

```
private void writeObject(java.io.ObjectOutputStream out) throws IOException
private void readObject(java.io.ObjectInputStream in) throws IOException,
    ClassNotFoundException;
```

When the serialization mechanism starts to write out an object, it will check to see whether the class implements writeObject( ). If so, the serialization mechanism will not use the default mechanism and will not write out any of the instance variables. Instead, it will call writeObject( ) and depend on the method to store out all the important state. Here is ArrayList's implementation of writeObject( ):

```
private synchronized void writeObject(java.io.ObjectOutputStream stream) throws java.
    io.IOException {
    stream.defaultWriteObject();
    stream.writeInt(elementData.length);
    for (int i=0; i<size; i++)
        stream.writeObject(elementData[i]);
}
```

The first thing this does is call defaultWriteObject( ). defaultWriteObject( ) invokes the default serialization mechanism, which serializes all the nontransient, nonstatic instance variables. Next, the method writes out elementData.length and then calls the stream's writeObject( ) for each element of elementData.

There's an important point here that is sometimes missed: readObject( ) and writeObject( ) are a pair of methods that need to be implemented together. If you do any customization of serialization inside one of these methods, you need to implement the other method. If you don't, the serialization algorithm will fail.

Unit Tests and Serialization

Unit tests are used to test a specific piece of functionality in a class. They are explicitly not end-to-end or application-level tests. It's often a good idea to adopt a unit-testing harness such as JUnit when developing an application. JUnit gives you an automated way to run unit tests on individual classes and is available from *http://www.junit.org*.

If you adopt a unit-testing methodology, then any serializable class should pass the following three tests:

- If it implements readObject( ), it should implement writeObject( ), and vice-versa.
- It is equal (using the equals( ) method) to a serialized copy of itself.
- It has the same hashcode as a serialized copy of itself.

Similar constraints hold for classes that implement the Externalizable interface.

Declaring serialPersistentFields

The final option that can be used is to explicitly declare which fields should be stored by the serialization mechanism. This is done using a special static final variable called serialPersistentFields, as shown in the following code snippet:

```
private static final ObjectStreamField[] serialPersistentFields = { new
    ObjectStreamField("size", Integer.TYPE), .... };
```

This line of code declares that the field named size, which is of type int, is a serial persistent field and will be written to the output stream by the serialization mechanism. Declaring serialPersistentFields is almost the opposite of declaring some fields transient. The meaning of transient is, "This field shouldn't be stored by serialization," and the meaning of serialPersistentFields is, "These fields should be stored by serialization."

But there is one important difference between declaring some variables to be transient and others to be serialPersistentFields. In order to declare variables to be transient, they must be locally declared. In other words, you must have access to the code that declares the variable. There is no such requirement for serialPersistentFields. You simply provide the name of the field and the type.

 What if you try to do both? That is, suppose you declare some variables to be transient, and then also provide a definition for serialPersistentFields? The answer is that the transient keyword is ignored; the definition of serialPersistentFields is definitive.

So far, we've talked only about instance-level state. What about class-level state? Suppose you have important information stored in a static variable? Static variables won't get saved by serialization unless you add special code to do so. In our context, (shipping objects over the wire between clients and servers), statics are usually a bad idea anyway.

Make Sure That Superclass State Is Handled Correctly

After you've handled the locally declared state, you may still need to worry about variables declared in a superclass. If the superclass implements the Serializable interface, then you don't need to do anything. The serialization mechanism will handle everything for you, either by using default serialization or by invoking writeObject( )/readObject( ) if they are declared in the superclass.

If the superclass doesn't implement Serializable, you will need to store its state. There are two different ways to approach this. You can use serialPersistentFields to tell the serialization mechanism about some of the superclass instance variables, or you can use writeObject( )/readObject( ) to handle the superclass state explicitly.

Both of these, unfortunately, require you to know a fair amount about the superclass. If you're getting the *.class* files from another source, you should be aware that versioning issues can cause some really nasty problems. If you subclass a class, and that class's internal representation of instance-level state changes, you may not be able to load in your serialized data. While you can sometimes work around this by using a sufficiently convoluted readObject( ) method, this may not be a solvable problem. We'll return to this later. However, be aware that the ultimate solution may be to just implement the Externalizable interface instead, which we'll talk about later.

Another aspect of handling the state of a nonserializable superclass is that nonserializable superclasses must have a zero-argument constructor. This isn't important for serializing out an object, but it's incredibly important when deserializing an object. Deserialization works by creating an instance of a class and filling out its fields correctly. During this process, the deserialization algorithm doesn't actually call any of the serialized class's constructors, but does call the zero-argument constructor of the first nonserializable superclass. If there isn't a zero-argument constructor, then the deserialization algorithm can't create instances of the class, and the whole process fails.

 If you can't create a zero-argument constructor in the first nonserializable superclass, you'll have to implement the Externalizable interface instead.

Simply adding a zero-argument constructor might seem a little problematic. Suppose the object already has several constructors, all of which take arguments. If you simply add a zero-argument constructor, then the serialization mechanism might leave the object in a half-initialized, and therefore unusable, state.

However, since serialization will supply the instance variables with correct values from an active instance immediately after instantiating the object, the only way this problem could arise is if the constructors actually do something with their arguments—besides setting variable values.

If all the constructors take arguments and actually execute initialization code as part of the constructor, then you may need to refactor a bit. The usual solution is to move the local initialization code into a new method (usually named something like initialize( )), which is then called from the original constructor:

```
public MyObject(arglist) {
// set local variables from arglist
// perform local initialization
}
```

to something that looks like:

```
private MyObject( ) {
    // zero argument constructor, invoked by serialization and never by any other
    // piece of code.
```

```
        // note that it doesn't call initialize()
}

    public void MyObject(arglist) {
    // set local variables from arglist
        initialize();
    }

    private void initialize() {
    // perform local initialization
    }
```

After this is done, writeObject()/readObject() should be implemented, and readObject() should end with a call to initialize(). Sometimes this will result in code that simply invokes the default serialization mechanism, as in the following snippet:

```
    private  void writeObject(java.io.ObjectOutputStream stream) throws
        java.io.IOException {
        stream.defaultWriteObject();
    }

    private  void readObject(java.io.ObjectInputStream stream) throws
        java.io.IOException {
        stream.defaultReadObject();
        intialize();
    }
```

 If creating a zero-argument constructor is difficult (for example, you don't have the source code for the superclass), your class will need to implement the Externalizable interface instead of Serializable.

Override equals( ) and hashCode( ) if Necessary

The default implementations of equals() and hashCode(), which are inherited from java.lang.Object, simply use an instance's location in memory. This can be problematic. Consider our previous deep copy code example:

```
ByteArrayOutputStream memoryOutputStream = new ByteArrayOutputStream();
ObjectOutputStream serializer = new ObjectOutputStream(memoryOutputStream);
serializer.writeObject(serializableObject);
serializer.flush();

ByteArrayInputStream memoryInputStream = new ByteArrayInputStream(memoryOutputStream.
    toByteArray());
ObjectInputStream deserializer = new ObjectInputStream(memoryInputStream);
Object deepCopyOfOriginalObject = deserializer.readObject();
```

The potential problem here involves the following boolean test:

```
serializableObject.equals(deepCopyOfOriginalObject)
```

Sometimes, as in the case of Money and DocumentDescription, the answer should be true. If two instances of Money have the same values for _cents, then they are equal. However, the implementation of equals( ) inherited from Object will return false.

The same problem occurs with hashCode( ). Note that Object implements hashCode( ) by returning the memory address of the instance. Hence, no two instances ever have the same hashCode( ) using Object's implementation. If two objects are equal, however, then they should have the same hashcode. So if you need to override equals( ), you probably need to override hashCode( ) as well.

 With the exception of declaring variables to be transient, all our changes involve adding functionality. Making a class serializable rarely involves significant changes to its functionality and shouldn't result in any changes to method implementations. This means that it's fairly easy to retrofit serialization onto an existing object hierarchy. The hardest part is usually implementing equals( ) and hashCode( ).

Making DocumentDescription Serializable

To make this more concrete, we now turn to the DocumentDescription class from the RMI version of our printer server, which we implemented in Chapter 4. The code for the first nonserializable version of DocumentDescription was the following:

```java
public class DocumentDescription implements PrinterConstants {
    private InputStream _actualDocument;
    private int _length;
    private int _documentType;
    private boolean _printTwoSided;
    private int _printQuality;

    public DocumentDescription(InputStream actualDocument)  throws IOException {
        this(actualDocument, DEFAULT_DOCUMENT_TYPE, DEFAULT_PRINT_TWO_SIDED,
            DEFAULT_PRINT_QUALITY);
    }

    public DocumentDescription(InputStream actualDocument, int documentType, boolean
        printTwoSided, int printQuality)
        throws IOException {
        _documentType = documentType;
        _printTwoSided = printTwoSided;
        _printQuality = printQuality;
        BufferedInputStream buffer = new BufferedInputStream(actualDocument);
        DataInputStream dataInputStream = new DataInputStream(buffer);
        ByteArrayOutputStream temporaryBuffer = new ByteArrayOutputStream( );
        _length = copy(dataInputStream, new DataOutputStream(temporaryBuffer));
        _actualDocument = new DataInputStream(new
            ByteArrayInputStream(temporaryBuffer.toByteArray( )));
    }

    public int getDocumentType( ) {
        return _documentType;
    }
```

```
public boolean isPrintTwoSided( ) {
    return _printTwoSided;
}

public int getPrintQuality( ) {
    return _printQuality;
}

private int copy(InputStream source, OutputStream destination) throws
    IOException {
    int nextByte;
    int numberOfBytesCopied = 0;
    while(-1!= (nextByte = source.read( ))) {
        destination.write(nextByte);
        numberOfBytesCopied++;
    }
    destination.flush( );
    return numberOfBytesCopied;
}
}
```

We will make this into a serializable class by following the steps outlined in the previous section.

Implement the Serializable interface

This is easy. All we need to do is change the class declaration:

```
public class DocumentDescription implements Serialiazble, PrinterConstants
```

Make sure that instance-level, locally defined state is serialized properly

We have five fields to take care of:

```
private InputStream _actualDocument;
private int _length;
private int _documentType;
private boolean _printTwoSided;
private int _printQuality;
```

Of these, four are primitive types that serialization can handle without any problem. However, _actualDocument is a problem. InputStream is not a serializable class. And the contents of _actualDocument are very important; _actualDocument contains the document we want to print. There is no point in serializing an instance of DocumentDescription unless we somehow serialize _actualDocument as well.

If we have fields that serialization cannot handle, and they must be serialized, then our only option is to implement readObject( ) and writeObject( ). For Document-Description, we declare _actualDocument to be transient and then implement readObject( ) and writeObject( ) as follows:

```
private transient InputStream _actualDocument;

private void writeObject(java.io.ObjectOutputStream out) throws IOException {
    out.defaultWriteObject( );
```

```
            copy(_actualDocument, out);
        }

        private void readObject(java.io.ObjectInputStream in) throws IOException,
            ClassNotFoundException {
            in.defaultReadObject();
            ByteArrayOutputStream temporaryBuffer = new ByteArrayOutputStream();
            copy(in, temporaryBuffer, _length);
            _actualDocument = new DataInputStream(new
                ByteArrayInputStream(temporaryBuffer.toByteArray()));
        }
        private void copy(InputStream source, OutputStream destination, int length)
            throws IOException {
            int counter;
            int nextByte;
            for (counter = 0; counter <length; counter++) {
                nextByte = source.read();
                destination.write(nextByte);
            }
            destination.flush();
        }
```

Note that we declare _actualDocument to be transient and call defaultWriteObject()
in the first line of our writeObject() method. Doing these two things allows the standard serialization mechanism to serialize the other four instance variables without
any extra effort on our part. We then simply copy _actualDocument to the stream.

Our implementation of readObject() simply calls defaultReadObject() and then
reads _actualDocument from the stream. In order to read _actualDocument from the
stream, we used the length of the document, which had previously been written to
the stream. In essence, we needed to encode some metadata into the stream, in order
to correctly pull our data out of the stream.

This code is a little ugly. We're using serialization, but we're still forced to think
about how to encode some of our state when we're sending it out of the stream. In
fact, the code for writeObject() and readObject() is remarkably similar to the marshalling code we implemented directly for the socket-based version of the printer
server. This is, unfortunately, often the case. Serialization's default implementation
handles simple objects very well. But, every now and then, you will want to send a
nonserializable object over the wire, or improve the serialization algorithm for efficiency. Doing so amounts to writing the same code you write if you implement all
the socket handling yourself, as in our socket-based version of the printer server.

 There is also an order dependency here. The first value written must
be the first value read. Since we start writing by calling
defaultWriteObject(), we have to start reading by calling default-
ReadObject(). On the bright side, this means we'll have an accurate
value for _length before we try to read _actualDocument from the
stream.

Make sure that superclass state is handled correctly

This isn't a problem. The superclass, `java.lang.Object`, doesn't actually have any important state that we need to worry about. Since it also already has a zero-argument constructor, we don't need to do anything.

Override equals() and hashCode( ) if necessary

In our current implementation of the printer server, we don't need to do this. The server never checks for equality between instances of `DocumentDescription`. Nor does it store them in a container object that relies on their hashcodes.

Did We Cheat When Implementing Serializable for DocumentDescription?

It may seem like we cheated a bit in implementing `DocumentDescription`. Three of the five steps in making a class serializable didn't actually result in changes to the code. Indeed, the only work we really did was implementing `readObject( )` and `writeObject( )`. But it's not really cheating. Serialization is just designed to be easy to use. It has a good set of defaults, and, at least in the case of value objects intended to be passed over the wire, the default behavior is often good enough.

The Serialization Algorithm

By now, you should have a pretty good feel for how the serialization mechanism works for individual classes. The next step in explaining serialization is to discuss the actual serialization algorithm in a little more detail. This discussion won't handle all the details of serialization.[*] Instead, the idea is to cover the algorithm and protocol, so you can understand how the various hooks for customizing serialization work and how they fit into the context of an RMI application.

The Data Format

The first step is to discuss what gets written to the stream when an instance is serialized. Be warned: it's a lot more information than you might guess from the previous discussion.

An important part of serialization involves writing out class-related metadata associated with an instance. Most instances are more than one class. For example, an instance of `String` is also an instance of `Object`. Any given instance, however, is an

---

[*] Though we'll come close.

instance of only a few classes. These classes can be written as a sequence: C1, C2...CN, in which C1 is a superclass of C2, C2 is a superclass of C3, and so on. This is actually a linear sequence because Java is a single inheritance language for classes. We call C1 the *least superclass* and CN the *most-derived class*. See Figure 10-4.

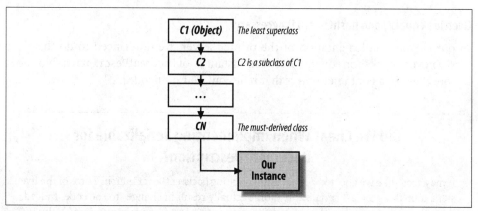

Figure 10-4. Inheritance diagram

After writing out the associated class information, the serialization mechanism stores out the following information for each instance:

- A description of the most-derived class.
- Data associated with the instance, interpreted as an instance of the least superclass.
- Data associated with the instance, interpreted as an instance of the second least superclass.

And so on until:

- Data associated with the instance, interpreted as an instance of the most-derived class.

So what really happens is that the type of the instance is stored out, and then all the serializable state is stored in discrete chunks that correspond to the class structure. But there's a question still remaining: what do we mean by "a description of the most-derived class?" This is either a reference to a class description that has already been recorded (e.g., an earlier location in the stream) or the following information:

- The version ID of the class, which is an integer used to validate the .*class* files
- A boolean stating whether writeObject( )/readObject( ) are implemented
- The number of serializable fields
- A description of each field (its name and type)
- Extra data produced by ObjectOutputStream's annotateClass( ) method
- A description of its superclass if the superclass is serializable

This should, of course, immediately seem familiar. The class descriptions consist entirely of metadata that allows the instance to be read back in. In fact, this is one of the most beautiful aspects of serialization; the serialization mechanism automatically, at runtime, converts class objects into metadata so instances can be serialized with the least amount of programmer work.

A Simplified Version of the Serialization Algorithm

In this section, I describe a slightly simplified version of the serialization algorithm. I then proceed to a more complete description of the serialization process in the next section.

Writing

Because the class descriptions actually contain the metadata, the basic idea behind the serialization algorithm is pretty easy to describe. The only tricky part is handling circular references.

The problem is this: suppose instance A refers to instance B. And instance B refers back to instance A. Completely writing out A requires you to write out B. But writing out B requires you to write out A. Because you don't want to get into an infinite loop, or even write out an instance or a class description more than once,[*] you need to keep track of what's already been written to the stream.

ObjectOutputStream does this by maintaining a mapping from instances and classes to handles. When writeObject() is called with an argument that has already been written to the stream, the handle is written to the stream, and no further operations are necessary.

If, however, writeObject() is passed an instance that has not yet been written to the stream, two things happen. First, the instance is assigned a reference handle, and the mapping from instance to reference handle is stored by ObjectOutputStream. The handle that is assigned is the next integer in a sequence.

 Remember the reset() method on ObjectOutputStream? It clears the mapping and resets the handle counter to 0x7E0000 .RMI also automatically resets its serialization mechanism after every remote method call.

Second, the instance data is written out as per the data format described earlier. This can involve some complications if the instance has a field whose value is also a serializable instance. In this case, the serialization of the first instance is suspended, and the second instance is serialized in its place (or, if the second instance has already

---

[*] Serialization is a slow process that uses the reflection API quite heavily in addition to the bandwidth.

been serialized, the reference handle for the second instance is written out). After the second instance is fully serialized, serialization of the first instance resumes. The contents of the stream look a little bit like Figure 10-5.

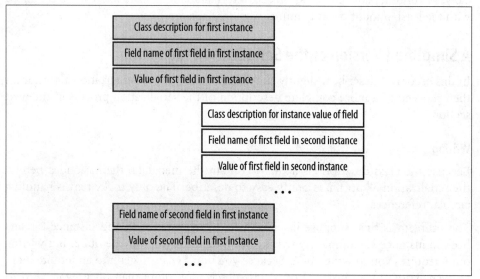

Figure 10-5. Contents of Serialization's data stream

Reading

From the description of writing, it's pretty easy to guess most of what happens when readObject( ) is called. Unfortunately, because of versioning issues, the implementation of readObject( ) is actually a little bit more complex than you might guess.

When it reads in an instance description, ObjectInputStream gets the following information:

- Descriptions of all the classes involved
- The serialization data from the instance

The problem is that the class descriptions that the instance of ObjectInputStream reads from the stream may not be equivalent to the class descriptions of the same classes in the local JVM. For example, if an instance is serialized to a file and then read back in three years later, there's a pretty good chance that the class definitions used to serialize the instance have changed.

This means that ObjectInputStream uses the class descriptions in two ways:

- It uses them to actually pull data from the stream, since the class descriptions completely describe the contents of the stream.

- It compares the class descriptions to the classes it has locally and tries to determine if the classes have changed, in which case it throws an exception. If the class descriptions match the local classes, it creates the instance and sets the instance's state appropriately.

RMI Customizes the Serialization Algorithm

RMI doesn't actually use `ObjectOutputStream` and `ObjectInputStream`. Instead, it uses custom subclasses so it can modify the serialization process by overriding some protected methods. In this section, we'll discuss the most important modifications that RMI makes when serializing instances. RMI makes similar changes when deserializing instances, but they follow from, and can easily be deduced from, the description of the serialization changes.

Recall that `ObjectOutputStream` contained the following protected methods:

```
protected void annotateClass(Class cl)
protected void annotateProxyClass(Class cl)
protected boolean enableReplaceObject(boolean enable)
protected Object replaceObject(Object obj)
protected void drain( )
protected void writeObjectOverride(Object obj)
protected void writeClassDescriptor(ObjectStreamClass classdesc)
protected void writeStreamHeader( )
```

These all have default implementations in `ObjectOutputStream`. That is, `annotateClass( )` and `annotateProxyClass( )` do nothing. `enableReplaceObject( )` returns `false`, and so on. However, these methods are still called during serialization. And RMI, by overriding these methods, customizes the serialization process.

The three most important methods from the point of view of RMI are:

```
protected void annotateClass(Class cl)
protected boolean enableReplaceObject(boolean enable)
protected Object replaceObject(Object obj)
```

Let's describe how RMI overrides each of these.

annotateClass( )

`ObjectOutputStream` calls `annotateClass( )` when it writes out class descriptions. Annotations are used to provide extra information about a class that comes from the serialization mechanism and not from the class itself. The basic serialization mechanism has no real need for annotations; most of the information about a given class is already stored in the stream.

> RMI's dynamic classloading system uses `annotateClass( )` to record where *.class* files are stored. We'll discuss this more in Chapter 19.

RMI, on the other hand, uses annotations to record *codebase information*. That is, RMI, in addition to recording the class descriptions, also records information about the location from which it loaded the class's bytecode. Codebases are often simply locations in a filesystem. Incidentally, locations in a filesystem are often useless information, since the JVM that deserializes the instances may have a very different filesystem than the one from where the instances were serialized. However, a codebase isn't restricted to being a location in a filesystem. The only restriction on codebases is that they have to be valid URLs. That is, a codebase is a URL that specifies a location on the network from which the bytecode for a class can be obtained. This enables RMI to dynamically load new classes based on the serialized information in the stream. We'll return to this in Chapter 19.

replaceObject( )

The idea of replacement is simple; sometimes the instance that is passed to the serialization mechanism isn't the instance that ought to be written out to the data stream. To make this more concrete, recall what happened when we called rebind( ) to register a server with the RMI registry. The following code was used in the bank example:

```
Account_Impl newAccount = new Account_Impl(serverDescription.balance);
Naming.rebind(serverDescription.name, newAccount);
System.out.println("Account " + serverDescription.name + " successfully launched.");
```

This creates an instance of Account_Impl and then calls rebind( ) with that instance. Account_Impl is a server that implements the Remote interface, but not the Serializable interface. And yet, somehow, the registry, which is running in a different JVM, is sent something.

What the registry actually gets is a stub. The stub for Account_Impl, which was automatically generated by rmic, begins with:

```
public final class Account_Impl_Stub extends java.rmi.server.RemoteStub
```

java.rmi.server.RemoteStub is a class that implements the Serializable interface. The RMI serialization mechanism knows that whenever a remote server is "sent" over the wire, the server object should be replaced by a stub that knows how to communicate with the server (e.g., a stub that knows on which machine and port the server is listening).

Calling Naming.rebind( ) actually winds up passing a stub to the RMI registry. When clients make calls to Naming.lookup( ), as in the following code snippet, they also receive copies of the stub. Since the stub is serializable, there's no problem in making a copy of it:

```
_account = (Account)Naming.lookup(_accountNameField.getText( ));
```

In order to enable this behavior, `ObjectOutputStream` calls `enableReplaceObject()` and `replaceObject()` during the serialization process. In other words, when an instance is about to be serialized, `ObjectOutputStream` does the following:

1. It calls `enableReplaceObject()` to see whether instance replacement is enabled.

2. If instance replacement is enabled, it calls `replaceObject()`, passing in the instance it was about to serialize, to find out which instance it should really write to the stream.

3. It then writes the appropriate instance to the stream.

Maintaining Direct Connections

A question that frequently arises as distributed applications get more complicated involves message forwarding. For example, suppose that we have three communicating programs: A, B, and C. At the start, A has a stub for B, B has a stub for C, and C has a stub for A. See Figure 10-6.

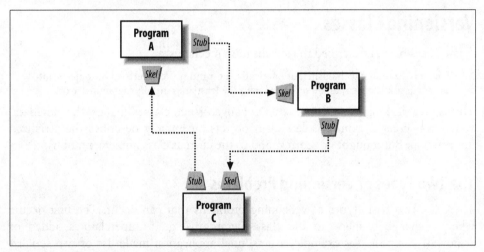

Figure 10-6. Communication between three applications

Now, what happens if A calls a method, for example, `getOtherServer()`, on B that "returns" C? The answer is that A gets a deep copy of the stub B uses to communicate with C. That is, A now has a direct connection to C; whenever A tries to send a message to C, B is not involved at all. This is illustrated in Figure 10-7.

This is very good from a bandwidth and network latency point of view. But it can also be somewhat problematic. Suppose, for example, B implements load balancing. Since B isn't involved in the A to C communication, it has no direct way of knowing whether A is still using C, or how heavily. We'll revisit this in Chapters 16 and 17, when we discuss the distributed garbage collector and the `Unreferenced` interface.

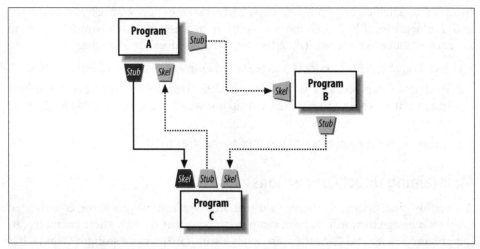

Figure 10-7. Improved communication between three applications

Versioning Classes

A few pages back, I described the serialization mechanism:

> The serialization mechanism automatically, at runtime, converts class objects into metadata so instances can be serialized with the least amount of programmer work.

This is great as long as the classes don't change. When classes change, the metadata, which was created from obsolete class objects, accurately describes the serialized information. But it might not correspond to the current class implementations.

The Two Types of Versioning Problems

There are two basic types of versioning problems that can occur. The first occurs when a change is made to the class hierarchy (e.g., a superclass is added or removed). Suppose, for example, a personnel application made use of two serializable classes: Employee and Manager (a subclass of Employee). For the next version of the application, two more classes need to be added: Contractor and Consultant. After careful thought, the new hierarchy is based on the abstract superclass Person, which has two direct subclasses: Employee and Contractor. Consultant is defined as a subclass of Contractor, and Manager is a subclass of Employee. See Figure 10-8.

While introducing Person is probably good object-oriented design, it breaks serialization. Recall that serialization relied on the class hierarchy to define the data format.

The second type of version problem arises from local changes to a serializable class. Suppose, for example, that in our bank example, we want to add the possibility of

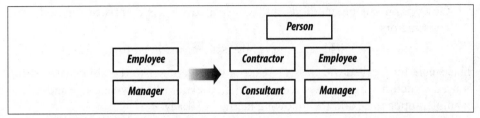

Figure 10-8. Changing the class hierarchy

handling different currencies. To do so, we define a new class, Currency, and change the definition of Money:

```
public class Money extends ValueObject {
    public float amount;
    public Currency typeOfMoney;
}
```

This completely changes the definition of Money but doesn't change the object hierarchy at all.

The important distinction between the two types of versioning problems is that the first type can't really be repaired. If you have old data lying around that was serialized using an older class hierarchy, and you need to use that data, your best option is probably something along the lines of the following:

1. Using the old class definitions, write an application that deserializes the data into instances and writes the instance data out in a neutral format, say as tab-delimited columns of text.

2. Using the new class definitions, write a program that reads in the neutral-format data, creates instances of the new classes, and serializes these new instances.

The second type of versioning problem, on the other hand, can be handled locally, within the class definition.

How Serialization Detects When a Class Has Changed

In order for serialization to gracefully detect when a versioning problem has occurred, it needs to be able to detect when a class has changed. As with all the other aspects of serialization, there is a default way that serialization does this. And there is a way for you to override the default.

The default involves a hashcode. Serialization creates a single hashcode, of type long, from the following information:

- The class name and modifiers
- The names of any interfaces the class implements

- Descriptions of all methods and constructors except `private` methods and constructors
- Descriptions of all fields except `private`, `static`, and `private transient`

This single `long`, called the class's stream unique identifier (often abbreviated suid), is used to detect when a class changes. It is an extraordinarily sensitive index. For example, suppose we add the following method to `Money`:

```
public boolean isBigBucks( ) {
    return _cents > 5000;
}
```

We haven't changed, added, or removed any fields; we've simply added a method with no side effects at all. But adding this method changes the suid. Prior to adding it, the suid was `6625436957363978372L`; afterwards, it was `-3144267589449789474L`. Moreover, if we had made `isBigBucks( )` a protected method, the suid would have been `4747443272709729176L`.

 These numbers can be computed using the serialVer program that ships with the JDK. For example, these were all computed by typing `serialVer com.ora.rmibook.chapter10.Money` at the command line for slightly different versions of the `Money` class.

The default behavior for the serialization mechanism is a classic "better safe than sorry" strategy. The serialization mechanism uses the suid, which defaults to an extremely sensitive index, to tell when a class has changed. If so, the serialization mechanism refuses to create instances of the new class using data that was serialized with the old classes.

Implementing Your Own Versioning Scheme

While this is reasonable as a default strategy, it would be painful if serialization didn't provide a way to override the default behavior. Fortunately, it does. Serialization uses only the default suid if a class definition doesn't provide one. That is, if a class definition includes a `static final long` named `serialVersionUID`, then serialization will use that `static final long` value as the suid. In the case of our `Money` example, if we included the line:

```
private static final long serialVersionUID = 1;
```

in our source code, then the suid would be 1, no matter how many changes we made to the rest of the class. Explicitly declaring `serialVersionUID` allows us to change the class, and add convenience methods such as `isBigBucks( )`, without losing backwards compatibility.

serialVersionUID doesn't have to be private. However, it must be static, final, and long.

The downside to using serialVersionUID is that, if a significant change is made (for example, if a field is added to the class definition), the suid will not reflect this difference. This means that the deserialization code might not detect an incompatible version of a class. Again, using Money as an example, suppose we had:

```
public class Money extends ValueObject {
    private static final long serialVersionUID = 1;
    protected int _cents;
```

and we migrated to:

```
public class Money extends ValueObject {
    private static final long serialVersionUID = 1;
    public float amount;
    public Currency typeOfMoney;
}
```

The serialization mechanism won't detect that these are completely incompatible classes. Instead, when it tries to create the new instance, it will throw away all the data it reads in. Recall that, as part of the metadata, the serialization algorithm records the name and type of each field. Since it can't find the fields during deserialization, it simply discards the information.

The solution to this problem is to implement your own versioning inside of readObject( ) and writeObject( ). The first line in your writeObject( ) method should begin:

```
private void writeObject(java.io.ObjectOutputStream out) throws IOException {
    stream.writeInt(VERSION_NUMBER);
    ....
}
```

In addition, your readObject( ) code should start with a switch statement based on the version number:

```
private void readObject(java.io.ObjectInputStream in) throws IOException,
    ClassNotFoundException {
    int version = in.readInt();
    switch(version) {
    // version specific demarshalling code.
    ....}
}
```

Doing this will enable you to explicitly control the versioning of your class. In addition to the added control you gain over the serialization process, there is an important consequence you ought to consider before doing this. As soon as you start to explicitly version your classes, `defaultWriteObject( )` and `defaultReadObject( )` lose a lot of their usefulness.

Trying to control versioning puts you in the position of explicitly writing all the marshalling and demarshalling code. This is a trade-off you might not want to make.

Performance Issues

Serialization is a generic marshalling and demarshalling algorithm, with many hooks for customization. As an experienced programmer, you should be skeptical—generic algorithms with many hooks for customization tend to be slow. Serialization is not an exception to this rule. It is, at times, both slow and bandwidth-intensive. There are three main performance problems with serialization: it depends on reflection, it has an incredibly verbose data format, and it is very easy to send more data than is required.

Serialization Depends on Reflection

The dependence on reflection is the hardest of these to eliminate. Both serializing and deserializing require the serialization mechanism to discover information about the instance it is serializing. At a minimum, the serialization algorithm needs to find out things such as the value of `serialVersionUID`, whether `writeObject( )` is implemented, and what the superclass structure is. What's more, using the default serialization mechanism, (or calling `defaultWriteObject( )` from within `writeObject( )`) will use reflection to discover all the field values. This can be quite slow.

 Setting `serialVersionUID` is a simple, and often surprisingly noticeable, performance improvement. If you don't set `serialVersionUID`, the serialization mechanism has to compute it. This involves going through all the fields and methods and computing a hash. If you set `serialVersionUID`, on the other hand, the serialization mechanism simply looks up a single value.

Serialization Has a Verbose Data Format

Serialization's data format has two problems. The first is all the class description information included in the stream. To send a single instance of `Money`, we need to send all of the following:

- The description of the `ValueObject` class
- The description of the `Money` class
- The instance data associated with the specific instance of `Money`.

This isn't a lot of information, but it's information that RMI computes and sends with every method invocation.* Even if the first two bullets comprise only 100 extra bytes of information, the cumulative impact is probably significant.

The second problem is that each serialized instance is treated as an individual unit. If we are sending large numbers of instances within a single method invocation, then there is a fairly good chance that we could compress the data by noticing commonalities across the instances being sent.

It Is Easy to Send More Data Than Is Required

Serialization is a recursive algorithm. You pass in a single object, and all the objects that can be reached from that object by following instance variables, are also serialized. To see why this can cause problems, suppose we have a simple application that uses the Employee class:

```
public class Employee implements Serializable {
    public String firstName;
    public String lastName;
    Public String socialSecurityNumber;
}
```

In a later version of the application, someone adds a new piece of functionality. As part of doing so, they add a single additional field to Employee:

```
public class Employee implements Serializable {
    public String firstName;
    public String lastName;
    Public String socialSecurityNumber;
    Public Employee manager;
}
```

What happens as a result of this? On the bright side, the application still works. After everything is recompiled, the entire application, including the remote method invocations, will still work. That's the nice aspect of serialization—we added new fields, and the data format used to send arguments over the wire automatically adapted to handle our changes. We didn't have to do any work at all.

On the other hand, adding a new field redefined the data format associated with Employee. Because serialVersionUID wasn't defined in the first version of the class, none of the old data can be read back in anymore. And there's an even more serious problem: we've just dramatically increased the bandwidth required by remote method calls.

---

* Recall that RMI resets the serialization mechanism with every method call.

Suppose Bob works in the mailroom. And we serialize the object associated with Bob. In the old version of our application, the data for serialization consisted of:

- The class information for Employee
- The instance data for Bob

In the new version, we send:

- The class information for Employee
- The instance data for Bob
- The instance data for Sally (who runs the mailroom and is Bob's manager)
- The instance data for Henry (who is in charge of building facilities)
- The instance data for Alison (Director, Corporate Infrastructure)
- The instance data for Mary (VP in charge of IT)

And so on...

The new version of the application isn't backwards-compatible because our old data can't be read by the new version of the application. In addition, it's slower and is much more likely to cause network congestion.

The Externalizable Interface

To solve the performance problems associated with making a class Serializable, the serialization mechanism allows you to declare that a class is Externalizable instead. When ObjectOutputStream's writeObject( ) method is called, it performs the following sequence of actions:

1. It tests to see if the object is an instance of Externalizable. If so, it uses externalization to marshall the object.

2. If the object isn't an instance of Externalizable, it tests to see whether the object is an instance of Serializable. If so, it uses serialization to marshall the object.

3. If neither of these two cases apply, an exception is thrown.

Externalizable is an interface that consists of two methods:

```
public void readExternal(ObjectInput in);
public void writeExternal(ObjectOutput out);
```

These have roughly the same role that readObject( ) and writeObject( ) have for serialization. There are, however, some very important differences. The first, and most obvious, is that readExternal( ) and writeExternal( ) are part of the Externalizable interface. An object cannot be declared to be Externalizable without implementing these methods.

However, the major difference lies in how these methods are used. The serialization mechanism always writes out class descriptions of all the serializable superclasses.

And it always writes out the information associated with the instance when viewed as an instance of each individual superclasses.

Externalization gets rid of some of this. It writes out the identity of the class (which boils down to the name of the class and the appropriate serialVersionUID). It also stores the superclass structure and all the information about the class hierarchy. But instead of visiting each superclass and using that superclass to store some of the state information, it simply calls writeExternal() on the local class definition. In a nutshell: it stores all the metadata, but writes out only the local instance information.

 This is true even if the superclass implements Serializable. The metadata about the class structure will be written to the stream, but the serialization mechanism will not be invoked. This can be useful if, for some reason, you want to avoid using serialization with the superclass. For example, some of the Swing classes,[*] while they claim to implement Serializable, do so incorrectly (and will throw exceptions during the serialization process). If you really need to use these classes, and you think serialization would be useful, you may want to think about creating a subclass and declaring it to be Externalizable. Instances of your class will be written out and read in using externalization. Because the superclass is never serialized or deserialized, the incorrect code is never invoked, and the exceptions are never thrown.

Comparing Externalizable to Serializable

Of course, this efficiency comes at a price. Serializable can be frequently implemented by doing two things: declaring that a class implements the Serializable interface and adding a zero-argument constructor to the class. Furthermore, as an application evolves, the serialization mechanism automatically adapts. Because the metadata is automatically extracted from the class definitions, application programmers often don't have to do anything except recompile the program.

On the other hand, Externalizable isn't particularly easy to do, isn't very flexible, and requires you to rewrite your marshalling and demarshalling code whenever you change your class definitions. However, because it eliminates almost all the reflective calls used by the serialization mechanism and gives you complete control over the marshalling and demarshalling algorithms, it can result in dramatic performance improvements.

To demonstrate this, I have defined the EfficientMoney class. It has the same fields and functionality as Money but implements Externalizable instead of Serializable:

```
public class EfficientMoney extends ValueObject implements Externalizable {
    public static final long serialVersionUID = 1;
    protected int _cents;
```

---

[*] JTextArea is one of the most egregious offenders.

```
        public EfficientMoney(Integer cents) {
            this(cents.intValue());
        }

        public EfficientMoney(int cents) {
            super(cents + " cents.");
            _cents = cents;
        }

        public void readExternal(ObjectInput in) throws IOException,
            ClassNotFoundException {
            _cents = in.readInt();
            _stringifiedRepresentation = _cents + " cents.";
        }

        public void writeExternal(ObjectOutput out) throws IOException {
            out.writeInt(_cents);
        }
    }
```

We now want to compare Money with EfficientMoney. We'll do so using the following application:

```
public class MoneyWriter {
    public static void main(String[] args) {
        writeOne();
        writeMany();
    }

    private static void writeOne() {
        try {
            System.out.println("Writing one instance");
            Money money = new Money(1000);
            writeObject("C:\\temp\\foo", money);
        }
        catch(Exception e){}
    }

    private static void writeMany() {
        try {
            System.out.println("Writing many instances");
            ArrayList listOfMoney = new ArrayList();
            for (int i=0; i<10000; i++) {
                Money money = new Money(i*100);
                listOfMoney.add(money);
            }
            writeObject("C:\\temp\\foo2", listOfMoney);
        }
         catch(Exception e){}
    }

    private static void writeObject(String filename, Object object) throws
        Exception {
```

```
            FileOutputStream fileOutputStream = new FileOutputStream(filename);
            ObjectOutputStream objectOutputStream = new
                ObjectOutputStream(fileOutputStream);
            long startTime = System.currentTimeMillis( );
            objectOutputStream.writeObject(object);
            objectOutputStream.flush( );
            objectOutputStream.close( );
            System.out.println("Time: " + (System.currentTimeMillis( ) - startTime));
        }
    }
```

On my home machine, averaging over 10 trial runs for both `Money` and `EfficientMoney`, I get the results shown in Table 10-1. [*]

Table 10-1. Testing Money and EfficientMoney

Class	Number of instances	File size	Elapsed time
Money	1	266 bytes	60 milliseconds
Money	10,000	309 KB	995 milliseconds
EfficientMoney	1	199 bytes	50 milliseconds
EfficientMoney	10,000	130 KB	907 milliseconds

These results are fairly impressive. By simply converting a leaf class in our hierarchy to use externalization, I save 67 bytes and 10 milliseconds when serializing a single instance. In addition, as I pass larger data sets over the wire, I save more and more bandwidth—on average, 18 bytes per instance.

> Which numbers should we pay attention to? The single-instance costs or the 10,000-instance costs? For most applications, the single-instance cost is the most important one. A typical remote method call involves sending three or four arguments (usually of different types) and getting back a single return value. Since RMI clears the serialization mechanism between calls, a typical remote method call looks a lot more like serializing 3 or 4 single instances than serializing 10,000 instances of the same class.

If I need more efficiency, I can go further and remove `ValueObject` from the hierarchy entirely. The `ReallyEfficientMoney` class directly extends `Object` and implements `Externalizable`:

```
    public class ReallyEfficientMoney implements Externalizable {
        public static final long serialVersionUID = 1;
        protected int _cents;
        protected String _stringifiedRepresentation;
```

---

[*] We need to average because the elapsed time can vary (it depends on what else the computer is doing). The size of the file is, of course, constant.

```
    public ReallyEfficientMoney(Integer cents) {
        this(cents.intValue());
    }

    public ReallyEfficientMoney(int cents) {
        _cents = cents;
        _stringifiedRepresentation = _cents + " cents.";
    }

    public void readExternal(ObjectInput in) throws IOException,
        ClassNotFoundException {
        _cents = in.readInt();
        _stringifiedRepresentation = _cents + " cents.";
    }

    public void writeExternal(ObjectOutput out) throws IOException {
        out.writeInt(_cents);
    }
}
```

ReallyEfficientMoney has much better performance than either Money or
EfficientMoney when a single instance is serialized but is almost identical to
EfficientMoney for large data sets. Again, averaging over 10 iterations, I record the
numbers in Table 10-2.

Table 10-2. Testing ReallyEfficientMoney

Class	Number of instances	File size	Elapsed time
ReallyEfficientMoney	1	74 bytes	20 milliseconds
ReallyEfficientMoney	10,000	127 KB	927 milliseconds

Compared to Money, this is quite impressive; I've shaved almost 200 bytes of bandwidth and saved 40 milliseconds for the typical remote method call. The downside is
that I've had to abandon my object hierarchy completely to do so; a significant percentage of the savings resulted from not including ValueObject in the inheritance
chain. Removing superclasses makes code harder to maintain and forces programmers to implement the same method many times (ReallyEfficientMoney can't use
ValueObject's implementation of equals() and hashCode() anymore). But it does
lead to significant performance improvements.

One Final Point

An important point is that you can decide whether to implement Externalizable or
Serializable on a class-by-class basis. Within the same application, some of your
classes can be Serializable, and some can be Externalizable. This makes it easy to

evolve your application in response to actual performance data and shifting requirements. The following two-part strategy is often quite nice:

- Make all your classes implement Serializable.
- After that, make some of them, the ones you send often and for which serialization is dramatically inefficient, implement Externalizable instead.

This gets you most of the convenience of serialization and lets you use Externalizable to optimize when appropriate.

Experience has shown that, over time, more and more objects will gradually come to directly extend Object and implement Externalizable. But that's fine. It simply means that the code was incrementally improved in response to performance problems when the application was deployed.

CHAPTER 11

Threads

Threads are simple. They allow a program running on a single computer to perform more than one task at a time in much the same way that an operating system allows more than one program to run at the same time. Using threads, however, can involve some subtlety. The Java programming language has extensive support for threading, both in the programming language and in the libraries that come with the JDK. In this chapter, we'll discuss why threading is important in distributed programming and cover the fundamentals of using threads in Java.

More Than One Client

In our previous discussions on deciding on a server, I talked briefly about several issues related to scalability. The goal of those discussions was simple: we wanted to guarantee that our systems will be able to simultaneously support many different users, all of whom are attempting to perform different tasks.

But those discussions carefully dodged a very difficult question: how do we build a server that can handle more than one request at once? Consider the bank system we built in Chapter 9. If we take the existence of multiple clients into account, we wind up with the architecture diagram shown in Figure 11-1.

This has an important implication: the possibility exists that two separate clients will receive stubs for the same instance of Account (e.g., they request the same server from the registry) and then simultaneously attempt to perform banking operations on it. This could be undesirable, for example, if both clients attempt to withdraw money from the same account at the same time.

This seems like an easily solved problem. It's analogous, in the real world, to having more than one client in the bank at the same time. In the real world, the clients form a line and wait until a teller becomes available. And, at first glance, that seems like what we did with the socket-based printer server. Recall how we implemented the method that accepted print requests:

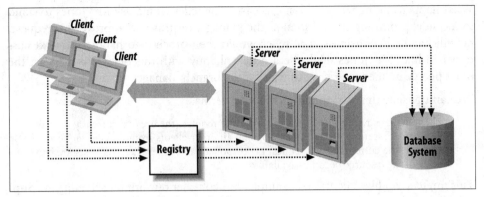

Figure 11-1. Architecture diagram for the bank system

```
public void accept( ) {
    while (true) {
        Socket clientSocket = null;
        try {
            clientSocket = _serverSocket.accept( ); // blocking call
            processPrintRequest(clientSocket);
            ....
    }
```

When one client connects, the request is processed, and our code resumes listening for other connections. Consequently, while a print request is processed, all the other print requests simply wait. The requests are trapped in the operating-system layer and never even get to the server until the server is ready to handle them.

However, this similarity is deceptive. There are two crucial differences between what happens in the bank and what we implemented. The first is that we never really implemented any sort of "next in line" functionality. That is, our socket-based printer server doesn't guarantee a first-come, first-served policy (unless the operating system does). Moreover, if a request is complex and ties up the printer server for a significant period of time, most of the client requests will simply time out.

The second difference is similar: the server offers no feedback. In the real world, you can see how long the line is, and how fast the line is moving. Based on that information, you can decide to do something else. The socket code simply offers you the opportunity to wait, without knowing how long you'll wait or whether you'll eventually time out.

In general, the "put all the clients in a queue solution" isn't even a good policy in the real world. Consider our real-world bank example and suppose that the following situation occurs:

> Mr. Jones steps up to the teller's window. He attempts to withdraw $100,000, a sum large enough to require a branch manager's approval before being processed. The branch manager, however, has stepped out to the corner store to buy some cigarettes.

What happens in the real world in this case? The teller would ask Mr. Jones to stand to the side, promising that as soon as the manager returns and approves his request, he will handle his business. The teller would then proceed to handle the next customer in line. Mr. Jones might be a little unhappy with this delay, but at least the other people in line won't have to wait for the branch manager as well.

We can translate this scenario into computer terms:

> A client makes a request on a remote server that requires the use of a currently unavailable (scarce) resource. Rather than blocking all other clients from making requests of the server, the current client's request is postponed, and other client requests are handled until the resource becomes available.

This might seem like a contrived example, but consider our printer server again. Suppose that a client submits a complex 37-page document that will take 11 minutes to print. The "wait-in-line" solution then says: no one else can submit print jobs for the next 11 minutes. What we'd really rather have happen is:

1. The first client attempts to submit the print job.
2. The server accepts the print job and starts printing the document.
3. The second client submits its print job.
4. The server accepts the second print job but also informs the second client that the current wait is rather long, giving the client an estimate as to when the printed document will be available.
5. The client can then monitor the printer's status, sending more method calls to the printer while the printer is still printing other documents, and perhaps cancel its request.

Nailing this down a little further, what we really want in this scenario is an implementation of the following rough description:

> When a print request is received, take the entire document and put it into a print queue on the server machine. Immediately return to handle the next remote method call. At the same time, since marshalling and demarshalling a document can be a lengthy process, and since the document may take a long time to be sent over the network, continue to simultaneously accept other documents and respond to method calls that are querying the server's status.

The second part of this description ("At the same time...") may still seem a little unmotivated. Why do we need to be able to accept more than one document simultaneously? The reason is that our application is a distributed application. Network latency and partial failure can cause difficulties, as in the following scenario:

> Bob is working from home this morning on an important presentation. He puts the finishing touches on it, connects to the Internet, and sends the document to the company printer. He then heads out for lunch, planning to pick up the printed document later in the day.

In this scenario, network latency can cause the printer to become unavailable for long periods of time. Bob's presentation is probably quite large. And sending it over the Internet, from a dialup connection, might take a long time. If we don't insist that the printer handle simultaneous connections, then while Bob is sending the document, the printer will be idle and not accept other documents. Not only do we have the feedback problems we mentioned earlier (i.e., other clients don't have any idea when, and if, they will be able to submit documents), this is also an inefficient use of the printer.

The partial failure scenario causes a similar problem. Bob's connection could go down for a little while before the printer server realizes anything is wrong. In which case, not only does the printer server not accept documents, it no longer receives Bob's print request.

As you can see, the ability to service requests from more than one client, and to do so at the same time, is crucial in the world of distributed applications. And the way it is done is by the use of *threads*.*

Basic Terminology

To understand threads, we need to step back for a moment and recall some basic ideas from computer science. In particular, we need to talk for a moment about the stack and the heap.

 Readers who feel comfortable with the basic concepts that underly threading might want to jump ahead to "Applying This to the Printer Server."

The Calling Stack

A stack is a data structure that serves as a container. You can insert and remove items from a stack. The only restriction is that the only item that can be removed is the item that was most recently inserted. Stacks are often visualized as a pile of items. You insert items† by placing them on the top of the stack; you can remove only the item on top of the pile. See Figure 11-2.

While running, a program maintains a calling stack of methods that it is currently "in." Consider the following code:

```
private class GetBalanceAction implements ActionListener {
    public void actionPerformed(ActionEvent event) {
        try {
            getAccount();
            resetBalanceField();
```

---

* "Thread" is shorthand for "thread of execution." With the exception of overly zealous undergraduates, very few people use the full name.

† These items are often called "stack frames." I will use the terminology interchangeably.

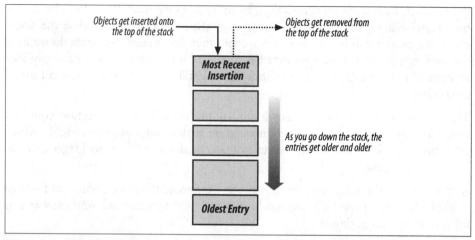

Figure 11-2. The calling stack

```
            releaseAccount( );
      }
  .....
      }
  }
```

When `actionPerformed( )` is called, the top element of the stack corresponds to the `actionPerformed( )` method. When `getAccount( )` is called, information corresponding to `getAccount( )` is placed on top of the calling stack. When `getAccount( )` returns, the stack frame corresponding to `getAccount( )` is removed from the calling stack, and the information corresponding to `actionPerformed( )` is once again at the top of the calling stack. Most Java programmers are familiar with the depiction of a calling stack shown in Figure 11-3.

```
C:\WINNT\system32\java.exe
java.lang.Throwable
        at com.ora.rmibook.chapter6.applications.BankClientFrame.getAccount(BankClientFrame.java:80)
        at com.ora.rmibook.chapter6.applications.BankClientFrame.access$0(BankClientFrame.java:12)
        at com.ora.rmibook.chapter6.applications.BankClientFrame$GetBalanceAction.actionPerformed(Ba
nkClientFrame.java:119)
        at javax.swing.AbstractButton.fireActionPerformed(Unknown Source)
        at javax.swing.AbstractButton$ForwardActionEvents.actionPerformed(Unknown Source)
        at javax.swing.DefaultButtonModel.fireActionPerformed(Unknown Source)
        at javax.swing.DefaultButtonModel.setPressed(Unknown Source)
        at javax.swing.plaf.basic.BasicButtonListener.mouseReleased(Unknown Source)
        at java.awt.Component.processMouseEvent(Unknown Source)
        at java.awt.Component.processEvent(Unknown Source)
        at java.awt.Container.processEvent(Unknown Source)
        at java.awt.Component.dispatchEventImpl(Unknown Source)
        at java.awt.Container.dispatchEventImpl(Unknown Source)
        at java.awt.Component.dispatchEvent(Unknown Source)
        at java.awt.LightweightDispatcher.retargetMouseEvent(Unknown Source)
        at java.awt.LightweightDispatcher.processMouseEvent(Unknown Source)
        at java.awt.LightweightDispatcher.dispatchEvent(Unknown Source)
        at java.awt.Container.dispatchEventImpl(Unknown Source)
        at java.awt.Window.dispatchEventImpl(Unknown Source)
        at java.awt.Component.dispatchEvent(Unknown Source)
        at java.awt.EventQueue.dispatchEvent(Unknown Source)
        at java.awt.EventDispatchThread.pumpOneEvent(Unknown Source)
        at java.awt.EventDispatchThread.pumpEvents(Unknown Source)
```

Figure 11-3. An exception stack trace

Stack traces are one of the single most useful debugging tools around; they're often very useful in tracking program flow even when an exception hasn't been thrown. The stack trace shown earlier was generated by adding (new Throwable()).printStackTrace(); to the bank example's client application.

This stack is important because it lets us attach information to the program's flow of execution. In particular, it is useful to think of the stack as containing the following information:

The arguments to the method being called. Primitive arguments are passed by value, and objects are passed by reference. This means that if you pass an integer into a method, and the method changes the value, the change isn't visible to the calling method. However, if you pass an object to a method, any changes to the object are visible to the calling method.

Locally scoped variables with primitive types. When an int or float is declared within a method, that variable is accessible only while that particular method is on top of the stack. Furthermore, locally scoped variables are accessible by only one particular stack frame. If a method appears twice in the calling stack, there are two distinct and independent sets of local variables.

Synchronization information. I haven't explained this yet. And, technically speaking, this information isn't stored in the stack frames. But, nonetheless, it is often useful to associate synchronization information with the method with which it is acquired (and eventually released).

The Heap

We explicitly limited the stack information to locally scoped primitive variables. One reason for this is because objects in Java never have local scope. That is, the Java VM stores all the objects for a single application in a single data structure, often referred to as the application's heap. Since all stack frames have access to the application heap, storing objects in a single heap makes it easier to return objects from method calls.

In other languages, care has to be taken as to whether an object was allocated on the stack or on the heap. Objects allocated on the stack have local scope; they are part of the stack frame and will be thrown away when the stack frame is removed from the calling stack. That is, limiting the scope makes memory management easier.

Objects allocated on the heap, on the other hand, can be referenced from any stack frame and hence can be used as return values from method calls. But figuring out when the object is no longer useful and can be destroyed is much more difficult. Java solves this problem by making garbage collection, which is the automatic cleanup of the heap to remove objects that are no longer referenced, part of the basic language specification.

Threads

A thread is basically two things, plus some glue:

- A calling stack
- A thread-specific cache that contains local copies of some of the heap objects that I will sometimes, in a flagrant abuse of terminology, call the *local heap*.

The idea is simple: if you want a program to perform more than one operation at a time, you ought to keep the information for each thing the program does. A thread is simply the name for the data structure that does this.

 There is a slight problem here. Namely, in a single-processor machine, how can a program be capable of doing more than one thing at a time? The answer is that either the JVM (via so-called *green threads*) or the operating system (via *native threads*) is responsible for making sure that each thread is occasionally active. That is, either the JVM or the OS manages the threads and makes sure that each thread can use a percentage of the processor's time. The process of doing this is often called *time-slicing* or *context-switching*; the piece of code that does it is often called the *thread-scheduler*. Time-slicing is a rather expensive process. The price you pay for doing two things at once is the cost of switching between the associated threads and, occasionally, of copying the local caches to the heap.

All of this terminology is conveniently, if slightly inaccurately, summed up in the JVM's internal structure illustrated in Figure 11-4.

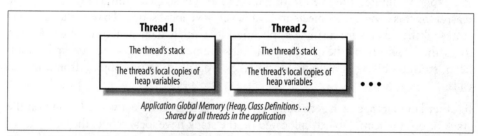

Figure 11-4. Internal structure of the JVM

Mutexes

The final piece of threading terminology we need is the idea of a *mutex variable*, or *mutex*.[*] A mutex, short for "mutual exclusion," is a locking mechanism. Mutex variables have the following three properties:

1. They support at least two operations: lock and unlock (often referred to as get and release).

2. Both lock and unlock are unary operations. That is, at most, one call to lock will succeed. After which, all calls to lock will fail until the thread that locked the mutex variable calls unlock.

3. They are global in scope. That is, mutex variables aren't copied into local caches of threads.

Applying This to the Printer Server

Let's return to our description of the printer server for a moment. We said we wanted the following behavior:

> When a print request is received, take the entire document and put it into a print queue on the server machine. Immediately return to handle the next remote method call. At the same time, since marshalling and demarshalling a document can be a lengthy process, and since the document may take a long time to be sent over the network, continue to simultaneously accept other documents and respond to method calls that are querying the server's status.

This can be split into three simultaneous tasks:

1. Actual printing, which removes documents from the printer queue and sends them to the printer

2. Answering questions about the status of the printer server

3. Receiving documents

And this naturally leads to a thread-based decomposition of the application:

- A single thread for actual printing. Because you can't simultaneously print more than one document, more threads would simply cause problems.

- A single thread for answering questions about the status of the printer server. This is likely to be a really fast operation, and there aren't going to be many questions in a typical use scenario. Since threads do cost us resources, we should probably have only a single thread here, at least until we discover we need more.

---

[*] Mutexes are also frequently referred to as locks, and I will occasionally do so when the meaning is clear. However, because there are many possible meanings for "lock," I'll stick with mutex most of the time.

- Many threads for receiving documents. Since you need to receive more than one document at once, and because receiving a single document isn't likely to stress the server (the bottleneck is much more likely to be either the client or the network between the client and the server), you should allocate multiple threads for receiving documents.

The last point is slightly deceptive. Even if the server was a bottleneck, and even if introducing threading to respond to multiple print requests at once substantially slowed down the server, it's still almost always a good idea to do so. Basically, the decision boils down to choosing one of the following alternatives:

The faster application
> Uses only a single thread to receive documents. There's less context-switching going on, and the overall amount of processor time devoted to receiving documents is fairly high. However, if a client tries to send a document, and the server is busy, the client simply waits with no feedback.

The slower application
> Uses multiple threads to receive documents. There's more context-switching going on, and, subsequently, there's less processor time devoted to receiving documents. On the other hand, the client application can display a progress bar to let the user know what percentage of the document has been transmitted.

While this may not seem terribly relevant with a simple printer server, this particular design trade-off is ubiquitous in distributed computing. You can maximize application performance, or you can trade some performance in order to tell the user what's going on. It might seem counterintuitive; the faster application is the less-responsive one, but there you have it.

Threading Concepts

> Writing a multi-threaded program is hard.
>
> Writing a correct multi-threaded program is impossible.
>
> —seen in an email signature

So far, this all seems reasonable. A program is attempting to do several things at once. It's connected to a set of clients and devices. Since the clients and devices are acting independently of each other, it makes sense that the program's runtime structure reflects this. Threads are simply a nice abstraction that helps keep the clutter down. Why, then, do threads have such a bad reputation? Why do most people frequently make mistakes when they try to write multithreaded code?*

---

* The author included.

The vocabulary associated with threading can be confusing. In this book, I use the term *multithreaded code* to refer to code that necessarily has several threads running through it and still executes correctly. I call code that can have multiple threads running through it, but doesn't necessarily involve more than one thread, *threadsafe*. Furthermore, I will frequently say that a thread is *in* an object or method, or *active in* an object or method. This simply means that the top frame of the calling stack involves that particular instance and method.

The problem with threads is that they can interfere with each other. Consider our bank account example again. Account_Impl contains the following code:

```
public class Account_Impl extends UnicastRemoteObject implements Account {
    private Money _balance;
    public Account_Impl(Money startingBalance) throws RemoteException {
        _balance = startingBalance;
    }

    public Money getBalance( ) throws RemoteException {
        return _balance;
    }

    public void makeDeposit(Money amount) throws RemoteException,
        NegativeAmountException {
        checkForNegativeAmount(amount);
        _balance.add(amount);
        return;
    }

    public void makeWithdrawal(Money amount) throws RemoteException,
        OverdraftException, NegativeAmountException {
        checkForNegativeAmount(amount);
        checkForOverdraft(amount);
        _balance.subtract(amount);
        return;
    }
    ...
}
```

Our banking application was structured as a collection of many instances of Account_Impl. These instances were bound into the registry as independent servers but ran inside a single JVM. Suppose we tried to make this a multithreaded application by simply adding some request-processing threads. In this scenario, each request-processing thread can handle a request from a client. That is, when a client invokes a method on a server, the request is handled by one of our request-handling threads. Problems can occur when two or more clients try to modify the same account. Consider the following scenario:

> Rachel and Mary are celebrating their fifth anniversary together. Rachel decides to buy Mary a diamond necklace as a surprise gift. Meanwhile, Mary decides to surprise Rachel with a weekend ski vacation. Because they both work in the computer industry, and hence have very little free time, they wind up buying the gifts during their lunch hours. But first, each of them heads to an ATM to get some cash.

What happens? Well, if they own a joint account, we could very well see the following sequence of events:

1. Mary's client application asks what the account balance is. As a result, the thread that processes Mary's requests makes a copy of the appropriate instance of Account_Impl and puts it in the thread's local cache.

2. Rachel's client application asks what the account balance is. As a result, the thread that processes Rachel's requests makes a copy of the appropriate instance of Account_Impl and puts it in the thread's local cache.

3. Mary withdraws $1,200 of the $1,400 in the account. This transaction is processed by her request-handling thread, using the cached copy of the instance of Account_Impl.

4. Rachel withdraws $900 of the $1,400 in the account. This transaction is processed by her request-handling thread, using the cached copy of the instance of Account_Impl.

5. Eventually, both threads flush their caches. At the end of all of this, Mary and Rachel have withdrawn $2,100 from the account, and the account has either $200 or $400 left in it (either result is erroneous).

Note that while the problem is easy to understand because of the caches, it isn't actually caused by the cache. Even if there was only one instance of Account_Impl that both threads were using, a similar problem could easily occur. For example:

1. Mary starts to withdraw $1,200 of the $1,400 in the account. The thread that services her request gets part of the way through before being switched out by the time-slicer. In particular, it gets past the line checkForOverdraft( ) and is about to call _balance.subtract( ) when another thread becomes active:

```
public void makeWithdrawal(Money amount) throws RemoteException,
    OverdraftException, NegativeAmountException {
    checkForNegativeAmount(amount);
    checkForOverdraft(amount);
    _balance.subtract(amount);  // (*) calls the method below.
    return;
}

// next method is from Money object. This is the method called by the previous
// line marked (*).
```

```
    public void subtract(Money otherMoney) {
        _cents --= otherMoney.getCents( );
    }
}
```

2. The thread that becomes active is the one handling Rachel's request to withdraw $900. This transaction completes, and _balance is now $500.

3. Mary's request now completes (since _balance.subtract( ) doesn't actually validate its argument). At the end of this, Mary and Rachel have withdrawn $2,100 from their account, and their account shows a balance of $–700.

 Actually, the bank example already is a multithreaded application. RMI automatically allocates a set of threads (roughly, one per open socket), which listen for remote method invocations. The scenario I described can actually happen if you try to run the bank example, as it was implemented in Chapter 9, with more than one client.

As these examples show, what is needed is a way to coordinate the actions undertaken by distinct threads. In particular, we need four pieces of functionality:

- A way to control individual threads
- A way to coordinate thread activities
- A way to manage a thread's cache
- A way to assign priorities to threads

I'll now drill down on each of these four categories, explaining exactly what they mean and why they're required. Then, in the next section, I'll explain how Java implements each of these pieces of functionality.

Controlling Individual Threads

A thread has a lifecycle. From when it is first created until it is destroyed, it is in one of the following states:

New
> The thread exists, but hasn't begun to do anything.

Running and active
> A thread is running if it is in the middle of performing operations. It is active if it is running and actually occupies a processor at the current time. We also refer to this state as, simply, *active*.

Running and inactive
> A thread is running and inactive if it is in the middle of performing operations but does not actually occupy a processor at the current time. We also refer to this state as, simply, *inactive*.

Suspended

A thread is suspended if it cannot simply start processing. That is, it isn't running (and wouldn't be able to use the processor even if it were given some CPU time). But it will, at some point in the future, run once again.

Dead

A thread is dead if it has no further operations to perform.

 It is very hard, inside a program, to distinguish between active and inactive threads. The problem is this: suppose you had some way of determining whether a thread was active. By the time you got around to taking action based on this information, the answer might very well have changed.

From the point of view of thread management, the important distinction is between running and suspended. The three operations you need most are:

- Suspend a thread for a period of time and then have it resume running. This is frequently useful when applications are *polling* a source of information. For example, an email client will occasionally check to see whether more email has arrived. It doesn't need to do so very often, so suspending the thread that checks for new email can be a useful thing to do.

- Suspend a thread until a particular mutex becomes available, and then have it grab the mutex and resume running. This is exactly what we want for our bank example.

- Suspend a thread until another thread has died. This is often used for reporting back on the outcome of a task. For example, generating a monthly report on a database might involve two threads: one that actually does the computation and another that waits for that thread to finish so it can tell the world that the monthly report is available.

Coordinating Thread Activities

An operation is sometimes called an atomic operation if it can't be interrupted. That is, if a thread is active and performing the operation, it cannot be deactivated until the operation is completed. In a single-processor machine, this also means that no other thread can become active until the operation is completed. The Java programming language provides a small set of atomic operations. Many of the atomic operations deal with things such as variable assignments. For example, a thread executing the following line of code cannot be deactivated until the assignment is complete:

```
int i = 7;
```

You can see why this needs to be atomic; if a thread begins to set a variable, it should finish doing so before relinquishing the processor.

The other important atomic operations involve mutexes. Getting or releasing a mutex is guaranteed to be atomic.

People new to threading often think that most problems can be solved if we make other, larger operations atomic. To see why this isn't the case, consider the case of Mary and Rachel performing multiple withdrawals. If we had an atomic keyword, the code might be:

```
public atomic void  makeWithdrawal(Money amount) throws RemoteException,
    OverdraftException, NegativeAmountException {
    checkForNegativeAmount(amount);
    checkForOverdraft(amount);
    _balance.subtract(amount);  // (*) calls the method below.
    return;
}
```

This only solves the problem while the code is running on a single-processor machine. As soon as the server moves to a multiple-processor computer, the problem returns. Mary's request is handled in one processor, and Rachel's is handled in another. Neither thread gets deactivated and too much money is withdrawn.

Moreover, making operations atomic has a fairly strong practical limitation—if a thread cannot be deactivated, then nothing else can run on a processor. This means that if an operation can block, or might take a long time, it should not be atomic.

The key point is that atomic operations "lock" a processor and guarantee that the processor will do nothing else until the operation completes. But what we really need is a way to "lock" a piece of program state and guarantee that no other thread will be able to modify that piece of program state. Traditionally, such locks are created through the use of *mutex variables*.

Mutex variables allow a thread to prevent other threads from interfering with it. Suppose the withdrawal code in our bank example had the following logic:

1. Get a mutex associated to the account. If we can't, wait until we can.

2. Make the withdrawal.

3. Release the mutex.

Now, we know that at most one thread will be performing a withdrawal on any given bank account at a time because the withdrawing thread will lock the other threads out. If we add similar logic to the other operations, we guarantee that only one thread is performing an operation on a specific account at any given time. Let's examine each of these in more detail.

Cache Management

Unfortunately, this isn't quite enough to prevent data corruption. Consider Mary's scenario again. It began with:

> Mary's client application asks what the account balance is. As a result, the thread that processes Mary's requests makes a copy of the appropriate instance of Account_Impl and puts it in the thread's local cache.

If we add in locking functionality, what we end up with is the following guarantee:

> As long as the thread that processes Mary's requests is performing a banking operation on its local cached copy of the instance of Account_Impl, no other thread may perform a banking operation on other local cached copies of the same instance of Account_Impl.

That is, other threads are still free to make copies of Account_Impl. When the lock becomes available, they will still modify their local copies.

In order to get around this problem, we also need a way to manage the thread's local cache. That is, what we really want is for our withdrawal logic to look like the following:

1. Get the mutex associated with the account. If we can't, wait until we can.
2. Refresh our copy of Account_Impl.
3. Make the withdrawal.
4. Flush our copy of Account_Impl back to the heap.
5. Release the mutex.

If we could do these, we would completely eliminate our multiple-withdrawal problems.

Assigning Priorities to Threads

The last thing on our wish list is a way to assign priorities to threads. It is simply the case that some tasks are more important than others. The thread-scheduler is responsible for making sure each thread gets processor time so each task can move forward. However, it is not required to give each thread equal time in the processor. Higher-priority threads can get either larger time slices or more time slices, depending on the implementation of the scheduler.

There are usually a number of background threads running in any distributed application to handle "maintenance functions," such as garbage-collection or rebuilding indices into a data structure.* And there are high-priority threads that service actual requests from clients. What winds up happening is:

---

* For example, rebalancing a b-tree, an operation that's fairly expensive, can be done incrementally and is rarely urgent—a perfect thing to do in the background.

- When there are no client requests, the high-priority threads become inactive, and the low-priority threads get the lion's share of processor time.
- When there are client requests, they get most of the processor time because they have higher priority.

Support for Threads in Java

Now that we've discussed why we need threads, and what sort of control we need over them, we can discuss how to use threads in Java. Java is almost unique among programming languages in that it has explicit, and fairly extensive, support for threading built into the language. This support is in three main forms:

- A mutex variable is associated with every object. Java provides the synchronized keyword as a way to lock and unlock these mutex variables.
- In addition, there is a set of methods defined on Object that support more finely grained coordination of related actions taken by threads.
- A set of classes, defined in the java.lang package, that enables programmers to create new threads and manage their lifetimes.

 There are other forms of support for threading in Java. One example is the volatile keyword. We don't cover these other threading mechanisms because this is a chapter on threading, not a book on threading. The preceding forms of support constitute the core of what you need to know in order to write threadsafe code.

Objects Have Associated Mutex Variables

Every instance in a Java program has an associated lock, including class objects that are instances of java.lang.Class. In order to request a lock, you simply use the synchronized keyword, as in the following code snippet:

```
// declarations
Object foo;
// ....
synchronized(foo) {
// processing that occurs once the lock is granted
}
```

That is, you create a *synchronized block* by using the keyword synchronized in conjunction with a particular object instance. When this code is executed, the executing thread will attempt to get the lock associated with foo. If the lock is available, the thread will get the lock and then proceed to execute the code inside the synchronized block. When the thread exits the synchronized block, it will release the lock associated with foo.

If, however, the mutex is not available (e.g., if some other thread has already locked foo), a thread attempting to execute this code will block on the line:

```
synchronized(foo);
```

and wait until the lock becomes available. Once the lock becomes available, the thread will proceed as in the previous case (e.g., it will lock foo and then execute the synchronized block of code).

So, for example, we can make sure that only one thread is executing makeWithdrawal( ) on a particular account by changing the code slightly:

```
public void makeWithdrawal(Money amount) throws RemoteException, OverdraftException,
    NegativeAmountException {
    synchronized(this) {
        checkForNegativeAmount(amount);
        checkForOverdraft(amount);
        _balance.subtract(amount);  // (*) calls the method below.
        return;
    }
}
```

Of course, there's no requirement that methods synchronize using the instance variable this. If we want only one withdrawal to occur at a time, regardless of which account is accessed, we could synchronize on the class variable, as in the following example:

```
public void makeWithdrawal(Money amount) throws RemoteException, OverdraftException,
    NegativeAmountException {
    synchronized(this.getClass( )) {
        checkForNegativeAmount(amount);
        checkForOverdraft(amount);
        _balance.subtract(amount);  // (*) calls the method below.
        return;
    }
}
```

Keep in mind that, even as the thread is executing the checkForOverDraft( ) method, it still keeps the lock within the synchronized block associated with makeWithdrawal( ). Locks are relinquished only when code exits synchronized blocks, either normally or via exceptions. This is why I said earlier that it's useful to think of synchronization information as belonging to the stack frames.

Methods can also be declared as synchronized methods. Declaring a method as synchronized is equivalent to placing it inside a single synchronized block, which is synchronized on this. The following code is equivalent to the previous example that used synchronized(this):

```
public synchronized void makeWithdrawal(Money amount) throws RemoteException,
    OverdraftException, NegativeAmountException {
    checkForNegativeAmount(amount);
    checkForOverdraft(amount);
    _balance.subtract(amount);
```

```
        return;
    }
```

 Synchronization is not part of the method signature. A method can be synchronized in a superclass and not synchronized in a subclass. Similarly, methods declared in an interface cannot be declared synchronized.

There's a very important point here: synchronization only affects the code in synchronized blocks or inside a synchronized method. Suppose, for example, we synchronize two out of the three public methods in `Account_Impl`, as in the following declarations:

```
public Money getBalance( ) throws RemoteException
public synchronized void makeDeposit(Money amount) throws RemoteException,
    NegativeAmountException
public synchronized  void makeWithdrawal(Money amount) throws RemoteException,
    OverdraftException, NegativeAmountException
```

This has the following effects:

- Any number of threads can be executing the `getBalance( )` method at any time. There are no restrictions whatsoever on the number of threads that can execute `getBalance( )`.

- At most, one thread can be executing either the `makeDeposit( )` or `makeWithdrawal( )` methods.

- If a thread is executing `makeDeposit( )`, then no thread can execute `makeWithdrawal( )`.

- If a thread is executing `makeWithdrawal( )`, then no thread can execute `makeDeposit( )`.

The effects of synchronization on the thread's local cache

Synchronizing on an object also affects a thread's local cache. Any time a thread synchronizes on an object, its cache is partially invalidated. That is, the first time a thread accesses a variable after acquiring a lock, it must load or reload that variable from main memory.

Unlocking has a similar effect. Any time a thread releases a lock, any variables in its local cache it has changed since acquiring that particular lock must be flushed to the main heap. It is important to note that this flushing occurs *before* the lock is released.

Unfortunately, this isn't quite as powerful as you might think. If two threads synchronize on different objects, then they might interfere with each other. Suppose, for example, we implemented a simple logging facility in our bank example. All this does is increment a static variable that tells us the number of transactions we handled:

```
public class Account_Impl extends UnicastRemoteObject implements Account {
    private static int _numberOfTransactions = 0;
    private Money _balance;
```

```
public syncrhonized void makeDeposit(Money amount) throws RemoteException,
    NegativeAmountException {
    checkForNegativeAmount(amount);
    _balance.add(amount);
    _numberOfTransactions++;
    return;
}
```

Suppose two customers made deposits to different accounts. We know that:

- Customer 1 synchronized on her account and then accessed _numberOfTransactions before releasing the lock.

- Customer 2 synchronized on his account and then accessed _numberOfTransactions before releasing the lock.

But we don't have any particular guarantees about the order in which the operations executed. Suppose before either transaction that _numberOfTransactions was 13. The following sequence might have occurred:

1. The thread associated to customer 1 synchronized and loaded the value of _numberOfTransactions (13) into its local cache.

2. The thread associated to customer 2 synchronized and loaded the value of _numberOfTransactions (13) into its local cache.

3. The thread associated to customer 1 finished executing makeDeposit( ) and, before releasing its lock, stored the value of the local copy of _numberOfTransactions (14) out to the main heap.

4. The thread associated to customer 2 finished executing makeDeposit( ) and, before releasing its lock, stored the value of the local copy of _numberOfTransactions (14) out to the main heap.

Another, equally possible, sequence:

1. The thread associated to customer 1 synchronized and loaded the value of _numberOfTransactions (13) into its local cache.

2. The thread associated to customer 1 finished executing makeDeposit( ) and, before releasing its lock, stored the value of the local copy of _numberOfTransactions (14) out to the main heap.

3. The thread associated to customer 2 synchronized and loaded the value of _numberOfTransactions (14) into its local cache.

4. The thread associated to customer 2 finished executing makeDeposit( ) and, before releasing its lock, stored the value of the local copy of _numberOfTransactions (15) out to the main heap.

In one case, _numberOfTransactions increments correctly. In the other, it does not. The point is that if threads share state, they need to coordinate their caches. The only way for them to do this is to synchronize on the *same* lock. For example, we could replace the line:

```
_numberOfTransactions++;
```

with an invocation of the static method incrementNumberOfTransactions():

```
public static synchronized void incrementNumberOfTransactions() {
    _numberOfTransactions++;
}

public synchronized void makeDeposit(Money amount) throws RemoteException,
    NegativeAmountException {
    checkForNegativeAmount(amount);
    _balance.add(amount);
    incrementNumberOfTransactions();
    return;
}
```

 Declaring a static method as synchronized simply means that it synchronizes on the lock associated with the class object (rather than on the lock associated with a particular instance). This is a very useful way of coordinating behavior between instances of the same class.

Now, each thread synchronizes on the class object just before incrementing _numberOfTransactions. This means that each request-handling thread is forced to (re)load _numberOfTransactions after obtaining the lock associated with the class object. Moreover, they write the value out to the main heap before relinquishing the lock associated with the class object.

This extra layer of synchronization guarantees that _numberOfTransactions will be correctly incremented.

Acquiring the same lock more than once

All of the previous analysis has been about conflicting threads; if a thread synchronizes on an object, then no other thread can synchronize on that object, and hence, we can coordinate multiple threads.

A single thread, however, can acquire the same lock more than once. Suppose, for example, we made checkForNegativeAmount() a synchronized method, as in the following code snippet:

```
public synchronized void makeDeposit(Money amount) throws RemoteException,
NegativeAmountException {
    checkForNegativeAmount(amount);
    _balance.add(amount);
    _numberOfTransactions++;
    return;
}

public synchronized void checkForNegativeAMount(Money amount) throws
    NegativeAmountException {
// ...
}
```

This will work. What's more, the thread executing makeDeposit( ) will keep the lock until makeDeposit( ) is exited. Java's locking mechanism keeps a reference count of the number of times a lock is acquired by a particular thread and only releases the lock when the count returns to 0.

Thread Manipulation Methods Defined on Object

In addition to the synchronized keyword, the core Java libraries include a number of methods defined on Object to help manage locks and coordinate the actions of multiple threads. These methods are:

```
public void notify( )
public void notifyAll( )
public void wait( )
public void wait(long timeout)
public void wait(long timeout, int nanoseconds)
```

All of these methods require the code calling them to already have the lock associated with the instance on which they are being called. For example:

```
foo.wait( );
```

will throw an exception unless the call is made by a thread that currently owns the lock associated with foo. This is because these methods are used for interthread communications based on an event model. This event model is easily described: some threads wait for an event; other threads notify the waiting threads that the event has occurred.

The wait methods

With the wait methods, a thread waits to be notified that an event has occurred. In the no-argument version of wait( ), a thread can wait forever. Furthermore, the wait methods actually relinquish the lock and proceed to block. That is, the following code will block immediately after the wait( ) and not execute println until later, when the thread resumes (we'll discuss how this happens later in the chapter):

```
synchronized(this) {
    wait( );// blocked
    System.out.println("We don't get here right away");
}
```

In the versions of wait( ) that take arguments, the thread will wait for, at most, the duration of the arguments. After which, it will attempt to reaquire the lock it gave up when it called wait( ), and continue processing.

In either case, whether because it was notified or because time expired, the thread will then attempt to reacquire the lock; because it is inside a synchronized block, it needs to acquire the lock to continue processing. This means that, after waiting, the thread will block until the lock becomes available, just as if it had recently executed synchronized( ).

The wait methods surrender only the locks associated with the instances on which they called wait( ). If a thread has locks associated with 14 different instances and calls wait( ) on one of those instances, the sleeping thread still holds on to the other 13 locks.

The notify methods

With the notify methods, a thread sends a simple event ("Wake up!") to one or more threads that have previously called one of the wait( ) methods on the same instance. notify( ) wakes up a single waiting thread; notifyAll( ) wakes up all waiting threads.

All of the awakened threads immediately block because the thread that called the notify method still holds the lock associated with the instance. Until the thread that called notify relinquishes the lock, the awakened threads will not be able to continue processing.

Classes

So far, we've discussed how to prevent threads from interfering with each other, and how to loosely coordinate threads by using an object's associated lock. We still need to discuss how to start and stop a thread. But before we do this, we need to discuss the Thread class and the Runnable interface, both of which are defined in the java.lang package.

Thread is a class whose instances correspond to threads. The point of using classes to represent threads is simple: it gives us a way to refer to specific threads. That is, an instance of java.lang.Thread corresponds exactly to a thread in the way we've used it up until now. By creating and calling methods on an instance of Thread, we will be able to start, stop, and achieve fine-grained coordination between threads.

It's unfortunate that the word "thread" has two distinct but related meanings in Java. One meaning is that which we've been discussing all along: something that has a stack and a cache and executes code. The other is just an instance of a class. This can make discussions a little confusing.

The Thread class is a large and complicated class; it has 28 nondeprecated methods, some of which are well beyond the scope of this book. Rather than provide an exhaustive listing of the methods and their usage, I'll start with some simple uses that illustrate the basics of creating, using, and terminating a thread.

Starting a thread is easy

To create a thread, you must provide two things: something for the thread to do and a way for the thread to know when it's done. These are usually done at the same time, within a single method known as the run( ) method.

Notify Versus NotifyAll

People frequently wonder when to use notify( ) and when to use notifyAll( ). Both are used to announce that an event has occurred to waiting threads. Since notify( ) wakes up a single waiting thread, and notifyAll( ) wakes up all the waiting threads (most of which immediately block), it's clearly more efficient to use notify( ). However, there are situations when notifyAll( ) is absolutely the correct choice.

One example is when there is more than one type of thread that needs to know about an event. For example, in a distributed chat room application, we might make the following design decisions:

1. There is a single centralized WhiteBoard object, which contains the transcript of the conversation.

2. Every remote participant is assigned a thread that sends new lines of text.

3. Posting a new piece of text involves locking the whiteboard, adding the text to the whiteboard and then calling notifyAll( ). Each thread grabs the change and sends it out.

Another example occurs when the same lock is used to signal more than one type of event (and different types of events are handled by different types of waiting threads). For example, in a stockticker application, we may not want lots of information to pile up, waiting to be sent. One possible design uses a fixed-length queue to control communication. This involves the following design decisions:

- There is a fixed-length queue and two threads. One thread sends messages out to the recipient, pulling them off the queue. Another thread gets messages from the sender and puts them on the queue.

- Because the queue is fixed-length, however, both threads also need to wait on the queue when they get ahead. The client thread will wait for messages to come into the queue. The server thread will wait for messages to be sent, so that more space is available on the queue.

- There is only one lock, but there are two events ("message put in queue" and "message removed from queue"), each intended for a different thread. Therefore, notifyAll( ) must be used.

But, even beyond the cases when notifyAll( ) is absolutely required, there's a simple fact that causes many programmers to use it as the default: at any point where notify( ) can be used, notifyAll( ) can also be used. You may need to add a check or two, but that's it; at worst, the program will be a little less efficient.

On the other hand, if notifyAll( ) is required, and you use notify( ), the program will simply be incorrect, and there's usually no way to fix it (other than to use notifyAll( )). This line of reasoning leads many programmers to simply use notifyAll( ) whenever they need to alert a waiting thread.

The run( ) method is either placed in a separate class that implements the Runnable interface, or is defined in a subclass of Thread. In the first case, the code to start a thread running simply looks like:

```
Thread thread = new Thread(new MyRunnable( ));
thread.start( );
```

and in the second case, the code to start the thread running looks like:

```
Thread thread = new ThreadSubclass( );
thread.start( );
```

The first line in both of these cases creates and allocates the thread. The second actually starts the thread running.

Stopping a thread is harder

This thread will terminate in either of two cases:

- You explicitly terminate the thread by calling the stop( ) method on the instance of Thread that you created.

- The run( ) method exits.

The first choice here, calling stop( ), is a rather drastic action. It causes the thread to immediately stop and throw an instance of ThreadDeath. ThreadDeath is a subclass of Error, but not of Exception, and hence, most of your code won't even try to catch it.[*] The stack will unwind, which means that all the locks the thread was holding will be released. However, a crucial point should be made: since ThreadDeath usually isn't caught, no finally blocks will be executed, and no cleanup code will run. This has the potential to be really nasty. Consider, for example, the following snippet of code:

```
public boolean updateDatabase( ) {
    try {
        openConnection( );
        executeUpdate( );
    }
    catch (SQLException databaseError) {
        logDatabaseErrror(databaseError);
    }
    finally {
        closeConnection( );// always release database resources
    }
}
```

This is a simple method that tries to update a table in a database. Note that the SQL code has been abstracted out into submethods.

---

[*] "An Error is a subclass of Throwable that indicates serious problems that a reasonable application should not try to catch."—the JavaDoc.

Suppose this is running in a thread that gets stopped while in the middle of the executeUpdate( ) method. There are two issues that can arise:

- We're not sure what the status of the database is. Did the database get updated? There's no way to know.

- We're not going to ever enter that finally block and release the database connection. This may not be a significant resource drain in the client application, but it may be significant for the database server, especially if we have a database license that allows only a limited number of concurrent connections.

For these reasons, Javasoft deprecated stop( ) in JDK1.1 and instead recommended that people use a boolean flag inside their implementation of run( ). Here, for example, is a simple schema for subclassing Thread:

```
public abstract class StoppableThread extends Thread {
    // ... many constructors, we've only included one
    public StopppableThread(String threadName, Object arg1, OObject arg2) {
        super(threadName);
    // use arg1, arg2, ... to initialize thread state
        start( );
    }

    private boolean _shouldStopExecuting;
    public void setShouldStopExecuting(boolean shouldStopExecuting) {
        _shouldStopExecuting = shouldStopExecuting;
    }
    public boolean getShouldStopExecuting( ) {
        return _shouldStopExecuting;
    }

    public void run( ) {
        while (!_shouldStopExecuting) {
            performTask( );
        }
    }

    protected abstract void performTask( );
}
```

This defines an abstract method, performTask( ), and puts it inside a potentially infinite loop. As long as the instance's setShouldStopExecuting( ) method isn't called with a value of true, the loop will continue, and performTask( ) will be executed repeatedly.

Using Runnable instead of subclassing Thread

The preceding example used a subclass of Thread to implement the run( ) method. Another way to accomplish this is to pass in an object to Thread's constructor. This object needs to implement the Runnable interface, which consists of a single method:

```
public void run( );
```

Generally speaking, people prefer to do this for two reasons. The first is that it's slightly cleaner—it separates what the thread does from the instance that represents the thread. The second reason is that it preserves flexibility. In Java, a class can extend only one other class. If the class that implements run( ) extends Thread, it cannot extend another class in your application. This can be annoying.

Useful methods defined on the Thread class

In addition to providing the ability to start and stop threads, the Thread class also contains some useful methods that enable you to have a much finer degree of control over individual threads than wait( )/notify( ) provide. The most important of these methods are:

```
public static Thread  currentThread();
public static void sleep(long millis);
public static void yield();
public String getName();
public void setName(String name);
public boolean isAlive();
public int getPriority();
public void setPriority(int newPriority);
```

The static methods all operate on the currently executing thread. currentThread( ) returns the instance of Thread corresponding to the currently executing thread. sleep( ) causes the calling thread to become inactive for at least millis (and quite possibly longer). Note that, while asleep, the thread retains any locks it has. And yield( ) is a milder form of sleep( )—it causes the thread to become momentarily inactive, but does not guarantee that the thread will remain inactive for any length of time.

One of the more frequent programming errors using threads involves calling sleep( ) on an instance of Thread. Java allows you to call static methods on instances of a class (and simply redirects the call to the class object). This can be problematic, as programmers sometimes write lines of code such as:

```
instanceOfthread.sleep();
```

which are intended to cause the instance of Thread to sleep for awhile. But this invokes the static method sleep( ) defined on the Thread class, which will put the calling thread to sleep.

setName( ) and getName( ) enable you to name a specific thread and find the name of a thread, respectively. These don't actually alter program functionality in any significant way but can be tremendously useful when debugging. Frequently, the first thing you need to do when something goes wrong is find out which thread is screwing up. If you've given your threads descriptive names, this becomes much easier. For example, the following line of code can be very convenient:

```
System.out.println("Thread named " + Thread.currentThread().getName() + " is going
    haywire");
```

isAlive( ) is a method that returns true if, when it is called, the thread associated with the instance is still alive. There is no guarantee, however, that the thread is still alive when the calling thread acts on the information. Consider, for example, the following code:

```
if (threadInstance.isAlive( )) {
    // do something
}
```

We could have the following sequence occur in our program:

1. The test is executed and returns true.

2. The thread associated to threadInstance expires.

3. The body of the if statement is executed.

This is usually not what we want to happen. On the other hand, a return value of false, indicating that the thread has died, is reliable. Threads do not restart once dead, and once isAlive( ) returns false, it will always return false.

The final pair of useful methods is getPriority( ) and setPriority( ). A thread with a higher priority usually gets more processor time. Conversely, a thread with a lower priority usually gets a smaller percentage of the processor's time. However, there aren't any hard and fast guarantees about this. In all of *The Java Language Specification, 2nd Edition* edited by Bill Joy (Addison-Wesley), there is exactly one paragraph devoted to thread priorities:

> Every thread has a priority. When there is competition for processing resources, threads with higher priority are generally executed in preference to threads with lower priority. Such preference is not, however, a guarantee that the highest priority thread will always be running, and thread priorities cannot be used to reliably implement mutual exclusion.

This means that you can't rely on priorities to guarantee program correctness. You can, however, use them as a way to hint to the JVM which threads are more important to you. And doing so is often useful.

 Thread has many other methods that can be useful in certain situations. And there are other classes that can be used when dealing with sets of threads. (The two most useful are ThreadGroup and ThreadLocal. Both are defined in java.lang.) Covering the additional methods and classes, however, is just a little too far outside the scope of this book.

Deadlock

My boss came into my office a couple of weeks ago. "The database metrics aren't being recorded again. I think the storage thread is running into a deadlock."

"Why?" I asked.

"Server problems are always deadlocks," he replied.

Technically, he was, of course, incorrect. Servers experience many other types of problems. But there was, nonetheless, a kernel of truth to what he said. Deadlock, a situation in which two (or more) threads block each other and force each other to wait forever, is far and away the single most common serious mistake made in writing multithreaded code.

The simplest deadlock scenario involves two threads and two locks. The first thread already has the first lock and is trying to acquire the second lock. The second thread has the second lock and is trying to acquire the first lock.

For example, this could be caused by two methods with the following structure:

```
public synchronized void method1(...) {
    otherObject.method2( );}
}

public synchronized void method2(...) {
    otherObject.method1( );}
}
```

If there are two methods like this in your code, the following situation can arise:

1. The first thread enters method1 on object1. As part of doing so, it grabs the lock associated with object1. It then prepares to call method2 on another object (which we'll refer to as object2).

2. At which point, the thread scheduler deactivates the first thread and activates the second thread. The second thread calls method2 on object2, and as part of doing so, grabs the lock associated with object2.

At this point, neither thread can proceed. The first thread is blocked because it cannot acquire the lock associated with object2. And the second thread cannot proceed because it needs the lock associated with object1. Each thread blocks the other from continuing. And neither thread will ever do anything ever again. They are *deadlocked*. See Figure 11-5.

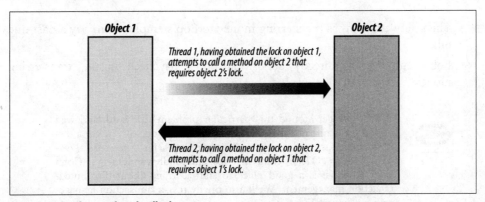

Figure 11-5. The simplest deadlock

Deadlock situations require at least two threads with at least two locks in common. A single thread cannot deadlock itself, nor can two threads block each other when there is only one lock involved (the thread that has the lock gets to keep going). But beyond this, it is hard to state general rules about deadlock. It's also difficult to detect in code and to guarantee that your code doesn't, at least in one place, have a potential deadlock.

The key thing is to be aware of the possibility of deadlock. Whenever you're writing code that involves two different threads communicating with each other, you should be aware of the possibility of deadlock, and try to design your code to avoid it. For example, in our bank example there's a very real possibility that extending the Account interface to include the transferMoney( ) function could lead to a deadlock in the implementation. Suppose transferMoney( ) is implemented naively, as in the following code snippet:

```
public syncrhonized void transferMoney(Account source, Account destination, Money
    amount) {
    makeWithdrawal(amount);
    destination.makeDeposit(amount);
    return;
}
public synchronized void makeDeposit(Money amount) throws RemoteException,
    NegativeAmountException {
    checkForNegativeAmount(amount);
    _balance.add(amount);
    return;
}

public synchronized void makeWithdrawal(Money amount)  {
// ... similar implementation
}
```

The following three-way transaction can cause deadlock:

- Bob tries to pay his electric bill by transferring money into the utility company's account.

- The utility company is transferring money to Bob's employer, to pay a past-due bill.

- Bob's employer is directly depositing Bob's paycheck (again, transferring money).

 How do we get around this particular problem? It's hard, and well beyond the scope of this book. The best way to do so is to use a distributed-transaction manager. *Programming with Enterprise Java-Beans, JTS, and OTS* by Andreas Vogel and Madhavan Rangarao (John Wiley & Sons) is a good place to start learning about distributed-tranaction management. We'll also briefly revisit transaction management in Chapter 17.

Threading and RMI

Given that I opened this chapter by talking about the need for multithreaded servers, and given that we've spent 30 pages or so on the basic thread manipulation operations in Java, you might think that the RMI specification goes heavy on the details of the threading model. You'd be wrong.

Here's all of what the RMI specification says about threading:

3.2 Thread Usage in Remote Method Invocations

A method dispatched by the RMI runtime to a remote object implementation may or may not execute in a separate thread. The RMI runtime makes no guarantees with respect to mapping remote object invocations to threads. Since remote method invocations on the same remote object may execute concurrently, a remote object implementation needs to make sure its implementation is threadsafe.

In practice, threading in RMI is fairly simple. On the client side, RMI adds no threading complications. Remote method invocations on the client side consist, more or less, of code that behaves exactly like our socket code. That is, a request is marshalled and sent through a socket. The thread sending the request then tries to read a response back from the server, over the socket. This means that the calling thread (on the client) blocks until the server sends a response.

This model of remote method invocation is nice because it corresponds to what happens with local method invocation. That is, we have:

Local method invocation
> A new frame is put on the stack, corresponding to the new method call. Processing in the previous method call stops (the thread is executing the new stack frame). Eventually, a value is returned, and processing resumes in the original stack frame.

Remote method invocation
> A new frame isn't put on the stack. Instead, processing blocks at the socket level, waiting for the return value. Meanwhile, on the server, a different thread attempts to handle the request and return a value. As part of this, a request-handling thread executes a local method invocation.

In essence, the RMI messaging model simply puts part of the stack on the server side.

 This is often referred to as a synchronous messaging model.

Meanwhile, on the server, things are more complicated. The following sequence of operations occurs in every RMI server whenever a request is made:

1. When a remote request comes in, it is immediately demarshalled into a request object that encapsulates the method invocation. This request object, which is an

instance of a class implementing the `RemoteCall` interface, has a reference to the socket's output stream. This means that, although RMI shares sockets, a socket is used only for one remote method invocation at a time.

2. The thread that received the request from the socket finds the intended remote object for the method invocation, finds the skeleton associated with that remote object, and invokes that skeleton's `dispatch( )` method. The dispatch method has the following signature:

```
public void dispatch(java.rmi.Remote obj, java.rmi.server.RemoteCall call, int
        opnum, long hash) throws java.lang.Exception
```

3. The skeleton's `dispatch( )` method invokes the right method on the server. This is where the code you wrote is actually executed.

4. The server method returns a value, which is eventually propagated back through the socket on which the original request was received.

There are two important points to note. The first, and by far the more important, is that your server code *must* be threadsafe. RMI allows many threads to enter a server object. But, if your server is too heavily synchronized, you will either wind up deadlocked or locking out a lot of the threads for extended periods of time. Hence, you run the risk of timing out a significant percentage of the remote method invocations.

The second point concerns socket allocation. RMI shares on sockets. This means that it tries to reuse sockets between the client JVM and the server JVM whenever possible. But when a socket is being used by a remote method invocation, it is not available for reuse. This means that the number of sockets allocated to a client is really equal to the number of simultaneous requests a client is making. Since the number of sockets available to an RMI server is limited, and socket allocation is expensive, this can affect scalability.

 Congratulations! Between the early socket chapters, in which you learned how to send data over the wire; Chapter 10, in which you learned how to marshall objects using serialization; and this chapter, in which I covered threading and the details of handling remote method invocations in a server, you now know enough to write an RMI implementation.[*]

---

[*] I wouldn't recommend it, though. Life's too short.

CHAPTER 12

Implementing Threading

In Chapter 11, we discussed the support Java provides for threading, both in the language and in the core libraries. In this chapter, we take a much more pragmatic point of view. The heart of this chapter is a set of idioms and usage guidelines intended to help you use threads safely and effectively in your applications. As part of this, we'll reimplement the bank example as a threadsafe application and, as a final example, talk about how to implement a general-purpose pooling mechanism. By the end of this chapter, you should have a complete understanding of how to use threads in a distributed application.

The Basic Task

Let's walk through the bank example again, this time looking at everything from the point of view of threads. The first problem is, of course, to discover where the threads are. Recall that we have three basic executing pieces of code: the server, the client, and the launch code.

Of these, the server must be absolutely threadsafe. As we discussed in Chapter 11, RMI creates multiple threads. It will gleefully dispatch multiple threads into a single server object if multiple clients simultaneously make method calls on it. If you don't take this into account while implementing the server objects, the application will fail.

The launch code, on the other hand, rarely needs to use multiple threads. It's executed once to configure and launch the application. Launch code is not complex, nor does it need to handle multiple tasks simultaneously. Making launch code thread-safe is usually a waste of time.

Client code occupies the middle ground. Many clients are fairly simple programs and are single-threaded, or in the case of Java Swing, dual-threaded. However, in the typical client program, most activity occurs as a response to user interaction. The user clicks a button or slides a slider, and then something happens. Consequently, threading is not an issue for *most* clients. There are three important exceptions to this: when a client needs to receive an asynchronous callback from a server, when a client wishes to download a large data set in the background, and when a remote method call takes a substantial amount of time. In the final case, you probably don't want the GUI to stop responding simply because a remote method call is executing. We'll discuss these in more detail in Chapter 21.

Having said that, in order to make the bank example threadsafe, we'll worry only about objects that are in the server's JVM. In particular, this means we need to focus on Account_Impl. However, it also implies that we need to pay attention to our data objects. Instances of Money are required by our remote interface and are used in both the client and the server.

 As a rule of thumb, data objects should always be made threadsafe. This is because the client and server are likely to evolve independently, and, over time, they will use the data objects in different contexts. It is quite possible that in some future version of your application there will be multiple threads accessing a data object at the same time, even if this isn't the case in the current version of the application. In general, data objects shouldn't make assumptions about how they are going to be used in either the server or the client. And this means that, unless it requires significant effort, they should be made threadsafe as a default development procedure.

Guidelines for Threading

This section contains some basic guidelines and tips for writing multithreaded code. These guidelines are similar to the design questions from Chapters 6 and 7 in that they form a starting point for design. They're different, however, in that they're not questions that lead to a clean design. Instead, they are rules of thumb for using threads in everyday code. Because they're fairly general guidelines, I've interleaved applications to the banking example throughout this section.

Start with Code That Works

It's all too easy to say something such as:

> I need to build a server that meets all these requirements and simultaneously scales to 150 clients.

Once you start trying to design for all the features in one shot, including thread safety and scalability, you're doomed. Instead, the preceding situation is really three tasks that should be performed sequentially:

> I need to build a server that meets all these requirements *for a single client*.
>
> Then I need to make it threadsafe (so it can be used by three clients).
>
> Then I need to make it scale.

If you approach the job of building a distributed application this way, you have a better chance of succeeding than if you try to satisfy all the requirements at once. Doing the latter is a sure way to fail.

Above All Else, Ensure Data Integrity

The first rule of threading is that it's better to be threadsafe than sorry. However, there's a trade-off in thread management. First, synchronizing large blocks of code that need to be executed by a large percentage of method calls can introduce performance bottlenecks, as most threads will wind up waiting to enter the synchronized block. This leads to inadequate performance. Second, synchronizing large blocks of code increases the risk of deadlock.*

In spite of this, enthusiastically synchronizing code blocks is a good way to start making your code threadsafe. To see why, think about the types of problems that arise in extreme cases:

Excessive synchronization
> The servers are slow and bottlenecked; they lurch from request to request like a 400-pound person dancing the lead in Swan Lake. And clients occasionally just hang. These problems are immediately noticed, and users complain loudly until they're fixed. However, the application is still somewhat usable in the interim, until the problems get solved.

Inadequate synchronization
> The application is fast, and problems aren't immediately obvious. Instead, over time, more and more data gets corrupted, until someone finally notices the problems, at which point recovery may or may not be possible.

There are two additional reasons to start by ensuring data integrity. The first is that a simple data-integrity strategy is often fairly easy to formulate and performs well enough so you can possibly be done with the purchase of a fast server. After all, these days processors are cheap, and memory is even cheaper.

The second reason is a slight variation on our first rule of thumb: once you have such a strategy in place, it becomes easier to modify it. Starting with threadsafe code and gradually modifying it to improve performance is a lot easier to do than trying, in one conceptual leap, to design high-performance, threadsafe code.

Applying this to the bank example

A first attempt at ensuring data integrity in the bank example is simply to synchronize all the public methods. If only one thread can access an object at any given time, then there will not be any problems with data integrity when deposits or withdrawals

---

* Though, in my experience, deadlocks most often arise when I try to be a little too clever in my thread management.

are made. There may be larger data-integrity problems arising from sequences of calls, but the actual call to makeDeposit( ) or makeWithdrawal( ) will be fine:

```
public synchronized Money getBalance() throws RemoteException {
    return _balance;
}

public synchronized  void makeDeposit(Money amount) throws RemoteException,
    NegativeAmountException {
    checkForNegativeAmount(amount);
    _balance.add(amount);
    return;
}

public synchronized void makeWithdrawal(Money amount) throws RemoteException,
    OverdraftException, NegativeAmountException {
    checkForNegativeAmount(amount);
    checkForOverdraft(amount);
    _balance.subtract(amount);
    return;
}
```

There is, however, a potential problem. Namely, many people check their balance before deciding how much money to withdraw. They perform the following sequence of actions:

1. Check balance. This is a call to getBalance( ). As such, it locks the instance of Account_Impl and is guaranteed to return the correct answer.

2. Get money. This is a call to makeWithdrawal( ). As such, it locks the instance of Account_Impl before processing the withdrawal.

The problem is that the client doesn't keep the lock between the two method invocations. It's perfectly possible for a client to check the balance, find that the account has $300 in it, and then fail to withdraw $300 because, in the time between the first and second steps, another client withdrew the money. This can be frustrating for end users.

The solution is to have the client maintain a lock between the steps. There are two basic ways to do this. The first is to simply add in extra remote methods so the client can explicitly manage the synchronization on Account_Impl. For example, we could add a pair of methods, getLock( ) and releaseLock( ), to the interface. We also need another exception type, LockedAccountException, so the server can tell the client when it has attempted to make an operation on an account that another client has locked.

This is implemented in the following code snippets:

```
public interface Account2 extends Remote {
    public void getLock() throws RemoteException, LockedAccountException;
    public void releaseLock() throws RemoteException;
    public Money getBalance() throws RemoteException, LockedAccountException;
```

```
        public void makeDeposit(Money amount) throws RemoteException,
            NegativeAmountException, LockedAccountException;
        public void makeWithdrawal(Money amount) throws RemoteException,
            OverdraftException, LockedAccountException, NegativeAmountException;
}

public class Account2_Impl extends UnicastRemoteObject implements Account2 {
    private Money _balance;
    private String _currentClient;

    public Account_Impl2(Money startingBalance) throws RemoteException {
        _balance = startingBalance;
    }

    public synchronized void getLock() throws RemoteException,
        LockedAccountException{
        if (false==becomeOwner()) {
            throw new LockedAccountException();
        }
        return;
    }

    public synchronized void releaseLock() throws RemoteException {
        String clientHost = wrapperAroundGetClientHost();
        if ((null!=_currentClient) && (_currentClient.equals(clientHost)))  {
            _currentClient = null;
        }
    }

    public syncrhonized Money getBalance() throws RemoteException,
        LockedAccountException {
        checkAccess();
        return _balance;
    }

    public synchronized void makeDeposit(Money amount) throws RemoteException,
        LockedAccountException, NegativeAmountException {
        //.....
    }

    public syncrhonized void makeWithdrawal(Money amount) throws RemoteException,
        OverdraftException, LockedAccountException, NegativeAmountException {
    // ...
    }

    private boolean becomeOwner() {
        String clientHost = wrapperAroundGetClientHost();
        if (null!=_currentClient) {
            if (_currentClient.equals(clientHost)) {
                return true;
            }
        }
        else {
            _currentClient = clientHost;
```

```
            return true;
        }
        return false;
    }

    private void checkAccess() throws LockedAccountException {
        String clientHost = wrapperAroundGetClientHost();
        if ((null!=_currentClient) && (_currentClient.equals(clientHost))) {
            return;
        }
        throw new LockedAccountException();
    }

    private String wrapperAroundGetClientHost() {
        String clientHost = null;
        try {
            clientHost = getClientHost();
        }
        catch (ServerNotActiveException ignored) {}
        return clientHost
    }

// ....other private methods
}
```

This is intended to work as follows:

1. The client program begins a session by calling getLock( ). If the lock is in use, a
   LockedAccountException is thrown, and the client knows that it does not have
   permission to call any of the banking methods.

   An alternative implementation might be to make getLock( ) a blocking operation. In this scenario, clients wait inside getLock( ) until the account becomes
   available, as in the following code example:

   ```
   public synchronized void getLock() throws RemoteException {
       while (false==becomeOwner()) {
           try {
               wait();
           } catch (Exception ignored) {}
       }
       return;
   }

   public synchronized void releaseLock() throws RemoteException {
       String clientHost = wrapperAroundGetClientHost();
       if ((null!=_currentClient) && (_currentClient.equals(clientHost)))  {
           _currentClient = null;
           notifyAll();
       }
   }
   ```

2. Once it has the lock, the client program can perform banking operations such as
   getBalance( ) and makeWithdrawal( ).

3. After the client program is done, it *must* call releaseLock( ) to make the server available for other programs.

This design has quite a few problems. Among the most significant:

An increase in the number of method calls
Recall that, in Chapter 7, one of our interface design questions was, "Is each conceptual operation a single method call?" This design, in which getting an account balance actually entails three method calls, is in direct violation of that principle.

Vulnerability to partial failure
Suppose that something happens between when the client gets the lock and when the client releases the lock. For example, the network might go down, or the client's computer might crash. In this case, the lock is never released, and the account is no longer accessible from any location.* What makes this even more galling is that the integrity of the entire system depends on the client behaving properly. A program running on an unknown machine somewhere out there on a WAN simply should not have the ability to cause server failures.

This design may have other major faults, depending on how the application is deployed. For example, it assumes that there is at most one client program running on any given host. This may or may not be reasonable in any given deployment scenario. But it's an assumption that should be verified.

On the other hand, this version of Account does solve the original problem: a correctly written and noncrashing client program running on a reliable network does get to keep a lock on the account. During a single session, the client program is guaranteed that no other client program can change or even access the account data in any manner at all.

Our goal is to achieve this with neither the extra method calls nor the increased vulnerability to partial failure. One solution is to automatically grant a lock and use a background thread to expire the lock when the client hasn't been active for a while. An implementation of this looks like the following:

```
public interface Account3 extends Remote {
    public Money getBalance( ) throws RemoteException, LockedAccountException;
    public void makeDeposit(Money amount) throws RemoteException,
        NegativeAmountException, LockedAccountException;
    public void makeWithdrawal(Money amount) throws RemoteException,
        OverdraftException, LockedAccountException, NegativeAmountException;
}

public class Account3_Impl extends UnicastRemoteObject implements Account3 {
    private static final int TIMER_DURATION = 120000; // Two minutes
```

---

* Well, until someone figures out what's wrong and restarts the client application, on the same computer, to release the lock.

```java
private static final int THREAD_SLEEP_TIME = 10000; // 10 seconds
private Money _balance;
private String _currentClient;
private int _timeLeftUntilLockIsReleased;

public Account3_Impl(Money startingBalance) throws RemoteException {
    _balance = startingBalance;
    _timeLeftUntilLockIsReleased = 0;
    new Thread(new CountDownTimer()).start();
}

public synchronized Money getBalance() throws RemoteException,
    LockedAccountException {
    checkAccess();
    return _balance;
}

public synchronized void makeDeposit(Money amount) throws RemoteException,
    LockedAccountException, NegativeAmountException {
    checkAccess();
// ...
}

public synchronized void makeWithdrawal(Money amount) throws RemoteException,
    OverdraftException, LockedAccountException, NegativeAmountException {
    checkAccess();
// ...
}

private void checkAccess() throws LockedAccountException {
    String clientHost = wrapperAroundGetClientHost();
    if (null==_currentClient) {
        _currentClient = clientHost;
    }
    else {
        if (!_currentClient.equals(clientHost)) {
            throw new LockedAccountException();
        }
    }
    resetCounter();
    return;
}

private void resetCounter() {
    _timeUntilLockIsReleased = TIMER_DURATION;
}

private void releaseLock() {
    if (null!=_currentClient) {
        _currentClient = null;
    }
}
```

```
//...

    private class CountDownTimer implements Runnable {
        public void run( ) {
            while (true) {
                try {
                    Thread.sleep(THREAD_SLEEP_TIME);
                }
                catch (Exception ignored) {}
                synchronized(Account3_Impl.this) {
                    if (_timeUntilLockIsReleased > 0) {
                        _timeUntilLockIsReleased -= THREAD_SLEEP_TIME;
                    }
                    else {
                        releaseLock( );
                    }
                }
            }
        }
    }
}
```

This works a lot like the previous example. However, there are two major differences. The first is that when a method call is made, the server automatically attempts
to acquire the lock on behalf of the client. The client doesn't do anything except
catch an exception if the account is locked.

The second difference is that the server uses a background thread to constantly check
whether the client has sent any messages recently. The background thread's sole mission in life is to expire the lock on the server. In order to do this, the background
thread executes the following infinite loop:

1. Sleep 10 seconds.

2. See if the lock needs to be expired. If it does, expire the lock. Otherwise, decrement _timeLeftUntilLockIsReleased by 10 seconds.

3. Return to step 1.

Meanwhile, every time a banking operation is invoked, _timeLeftUntilLockIs-
Released is reset to two minutes. As long as the client program is executing at least
one banking operation every two minutes, the lock will automatically be maintained. However, if the client finishes, if the network crashes, or if the client computer crashes, the lock will expire automatically within two minutes, and the server
will once again be available.

This is convenient; it solves our original problem by allowing the client to lock an
account across multiple remote method invocations. In addition, it does so without
any extra client overhead—it simply automatically grants short-term locks to clients
whenever it is possible to do so.

It's worth stopping to make sure you fully understand how this works. Using background threads to perform maintenance tasks is an important technique in distributed programming. And the idea of granting short-term privileges to clients, which must be occasionally renewed, is at the heart of RMI's distributed garbage collector.

There are, however, two significant downsides to this new approach:

The code is more complicated
> Using a background thread to expire a remote lock is not an entirely intuitive idea. Moreover, any new method, such as the transferMoney( ) method we discussed in previous chapters, will have to somehow accommodate itself to the background thread. At the very least, it will need to call checkAccess( ) before attempting to do anything.

Threads are expensive
> They consume both memory and system resources. Moreover, most operating systems limit the number of threads available to a process. When most JVM's have only a limited number of threads available, using an extra thread per account server can be an unacceptable design decision.

Of course, we can solve the second problem by making the first a little worse. For example, a single background thread can check the locks on all instances of Account3_Impl. That is, instead of creating a thread inside each instance of Account3_Impl, we can simply register the instance with a pre-existing thread that expires locks for all instances of Account3_Impl. Here's the constructor for this new implementation of the Account3 interface, Account3_Impl2:

```
public Account3_Impl2(Money startingBalance) throws RemoteException {
    _balance = startingBalance;
    _timeLeftUntilLockIsReleased = 0;
    (Account3_Impl2_LockThread.getSingleton( )).addAccount(this);
        //  register with the lock-expiration thread
}
```

The background thread simply loops through all the registered instances of Account3_Impl2, telling them to decrement their lock timers. To do this, we need a new method in Account3_Impl2, decrementLockTimer( ):

```
protected synchronized void decrementLockTimer(int amountToDecrement) {
    _timeLeftUntilLockIsReleased -= amountToDecrement;
    if (_timeLeftUntilLockIsReleased <0) {
        _currentClient = null;
    }
}
```

And, finally, we need to implement the background timer:

```
public class Account3_Impl2_LockThread extends Thread {
    private static final int THREAD_SLEEP_TIME = 10000;// 10 seconds
    private static Account3_Impl2_LockThread _singleton;
```

```
public static synchronized Account3_Impl2_LockThread getSingleton( ) {
    if (null==_singleton) {
        _singleton = new Account3_Impl2_LockThread( );
        _singleton.start( );
    }
    return _singleton;
}

private ArrayList _accounts;

private Account3_Impl2_LockThread( ) {
    _accounts = new ArrayList( );
}

public synchronized void addAccount(Account3 newAccount) {
    _accounts.add(newAccount);
}

public void run( ) {
    while (true) {
        try {
            Thread.sleep(THREAD_SLEEP_TIME);
        }
        catch (Exception ignored) {}
        decrementLockTimers( );
    }
}

private synchronized void decrementLockTimers( ) {
    Iterator i = _accounts.iterator( );
    while (i.hasNext( )) {
        Account3_Impl2 nextAccount = (Account3_Impl2) i.next( );
        nextAccount.decrementLockTimer(THREAD_SLEEP_TIME);
    }
}
}
```

Minimize Time Spent in Synchronized Blocks

This guideline may seem rather obvious. After all, the whole reason for using the synchronized keyword is to force threads to temporarily suspend execution. If a single thread holds on to a synchronization lock for a very long time, then the other threads will halt for a very long time. This often results in unresponsive applications that "feel sluggish"—at least to the clients whose threads are halted.

However, a tip that says to "minimize time" may be too abstract a rule of thumb, so let's break that rule down into three very concrete sub-tips: synchronize around the smallest possible block of code, don't synchronize across device accesses, and don't synchronize across secondary remote method invocations.

Synchronize around the smallest possible block of code

Of the three concrete sub-rules, this is both the most obvious and the vaguest. The essence of it is looking at each synchronized method and trying to see whether all of the code in that method needs to be synchronized. Consider our synchronization of Account3_Impl2 earlier:

```
public synchronized Money getBalance( ) throws RemoteException,
    LockedAccountException {
    checkAccess( );
    return _balance;
}

public synchronized void makeDeposit(Money amount) throws RemoteException,
    LockedAccountException, NegativeAmountException {
    checkAccess( );
// ...
}

public synchronized void makeWithdrawal(Money amount) throws RemoteException,
    OverdraftException, LockedAccountException, NegativeAmountException {
    checkAccess( );
// ...
}
private void checkAccess( ) throws LockedAccountException {
    String clientHost = wrapperAroundGetClientHost( );
    if (null==_currentClient) {
        _currentClient = clientHost;
    }
    else {
        if (!_currentClient.equals(clientHost)) {
            throw new LockedAccountException( );
        }
    }
    resetCounter( );
    return;
}
```

The way this works is we synchronize on the three public interface methods. As a result, each call to checkAccess( ) occurs within a synchronized block, and only one thread can execute the checkAccess( ) method at any given time.

Suppose we know that any given computer makes only a single request at a time (which is, in fact, the case for dedicated ATMs). We may be able to take advantage of this by using only checkAccess( ) to control synchronization. For example, since checkAccess( ) either grants a lock or throws a LockedAccountException, we could simply rewrite this as:

```
public Money getBalance( ) throws RemoteException, LockedAccountException {
    checkAccess( );
    return _balance;
}
// ...
private synchronized void checkAccess( ) throws LockedAccountException {
```

```
        String clientHost = wrapperAroundGetClientHost();
    // ...
    }
```

Now, each time a remote method call is made, checkAccess() is called. Because it's synchronized, the server-locking mechanism almost works. The only difficulty is that because this is a multithreaded application, the body of an Account3_Impl2 public method could take longer than two minutes. If so, the lock might be released and two clients can access the account simultaneously. We can fix this with one extra boolean flag, _decrementTimerOn, as in the following code:

```
public  void makeWithdrawal(Money amount) throws RemoteException, OverdraftException,
    LockedAccountException, NegativeAmountException {
        checkAccess();
    // ...
    _decrementTimerOn= true;
    }

private synchronized void checkAccess() throws LockedAccountException {
        String clientHost = wrapperAroundGetClientHost();
        if (null==_currentClient) {
            _currentClient = clientHost;
        }
        else {
            if (!_currentClient.equals(clientHost)) {
                throw new LockedAccountException();
            }
        }
        _decrementTimerOn = false;
        resetCounter();
        return;
    }
protected synchronized void decrementLockTimer(int amountToDecrement) {
        if  (false == _decrementTimerOn) {
            return;
        }
        _timeLeftUntilLockIsReleased -= amountToDecrement;
        if (_timeLeftUntilLockIsReleased <0) {
            _currentClient = null;
        }
    }
}
```

Here's a summary. As part of the checkAccess() method, which is synchronized, _decrementTimerOn is set to false. Since the method decrementLockTimer() is also synchronized, we know that the next time it is called, the thread that calls it will retrieve the new value of _decrementTimerOn and place it in its cache. Hence, it won't actually start the timer going until _decrementTimerOn is set to true once more. Since the only place where _decrementTimerOn is set to true is at the end of the public interface methods, this means the lock won't be relinquished while a public interface method is being executed.

The trade-off? We traded a single boolean flag for less code inside the synchronized block. Moreover, we have only two synchronized methods at this point. We've reduced the number of synchronized blocks of code, which makes the code much easier to understand.

Now, it's much easier to think about how to remove even more synchronization. The method:

```
private synchronized void checkAccess( ) throws LockedAccountException {
    String clientHost = wrapperAroundGetClientHost( );
    if (null==_currentClient) {
        _currentClient = clientHost;
    }
    else {
        if (!_currentClient.equals(clientHost)) {
            throw new LockedAccountException( );
        }
    }
    _decrementTimerOn = false;
    resetCounter( );
    return;
}
```

doesn't need to be fully synchronized. In particular, the method wrapperAround-GetClientHost( ), which is simply a wrapper around a threadsafe static method in RemoteServer, doesn't need to be synchronized. However, at this point, we're reaching diminishing returns; there's a certain value in simply having a few core methods that are entirely synchronized.

 Remember, these last few rewrites are valid only if client computers send a single request at a time. For example, checkAccess( ) isn't nearly sophisticated enough to differentiate between two clients running at the same IP address. If we need to distinguish between two such clients, the client will probably have to pass in a unique identifier (we'll actually do this when we discuss testing in Chapter 13). In general, reducing the number of synchronization blocks often involves making assumptions about client behavior. It's a good idea to document those assumptions.

Don't synchronize across device accesses

There are times, however, when no matter how small the method or how crucial the data in it, you should still avoid synchronizing the method. The most common situation is when the method accesses a physical device with uncertain latency. For example, writing a log file to a hard drive is a very bad thing to do within a synchronized method. The reason for this is simple. Suppose we're in a scenario with many instances of Account, and they all log their transactions to a log file,[*] as shown in Figure 12-1.

---

[*] Or to a database. The discussion applies equally to a database.

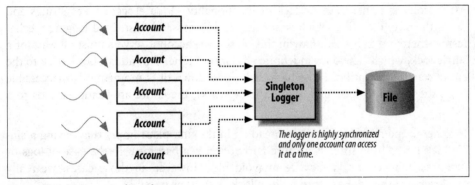

Figure 12-1. Using a singleton logger

A simple version of this is quite easy to implement:

```
package com.ora.rmibook.chapter12;
import java.io.*;

public interface Logger {
    public void setOutputStream(PrintStream outputStream);
    public void logString(String string);
}
```

```
package com.ora.rmibook.chapter12;
import java.io.*;

public class SimpleLogger implements Logger {
    private static SimpleLogger _singleton;
    public synchronized static SimpleLogger getSingleton() {
        if (null==_singleton) {
            _singleton = new SimpleLogger();
        }
        return _singleton;
    }

    private PrintStream _loggingStream;
    private SimpleLogger() {
        _loggingStream = System.err;// a good default value
    }

    public void setOutputStream(PrintStream outputStream) {
        _loggingStream = outputStream;
    }

    public synchronized void logString(String string) {
        _loggingStream.println(string);
    }
}
```

Note that the static method getSingleton( ) must be synchronized. Otherwise, more than one instance of SimpleLogger can be created.

Aside from its rather pathetic lack of functionality—SimpleLogger takes strings and sends them to a log file, which is not the world's most sophisticated logging mechanism—there is a significant flaw in this object: the account servers must all wait for a single lock, which is held for indefinite amounts of time. This adds a bottleneck to the entire server application. If the hard disk slows down or is momentarily inaccessible (e.g., the log file is mounted across the network), the entire application grinds to a halt.

In general, the reasons for using threading in the first place imply that having a single lock that all the threads acquire fairly often is a bad idea. In the case of logs or database connections, it may be unavoidable. However, in those cases, we really need to make the time a thread holds a lock as short as possible.

One common solution is to wrap the actual logging mechanism in an outer shell, which also implements the Logger interface, as shown in Figure 12-2.

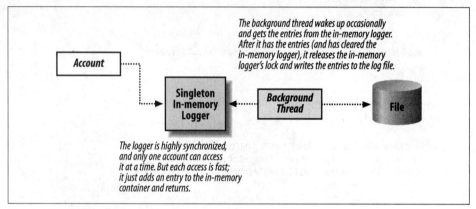

Figure 12-2. An improved singleton logger

The way this works is that a piece of code calls logString( ). The wrapper class takes the string that is supposed to be logged and simply places it in a container, after which, the method returns. This is a very fast operation.

Meanwhile, the background thread executes the following loop:

1. Sleep for awhile.
2. Wake up and get all the available strings from the wrapper class.
3. Send the strings to the real logging mechanism.
4. Return to step 1.

The code for this logger isn't all that complicated either. In the following example, we've implemented the background thread as an inner class:

```
public class ThreadedLogger implements Logger {
    private SimpleLogger _actualLogger;
    private ArrayList _logQueue;
```

```java
    public ThreadedLogger(SimpleLogger actualLogger) {
        _logQueue = new ArrayList();
        (new BackgroundThread()).start();
    }

    public void setOutputStream(PrintStream outputStream) {
        _actualLogger.setOutputStream(outputStream);
    }

    public synchronized void logString(String string) {
        _logQueue.add(string);
    }

    private synchronized Collection getAndReplaceQueue() {
        ArrayList returnValue = _logQueue;
        _logQueue = new ArrayList();
        return returnValue;
    }

    private class BackgroundThread extends Thread {
        public void run() {
            while(true) {
                pause();
                logEntries();
            }
        }

        private void pause() {
            try {
                Thread.sleep(5000);
            }
            catch (Exception ignored){}
        }

        private void logEntries() {
            Collection entries = getAndReplaceQueue();
            Iterator i = entries.iterator();
            while(i.hasNext()) {
                String nextString = (String) i.next();
                _actualLogger.logString(nextString);
            }
        }
    }
}
```

We still have the problem in which different account servers may want to write to the log at the same time, and an instance of Account may be forced to wait. We've simply replaced a potentially slow and high-variance bottleneck with a fast and low-variance bottleneck.

This may still be unacceptable for some. If instances of Account are constantly accessing the log, though each individual logString( ) operation is quick, each instance of Account still waits for many other instances to execute logString( ). For example, suppose that an average of 30 instances of Account are waiting to use the log file.

Then the logString( ) method is really 30 times slower than it appears to be at first glance.

Think about that sentence again. What I just asserted is this: the "real time" it takes to log a string is approximately the time it takes to log a string multiplied by the number of accounts waiting to log a string. However, suppose we have a burst of activity. The number of accounts waiting to log strings may increase, which means that every instance of Account becomes slower. This is pretty nasty; our system will slow down by more than a linear factor during burst periods.

 How nasty is this? Run a profiler and find out. That's really the only way to tell why a program isn't performing well.

If this is a problem, and we need to eliminate the bottleneck entirely, a variant of the preceding technique often works. Namely, we make the following three changes:

- Each server has a separate log object into which it stores logging information.
- Each of these logs registers with the background thread.
- The background thread now visits each of the logs in sequence, getting the entries and sending them to the real logging mechanism.

This effectively means that accounts cannot interfere with each other. Each instance of Account writes to a distinct logging object. The instance of Account may be forced to wait momentarily while the background thread gets the entries from its log. However, that wait is bounded and small. See Figure 12-3.

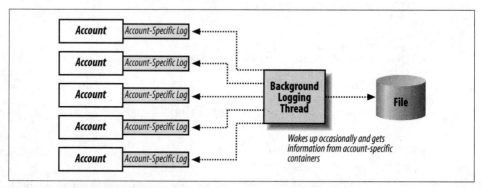

Figure 12-3. A more complex logging example

This approach to logging and other forms of device access is often called *using a batch thread*. Our logging code is remarkably similar to our implementation of automatic lock maintenance using a background thread. You may start to see a pattern here.

Don't synchronize across secondary remote method invocations

This is really the same admonition as the previous one. It is illustrated in Figure 12-4.

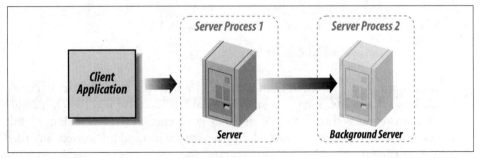

Figure 12-4. Don't synchronize across remote invocations

The point is that there's very little difference between a device and a remote server. If we synchronize a block of code in a server, and that block of code calls on a method in another server, we may wind up waiting a long time for a response. And, while we're waiting, the first server is locked.

The transferMoney( ) method now looks like a very dangerous method. If we wind up synchronizing the entire method (e.g., if we can't simply synchronize on checkAccess( ) as in the preceding example), then the implementation of transferMoney( ) will necessarily involve synchronizing across a remote method invocation. On the other hand, this isn't nearly so bad as logging. While the transferMoney( ) method has the potential to lock a single instance of Account for a long time, it won't block other remote method calls dealing with other accounts. Depending on the account, this might not be an issue.

Be Careful When Using Container Classes

The JDK comes with a fairly nice group of container classes. These container classes can be grouped into two sets: those that claim to be threadsafe and those that don't claim to be threadsafe.

Vector and Hashtable are the containers that claim to be threadsafe. They achieve this by synchronizing every method. If you peek inside Vector, you'll see code such as:

```java
public synchronized void copyInto(Object anArray[]) {
    System.arraycopy(elementData, 0, anArray, 0, elementCount);
}

public synchronized void trimToSize() {
    modCount++;
    int oldCapacity = elementData.length;
    if (elementCount < oldCapacity) {
        Object oldData[] = elementData;
```

```
        elementData = new Object[elementCount];
      System.arraycopy(oldData, 0, elementData, 0, elementCount);
      }
  }

  public synchronized void ensureCapacity(int minCapacity) {
      modCount++;
      ensureCapacityHelper(minCapacity);
  }
```

Because only one thread can modify an instance of Vector at a time, Vector is, technically speaking, threadsafe. I say "technically speaking" because while each individual method of Vector is threadsafe, this is rarely good enough. Just as with our bank accounts, you will often need to hold a lock over several method invocations in order to use Vector correctly.

For example, suppose we only want to put an object into Vector if it isn't already in Vector. The following code is incorrect:

```
  public void insertIfAbsent(Vector vector, Object object) {
      if (vector.contains(object)) {
          return;
      }
      vector.add(object);
  }
```

If more than one thread is executing inside this method, then the same object can wind up being added to the Vector more than once. How? More than one thread can make the test before any of the threads add the object. It's not even enough to synchronize the method, as in the following version:

```
  public synchronized void insertIfAbsent(Vector vector, Object object) {
      if (vector.contains(object)) {
          return;
      }
      vector.add(object);
  }
```

because this code implicitly assumes that there is only one instance of the class that contains the method. If there are two instances of the class, then there are two synchronization locks, one for each instance. Hence, the same object may be added to the instance of Vector twice. If there will be more than one thread manipulating an instance of Vector, you probably need to synchronize on the instance of Vector, as in the following code:

```
  public void insertIfAbsent(Vector vector, Object object) {
      synchronized(vector) {
          if (vector.contains(object)) {
              return;
          }
          vector.add(object);
      }
  }
```

Concurrent modification exceptions

The previous example may seem a little contrived. However, consider the following piece of generic "event-broadcasting" code, which is similar to the code used to broadcast user-interface events in the JDK 1.1 event model:

```
private void broadcastAnnouncement( ) {
    Enumeration e = _listeners.elements( );
    while (e.hasMoreElements( )) {
        (Listener) nextListener = (Listener) e.nextElement( );
        nextListener.changeOccurred( );
    }
}
```

This isn't threadsafe either. We could easily wind up throwing an instance of NullPointerException if _listeners is being changed while the enumeration is in progress. And simply synchronizing on _listeners, as in the following version, doesn't quite solve the problem:

```
private void broadcastAnnouncement( ) {
    syncrhonized(_listeners) {
        Enumeration e = _listeners.elements( );
        while (e.hasMoreElements( )) {
            (Listener) nextListener = (Listener) e.nextElement( );
            nextListener.changeOccurred( );
        }
    }
}
```

This is because the same thread that owns the synchronization lock can still alter _listeners. That is, if the call to nextListener.changeOccurred( ) results in a change to _listeners, and that change is made from within the same thread, then the lock won't prevent the change from happening.

In Java 2, this problem is called a *concurrent modification error*. The newer Collection classes attempt to detect it and throw instances of ConcurrentModificationException when it occurs. For more information, see the description of the ConcurrentModificationException class in the java.util package and some of the discussions about *fail-fast* iterators found on the Internet.

Preventing this sort of error can be difficult to do efficiently. A good, if slightly inefficient solution, is to simply make a local copy of the container in the methods that alter the container, as in the following code:

```
public void addListener(Listener listener) {
    Vector copy;
    synchronized(_vector) {
        copy = (Vector) _vector.clone( );
        _vector = copy;
    }
}
private void broadcastAnnouncement( ) {// no change necessary to this code.
    syncrhonized(_vector) {
```

```
        Enumeration e = _listeners.elements();
        while (e.hasMoreElements()) {
            (Listener) nextListener  = (Listener) e.nextElement();
            nextListener.changeOccurred();
        }
    }
}
```

This makes the modification to a new copy of _listeners. Meanwhile, the enumeration continues to use the old instance of Vector, which means that the instance of Vector the enumeration is using is not changing and cannot have a concurrent modification error. On the other hand, this can result in the creation of a large number of new objects. If the vector is modified frequently, this can be an expensive technique.

The other containers

The other container objects defined in the java.util package don't even synchronize their methods. The warnings stated earlier also hold true for them. In addition, since the fine-grained methods aren't synchronized, you need to be careful if you use an ArrayList in a multithreaded environment.

 There are some helpful static methods defined on java.util. Collections. For example, the synchronizedCollection() method takes a collection as an argument and returns a collection with the same contents, all of whose methods are synchronized.

Use Containers to Mediate Interthread Communication

Another way to write threadsafe code is to try to guarantee that any given instance is used by only a single thread. The problem with attempting to do this is that it's realisticly impossible; if you succeed, the threads would execute separate programs. To the extent that threads need to communicate, objects are touched by more than one thread.

However, phrasing the goal this way leads to an interesting idea: instead of trying to build many threadsafe classes, we can try to design our program so that threads have very few instances in common. One of the best ways to achieve this is to encapsulate messages between threads in a container object (which, of course, must be very safe). For example, consider our PrinterServer again.

The PrinterServer is much like the previous Logger example. The printer is a device, and we'd really like responses to the client to be fast, rather than wait for the printer to actually handle the print request. So we'll do the same thing we did in the Logger example, but with two minor differences. The first is that instead of putting strings in the intermediate container, we'll insert instances of DocumentDescription. The second is that the thread, instead of receiving everything in the container when it picks up information, will remove only one instance of DocumentDescription at a time. See Figure 12-5.

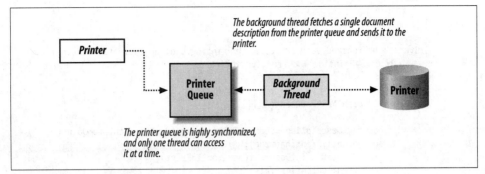

The background thread fetches a single document description from the printer queue and sends it to the printer.

Printer

Printer Queue

Background Thread

Printer

The printer queue is highly synchronized, and only one thread can access it at a time.

Figure 12-5. Making PrinterServer more responsive

This is a fairly general, and quite useful, technique for communicating between threads. For the most part, the threads operate independently and use different sets of instances (which, because they are used by only a single thread, don't need to be threadsafe). In order to communicate with each other, the threads have a highly synchronized and threadsafe container in common. They either place data objects in the container or remove data objects from the container.

Here's the implementation of BatchingPrinter:

```
package com.ora.rmibook.chapter12.printer.printers;
import com.ora.rmibook.chapter12.printer.*;
import java.io.*;
import java.rmi.*;
import java.rmi.server.*;
import java.util.*;

public class BatchingPrinter extends UnicastRemoteObject implements Printer {
    private LinkedList _printQueue;
    private Printer _realPrinter;
    private Object _printerLock = new Object( );
    private boolean _currentlyPrinting;

    public BatchingPrinter(Printer realPrinter) throws RemoteException {
        _printQueue = new LinkedList( );
        _realPrinter = realPrinter;
        (new BackgroundThread()).start( );
    }

    public synchronized boolean printerAvailable( ) throws RemoteException {
        if (_currentlyPrinting) {
            return false;
        }
        return _realPrinter.printerAvailable( );
    }

    public synchronized boolean printDocument(DocumentDescription document) throws
        RemoteException, PrinterException {
        _printQueue.add(document);
        notifyAll( );
```

```
            return true;
        }

        private synchronized void setCurrentlyPrinting(boolean currentlyPrinting) {
            _currentlyPrinting = currentlyPrinting;
        }

        private void printNextDocument() {
            try {
                DocumentDescription documentToPrint = getNextDocumentFromQueue();
                setCurrentlyPrinting(true);
                _realPrinter.printDocument(documentToPrint);
                setCurrentlyPrinting(false);
            }
            catch (Exception ignored) {
        /* This is a real issue-- what do we do with PrinterExceptions when we've batched
            things up like this. */
            }
        }

        private synchronized DocumentDescription getNextDocumentFromQueue() {
            while (0==_printQueue.size()) {
                try {
                    wait();
                }
                catch(Exception ignored) {}
            }
            DocumentDescription nextDocument = (DocumentDescription)_printQueue
                remove(0);
            return nextDocument;
        }

        private class BackgroundThread extends Thread {
            public void run() {
                while(true) {
                    printNextDocument();
                }
            }
        }
    }
```

There are three nice things about building our networked printer this way. The first is, obviously, that we've greatly improved client performance. Submitting a print request to BatchingPrinter returns almost immediately, even if the actual printer is busy at the time.

The second nice aspect is that most of the threadsafe (and thread-aware) code is in a single object. We don't have to worry about the actual printer code being thread-safe. Since the printer probably uses native libraries and legacy code, this is a good thing. It's easy to tell that the application is threadsafe, because most of the application has only a single thread running through it.

The final point is that this decomposition is good object-oriented design. By explicitly representing the print queue, we've made it easier to build additional functionality into the application. We have an object whose explicit role is to handle dispatching print requests. This means we have a place to store things such as the results of all print requests and a place to implement additional methods. Recall that in Chapter 3, our list of probable extensions included:

> Users will want to have a print queue. Important documents should be moved to the top of a print queue; less urgent jobs should wait until the printer isn't busy.

> If we're going to have a print queue it would be nice to be able to explicitly access the queue, both to see the entire queue and to make queries about our job. It should also be possible to cancel a print request that is in the queue but hasn't already been sent to the printer.

The fact that increasing network performance and building in thread safety leads to this last benefit is a sure hint that we've done something correctly.

Note that we've made a big trade-off here. In essence, we've replaced synchronous with asynchronous method calls to allow batching. This means that the return values aren't meaningful. In addition, in our current framework there's no way to tell the client if something goes wrong—we can't throw a `PrinterException` after the method call has already returned.

If the client really needs to know whether the print request succeeded, the client must either make a second method call later on to explicitly ask about the status of the print request or register for a callback. We'll cover the latter technique in Chapter 21.

You may have noticed that several of our threading principles are actually concrete versions of a abstract principle for organizing code:

> Things that are logically distinct should not interact with each other.

"Ensure Data Integrity" was about preventing catastrophic interference. "Minimize Time Spent in Synchronized Blocks" was about reducing the amount of time distinct tasks spend waiting for each other to finish, and so on. It's apparent that I'm a big fan of eliminating unneccesary interactions whenever, and wherever, possible. Even if it results in more code in the short-term, doing so will simplify debugging and long-term maintenance.

Immutable Objects Are Automatically Threadsafe

This is an obvious point that people often overlook. If you can guarantee that an object's state will never change, then you have guaranteed that the object is thread-safe. The `String` class, for example, is immutable. Once created, an instance of `String` does not change. Instead, methods such as `concat( )` have the following signature:

```
public String concat(String str)
```

This method returns a brand new string, which is the concatenation of the two older strings, both of which remain unchanged. This means that `String` is threadsafe.

If we needed to, we could apply this to our Money class as well. The current implementation of subtract( ) is:

```
public void subtract(Money otherMoney) {
    _cents -= otherMoney.getCents();
}
```

This could easily be changed to:

```
public Money subtract(Money otherMoney) {
    int resultCents -= _cents - otherMoney.getCents();
    return new Money( resultCents);
}
```

If we performed a similar transformation on Money's add( ) method, Money would become a threadsafe class, without a need to synchronize any of the methods or think about whether they are synchronized correctly.

Of course, once we've changed Money, we must change our implementation of Account as well to reflect the new behavior. But have no fear. If we forget to do this, the testing framework we'll build in Chapter 13 will help to detect the error.

 A special case of this rule of thumb is the stateless object; if an object has no state, its state cannot change. Hence, stateless objects are automatically threadsafe.

Always Have a Safe Way to Stop Your Threads

I mentioned this in Chapter 11. Threads, especially background threads, are usually set up to run for a very long period of time. For example, the lock expiration threads we implemented a few pages back ran in an infinite loop. Similarly, threads that automatically serialize objects to a datastore often run in the background in an infinite loop. Another example is a thread that automatically polls for external events, such as the thread in my mailreader that indefinitely checks for new mail every two minutes.

What happens when you want to stop a thread? The Java language allows you to stop a thread simply by calling stop( ). However, as we discussed in Chapter 11, this method is deprecated, and doing so can leave your program in an inconsistent state. It's much better to use a boolean stop variable in your run( ) method. Implement your run( ) method as a loop that only continues if the stop variable is set correctly. The following code snippet is from Chapter 11, but it's worth repeating:

```
public abstract class StoppableThread extends Thread {
    // ... many constructors, we've only included one
    public StopppableThread(String threadName, Object arg1, OObject arg2) {
        super(threadName);
        // use arg1, arg2, ... to initialize thread state
```

```
        start();
    }

    private boolean _shouldStopExecuting;
    public void setShouldStopExecuting(boolean shouldStopExecuting) {
        _shouldStopExecuting = shouldStopExecuting;
    }
    public boolean getShouldStopExecuting() {
        return _shouldStopExecuting;
    }

    public void run() {
        while (!_shouldStopExecuting) {
            performTask();
        }
    }

    protected abstract void performTask();
}
```

Background Threads Should Have Low Priority

In Java, threads can be assigned a priority. Priorities are integers that tell a JVM how important a particular thread's tasks are. In general, the JVM schedules more processor time for higher-priority threads.

There are three distinguished, and predefined priorities: MAX_PRIORITY, NORM_PRIORITY, and MIN_PRIORITY. MAX_PRIORITY is equal to 10, NORM_PRIORITY is equal to 5, and MIN_PRIORITY is equal to 1.

 When you create a thread, it gets the same priority as the thread which created it.

Background threads perform secondary tasks. Logging into a file, while important, does not need to be done right away. It can wait until the processor has more time available. On the other hand, servicing a client request is important and needs to be done quickly. So the general rule is background tasks get low priorities; client tasks get high priorities.

Applying this to the bank example

A very nice illustration of this idea can be shown in the bank example by implementing a persistence layer. The goal of a persistence layer is to take server state, which is stored in RAM, and place it in a much more secure and dependable location on a disk. If the computer crashes, the contents of RAM are gone forever. Whatever's on the hard drive is much more likely to be recovered. We thus have two different strategies for where to store a single account's state:

The in-memory strategy
> State is easily accessible, and the server is incredibly fast and responsive. It can handle thousands of operations per minute, and as long as the server doesn't crash, data integrity isn't a problem.

The on-disk strategy
> This is much slower and much less responsive. It can handle tens of operations per minute, but is much more resilient in the face of system failures. Furthermore, if the data is stored in a database (or database-like system), it can be accessed by other applications.

Moreover, these are characteristics of the entire system. If all the servers store their state to disk constantly, then the entire system is only as responsive as the hard drive, since individual Accounts will conflict when they attempt to read from the hard drive. If, on the other hand, all the Accounts store their state in memory, then the system will be much more responsive.

Clearly, neither of these is a particularly desirable situation. Fortunately, there is a fairly nice compromise strategy: implement a persistence layer. Use the in-memory strategy for active servers. However, when a server has been inactive for awhile, when clients are not accessing it and haven't done so for some predetermined amount of time, surreptitiously make a copy of the server's state and store it on a disk.

The most common place to store a server's state is, of course, in a relational database. But that's a detail. The important aspect of the strategy is the compromise it effects between the fast response time necessary for active servers and the long-term data integrity necessary for a successful enterprise application.

Persistence is usually implemented in a way that's fairly similar to the background lock-maintenance threads we examined earlier. The design strategy is something like:

- A background thread is decrementing a timer, using the "sleep for a while, then wake up and decrement the count" implementation that the lock strategy used. This is a low-priority thread.

- When a server object has been inactive long enough, the background thread registers the server with a container that holds objects eligible for persisting.

- When the server JVM isn't busy, a persistence thread makes a permanent copy of the registered servers. This persistence thread is also a low-priority thread.

Pay Careful Attention to What You Serialize

Recall how serialization, the default mechanism for marshalling and demarshalling objects, works. It starts with a single instance and records all the information associated with that instance. Some of the attribute values of the instance may themselves be instances of other classes. Those instances also get serialized, and so on. Serialization traverses all the instances reachable from the first instance, and records all the information associated with each.

I previously mentioned that serialization uses the reflection API quite extensively and is rather slow. In the world of multithreaded servers, however, serialization has another flaw that is much more serious: serialization essentially assumes that the object graph is static.

To see what I mean, assume, for a moment, that our instances of Account also keep records. That is, in addition to recording the new balance after every operation, they store a list of transactions to track the individual operations that occur:

```
public class Transaction implements Serializable {
    public Money amount;
    public int typeOfTransaction;
    public time whenMade;
}
```

In addition, assume we have a persistence layer that serializes out the instance of Account every now and then (using a background thread).

At first glance, this seems quite nice. Money needs to implement Serializable anyway to pass over the wire. By adding the words "implements Serializable" to our implementation of Account and implementing a simple background thread, we can restore accounts when the system crashes and restart accounts on different servers quite easily.

However, care needs to be taken when we do this. Suppose that we do serialize a server in a background thread, and suppose that a client makes a request on the server while serialization is occurring. Unless we are careful, scenarios such as the following can happen:

1. Serialization starts. The balance is recorded by the serialization mechanism, and we begin serializing each of the transactions.

2. A request comes in, the balance changes, and a transaction is added to the end of the list of transactions.

3. Serialization finishes recording all the transactions, including the one that was just registered.

This is a problem. The balance we stored is inconsistent with the list of transactions we wrote—it's the balance from before the final request came in. The serialized copy of our implementation of Account that we saved, which is intended to be a correct copy of our server, is flawed because another thread changed the data while serialization was occurring.

What makes this problem especially insidious is that it doesn't crash the server. It simply corrupts the backup copy of your data. So when the server crashes due to some other problem, you won't be able to recover.

In practice, there's really only one solution to this problem. While the serialization is going on, we need to block all operations that alter the state of the objects being serialized. Since serialization is slow, and can traverse a large number of instances, this can be a problem.

 In the case of the bank example, this solution doesn't really cause a problem. If we serialize only instances of Account that haven't been active for a while, the risks of locking out a client who wants to access her money are minimal. However, in other applications, using serialization for persistence can lead to serious problems.

In practice, serialization is fine for client applications. It's quite easy to design data objects so they are fast to serialize and involve passing small amounts of information over the wire. Furthermore, most clients are single-threaded anyway; since the serialization algorithm's data-corruption problems occur only when multiple threads are running, they rarely occur on the client side.

Yet if you use serialization for persistence, logging, or to pass state between servers, you need to be careful. The rules are simple:

Make serialization fast
Limit the number of instances that can be reached by the serialization algorithm from any serializable instance.

Make serialization safe
Make sure that the objects being serialized are locked during the serialization algorithm.

Use Threading to Reduce Response-Time Variance

A typical remote method invocation embodies three distinct types of code:

- Resource allocation code
- Actual requested functionality
- Cleanup code

One of the key observations about threads is that, to a large extent, they allow us to isolate these three types of code in different threads. The upcoming pool example shows how this is done. What I want to emphasize here is that when we move functionality into worker threads, we not only get a more robust server, we get a more responsive and predictable client. The less we do inside any given client method invocation, the more predictable the outcome will be.

For example, consider what we did in our printer example. We moved the actual printing into a separate thread. The client threads, which used to print the document, simply drop off an object in a container and return. Every client thread does the same things in the same order, and they never block while waiting for resources.

Similarly, when we implemented logging as a background thread, one of the major gains was that client threads didn't have to wait for a resource to become available. We turned a variable-length operation (waiting for the log file) into a faster, fixed-length operation (putting an object into a container). The servers aren't necessarily faster or more efficient as a result of these transformations, but the client application feels faster and has a much more uniform response time as a result.

Limit the Number of Objects a Thread Touches

The next tip in using threads is almost an emergent tip. If you use containers to mediate thread communication, use background threads to perform resource allocation and cleanup tasks, and carefully limit the number of objects that serialization will visit, you'll notice something else happening. Each thread will only ever visit a small number of objects.

 There's a slight exception to this. Since RMI reuses the same thread across multiple client requests, that thread may eventually wind up visiting many instances. But during any given remote method invocation, it will only visit a few.

This is an important and useful consequence. It's so important and so useful that it deserves to be a design guideline of its own instead of just a consequence of the others. If all of your threads touch only a few objects, then your code will be much easier to debug, and you can think about thread interaction problems such as deadlock. If, on the other hand, a given thread can execute any method in your code, then you'll have a hard time predicting when thread-interaction problems will occur and which threads caused a particular problem.

Acquire Locks in a Fixed Order

Recall that deadlock is a situation when a set of threads acquire locks in such a way that none of them can continue processing. The simplest example requires two threads and two locks and involves the following sequence of actions:

1. Thread 1 acquires Lock 1.
2. Thread 2 acquires Lock 2.
3. Thread 1 attempts to acquire Lock 2 and blocks (because Thread 2 has Lock 2).
4. Thread 2 attempts to acquire Lock 1 and blocks (because Thread 1 has Lock 1).

The basic idea behind ordering locks is simple. Deadlock depends on locks being acquired in different orders. In our example scenario, Thread 1 acquires Lock 1 and then Lock 2. And Thread 2 acquires Lock 2 and then Lock 1. However, if both threads acquire the locks in the same order, then deadlock doesn't occur. Instead, one of the threads blocks until the other thread completes, as in the following variant scenario:

1. Thread 1 acquires Lock 1.
2. Thread 2 attempts to acquire Lock 1 and blocks because Thread 1 has Lock 1.
3. Thread 1 attempts to acquire Lock 2 and succeeds. After awhile, it relinquishes both locks.
4. Thread 2 then acquires Lock 1 and continues.

Of course, it's often very difficult to define a global order on all the locks. If there are a large number of objects being locked, and if the codebase is large enough, enforcing a global ordering turns out to be a difficult task.

Often, however, you can impose an ordering on the types of locks. A rule as simple as:

> Synchronize on instances of class X before synchronizing on instances of class Y.

often has the same effect as imposing a global ordering on all instances. For example, "Synchronize on instances of Logfile before synchronizing on instances of Account."

Use Worker Threads to Prevent Deadlocks

Another common trick to prevent deadlocks is to use worker threads to reduce the number of locks any given thread has. We've already briefly discussed worker threads. Among other examples, we discussed log files. Our example began with:

> A single thread that both received and handled a request and, in the course of doing so, logged information to the log file.

We transformed this into:

> Two threads. One thread received the request and encapsulated the request in an object that was dropped off in a container. The second (worker) thread, pulled these objects from the container and registered them in a log.

The main reason I gave for doing this was to prevent clients from blocking each other, or waiting for an external device to become available. Logging is something that can often be done independently of the actual client request. But there's another benefit. In the first scenario, a single thread holds two distinct types of locks: locks associated with the actual client request and incidental locks associated with the logging mechanism. Using a logging thread changes this in a very significant way:

> There is only one lock associated with logging that the request thread ever acquires (namely, the lock associated with the container used to communicate with the worker thread).

Moreover, the lock associated with the container doesn't count when you're reasoning about deadlock. This is because the container lock has the following two properties:

- If another lock is acquired before the container lock, that other lock will be released after the container lock is released.
- No locks are acquired between when the container lock is acquired and when the container lock is released.

Any lock with these two properties cannot add a deadlock to a system. It can block threads (as the container lock does in order to ensure data integrity), but it cannot deadlock threads.

Pools: An Extended Example

At this point, you've read some 70 or so pages of reasonably plausible material on threading. But, speaking from personal experience, it's almost impossible to read 70 pages of material on threading and actually understand all of it on the first reading.

The point of this section is to introduce a fairly complex and sophisticated piece of code that involves threading. If you understand this example, how it works, and why it's built the way it is, then you've got a reasonable grasp of this material and how to use threads in your applications. If, however, this seems like an incredibly byzantine and opaque piece of code, then you may want to reread those 70 pages or grab a copy of one of the references.

The Idea of a Pool

Pooling is an important idiom in designing scalable applications. The central idea is that there is a resource, encapsulated by an object, with the following characteristics:

- It is difficult to create the resource, or doing so consumes other scarce resources.
- The resource can be reused many times.
- You frequently need more than one instance of the resource because there are many threads that perform tasks involving this type of resource (I will call these threads the *client threads*).

The canonical example of a resource that ought to be pooled is a database connection. In Java, database connections are embodied as instances of an implementation of the java.sql.Connection interface. A database vendor will supply a class that implements the Connection interface and is used to communicate with the vendor's database server.

Database connections almost always involve a socket connection to the database server. Socket connections to the database server are expensive for two reasons. First, the database has a limited number of sockets it can vend. Second, establishing a connection often involves logging into the database and establishing a secure communications channel. Performing the security check is time-consuming and is something you don't want to repeat every time you need to make a query against a database.

Two Interfaces That Define a Pool

Our goal is to define a generic and reusable pooling mechanism. To do so, we start by defining two interfaces: Pool and PoolHelper. These are very simple interfaces, defined in the com.ora.rmibook.chapter12.pool package:

```
public interface Pool{
    public Object getObject();
    public void returnObject(Object object);
}
public interface PoolHelper
{
    public Object create();
    public boolean dispose(Object object);
    public boolean isObjectStillValid(Object object);
}
```

Pool and PoolHelper encaspulate everything that the client threads (which simply use the pooling mechanism) need to know. Pool defines only two methods: getObject() lets a client thread get an object from the pool, and returnObject() returns an object to the pool (thereby making it available for other client threads to use).

The second interface helps us build a generic and reusable pool class. Since there's no way an implementation of the Pool interface could know how to construct the objects in the pool, or how to make sure they're still valid, we need to provide a way for the generic pooling mechanism to create and validate individual objects in the pool. For example, database connections have a tendency to fail over time. The pooling mechanism should occasionally check them and make sure they still work. We build this into our system by defining the PoolHelper interface. Users of the pooling mechanism will implement PoolHelper's three methods in order to customize the pool to their specific needs.

A First Implementation of Pooling

Our first implementation of Pool, called SimplePool, is a basic implementation of Pool. It does the following:

- In the constructor, it gets a PoolHelper, a starting size for the pool, and a maximum size. SimplePool immediately creates a set of available objects. The size of the set is the starting size of the pool.

- Whenever getObject() is called, it checks to see whether it has an object. If it does, it returns one (first removing it from the set of available objects). If the pool has no available objects, it calls its helper's create() method.

- Whenever returnObject( ) is called, the object is put back into the set of available objects if two conditions are met: the set of available objects isn't already at the maximum size (e.g., the pool isn't already full), and the object is still valid, which the pool checks by calling the helper's isObjectStillValid( ) method.

Here's the code for SimplePool in its entirety:

```java
public class SimplePool implements Pool {
    private int _maximumIndex;
    private int _currentPosition;
    private PoolHelper _helper;
    private Object[] _availableObjects;
    public SimplePool(int startingSize, int maximumSize, PoolHelper helper) {
        _maximumIndex = maximumSize -1;
        _helper = helper;
        buildInitialObjects(startingSize, maximumSize);
    }

    public synchronized Object getObject( ) {
        if (_currentPosition == -1) {
            return _helper.create( );
        }
        return getObjectFromArray( );
    }

    private Object getObjectFromArray( ) {
        Object returnValue = _availableObjects[_currentPosition];
        _availableObjects[_currentPosition] = null;
        _currentPosition--;
        return returnValue;
    }

    public synchronized void returnObject(Object object) {
        if (_currentPosition == _maximumIndex) {
            _helper.dispose(object);
            return;
        }
        if (!_helper.isObjectStillValid(object)) {
            _helper.dispose(object);
            return;
        }
        _currentPosition++;
        _availableObjects[_currentPosition] = object;
    }

    private void buildInitialObjects(int startingSize, int maximumSize) {
        _availableObjects = new Object[maximumSize];
        int counter;
        for (counter = 0; counter < startingSize; counter++) {
            _availableObjects[counter] =_helper.create( );
        }
        _currentPosition = startingSize -1;
    }
}
```

Problems with SimplePool

SimplePool has a number of nice attributes. The first is that, as advertised, the code is straightforward. Another is threadsafety. Since both getObject( ) and returnObject( ) are synchronized, SimplePool is threadsafe. Moreover, because only one thread ever gets to _helper at a time, SimplePool is threadsafe independent of the implementation of PoolHelper.

However, SimplePool also has four major problems. First, there is no effective bound on the number of pooled objects that are created. If all the pooled objects are checked out, then another object is created. This can be unfortunate. When our server is really busy, it may spend an inordinate amount of time and resources creating pooled objects that it will then throw away. In the case of database connections, it may swamp the database server as well.

The second problem is that getObject( ) and returnObject( ) are both synchronized. Thus, at most, one thread can either get or return an object. This, in turn, has two effects. First, returning an object to the pool, an operation that ought to be quite fast for the client threads, may take a long time. Second, it's quite possible that instances of SimplePool will not achieve efficient reuse during peak usage periods. Suppose, for example, that all the pooled objects have been vended, and 15 more requests for objects come in. It's possible that 15 new objects will be created, even if during that same time period, 11 client threads were attempting to return pooled objects.

The third major problem with SimplePool is that the validity checks, and the destruction of surplus pooled objects, are done in the calling thread. One of the big benefits of using a pool is that it makes the client threads more responsive by offloading most of their work to the pool. We'd certainly like to move validation and destruction out of the client threads as well.

The last major defect with SimplePool is that the pool doesn't shrink during quiet times. Once the pool is at maximum size, it will keep all of its allocated objects forever. Given that pooled objects are usually scarce resources, we'd probably like a way to gradually shrink the pool when it's not often being used and release those scare resources for other uses.

Each of these problems cries out for background threads inside our pooling mechanism. In particular, we will implement three threads: one that handles object creation, another that handles returning objects to the pool, and a third that handles shrinking the pool over time.

The Creation Thread

The first step in solving SimplePool's problems is to add a separate thread to handle object creation. This will enable us to solve the first two problems mentioned earlier. The basic idea is:

- A separate thread handles object-creation requests. It does so one at a time.
- When calls to getObject( ) are made, the pool first checks its local storage. If no object is available, it sends a message to the object-creation thread, requesting that a single object be created, and then waits.
- When the object-creation thread receives the message, it creates a single object (if the pool hasn't exceeded its maximum size limit) and notifies a waiting thread. If the pool is already at its maximum size, the object-creation thread does nothing.
- When objects are checked into the pool, notification also occurs. This accomplishes two things. First, it handles the problems caused by the object-creation thread's refusal to create objects when the pool is already at maximum size. Second, it increases the likelihood that waiting creation requests will be able to reuse objects that were checked in while they were waiting.

The code to implement this version of Pool isn't much longer than that for SimplePool. But it's much trickier. Avoiding a deadlock between the threads calling getObject( ) and the object creation thread requires some thought. In addition, making sure that all the getObject( ) calls are eventually satisfied also requires some work.

Here's the code for ThreadedPool1:

```
public class ThreadedPool1 implements Pool {
    private int _maximumSize;
    private Vector _availableObjects;
    private int _totalNumberOfObjects;
    private PoolHelper _helper;
    private ObjectCreator _creator;

    public ThreadedPool1(String poolName, int maximumSize, PoolHelper helper) {
        _maximumSize = maximumSize;
        _helper = helper;
        _availableObjects = new Vector();
        startCreatorThread(poolName);
    }

    public Object getObject() {
        Object returnValue = null;
        while (null== (returnValue = getLocallyAvailableObject())) {
```

```
                _creator.askForObject();
                waitForAvailableObject();
            }
        return returnValue;
    }

    public void returnObject(Object object) {
        if (_helper.isObjectStillValid(object)) {
            _availableObjects.add(object);
            notifyWaitingGets();
        }
        else {
            _helper.dispose(object);
            _totalNumberOfObjects--;
        }
        return;
    }

    protected void createAndAddObject() {
        Object createdObject = null;
        if (_totalNumberOfObjects < _maximumSize) {
            Object newObject = _helper.create();
            _availableObjects.add(newObject);
            _totalNumberOfObjects++;
        }
        if (null!=createdObject) {
            notifyWaitingGets();
        }
        return;
    }

    private synchronized void waitForAvailableObject() {
        try {
            wait();
        }
        catch (InterruptedException ignored) {}
    }

    private synchronized void notifyWaitingGets() {
        notify();
    }

    private Object getLocallyAvailableObject() {
        // Locks the container while we check for values.
        // That way, we don't simultaneously vend the same object
        // to two different requests
        synchronized(_availableObjects) {
            if (!_availableObjects.isEmpty()) {
                int lastPosition = _availableObjects.size()-1;
                _return _availableObjects.remove(lastPosition);
            }
        }
        return null;
    }
```

```
        private void startCreatorThread(String poolName) {
            _creator = new ObjectCreator(this);
            Thread creatorThread = new Thread(_creator, poolName + " creation thread");
            creatorThread.setPriority(Thread.NORM_PRIORITY-2);
            creatorThread.start();
        }
    }
```

There are two important points to note here. The first is that we deliberately choose to use Vector instead of ArrayLists. Vectors are a slightly slower container structure, but they have one important advantage: all method calls on an instance of Vector are synchronized. This means that some of the problems are solved for us because we don't have to worry about two different add( ) operations being performed simultaneously.

The second important point is that object creation is given a lower priority. Object creation is important—we've offloaded it to a background thread—but the last thing we want is for that thread to get priority. Given our druthers, we'd rather reuse an object. So, we make creation a slightly lower priority and hope that returned objects satisfy most of the pending requests.

We use a separate class, ObjectCreator, to implement the Runnable interface. All Runnable does is wait for requests to come in and then call ThreadedPool1's createAndAddObject( ) method:

```
    public class ObjectCreator implements Runnable {
        private ThreadedPool1 _owner;
        private boolean _requestPending;
        public ObjectCreator(ThreadedPool1 owner) {
            _owner = owner;
        }

        public void run( ) {
            boolean needToCreate = false;
            while (true) {
                synchronized(this) {
                    while (!_requestPending) {
                        try {
                            wait( );
                        } catch (InterruptedException ignored){}
                    }
                    needToCreate = _requestPending;
                    requestPending = false;
                }
                if (needToCreate) {
                    needToCreate = false
                    _owner.createAndAddObject( );
                }
            }
        }

        public synchronized void askForObject( ) {
            _requestPending = true;
```

```
            notify();
        }
    }
```

Adding a Return Thread

Adding a creation thread partially solved two of the four problems we noticed with SimplePool. There is now an upper bound on the number of objects created (_maximumSize is used to limit the total number of objects created, as well as the total number of objects stored). And, while creation requests are queued and waiting, objects can still be returned to the pool and will immediately be available to getObject( ) requests.

This did not, however, completely solve our second problem. Returning an object involves synchronizing, and thus may block for an extended period of time. To solve this problem, we'll add another thread, which will return objects to the pool. Moreover, in doing so, we will solve our third problem:

> The third major problem with SimplePool is that the validity checks, and the destruction of surplus pooled objects, are done in the calling thread. One of the big benefits of using a pool is that it makes the client threads more responsive by offloading most of their work to the pool. We'd certainly like to move validation and destruction out of the client threads as well.

Adding this thread involves a few small changes to the actual pool object. In particular, in the class ThreadedPool2, we rewrote returnObject( ) to simply delegate all of its functionality to the background thread. We also added a new method, startReturnerThread( ), which is called by ThreadedPool2's constructor. ThreadedPool2 is otherwise almost identical to ThreadedPool1:

```
public void returnObject(Object object)  {
    _returner.validateAndReturn(object);
}

protected void returnObjectToPool(Object object) { // called from background thread
    if (_helper.isObjectStillValid(object))  {
        _availableObjects.add(object);
        notifyWaitingGets();
    }
    else {
        _helper.dispose(object);
        _totalNumberOfObjects--;
    }
    return;
}

private void startReturnerThread(String poolName) {
    _returner = new ObjectReturner(this);
    Thread returnerThread = new Thread(_returner, poolName + " returner thread");
    returnerThread.setPriority(Thread.NORM_PRIORITY+2);
    returnerThread.start();
}
```

There's a general programming pattern here. Grady Booch is generally credited with the aphorism, "If the design of your program is too complicated, add more objects." Similarly, if you are having threading or synchronization problems, the solution is usually to add more threads. Both statements are ludicrous and counterintuitive. But they're also both true, and moreover, they're both really specializations of the old saw that "adding another level of indirection never hurt anything."

The returner thread has a fairly high priority because we're biased towards returning objects to the pool and reusing them. We don't want client threads to perform the return and validation operations, but we definitely want the return thread to return objects to the pool as quickly as possible. For example, if validating an object requires calling a database, we'd rather not have the client thread wait for that operation to complete.

_returner is an instance of the ObjectReturner class. What happens inside ObjectReturner is simple. When validateAndReturnObject( ) is called, the instance of ObjectReturner places the argument inside a vector and notifies the background thread. The background thread handles all the validation and reclamation work by calling the pool's protected returnObjectToPool( ) method. Meanwhile, the original calling thread, presumably a client thread, returns from validateAndReturnObject( ) and can continue processing without anymore delays:

```java
public class ObjectReturner implements Runnable {
    private Vector _objectsToReturn;
    private ThreadedPool2 _owner;
    public ObjectReturner(ThreadedPool2 owner) {
        _owner = owner;
        _objectsToReturn = new Vector( );
    }

    public void run( ) {
        while (true) {
            Object objectToReturn;
            while (0==_objectsToReturn.size( )) {
                synchronized (_objectsToReturn) {
                    try {
                        _objectsToReturn.wait( );
                    } catch (InterruptedException e){}
                }
            }
            int lastIndex = _objectsToReturn.size( ) -1;
            objectToReturn = _objectsToReturn.remove(lastIndex);
            _owner.returnObjectToPool(objectToReturn);
        }
    }

    public void validateAndReturn(Object object) {
        synchronized(_objectsToReturn) {
            _objectsToReturn.add(object);
```

```
                    if (1== _objectsToReturn.size( )) {
                        _objectsToReturn.notify( );
                    }
                }
            }
        }
```

Gradually Shrinking the Pool

The last feature we want to add to our pool is the ability to shrink the pool gradually over time. If you look at pool utilization you'll notice an interesting fact: it is usually "bursty." That is, most of the time, a small number of pooled objects will suffice. However, during peak usage times, far more objects will be required. This makes the design of ThreadedPool2 rather awkward. In particular, we're faced with one of the following choices:

- Pass in a large maximum size to the constructor. This means that client threads don't have to wait very long during peak usage. However, this also means that we're carrying around a lot of extra baggage during ordinary usage times (our pool will almost always have many extra objects in it).

- Pass in a smaller maximum size to the constructor and have client threads wait inside the getObject( ) method for a pooled object to become available during peak usage.

A compromise solution to this problem is to pass in two values: a maximum size and a "steady-state size." They are used to implement the following behavior:

- During peak usage, the pool expands to the maximum size and stays that size as long as there is demand for that many pooled objects.

- As demand recedes, objects are gradually removed from the pool until the steady-state size is reached.

Of course, implementing this behavior requires yet another background thread to remove objects from the pool. This thread is a lot like the lock maintenance and persistence threads we saw earlier in the chapter. In other words, it's a background thread that operates on a timer. If enough time has passed without the pool ever being completely emptied, then the background thread removes the "surplus" object and resumes waiting.

This is the final version of our threaded pool:

```java
public class ThreadedPool_Final implements Pool {
    private int _maximumSize;
    private int _steadyStateSize;
    private Vector _availableObjects;
    private int _totalNumberOfObjects;
    private PoolHelper _helper;
    private ObjectCreator _creator;
    private ObjectReturner _returner;
    private PoolShrinker _shrinker;
```

```java
public ThreadedPool_Final(String poolName, int steadyStateSize, int maximumSize,
    PoolHelper helper) {
    _steadyStateSize = steadyStateSize;
    _maximumSize = maximumSize;
    _helper = helper;
    _availableObjects = new Vector();
    startCreatorThread(poolName);
    startReturnerThread(poolName);
    startShrinkingThread(poolName);
}

public Object getObject() {
    Object returnValue = null;
    while (null== (returnValue = getLocallyAvailableObject())) {
        _creator.askForObject();
        waitForAvailableObject();
    }
    return returnValue;
}

public void returnObject(Object object) {
    _returner.validateAndReturn(object);
}

protected void returnObjectToPool(Object object) {
    if (_helper.isObjectStillValid(object)) {
        _availableObjects.add(object);
        notifyWaitingGets();
    }
    else {
        _helper.dispose(object);
        _totalNumberOfObjects--;
    }
    return;
}

protected void createAndAddObject() {
    Object createdObject = null;
    if (_totalNumberOfObjects < _maximumSize) {
        Object newObject = _helper.create();
        _availableObjects.add(newObject);
        _totalNumberOfObjects++;
    }
    if (null!=createdObject) {
        notifyWaitingGets();
    }
    return;
}

protected void removeAnObject() {
    if (_totalNumberOfObjects < _steadyStateSize) {
        return;
    }
    Object objectToRemove = getLocallyAvailableObject();
    if (null!=objectToRemove) {
```

```
                _helper.dispose(objectToRemove);
        }
    }

    private synchronized void waitForAvailableObject( ) {
        _shrinker.pause( );// if we have to wait, the pool is at full utilization
        try {
            wait( );
        }
        catch (InterruptedException e) {/*ignored*/}
        _shrinker.resume( );// if we had to wait, the pool is at full utilization
    }

    private synchronized void notifyWaitingGets( ) {
        notify( );
    }

    private Object getLocallyAvailableObject( ) {
        // Locks the container while we check for values.
        // That way, we don't simultaneously vend the same object
        // to two different requests
        synchronized(_availableObjects) {
            if (!_availableObjects.isEmpty( )) {
                int lastPosition = _availableObjects.size( )-1;
                return _availableObjects.remove(lastPosition);
            }
        }
        return null;
    }

    private void startCreatorThread(String poolName)  {
        _creator = new ObjectCreator(this);
        Thread creatorThread = new Thread(_creator, poolName + " creation thread");
        creatorThread.setPriority(Thread.NORM_PRIORITY-2);
        creatorThread.start( );
    }

    private void startReturnerThread(String poolName)  {
        _returner = new ObjectReturner(this);
        Thread returnerThread = new Thread(_returner, poolName + " returner
            thread");
        returnerThread.setPriority(Thread.NORM_PRIORITY+2);
        returnerThread.start( );
    }

    private void startShrinkingThread(String poolName)  {
        _shrinker = new PoolShrinker(this);
        Thread shrinkerThread = new Thread(_shrinker, poolName + " shrinking
            thread");
        shrinkerThread.setPriority(Thread.NORM_PRIORITY-2);
        shrinkerThread.start( );
    }
}
```

And the code for PoolShrinker is:

```
public class PoolShrinker implements Runnable {
    private static final int DEFAULT_TIME_TO_WAIT = 120000;
    private static final int DEFAULT_TIME_INTERVAL = 5000;
    private ThreadedPool_Final _owner;
    private int _timeLeftUntilWeShrinkThePool;
    private boolean _paused;

    public PoolShrinker(ThreadedPool_Final owner) {
        _owner = owner;
        _timeLeftUntilWeShrinkThePool = DEFAULT_TIME_TO_WAIT;
    }

    public synchronized void pause() {
        _paused = true;
    }

    public synchronized void resume() {
        _timeLeftUntilWeShrinkThePool = DEFAULT_TIME_TO_WAIT;
        _paused = false;
    }

    public void run() {
        while (true) {
            try {
                Thread.sleep(DEFAULT_TIME_INTERVAL);
            }
            catch (InterruptedException e) {/* ignored*/}
            if (!_paused) {
                decrementClock();
                if (0==_timeLeftUntilWeShrinkThePool) {
                    _owner.removeAnObject();
                    resetClock();
                }
            }
        }
    }

    private synchronized void resetClock() {
        _timeLeftUntilWeShrinkThePool = DEFAULT_TIME_TO_WAIT;
    }

    private synchronized void decrementClock() {
        _timeLeftUntilWeShrinkThePool-= DEFAULT_TIME_INTERVAL;
        if (0> _timeLeftUntilWeShrinkThePool) {
            _timeLeftUntilWeShrinkThePool = 0;
        }
    }
}
```

The last thread we added, which shrinks the pool, is somewhat inefficient. It counts constantly, even if the pool has already been reduced to its steady-state size. It can be easily argued that having a thread do nothing, and do nothing repeatedly, is a bad design.

This suggests two possible modifications to our design. The first is that we make the thread wait once steady state is reached. That is, we add a lock object and have the shrinking thread wait on it (the thread would get notified the next time an object is actually created). This can easily be implemented within ThreadPool_Final.

A second, more interesting design change, is to eliminate the idea of a steady-state size entirely. Right now, the shrinker thread checks two things: whether the pool has had objects in it continually for a long period of time and whether the pool is larger than its steady state. If so, an object is pulled from the pool and destroyed. We could easily change this behavior so that the thread monitors the pool constantly and removes any objects it thinks are surplus, regardless of the pool's size.

Two Additional Considerations When Implementing a Pool

While this example has gone on long enough, there are two additional factors you should consider when implementing a pool: the initial-resource creation strategy and the difference between the steady-state size and the maximum-pool size.

The initial-resource creation strategy

In our example, we used a lazy creation strategy and only created objects when they were needed. That is, when the pool is created, it contains no objects. And it will continue to be empty until a client thread makes a request for a resource. The alternative strategy is to have the creation thread fill the pool immediately by creating resource objects.

This doesn't make much of a difference in practice. I prefer a lazy creation strategy simply because I'd rather not create a lot of extra objects when the server launches (or in servers that are lightly used). But, if you think that a lazy creation strategy may have a noticeable impact on either perceived or actual server performance, you should consider either immediately filling the pool up to its steady-state size, or adding a third variable to control how many objects to immediately create when the pool is created.

The difference between the steady-state size and the maximum-pool size

Suppose you implement a database connection pool with a steady-state size of 10 connections and a maximum size of 15 connections. Further suppose that, at some point, your server already has 10 transactions open and needs to use another database connection. In all the implementations we've discussed, the pool will create the database connection right away.

The problem is this: it's quite possible that your server needs the extra database connection because it's currently handling an unusually heavy load. In which case, creating extra database connections may be a really bad idea—it amounts to deciding that the currently pending requests ought to slow down while extra database connections are created. A better strategy might be:

> If the server is really busy, all new database requests are put on hold (and not serviced by additional database connections).

If you decide to use the second strategy, you can implement it easily enough—just set the steady-state size equal to the maximum-pool size.

Some Final Words on Threading

Writing multithreaded programs is incredibly difficult to do well; it is perhaps the most subtle task you will be called upon to do as a server developer. We've spent two chapters on a topic that could easily consume a dozen books.

Once you've mastered this material, you should read more. Good references include *Concurrent Programming in Java, Second Edition* by Doug Lea (Addison-Wesley) and *Concurrent Programming: Principles and Practice* by Gregory Andrews (Addison-Wesley).

CHAPTER 13
Testing a Distributed Application

In the previous two chapters, we discussed threading in detail. Now that we have threading under our belts, it's time to return to the idea of testing our distributed application. In this chapter, we'll discuss the basics of building a testing framework, and walk through a set of minimal tests for the bank application.

When you think about the amount of code, and the number of independent pieces that must perform correctly in order for a distributed application to work, it's very easy to feel a certain amount of despair. Consider that each computer running part of the application has at least four layers of independently written code: the BIOS, the operating system, the JVM, and the application. Remote method invocations are sent from one machine to another, forwarded by other computers and network devices. Persistence is achieved through the user of relational database management systems, which are themselves huge and complex pieces of code that run on independent servers.

The complexity involved is incredible. The number of subtle errors that can be made, by any of the developers involved, is incomprehensible. There is no way to be certain the piece of code you've written is solid in itself, much less that it behaves well as part of the larger system. In the face of all the potential errors, and the uncertainty that they produce, the best thing you can do is test your code. Test early, test often, and always remember that until the code is tested, you don't know whether it actually works.*

In this chapter, the focus will be on testing the distributed aspects of the bank example (e.g., focusing on how our system functions when there are multiple clients). If we were actually writing a real application to be deployed to actual desktops, the testing suite would be far more extensive; the fact that don't talk about how to test the GUI or the business logic should not be taken as evidence that such tests aren't important. The testing suite is limited because this is a book about how to build distributed

---

* Strictly speaking, we won't *know* afterwards either. But we're more likely to believe that it will work, and that's worth something.

applications, and discussing testing in general is simply outside the scope of this book.

 In general, as soon as the framework is in place, and the application can be run as a distributed application, testing should commence. Writing the test code as soon as is feasible, and running the tests as often as is reasonable, helps guarantee that mistakes will be spotted quickly. This, in turn, helps make them easier to repair.

Testing the Bank Application

After all of the alterations in Chapters 11 and 12, we now have a version of the bank example that we think is threadsafe and scalable.[*] If you can make a claim, you should be able to provide evidence that the claim is correct. So we will now proceed to test the code we've put in place.

What We're Testing

Any reasonable set of tests checks two different things: correctness and scalability. *Correctness* is a simple property; we're testing whether, for an isolated client, the application actually works. The questions we have to ask ourselves are:

- Can the client connect to the server?
- Can the client perform remote method calls?
- Does the server do the right thing when the client makes a method call?

Scalability, on the other hand, is a more subtle property. Basically, we're concerned about the behavior of the application as the load increases. This encompasses five basic questions. In order of descending importance they are:

Is the application still correct (from the point of view of a single client)? If the application no longer functions correctly when there are multiple clients, then we've got a serious problem. It's probably thread related; we probably have two client requests that interfere with each other.

Is the application's performance under typical client loads acceptable? This is the single most important performance test. If the user can't use the application because it's too slow, then the application is useless.

Can the application handle peak loads? The application is allowed to get slower when usage unexpectedly spikes. But it shouldn't crash, or consume disproportionate amounts of server resources.

[*] Contained in the package com.ora.rmibook.chapter12.bank.scale and its subpackages.

***How does the application's response time degrade as the number of clients
increases?*** The application's performance will degrade as we add clients. The goal is
to have the performance degrade gracefully. Typically, the way you measure this
is in terms of average response time versus the number of users (e.g., "When
there are 30 users, the average response time is 134 milliseconds for a withdrawal"). What we'd love is a flat relationship: constant response time as the
number of users increase. But since each additional user will consume extra
resources and computing time, that's impossible once a server starts to get busy.
The best we can hope for is a linear relationship between the number of users
and the the response time. This is hard to achieve.

How does the application behave over long-term usage? The issues here revolve
around the performance of the server when you leave it running for an extended
period of time. Does it leak memory? Does it gradually lose the ability to
respond? The memory and resource footprint of the server when it has no clients should be the same, no matter how long the server's been running. And the
server should have the same performance characteristics after five weeks in operation as when it was first started. If this isn't the case, and there is no explanation for why the server's profile has changed, then the server is not ready to be
deployed.

How to Test a Server

Testing all of this stuff might seem like a tall order, requiring lots of code and an
advanced degree in mathematical statistics. And the truth is that it does involve a fair
amount of code. However, it's also the case that a little bit of work can go a long
way. Coding up some simple tests, and checking them repeatedly during the development cycle, can save a great deal of time and effort later on.

The basic testing strategy involves the following seven steps:

1. Build simple test objects. These are objects that test if a single server object
   works correctly and measure the time a given operation takes.

   An important, and often overlooked, point is that it's not enough to test that the
   server functions correctly when "good" arguments are passed in. The server
   must be able to detect incorrect method calls and respond appropriately.

    In this section, I'm coming awfully close to advocating what the pro-
   ponents of *Extreme Programming* (XP) refer to as *unit testing*. If this
   was a general methodology book, I would strongly advocate unit testing. But, since this book is about RMI, I'll simply refer you to the
   definitive XP web site for more information. It can be found at *http://
   www.xprogramming.com/*.

2. Build aggregate tests that test entire use cases. For complex applications, it is
   often useful to build aggregate tests that correspond to the use cases. Just as a

use case is a sequence of user actions, an aggregate test is a sequence of simple tests.

3. Build a threaded tester that repeatedly performs these tests. This is usually just a subclass of Thread that knows how to repeatedly perform tests. It's not very complex, but it does need to be in a separate thread because the tester is, more or less, analogous to a sequence of users.

4. Build a container that launches many testers and stores the results of the test in an indexed structure. The next step, now that you've built a threaded tester that can perform lots of tests, one after the other, is to add a piece of code that launches many testers. Once this is done, you have the ability to perform many concurrent operations over a long period of time. That is, you can perform a crude simulation of a large client load.

5. Build a reporting mechanism. Testing is useless unless you can access the results. This can be a simple GUI that says "tests succeeded," or it can be a complex database containing all sorts of information about each test performed. The complex database can be a great idea if you're interested in finding out how performance and scalability change over time. If you're just interested in making sure the application works, it's usually not necessary.

6. Run the tests repeatedly. You should run simple, low-load tests very often to test whether the server objects are still correct, preferably as part of a daily build process. Scalability tests, in which you simulate hundreds of clients and watch the system try to cope, should also be run often. However, since they're not quite as important for day-to-day development and consume more resources, they don't need to be run as frequently.

7. Profile using your scale tester. If you run the servers inside a profiler, and then launch a large-scale test, you will find where your application bottlenecks are located. Profilers are really the only way to learn about application performance, and the beauty of a testing framework is that it lets you do intensive profiling of your application under load without deploying it.

Testing the Bank Application

The first thing we need to do, in the case of the bank application, is alter the infrastructure slightly. There are two changes we need to make:

- Up until now, the launch code has been taking a set of command-line arguments that list the accounts that will be launched. This is obviously unrealistic and not at all useful for large-scale testing. We added a NameRepository object that automatically generates names for us.

- The second change is to the Account3 interface. We need to add an argument, clientIDNumber, to each method. This argument is used, instead of the client's IP address, inside the checkAccess() method; it allows us to simulate multiple clients from a single machine:

```
public interface Account3 extends Remote {
    public Money getBalance(String clientIDNumber) throws RemoteException,
        LockedAccountException;
    public void makeDeposit(String clientIDNumber, Money amount) throws
        RemoteException, NegativeAmountException, LockedAccountException;
    public void makeWithdrawal(String clientIDNumber, Money amount) throws
        RemoteException, OverdraftException, LockedAccountException,
        NegativeAmountException;
}
```

What we're building is a very simple test application. It launches a number of testers, each of which simply does the following:

1. Gets a random account

2. Performs a random operation

3. Repeats

After all the threads are done, a GUI displays the results, as shown in Figure 13-1.

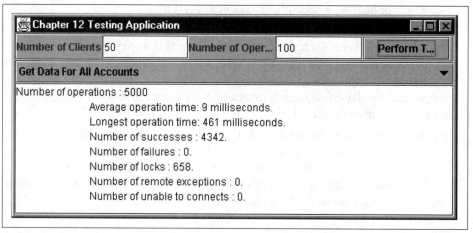

Figure 13-1. GUI testing framework for our distributed application

Note that this isn't particularly detailed information. We find out whether the servers worked correctly under testing and some preliminary information about the behavior under loads. More accurately, we find out the average response time, the longest response time, and how many requests ran into locks on an account.

Ideally, we'd like to analyze the data further. For example, we'd like to know more about the distribution of response times. If 10 percent of the responses were very slow, and 90 percent were very fast, then we probably ought to investigate further. Similarly, we should run the tests with varying numbers of clients to see how the performance changes as we change the load.

However, even without that, running this test every night and seeing that the code performs similarly (no failures, small average response time) is a good and useful thing to do. Certainly, if I were project lead, and I knew that new tests were added every time remote functionality was added, I'd be thrilled to get this sort of information every morning.

We will now walk through the design and implementation of our testing application in more detail, following the first five steps outlined earlier.

Build simple test objects

There are three methods we can call, each of which needs to be tested. In addition, we need to test the ability of clients to find and connect with servers. We do this by building four classes: an abstract class named Test and three concrete subclasses corresponding to the three methods we can invoke remotely.

Test is responsible for three things: it connects to an individual account server, it defines a set of possible outcomes (things such as, "The account was locked"), and it keeps track of how long a remote invocation takes. In addition, Test implements the Comparable interface so that instances of Test can be sorted. The concrete subclasses handle the details of invoking a particular method.

The time information that Test keeps track of isn't particularly accurate. Test uses System.currentTimeMillis(), which is accurate only to 50 milliseconds. Nonetheless, the rough order of magnitude calculations are quite nice.

Here is the source code for Test:

```
public abstract class Test implements Comparable {
    public static final String UNABLE_TO_CONNECT = "Unable to connect";
    public static final String ACCOUNT_WAS_LOCKED = "Account was locked";
    public static final String REMOTE_EXCEPTION_THROWN =
        "A remote exception was thrown";
    public static final String FAILURE = "Operation completed with incorrect result";
    public static final String SUCCESS = "Everything was cool";

    public String status;
    public long duration;
    public long startTime;
    public String accountName;

    private NameRepository _nameRepository;
    private String _className;

    protected abstract String performActualTest(String idNumber, Account3 account);
    protected abstract String describeOperation();

    public Test(NameRepository nameRepository) {
        _nameRepository = nameRepository;
        _className = getClass().getName();
    }
```

```
public void performTest(String idNumber) {
    accountName = _nameRepository.getAName( );
    Account3 account = null;
    try {
        account = (Account3)Naming.lookup(accountName);
    }
    catch (Exception e) {}
    if (null==account) {
        status = UNABLE_TO_CONNECT;
        duration = 0;
        return;
    }
    startTime = System.currentTimeMillis( );
    status = performActualTest(idNumber, account);
        // abstract method implemented in subclasses
    duration =  System.currentTimeMillis( )- startTime;
    return;
}

public String describeOutcome( ) {
    return "Attempted to " + describeOperation( ) + " account " + accountName + "
        at " + startTime +". \n\t The operation took " + duration + "
            milliseconds and the result was : " + status +"\n";
}

public int compareTo(Object object) {
/*  first sort is alphabetical, on class name, second test is on account name
    third test is by startTime, fourth test uses object's hashcode
*/
    // ....
}

protected Money getRandomMoney( ) {
    /*
    Sometimes the money will be negative. But, most of the time, we'll send in
        positive amounts.
    */
        int cents = -2000 + (int) (Math.random( ) * 100000);
        return new Money(cents);
    }
}
```

Given the implementation of Test, the actual test objects are as simple as they can
be—they simply test a single method to see whether it functions correctly. Here, for
example, is the source code for MakeWithdrawal:

```
public class MakeWithdrawal extends Test {
    public MakeWithdrawal(NameRepository nameRepository) {
        super(nameRepository);
    }

    protected String describeOperation( ) {
        return "make a widthdrawal from ";
    }
```

```
protected String performActualTest(String idNumber, Account3 account) {
    Money balance = null;
    Money amountToWithdraw = getRandomMoney( );
    Money correctResult;
    Money actualResultingBalance;
    try {
        balance = account.getBalance(idNumber);
        correctResult = balance.subtract(amountToWithdraw);
        account.makeWithdrawal(idNumber, amountToWithdraw);
        actualResultingBalance = account.getBalance(idNumber);
    }
    catch (RemoteException remoteException) {
        return REMOTE_EXCEPTION_THROWN;
    }
    catch (OverdraftException overdraftException) {
        if(amountToWithdraw.greaterThan(balance)) {
            return SUCCESS;
        }
         else {
            return FAILURE;
        }
    }
    catch (LockedAccountException lockedAccountException) {
        return ACCOUNT_WAS_LOCKED;
    }
    catch (NegativeAmountException negativeAmountException) {
        if (amountToWithdraw.isNegative( )) {
            return SUCCESS;
        }
        else {
            return FAILURE;
        }
    }
    if(amountToWithdraw.greaterThan(balance)) {
        return FAILURE;
    }
    if (amountToWithdraw.isNegative( )) {
        return FAILURE;
    }
    if (correctResult.equals(actualResultingBalance)) {
        return SUCCESS;
    }
    else {
        return FAILURE;
    }
}
}
```

There are two things to note here. The first is that we really are using our distributed exceptions quite heavily. It's important to make sure that the server really does catch improper arguments (e.g., an attempt to withdraw a negative amount), and that when the server does throw an exception, it is does so for the correct reasons.

The second point to note is that it's not entirely obvious what a failure means. Suppose performActualTest( ) fails. This could be due to either of the following reasons:

- The lock wasn't set, and another client thread managed to perform an operation.
- The actual withdrawal code is flawed.

The right way to distinguish between these is to write additional tests that check only the locking mechanism. If the locking mechanism works, then we know the withdrawal code must be flawed. In our case, it's not such a big deal; our codebase is small enough to simply spot errors once we have a good hint. However, in larger applications, distinguishing between possible causes of error is incredibly useful.

 This is an important point. When you're building fine-grained tests, they rely, to a large extent, on the existence of many other fine-grained tests. Every test you add makes the others work better, and makes the testing suite more effective. The general rule of thumb: if you can talk about something and have a name for it (e.g., "the locking mechanism"), you should be able to test it.

Build aggregate tests that test entire use cases

The use case we've been relying on, first defined in Chapter 5, basically consists of a sequence of simple tests performed on the same account. If this were an industrial application, we'd implement this as a single test for the reasons outlined in the next section. However, the code to do so is quite similar to the code for our other tests, and doing so so only serves to make the testing framework more complex; it serves no pedagogical purpose at all.

Build a threaded tester that repeatedly performs these tests

The next step is to build an object that can repeatedly invoke tests. In our case, we've chosen to do this by extending Thread. Instances of TestThread repeatedly create tests purely at random, invoke the test, and then store the test object in an instance of TestResultHolder. After doing this a predetermined number of times (the argument numberOfOperations is passed into TestThread's constructor), the thread notifies its owner, an instance of TestAppFrame, that it is done:

```
public class TestThread extends Thread {
    private static final int MILLISECONDS_TO_PAUSE = 2000;
    private static int _idNumberCounter;
    private NameRepository _nameRepository;
    private TestResultHolder _testResultHolder;
    private int _numberOfOperationsLeft;
    private TestAppFrame _owner;
    private String _idNumber;

    public TestThread(NameRepository nameRepository, int numberOfOperations,
        TestResultHolder testResultHolder, TestAppFrame owner) {
```

```
        _testResultHolder = testResultHolder;
        _nameRepository = nameRepository;
        _numberOfOperationsLeft = numberOfOperations;
        _owner = owner;
        _idNumber = String.valueOf(_idNumberCounter++);
    }

    public void run() {
        while(_numberOfOperationsLeft > 0) {
            Test testToPerform = getRandomTest();
            testToPerform.performTest(_idNumber);
            _testResultHolder.addResult(testToPerform);
            try {
                Thread.sleep(MILLISECONDS_TO_PAUSE);
            }
            catch (Exception ignored){}
            _numberOfOperationsLeft--;
        }
        _owner.testThreadFinished(this);
    }

    private Test getRandomTest() {
        double choice = Math.random();
        if (choice <.1)  {
            return new GetBalance(_nameRepository);
        }
        if(choice < .6) {
            return new MakeDeposit(_nameRepository);
        }
        return new MakeWithdrawal(_nameRepository);
    }
}
```

The only curious thing here is how we determine what test to use. The answer is that we randomly pick one. At first, this might seem a little disturbing. It may make for more convincing testing if we followed scripts or what we think an actual user session would be like.

The answer to this objection is twofold. The first is that, to a large extent, if we'd encoded the use cases as tests, those tests would be scripts and would reflect what we think an actual user session would be like. However, even past that, random testing has a significant positive aspect. If an application can handle random method invocations well, it can handle pretty much anything that gets thrown at it. If, on the other hand, our tests reflect what we think the user will do, we haven't really tested how robust the application is at all.

This leads to a compromise. We can make TestThread an abstract class with a single abstract method:

```
    protected abstract Test getRandomTest()
```

Then, we create two concrete subclasses of `TestThread`:

getRandomThread( ) *(Type 1)*
> Randomly chooses from among all the tests available.

getRandomThread( ) *(Type 2)*
> Also makes random choices. But Type 2 chooses only from among the use-case tests in an attempt to simulate the real world more accurately.

The reason for having two subclasses of `TestThread` is simple. They actually return slightly different types of information. Type 1 ensures that the application functions correctly and is reasonably bulletproof. Type 2 can give much more accurate information about application performance and scalability. In our case, since we have no use-case tests, we've implemented only Type 1.

Build a thread container that launches many threads and stores the results of the test in an indexed structure

In our case, this is the main GUI component, `TestAppFrame`. The Perform Test button has the following action listener attached to it:

```java
private class TestLauncher implements ActionListener  {
    public void actionPerformed(ActionEvent event) {
        try {
            reset();
            numberOfThreads = (Integer.valueOf(_numberOfThreadsField.getText()))
                intValue();
            int numberOfOperations = (Integer.valueOf(_numberOfOperationsField
                getText())).intValue();
            int counter;
            for (counter = 0; counter < _numberOfThreads; counter++)  {
                TestThread nextThread = new TestThread(_nameRepository,
                    numberOfOperations, _testResultHolder, TestAppFrame.this);
                nextThread.start();
                Thread.sleep(100);// wait a little bit to spread out the load
            }
            while (someThreadsNotFinished()) {
                Thread.sleep(10000); // 10 seconds. It's not bad
            }
        }
        catch (Exception exception) {}
        finally {resetGUI();}
    }
}
```

This resets all the data structures in `TestAppFrame` by calling `TestAppFrame`'s `reset( )` method:

```java
private void reset() {
    _testResultHolder = new TestResultHolder();
    _numberOfFinishedThreads = 0;
}
```

After this is done, TestLauncher creates a number of instances of TestThread, based on the value the user typed into _numberOfThreadsField, and starts them running. Finally, when all the threads have finished, TestLauncher calls TestAppFrame's resetGUI() method, which simply computes the very simple statistics we display in the main text area:

```
private void resetGUI() {
    _testResultHolder.sortResults();
    _accountChooser.removeActionListener(_chooserListener);
    _accountChooser.removeAllItems();
    _accountChooser.addItem(ALL_ACCOUNTS);
    Iterator i = (_testResultHolder.getAccountNames()).iterator();
    while(i.hasNext()) {
        _accountChooser.addItem(i.next());
    }
    _resultsArea.setText("");
    _accountChooser.addActionListener(_chooserListener);
    computeSummaryforAllAccounts();
}
```

Build a reporting mechanism

We chose not to do this, instead relying on displaying information in a JTextArea. Ideally, you'd want to do something much more sophisticated. For example, a relational database is an ideal storage mechanism. The following two tables would be a fairly nice storage mechanism that would allow for sophisticated data analysis when required:

IndividualTests
> Corresponds to the definition of the Test class. Namely, it has columns for the public variables: status, duration, startTime, and accountName. It also has two additional columns: test type (in our case, there are three different types of tests) and run identifier, which is a foreign key into the second table

TestRuns
> Each row in this table records the metadata for a particular test. It should store all of the following information: who ran the test, when the test was run, how many clients were used, how many operations per client, and the version of the codebase tested.

From this information, all of which is already present in our application, we can answer arbitrary questions about the sophistication of our application's performance as a distributed application. You still need to do other things to check resource allocation and memory utilization. But how to do that is outside the scope of this book.

CHAPTER 14

The RMI Registry

RMI provides a simple naming service called the RMI registry, which we've already used in our examples. Now that we've built a few distributed applications and understand threading, it's time to revisit the RMI registry. After a preliminary discussion of naming services, we'll spend most of this chapter examining the RMI registry in detail, discussing both how it works and how to use it in applications. By the end of this chapter, you will not only understand how to use the RMI registry, you'll have a basic understanding of naming services as well.

Why Use a Naming Service?

The first step in discussing naming services is to be a little clearer about what they are and what problems they solve. A first attempt at a definition may look something like the following:

> A naming service is a centralized resource that a number of applications use as a "phone book"-like resource. That is, it is an easily locatable and well-known application that maps logical names to actual servers so client programs can easily locate and use appropriate server applications.

This definition is intentionally vague on two points. First, it doesn't define what is meant by "phone book" or "logical names." And second, it doesn't specify what a naming service returns. This is because there are a wide range of servers that claim to be naming services. And many of these services use slightly different meanings for these two points. For example, in the case of the RMI registry, we have:

- The "phone book" is a white-pages-style phone book, and "logical names" are strings. Finding means retrieval based on case-sensitive string equality.

- You get back a stub that encapsulates information about the machine on which the server runs and the port on which it listens. The stub hides this information from the client program and simply exposes the remote methods that can be called on the server.

Naming services have one other property that, while not really part of the definition of the server's functionality, often helps when trying to understand how they are designed:

> A naming service is a generic piece of code. It is not intended to solve a particular problem in a particular application. Rather, it is intended to be a reusable component that solves a generic problem that recurs in a wide variety of applications and domains.

Because of this, a naming service is often a little awkward to use in any given application. The client code that finds a server is often a little convoluted and has to cast the returned stub to the right type. Even in our simple RemotePrinter application, we had to cast the return value from the naming service to Printer:

```
Printer printer = (Printer) Naming.lookup(DEFAULT_PRINTER_NAME);
printer.printDocument(documentDescription);
```

Bootstrapping

The bootstrapping problem is simple: in a distributed application, clients running on one machine need to connect with servers running on another machine. On a large network, there are really only three ways to solve this problem:[*]

- The client knows in advance where the server is. Either the server location is actually compiled into the client application or, more typically, the location of the server is stored in a secondary resource (for example, in an easily edited text file distributed with the client application).

- The user tells the client application where the server is. The client might then store this value. For example, in an email client, one part of configuration the user is usually required to enter is the address of the mail server. The location of the mail server is then stored, or the user may have to enter the value repeatedly, such as with web browsers.

- A standard server in a well-known location serves as a point of indirection. In this scenario, the client queries a network service to find out where the server is. This is the solution that naming services provide. The client has to know how to find the naming service, but then asks the naming service for information about how to connect to the server applications it requires.

Installing a new printer

To illustrate this, consider our printer server. Look what happens in each case when we move an existing printer to a new location on the network:

The client knows in advance where the server is.   In this case, we need to update each client application or change the secondary resource to reflect the new

---

[*] On smaller networks, automatic discovery by multicasting is also an option. See *Java Network Programming, Second Edition* by Elliotte Rusty Harold (O'Reilly) and *Jini in a Nutshell* by Scott Oaks and Henry Wong (O'Reilly) for more information on multicasting and automatic discovery, respectively.

information when we move the printer. If we were clever, and stored the list of printers in a single file to which all machines on the network had access, this might not be so bad. On the other hand, arranging to have a single machine mounted by all the client computers on a large network is a difficult chore. Moreover, having a single file with all the printers listed in it comes awfully close to having a form of centralized indirection and is a hint that we probably want to use a naming service anyway.

The user tells the client application where the server is. In this scenario, when the user runs the application, the user enters the information about the new printer (or the new location of the old printer). This is, more or less, an unworkable solution. End users don't want to do this, and a significant percentage of them will get it wrong.

The client makes a query to a network service to find out where the server is.
When the printer is installed or moved, the naming service is updated to reflect the new information. When clients launch, they query the naming service. The clients are always up-to-date, the client machines didn't need to be modified in any way, and the end users didn't have to do anything.

When Are Naming Services Appropriate?

Each of the three approaches to the bootstrapping problem has advantages and disadvantages, depending on the application being written. Servers in a typical client-server application have many properties, which suggests that the flexibility provided by naming services is worth having. Among them are:

Servers migrate. Servers sometimes overwhelm the machine on which they're initially deployed. Sometimes, server hardware is retired or repurposed. Sometimes network administrators install a firewall, and the server applications must be moved to another machine. For whatever reason, server applications are often moved from machine to machine over the application's lifetime.

There may be many servers. This is obvious in the case of network services such as printers. Every floor may have a printer. However, it's also true for our bank example; there are thousands of servers, and each client needs to be able to access each one.

Servers get partitioned and replicated. One response to overwhelming demand is to replicate servers. We discussed partitioning briefly in the bank example; the idea was to move some of the instances of Account to another machine if the server response time was unacceptable. In addition, read-only requests can be farmed out to any number of replicated servers.

There may be many servers running on one machine. A single machine can run many servers. Some of these servers may have reserved well-known ports (for example, port 80 is reserved for web servers). However, reserving ports is a risky strategy because the more ports that are reserved, the greater the chance of having reservations conflict. A much better strategy is for servers to randomly grab an available port number when it launches.

Note that the bank example exhibits all of these properties. In contrast, consider the prototypical naming service. It's implemented once and reused. It never evolves. There's usually only one, and it doesn't get partitioned. And it's a simple enough piece of code that an implementation can usually handle large numbers of requests quite robustly. If you have to hardwire a server's location into your client (or as a parameter in a configuration file), hardwiring the location of a naming service involves the least risk of having to update the client.

All of the preceding points are arguments for indirection. If many of them apply to an application, then the design should include a level of indirection when clients connect to a server. A naming service provides this indirection in a very simple manner: clients call a stable and well-known server whose sole responsibility is to direct them to the server that they really need. That is:

- Servers are registered ("bound into") the naming service using logical names.
- Clients know the location of the naming service and the logical names of the servers they require. From this information, they can find the servers at runtime.

The RMI Registry

We've done three things with the RMI registry: we've launched the actual registry server, we've bound objects into the registry using strings for names, and we've looked up objects in the registry.

All of the code we've written has used static methods on the java.rmi.Naming class to accomplish these tasks. In particular, Naming defines the following five static methods:

```
public static void bind(String name, Remote obj)
public static void rebind(String name, Remote obj)
public static void unbind(String name)
public static String[] list(String name)
public static Remote lookup(String name)
```

These methods naturally divide into two sets: those called by the launch code and those called by clients. The launch-code methods, bind( ), unbind( ), and rebind( ), deal with the mechanics of inserting and removing servers from a registry. The client methods, list( ) and lookup( ), deal with querying a registry to find a server.

bind( ), rebind( ), and unbind( )

These three methods deal with binding or unbinding a server into the registry. Each of them takes a string argument called name. In addition, bind( ) and rebind( ) take an instance of a class that implements the Remote interface. The first thing that any of them do is parse name to find out where the registry is running. name is a combination of the location of the RMI registry and the logical name of the server. That is, it is a URL with the following format:

```
//registryHost:port/logical_name
```

Both host and port are optional. host defaults to the machine that makes the call, and port defaults to 1099.

After parsing name, these methods form a socket connection to the actual registry. The registry is an RMI server running on the named host machine and listening on the indicated port. In the case of bind and rebind, they serialize the remote object (e.g., serialize the stub that implements the Remote interface) and pass it, along with logical_name, to the registry. The registry then proceeds to do one of two things:

Reject the request
    If a bind was requested, and another object has already been bound to logical_name, the request will be rejected.

Bind the object
    Otherwise, logical_name will be associated to the deserialized object that was received.

 There's an interesting point here. What the registry receives is not the object itself, but the output of RMI's customized version of the serialization mechanism. That is, the registry deserializes a stub that knows how to communicate with the original server.

In the case of unbind( ), the URL is parsed, and the registry is told to forget about whatever object was bound to logical_name.

lookup( ) and list( )

lookup( ) and list( ) are similar to each other. Each begins by parsing their argument. In the case of lookup( ), name is a URL with the same format as the URL passed to bind( ), rebind( ), and unbind( ). In the case of list( ), the argument should be shorter, specifying only the machine and port for the RMI registry, but not a specific server.

After parsing the URL, each opens a socket connection to the indicated registry and makes a method invocation. In the case of lookup( ), logical_name is passed; in the case of list( ), there are no arguments to send.

lookup( ) either throws an exception or returns a single stub to the calling application. This stub is a serialized copy of the stub bound into the registry under logical_name. And, hence, the client can use this stub to directly call methods on the server, without using the registry ever again.

list( ) returns an array of strings. These strings are the complete URLs, not just the logical names, of all the servers bound into the registry.

The RMI Registry Is an RMI Server

The RMI registry is implemented as an RMI server. Underlying Naming's static methods is an interface that extends Remote and an implementation of that interface. In Java 2, these are:

The java.rmi.registry.Registry interface
> This extends Remote and defines the methods an implementation of Registry must implement.

The sun.rmi.registry.RegistryImpl implementation class
> This is an actual RMI server that implements the Registry interface.

The Registry interface is straightforward. It defines five methods, each of which maps directly to one of the static methods defined in Naming:

```
public interface Registry extends Remote {
    public static final int REGISTRY_PORT = 1099;
    public Remote lookup(String name) throws RemoteException, NotBoundException,
        AccessException;
    public void bind(String name, Remote obj) throws RemoteException,
        AlreadyBoundException, AccessException;
    public void unbind(String name) throws RemoteException, NotBoundException,
        AccessException;
    public void rebind(String name, Remote obj) throws RemoteException,
        AccessException;
    public String[] list( ) throws RemoteException, AccessException;
}
```

Bootstrapping the Registry

Given that the RMI registry is an RMI server, with both an interface and an implementation, many people wonder why Naming was defined. Why go through the trouble of making static methods that simply redirect to a standard implementation?

The answer is that we use Naming and the static methods because the bootstrapping problem exists for any server, even a naming service. The problem the designers of RMI had to overcome was enabling a client to get an initial reference to the RMI registry.

Their solution was to define two additional classes: Naming and LocateRegistry. Naming and LocateRegistry play the following roles:

- Naming serves as a static and public mirror of every registry. Because the methods are static, you don't need to create an instance of Naming. Instead, you simply call class methods.

- LocateRegistry handles the initial connection to a running Registry. That is, LocateRegistry is a class that knows how to create a stub for Registry.

LocateRegistry is defined in the java.rmi.registry package and implements the following seven static methods:

```
public static Registry createRegistry(int port)
public static Registry createRegistry(int port, RMIClientSocketFactory csf,
    RMIServerSocketFactory ssf)
public static Registry getRegistry()
public static getRegistry(int port)
public static Registry getRegistry(String host)
public static Registry getRegistry(String host, int port)
public static Registry getRegistry(String host, int port, RMIClientSocketFactory csf)
```

The create methods all create and return a running instance of the class RegistryImpl, defined in the sun.rmi.registry package. The get methods attempt to establish a connection to an already existing registry. If the registry exists, the get methods return a stub.

Given Naming and LocateRegistry, the RMI solution to the bootstrapping problem works as follows:

1. A static method on Naming, which has the same name as a method defined in the Registry interface, is handed a URL.

2. The URL is parsed, and the machine/port information is forwarded to LocateRegistry, which returns a stub for the registry running on that machine and port.

3. Naming uses the stub returned by LocateRegistry to invoke the correct method on the registry.

We'll discuss LocateRegistry's create() methods in more detail later.

Examining the Registry

bind(), lookup(), rebind(), and unbind() are all straightforward and easy to understand. However, list() is a somewhat stranger method. It enables a client application to find the URLs of all the servers bound into a particular registry. At first glance, this isn't particularly useful. There are, however, two cases when this can be a very useful property.

The first case occurs when the results of querying the RMI registry are combined with reflection. That is:

- list() enables a client to find all the servers in the registry.

- Java's support for reflection enables the client to discover the interfaces each server implements and thus find a particular server (or give the user a choice of appropriate servers).

The second case when list() is useful occurs when the registry isn't used as a general-purpose registry, but is instead application-specific. Note that this second case is really a special case of the first, in which we don't need reflection. That is, in the first case we use reflection to find a subset of the servers that meet our application-specific criteria. In the second case, we know in advance, because we are using a specific registry with a specific purpose, that the servers returned by list( ) meet our application-specific criteria.

To make this more concrete, consider our remote printer application once again. Suppose we decide on a logical naming convention consisting of the following three components:

- Location. A human-readable string describes the location of the printer.
- A separator consisting of two colons.
- Either the word "Color" or the words "Black and White."

This leads to logical names such as:

> Bob's office::Color
> Room 445::Black and White

Now we can register these printers in a registry, either a global registry or a registry devoted only to remote printers. If we use a global registry, the client will wind up using the reflection API to determine which servers are printers. In the second case, this information is inherent in the fact that the server is registered. In either case, when the end user wants to print a document, the client application can display a list of printers and have the end user select a printer from among the available printers.

Let's implement programs that illustrate both of these approaches.

Querying the Registry

RegistryExplorer, defined in the com.ora.rmibook.chapter14.registry package, is a simple application that lists each server in the registry, along with all the interfaces it implements. A screenshot of its user interface is shown in Figure 14-1. Note that this screenshot was taken immediately after running Example 9-2.

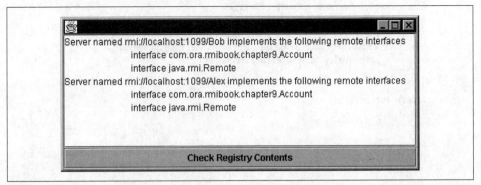

Figure 14-1. The RegistryExplorer user interface

The important part of this application is the listener attached to the Check Registry Contents button. The listener calls list( ) to get all the URLs from the registry and then displays the information for each URL in the registry:

```
private class QueryRegistry implements ActionListener {
    public void actionPerformed(ActionEvent event) {
        try {
            String[] names = Naming.list("//localhost:1099");
            if ((null==names) || (0==names.length)) {
                _resultsArea.setText("The Registry is Empty");
                return;
            }
            _resultsArea.setText("");
            for (int counter=0;counter<names.length;counter++) {
                displayInformationForName(names[counter]);
            }
        }
        catch (Exception ignored) { }
    }
}
```

The displayInformation( ) method takes a single URL, retrieves the stub associated with the URL and then uses reflection to find out which remote interfaces the stub implements:

```
private void displayInformationForName(String name) throws Exception {
    Object value = Naming.lookup(name);
    Collection interfaces = getRemoteInterfacesForObject(value);
    _resultsArea.append("Server named " + name +
        " implements the following remote interfaces\n");
    Iterator i = interfaces.iterator();
    while (i.hasNext( )) {
        _resultsArea.append("\t" + i.next( ) + "\n");
    }
    return;
}

private Collection getRemoteInterfacesForObject(Object object) {
    Class objectType = object.getClass( );
    Class[] interfaces = objectType.getInterfaces( );
    Class remoteInterface = Remote.class;
    ArrayList returnValue = new ArrayList( );
    for (int counter=0; counter < interfaces.length; counter++) {
        if (remoteInterface.isAssignableFrom(interfaces[counter])) {
            returnValue.add(interfaces[counter]);
        }
    }
    return returnValue;
}
```

Launching an Application-Specific Registry

Another approach to the same problem is to simply launch more than one registry. There are two ways to do this:

- Using the rmiregistry program supplied with the JDK and specifying a particular port
- From within your application (via code)

The first approach is easy; the rmiregistry application takes an integer argument, which is the port that the registry should use. If you omit the port, the default port 1099 is used. Thus, either of the following two command-line invocations produce the same result:

```
rmiregistry
rmiregistry 1099
```

However, you can also specify another port. For example, the following command-line invocation will launch an instance of the RMI registry listening on port 10345:

```
rmiregistry 10345
```

The second approach, launching a registry from within an application, is only slightly more difficult. You simply use a static method from the LocateRegistry class. Either of the following will create a registry (we'll discuss the second method in more detail in Chapter 18):

```
public static Registry createRegistry(int port)
public static Registry createRegistry(int port, RMIClientSocketFactory csf,
    RMIServerSocketFactory ssf)
```

 The Sun Microsystems, Inc. implementation of the RMI registry uses static variables in order to help solve the bootstrapping problem. These static variables effectively limit you to creating only one registry per JVM.

Limitations of the RMI Registry

At first glance, the RMI registry might seem like a nice solution to the problem of bootstrapping a distributed application. As a piece of software, it has many nice properties. Among its chief virtues:

It's easy to administer
> The standard download of the JDK provides an application called rmiregistry. To launch the RMI registry, you simply run that application. After which, you don't need to do anything else.

It's easy for clients to find
> The RMI registry has a standard port (1099) on which it usually runs. Moreover, clients don't need to get a stub to the registry—they simply use static

methods defined in the java.rmi.Naming class. All the client really needs to know about the RMI registry is the machine on which it runs.

It's easy for clients to use

The interface to the RMI registry consists of just five easily understood methods. In addition, these methods have reasonable default arguments.

It's fast

The five methods are all very fast.

These are all good for an important piece of infrastructure[*] such as a naming service to provide. The question, however, remains: is the RMI registry a good naming service?

In order to answer this question, consider the printer client again. Suppose we want to print a document. To do this, our application needs to do two things. It must find a printer server and then send a document to the printer server.

In the last section, we discussed how to find a printer from a registry using the list( ) and lookup( ) methods. The problem is that designing an application to use either of these approaches inevitably runs afoul of the design guidelines we outlined in Part I—unless the user knows the exact name of the printer we want in advance, finding a printer using the RMI registry is incredibly clumsy.

---

[*] Or any server, for that matter.

If we don't use a printer-specific registry, we need to get the list of all the entries in the RMI registry and then iterate through them, checking to see whether we've found a printer. Not only is this code ugly, it involves:

- Getting the names of all the entries in the registry.
- Retrieving lots of potentially irrelevant information. For example, most of the calls to Naming.lookup( ) will retrieve stubs for servers that aren't instances of Printer.

Taken together, these are an inordinate waste of bandwidth. And there is an absolutely horrible failure case: what if the registry doesn't have a printer? The client will download the entire contents of the registry and then tell the user, "No Printers." Even if we use a printer-specific registry, there may be a significant problem: we still wind up downloading stubs for all the printers, in order to ask the user which one she wants to use.

This isn't so bad if we store the user's choice locally and then reuse it whenever possible. That is, during configuration, have the user select a default printer (this may involve downloading all the printers) and then store the logical name of the printer the user selects. Afterwards, unless the user specifically indicates she wants to use a different printer, or the default printer is no longer registered, the program simply uses the default printer, using the stored logical name to find it.

But what about other types of applications and other types of users? Suppose, for example, you have dozens of printers, and users want to select a printer based on the following criteria:

- The print quality you want
- The type of file you're printing
- The location of the printer

That is, if I'm in building C and I'm trying to print a PDF file for a meeting I'm attending in building A, I probably don't want to send it to a dot-matrix printer in building D.

Since a substantial portion of this functionality is almost completely generic (it is required whenever a client program can contact more than one server), we should probably add more functionality to our naming service, and make it capable of handling these requests.

The upshot of this discussion is that whenever you have many similar servers between which the users choose on a regular basis (e.g., when there is no stable notion of a default server), the RMI registry's design choices are almost certainly inadequate.

Directories and Entries

Recall how we defined a naming service:

> A naming service is a centralized resource that a number of applications use as a "phone book"-like resource. That is, it is an easily locatable and well-known application that maps logical names to actual servers so client programs can easily locate and use appropriate server applications.

> The "phone book" is a white-pages-style phone book, and "logical names" are strings. Finding means retrieval based on case-sensitive string equality.

That the design choices inherent in the RMI registry are often inadequate doesn't tell us much about how to fix them. Fortunately, we have several decent models available. In particular, either the file systems or the yellow pages approach will work.

Filesystems

A filesystem is usually built out of two basic abstractions:

Files

A file typically has two types of properties: access properties and content-description properties. Access properties include information such as who has permission to edit the file and when the file was last modified. Content-description properties describe what sort of data the file contains.

 Some operating systems, like Windows, don't really store much in the way of content description. Other operating systems store much more information. For example, BeOS stores a MIME type for each file.

Directories or folders

A directory (sometimes called a folder) is something that contains and organizes other things, including files and other directories. Most of the properties associated with a directory are access properties and apply to all the files in the directory.

Yellow pages

The yellow pages are an index to goods-and-services providers, located in the back of most phone books. They're organized as follows:

Entries

An entry in the yellow pages consists of the name of an organization or company, the company's main address, and a phone number. In recent years, some yellow pages have also begun including a line of text. Here, for example, is an entry from the yellow pages for Mountain View, California:

AQC: Air Quality Control Inc.
Cleaning and Decontamination Services
1-800-433-7117

Topics

A topic is a logical grouping of entries according to similarity of goods or services provided by the entries. For example, "Cleaners" is a topic. Topics have only one property: an empty topic can refer you to another topic. Thus, for example, the following topic is empty in my local yellow pages:

Swing Sets
See: Playground Equipment

Unlike directories, which can be nested, topics don't contain other topics. Instead, topics are ordered alphabetically, to make it easier for a human being to search the yellow pages.

The general idea of directories and entries

What's good enough for the yellow pages and filesystems is most likely good enough for a naming service. That is, naming services for distributed applications usually consist of two basic abstractions:

Entries

An entry is a name, a set of name-value pairs, and enough information to construct a stub.

Contexts[*]

A context is analogous to a directory or a topic. It contains other contexts, and entries as well. Contexts are named and are often allowed to have properties. In addition, there is usually a single "base context" from which all entries can be reached, either directly or by accessing a context contained in the base context.

In addition, we need to define the idea of a "logical name." A logical name is neither an entry nor a context. It consists of the following information, rendered in a suitable format:

- The machine running the naming service containing the base context and the port to which the server listens
- A set of context names that form a "path" (e.g., the first name in the path is the name of a context contained in the base context, the second name in the path is the name of a context contained in the first context, and so on)
- An entry name

In Chapter 15, when we build a naming service to replace the RMI registry, we will implement this sort of hierarchical structure.

---

[*] The word "context" is, unfortunately, the standard term.

Security Issues

The last thing we need to discuss about the RMI registry involves security. The archetypal bad case is something like the following:

> A hacker has written a program that scans the Internet looking for RMI registries. It does this by simply trying to connect to every port on every machine it finds. Whenever the program finds a running RMI registry, the program immediately uses the list( ) method to find the names of all the servers running on the registry. After which, the program calls rebind( ) and replaces each stub in the registry with a stub that points to his server.

The point: if you don't restrict access to a naming service, then your network becomes incredibly vulnerable. Even if each individual server is secure (e.g., each individual server requires the clients to log in), the naming service itself is a vulnerable point and needs to be protected.

The solution the RMI registry adopted was quite simple: any call that binds a server into the registry must originate from a process that runs on the same machine as the registry. This doesn't prevent hackers from finding out which servers are running, or calling methods on a given server, but it does prevent them from replacing any of the servers, and thus prevents them from altering the structure of client-server applications, which depend on the registry.

CHAPTER 15

Naming Services

In Chapter 14, we discussed the RMI registry. In this chapter, we'll build on that discussion to explore naming services in general. The goal of the chapter is to help you understand just what a naming service is, and how they're used in distributed computing. We'll also implement a new and more flexible naming service. As part of doing so, we'll discuss threading and bootstrapping issues again, this time from an applied perspective. And finally, I'll introduce an important design technique known as federation. By the end of this chapter, you'll have a much better understanding of naming services and of how to build multithreaded servers.

Naming services have a long and varied history in distributed computing. Examples of modern naming services include:

The Domain Name System (DNS)
> This is how the Internet resolves logical names such as "www.oreilly.com" into IP addresses. Because it is used everywhere, and must handle extraordinary loads, DNS is a very simple protocol with limited query functionality. But it does map logical names to IP addresses and is, more or less, the definitive example of a naming service.

The Lightweight Directory Access Protocol (LDAP)
> This is a protocol and API definition developed at the University of Michigan. It is commonly used in large enterprises for authentication (e.g, for storing information about employees in a way that's easily accessed by computer applications).

The COSNaming Service
> This is defined as part of the Common Object Request Broker Architecture (CORBA) standard. CORBA is a specification for building cross-language distributed systems. That is, CORBA implementations are frameworks used to build a certain type of distributed application. And, as such, CORBA requires a naming service to solve the bootstrapping problem.

These three examples define three distinct points on the performance/flexibility curve. DNS is the most limited. It can resolve names to IP addresses but nothing else, and it doesn't support any advanced query capabilities at all.

LDAP has extensive support for attributes. However, it doesn't really support the idea of storing servers, or stubs to servers. Instead, it's intended to support fast queries for predefined records, such as static data structures. Cameron Laird (in *Sunworld*, July 1999, "Lighting up LDAP: A programmer's guide to directory development, Part 1") gave the following motivating example for LDAP:

> Directories are the online telephone books that keep such information as e-mail addresses, printers' room locations, and the fax numbers of businesses' purchasing departments.

COSNaming, on the other hand, is designed specifically for distributed systems. COSNaming stores only references to CORBA servers. On the other hand, while it supports hierarchical structures and expects servers to be bound and unbound fairly frequently, it doesn't have much support for querying either.

Figure 15-1 shows the performance of each of these approaches, graphed with their flexibility.

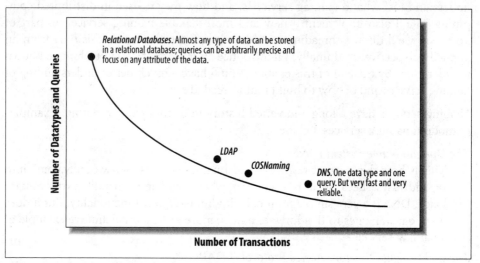

Figure 15-1. The performance/flexibility curve

The fact that all of these (and the RMI registry) are all easily recognized as embodying the same idea suggests two basic conclusions:

- Naming services show up in many forms in many types of distributed applications and are among the most useful server components. Therefore, an understanding of how they are used, and the basic terminology used when referring to a naming service, is quite useful when building distributed systems.

- Naming services are fairly prototypical servers in many ways. They have well-understood functional requirements and need to be very scalable. Therefore, the architecture of a naming service (e.g., how a naming service is built, the basic architectural ideas and trade-offs that are frequently made) can be a useful example for people learning distributed programming.

The rest of this chapter attempts to weave these two themes together. We start by discussing in more detail how naming services are used and finish by implementing a full-fledged naming service in RMI. Along the way, we'll deal with threading and bootstrapping issues again, and tackle the idea of scalability head on.

Basic Design, Terminology, and Requirements

For the most part, our requirements follow from the discussion in Chapter 14, where we discussed the RMI registry in detail. The RMI registry has two major shortcomings: it uses a flat namespace instead of hierarchically organizing entries, and entries are names of servers, without any further information or query capability. In addition to our desire to have hierarchies and a more extensive querying capability, we also have a requirement that our naming service be as backwards-compatible with the RMI registry as is possible.

Hierarchies

Basically, we want to define a way to make the naming service look more like a directory structure. That is, it should have multiple directories or folders, each of which contains a small percentage of the logical names that have actually been registered with the naming service.

The primary motivation for using hierarchies is the same one that leads me to have 30 top-level directories on my C: drive. I have close to 30,000 files on a single hard disk; arranging them in a single list would be a catastrophic organizational scheme. Similarly, naming services use hierarchies to enable different types of servers to be grouped with each other and apart from other servers. Some common grouping criteria:

By application/functionality
   All servers that perform a similar function are grouped together. For example, "All the publicly available printers are grouped together under the name *Printers*."

By ownership
   Applications that are run by, or are frequently used by, a single group or department. For example, "These are the stubs for the servers associated with the Accounting IT Group."

By geographic location
   Servers located in a particular area, or even a building. For example, "Servers located in California."

The terminology associated with hierarchical structures can be a little confusing. Here are some of the most important definitions:

Context

The traditional name for the "container" structure. It plays a role analogous to a directory in a filesystem.

Direct subcontext

A context that has been directly registered with another context. Usually, there are two operations. bind( ) is much like the registry operation of the same name; it registers objects within a context. And there is a special form of bind( ) that registers subcontexts within a context.

Path

A sequence of contexts, each of which is a direct subcontext of the previous context. Usually, we denote paths as if they are in a filesystem: */context1/context2/...* (the first / denotes a base context).

Thus, if we form a path from the strings usr, bin, and games (which we denote by */usr/bin/games*) we make the following assertions: there is a context named usr; if we list the subcontexts of usr, we will find a subcontext named bin; if we list the subcontexts of bin, we will find a context named games.

Subcontext

A context is a subcontext of another context if it is either a direct subcontext or a subcontext of a context that is a subcontext of the containing context.

Local

A server is local to a context if it has been directly bound into the context.

Contained

A server is contained by a context if it is local to the context or to one its subcontexts.

Figure 15-2 demonstrates how contexts and paths are used.

Operations on contexts

Contexts have four main types of operations, corresponding to the following two ways of classifying an operation:

Binding/unbinding and querying

A binding operation is an operation that adds another server or context to the list of servers or contexts a particular context knows. Querying operations enable a client to find a particular server or context. These operations are very similar to the methods present in the RMI registry. They usually take a path as an argument and resolve the path appropriately by forwarding the binding or querying operation to the appropriate subcontext.

Context versus ordinary server

Subcontexts are usually treated differently from other types of servers. The basic idea here is that contexts can be bound in as ordinary servers, or they can be

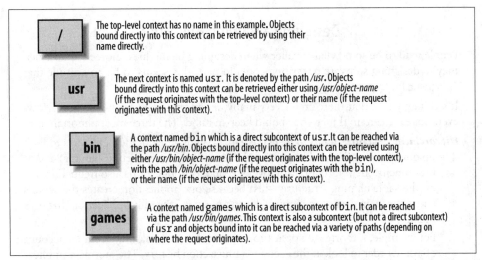

The top-level context has no name in this example. Objects bound directly into this context can be retrieved by using their name directly.

The next context is named usr. It is denoted by the path /usr. Objects bound directly into this context can be retrieved either using /usr/object-name (if the request originates with the top-level context) or their name (if the request originates with this context).

A context named bin which is a direct subcontext of usr. It can be reached via the path /usr/bin. Objects bound directly into this context can be retrieved using either /usr/bin/object-name (if the request originates with the top-level context), with the path /bin/object-name (if the request originates with the bin), or their name (if the request originates with this context).

A context named games which is a direct subcontext of bin. It can be reached via the path /usr/bin/games. This context is also a subcontext (but not a direct subcontext) of usr and objects bound into it can be reached via a variety of paths (depending on where the request originates).

Figure 15-2. Contexts and paths

bound in as subcontexts. In the first case, they can be retrieved by query operations but are not counted as subcontexts when paths are resolved. In the second case, they aren't returned as answers to the standard query operations but are used when paths are resolved.

Query by Attribute

Generally, a naming service is not quite static, but a "sticky" data structure instead. Once servers are bound under a particular logical name, they tend to be bound under that name for awhile. Binding and unbinding are relatively rare operations.

Query operations, on the other hand, occur far more frequently than binding or unbinding. Every time a client needs to find a server, it needs to issue a query to the naming service.

This implies three basic design requirements:

- The naming service has to respond quickly to queries.
- Queries from distinct clients should not block each other. It's very important to minimize the use of synchronization in query methods.
- The query functionality should be expressive enough to pick out a single server from the ones bound into the naming service. If the naming service often returns a list of servers that the client then narrows down, presumably by querying the server, then using the naming service will be incredibly inefficient.

Attributes are string-valued, name-value pairs

One fairly traditional way to implement a query capability is to allow server entries to be annotated with a set of attributes that describe the server. These attributes are

Designing a Naming Hierarchy

People tend to be somewhat cavalier when designing hierarchies, more so than when they're designing software or writing code. In part, this seems to be an attitude that "it's just a lookup mechanism."

It's certainly true that there aren't very many design principles for hierarchies. However, there are certain things you should keep in mind. The three most important are:

Hierarchical structures tends to be persistent. Naming hierarchies and ways to look up objects are embedded in your application, both in the client (querying) and in the launch code (binding). Moreover, secondary applications also frequently rely on the same naming structure—just because one application creates the servers and is the main user of the servers doesn't mean it's the only application that uses them.

For example, a mortgage application analysis at our bank may fetch an account object in order to look at the account's transaction history. The mortgage application isn't the primary user of the servers, and the code may have been implemented by another group entirely. However, it still uses the hierarchical structure.

You need to decide whether you're designing for humans or for machines. There is often a convenient logical structure for servers, and then there is a hierarchical structure that humans can navigate. Humans typically prefer descriptive names and longer paths. On the other hand, flatter hierarchies generally require less code and are easier for programmers and systems administrators to maintain. The ultimate example of this is RMI's flat namespace. It quickly becomes unreadable. But the code that interacts with the RMI registry is very simple.

The longer the path, the more opportunities you have for federating the naming service. We'll talk more about federation later. For now, it's enough to say that federation is a way of moving subcontexts to another machine to enable naming services to scale.

metadata that help describe the server and enable the clients to choose a server quickly and easily.

Consider our printer application again. We have a document we need to print. It's a color PostScript file for an 18" × 24" poster. To find the correct printer in the RMI registry, we must:

1. Get all the servers by using list( ).

2. Find out which servers are printers. This involves retrieving the stubs (using a lookup( ) method for each name) and then using the instanceof keyword to discard the stubs that aren't associated with printers.

3. Query each printer we find to discover what sorts of jobs it can handle. Note that even if we subclassed the `Printer` interface by defining, for example, `ColorPrinter` or `PostscriptPrinter`, we'd probably still wind up asking it about the paper sizes the printer can handle, and whether the printer is in a nearby location.

Surprisingly enough, hierarchies help, but they don't solve this problem entirely. For example, we could define the following printer hierarchy:

/printers/postscript
/printers/pdf
/printers/pcl

Assuming we know the hierarchy (e.g., the first classification is based on the printer formatting language and not on whether the printer can handle color), we can easily find a potential match. But hierarchy has its limits. Consider what happens when we add location, paper size, and resolution to the preceding tree. We may wind up with hierarchical paths such as:

/building47/printers/postscript/A12Paper/1200DPI/Color

This type of hierarchy is awful, for a number of reasons. Here are three of the most important:

- Many servers are entered multiple times. A server that can print either black-and-white or color documents and can handle either ordinary or legal paper is entered four times in four different contexts in the hierarchy. When the printer gets moved, it needs to be removed from those four contexts and put in four different contexts. This is unmanageable.

- The client needs to hardwire in a great deal of assumptions about the hierarchical structure being used. In this example, the top-level context is named `printers`. The second-level context is used to describe a file format. The third-level context is used to describe whether color documents can be printed, and so on. Hardwiring in all these assumptions about the structure of the naming service leads to brittle code.

- All information that can ever be used in a query must be known and expressed in the hierarchal structure. Moreover, the queries must have a value for every possibility. There is no way, in the preceding hierarchy, to express, "I need a color printer in building A." Instead, making this query involves multiple calls to the naming service.

Reasons such as these lead to the idea of using attributes instead of a hierarchical structure. Attributes are simply name-value pairs, in which both name and value are strings. So for example, we may choose to have a two-tier context structure:

/printers/building-name

And then within the building-name context, we may choose to annotate printers with the following three attributes:

- Document-type (values: PCL, PostScript, PDF)
- Color-resolution (values: color, black-and-white)
- Dots-resolution (values: high, medium, low)

The idea is that a client must specify the attributes it cares about, and isn't required to specify the rest, nor does the order in which the client specifies the attributes matter. Thus, by passing in a value for the document-type and color-resolution attributes, the client can say, "I want a printer that handles color PDF files, but any resolution value is fine." This is a much more natural way to think about servers in a lot of situations.

Moreover, it greatly simplifies versioning problems. If all the important server properties were reflected in the hierarchical structure, there would be two problems:

All client applications would need to know about all the server properties. Because the properties were encoded in the path, there would be no way to hide the properties.

New server properties (for example, a new paper size) would involve a change to the hierarchy and may break existing code. Because attributes work on partial matches, on the other hand, adding a new attribute is invisible to applications that don't know about the attribute.

 There is a trade-off here. A naming service has to be very fast and highly reliable. This means that, while we want to implement some sort of querying functionality, it's going to be fairly limited. After all, a naming service is not a database. We'll add enough functionality and flexibility to handle printers nicely (since they're a pretty typical case), but we won't go much further.

Requirements for Our Naming Service

The first requirement is to be backwards-compatible with already existing naming services. The second is that future versions of the naming service can be backwards-compatible with our naming service.

Unfortunately, there isn't really a reliable way to be backwards-compatible with the RMI registry. First, any calls to static methods on classes in the Javasoft packages are out of our control. Therefore, client code that makes calls to Naming will either communicate with an instance of the RMI registry or not work at all. Second, we will directly support concepts that just aren't present in RMI (namely, hierarchical structures and attributes). This means that the best we can do is use the same method

When to Use an Attribute

Given that I've already said there aren't very many design principles for hierarchies, it's reasonable to wonder if there are any design principles for when to encode structure as an attribute and when to use a hierarchy. The following loose guidelines might be helpful.

There are three fairly good design principles for when something ought to be encoded in a hierarchy:

- Mutually exclusive possibilities tend to be hierarchical.
- Attributes that must be specified, or which are specified in all the use cases, tend to be encoded in a hierarchy.
- If the subcontexts can be thought of as a way to cache answers to queries that clients ask often, then having subcontexts (and using the stub for them directly from the client side) is often a good idea.

Thus, for example, location tends be encoded in hierarchical structures. It meets all three of these criteria—a printer can be in only one location, most users really care about the location of the printer, and a given user will likely revisit the location subcontext repeatedly. (There are other reasons to make locations a subcontext as well—if we encode location in the hierarchy, we can federate on the basis of location. And that's a potentially huge win in the fight against network latency.)

On the other hand, the negations of the first two design principles are also fairly good indicators for when a piece of metadata ought to be encoded as an attribute:

- If the metadata can have multiple, meaningful, values, it might be better expressed as an attribute.
- If the metadata can be easily ignored, or not specified in a query, it might be better specified as an attribute.

Thus, for example, the resolution of a printer is probably best left as an attribute.

Of course, even in the world of printers, there are borderline cases; for example, color. Generally speaking, color printers can print black-and-white documents. But most organizations have fewer color printers than black-and-white ones. And color printers are far more expensive in terms of cost-per-page than black-and-white printers.

This means that, while color/black-and-white meets the criteria for an attribute (both values are possible; if I'm printing a black-and-white document, I may very well ignore it since color printers can handle my request), an organization might decide to encode color within the hierarchy anyway.

names (bind( ), unbind( ), etc.) to make it easier for a programmer to translate the client code.

As for the second compatibility requirement, there are a few things we can do to make it more likely. The easiest is to simply use objects for arguments. When you use objects, you make it easier to update and alter an interface. Even though a path is, for the most part, a sequence of strings, and attributes are simply name-value pairs, we actually define a class called `Path` and a class called `AttributeSet`. This means our methods look like the following `bind()` method:

```
public void bind(Path path, String name, AttributeSet attributes, Remote server)
```

This will enable us to broaden the definition of either "path" or "attribute" in future versions of the application simply be defining new subclasses of `Path` and `AttributeSet`. The old client code will still work fine.

Of course, creating a new subclass of `Path` may require substantial changes to the server, especially if we have to support the old definition of `Path` as well. That's okay. For a generic server interface, such as a naming service, first remember that there are probably many client applications out there, several of which aren't under the control of the server developer. Second, from a testing and deployment perspective, it's much easier to make large-scale changes to a single server application than it is to make small-scale changes to many client applications.

Our Use Case

Our use case centers around the bank example once more. In this scenario, we have different types of accounts. We have *checking accounts*, we have *savings accounts*, we have *money market accounts*, and so on. Every one of our customers have one of each of these accounts.* We want our naming service to reflect this structure. In particular, we need to support the following two scenarios:

- Using the hierarchy to reflect the account type. In this scenario, the base context has a subcontext for each particular type of account.

- Using an account-type attribute to encode the account type. In this scenario, we have a flat hierarchy and simply use the attributes to encode all the information.

If we can support both of these, and the related query ability ("Get me the server named 'foo,' which is of type 'checking'"), in a scalable fashion, we'll have implemented a fairly significant piece of code.

Federation and Threading

One of the most interesting characteristics of hierarchies is that contexts both simplify the design task and make the naming service much more flexible. To see why, we need to make two fairly plausible usage assumptions:

- Contexts will be small (usually containing fewer than 100 local entries and 10 subcontexts).

In the real world, they may have more than one. But remember—this is a contrived example in a book about programming.

- Most servers for a given application are equally desirable. That is, if an application has multiple servers, they probably all handle similar numbers of requests.

The truth is that neither of these assumptions really holds in practice. However, they almost hold, in the same way that a red-black tree is almost a black tree. And they immediately lead to the following conclusion: contexts are the perfect first pass at thread locks.

For example, suppose a a request comes into a context. The context looks at the request and does one of two things: it either finds a server that has been bound into the context and that satisfies the request, or it forwards the request to the appropriate subcontext. See Figure 15-3.

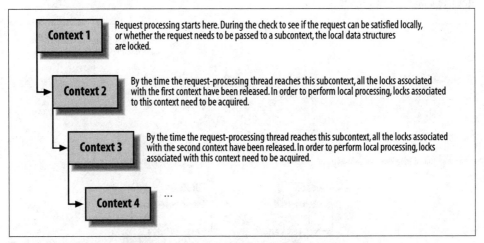

Figure 15-3. Contexts, request forwarding, and locking

Let's now restate this in a slightly more detailed way. The context must:

1. Analyze the request to determine whether it should be handled locally or should be forwarded.

2. Find the local server or the appropriate subcontext.

3. Either return the server or forward the message.

Let's look at the state information required for each of these steps:

1. Requires only the information passed in as request arguments. Therefore, requires no local state. Therefore, can be written to be threadsafe without any synchronization.

2. Requires use, and potentially modification, of local indices. Therefore, needs synchronization.

3. Requires no local state and can therefore be written to be threadsafe without any synchronization.

Now consider a first pass at a context method. The method examines the request and figures out whether the request is local (e.g., refers to an object stored directly in the context). If so, it obtains the lock associated with the context and takes the required actions. After which, it unlocks the context.

If the request isn't local (e.g., should be forwarded to a subcontext), it locks the context and then uses an index structure to find the right subcontext. After it finds the right subcontext, it unlocks the context and forwards the request to the subcontext.

This means that two requests can block each other only to the extent that they share a path structure. For example, if you attempt to retrieve an account from */UnitedStates/Utah/Provo*, and I attempt to retrieve one from */UnitedStates/Nevada/Reno*, we get the diagram in Figure 15-4.

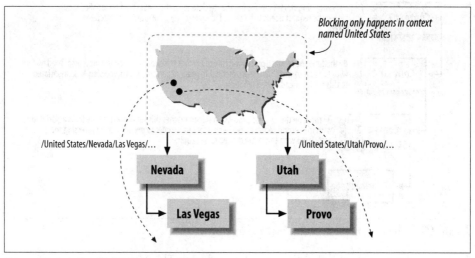

Figure 15-4. A geographic example of locking

However, this isn't so bad and is possibly quite good. In particular, there are two benefits:

- This is a provable threadsafe locking scheme with no deadlocks. Every request has at most one lock at any given time.
- To the extent that the hierarchical structure reflects our plausible assumptions, most threads won't interfere with most other threads, except possibly at the topmost level.

Even more importantly, this scenario immediately leads to the concept of federation.

Federation

A *federated architecture* is one in which multiple servers all support the same set of interfaces and are linked to each other. The linking is done in a way that is essentially transparent to a client but enables the servers to route requests to the server best suited to respond to it.[*]

That might seem like a mouthful, but we have a very simple illustration at hand. We've already got the idea of a context, and it's pretty obvious that a context will be a Java object in our implementation of a naming service. The next step is simple: let's make each context an RMI server.

We already know that when the client passes in a path to the context, the context will find the appropriate subcontext and forward the request. There's no reason why the request can't go to another server, running on another machine entirely.

The ability to federate contexts, and to do so in a way that's transparent to the client, is a fairly impressive feature that can offer substantial benefits. Consider, for example, a company with four offices in Tokyo, Bangkok, San Francisco, and Reykjavik. Each office maintains a naming context with all the servers for that office, and the contexts are bound into each other as subcontexts. So, for example, the hierarchical structure for Reykjavik looks like Figure 15-5.

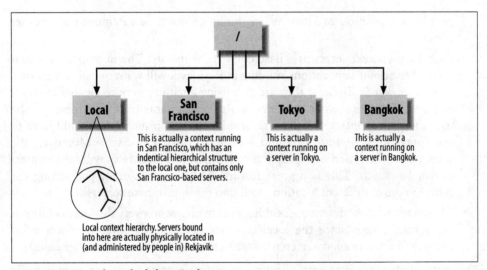

Figure 15-5. How things look from Reykjavic

The hierarchical structure for Bangkok looks like Figure 15-6.

This is helpful for several reasons:

- The local contexts are managed locally by the local systems administrators and developers. It's much better if the naming-service information is maintained by

---

[*] At least, that's what *I* think it means. One of the great benefits of writing a book like this is that you get to make up definitions for all the terms everybody uses but that don't have a canonical definition yet.

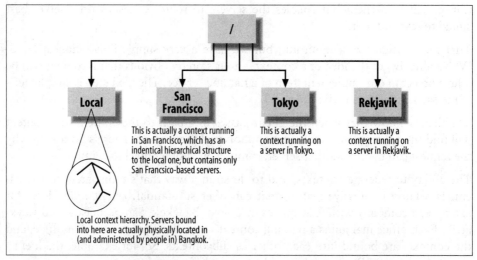

Figure 15-6. How things look from Bangkok

people in a position to know when things go down or get moved to another server.

- Each local context serves as a base context for its city. The anticipation is that most of the client applications running in Reykjavik will want to call servers running in Reykjavik. Because they are also using a naming service located in Reykjavik, it follows that when someone in Reykjavik wants to find a printer, if she uses the path */printers*, it will be resolved to a local printer (she would have to use */San Francisco/printers* to find a printer in San Francisco). Moreover, the same path, when used by a program running in San Francisco, will find printers in San Francisco. This is a great feature. The same program, performing the same lookup in different locations, will find the appropriate servers.

- All servers worldwide are accessible, worldwide. Moreover, this accessibility is easily maintained (since the local contexts have exactly three nonlocal references, and those nonlocal references are to naming services in the other cities).

Of course, federation isn't just a feature of our naming service, nor does it really require contexts. DNS is an incredibly federated system (there is no other way to scale a naming service to the Internet) that doesn't support the idea of contexts at all. See *DNS and Bind, Fourth Edition* by Paul Albitz and Cricket Liu (O'Reilly) for more details on DNS.

The Context Interface

After all these preliminaries, it's time to discuss the actual Context interface. Context contains quite a few more methods than the RMI registry does. But, all in all, it should look reasonably familiar. Here's the entire interface:

```
public interface Context extends Remote {
// Basic binding functionality

    public void bind(Path path, String name, AttributeSet attributes, Remote server)
        throws RemoteException, NamingException;
    public void rebind(Path path, String name, AttributeSet attributes, Remote
        server) throws RemoteException, NamingException;
    public void unbind(Path path, String name, AttributeSet attributes) throws
        RemoteException, NamingException;

    // Basic querying functionality
```

```
public Remote lookup(Path path, String name, AttributeSet attributes) throws
    RemoteException, NamingException;
public Remote[] list() throws RemoteException, NamingException;
public Remote[] list(AttributeSet attributes) throws RemoteException,
    NamingException;
public Remote[] list(String name, AttributeSet attributes) throws
    RemoteException, NamingException;
public Remote[] list(Path path, String name, AttributeSet attributes) throws
    RemoteException, NamingException;

// Context-level API

public Context lookupSubContext(Path path, String name) throws RemoteException,
    NamingException;
public ContextList listSubContexts() throws RemoteException, NamingException;
public ContextList listSubContexts(Path path) throws RemoteException,
    NamingException;
public Context createSubContext(Path path, String name) throws RemoteException,
    NamingException;
public void bindSubContext(Path path, String name, Context context) throws
    RemoteException, NamingException;
public void rebindSubContext(Path path, String name, Context context) throws
    RemoteException, NamingException;
public void unbindSubContext(Path path, String name) throws RemoteException,
    NamingException;
}
```

This interface is actually fairly simple. It consists of 15 methods neatly grouped into three distinct types of functionality. In addition, it looks a lot like the Registry interface, even if it is not immediately apparent exactly what the arguments to:

```
public Remote[] list(Path path, String name, AttributeSet attributes) throws
    RemoteException, NamingException;
```

mean, it is fairly clear that Context's list( ) methods are all related to each other and to the RMI registry's list( ) method.

However, even in such a simple interface, there are a significant number of design decisions that may not be obvious. In the remainder of this section, we'll explore some of the decisions made while designing Context. Some of them are implied by the interface; some are just arbitrary decisions that had to be made. Most of them could have been done differently; the key is to know in advance what we're building so we're confident it will meet our needs, and so we can test it.

Value Objects Represent Sets and Lists

Most of the arguments are objects that we need to define. Even in a method such as bind( ), in which we try to be as similar as possible to the registry's bind( ) method:

```
public void bind(Path path, String name, AttributeSet attributes, Remote server)
```

we use two new objects, `Path` and `AttributeSet`. When we get to the context-specific API, even the return values are new objects:

```
public ContextList listSubContexts() throws RemoteException, NamingException;
```

Moreover, we've explicitly chosen not to use object arrays or the Javasoft container classes. For example, we could have defined `bind( )` to have either of the following signatures:

```
public void bind(Path path, String name, Attribute[] attributes, Remote server)
public void bind(Path path, String name, ArrayList attributes, Remote server)
```

There are two reasons for designing the interface using `AttributeSet` instead of `Attribute[]`. First, it preserves flexibility at very little cost. If you use array types or classes defined by a third party, then you limit your future options. We can always add fields, or functionality, to `AttributeSet`. We cannot add fields or functionality to either `java.util.ArrayList` or `Attribute[]`.

Second, it allows for validation on the client side. When you try to construct an instance of `Path` or `AttributeSet`, the objects can validate their member variables. For example, `Path` has a private constructor and a static `buildPath( )` method:

```
public static Path buildPath(String[] components) {
    ArrayList arrayList = new ArrayList(components.length);
    for (int i = 0; i < components.length; i++) {
        if ((null != components[i]) && (0!=components[i].length())) {
            arrayList.add(components[i]);
        }
    }
    return new Path(arrayList);
}
```

This way of constructing paths has two nice consequences:

- All the path components are instances of `String`.
- None of the path components are empty strings (and we could easily extend this to enforce other name-formatting conventions, should we so desire).

Paths, Names, and Attributes Are All Distinct

Given that attributes can be omitted, it's not very surprising that attributes are treated differently from paths and names in a methods such as:

```
public Remote lookup(Path path, String name, AttributeSet attributes) throws
    RemoteException, NamingException;
```

However, the fact that server names are treated differently from context names might seem a bit surprising. When I defined paths, I said:

> If we form a path from the strings usr, bin, and games (which we denote by /usr/bin/ games) we make the following assertions: there is a context named usr; if we list the subcontexts of usr, we will find a subcontext named bin; if we list the subcontexts of bin, we will find a context named games.

The meaning of the separation of path from name is that specifying the path */usr/bin/ games*, which specifies a subcontext of the base context, is different than specifying the name games and the path */usr/bin*, which specifies a server bound locally into the context specified by */usr/bin*.

It's worth repeating this in a slightly different way: the namespace for subcontexts is different than the namespace for locally bound servers. That means the following four queries, written in pseudocode, can all return different results:

`lookup(/usr/bin/games, tank, null)`
> Returns all servers named tank in the context specified by the path */usr/bin/games*.

`lookup(/usr/bin/games/tank, null, null)`
> Returns all servers from the context specified by the path */usr/bin/games/tank*. The server is guaranteed to match the name and attribute properties. However, since they're null, any server from the context will do.

`lookupSubContext(/usr/bin/games/tank, null)`
> Returns all subcontexts of the context specified by the path */usr/games/bin/tank*.

`lookupSubContext(/usr/bin/games, tank)`
> Returns the subcontext named tank of the context specified by */usr/bin/games*.

 This design decision is rather arbitrary. I feel the last two points are really separate cases, and the first two just fell out of how I think about things. Other design decisions are quite possible (and indeed, may be the usual case) here.

Null Arguments Are Okay

An important feature of the query functionality is that null arguments are perfectly okay. If a client doesn't care about any attributes, it can pass in a null value for the attributes argument, or call a variant of the method that doesn't even have an attributes argument.

Similarly, if any server will do, the name can be null. It's perfectly reasonable for someone to say, "I want a printer that supports color PDF files." The naming service equivalent of this is, "Go to the subcontext named Printers and query solely on attribute values."

Attributes Are Single Valued

For ease of implementation, and because it's not entirely clear what multiple valued attributes mean when querying, attributes are single valued in the current implementation. This works quite well in our use case involving the bank example but isn't quite flexible enough to make the printer example feel natural. For example, consider document-types. Our printer example currently has three: PDF, PostScript, and PCL.

We have two options:

- We can encode this as delimited strings. For example, we can say that the document type attribute takes one of the following values: "pdf," "postscript," "pcl," "pdf, postscript," "postscript, pcl," "pdf, pcl," or "pdf, postscript, pcl."
- Alternatively, we can encode this as boolean-valued attributes: "handles pdf," "handles postscript," and "handles pcl."

 This might be the first requirements-level decision reversed in Version 2.0.

Contexts Are Handled by a Separate Set of Methods

Recall that contexts can be bound into other contexts without being subcontexts. In order to fully support this, we need to have a separate set of context-specific methods. Calling:

```
public void bind(Path path, String name, AttributeSet attributes, Remote server)
```

and passing in an instance of Context is semantically distinct from calling:

```
public void bindSubContext(Path path, String name, Context context) throws
    RemoteException, NamingException;
```

and passing in the same arguments. (Note that in order to pass in "the same" arguments, the attribute set has to be null in the first call.) This extra bit of flexibility is rarely used, but is traditional.*

Contexts, When Bound as Contexts, Have No Attributes

Consider what happens when we call:

```
public Remote lookup(Path path, String name, AttributeSet attributes) throws
    RemoteException, NamingException;
```

Now consider what happens in the printer example, when we have a location context and attributes that specify the printer more fully. Those attributes don't really apply to the contexts along the path; they really only describe the final server.

If we want to associate attributes with contexts, we must associate an AttributeSet with every component of the path. While this is possible, it is rarely useful, and the extra functionality doesn't seem worth the extra complexity, both in server implementation and in client-side coding.

---

* "Traditional" in distributed computing often means, as it does here, "The people who designed CORBA did it this way, and I can't think of a good reason to change it."

Contexts Can Create Subcontexts Directly

Recall one of the design points we discussed in the sidebar, "When Should a Subcontext Be Federated?":

> Frequently accessed servers should be accessed via paths that stay inside a single naming service.

The basic idea is that you should avoid network latency whenever reasonable. Related contexts and paths that are frequently accessed as units should exist on a single machine, and should probably exist inside a single JVM. This means that, in daily use of a naming service with a well-structured context hierarchy, the following case holds:

> Most of the frequently accessed subcontexts of any given context will be objects inside the same JVM.[*]

In order to support this in a flexible way, a context needs to be able to create subcontexts directly; since bind( ) cannot create an object inside another JVM, we need the createSubContext( ) method. createSubContext( ) also implicitly binds the created subcontext.

There Are No Remote Iterators

This is another decision based on past experience and anticipated usage and may be removed quickly in Version 2.0. Basically, the idea is that with the addition of a well-designed set of attributes, queries should have very few return values (of which, even fewer are superfluous). This means, in the general case, iterators would make the clients more complex without saving us much bandwidth.

For now, the interface seems complicated enough.

The Value Objects

There are three value objects: AttributeSet, Path, and ContextList. As I mentioned earlier, one of the reasons for implementing our own container objects is to preserve flexibility. However, these objects—especially AttributeSet—also have other functionalities.

AttributeSet

An instance of AttributeSet represents a set of name-value pairs which can be queried. That is, when a client calls:

```
public Remote[] list(Path path, String name, AttributeSet attributes) throws
    RemoteException, NamingException;
```

---

[*] That is, "Federation is very useful and rarely used."

the server is supposed to do the following:

- Find the context associated with path.
- Find all the objects that were bound into the path context as servers (not as contexts) using name. There can be more than one, as long as the attributes are different.
- From those objects, pull out the ones that match attributes. By "match," I mean, "It has the same values for all individual name-value pairs set in attributes. But the match may have additional name-value pairs that are not defined in attributes."

In order to do this, we've made AttributeSet into a fairly sophisticated object with four main features:

- An instance of AttributeSet stores name-value pairs.
- AttributeSet implements Serializable.
- AttributeSets are comparable and can be sorted.
- An instance of AttributeSet can tell whether it is a superset of another instance of AttributeSet in a reasonably efficient way.

The first two features are easy to implement. The last two are more difficult, and the implementation is a little complicated. We start by storing all the name-value pairs inside an instance of TreeMap:

```
public class AttributeSet implements Serializable, Comparable {
    private TreeMap _underlyingMap;

    public AttributeSet( ) {
        _underlyingMap = new TreeMap( );
    }

    public synchronized void add(String name, String value) {
        if (null==name)  {
            return;
        }
        if (null==value) {
            _underlyingMap.remove(name);
        }
         else {
            _underlyingMap.put(name, value);
        }
    }

    public synchronized void remove(String name) {
        _underlyingMap.remove(name);
    }

    public synchronized int getSize( ) {
        return _underlyingMap.size( );
    }
```

```
public synchronized Iterator getNames() {
    return _underlyingMap.keySet().iterator();
}

public synchronized String getValue(String name) {
    return (String) _underlyingMap.get(name);
}

public synchronized boolean contains(String name) {
    return (null!=_underlyingMap.get(name));
}

public synchronized boolean contains(String name, String value) {
    String internalValue = (String) _underlyingMap.get(name);
    if (null!=internalValue) {
        return internalValue.equals(value);
    }
    return null==value;
}
// ....
}
```

TreeMap

TreeMap is a class in the java.util package that implements the Map interface. Map itself is pretty simple. It's just an interface version of the methods that were defined on Hashtable in JDK1.02. In particular, most uses of a map boil down to using five methods:

```
public Object get(Object key)
public boolean isEmpty()
public Set keySet()
public Object put(Object key, Object value)
public Collection values()
```

TreeMap implements Map by using a tree data structure internally. As such, it has the following features:

- It sorts entries internally, using either a Comparator or assuming the entries implement the Comparable interface (also defined in the java.util package).

- Iterating over the keys or values of a TreeMap is fast, especially compared to the same operations done using HashMap.

- Insertion, removal, and lookup operations are O(nlog(n)), where n is the number of entries in the TreeMap.

Also note that TreeMap implements Serializable, as do most of the Collections classes.

Once we have the data in place, we need to implement comparison operations. In particular, we need to be able to tell the following three things:

- Whether two instances of AttributeSet are equal
- Whether one instance of AttributeSet is a subset of another
- Whether one instance of AttributeSet is less than another, using an artificial ordering we impose to help with lookups

These first two are pretty straightforward. Two instances of AttributeSet are equal if they consist of the same name-value pairs. In addition, AttributeSet A is a subset of AttributeSet B if every name-value pair in A is also in B.

The third of these bulleted properties isn't logically necessary. We need it because we want to be able to use instances of TreeMap to store bindings in our naming service. TreeMap offers a nice compromise between fast lookup/removal/insertion and the ability to enumerate. However, in order to use them, we need the objects we insert to be ordered.

It'd be nice to define an order on AttributeSets such that if A is greater than B, then A cannot be a partial match for B—that would make our query functionality significantly faster than it is currently. Unfortunately, such an example would be far too complicated for this book.

Here's the rest of the code for AttributeSet:

```
public synchronized boolean equals(Object object) {
    if (false == (object instanceof AttributeSet)) {
        return false;
    }
    return (0 == compareTo (object));
}

public synchronized boolean subsetOf(AttributeSet otherAttributeSet) {
    Iterator i = getNames();
    while (i.hasNext()) {
        String name = (String) i.next();
        String value = getValue(name);
        if (false == otherAttributeSet.contains(name, value)) {
            return false;
        }
    }
    return true;
}

public synchronized int compareTo(Object object) {
    AttributeSet otherAttributeSet = (AttributeSet)object;
    int sizeDifferential = _underlyingMap.size()- otherAttributeSet.getSize();
    if (0!=sizeDifferential) {
```

```
        return (sizeDifferential > 0) ? -1 :  1 ;    // doesn't matter as long as
                                                     // we're consistent.
    }
    Iterator otherIterator = otherAttributeSet.getNames( );
    Iterator internalIterator = getNames( );
    while (otherIterator.hasNext( )) {
        String foreignName = (String) otherIterator.next( );
        String internalName = (String)internalIterator.next( );
        int firstComparison = internalName.compareTo(foreignName);
        if (0 != firstComparison) {
            return firstComparison;
        }
        String foreignValue =  otherAttributeSet.getValue(foreignName);
        String internalValue = getValue(foreignName);
        int secondComparison = internalValue.compareTo(foreignValue);
        if (0 != secondComparison) {
            return secondComparison;
        }
    }
    return 0;
}
```

Path and ContextList

Path and ContextList are simpler objects than AttributeSet. They are both sub-classes of SerializableList and are designed to hold an ordered sequence of values. In the case of Path, the ordered sequence is a sequence of instances of String; in the case of ContextList, the sequence is a sequence of instances of Context.

SerializableList is a container whose main role is to provide a wrapper around ArrayLists. Recall that we don't want our Remote interfaces to directly use the Javasoft collection classes and provide an implementation of equals( ). This implementation of equals( ) is a little strange in one respect—order is very important. Paths are more than a collection of strings; the path */usr/games/bin* is different than the path */usr/bin/games* (and they are not equal).

Here's the code for SerializableList:

```
public abstract class SerializableList implements Serializable {
    protected ArrayList _containedObjects;
    public SerializableList( ) {/* here so we can deserialize */}
    public SerializableList(Collection objects) {
        _containedObjects = new ArrayList(objects.size( ));
        Iterator i = objects.iterator( );
        while (i.hasNext( )) {
            _containedObjects.add(i.next( ));
        }
    }

    public synchronized int getSize( ) {
        return _containedObjects.size( );
    }
```

```
public synchronized Object get(int index) {
    return _containedObjects.get(index);
}

public synchronized boolean equals(Object otherObject) {
    if (false == (containerIsOfSameType(otherObject))) {
        return false;
    }
    SerializableList otherComparableList = (SerializableList) otherObject;
    int size = _containedObjects.size();
    if (size != otherComparableList.getSize()) {
        return false;
    }
    for (int i = 0; i <size; i++) {
        if (false == equalObjects(_containedObjects.get(i), otherComparableList
            get(i))) {
            return false;
        }
    }
    return true;
}

protected abstract boolean containerIsOfSameType(Object object);
protected abstract boolean equalObjects(Object firstObject, Object secondObject);
}
```

Once we have SerializableList, ContextList is simple. ContextList simply provides the obvious implementations of containerIsOfSameType( ) and equalObjects( ). Here's the entire implementation of ContextList:

```
public class ContextList extends SerializableList {
    private ContextList() {/* here so we can deserialize */}
    public ContextList(List components) {
        super(components);
    }

    protected boolean containerIsOfSameType(Object object) {
        return (object instanceof ContextList);
    }

    protected boolean equalObjects(Object firstObject, Object secondObject) {
        Context firstContext = (Context) firstObject;
        Context secondContext = (Context) secondObject;
        return firstContext.equals(secondContext);
    }
}
```

Path is only slightly more complicated. In addition to extending SerializableList, Path needs to support two additional list operations, corresponding to the path resolution operations used by contexts. Namely, an instance of Path needs to be able to return its first path component, which is a string, and the remainder of the path. For example, /usr/bin/games/ has as its first path component usr, and /bin/games as the remainder. In addition, Path has a static convenience method to make it easy to assemble instances of Path from strings.

Here's the code for Path:

```java
public class Path extends SerializableList {
    public static Path buildPath(String[] components) {
        ArrayList arrayList = new ArrayList(components.length);
        for (int i = 0; i < components.length; i++) {
            if ((null != components[i]) && (0!=components[i].length())) {
                arrayList.add(components[i]);
            }
        }
        return new Path(arrayList);
    }

    private Path() {/* here so we can deserialize */}
    public Path(List components) {
        super(components);
    }

    public synchronized String getFirstComponent() {
        if (_containedObjects.size() == 0) {
            return null;
        }
        return (String) _containedObjects.get(0);
    }

    public synchronized Path getSubPath() {
        if (_containedObjects.size() == 0) {
            return null;
        }
        ArrayList subPathComponents = new ArrayList(_containedObjects);
        subPathComponents.remove(0);
        return new Path(subPathComponents);
    }

    public synchronized boolean isEmpty() {
        return (0==getSize());
    }

    protected boolean containerIsOfSameType(Object object) {
        return (object instanceof Path);
    }

    protected boolean equalObjects(Object firstObject, Object secondObject) {
        String firstString = (String) firstObject;
        String secondString = (String) secondObject;
        return firstString.equals(secondString);
    }

    protected int compareObjects(Object firstObject, Object secondObject) {
        String firstString = (String) firstObject;
        String secondString = (String) secondObject;
        return firstString.compareTo(secondString);
    }
}
```

Note that Path suffers from the same bandwidth problems that AttributeSet has. Yet the same solution works: we could replace all the instances of String with instances of Integer and boost Path's performance significantly. The trick of replacing strings with their hashcodes is well worth remembering.

ContextImpl

Now that we have our interface and value objects firmly in place, it's time to move on to the main object. ContextImpl is our implementation of Context. Our implementation uses two delegate objects to actually maintain the indexes, along with a special-purpose object used to associate a name with an AttributeSet. That is, our implementation of Context really consists of the following four objects:

ContextImpl
> This implements the Context interface. It has very little direct state, a reference to ContextHolder and a reference to RemoteHolder, and is completely unsynchronized. Its role is to implement the Context interface by forwarding method calls to the appropriate object, either a subcontext or one of the two delegates.

ContextHolder
> This is a delegate object whose role is to hold, and index, direct subcontexts. All of its methods are synchronized.

RemoteHolder
> This is a delegate object whose role is to hold, and index, locally contained references to servers. All of its methods are synchronized.

NameAttrributeSetPair
> This is a class that combines a name and an attribute set in an indexable object. It also implements the Comparable interface so that it can be used by RemoteHolder.

The runtime structure looks something like Figure 15-7.

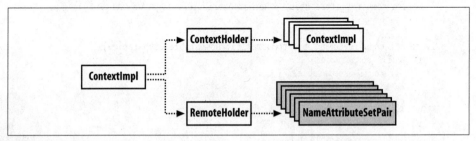

Figure 15-7. The runtime structure

Let's look at each of these objects in a little more detail.

NameAttributeSetPair

NameAttributeSetPair is a class that holds both a String (the name) and an AttributeSet. Perhaps the most important piece of functionality in NameAttribute-SetPair is that it has the ability to detect partial matches between two instances.

Here is the query-matching method:

```
public boolean matchesQueryObject(NameAttributeSetPair query) {
    String otherName = query.getName();
    if ((null!=otherName) && (false == otherName.equals(_name))) {
        return false;
    }
    AttributeSet otherAttributes = query.getAttributes();
    if (null!=otherAttributes) {
        return otherAttributes.subsetOf(_attributes);
    }
    return true;
}
```

All this does for a given instance of NameAttributeSetPair is make sure that if query has a name, or defines a particular attribute value, then the same value holds for the instance of NameAttributeSetPair being queried. That is, it gives us the ability to perform partial matching and easily answer queries of the form, "Find all servers with a given set of attribute values."

In addition, NameAttributeSetPair also implements the Comparable interface. This allows RemoteHolder to store instances of NameAttributeSetPair in a TreeMap. The implementation simply compares names. If the names are equal, it then compares AttributeSets:[*]

```
public int compareTo(Object object) {
    NameAttributeSetPair otherNameAttributePair = (NameAttributeSetPair) object;
    int returnValue;
    returnValue = compare(_name, otherNameAttributePair.getName());
    if (0!=returnValue) {
        return returnValue;
    }
    return compare(_attributes, otherNameAttributePair.getAttributes());
}

private int compare(Comparable comparable1, Comparable comparable2) {
    if (null==comparable1) {
        if (null==comparable2) {
            return 0;
        }
        return -1; // null is less than non-null
    }
    if (null == comparable2) {
        return 1;
    }
```

---

[*] Recall that AttributeSet implemented the Comparable interface as well.

```
        return comparable1.compareTo(comparable2);
    }
```

RemoteHolder

RemoteHolder's sole responsibility is to maintain a collection of the servers that have
been directly bound into a context. In order to do this, it uses a TreeMap, called _ourTree,
which maps instances of NameAttributeSetPair to server stubs. Here, for example, is
how RemoteHolder performs local binding operations:

```
protected synchronized void bind(String name, AttributeSet attributes, Remote server)
    throws BindingException {
    NameAttributeSetPair nameAttributePair = new NameAttributeSetPair (name,
        attributes);
    Object alreadyBoundObject = _ourTree.get(nameAttributePair);
    if (null!=alreadyBoundObject)  {
        throw new BindingException("Object already bound to " + name);
    }
    _ourTree.put(nameAttributePair, server);
}
```

This uses the arguments to create a NameAttributeSetPair and then looks to see if
there is already a server bound to that name and those attributes. If there is, an exception is thrown.* Otherwise the server is bound into the instance of RemoteHolder.

Querying is slightly more complex. Because the client may specify a set of attributes
for which many matches are possible, we need to iterate through all the entries
bound into the instance of RemoteHolder. Here's the code that does this:

```
protected synchronized Remote[] list(String name, AttributeSet attributes) throws
    RemoteException, NamingException {
    NameAttributeSetPair queryObject = new NameAttributeSetPair (name, attributes);
    ArrayList returnValues = new ArrayList();
    Iterator i = _ourTree.keySet().iterator();
    while(i.hasNext()) {
        NameAttributeSetPair next = (NameAttributeSetPair) i.next();
        if (next.matchesQueryObject(queryObject)) {
            returnValues.add(_ourTree.get(next));
        }
    }
    return convertCollectionToRemoteArray(returnValues);
}

private Remote[] convertCollectionToRemoteArray(Collection remotes)  {
    Iterator iterator = remotes.iterator();
    Remote[] returnValue = new Remote[remotes.size()];
    int counter = 0;
    while (iterator.hasNext()) {
        returnValue[counter] = (Remote) iterator.next();;
```

---

* The exception is thrown because this is an implementation of bind( ). rebind( ) doesn't throw an exception.

```
        counter ++;
    }
    return returnValue;
}
```

ContextHolder

ContextHolder is a much simpler class than RemoteHolder. First, subcontexts don't have attributes. This means that, instead of instances of NameAttributeSetPair, we can simply use the subcontext name as a key into our indexing mechanism. Second, there isn't a general query mechanism for contexts. The only query method that the Context interface supports is list( ), which returns all the direct subcontexts of a context. Taken together, these enable us to implement ContextHolder as a simple wrapper around an instance of HashMap. Here, for example, is ContextHolder's bind( ) method:

```
public synchronized void bind(String name, Context context) throws BindingException {
    if ((null==name) || (null==context)) {
        return;
    }
    Object priorValue = _namesToContexts.get(name);
    if (null!=priorValue) {
        throw new BindingException( "Attempt to bind context to an already bound
            name.");
    }
    _namesToContexts.put(name, context);
    return;
}
```

ContextImpl

Rather than give the complete source code for ContextImpl, I will go over just a few representative methods. The rest of the code is similar, and including it in the body of the text would serve no purpose.

The class itself has a very simple declaration and constructor:

```
public class ContextImpl extends UnicastRemoteObject implements Context {
    private RemoteHolder _remoteHolder;
    private ContextHolder _contextHolder;

    public ContextImpl(int portNumber) throws RemoteException {
        super(portNumber);
        _remoteHolder = new RemoteHolder();
        _contextHolder = new ContextHolder(this);
    }
    /// ...
}
```

This is reasonable—most of the work is actually done in the delegate objects. All ContextImpl does is figure out how a request should be handled. Here, for example, is the implementation of bind( ):

```
public void bind(Path path, String name, AttributeSet attributes, Remote server)
        throws RemoteException, NamingException
{
    checkNameForBindingOperation(name);
    if ((null==path) || (path.isEmpty())) {
        _remoteHolder.bind(name, attributes, server);
    }
    else {
        String firstPathComponent = path.getFirstComponent();
        Context subContext = _contextHolder.lookup(firstPathComponent);
        if (null==subContext) {
            throw new InvalidPathException( "The specified path in the naming" +
                "hierarchy does not exist. In particular " + firstPathComponent + "
                is not a valid context name.");
        }
        subContext.bind(path.getSubPath( ), name,  attributes, server);
    }
}

private void checkNameForBindingOperation(String name) throws InvalidNameException {
    if ((null==name) || (name.equals(""))) {
        throw new InvalidNameException("Name cannot be null");
    }
}
```

There are several points to note about this. The most important is that bind( ) is almost entirely a dispatch method. It uses path to determine whether the method call refers to the current context or to a subcontext. Then it either performs a local bind using _remoteHolder, or modifies path and forwards the request to a subcontext.

The way it modifies path is also straightforward. It removes the first path component and then sends the request to the subcontext associated with the first path component. So, if the path is */usr/bin/games*, ContextImpl creates the path */bin/games* and then passes the entire request on to the subcontext associated with the name usr.

Another important point is that the behavior inside the bind( ) method depends entirely on the arguments passed in. Since all the methods in both ContextHolder and RemoteHolder are threadsafe, this method is threadsafe without being synchronized. This is by design, and is part of a larger threading strategy. Here's the sequence of lock requests and releases associated with a bind that starts with a path equal to */usr/bin/games*:

In the base context

_contextHolder is momentarily locked while the name usr is mapped to a subcontext. This lock is obtained and subsequently released automatically because all the methods in ContextHolder are synchronized.

In the context associated with usr

When the request is forwarded here, no locks are held by the request. Once again, the lock associated with an instance of `ContextHolder` is momentarily acquired while `bin` is resolved.

In the context associated with bin

When the request is forwarded here, no locks are held by the request. Once again, the lock associated with an instance of `ContextHolder` is momentarily acquired and released—this time, while `games` is resolved.

In the context associated with games

When the request is forwarded here, no locks are held by the request. Since the bind is now local to the context, an instance of `RemoteHolder` is locked while the actual binding occurs (this happens automatically because the methods in `RemoteHolder` are synchronized). After that, the lock is released, and the call returns.

There are several important points here:

- At most, one lock is held by a request at any given time. Requests can block other requests for a limited period of time. However, two requests cannot block each other or cause a deadlock.

- Locks are held for limited periods of time.

- Locks are local. No locks are held across contexts. This means that when a request is forwarded to a subcontext, the request has no locks. Therefore, a request can only block another one while they are both trying to operate on the same context. A request with path */usr/bin/games* blocks only a request with path */etc/bin* while it makes a single call on the base context's `_contextHolder`. Once the first request has moved on to the subcontext associated with `usr`, the second request is no longer blocked at all.

  Moreover, if we choose to federate our naming service, no locks are held while a remote method invocation occurs.

The other representative methods of `ContextImpl` that we will discuss are a pair of context operations:

```
public Context createSubContext(Path path, String name) throws RemoteException,
    NamingException  {
    checkNameForBindingOperation(name);
    Context newSubContext = new ContextImpl();
    bindSubContext(path, name, newSubContext);
    return newSubContext;
}

public void bindSubContext(Path path, String name, Context context) throws
    RemoteException, NamingException {
    checkNameForBindingOperation(name);
    if ((null==path) || (path.isEmpty())) {
        _contextHolder.bind(name, context);
```

```
        return;
    }
    String firstPathComponent = path.getFirstComponent();
    Context subContext = _contextHolder.lookup(firstPathComponent);
    if (null==subContext) {
        throw new InvalidPathException( "The specified path in the naming hierarchy
            " + " does not exist. In particular " + name + " is not a valid context
            name.");
    }
    subContext.bindSubContext(path.getSubPath( ), name, context);
    return;
}
```

The first thing to note is that bindSubContext( ) has the same threading and locking strategy as bind( ). Once again, at most, one lock is held at a time, and it's held only for brief intervals.

There's also an interesting performance optimization hidden in our implementation of createSubContext( ). Recall that we added createSubContext( ) to the Context interface because of the following usage assumption:

> Most of the frequently accessed subcontexts of any given context will be objects inside the same JVM.

Adding createSubContext( ) lets us use paths without worrying that each time a request is forwarded to a subcontext, a remote method invocation is implicitly invoked.

However, our implementation does one more thing: it binds the subcontext itself, rather than a stub. In other words, when a client application calls bindSubContext( ), a stub to a context is bound into _contextHolder. createSubContext( ), on the other hand, binds an actual instance of ContextImpl into _contextHolder.

This results in a substantial performance improvement because it eliminates the entire stub/skeleton framework from internal context operations. Locally created contexts are messaged directly using the Java standard method of dispatching. If we had bound in the stubs instead, forwarding a request would have involved the following three steps:

1. Serializing the arguments in the stub
2. Sending the data through local socket connections
3. Deserializing the arguments in the skeleton

And while the network latency involved in step 2 might be minimal, we still have the following associated costs:

1. The cost of serializing
2. The cost of passing data out of the JVM to the operating system through the socket layer, and getting the data back
3. The cost of deserializing the data

This is considerably more expensive than directly calling the method.

This analysis applies to any potentially federated architecture. Federated architectures frequently break down into local servers and remote servers, just as our contexts do. Keeping track of which servers are local, and sending messages directly to them, can result in a substantial performance improvement.

 Avoiding RMI for making method calls inside a JVM is often a good idea. But there are two things to watch out for. The first is that servers often make the assumption that they own their arguments (which is reasonable in most cases, because the server is passed a serialized copy of the original argument by the RMI runtime. But, if the method call is local, the server gets a reference to the original argument and not a reference to an object it owns). The second thing to watch out for is that RMI's logs don't track messages that don't go through the RMI runtime. Bypassing the RMI infrastructure also means bypassing the RMI logging mechanism, which means that, if you're relying on RMI's logs to help you trace sequences of method calls, you're relying on incomplete data.

Bootstrapping

What we've implemented so far is quite nice. We have a very usable interface: Context. Our value objects are flexible and expressive, and we know how to optimize them if we need to. Finally, ContextImpl, with the help of ContextHolder and RemoteHolder, gives us a fast, threadsafe, and scalable implementation of the whole naming service. There's just one problem: it doesn't bootstrap yet. We haven't implemented a way for the client to connect to an initial context.

One solution is to require an RMI registry for that. If we register an initial context with an instance of the RMI registry, we can use the static methods on Naming to establish the first connection with a base context.

I'm not fond of that solution. It introduces an extra server, and makes the client code a little more complicated (the client code has to know about two different naming services). We can do better. Unfortunately, in order to do so, we will have to revert to socket-level programming for a bit. The bootstrapping process requires a first step. In this case, the first step is to use a socket. Here's the plan:

- We'll create a subclass of ContextImpl called BaseContextImpl. Since it's a subclass of ContextImpl, it implements Context. However, it will also create instances of two helper classes, StubSender and StubSocketListener.

- StubSocketListener opens up an instance of ServerSocket and waits. Whenever a client connects to it, StubSocketListener immediately hands the client off to StubSender and resumes listening.

- StubSender maintains a queue of clients. It sends an RMI stub to the established instance of BaseContextImpl to each client in the queue, and then closes the connection.

- In order to make this all work, we'll also define a pair of static methods on BaseContextImpl that the client can use to establish a connection to the running server.

 Got all that? Then stop and do the Yes-I-Am-So-Cool dance. The code I just described uses sockets for network communication, a background thread that listens on a ServerSocket, a background thread for scalability, and object serialization to send the stub. Moreover, it solves a fairly subtle problem. Think back to what you knew when you started reading Chapter 1. Odds are that you've come a *long* way.

Here's the first step in this process, the code for BaseContextImpl:

```
public class BaseContextImpl extends ContextImpl implements Context {
    public static final int BOOTSTRAP_PORT_NUMBER = 1066;
    public static final int DEFAULT_PORT_NUMBER = 1967;

    public static Context getStubFromServer(String serverName) {
        return getStubFromServer(serverName, BOOTSTRAP_PORT_NUMBER);
    }

    public static Context getStubFromServer(String serverName, int portNumber) {
        Context returnValue = null;
        try {
            Socket socket = new Socket(serverName, portNumber);
            ObjectInputStream objectInputStream= new ObjectInputStream(socket
                getInputStream( ));
            returnValue = (Context)objectInputStream.readObject( );
        }
        catch (Exception e) {
            System.out.println("Stub not available");
            e.printStackTrace( );
        }
        return returnValue;
    }

// constructors omitted

    public void vendStubViaSocket(int portNumber)  {
        StubSender stubSender = new StubSender(this);
        Thread stubSenderThread = new Thread(stubSender);
        stubSenderThread.setName("Stub sender thread");
        stubSenderThread.start( );
        StubSocketListener socketListener = new StubSocketListener(portNumber,
            stubSender);
```

```
        Thread socketListenerThread = new Thread(socketListener);
        socketListenerThread.setName("Socket Listener thread");
        socketListenerThread.start();
    }
}
```

The way it works is this: the launch code will create an instance of BaseContextImpl. Because BaseContextImpl is a subclass of ContextImpl, it is also a subclass of UnicastRemoteObject. This means that as soon as the instance is created, it is up and running as an RMI server. A stub created using the instance of BaseContextImpl will have all the information necessary to communicate with the instance.

The launch code must then call vendStubViaSocket() with a port number. This method is the crucial one—it creates the servant objects and starts the socket-level code going. In particular, it creates an instance of StubSender and an instance of StubSocketListener.

StubSocketListener is straightforward; it implements the Runnable interface as follows:

```
public class StubSocketListener implements Runnable {
    private int _port;
    private StubSender _sender;
    public StubSocketListener(int portNumber, StubSender sender) {
        _port = portNumber;
        _sender = sender;
    }

    public void run() {
        ServerSocket serverSocket;
        try {
            serverSocket = new ServerSocket(_port);
        }
        catch (Exception e) {
            System.out.println("Unable to vend on port " + _port);
            return;
        }
        while(true) {
            try {
                Socket socket = serverSocket.accept();
                _sender.add(socket);
            }
            catch (Exception ee) { ee.printStackTrace(); }
        }
    }
}
```

All this does is listen for connections. When a connection is established, it immediately forwards the connection to an instance of StubSender for further handling. After handing off the connection, StubSocketListener immediately returns to listening for connections on its socket.

StubSender is slightly more complicated. It queues up the requests for stubs so that StubSocketListener can immediately return. Then, in a separate thread, it sends out the stubs that reference the initial instance of BaseContextImpl. Here's the code for StubSender:

```java
public class StubSender implements Runnable {
    private ArrayList _customers = new ArrayList();
    private BaseContextImpl _server;
    public StubSender(BaseContextImpl server) {
        _server = server;
    }

    public void run() {
        while(true) {
            sendStub();
        }
    }

    public synchronized void add(Socket socket) {
        _customers.add(socket);
        notifyAll();
    }

    private synchronized Socket getNextSocket() {
        int size = _customers.size();
        if (0==size) {
            return null;
        }
        size--;
        Socket returnValue = (Socket) _customers.remove(size);
        return returnValue;
    }

    public void sendStub() {
        Socket nextSocket = getNextSocket();
        if (null==nextSocket) {
            waitForSocket();
            return;
        }
        else {
            try {
                RemoteStub stub = (RemoteStub) RemoteStub.toStub(_server);
                OutputStream output = nextSocket.getOutputStream();
                ObjectOutputStream objectOutputStream= new
                    ObjectOutputStream(output);
                objectOutputStream.writeObject(stub);
                objectOutputStream.close();
            }
            catch (Exception e) { e.printStackTrace(); }
        }
    }

    private synchronized void waitForSocket() {
        if (0==_customers.size()) {
            try {
                wait();
            }
```

```
                    catch (InterruptedException e) { e.printStackTrace( ); }
            }
        }
    }
```

There are five points worth noting about this solution:

- From the client's point of view, this is equivalent to the RMI bootstrapping solution. In order to use the static methods defined on Naming, a client needs to know the machine on which the RMI registry runs, and the port to which it listens. This is the same information required by BaseContextImpl's getStubFromServer( ).

- It could be made much more efficient. In particular, StubSender would be much more efficient if it cached the result of object serialization, instead of redoing the serialization each time. The trade-off is that if the server unexports itself and then re-exports itself on another port, the cached stub will be incorrect. Since naming services are rarely taken offline, it's probably worth making the effort.

- This is actually a generic solution. You could adapt this solution to any RMI server that you didn't want to, or couldn't, register in a naming service.

- This doesn't actually rely on sockets. It really depends only on streams. Thus, for example, the stub for BaseContextImpl could be serialized to a file or to a relational database.*

- As written, this is tremendously insecure. Any application that connects to the port gets a stub. If you're planning on using this code in an actual application, you'll probably want to redo the bootstrapping mechanism to be more secure.

Version 2.0

There are many features we've left out of our naming service. Among them:

- Support for strongly typed attributes. Our attribute values are all strings. In the future, we may want to support integer, boolean, or float-valued attributes.

- Support for multivalued attributes. Currently, our attributes can have no value or one value. It's certainly more natural, in the case of some attributes, to have multiple values (e.g., the paper sizes a printer supports).

- The ability to encode "not" and "or" within our search parameters. Suppose we generated a file in either PDF or PostScript, but we definitely needed a color printer. Right now, this requires two calls to the naming service: one to ask about PostScript printers and one to ask about PDF printers. Making this into a single query by allowing boolean operators such as "or" would make the naming service easier to use.

- Access to attribute sets as part of the return value. Suppose we were able to make the query from the previous bullet item, and we get back a single stub. Do

---

* Presumably as a BLOB in the case of databases.

we send it the PostScript version of the file? Or the PDF version? More generally, we probably want an ability to find out (and alter) the attributes associated with a particular server.

- Remote iterators. Results are currently returned as either an instance of Remote or as ContextList. This might be a bad design for the reasons outlined in Chapter 7.

All of these features are useful—there are naming services out there that support each one of these features. In addition, none of these are particularly hard to add to our naming service (though a seat-of-the-pants estimate is that including them all would double the code size). Our naming service is just one possible design choice among many.

Switching Between Naming Services

Now that we have another naming service, it's natural to wonder how much work it is to adapt our existing code to use it. The answer is that it's pretty easy to switch between naming services. In order to adapt an application, we need to do three things:

- Decide how we're going to store information in the naming service
- Rewrite the launch code to create the necessary contexts and store the stubs appropriately
- Rewrite the client's lookup code to reflect the new naming structure

There are two very important things you don't need to change:

- The actual servers. Neither the interfaces nor the implementations need to change at all.
- The distributed garbage collection strategy. Because leases are automatically maintained by RMI, binding stubs into this naming service will keep the associated servers alive, just as binding stubs into the RMI registry kept the associated servers alive.

Adapting the Bank Example

One way to adapt the bank example is to bind stubs into two different contexts, checking and savings. Stubs for checking accounts will be bound into checking and stubs for savings accounts will be bound into savings.

 Another way to accomplish this is to create an attribute called account_type and use two values (checking and savings).

Modifying the launch code

In order to gratuitously demonstrate federation in action, we will actually launch each of our contexts in a separate JVM. To do this, we will use the `AdditionalContextLauncher` class. Here's the code for it:

```java
public class AdditionalContextLauncher {
    public static void main(String[] args)  {
        for (int i = 0; i < args.length; i++)  {
            launchContext(args[0], args[i]);
        }
    }

    private static void launchContext(String baseContextMachine, String
        pathPlusName) {
        StringTokenizer tokenizer = new StringTokenizer(pathPlusName, "/", false);
        int numberOfPathTokens = tokenizer.countTokens( ) -1 ;
        Path path = null;
        if (0!=numberOfPathTokens) {
            String[] pathComponents = new String[numberOfPathTokens];
            for (int counter=0; counter < numberOfPathTokens; counter++) {
                pathComponents[counter] = tokenizer.nextToken( );
            }
            path = Path.buildPath(pathComponents);
        }
        String name = tokenizer.nextToken( );
        try {
            ContextImpl newContext = new ContextImpl( );
            Context startingContext = BaseContextImpl
                getStubFromServer(baseContextMachine);
            startingContext.bindSubContext(path, name, newContext);
        }
        catch (NamingException e) {
            System.out.println("Failed to launched context " + pathPlusName);
            System.out.println(e.getDescription( ));
            e.printStackTrace( );
        }
        catch (Exception ee) {
            ee.printStackTrace( );
        }
    }
}
```

This is a simple program that expects at least two, possibly more, arguments on the command line. The first argument is the machine where the base context is running, and the additional arguments are paths for the various contexts that should be added to the naming structure. Thus, the *launchcheckingcontexts.bat* batch file consists of the following single line:

```
start java -cp d:\classes -Djava.security.policy=c:\java.policy com.ora.rmibook
    chapter15.basicapps.AdditionalContextLauncher "127.0.0.1" checking
```

This isn't a particularly good way to bind subcontexts. Note that we don't use createsubContext() at all in AdditionalContextLauncher. In fact, all messages between contexts added by AdditionalContextLauncher go through RMI (through serialization and socket communication).

Once we've written the code and the batch files that create the contexts we will need, we need to modify the code that binds our servers into the naming service. Here, for example is the code from the ImplLauncher class in the com.ora.rmibook.chapter15. bank.applications package that binds a server into the naming service:

```
Account_Impl newAccount = new Account_Impl(serverDescription.balance);
Path path = Path.buildPath(new String[]{serverDescription.contextName});
if (null==baseContext) {
    getContext();
}
baseContext.bind(path, serverDescription.name, new AttributeSet(), newAccount);
System.out.println("Account " + serverDescription.name + " successfully launched.");
```

serverDescription is just an instance of a static inner class named AccountDescription:

```
private static class AccountDescription  {
    String name;
    Money balance;
    String contextName;
}
```

This compares quite favorably to the launch code that used the RMI registry— ImplLauncher has four more lines of code but binds stubs to subcontexts.

Modifying the client code

The hardest part of our modification is modifying the client code. As is usually the case, this is because we need to support a new user interface. Our new interface has an additional textbox to allow the user to enter a context, shown in Figure 15-8.

Once we have this, the lookup code is a breeze. It changes from:

```
_account = (Account)Naming.lookup(_accountNameField.getText());
```

under the RMI registry version of the bank example to:

```
Context baseContext = BaseContextImpl.getStubFromServer("127.0.0.1");
Path path = Path.buildPath(new String[]{_contextTextField.getText()});
_account = (Account)baseContext.lookup(path, _accountNameField.getText(), null);
```

using the new naming service.

The Java Naming and Directory Interface (JNDI)

This chapter has been something of a mixed bag. We first discussed the general idea of a naming service. This led to a discussion of the idea of federating, and from there

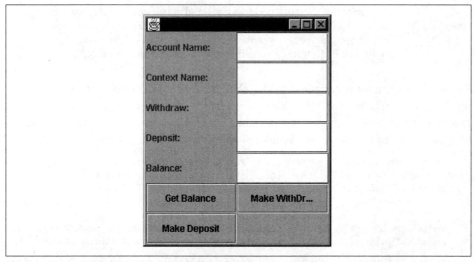

Figure 15-8. New user interface for the bank example

we implemented our own naming service. Implementing our own naming service served two purposes: it helped to make the idea that there are many different possible naming services, each with their own advantages and disadvantages, more concrete. It also served as a fully worked example of a highly threaded server; our naming service is significantly more complex that any version of `Account_Impl` that will appear in this book.

The final topic for this chapter is the Java Naming and Directory Interface (JNDI). JNDI consists of three things:

- A set of fairly generic interfaces that encapsulate the common operations performed on naming services. These interfaces are defined in the `javax.naming` and `javax.naming.directory` packages and include such interfaces as `Context`, `Attribute`, and `Name`.

- A generic way for client code to initialize a connection to a naming service that implements the JNDI interfaces. JNDI provides the `InitialContext` class, defined in the `javax.naming` package, to enable code to connect to a naming service. `InitialContext` works by using various system properties to create an instance of `Context` for client code.

- A "device-driver" model for naming service providers. Client code uses the interfaces and connects to a context using `InitialContext`. The last remaining piece involves connecting a naming service to JNDI. This requires two things: a set of classes that implement the JNDI interfaces and code that enables `InitialContext` and its supporting classes to create and configure the naming service.

The Context Interface

From the point of view of an application developer, the most important part of JNDI is the Context interface. At first glance, Context is intimidating: it defines 29 methods as opposed to the RMI registry's 5 methods or the 15 methods we defined in our naming service. However, when you take a closer look at them, Context becomes a much friendlier interface.

Here are the methods defined in Context:

```
public NamingEnumeration list(Name name) throws NamingException
public NamingEnumeration list(String name) throws NamingException
public NamingEnumeration listBindings(Name name) throws NamingException
public NamingEnumeration listBindings(String name) throws NamingException

public Object lookup(Name name) throws NamingException
public Object lookup(String name) throws NamingException
public Object lookupLink(Name name) throws NamingException
public Object lookupLink(String name) throws NamingException

public void bind(Name name, Object obj) throws NamingException
public void bind(String name, Object obj) throws NamingException
public void rebind(Name name, Object obj) throws NamingException
public void rebind(String name, Object obj) throws NamingException
public void unbind(Name name) throws NamingException
public void unbind(String name) throws NamingException
public void rename(Name oldName, Name newName) throws NamingException
public void rename(String oldName, String newName) throws NamingException

public Context createSubcontext(Name name) throws NamingException
public Context createSubcontext(String name) throws NamingException
public void destroySubcontext(Name name) throws NamingException
public void destroySubcontext(String name) throws NamingException

public void close( ) throws NamingException
public String getNameInNamespace( ) throws NamingException

public Object addToEnvironment(String propName, Object propVal) throws
    NamingException
public Hashtable getEnvironment( ) throws NamingException
public Object removeFromEnvironment(String propName) throws NamingException

public Name composeName(Name name, Name prefix) throws NamingException
public String composeName(String name, String prefix) throws NamingException
public NameParser getNameParser(Name name) throws NamingException
public NameParser getNameParser(String name) throws NamingException
```

Twenty-one of the 29 methods defined in Context are variations on methods we've already seen. There are minor changes, of course. For example, list( ) returns an instance of NamingEnumeration rather than an array of objects. And the process of unbinding a server and rebinding it under another name has been promoted to a full-fledged method called rename( ). However, all in all, most of this is fairly straightforward.

NamingEnumeration

NamingEnumeration is an interface that extends the Enumeration interface defined in the java.util package. Enumeration defines the following two methods:

```
public boolean hasMoreElements( )
public Object nextElement( )
```

And NamingEnumeration adds three additional methods:

```
public void close( ) throws NamingException
public boolean hasMore( ) throws NamingException
public Object next( ) throws NamingException
```

NamingEnumeration extends Enumeration for convenience—one piece of code can get NamingEnumeration and then pass it around to other objects as an instance of Enumeration (which is a more familiar interface). The implementations of hasMore( ) and hasMoreElements( ) are functionally equivalent—it's just that one throws a more detailed type of exception.

You may wonder why NamingEnumeration doesn't extend Remote. As it is defined, the instances of NamingEnumeration have to be serialized and passed by value over the wire. Why not instead use the following interface:

```
public interface NamingEnumeration extends Remote {
public void close( ) throws NamingException, RemoteException
public boolean hasMore( ) throws NamingException, RemoteException
public Object next( ) throws NamingException, RemoteException
}
```

This lets us use NamingEnumeration as a remote iterator (one of our design guidelines from Chapter 7). But it also leads to two significant problems:

- It makes JNDI RMI-centric. Other naming and directory services might not use RMI. Making the NamingEnumeration interface extend Remote, and declaring the methods to throw RemoteException, partially defeats the goal of a generic interface.

- It forces instances of NamingEnumeration to be servers. If there are only five return values for a list(...) query, the query probably shouldn't cause the creation of a short-lived remote iterator.

Instead, if we want to use a remote iterator for a particular response, we can create a subclass of NamingEnumeration that uses a stub on the remote iterator (and forwards method calls). In this case, the instance of the subclass of NamingEnumeration becomes a client-side proxy for the remote iterator.

The genuinely new functionality is contained in seven methods. The first three methods enable Context to store environment variables in an instance of Hashtable for easy retrieval:

```
public Object addToEnvironment(String propName, Object propVal) throws
    NamingException
public Hashtable getEnvironment( ) throws NamingException
public Object removeFromEnvironment(String propName) throws NamingException
```

There are two main differences between a name-value pair bound into a context and a name-value pair that defines an environment variable:

- When you use bind( ), there's an implicit understanding that what you're binding is a complex structure of some type. It doesn't necessarily have to be a server,* but it's usually an object with methods and structure.

- When you use bind( ), you're explicitly allowing for paths, complex names, and more general queries. For example, if the context you bind into is a subcontext of another context, the object that has been bound may be accessible via a path-based lookup. Environment variables are explicitly local and can only be retrieved by name.

It's not clear when environment variables are a good idea. They're often convenient (they're the conceptual equivalent of attaching a sticky note to the context), but they don't really add any functionality. And using such a weakly typed interface to store important information can only cause headaches.

The final four methods are:

```
public Name composeName(Name name, Name prefix) throws NamingException
public String composeName(String name, String prefix) throws NamingException
public NameParser getNameParser(Name name) throws NamingException
public NameParser getNameParser(String name) throws NamingException
```

These are an attempt to get around the fact that different naming services use different formatting conventions for their names. For example, the RMI registry uses strings with the following format:

```
rmi://host:port/humanReadableName
```

The naming service we implemented, on the other hand, doesn't use a URL format. Instead, it just uses a path-based notation to choose between contexts.

The NamingParser interface lets client code parse, and deal with components of names, without having to know the exact details of the format.

---

* In the case of RMI, the object being bound has to be a server. But with other JNDI contexts, the LDAP JNDI implementation for example, there are no restrictions at all.

JNDI Service Providers

A JNDI Service Provider Implementation is an implementation of the JNDI interfaces, including the code that enables Initial Context to find the naming service so specified. As of this writing, JDK 1.3 ships with two JNDI Service Provider implementations: one that wraps the RMI registry, and one that wraps the CORBA naming service.

In addition, you can download several additional service providers from Javasoft's web site. Currently, the Javasoft web site contains JNDI wrappers for DNS, LDAP, and the filesystem. Of course, third-party software companies such as Novell provide JNDI wrappers for their directory-based products.

Using JNDI with the Bank Example

Now that we've said all this, it's time to actually use JNDI. There is a wrapper around JNDI that allows us to use the JNDI interfaces to access the RMI registry. In order to use this, we'll need to make three minor changes to our application.

The first thing we need to do is change our batch files. We'll still be using the RMI registry, so that batch file is okay. However, the batch files that launch the client and the server need an additional command-line property.

Here's the server's batch file:

```
start java -Djava.naming.factory.initial=com.sun.jndi.rmi.registry.
    RegistryContextFactory com.ora.rmibook.chapter15.jndiaccounts.applications.
    ImplLauncher Bob 10000 Alex 1223
```

The only change is that we've set the java.naming.factory.initial property to be the name of the class that creates a JNDI wrapper around the RMI registry.

We could also have set this property from within our code. Either of the following two pieces of code would accomplish the same task. The first version simply sets the property from within the application, while the second overrides the system property temporarily, for the creation of a single Context:

```
// first version
System.properties.put(Context.INITIAL_CONTEXT_FACTORY, "com.sun.jndi.rmi.registry.
    RegistryContextFactory");

// second version
Hashtable environment = new Hashtable();
environment.put(Context.INITIAL_CONTEXT_FACTORY, "com.sun.jndi.rmi.registry.
    RegistryContextFactory");
return new InitialContext(environment);
```

Once we've changed our batch files, we need to alter our code to use JNDI. Here's the relevant part of the new version of our launch code:

```
public class ImplLauncher {
    private static Context namingContext;
```

```java
    public static void main(String[] args) {
        try {
            namingContext = new InitialContext( );
        }
        catch (Exception e) {
            System.out.println("Naming context unavailable");
            System.exit(0);
        }
        Collection nameBalancePairs = getNameBalancePairs(args);
        Iterator i = nameBalancePairs.iterator( );
        while(i.hasNext( )) {
            NameBalancePair nextNameBalancePair = (NameBalancePair) i.next( );
            launchServer(nextNameBalancePair);
        }
    }

    private static void launchServer(NameBalancePair serverDescription) {
        try {
            Account_Impl newAccount = new Account_Impl(serverDescription.balance);
            namingContext.rebind(serverDescription.name, newAccount);
            System.out.println("Account " + serverDescription.name + " successfully
                launched.");
        }
        catch(Exception e) {
            e.printStackTrace( );
        }
    }
// ....
}
```

This is almost identical to the our earlier code. The major difference is that we have to create an instance of InitialContext. The InitialContext class looks at the system property we set and uses the factory class to create the actual context we need (in this case an instance of com.sun.jndi.rmi.registry.RegistryContext), to which it then forwards all method calls. After we've created the instance of InitialContext, we use the JNDI declaration of rebind( ), rather than the version defined in the RMI registry's interface.

There is something tricky happening here. We call a method on an instance of InitialContext. That instance of InitialContext forwards the method call to the instance of com.sun.jndi.rmi.registry.RegistryContext. The instance of com.sun. jndi.rmi.registry.RegistryContext in turn forwards the method call to the RMI registry, which means that all the underlying limitations and assumptions of the RMI registry are still in place, and still in force.

In particular, the RMI registry is flat and has no ability to create subcontexts. In addition, it assumes that the objects bound into it are serializable. Therefore, attempts to use subcontexts or bind nonserializable objects will throw exceptions, even though the code might be perfectly valid JNDI code that works with other service providers. JNDI provides a common interface to different naming services.

However, you still need to be aware of the limitations of the underlying service providers your code uses.

The last change we need to make is to our client code. Like our launch code, it will need to create an InitialContext. It will then use the InitialContext to retrieve objects from the registry.

Here's the new implementation of getAccount( ):

```java
private void getAccount( ) {
    try {
        Context namingContext = new InitialContext( );
        _account = (Account) namingContext.lookup(_accountNameField.getText( ));
    }
    catch (Exception e) {
        System.out.println("Couldn't find account. Error was \n " + e);
        e.printStackTrace( );
    }
    return;
}
```

CHAPTER 16

The RMI Runtime

Before we can get to the last major design pattern in Chapter 17, factories, we need to take a short detour and discuss what we've been referring to as "the RMI runtime." This chapter is devoted to exploring the code that exists between, and manages the connection between, the stub and the skeleton. By the end of this chapter, you will understand how the distributed garbage collector works, how RMI maintains connections between clients and servers, how to use the RMI logging facilities, and how to customize RMI's behavior at runtime.

Reviewing the Mechanics of a Remote Method Call

The place to start is with a variation on the standard architecture diagram shown in Figure 16-1.

This picture is a little different from the previous ones in that we've included the RMI runtime on the client side of the wire as well as on the server side. This is not the graphical equivalent of a typo; the RMI runtime plays a significant role on the client side as well as on the server side. By the way, note that the RMI runtime, especially on the client side, is often referred to as "the transport layer."

In this architecture, the stub serves three distinct purposes:

- It is serialized and sent over the wire from the server to a client; it contains the data that enables the client to reliably send messages to that server.
- It is a proxy for the server; the client "thinks" of the stub as if it was the server.
- It enables socket pooling. The stubs ask the RMI runtime for a connection to a particular server with every method invocation. This lets the RMI runtime reuse sockets across multiple requests.

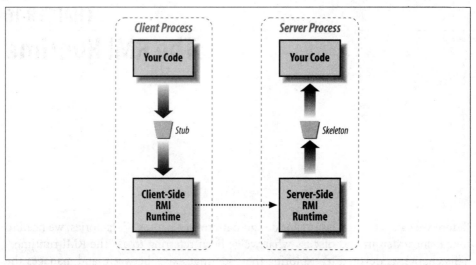

Figure 16-1. The layers in a remote call

This first two roles should be familiar; the last is implied by the fact that sockets are shared. However, it is worth looking at nonetheless. Here, for example, is the code from a stub method (from an Account_Impl stub):

```
public com.ora.rmibook.chapter9.valueobjects.Money getBalance() throws java.rmi
    RemoteException {
        try {
            if (useNewInvoke) {
                Object $result = ref.invoke(this, $method_getBalance_0, null,
                    8933230144580145706L);
                return ((com.ora.rmibook.chapter9.valueobjects.Money) $result);
            } else {
                java.rmi.server.RemoteCall call =
                    ref.newCall((java.rmi.server.RemoteObject) this, operations, 0,
                        interfaceHash);
                ref.invoke(call);
                com.ora.rmibook.chapter9.valueobjects.Money $result;
                try {
                    java.io.ObjectInput in = call.getInputStream();
                    $result = (com.ora.rmibook.chapter9.valueobjects.Money) in.
                        readObject();
                }
                } catch (java.io.IOException e) {
                    throw new java.rmi.UnmarshalException(
                        "error unmarshalling return", e);
                } catch (java.lang.ClassNotFoundException e) {
                    throw new java.rmi.UnmarshalException(
                        "error unmarshalling return", e);
                } finally {
                    ref.done(call);
                }
                return $result;
            }
```

```
        } catch (java.lang.RuntimeException e) {
            throw e;
        } catch (java.rmi.RemoteException e) {
            throw e;
        } catch (java.lang.Exception e) {
            throw new java.rmi.UnexpectedException("undeclared checked exception",
                e);
        }
    }
```

The first real line of code testing the boolean newInvoke. is a hook for the second version of the RMI protocol, which was introduced in Java 2. The new protocol is functionally equivalent to the old one. The older protocol is more explicit, though, and we'll center the discussion around it. If no exceptions are thrown, the lines of code that get executed are:

```
java.rmi.server.RemoteCall call = ref.newCall((java.rmi.server.RemoteObject) this,
    operations, 0, interfaceHash);
    ref.invoke(call);
    com.ora.rmibook.chapter9.valueobjects.Money $result;
    java.io.ObjectInput in = call.getInputStream();
    $result = (com.ora.rmibook.chapter9.valueobjects.Money) in.readObject();
    ref.done(call);
    return $result;
```

This is very similar to what we needed to do to send a reference to our new naming service over the wire in Chapter 15. Recall that we opened a socket with our naming service, acquired the streams associated with the socket, and then used serialization to send a stub over the wire. The only difference here is that, instead of a socket, a RemoteRef is used. RemoteRef exists for a single reason: to isolate the stub from the details of managing a socket connection. By doing so, the designers of RMI achieved two goals, one abstract and the other concrete. The abstract goal is that the definition of RMI is independent of TCP/IP. Technically speaking, all an implementation of RMI requires is a streams-based communication protocol.

The concrete goal is that sockets get reused. When ref.newCall() executes, the transport layer checks to see if an already existing socket is available (e.g., has no currently executing remote method invocations on it). If such a socket is available, it reuses the socket. Otherwise, a new socket connection to the server is created and used.

This leads to another problem. We effectively have the diagram in Figure 16-2.

If a socket is reused by several client stubs, each of which sends messages to a different server, those messages must get differentiated somehow. In RMI, this is managed through the use of the ObjID class, which is defined in the java.rmi.server package. The javadoc for ObjID says the following:

> An ObjID is used to identify remote objects uniquely in a VM over time. Each identifier contains an object number and an address space identifier that is unique with respect to a specific host. An object identifier is assigned to a remote object when it is exported. If the java.rmi.server.randomIDs property is true, then the object number

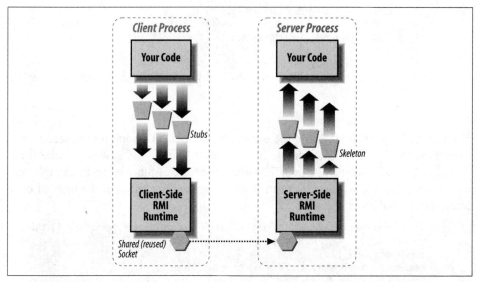

Figure 16-2. Sharing sockets

component (64 bits) of an ObjID created with the no argument constructor will contain a cryptographically strong random number.

Thus, an instance of ObjID uniquely identifies a particular server inside the server's JVM. The ObjID class implements the Serializable interface, and instances of it are serialized with every remote method call.

 We'll frequently refer to object identifiers or object identities. These simply refer to instances of ObjID.

On the server side, the RMI runtime uses the deserialized instance of ObjID to figure out for which skeleton the remote method invocation is intended.

How RMI Solves the Bootstrapping Problem

Most servers in ordinary use have randomly assigned instances of ObjID. However, there are three reserved identifiers: ACTIVATOR_ID, DGC_ID, and REGISTRY_ID. These three IDs correspond to the three main servers that RMI provides: the activation framework, the distributed garbage collector, and the RMI registry. We'll talk about the distributed garbage collector later in this chapter and the activation framework in Chapter 17.

The RMI registry needs a unique identifier, which is known in advance, in order to fully solve the bootstrapping problem. Recall that the RMI runtime tries to reuse sockets. RMI servers, even the registry, do not get dedicated sockets.

But now consider a client attempting to connect to the RMI registry for the first time. Unless it already knows the object identity associated with a server, a client cannot send a message to that server. That is, since the server's RMI runtime requires an instance of ObjID in order to determine the appropriate server for a request, the client needs to know the ObjID of the registry running in the server's JVM in order to connect to the registry.

In order to solve this problem, the designers of RMI decided to define a special instance of ObjID that is reserved—if a registry is running in a JVM, it uses REGISTRY_ID. Otherwise, no server is allowed to use REGISTRY_ID.

This solves the RMI bootstrapping problem. The static methods defined in the Naming class take a string that contains the address of a computer on the network and a port; the only additional information needed to construct a stub is the object ID of the server to which the stub connects. Since the registry always uses REGISTRY_ID, a stub for the registry can be constructed entirely on the client side, before connecting to the registry.

This strategy also means that there can only be one registry exported per JVM, since ObjIDs cannot be shared by more than one server. In comparison, we solved the bootstrapping problem for the naming service implemented in Chapter 15 by defining a second, more primitive protocol that was used only to establish initial connections. Each instance of BaseContextImpl had both its RMI behavior (achieved by extending UnicastRemoteObject) and a second port, which it used to vend stubs. This second port used a dedicated server socket that enabled our instances of BaseContextImpl to bypass the preceding problem. Since the message that establishes the initial connection doesn't go through RMI, the client doesn't need to know the identity of the BaseContextImpl in advance.

Distributed Garbage Collection

Another one of the three fixed object identifiers is DGC_ID. This is the object identifier associated with the distributed garbage collector built into RMI. The distributed garbage collector is useful and important in distributed applications built using RMI. It's also not very complicated. Before describing how the distributed garbage collector works, however, I will spend a few paragraphs explaining ordinary garbage collection.

Ordinary Garbage Collection

The motivation for garbage collection is simple: memory management is hard. Programmers are very good at creating new objects. But knowing when to release an object is much more difficult. Consider, for example, the following snippet of Java code:

```
public Money getBalance(String clientIDNumber) throws RemoteException,
    LockedAccountException {
```

```
        checkAccess(clientIDNumber);
        return _balance;
    }
```

The problem is that, without some form of automatic memory management, pro-grammers must somehow decide when _balance is freed. A consistent policy must be adopted across the entire codebase. Any failure, anywhere in the code, to abide by and enforce the policy, can lead to a memory leak. One such policy, for example, is:

> If a method returns an object, the returned object is the responsibility of the caller. The object whose method was called should not retain any references to returned objects.

This policy is easy enough to implement; it changes the preceding method into:

```
public Money getBalance(String clientIDNumber) throws RemoteException,
    LockedAccountException {
        checkAccess(clientIDNumber);
        Money returnValue = new Money(_balance);
        return rreturnValue;
    }
```

However, this has two sizable flaws. The first is that it leads to the creation of a lot of objects in cases where you don't really need to create objects. The second is that you can't actually universally adhere to this solution. You cannot simply make a copy of a socket or a file.

Of course, you can then create an addendum to the preceding policy, something like:

> Unless, of course, the returned object is a special object such as a socket or a file; spe-cial objects are treated according to the following rules...

Garbage collection is a much simpler solution. The basic idea is to define a set of reachable objects and then discard objects that are not reachable (the "garbage"). Reachable objects are defined recursively:

- Each active thread is currently in a method, in an instance of an unknown object. These instances, which threads are actually in, are reachable.

- There's a small set of objects that each thread can immediately find: the objects referenced by the method-level variables and the instance's fields. These objects are also reachable.

- From each of these immediately accessible objects, there are other objects that can be reached.

- And so on. In general, if a thread, starting from where it is currently, can eventu-ally find an object, that object is reachable.

Given the definition of reachable objects, any garbage collection algorithm does three things:

- It either maintains an index of, or knows how to find out about, the set of all currently allocated objects.

- It occasionally computes the set of objects that are reachable from the active threads.
- It reclaims ("garbage collects") objects that are not reachable.

This neatly solves the problem of when to free objects. We can use the first version of the code:

```
public Money getBalance(String clientIDNumber) throws RemoteException,
    LockedAccountException {
        checkAccess(clientIDNumber);
        return _balance;
```

and rely on the system to free _balance when _balance is no longer reachable.

Defining Network Garbage

Garbage collection works well inside a single JVM. However, a problem with stubs arises in a distributed system. If a client has a stub that references a server, then that server should be reachable. Since all the stub really has is an instance of ObjID, this means that the RMI runtime is really keeping references to all the active servers. In order to do garbage collection, the RMI runtime on a client machine must somehow let the RMI runtime on a server machine know when a stub is no longer being used.

The obvious way to do this is to use distributed reference counting. That is, force the stub on a client machine to send two additional messages to the server. One message is sent when the stub is instantiated, to let the server know that there is an active client. The other message is sent when the stub is freed, to let the server know when the client is finished using the server.

The RMI runtime on the server, meanwhile, simply keeps track of the number of active clients. When a stub sends the first message, the RMI runtime on the server increments the number of active clients. When a stub sends the second message, the RMI runtime on the server decrements the number of active clients. When there are no active clients, it removes the server from its indexing scheme and thus makes it possible for local garbage collection to reclaim the server.

This scheme, while an obvious first step, is very fragile. Each of the following problems makes distributed reference counting difficult:

- The client's garbage collection algorithm isn't guaranteed to reclaim the stub right away. If the client isn't running low on memory, and is busy performing a high-priority task, garbage collection may not happen for a while. During that time period, the client is implicitly forcing the server to hold on to unnecessary resources.
- The client can crash. This is a much more serious problem. If a client crashes, then the second message is never sent. The server's reference count never gets to 0, and the RMI runtime keeps the server object active forever.

- Network problems may arise. Even if the client is well-behaved and sends its message, the network may be down. In which case, the RMI runtime never decrements the server's reference count to 0, and the server object is kept active forever.

Leasing

Of these problems, the first is impossible to overcome. The Java language specification clearly states that local garbage collection is undependable. Garbage collection will happen, but you have no way to force it to happen within a certain time frame. Since you have no way of knowing that a stub is unreferenced until garbage collection runs, any distributed reference-counting architecture will simply have to live with the first problem. The second and third problems, however, can be eliminated by making all distributed references *temporary* references. This idea is known as *leasing*.

The basic algorithm is this:

1. A client calls the server and requests a lease for a period of time.
2. The server responds back, granting a lease for a period of time (not necessarily the original amount of time).
3. During this period of time, the distributed reference count includes the client.
4. When the lease expires, if the client hasn't requested an extension, the distributed reference count is automatically decremented.

Clients automatically try to renew leases as long as a stub hasn't been garbage collected. Given this, if we look at the problems with distributed reference counting, we'll see that the second and third problems have been neatly solved. If the client crashes, then the client application is no longer running, and therefore, the client application certainly isn't attempting to renew leases. Consequently, the lease won't be renewed, and the server is eventually garbage collected.

Similarly, if network problems prevent the client application from connecting to the server, the client application won't renew the lease. In this case, the lease won't be renewed and the server will eventually get garbage collected.

The default value of a lease is 10 minutes. This is configurable using the java.rmi.dgc.leasevalue property. We'll discuss in more detail how to configure the default value, and why you would do so, later in this chapter.

The Actual Distributed Garbage Collector

The distributed garbage collector is an RMI server that implements the DGC interface, which is defined in the java.rmi.dgc package. This interface has only two methods:

```
public void clean(ObjID[] ids, long sequenceNum, VMID vmid, boolean strong)
public Lease dirty(ObjID[] ids, long sequenceNum, Lease lease)
```

Both of these methods are automatically called by the client's runtime; you will never write code that calls either clean( ) or dirty( ).

clean( ) is called by the client runtime when it no longer needs a reference to a server. Strictly speaking, calls to clean( ) are unnecessary—the client runtime can accomplish the same task by simply failing to renew the lease. However, leasing should be viewed as a last-gasp server cleanup mechanism, in place to lessen the damage caused by network or client failures. If you lengthen the duration of leases (we'll discuss how to do this later), having well-behaved clients that notify servers when their references are no longer useful becomes enormously important.

A client runtime requests a lease with dirty( ). It passes in a suggested lease and gets back the lease that the server is willing to grant. dirty( ) doesn't need to pass a virtual machine ID (VMID)* directly because the instance of Lease that is passed in has a VMID.

More precise details of the DGC interface aren't very useful; we've covered enough that you will be able to customize the distributed garbage collectors behavior and read the RMI logs.

 Each JVM can have only one distributed garbage collector. It's important enough, and enough messages get sent to it, that it gets a special object identity: DGC_ID.

The Unreferenced Interface

The distributed garbage collector is responsible for maintaining leases. On the server side, when all the outstanding leases to a particular server object expire, the distributed garbage collector makes sure the RMI runtime does not retain any references to the server, thereby enabling the server to be garbage collected.

During the process, if the server implements the Unreferenced interface, the server can find out if there are no longer any open leases. Unreferenced consists of exactly one method:

    public void unreferenced( )

This can be useful when the server needs to immediately release resources instead of waiting for garbage collection to occur. It is also a convenient hook for persistence code—since the server knows that no remote methods will be called anymore, it can safely store its state to a more persistent medium (e.g., a relational database). We'll talk more about persistence in Chapter 17. For now, there are two important caveats to note.

---

* A VMID is exactly what it sounds like: a unique identifier for a JVM.

First, the RMI registry maintains leases on all the objects in it. Here's what the main method for our launch code looked like:

```
public static void main(String[] args)  {
        int numberOfServers = (Integer.valueOf(args[0])).intValue( );
        NameRepository nameRepository= new NameRepository(numberOfServers);
        Collection nameBalancePairs = getNameBalancePairs(nameRepository);
        Iterator i = nameBalancePairs.iterator( );
        while(i.hasNext( )) {
            AccountDescription nextNameBalancePair = (AccountDescription) i.next( );
            launchServer(nextNameBalancePair);
        }
}
```

Once main( ) exits (and it does), all the servers that were launched should go away. But they don't. This is because the RMI registry has stubs that refer to the servers. Therefore, the RMI runtime in the JVM running the registry keeps negotiating leases for the servers, and the distributed garbage collector keeps the servers alive.

 This is not some peculiar quirk of the RMI registry. Our naming service does the same thing. In general, if you have a stub, you have a lease. Thus, objects that are bound into either the registry or our naming service are reachable (in the sense of the distributed garbage collector) and will not be garbage collected.

The second caveat is that unreferenced( ) can be called more than once by the RMI runtime. Consider, for example, our naming service's BaseContextImpl. Recall that an instance of BaseContextImpl creates instances of StubSender and StubSocketListener to handle the bootstrapping problem. Also recall that these objects create a thread that listens on an instance of ServerSocket. This means that BaseContextImpl is never garbage collected (it is reachable from the thread that is listening on the instance of ServerSocket). However, if it implements Unreferenced, unreferenced( ) would be called every time there were no active stubs. This could happen quite a few times.

RMI's Logging Facilities

In addition to a distributed garbage collector, the RMI runtime also provides a fairly extensive logging facility that enables you to track the behavior of your applications. Unfortunately, RMI's logging is somewhat idiosyncratic. There are actually three different types of logs: the standard log, the specialized logs (there are five of these), and the debugging log.

The Standard Log

The standard log is easy to use. You turn it on and off using the java.rmi.server. logCalls system property. This is a boolean system property. Note that this property can either be set at the command line or in code. There is no functional difference between the command line invocation:

```
java -Djava.rmi.server.logCalls=true [other stuff]
```

and using:

```
java [same other stuff]
```

to invoke a program that contains the line:

```
System.getProperties().put("java.rmi.serverr.logCalls", "true");
```

Actually, this isn't quite true. At the command line, you always have permission to set system properties. Depending on your security policy, a program might not have permission to do so. We'll explore this more in Chapter 20.

Once you've turned logging on, you need to set the logging destination. This is done by using one of the static logging methods defined in the RemoteServer class, which is defined in the java.rmi.server package. The methods are:

```
public static PrintStream getLog()
public static void setLog(OutputStream out)
```

The first retrieves the stream currently used to do logging, and the second allows you to set it. The most common use of these is dumping to a simple log file, as in the following code snippet:

```
private void setLogFile() {
    try {
        FileOutputStream logFile = new FileOutputStream("C:\\temp\\foo");
        RemoteServer.setLog(logFile);
    }
    catch (Exception e) {
        System.out.println("Failed to open log file");
    }
}
```

By default, the logging system uses System.err. That is, if you enable standard logging but don't specify where the logging messages should go, they will show up on System.err.

You have to set the logging destination before you invoke any RMI methods. Once RMI starts logging to a particular PrintStream, it keeps logging to that PrintStream.

The standard log records method calls that went through RMI and exceptions that were thrown by the server in the thread that handled the method call. Here's some output from a fairly typical log file:*

```
Sun Oct 29 19:26:53 PST 2000:RMI:RMI TCP Connection(2)-127.0.0.1:[127.0.0.1: sun.rmi.
transport.DGCImpl[0:0:0, 2]: java.rmi.dgc.Lease dirty(java.rmi.server.ObjID[], long,
java.rmi.dgc.Lease)]
Sun Oct 29 19:26:53 PST 2000:RMI:RMI TCP Connection(2)-127.0.0.1:[127.0.0.1: sun.rmi.
transport.DGCImpl[0:0:0, 2]: java.rmi.dgc.Lease dirty(java.rmi.server.ObjID[], long,
java.rmi.dgc.Lease)]
Sun Oct 29 19:27:02 PST 2000:RMI:RMI TCP Connection(3)-127.0.0.1:[127.0.0.1: sun.rmi.
transport.DGCImpl[0:0:0, 2]: java.rmi.dgc.Lease dirty(java.rmi.server.ObjID[], long,
java.rmi.dgc.Lease)]
Sun Oct 29 19:27:02 PST 2000:RMI:RMI TCP Connection(3)-127.0.0.1:[127.0.0.1: com.ora.
rmibook.chapter9.Account_Impl[0]: public abstract strictfp com.ora.rmibook.chapter9.
valueobjects.Money com.ora.rmibook.chapter9.Account.getBalance( ) throws java.rmi.
RemoteException]
Sun Oct 29 19:27:22 PST 2000:RMI:RMI TCP Connection(3)-127.0.0.1:[127.0.0.1: sun.rmi.
transport.DGCImpl[0:0:0, 2]: java.rmi.dgc.Lease dirty(java.rmi.server.ObjID[], long,
java.rmi.dgc.Lease)]
Sun Oct 29 19:27:22 PST 2000:RMI:RMI TCP Connection(3)-127.0.0.1:[127.0.0.1: com.ora.
rmibook.chapter9.Account_Impl[1]: public abstract strictfp com.ora.rmibook.chapter9.
valueobjects.Money com.ora.rmibook.chapter9.Account.getBalance( ) throws java.rmi.
RemoteException]
```

Each of these lines records a method call and has a rather verbose format. The first line, for example, can be translated as follows:

> On Sunday Oct. 29, 19:26:53 PST 2000, a client called an instance of sun.rmi. transport.DGCImpl   (which had object identity [0;0:0:2]). The method dirty( ) was invoked, and no exception was thrown.

There are several interesting things here. The first is that the distributed garbage collector really is an RMI server; you can watch the distributed garbage collector, and see how it is behaving, simply by watching the method flow. The second interesting point is that there's an awful lot of leasing traffic going on here.

The problem is that you can't tell any of this from the method call log. Practically speaking, while you can watch the distributed garbage collector work, you can't get much information from the transcript.

For example, the leases being negotiated in this transcript are, in order, from:

- The registry, opening a lease for the server named "Bob"
- The registry, opening a lease for the server named "Alex"
- The client, opening a lease for the server named "Bob"
- The client, opening a lease for the server named "Alex"

---

* All of the logging output shown in this chapter was generated using the com.ora.rmibook.chapter16. LoggingImplLauncher class.

However, I was able to figure that out because I had a fair amount of other information about the servers which I used when looking at the log.

Method call logs are not particularly useful unless you're watching them under carefully controlled conditions (e.g., in which you do something and then immediately see associated entries in the log).

The Specialized Logs

In addition to the standard log, RMI has five different specialized logs that track particular aspects of the runtime. These logs are: the transport log, the proxy log, the loader log, the DGC log, and the TCP log. Each of these specialized logs is associated with an instance of java.rmi.server.LogStream. To get the Logstream associated with a log, call a static method defined in the LogStream class:

```
public static LogStream log(String name)
```

Once you have the instance of LogStream associated with a particular log, you can set the actual output stream for the log using the setOutputStream( ) method. Here, for example, is code that sets up five different log files, one for each of the five specialized logs:

```
private static void setLogFiles( ) {
    try {
        FileOutputStream transportLogFile = new FileOutputStream(
            "C:\\temp\\transportLogFile");
        FileOutputStream proxyLogFile = new FileOutputStream(
            "C:\\temp\\proxyLogFile");
        FileOutputStream tcpLogFile = new FileOutputStream(
            "C:\\temp\\tcpLogFile");
        FileOutputStream dgcLogFile = new FileOutputStream(
            "C:\\temp\\dgcLogFile");
        FileOutputStream loaderLogFile = new FileOutputStream(
            "C:\\temp\\loaderLogFile");
        LogStream.log("transport").setOutputStream(transportLogFile);
        LogStream.log("proxy").setOutputStream(proxyLogFile);
        LogStream.log("tcp").setOutputStream(tcpLogFile);
        LogStream.log("dgc").setOutputStream(dgcLogFile);
        LogStream.log("loader").setOutputStream(loaderLogFile);
    }
    catch (Exception e) {
        System.out.println("Failed to open log files");
    }
}
```

As with the standard log, you need to define these logs before logging actually begins. Otherwise, logging information might be sent to the wrong destination (which is usually System.err).

Note that LogStream, and the entire specialized logging system, has been deprecated in JDK 1.3. This means that, in a future version of RMI, it may not be supported. Until then, however, it can be very useful.

It's not entirely obvious how these logs are broken down; much of the information recorded in one log is related to information stored in another log (in particular, the transport and TCP logs are very strongly correlated). This is partially because the logs themselves aren't turned on or off. Instead, they are manipulated by six system properties, each of which takes one of three settings: "silent," "brief," or "verbose." Silent means that no information is recorded, brief means that too little information is recorded, and verbose means that far too much information is recorded.

Note that you can actually use the values "s," "b," and "v" as abbreviations for silent, brief, and verbose. The logging facility only checks the first character. I prefer to use the whole word because doing so makes the code easier to read.

The six system properties are the following:

`sun.rmi.server.dgcLevel`

When turned on, this stores information about distributed garbage collection. In particular, it stores information about lease grants, lease expirations, and lease renewals to the distributed garbage collection (DGC) log.

`sun.rmi.server.logLevel`

When turned on, this logs information about outgoing calls, including connection-reuse information. This information gets recorded in the transport log.

`sun.rmi.loader.logLevel`

When turned on, this records information about class names and codebases whenever RMI attempts to load a class as a result of unmarshalling an argument or return value. The information gets recorded in the loader log.

`sun.rmi.transport.logLevel`

This logs information about communications at an abstract level, in terms of streams and connections. The information is recorded in the transport log.

`sun.rmi.transport.tcp.logLevel`

This records detailed information about the TCP/IP protocol (e.g., the ports being used). This information is record in the TCP log.

`sun.rmi.transport.proxy.logLevel`

This records information about the creation of Sockets and ServerSockets. It sends some of the information to the proxy log and some to the transport log.

When we set each of these to verbose, either by using command-line arguments or setting system properties programmatically, we get quite a bit of information about what RMI is doing. For example, starting the bank server going with two accounts

("Bob" and "Alex"), and then requesting the balance for both accounts generated 15 KB of log files, is broken down as follows:

    1 KB in the standard log
    3 KB in the DGC log
    5 KB in the transport log
    6 KB in the TCP log

Incidentally, the volume of logging information that can be generated is one of the main reasons to use command-line properties rather than hardwiring logging in your code. You often want logging information when tracking down a subtle problem; you rarely want it for a production server. Turning logs on and off via the command line is often the easiest way to achieve this. On the other hand, setting the LogStream is something that must be done in code.

Here's a little bit of the TCP log:

```
Sun Oct 29 20:49:14 PST 2000:tcp:main:TCPEndpoint.<clinit>: localHostKnown = false,
localHost = 127.0.0.1
Sun Oct 29 20:49:14 PST 2000:tcp:main:TCPTransport.<init>: Version = 2, ep = [127.0.
0.1:0]
Sun Oct 29 20:49:14 PST 2000:tcp:main:TCPEndpoint.getLocalEndpoint: created local
endpoint for socket factory null on port 0
Sun Oct 29 20:49:14 PST 2000:tcp:main:TCPTransport(0).listen: create socket, port = 0
Sun Oct 29 20:49:14 PST 2000:tcp:main:TCPEndpoint.newServerSocket: creating server
socket on [127.0.0.1:0]
Sun Oct 29 20:49:14 PST 2000:tcp:main:TCPEndpoint.setDefaultPort: default port for
server socket factory null and client socket factory null set to 1946
```

The entries themselves aren't defined in any of the RMI specifications but aren't terribly hard to decipher either. For example, these entries deal with RMI setting up a default server socket so that new connections can be established. Port 1946 was used, and RMI began listening on it soon after.

It can be interesting to try and correlate the method calls in the standard log with the more detailed information presented in the specialized logs. For example, the standard log had this to say about garbage collection:

```
Sun Oct 29 20:49:15 PST 2000:RMI:RMI TCP Connection(2)-127.0.0.1:[127.0.0.1: sun.rmi.
transport.DGCImpl[0:0:0, 2]: java.rmi.dgc.Lease dirty(java.rmi.server.ObjID[], long,
java.rmi.dgc.Lease)]
Sun Oct 29 20:49:15 PST 2000:RMI:RMI TCP Connection(2)-127.0.0.1:[127.0.0.1: sun.rmi.
transport.DGCImpl[0:0:0, 2]: java.rmi.dgc.Lease dirty(java.rmi.server.ObjID[], long,
java.rmi.dgc.Lease)]
Sun Oct 29 20:49:23 PST 2000:RMI:RMI TCP Connection(3)-127.0.0.1:[127.0.0.1: sun.rmi.
transport.DGCImpl[0:0:0, 2]: java.rmi.dgc.Lease dirty(java.rmi.server.ObjID[], long,
java.rmi.dgc.Lease)]
Sun Oct 29 20:49:27 PST 2000:RMI:RMI TCP Connection(3)-127.0.0.1:[127.0.0.1: sun.rmi.
transport.DGCImpl[0:0:0, 2]: java.rmi.dgc.Lease dirty(java.rmi.server.ObjID[], long,
java.rmi.dgc.Lease)]
Sun Oct 29 20:54:15 PST 2000:RMI:RMI TCP Connection(4)-127.0.0.1:[127.0.0.1: sun.rmi.
transport.DGCImpl[0:0:0, 2]: java.rmi.dgc.Lease dirty(java.rmi.server.ObjID[], long,
java.rmi.dgc.Lease)]
```

The DGC log, on the other hand, provides a much more detailed view of what occurs. The first two lines of the standard log, in which the registry established leases on the two servers that were launched, correspond to the following DGC log entries:

```
Sun Oct 29 20:49:14 PST 2000:dgc:main:WeakRef.pin: strongRef = sun.rmi.transport.
DGCImpl@42719c
Sun Oct 29 20:49:14 PST 2000:dgc:main:ObjectTable.putTarget: add object [0:0:0, 2]
Sun Oct 29 20:49:14 PST 2000:dgc:main:ObjectTable.putTarget: add object [0]
Sun Oct 29 20:49:15 PST 2000:dgc:main:WeakRef.pin: strongRef = com.ora.rmibook.
chapter9.Account_Impl[RemoteStub [ref: [endpoint:[127.0.0.1:1946](local),objID:[0]]]]
Sun Oct 29 20:49:15 PST 2000:dgc:RMI TCP Connection(2)-127.0.0.1:DGCImpl.dirty: vmid
= 11d1def534ea1be0:5ffb18:e2843f60ce:-7fff
Sun Oct 29 20:49:15 PST 2000:dgc:RMI TCP Connection(2)-127.0.0.1:DGCImpl.dirty: id =
[0], vmid = 11d1def534ea1be0:5ffb18:e2843f60ce:-7fff, duration = 600000
Sun Oct 29 20:49:15 PST 2000:dgc:RMI TCP Connection(2)-127.0.0.1:Target.referenced:
add to dirty set: 11d1def534ea1be0:5ffb18:e2843f60ce:-7fff
Sun Oct 29 20:49:15 PST 2000:dgc:main:ObjectTable.putTarget: add object [1]
Sun Oct 29 20:49:15 PST 2000:dgc:main:WeakRef.pin: strongRef = com.ora.rmibook.
chapter9.Account_Impl[RemoteStub [ref: [endpoint:[127.0.0.1:1946](local),objID:[1]]]]
Sun Oct 29 20:49:15 PST 2000:dgc:RMI TCP Connection(2)-127.0.0.1:DGCImpl.dirty: vmid
= 11d1def534ea1be0:5ffb18:e2843f60ce:-7fff
Sun Oct 29 20:49:15 PST 2000:dgc:RMI TCP Connection(2)-127.0.0.1:DGCImpl.dirty: id =
[1], vmid = 11d1def534ea1be0:5ffb18:e2843f60ce:-7fff, duration = 600000
Sun Oct 29 20:49:15 PST 2000:dgc:RMI TCP Connection(2)-127.0.0.1:Target.referenced:
add to dirty set: 11d1def534ea1be0:5ffb18:e2843f60ce:-7fff
```

This may not seem terribly useful. In fact, most log entries aren't useful at all until they're suddenly needed to diagnose some weird problem. The main thing to take away from this example is that the log files are correlated and can be compared. If you watch the method calls, you see on which connection they came in, in this case Connection (2). Then you can correlate entries in the more detailed logs. For example, the DGC log will tell you which JVM is associated with a particular connection via the VMID argument.

Going further, here's what the transport log has to say about that same connection:

```
Sun Oct 29 20:49:15 PST 2000:transport:RMI TCP Connection(2)-127.0.0.1:
StreamRemoteCall.getInputStream
Sun Oct 29 20:49:15 PST 2000:transport:RMI TCP Connection(2)-127.0.0.1:Transport.
serviceCall: call dispatcher
Sun Oct 29 20:49:15 PST 2000:transport:RMI TCP Connection(2)-127.0.0.1:
StreamRemoteCall.getOutputStream
Sun Oct 29 20:49:15 PST 2000:transport:main:StreamRemoteCall.getInputStream
Sun Oct 29 20:49:15 PST 2000:transport:main:UnicastRef.done: free connection (reuse =
true)
```

And here's what the TCP log records:

```
Sun Oct 29 20:49:15 PST 2000:tcp:RMI TCP Connection(2)-127.0.0.1:TCPTransport.run:
accepted socket from [127.0.0.1:1948]
Sun Oct 29 20:49:15 PST 2000:tcp:RMI TCP Connection(2)-127.0.0.1:TCPTransport(1946).
run: suggesting 127.0.0.1:1948
Sun Oct 29 20:49:15 PST 2000:tcp:RMI TCP Connection(2)-127.0.0.1:TCPTransport(1946).
run: client using 127.0.0.1:0
Sun Oct 29 20:49:15 PST 2000:tcp:RMI TCP Connection(2)-127.0.0.1:TCPTransport(1946).
handleMessages: op = 80
Sun Oct 29 20:49:15 PST 2000:tcp:main:TCPChannel.free: reuse connection
Sun Oct 29 20:49:15 PST 2000:tcp:main:TCPChannel.free: create reaper
Sun Oct 29 20:49:15 PST 2000:tcp:main:TCPChannel.newConnection: reuse connection
Sun Oct 29 20:49:15 PST 2000:tcp:RMI TCP Connection(2)-127.0.0.1:TCPTransport(1946).
handleMessages: op = 82
Sun Oct 29 20:49:15 PST 2000:tcp:RMI TCP Connection(2)-127.0.0.1:TCPTransport(1946).
handleMessages: op = 80
Sun Oct 29 20:49:15 PST 2000:tcp:main:TCPChannel.free: reuse connection
```

The net effect is that, if you're diligent enough, you can deduce an enormous amount of information about your system's runtime behavior from the RMI logs.

The Debugging Log

The final log that RMI uses is the debugging log. Like the standard log, the debugging log is either on or off based on the boolean system property sun.rmi.log.debug. Unlike the standard log, however, the debugging log always records its information to System.err. The debugging log is used by the Activation daemon, which we'll discuss in Chapter 17.

Other JVM Parameters

We've now talked quite a bit about how RMI works. We've covered the basic mechanisms (sockets, streams, and serialization) and some of the higher-level facilities provided by the RMI runtime. In addition, we've mentioned system parameters that help to configure RMI's behavior.

Passing parameters to the JVM is, in fact, the main way to configure RMI. There are many parameters; most of the advanced features in RMI are highly configurable. In several of the subsequent chapters, we'll discuss additional parameters that can be used to configure the RMI runtime. In the remainder of this chapter, however, we will cover all the properties applicable to the discussion so far.

Passing Parameters to the Registry

Passing parameters via command-line flags may seem easy and convenient. However, there are still some things to watch out for. Consider the rmiregistry application that ships with the JDK. rmiregistry is a small executable that launches a Java virtual machine as part of its job. Similarly, activation will involve a small application (rmid, also called the activation daemon) that, while not a Java virtual machine, launches one.

To configure those secondary JVMs, an indirection flag is used. For the RMI registry, the indirection flag is -J. For example, the following command gives the RMI registry a maximum heap size of 256 MB of RAM and sets the security policy of the registry's JVM. This is is very important when using custom sockets, as we'll see in Chapter 18.

```
rmiregisty -J-Djava.security.policy=c:\temp\security.policy -J-Xmx256M
```

On the other hand, the activation daemon uses both -J and -C as indirection flags. -J is used as with RMI—to set flags for the activation daemon's JVM. To set the security policy for rmid's JVM, you would use:

```
rmid -J-Djava.security.policy=c:\temp\security.policy
```

The -C indirection flag, on the other hand, sets a parameter in any spawned JVM. For example:

```
rmid -C-Djava.security.policy=c:\temp\security.policy
```

This doesn't set any parameters for rmid's JVM, but does set the security policy for any JVM that rmid spawns.

Note that there is no space between -J or -C and the actual parameter that is set.

There are four basic types of parameters we'll discuss: basic Java parameters, basic RMI parameters, transport layer parameters, and parameters that affect distributed garbage collection.

 All the RMI parameters that specify a time (most often, a duration) do so in milliseconds.

Basic Java Parameters

The parameters in this section are not RMI-specific but are nonetheless important for RMI applications. At present, there are two major ones: Xms and Xmx. Both deal with the amount of memory that's available to a JVM, an issue that's fairly important to a server.

Xms

Xms specifies the starting size of the heap. In other words, it specifies how much memory the JVM consumes when it is started. The amount of memory can be specified in bytes, kilobytes or megabytes of RAM; it must be greater than 1 MB of RAM, and it must be a multiple of 1024 bytes. This flag is set according to the following pattern:

```
java [other VM arguments] -Xms###
java [other VM arguments] -Xms####K
java [other VM arguments] -Xms###M
```

A trailing M signifies megabytes, and a trailing K signifies kilobytes. Otherwise, the argument is in bytes. For example, the following three invocations are equivalent. All launch a JVM that immediately grabs 200 MB of memory:

```
java [other VM arguments] -Xms200M
java [same VM arguments] -Xms204800K
java [same VM arguments] -Xms209715200
```

The default starting heap size is 2 MB of RAM.

Xmx

The other memory allocation flag is Xmx. It has the same argument structure as Xms and similar restrictions on possible values. However, in addition to the restrictions on Xms, the value assigned to Xmx must be greater than the value assigned to Xms. This is because Xmx specifies the maximum heap size, rather than the starting heap size, and the maximum heap size has to be greater than the starting heap size.

The following three invocations are equivalent. All launch a JVM that has a maximum heap size of 200 MB of memory:

```
java [other VM arguments] -Xmx200M
java [same VM arguments] -Xmx204800K
java [same VM arguments] -Xmx209715200
```

The maximum heap size defaults to 64 MB of RAM.

Basic RMI Parameters

There are only two basic RMI parameters that we cover in this chapter: java.rmi.server.randomIDs and sun.rmi.server.exceptionTrace. The first makes a system a little more secure, and the second makes a system a little easier to debug. Neither, however, is very useful.

java.rmi.server.randomIDs

This is a boolean-valued parameter, set to either true or false. If it is set to true, it forces the RMI runtime to generate cryptographically secure object identifiers for newly exported servers. The default is false.

Because RMI shares sockets, stubs have to know the object identifier for servers to which they send messages. This means that the object identifier is encoded and sent over the wire. If a hostile entity can easily guess object identifiers, then they can more easily spoof RMI messages, and thus infiltrate a running application.

On the other hand, it's still pretty hard to spoof JRMP. In addition, it's not clear what benefit the hostile agent gets from doing so. If you are worried about hostile agents to the extent that you are considering setting this parameter to true, you should probably know more about security than this book could possibly cover.

sun.rmi.server.exceptionTrace

This is a boolean-valued parameter. It controls the behavior of the server's RMI runtime. The issue is this: suppose we have a remote method that is allowed to throw a set of exceptions. For example, our Account interface had:

```
public void makeDeposit(Money amount) throws RemoteException,
    NegativeAmountException;
```

Suppose an account server throws an instance of NegativeAmountException. The exception is caught by the RMI runtime, serialized, sent over the wire, and rethrown so that the client exception-handling mechanism can catch it and deal with it appropriately. RMI does all of this automatically.

Sometimes, however, you also want a record of the exceptions that were thrown on the server side. sun.rmi.server.exceptionTrace is designed to help in those situations. When it is set to true (it defaults to false), all thrown exceptions will be printed to System.err along with the stack traces.

When, on the other hand, un.rmi.server.exceptionTrace is set to false, nothing will be printed, and the server records will not contain any information about the exception that was thrown. In fact, they won't even indicate that an exception was thrown.

Transport Layer Parameters

Transport layer parameters are low-level parameters that directly affect RMI's use of sockets and configure RMI's use of TCP/IP. There are three transport layer parameters, all of which specify timeouts and are specific to Sun Microsystems' implementation of RMI. The transport layer parameters are: sun.rmi.transport.connectionTimeout, sun.rmi.transport.tcp.readTimeout, and sun.rmi.transport.proxy.connectTimeout.

All of the transport layer parameters are specified in milliseconds.

sun.rmi.transport.connectionTimeout

RMI attempts to reuse sockets. Between individual uses, a socket is dormant. Dormant sockets use resources. If a socket is unused for a long period of time, the benefit gained from reusing the socket might be outweighed by the resource commitment the socket requires. RMI therefore includes the sun.rmi.transport.connectionTimeout parameter, which specifies how long a socket will remain dormant before RMI closes it.

sun.rmi.transport.connectionTimeout defaults to 15 seconds (i.e., has a default value of 15,000). On slower networks, this value should be increased.

 You have to set this value on both the client and the server, since both are attempting to reuse the same socket. That is, if the server sets the value to 60 seconds and the client uses the default of 15 seconds, the client will close the socket after 15 seconds. In effect, the server's parameters are overruled by the client's parameters.

sun.rmi.transport.tcp.readTimeout

sun.rmi.transport.tcp.readTimeout is the value for the underlying socket's timeout. It controls how long RMI will wait while trying to read a byte before determining that the socket is no longer working. The value of this parameter is actually just passed directly to the socket (via the socket's setSoTimeout( ) method) whenever RMI creates a socket. If RMI attempts to read from the socket, and the socket times out, the socket will throw an instance of java.io.InterruptedIOException. RMI catches the instance of InterruptedIOException and throws a RemoteException on the client side.

sun.rmi.transport.tcp.readTimeout defaults to 2 hours (i.e., has a default value of 7,200,000).

sun.rmi.transport.proxy.connectTimeout

sun.rmi.transport.proxy.connectTimeout determines how long RMI will wait while attempting to establish a socket connection between two JVMs. If the timeout is exceeded, RMI will throw an instance of RemoteException on the client side—the client is always the JVM attempting to initiate the connection.

The default value of sun.rmi.transport.proxy.connectTimeout defaults to 15 seconds (i.e., has a default value of 15,000). On slower networks, this value should definitely be increased.

Parameters That Affect the Distributed Garbage Collector

There are five parameters that affect the behavior of the distributed garbage collector. The most important of these is java.rmi.dgc.leaseValue, which sets the duration of leases issued by the RMI runtime in a particular JVM. The other four configure how the system deals with expired leases.

java.rmi.dgc.leaseValue

This parameter only affects servers; it is used to set a standard duration for leases granted by a particular server. It is specified in milliseconds, and it defaults to 10 minutes (i.e., the default value is 600,000).

There are several factors to consider when altering this value. If leases last for a long time, the server runtime will keep references to servers for long periods of time when a client behaves badly. Since the point of distributed garbage collection is to enable the server to release resources, this may not be a good thing when either the client application or the intervening network are unstable.

On the other hand, short-lived leases have problems as well. They result in increased network traffic (leases must be renegotiated fairly often) and make the application much more sensitive to temporary network problems. For example, if the network goes down for longer than the duration of a lease, the server might very well clean up a server, even if the client is still trying to use the server.

This last point is especially important—your application may suffer performance problems if you grant long-lived leases. But the consequences of leases that are too short are almost certainly worse; it's not just performance that is affected, but functionality as well.

Also note that leases are intended to be much larger than the typical network latency for a request. Clients try to renew leases when they are halfway over. Suppose you tried to have a very short lease time, relative to your network latency. For example, you tried to grant 15-second leases on a slow, congested network. Something like the following sequence of events may occur:

1. The client runtime requests a lease.
2. Five seconds later, the server runtime gets the request and grants a 15-second lease.
3. Five seconds later, the client runtime gets the response and starts a timer going.
4. Seven seconds later, the client running attempts to renew the lease.
5. Five seconds later, the server runtime gets the renewal request. However, by this time, 17 seconds have elapsed since the server runtime granted the lease, and the server runtime may already have released the server for garbage collection.

This is undesirable; leases that are too short are, essentially, unrenewable. This can render an application unusable.

The fact that clients try to renew leases when they are halfway expired suggests another rule of thumb: if bandwidth is a concern, then the typical lease should be more than twice the length of an average client session. This minimizes the network overhead due to the client lease (in the average case, a single call to dirty( ) and a single call to clean( )) while still allowing the distributed garbage collector to do its work.

We should admit one further thing. Setting lease durations is very much fine-grained tuning of an application. It doesn't actually affect the design of your application and should only be done once the application is deployed and a problem is noticed.

sun.rmi.dgc.client.gcInterval

This parameter configures client runtime behavior. The basic question is this: how often does RMI check to see whether a stub is no longer referenced by the rest of the client application? Once a stub is not referenced by the rest of the client application, the client runtime is free to send a clean( ) message to the server runtime.

sun.rmi.dgc.client.gcInterval is specified in milliseconds and defaults to 1 minute (i.e., the default value is 60,000).

The trade-off here is client-side computational resources versus improved server latency. That is, decreasing this value will result in increased client overhead but potentially release server resources faster.

How does the runtime know when a stub is no longer referenced by the client application? The answer is complicated. But the basic idea is that the RMI runtime doesn't really retain references to the stub. Instead, it uses instances of WeakReference (defined in the java.lang.ref package). A weak reference is a reference that does not prevent an object from being garbage collected. That is, if the object referred to has no other references other than weak references, an attempt to get the actual reference from weak references will return null. Otherwise, the weak reference can be used to get a valid reference to the object. The RMI runtime retains weak references to stubs. If the weak reference resolves to null, the RMI runtime knows that no other part of the client application has a reference to the stub and that, therefore, it should call clean( ) on the server.

At a minimum, the RMI runtime checks whether the weak reference resolves to null before renewing a lease. However, the RMI runtime also does periodic checks of all the stubs to which it has weak references. That's what sun.rmi.dgc.client. gcInterval is really controlling.

sun.rmi.dgc.server.gcInterval

This is similar to sun.rmi.dgc.client.gcInterval; the difference is that this controls the server side's refresh rate for distributed garbage collection. The server receives a number of clean( ) messages and also occasionally expires leases. This parameter controls how often the server examines the consequences of these actions and attempts to determine whether unreferenced( ) should be called.

`sun.rmi.dgc.server.gcInterval` is specified in milliseconds and defaults to 1 minute (i.e., the default value is 60,000).

sun.rmi.dgc.checkInterval

This specifies how often RMI checks for expired leases. That is, the server runtime maintains a list of active leases, including the time they were granted. Every so often, a background thread goes through the list looking for leases that have expired.

`sun.rmi.dgc.checkInterval` is specified in milliseconds and defaults to 5 minutes (i.e., the default value is 300,000).

There is a relationship between this value and that of `java.rmi.dgc.leaseValue`: they should be reasonably proportional, taking into account the number of clients. That is, if you expect to have 5 clients with long-lived sessions, and they're consequently getting leases that last for 24 hours, it makes very little sense to set `sun.rmi.dgc.checkInterval` to check for expired leases every 5 seconds.

The rule of thumb: if you expect a lease to expire every n seconds, then you should set `sun.rmi.dgc.checkInterval` to approximately `1000*n` (1,000 because, like all the duration parameters, this is specified in milliseconds).

sun.rmi.dgc.cleanInterval

This is a retry parameter for clients. If a client calls `clean( )` and the operation fails (e.g., if the network is down), this parameter specifies how long the client waits before trying to call `clean( )` again. It defaults to 3 minutes (180,000 milliseconds). Of the parameters that affect distributed garbage collection, `sun.rmi.dgc.cleanInterval` is the least important.

CHAPTER 17

Factories and the Activation Framework

In Chapters 14 and 15, we discussed how to build a better naming service, one that has a great deal more flexibility than the RMI registry and enables easier lookup of specific servers. However, applications that could potentially have millions of servers still require more infrastructure to help them deal with resource management. In this chapter, we'll discuss the most common way of achieving this, the factory pattern, and how it is supported in RMI. To do this, we'll implement a basic factory directly, and then implement similar functionality using RMI's activation framework.

Resource Management

Our bank example has so far been a small-scale application. While Account is a fairly flexible interface, and you may think you can support millions of accounts using our new naming service and one of the implementations of Account that we've discussed, the fact of the matter is that more infrastructure is required.

To see why, consider the Bank of America advertisement quoted in Chapter 5:

> When traveling, take advantage of more than 13,000 Bank of America ATMs coast to coast. We're in 30 states and the District of Columbia. As a Bank of America Check Card or ATM cardholder, there's no ATM fee when you use an ATM displaying a Bank of America sign...
>
> —Bank of America advertisement

That's 13,000 dedicated client machines. Plus, there are the client applications running inside each branch of the bank, the central reporting and analysis applications each division of the bank runs, and all the new Internet services that our hypothetical bank wants to roll out over the next few years.

In short, we have the following situation:

A potentially unbounded number of client applications running over a period of time. Practically speaking, there won't be many more clients running than there are accounts. So a good upper boundary on the number of clients is the number of open accounts. For a large bank, this can be over 10 million.

Most servers will be active occasionally. Most people look at their account balances and information at least once a month. In addition, automatic bill-paying programs and other advanced services will probably require access to account information.

Most servers will be inactive most of the time. Most people don't look at their account balances and information more than once a day. Since such usage, along with monthly and weekly reporting functionality, is the vast majority of anticipated use, it follows that most accounts will be inactive most of the time.

Most clients want to access a small number of accounts for a short period of time. We're assuming our previous model of client-interaction is probably correct for most applications.

We also know that each JVM has a limited number of available sockets and, as a practical matter, will run into problems supporting large numbers of clients.

 How many clients can a JVM support? It depends on the application, of course. The absolute limit, based on the number of sockets a process can open, is around 1,000 for most operating systems. But reports from the trenches occasionally suggest that a more reasonable limit for an RMI server is between 150 and 200 simultaneous client connections from distinct client computers. Once past that, the RMI runtime apparently bogs down.

Suppose we take the current implementation and try to make it scale, using the following seat-of-the-pants assumptions:

* There are 10 million accounts.
* We launch 200 accounts per JVM.
* We run 25 JVMs per machine on our server farm.

Simple arithmetic leads us to conclude that we need 2,000 servers on our server farm, which is, quite honestly, a ridiculous number. Consuming vast amounts of resources to keep mostly idle servers available on a 24/7 basis is a bad idea.

Moreover, 2,000 server computers, running 50,000 JVMs, would completely overwhelm any distributed garbage collection scheme based on a centralized naming service. The fact of the matter is, we can't take our existing architecture, move servers to different JVMs, and then scale to millions of servers.

 Looking at the numbers reveals a surprising assumption: our calculations assume that a server computer is capable of handling 5,000 clients (25 JVMS times 200 clients per JVM). This is quite a bit on the high side. However, this is good for a seat-of-the-pants estimate. Replacing our numbers with more reasonable ones only leads to an increase in the number of computers required.

In Part I, we used multiple instances of Account for our servers. The main reason for this decision was that, by and large, smaller servers are easier to write, maintain, and verify.

However, the previous discussion may cause you to revisit that decision. After all, if we went with the bank option, servers wouldn't be account-specific. Instead, account identifiers would get passed in as arguments with each method call. This partially solves the resource problem we've been discussing. We can assume:

- There are 10 million accounts (but this is irrelevant).
- We launch 1 server per JVM.
- We run 25 JVMs per machine on our server farm.

Hence, the number of server machines we need is simply a function of our expected number of clients. Each computer in the server farm is capable of handling 5,000 simultaneous clients.[*] If we expect to handle 20,000 simultaneous client requests, then we need only 10 or so servers, building in a margin of error for peak activity.

This is a dilemma. As developers, we'd like to go with the account servers. But, from a deployment point of view, the bank option looks compelling.

Factories

Fortunately for us, this problem is easy to solve. All we have to do is find a crucial underlying assumption and then reject it utterly. In this case, the assumption is this: the server must already be running when the client attempts to connect to it.

At first glance, this seems like an eminently reasonable assumption to make. After all, the idea of client-server computing is based on the idea that the client and the server are programs running on different machines. This means that the client can't launch the server. Moreover, even if this was possible, allowing the client to do so would probably involve security holes you could drive a truck through.

What the client can do, however, is ask an intermediate server to start the account server running. This intermediate server is usually called the *factory*.

> In distributed computing, the term factory usually refers to a server whose sole purpose in life is to start, and shut down, other servers in response to client requests.

When we add a factory, our application architecture looks something like the diagram shown in Figure 17-1.

---

[*] Again, not really. See the note about unrealistic assumptions.

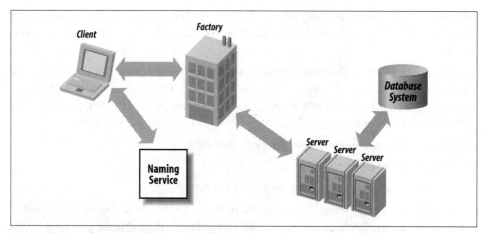

Figure 17-1. Application architecture with factories

The idea is that the client uses the factory in much the same way as it used a naming service. That is, we have the following three-step procedure for a client application:

1. The client calls the naming service to get a reference to the factory. The naming service isn't quite as necessary as it used to be, since there is only one factory (designs that involve multiple factories are few and far between). However, whether a naming service is used or not, the client must somehow obtain a reference to the factory.

2. The client calls the factory to get a reference to a particular account server. The factory, which is not at all generic, is obligated to return a reference to a server that implements Account. Because it acts as an intermediary for the client, however, it has the opportunity to launch an account server (and return a reference to the server that it just launched).

3. The client uses the account server.

Revisiting Our Basic Design

One consequence of our decision to use the Account interface has now become apparent. In order to reduce our application's resource consumption and enable it to scale, we need to write another server: our factory. This second server has nothing to do with the "business logic" we're attempting to implement. Instead, it serves as a sort of remote constructor.

This is fairly disturbing. If the factory is difficult to implement, or substantially complicates the implementations of the other components in the system, then maybe we should reconsider going with the bank option. Fortunately, factories are pretty simple pieces of code and can easily be added to our current system. We'll implement a basic factory in the next section; the actual factory code is straightforward, the server implementations don't need any changes at all, and using our factory requires relatively few changes to the client.

The fact that the factory has no business logic, and looks like a generic solution to a common problem, may seem to imply that RMI should have facilities for automatically doing this sort of thing. Actually, it does. In JDK 1.2 and beyond, you can use the RMI activation framework instead of implementing your own factory. We'll discuss the activation framework later in this chapter.

Moreover, the additional layer of indirection provided by a factory gives us three fairly substantial benefits:

Factories are the ideal places to insert extra querying functionality. To a client program, the factory looks a lot like a naming service: clients query the factory and receive stubs for a server. This means that a factory is an ideal place to put application-specific querying functionality, should the application require it.

Factories are very useful for tracking usage patterns (logging and debugging). A factory is, by definition, a place that all clients need to visit before they gain access to a server. If you want to track resource usage or client-behavior patterns, the factory is a wonderful place to start.[*]

Factories enable fine-grained control of the server lifecycle. Right now, our discussion centers around starting and stopping servers. But there's a lot more that a factory can do. In particular, questions about when to make data persistent are easier to resolve when you're using a factory-based architecture. We'll return to this topic a little later in the chapter.

Implementing a Generic Factory

In order to implement a factory for our bank example, we need to deal with three basic problems. The first, clearly, is actually implementing the factory. The second is adapting the existing code to use the factory. The third is revisiting some of the more esoteric functionality we implemented, such as the automatic locking mechanism in Chapter 12.

We will implement a generic factory first, in order to show the basic idea. In this simple factory, the client will request a server from the factory and tell the factory when it is no longer interested in the server.

A Basic Factory

The interface to our factory consists of two methods:

```
public interface BasicFactory extends Remote {
    public Account getAccount(String accountName) throws RemoteException;
```

---

[*] So is a naming service. There are two distinctions. First, a naming service isn't application-specific (and other applications might be using it). Second, factory code is easier to modify (it's project-specific).

```
        public void doneWithAccount(String accountName) throws RemoteException;
    }
```

The idea is this: because the client explicitly signals interest in a server and announces when it is done with a server, the factory will be able to directly manage the servers, shutting down those that are no longer active.

In order to implement this factory, we need to solve two basic problems:

- We need to store enough information in the factory so it can create the servers when they are requested.

- We need to make sure that, if the same account is simultaneously requested by two different clients, the factory doesn't create two different servers.

The first problem is nothing new. We had to solve it before in our launch code. In the real world, the factory would probably query a database to get the information. For the purpose of this chapter, however, we'll simply hardwire in some values:

```
public class BasicFactory_Impl extends UnicastRemoteObject implements Factory {
    private HashMap _namesToAccounts;
    private HashMap _accountsToSupport;
    private Integer _one = new Integer(1);

    public Factory_Impl() throws RemoteException {
        createServers();
        _accountsToSupport = new HashMap();
    }
    private void createServers() {
        _namesToAccounts = new HashMap();
        addAccount("Bob", 10000);
        addAccount("Alex", 1223);
        addAccount("Trish", 1894);
        addAccount("Pat", 3970);
        addAccount("David", 120056);
        addAccount("Mary", 21283);
    }

    private void addAccount(String name, int cents) {
        Integer Cents = new Integer(cents);
        try {
            Account_Impl newAccount = new Account_Impl(new Money(Cents));
            _namesToAccounts.put(name, newAccount);
        }
        catch (Exception e) {System.out.println(e);}
    }
```

What's going on here is simple. We create a HashMap of Account_Impl objects, which we will then query for the appropriate instance of Account_Impl.

 It's worth repeating that this is an ad hoc, hardwired solution to an application-specific problem. In reality, creating all the servers and storing them in a HashMap at launch time goes a long way towards defeating the whole purpose of a factory.

After this, it may seem that getAccount( )/doneWithAccount( ) should be straightforward. Here, for example, is what getAccount( ) must do:

1. Find the instance of Account_Impl associated with the request
2. Make this object available over the network, using UnicastRemoteObjects's exportObject( ) method
3. Return a stub so the client can communicate with the newly exported server

This is exactly what we do. The only complication comes from the objection I noted earlier: we don't want to export the same server more than once. We especially don't want to unexport it prematurely in the doneWithAccount( ) method. This means we need to keep track of the number of clients that are currently using the server. We do this using an instance of Hashmap, which maps server instances to instances of java.lang.Integer.

With that in mind, here's the implementation of getAccount( ) and doneWithAccount( ):

```java
public synchronized Account getAccount(String accountName) throws RemoteException {
    Account account = (Account) _namesToAccounts.get(accountName); // This
                                        should really create the server
    if (null==account) {
        return null;
    }
    Integer support = (Integer) _accountsToSupport.get(account);
    if (null==support) {
        try {
            RemoteStub stub = (RemoteStub) UnicastRemoteObject.
                exportObject(account);
            System.out.println("Account " + accountName + " successfully
                exported.");
            support = _one;
        }
        catch (Exception e) {
            System.out.println(e);
            return null;
        }
    }
    else {
        support = new Integer(support.intValue( ) +1);
    }
    _accountsToSupport.put(account, support);
    return account;
}

public void doneWithAccount(String accountName) throws RemoteException {
    Account account = (Account) _namesToAccounts.get(accountName);
    if (null==account) {
        return;
    }
    Integer support = (Integer) _accountsToSupport.get(account);
    if (null==support) {
        System.out.println("Attempt to unexport non-supported account");
```

```
            return;
        }
        int newSupportValue = support.intValue( ) - 1;
        if (newSupportValue>0)
            _accountsToSupport.put(account, new Integer(newSupportValue));
            return;
        }
        try {
            UnicastRemoteObject.unexportObject(account, true);
            System.out.println("Account " + accountName +
                " successfully unexported.");
            _accountsToSupport.remove(account);
        }
        catch (Exception e) {
            System.out.println(e);
        }
    }
}
```

When a server is first requested, _accountsToSupport contains an instance of Integer with a value of 1. Every additional client request for that server increments the value in accountsToSupport. When clients call doneWithAccount( ), the value is decremented. When the value reaches 0 again, the server is unexported. We should point out, however, that in this last step, when the client is unexported, a factory typically takes further action, instead of simply leaving the server object in a HashMap.

This is, in effect, a very crude version of garbage collection that relies on the client's good behavior. If clients don't call doneWithAccount( ), or call it too many times, bad things can happen. Also, second thoughts probably tell us that, for the bank example, reference counting in our application is probably a bad idea. We don't want to vend an account more than once.

Modifying the Existing Application

The various versions of our banking application have consisted of three distinct pieces of code: the client code, the server code, and the launch code. When examining the impact of an architectural change, it's often useful to try and gauge the impact separately for each of these pieces. If for no other reason, it lends some structure to the planning process.

The consequences for the client

From the client's point of view, this is a little more complicated than the first version of our application. The flow of control is:

1. The client contacts the naming service to get the factory's stub.

2. The client contacts the factory to get an account.

3. The client talks to the account.

4. The client then tells the factory it is done with the account.

However, this complexity, while it inserts another layer of abstraction into the client program, doesn't involve a lot of extra work. When you actually look at the code, the client really only needs a few extra lines of code, in the getAccount( ) and releaseAccount( ) methods. For example, the getAccount( ) method changes from:

```
private void getAccount( ) {
    try {
        _account = (Account)Naming.lookup(_accountNameField.getText( ));
    }
    catch (Exception e) {
        System.out.println("Couldn't find account. Error was \n " + e);
        e.printStackTrace( );
    }
    return;
}
```

to:

```
private void getAccount( ) {
    try {
        Factory factory = (Factory)Naming.lookup(ACCOUNT_FACTORY_NAME);
        _account = factory.getAccount(_accountNameField.getText( ));
    }
    catch (Exception e) {
        System.out.println("Couldn't find account. Error was \n " + e);
        e.printStackTrace( );
    }
    return;
}
```

The consequences for the naming service

The naming service has a much simpler task in this new application architecture. Instead of knowing about and keeping stubs for each and every account, the naming service simply needs to keep a single stub for the factory.

This doesn't actually involve a change in the naming service's functionality. However, it does mean that the application consumes a much smaller percentage of the naming service's resources. This means that we can probably use a single naming service, located and maintained on a central server, for multiple applications.

The consequences for the account servers

There are almost no consequences for the servers implementing the Account interface. We have chosen to use servers that don't extend UnicastRemote, in order to maximize control over exactly when an object listens for client connections. But the actual functionality we implemented in the account servers does not change at all. In other words:

> What changes in this new architecture is when the servers are launched and when they're shut down. The actual implementation of the account server doesn't need to change at all.

A Better Factory

Now that we've implemented a factory, and the basic idea of managing servers in response to client's actions doesn't seem so fearsome, it's time to think about automating the process. One of the points I've made more than once in this book is that the server should not rely on the client behaving correctly. This applies to arguments passed from the client to the server, which should always be validated, and even more strongly to the idea that clients will release a server when they're done with it.

In this section, we'll discuss how the factory is similar to some previously implemented pieces of code and use these to talk about how our factory can be improved.

Some Prior Art

In Chapter 12, we implemented an automatic locking mechanism for our servers. The basic idea can be summarized as follows:

> More than one client may want to access a particular account at a time. However, since a client could be making multiple calls (e.g., getting the balance and then making a withdrawal) from within a transaction, we need a way to lock an account when a client accesses it and relinquish the lock when the client is done with it.

Our first pass at this was to simply add two more methods to the Account interface.

```
public void getLock( ) throws RemoteException, LockedAccountException;
public void releaseLock( ) throws RemoteException;
```

Here, we relied on the client application to call getLock( ) and releaseLock( ) at the appropriate times.

After we implemented this, we then reimplemented the functionality using a background thread. In this second implementation, calling a method on the server automatically locked the server. And the lock was automatically released if the server was inactive for a long enough period of time. This latter implementation had two major advantages. First, it required less bandwidth and fewer remote method calls. Second, if a client crashed, or if the network failed, the server would eventually be unlocked again.

Building on the Account-Locking Mechanism

The point of discussing our account-locking scheme is that the current factory system, which uses reference counting, is a lot like locking accounts. Conceptually:

```
public void getLock( ) throws RemoteException, LockedAccountException;
public void releaseLock( ) throws RemoteException;
```

and:

```
public Account getAccount(String accountName) throws RemoteException;
public void doneWithAccount(String accountName) throws RemoteException;
```

are very closely related. What's more, they're both just slightly less complicated versions of the dgc interface we discussed in Chapter 6:

```
public void clean(ObjID[] ids, long sequenceNum, VMID vmid, boolean strong)
public Lease dirty(ObjID[] ids, long sequenceNum, Lease lease)
```

Indeed, our automatic locking mechanism, which extended the lock's duration whenever a method was called and then expired the lock after enough time elapsed, is very similar to leasing. We don't negotiate the duration of the lock, and the lock is automatically renewed, but the idea is the same.

Our goal is to improve our factory by taking advantage of this insight. Of course, as we do so, our new factory won't be quite as generic. In particular, we will do the following two things:

- Manage the account locks in the factory. Rather than have each account maintain a lock, we'll let the factory maintain the locks. When a client calls the factory, the factory knows whether the server is available or not. If the server has already been exported, the factory tells the client the server is unavailable (e.g., that it has been locked). Otherwise, the factory sends the stub to the client.

- Have the servers call the factory back when they're no longer referenced. That is, when an account server becomes unreferenced, it will call the factory to announce that it is, once again, available. This way, we don't have to implement a background thread and expire the lock when the server is no longer being accessed; instead we'll just use lease expiration to handle that detail.

This design has all the benefits of the locking mechanism we discussed in Chapter 12. It reduces the number of remote method calls the client has to make and safeguards the locking mechanism against either client or network failures. In addition, there's another fairly nice benefit: it enables a primitive form of distributed transaction management. Recall that one of the major problems with the transferMoney( ) method was that it required two servers to be locked. Therefore, two clients could wind up in a deadlock in the following situations:

- Client 1 wants to transfer money from account A to account B.
- Client 2 wants to transfer money from account B to account A.

We now have a central mechanism for requesting accounts, much like the one we used to request them from the naming service. However, there's no reason to restrict it to a request for a single account. We could, for example, create a new value object called ServerList and extend the interface with a single method called getAccounts( ):

```
public interface LockingFactory extends Remote {
    public Remote getAccount(String accountName) throws RemoteException;
    public ServerList getAccounts(String[] accountNames) throws RemoteException;
    public void serverNoLongerActive(String accountName) throws RemoteException;
}
```

If we require the clients to get all the relevant account stubs before they perform any transactions, we have, albeit in a fairly clumsy fashion, enabled the implementation of transferMoney( ) functionality.

The new factory

Because it no longer maintains a count of the number of times it has vended a server, our new factory is a bit simpler than the basic factory. Here's the code for the abstract superclass, LockingFactory_Impl:

```
public abstract class LockingFactory_Impl extends UnicastRemoteObject implements
    LockingFactory {
    protected abstract Remote _getAccount(String accountName);

    private HashMap _lockedaccountNames;
    public LockingFactory_Impl( ) throws RemoteException {
        _lockedaccountNames = new HashMap( );
    }

    public synchronized Remote getAccount(String accountName) throws RemoteException,
        LockedServerException {
        Remote returnValue = getAccount(accountName);
        _lockedaccountNames.put(accountName, accountName);
        return returnValue;
    }

    public synchronized Remote[] getAccounts(String[] accountNames) throws
        RemoteException, LockedServerException {
        Remote[] returnValue = new Remote[accountNames.length];
        int counter;
        for (counter = 0; counter < accountNames.length; counter ++) {
            try {
                checkLock(accountNames[counter]);
                Remote nextServer = getAccount(accountNames[counter]);
                returnValue[counter] = nextServer;
            }
            catch (LockedServerException serverLocked) {
                int returnCounter;
                for (returnCounter = 0; returnCounter < counter; returnCounter ++)
                {
                    serverNoLongerActive(accountNames[returnCounter]);
                }
            }
            throw serverLocked;
        }
        return returnValue;
    }

    public synchronized void serverNoLongerActive(String accountName) throws
        RemoteException {
        _lockedaccountNames.remove(accountName);
    }
```

```
                private synchronized void checkLock(String accountName) throws
                    LockedServerException {
                    if (null!=_lockedaccountNames.get(accountName)) {
                        throw new LockedServerException(accountName);
                    }
                    return;
                }
            }
```

There's one important subtlety in how this works. Because the entire locking mechanism relies upon the Unreferenced interface, the factory can never store a stub on any
account servers. If the factory held a stub to an account server, the factory would
maintain a lease to the server and, therefore, unreferenced( ) would never be called.
Hence, the account would never be unlocked.

This means that the protected method _getAccount( ) actually needs to create the
account servers (or cause them to be created), when it is called. For now, we'll ignore
this issue and simply hardwire the server creation code in a concrete subclass; the
Activation Framework provides a convenient way to handle automatically launching
servers.

Here's the code for LockingAccountFactory_Impl, a concrete subclass of LockingFactory_
Impl that simply creates accounts with random balances:

```
        public class LockingAccountFactory_Impl extends LockingFactory_Impl {
            public LockingAccountFactory_Impl( ) throws RemoteException {
            }

            protected Remote _getAccount(String accountName) {
                try {
                    Account returnValue = new Account_Impl(getRandomMoney( ), accountName);
                    returnValue.setFactory(this);
                    return returnValue;
                }
                catch (Exception ignored) {/* Creation of a local object should never fail*/

                    return null;
                }
            }

            private Money getRandomMoney( ) {
                int cents =  (int) (Math.random( ) * 100000);
                return new Money(cents);
            }
        }
```

The new account

Our new version of Account_Impl is one of the simpler implementations of Account
we've written. It needs two extra fields to store its name and a stub to the factory,
and it implements the Unreferenced interface, but other than those minor changes, it

is the same as the very first implementation of Account we wrote back in Chapter 8. Here's the code:

```
public class Account_Impl extends UnicastRemoteObject implements Account,
    Unreferenced {
    private Money _balance;
    private LockingFactory _factory;
    private String _accountName;

    public Account_Impl(Money startingBalance, String accountName) throws
        RemoteException {
        _balance = startingBalance;
        _accountName = accountName;
    }

    public synchronized Money getBalance() throws RemoteException {
        return _balance;
    }

    public synchronized void makeDeposit(Money amount) throws RemoteException,
        NegativeAmountException {
        checkForNegativeAmount(amount);
        _balance.add(amount);
        return;
    }

    public synchronized void makeWithdrawal(Money amount) throws RemoteException,
        OverdraftException, NegativeAmountException
    {
        checkForNegativeAmount(amount);
        checkForOverdraft(amount);
        _balance.subtract(amount);
        return;
    }

    public void setFactory(LockingFactory factory) throws RemoteException {
        _factory = factory;
    }

    private void checkForNegativeAmount(Money amount) throws NegativeAmountException
        {
        int cents = amount.getCents();
        if (0 > cents) {
            throw new NegativeAmountException();
        }
    }

    private void checkForOverdraft(Money amount) throws OverdraftException {
        if (amount.greaterThan(_balance)) {
            throw new OverdraftException(false);
        }
```

```
        return;
    }

    public void unreferenced( ) {
        if (null==_factory)  {
            return;
        }
        try {
            _factory.serverNoLongerActive(_accountName);
        }
        catch(RemoteException e) {/* Factory is having issues*/}
        _factory = null;
    }
}
```

The launch code and the client

The launch code and the client for this version of the bank example are essentially the same as they were for the version based on BasicAccountFactory_Impl. The only difference is that BankClientFrame's releaseAccount( ) method no longer needs to tell the factory that it is done with a particular account server. releaseAccount( ) is accordingly much simpler:

```
private void releaseAccount( )  {
    _account=null;
    return ;
}
```

Persistence and the Server Lifecycle

We've been talking about factories as convenient generalizations of the idea of a naming service: a factory is just a naming service that can launch servers. Another way to think about the idea of a factory server is that it's really a generalization of the idea of a class object. That is, the factories we've been implementing are objects with a set of constructors and maintain information about all the instances of Account, much the same way that a class object can have static information that is not specific to any particular instance of the class.

We've already come close to this idea with LockingFactory_Impl. It also allows a client to lock a set of servers in a single method call. The next step is to note that LockingFactory_Impl can also, should we so desire, control other aspects of the server's lifecycle.

Suppose, for example, we were to change the definition of serverNoLongerActive( ) to the following:

```
public void serverNoLongerActive(String accountName, Remote server) throws
    RemoteException;
```

The factory now gets both the name of the server and a stub to the server when the server is otherwise unreferenced. At which point, the factory can do things such as:

Implement a simple external persistence layer. That is, the factory can query the server for state information, which the factory then stores in a relational database before the server is garbage collected.

Tell the server to persist itself. This is a more object-oriented version of the first point. If there's no real reason the factory ought to know anything about the server's state, the persistence code probably belongs inside `Account_Impl`.

Keep the stub inside an indexed data structure in case it is needed again. By doing this, the factory keeps the server up and running. This is a potential performance optimization, based on the idea that a certain percentage of users forget to perform a transaction and wind up requesting the server a second time.

In this model, the factory tracks resource consumption and releases unused servers either after a significant period of time (e.g., they aren't being used by any client and haven't been requested in 20 minutes) or if resources become tight.

The essential point is simple: if you have something that creates objects, and knows when they're due for garbage collection, as `LockingFactory_Impl` does, then you have a perfect place to insert code that performs all sorts of secondary maintenance tasks.

 Really interested in this idea? Check out the Enterprise JavaBeans specification or see *Enterprise JavaBeans, Second Edition* by Richard Monson-Haefel (O'Reilly). An Enterprise JavaBeans "container" is a variation on this design, with explicitly labelled hooks for persistence and transactional control.

Activation

So far, we've sketched the basic motivation for factories, and talked a little bit about things such as distributed lock management and the basic functionality that a well-implemented factory can add to an application. We've waved our hands, however, at one of the harder parts: actually launching servers.

There's a good reason for this. As of Java 2, RMI includes a very generic and reusable factory implementation, called the Activation Framework, which handles the details of launching servers on remote machines quite nicely, and does so in a way that's completely transparent to clients.

The key to the activation framework is the *activation daemon*, a.k.a. the `rmid` program. The RMI activation daemon is an RMI server, just like the RMI registry, whose sole purpose is to launch Java servers. The topology of a distributed application is shown in Figure 17-2.

Note that when I say that the activation daemon is an RMI server, I mean precisely that. It is an RMI server that implements the `ActivationSystem` interface, has stubs

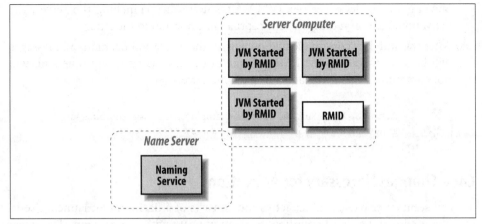

Figure 17-2. Topology for an application using activatable servers

and skeletons, passes serialized objects, and behaves according to the same rules and principles as any other RMI server. In fact, it's not a particularly complex server either; you know more than enough to implement it yourself at this point. The JVMs that are launched by the activation daemon also contain RMI servers, instances of ActivationGroup, that launch the actual servers.

On the client side, the Activation Framework works by using slightly smarter stubs. Ordinary RMI stubs have all the information necessary to send messages to an instance of a particular server. Activation stubs have all that information too. But they also have information about an instance of an activation daemon somewhere. And client-server communication works as follows:

1. When a stub for an activatable server is created and bound into a naming service, the stub has information only about the activation daemon and not about the server to which the stub will eventually refer. This is because that server has not been created yet. It will be created by the activation framework when clients start to send method calls to it.

2. When a client retrieves an activatable stub, the client doesn't know that the stub has no associated server. Activation is totally transparent to the client.

3. The first time the client makes a method call on its stub, the stub doesn't call the server (which may not be running yet). Instead, the stub calls the activation daemon (more precisely, it calls the instance of Activator within the daemon) and asks it for information about the server.

4. When the activation daemon is asked about a particular server, the daemon first checks to see if the server has already been launched. If the server hasn't already been launched, the daemon does so at this point. It is important to note that the activation daemon never launches a server in the rmid process. Instead, the activation daemon launches servers in other JVMs that it has also launched. (Note that many servers may reside in a single JVM. The activation daemon is not

launching a single server per JVM.) After it finishes launching the server, the activation daemon returns the appropriate information to the stub.

5. After the stub has communicated once with the activation daemon, all messages will be sent directly to the RMI runtime of the associated server. The stub will not communicate with the activation daemon ever again.

 Activation stubs are yet another example of a classic computer-programming maxim: *Got a problem? Add a layer of indirection.*

Code Changes Necessary for Activation

This all seems pretty reasonable; activation consists of a daemon that launches servers, along with stubs that know how to communicate with the daemon. The question then becomes: how do you incorporate activation into your application? The answer is that you have to do two things: modify the servers to become activatable objects and modify the launch code.

Making a server into an activatable object

All of our servers so far have used UnicastRemoteObject in order to be tied to the RMI runtime. This has happened in one of two ways. Either the server has extended UnicastRemoteObject, or the launch code has used one of the static export methods defined on UnicastRemoteObject to create a stub for the server.

In order to use a server with the activation framework, we need to change this. Instead of using UnicastRemoteObject, we need to extend the Activatable class (which is defined in the java.rmi.activation package) or use one of the static export methods defined on the Activatable class to create a stub for the server. That is, Activatable is used in a way that is exactly parallel to UnicastRemoteObject.

However, while Activatable is used in a way that's exactly parallel to UnicastRemoteObject, the methods that Activatable defines can take more, and more types of, arguments. Here, for example, are the constructors and export methods from Activatable:

```
protected Activatable(ActivationID id, int port)
protected Activatable(ActivationID id, int port, RMIClientSocketFactory csf,
    RMIServerSocketFactory ssf)
protected Activatable(String location, MarshalledObject data, boolean restart, int
    port)
protected Activatable(String location, MarshalledObject data, boolean restart, int
    port, RMIClientSocketFactory csf, RMIServerSocketFactory ssf)
public static Remote exportObject(Remote obj, ActivationID id, int port)
public static Remote exportObject(Remote obj, ActivationID id, int port,
    RMIClientSocketFactory csf,  RMIServerSocketFactory ssf)
public static ActivationID exportObject(Remote obj, String location, MarshalledObject
    data, boolean restart, int port)
```

```
public static ActivationID exportObject(Remote obj, String location, MarshalledObject
    data, boolean restart, int port, RMIClientSocketFactory csf,
    RMIServerSocketFactory ssf)
```

 For now, we'll continue ignoring the socket factories, a policy we first adopted in Chapter 8. Socket factories will be thoroughly covered in Chapter 18.

There are two new classes here: `ActivationID` and `MarshalledObject`. `ActivationID` is a globally unique identifier that contains the information the activation daemon needs to uniquely identify a particular server. In particular, it contains both an `ObjectID` for the server that will be activated (we discussed the `ObjectID` class in Chapter 16) and a reference to the activation daemon. For the most part, instances of `ActivationID` are created by the Activation Framework and passed into the Activation Framework without being altered by your code.

`MarshalledObject` is a wrapper class; an instance of `MarshalledObject` has only one purpose: encapsulating a serialized instance of another class. Instances of `MarshalledObject` are created by passing in an instance of a serializable class as an argument to the constructor. Once created, an instance of `MarshalledObject` has only one useful method, `get( )`, which is used to retrieve the instance stored in the instance of `MarshalledObject`.

The point of using `MarshalledObject` is that it defines a way for launch code to pass data to servers that will be launched at a later time. When instances of `MarshalledObject` are used to help create activatable servers, the following sequence occurs:

1. Instances of `MarshalledObject` are created by your launch code, which passes in a serializable object to `MarshalledObject`'s constructor. This object is serialized using RMI's customized version of the serialization mechanism.[*] The instance of `MarshalledObject` stores the output of serialization as a sequence of bytes.

2. The instances of `MarshalledObject` are passed into the Activation Framework. `MarshalledObject` is, itself, a serializable class.

3. The instances of `MarshalledObject` are stored by the Activation Framework. Eventually, when the servers are actually launched, copies of the instances of `MarshalledObject` are passed to the constructor of an activatable server. The activatable server is responsible for calling `get( )` on the instance of `MarshalledObject` (if appropriate), thereby getting deserialized copies of the original serialized object. This process is shown in Figure 17-3.

---

[*] See Chapter 10 for more details on this.

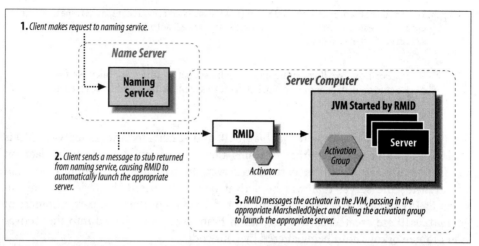

1. Client makes request to naming service.

Name Server

Naming Service

Server Computer

JVM Started by RMID

RMID

Activation Group

Server

Activator

2. Client sends a message to stub returned from naming service, causing RMID to automatically launch the appropriate server.

3. RMID messages the activator in the JVM, passing in the appropriate MarshelledObject and telling the activation group to launch the appropriate server.

Figure 17-3. Launching an individual server

Consider, for example, the constructor from the activatable version of `Account_Impl`:

```
public class Account_Impl extends Activatable implements Account {
    private Money _balance;
    public Account_Impl(ActivationID id, MarshalledObject data) throws
        RemoteException {
        super(id, 0);
        try {
            _balance = (Money) data.get();
        }
        catch (Exception e) {
        /* Both ClassNotFoundException and IOException can
            be thrown.*/
        }
    }
}
```

This calls the superclass constructor and then immediately attempts to initialize itself from the `MarshalledObject` by getting an instance of `Money` and setting it as the account balance.

The activatable constructor takes two arguments: an instance of `ActivationID` and an instance of `MarshalledObject`. This constructor must be present in order for the Activation Framework to work. That is, when the Activation Framework tries to launch a server, it looks for a two-argument constructor with precisely this signature and throws an exception if the constructor is not present.

Our constructor calls a similar superclass constructor that takes two arguments: an instance of `ActivationId` and a port. The port argument serves the same role as it does with `UnicastRemoteObject`: a value of 0 means that the associated server socket will listen on whatever port the RMI runtime finds convenient. Our code simply passes along the instance of `ActivationID` and lets RMI choose the port.

This is by far the most common way of writing an activatable server. Unless you have a good reason to do otherwise, extending `Activatable` and using a port with a value of 0 is convenient. The only problem arises when you need to pass a nonserializable argument to your server for initialization. However, that problem arises in any system that delays launching a server—you must find a way to store the initialization parameters until the server is launched. The second most common way uses the second constructor, which adds socket factories. We'll discuss reasons to use this second constructor in Chapter 18.

Apart from the constructor, our server code is exactly the same as it was before.

Modifying our launch code

The server itself isn't complex. However, our launch code is substantially more complicated than it used to be. The reason for this is simple: instead of simply launching our servers, we need to tell the Activation Framework how to launch our servers. This boils down to two things:

Describing a JVM
The first thing the Activation Framework will do when it needs to launch a server is check to see whether a suitable JVM has already been created. This is done by creating an instance of `ActivationGroup`.

Describing the actual server
After the Activation Framework creates the JVM the server will run in, it needs to create the server. In order to do so, it needs a complete description of the server object. (This is why we include an instance of `MarshalledObject` in our constructor; it makes things simpler for the Activation Framework.) This is done by creating an instance of `ActivationDesc`.

The first part of our launch code looks very familiar:

```
public static void main(String[] args) {
        try {
            ActivationGroup activationGroup = createActivationGroup( );
            createBankAccounts( );
        }
        catch (Exception e) {
            System.out.println("Utter Failure.");
            e.printStackTrace( );
            System.exit(0);
        }
        createBankAccounts( );
    }

    private static void createBankAccounts( ) {
        createBankAccount("Bob", getRandomMoney( ));
        createBankAccount("Tom", getRandomMoney( ));
        createBankAccount("Hans", getRandomMoney( ));
        createBankAccount("Bill", getRandomMoney( ));
```

```
                 createBankAccount("Yolanda", getRandomMoney( ));
                 createBankAccount("Dave", getRandomMoney( ));
        }


        private static Money getRandomMoney( ) {
                 int cents = (int) (Math.random( ) * 100000);
                 return new Money(cents);
        }
```

All the interesting things happen in createActivationGroup( ) and createBankAccount( ).
Here's createActivationGroup( ):

```
    private static ActivationGroup createActivationGroup( ) throws ActivationException,
        RemoteException {
                 Properties pList = new Properties( );
                 pList.put("java.security.policy", "d:\\java.policy");
                 ActivationGroupDesc.CommandEnvironment configInfo = null;
                 ActivationGroupDesc description = new ActivationGroupDesc(pList,
                         configInfo);
                 ActivationGroupID id = (ActivationGroup.getSystem( )).
                         registerGroup(description);
                 return ActivationGroup.createGroup(id, description, 0);
        }
```

Not surprisingly, this creates an instance of ActivationGroup, which corresponds to a
set of activatable servers. That is, you can think of that ActivationGroup as a "container" that contains a set of ActivatableServers.

Each ActivationGroup is associated with an instance of ActivationGroupDesc, which
corresponds to a JVM that the activation daemon will launch when required. One of
the most common ways to configure the JVM that the activation daemon will launch
is to pass it an instance of java.lang.Properties. The instance of Properties can set
any system parameters that you may want to pass to the JVM, including, for example, all of the parameters we defined in Chapter 16.

> The most important parameter given to an ActivationGroupDesc, or at
> least the one most commonly given, is the security policy of the JVM
> that will be created.

This code snippet creates a simple JVM description (i.e., setting a security policy, but
nothing else) and an instance of ActivationGroup. It then associates the two. When
the activation daemon needs to do something with this particular ActivationGroup, it
will use ActivationGroupDesc to create a JVM.

Now that we have a description of the JVM, we need to describe the individual servers. We do this in createBankAccount( ), as follows:

```
    private static void createBankAccount(String owner, Money money) {
             try {
                     ActivationDesc aD = createActivationDesc(owner, money);
                     Account account = (Account) Account_Impl.register(aD);
```

```
            Naming.rebind(owner, account);
        }
        catch (Exception e) {
            System.out.println("Failed to create account for " + owner);
            e.printStackTrace();
        }
    }

    private static ActivationDesc createActivationDesc(String owner, Money
        moneyToStart) throws ActivationException, RemoteException, IOException
    {
        return new ActivationDesc("com.ora.rmibook.chapter17.activation.
            Account_Impl", "file:/D:/Classes/", new
            MarshalledObject(moneyToStart));
    }
}
```

 The URL for finding classes (in this example, "file:/D:/Classes/")
specifies a directory (or an HTTP path) and must, therefore, end with
a /. If it doesn't, the class files won't be found.

If we unroll the code a little, we see that, for each activatable server we wish to create, the following lines of code are executed:

```
new ActivationDesc("com.ora.rmibook.chapter17.activation.Account_Impl",
    "file:/D:/Classes/", new MarshalledObject(moneyToStart));
Account account = (Account) Account_Impl.register(aD);
Naming.rebind(owner, account);
```

Each of these lines accomplishes a different task. The first line creates an object that contains enough information to create a server. In particular, when we examine the arguments passed into the constructor of ActivationDesc, we see:

- The complete name, including the package, of the server class
- A URL where the class file can be found or downloaded
- An instance of MarshalledObject containing all the initialization information that our instance of Account requires

This is enough information to create an instance of Account_Impl. Recall that the Activation Framework insists that any activatable server has a two-argument constructor that takes an instance of ActivationID and an instance of MarshalledObject. The Activation Framework will create an instance of ActivationID at launch time, invoke the constructor using the URL and classname to find the *.class* file, and then pass in a copy of the instance of MarshalledObject.

The second line of code calls a static method, register(), defined on the Activatable class. register() actually makes a remote call to the activation daemon, passing it ActivationDesc (ActivationDesc implements Serializable), and getting a stub in return. Since the activation daemon received a copy of the ActivationDesc, it has enough information to launch the server when necessary.

Note that the returned stub is an instance of `Account_Impl_Stub`, which is the stub class generated by `rmic`. You still need to run `rmic` on your servers in order to use activation.

The third line of code binds the stub returned by the activation daemon into the RMI registry so that the server is available to clients.

 This all works with our naming service as well. Nothing in the Activation Framework assumes that the naming service from which the client retrieves stubs is the RMI registry. In fact, nothing in the Activation Framework assumes that a naming service is involved at all. There's a very nice synergy between our second implementation of factories and the Activation Framework. The application-specific factory provides client-friendly methods for lookup and adds things such as persistence and lock management. However, it delegates the actual launching of the servers to the activation daemon.

Deploying an Activatable System

It has been observed by many people on numerous occasions that the activation daemon takes a while to get going. It's not exactly clear what's going on while the activation daemon launches, but the best policy is to wait a while for things to settle down before registering any activatable objects. That is, do something such as the following:

1. Start the naming service.
2. Start the activation daemon.
3. Wait two minutes.
4. Create the activatable objects.

In the case of our bank example, the entire launch sequence including a client application is:

1. `rmiregistry -J-Djava.security.policy=java.policy`.
2. `rmid -C-Djava.security.policy=java.policy`.
3. `-J-Djava.security.policy=java.policy`.
4. Wait two minutes.
5. `java com.ora.rmibook.chapter17.activation.applications.ActivationLauncher`.
6. `java com.ora.rmibook.chapter17.activation.applications.BankClient`.

 The security policies are necessary. I'll explain why in Chapter 18.

This launch sequence requires us to have at least two Java processes, the activation daemon and the registry, running in addition to our servers. Sometimes, especially in the case of smaller systems, the extra overhead of an additional Java process can be a bit annoying. If this is the case with your application, and you want to eliminate one of the processes, you can take advantage of the activation daemon's internal registry.

The activation daemon has a registry to enable clients to connect with it. We talked about how the activation system uses smarter stubs, and how these stubs first contact the activation daemon before connecting to the actual server. In addition, our launch code contacts the activation daemon indirectly when it registers the activation groups and descriptions.

In order for this to happen, the activation daemon itself must be registered in a naming service so external code can get a stub. There are two basic possibilities: either the activation daemon registers itself in an external naming service, or it provides a naming service on a well-known port.

The designers of RMI chose the second path. When you run rmid, the activation daemon creates an RMI registry on port 1098. This is a fully functional registry, created using LocateRegistry.createRegistry( ), and available on the network. Moreover, the activation daemon's registry is fairly empty—if you examine it using the RegistryExplorer program from Chapter 14, you'll find that only one server is bound into it. See Figure 17-4.

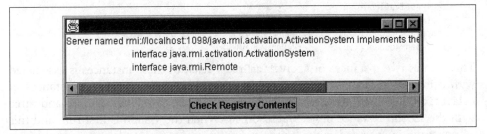

Server named rmi://localhost:1098/java.rmi.activation.ActivationSystem implements the interface java.rmi.activation.ActivationSystem
interface java.rmi.Remote

Check Registry Contents

Figure 17-4. Using the RegistryExplorer program on the activation daemon's registry

This means that on any server running an activation daemon, there is already a fairly empty RMI registry running on a well-known port, which you can use instead of a standalone registry.

ActivationDesc, ActivationGroupDesc, and ActivationGroup in More Detail

So far, we've covered the basics of how to describe a server to the Activation Framework. The objects involved are:

ActivationGroupDesc
> Instances of ActivationGroupDesc describe a JVM, which is configured as a server JVM. Usually, this means that a security policy is set, and the RMI runtime is configured through the use of the RMI-specific flags discussed in Chapter 16 and throughout the book.

ActivationGroup

>This is a container class. Instances of `ActivationGroup` describe a related set of activatable servers. Every instance of `ActivationGroup` is associated with a single instance of `ActivationGroupDesc`, although instances of `ActivationGroupDesc` can be associated with more than one `ActivationGroup`.

ActivationDesc

>Instances of `ActivationDesc` describe a single activatable server. An instance of `ActivationDesc` is associated with a single `ActivationGroup`, although instances of `ActivationGroup` can be associated with many instances of `ActivationDesc`.

You'll note that our code didn't actually associate the instances of `ActivationDesc` we created with the instance of `ActivationGroup`. If an instance of `ActivationDesc` isn't explicitly associated with an instance of `ActivationGroup`, it is automatically associated with the last created `ActivationGroup`.

To make this all a little more concrete, consider the following code example, which uses the private methods defined earlier:

```
createActivationGroup();
createBankAccount("Erik", getRandomMoney());
createBankAccount("Eugene", getRandomMoney());
createBankAccount("Earle", getRandomMoney());
createActivationGroup();
createBankAccount("Jim", getRandomMoney());
createBankAccount("Jack", getRandomMoney());
createBankAccount("Julie", getRandomMoney());
```

This creates two instances of `ActivationGroup`. Each of these instances is associated with a unique instance of `ActivationGroupDesc`. This code creates six instances of `ActivationDesc`, three associated with the first instance of `ActivationGroup` and three with the second instance of `ActivationGroup`. When the system is first run, and this launch code is executed, none of the servers are running, and neither of the two JVMs has been started.

Now suppose that the following client actions occur:

1. A client gets Julie's account balance.
2. A client withdraws money from Earl's account.
3. A client deposits money to Eugene's account.

These cause the following actions by the activation daemon:

1. A client gets Julie's account balance. The activation daemon checks to see whether the server associated with Julie's account has been launched. It hasn't, and so the activation daemon has no stub. The daemon then checks to see whether the JVM associated with the server associated with Julie's account has been started. The JVM hasn't been started either.

   The activation daemon starts the JVM. As part of this process, it starts an activation server (an implementation of the `Activator` interface) running within the new JVM. The activation daemon then passes in the `ActivationDesc` associated with Julie's account to the activation server within the newly created JVM.

The activation server within the newly created JVM uses the `ActivationDesc` to create the actual instance of `Account_Impl`. It then returns a stub for this newly created server to the activation daemon.

The activation daemon records all of this information internally (e.g., it records a map from `ActivationDesc` to the associated JVM, and from `ActivationID` to the stub for Julie's account) and then returns the stub to the client.

2. A client withdraws money from Earl's account. Earl's and Julie's instances of `ActivationDesc` were associated with different instances of `ActivationGroup`, and their associated instances of `ActivationGroup` were themselves associated with different instances of `ActivationGroupDesc`. This means that the entire process must be repeated; the activation daemon must launch a JVM, connect to the activation server in the new JVM, and request that the server associated with Eugene's account be created. After this, the activation daemon records all the necessary information internally and then returns the stub to the client.

3. A client deposits money to Eugene's account. Because Eugene's and Earl's instances of `ActivationDesc` were associated with the same `ActivationGroup`, the activation daemon doesn't need to create another JVM. Instead, it simply calls the activation server running in the already existing JVM, and passes it the `ActivationDesc` associated with Earl's account.

The activation server that receives the `ActivationDesc` creates the server for Eugene's account and returns the stub. After that, the activation daemon records all the necessary information internally and then returns the stub to the client.

This isn't as complicated as it seems. Figures 17-5 and 17-6 should help you keep it straight. Figure 17-5 illustrates the relationship between the objects created by launch code, and Figure 17-6 illustrates the corresponding server topology.

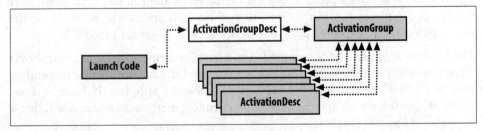

Figure 17-5. Launch code

Shutting Down an Activatable Server

So far, we've talked about how to automatically launch a server using the Activation Framework. However, there's another equally important task that needs to be done: servers need to be shut down when they're no longer being used. If we didn't shut

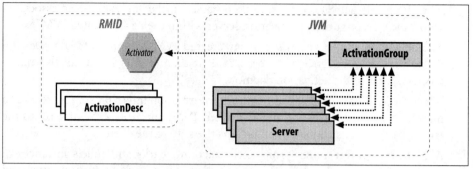

Figure 17-6. Runtime structure

down the servers, then over the course of a few weeks we'd wind up with all our servers up and running!

Fortunately, shutting down an activatable server is almost as easy as shutting down an ordinary RMI server. You need to do two things:

1. Unexport the server. Unexporting an activatable server does the same thing as unexporting an ordinary RMI server. That is, it tells the RMI runtime that the server is no longer accepting remote method invocations. The RMI runtime will then discard all references it has to the server, and the server will become eligible for garbage collection.

2. Clean things up with the activation daemon. At this point, the activation daemon thinks the server is up and running. It needs to be told otherwise.

Both of these steps are easily handled using static methods on the Activatable class. In particular, the two methods we need to use are:

```
public static boolean unexportObject(Remote obj, boolean force)
public static boolean inactive(ActivationID id)
```

The first of these, unexport( ), unexports the server. If the call succeeds, then, after the call is completed, no further remote method invocations will be made on the server, unless it is re-exported using one of Activatable's export( ) methods.

The boolean argument force is intended to allow for a finer degree of control over when the object is unexported. If force is false, and if there are current or pending remote method invocations, the attempt to unexport will fail. If force is true, unexport( ) will succeed, and the current and pending method invocations will throw instances of RemoteException.

inactive( ) tells the activation daemon that the server is no longer active. This lets the activation daemon reset its records so that, the next time a client tries to access the server, the server will be launched again.

A typical code sequence that shuts down a server looks like the following:

```
if (Activatable.unexport(server, true)) {
    Activatable.inactive(server.getID());
}
```

In addition, if the server should never be restarted, it also needs to be unregistered as in the following code snippet:

```
if (Activatable.unexport(server, true)) {
    ActivationID serverID = server.getID();
    Activatable.inactive(serverID);
    Activatable.unregister(serverID);
}
```

Unregistering a server with the activation daemon does not cause the server to stop listening for remote method invocations. It merely means the activation daemon won't restart the server if it goes down. You really do need to call all three methods in order to completely shut down a server so it won't be reactivated.

rmid Command-Line Arguments

The activation daemon accepts four command-line arguments. Three affect the activation daemon, and one affects the JVMs created by the activation daemon. The arguments that affect the activation daemon are: -port, -log, and -stop. -C affects the JVMs launched by the activation daemon.

-port

When the activation daemon launches a JVM, it also launches an RMI server inside the new JVM, which handles the details of creating server objects inside the newly launched JVM. The activation daemon and the server need to send messages to each other.

This communication is bootstrapped by an instance of an RMI registry inside the activation daemon. The actual instance of ActivationSystem that provides that activation daemon's core functionality is bound into this registry under the name java.rmi.activation.ActivationSystem.

The -port property specifies the port on which activation daemon's registry listens. Thus, if you know the port, you can communicate with the activation system directly, as in the following code snippet:

```
ActivationSystem system;
system = (ActivationSystem)Naming.lookup("//:port/java.rmi.activation.
    ActivationSystem");
```

The static methods on the Activatable class essentially do this. That is, there is no functional difference between calling a static method on Activatable that registers an

ActivationDesc with the activation daemon and getting a direct handle to the ActivationSystem yourself. We used the following three lines of code to register an account with the activation daemon:

```
ActivationDesc aD = createActivationDesc(owner, money);
Account account = (Account) Account_Impl.register(aD);
Naming.rebind(owner, account);
```

We could have, instead, done the following:

```
ActivationSystem system;
system = (ActivationSystem)Naming.lookup("//:1098/java.rmi.activation.
    ActivationSystem");
ActivationDesc aD = createActivationDesc(owner, money);
system.register(aD);
Naming.rebind(owner, account);
```

This flag takes an argument, as follows:

```
rmid -port 1967
```

If no value is specified for -port, it defaults to 1098.

-log

rmid automatically creates and writes to a log file. In fact, you can't prevent rmid from doing so. The only control you have over the rmid log is the directory in which it will be written. This is what the -log parameter specifies.

```
rmid -log directory-to-put-log-file-in
```

If you don't specify a directory, the log file will be written to the current working directory when the activation daemon was started.

The rmid log always has a name of the form Logfile.#, where # is an integer. The first time you run rmid with a particular directory for logging, rmid will create and use a log file named Logfile.1. On subsequent executions, rmid will create files named Logfile.2, Logfile.3, and so on.

-stop

Unlike -log and -port, -stop doesn't take a value. All it does is shut down an activation daemon. For example,

```
rmid -port 1967 -stop
```

shuts down the activation daemon using port 1967 for its internal registry.

There's a subtle implication here: you can have more than one activation daemon running on a machine. The question then becomes: how would the following code know which daemon to communicate with:

```
ActivationDesc aD = createActivationDesc(owner, money);
Account account = (Account) Account_Impl.register(aD);
Naming.rebind(owner, account);
```

The answer is that the static method really does perform a lookup as in the rewritten version of the code:

```
ActivationSystem system;
system = (ActivationSystem)Naming.lookup("//:port/java.rmi.activation.
    ActivationSystem");
ActivationDesc aD = createActivationDesc(owner, money);
system.register(aD);
Naming.rebind(owner, account);
```

And the value of the port in the second line is specified by the system parameter java.rmi.activation.port.

-C

The last command line argument, -C, is a meta-argument. It doesn't affect rmid directly, but the value of it is passed along to all the JVMs launched by the activation daemon. The usage is simple:

```
rmid -Ccommand-line-argument
```

Note that there is no space between -C and *command-line-argument*. This will pass the *command-line-argument* to each JVM started by the activation daemon. For example, to configure logging in each of the server JVMs, you could use:

```
rmid -C-Djava.rmi.server.logCalls=true -C-Dsun.rmi.transport.proxy.logLevel=verbose
```

Activation Parameters

The Activation Framework has six configurable parameters that will help you tweak various aspects of its behavior. Two of them are part of the Java standard, and four are specific to Sun's implementation of the activatable classes. The parameters are:

```
java.rmi.activation.activator.class
java.rmi.activation.port
sun.rmi.activation.execTimeout
sun.rmi.activation.snapshotInterval
sun.rmi.rmid.maxstartgroup
sun.rmi.server.activation.debugExec.
```

java.rmi.activation.activator.class

This is the implementation class that the activation system should use to instantiate the Activator interface. The default value is sun.rmi.server.Activation$ActivatorImpl. It is extremely rare that this property is overridden.

java.rmi.activation.port

This is the port on which rmid will listen for incoming remote calls. The default value is 1098. This value is used by both rmid (it is the default for the -port command-line argument) and by the launch code that registers instances of `ActivationDesc` with `rmid`. If you decide to use a different port for your launch code, then you also need to set -port for `rmid` and vice-versa.

sun.rmi.activation.execTimeout

This is the time, in milliseconds, that the activation system will wait for a spawned activation group to start up. The default value is 30,000 ms (30 seconds). Because the activation group and the activation daemon are on the same server, there are no network latency issues involved in this timeout. Hence, this is another property that rarely needs to be changed.

sun.rmi.activation.snapshotInterval

In addition to its log, `rmid` also occasionally creates a snapshot of all of its entries. These snapshots are stored in the *log* directory and used by `rmid` to recover from crashes. That is, if `rmid` stops executing and is then restarted, it can automatically recover. You don't need to recreate all the entries.

`sun.rmi.activation.snapshotInterval` controls how often the activation daemon writes to its log file. Instead of writing to the log file every time something happens, the activation daemon waits for `sun.rmi.activation.snapshotInterval`'s many operations to happen before writing a new snapshot. An operation is defined as something that changes the number of registered servers or the number of active servers. Starting up, or shutting down, a server counts as an operation; renewing a lease does not.

The default value for `sun.rmi.activation.snapshotInterval` is 200 operations.

sun.rmi.rmid.maxstartgroup

`rmid` needs to occasionally launch JVMs, such as when a server is required, but the JVM for that server has not yet been launched. This parameter sets a limit on the maximum number of JVMs that `rmid` will be in the process of launching at any given time.

Note that this is not a limit on the number of JVMs launched by the activation daemon. Instead, it's just a limit on how many are being launched concurrently. The idea is to smooth out system performance by preventing a large number of really costly operations (such as spawning a JVM) from occurring at the same time.

The default value for `sun.rmi.rmid.maxstartgroup` is 3 ms.

sun.rmi.server.activation.debugExec

This is the simplest, and possibly the most useful, of the `rmid` parameters. It's boolean valued. If it's set to `true`, then the activation system will print out the command line used to create JVMs.

This can really help in debugging an activatable system. You get to see exactly what parameters and properties are set in the created JVMs.

The default for `sun.rmi.server.activation.debugExec` is `false`.

 In addition to these parameters, has some security-related parameters that we will discuss in Chapter 19

A Final Word About Factories

In this chapter, we discussed the idea of a factory. At its most fundamental level, a factory is a server that launches other servers in response to client demands. However, a factory is more than just a remote constructor; it's also a way to share resources among clients, and it's a very convenient place to insert code that manages the server lifecycle.

There's another interesting point lurking here. Factories simplify client applications by providing client applications with the illusion of persistent servers. Consider the typical account server in our example. From the client's point of view, this server is always up and always available. The client calls the factory, using a method call that looks quite a bit like a naming-system lookup call. In response, the client gets a stub to a server.

As long as the client holds on to the stub, the distributed garbage collector will keep the server alive, and the stub will be a valid reference. If the client discards the stub and then makes another request to the factory, the client will get another stub. It's quite possible that in the interim, the account server was shut down, and the new stub the client gets is actually for an entirely different instance of `Account` (but with the same state as the previous instance). However, this fact is completely hidden from the client application.

This can be summarized in two points:

- Factories enable the automatic launching and shutdown of servers and provide an ideal mechanism for inserting persistence code. As such, they greatly simplify the design and implementation of large sets of similar server objects.
- Factories enable clients to be written as if all the associated servers are up all the time. They also greatly simplify the design and implementation of client code.

These two points make factories an incredibly important and versatile tool in the fight against application complexity.

PART III

Advanced Topics

CHAPTER 18

Using Custom Sockets

One of the major themes of this book is that RMI, for all its power and convenience, is really just a layer implemented on top of the standard socket objects shipped with the JDK. In this chapter, I build on this theme by showing how to replace the standard (cleartext) sockets that RMI uses with other sockets. The fact that RMI allows you to do this, and to do this differently for each type of server, is a very powerful feature. By the end of this chapter, you'll understand how to change the sockets that RMI uses and know when doing so is an appropriate design strategy.

As I've mentioned countless times, RMI is built on top of sockets. This means that:

- Data sent between clients and servers (in both directions) is sent using a streams interface.

- Connections between clients and servers are created and maintained by using the socket classes defined in the `java.net` package.

- RMI doesn't make any assumptions about the underlying network infrastructure or communication protocol.

Understanding these points, and what they imply, is crucial for understanding how RMI works "under the covers." However, the strict separation they imply between RMI on the one hand, and the operating system and network transport protocol on the other, also leads quite naturally to the following thought:

> If I can define a new socket class, and my socket-level communications protocols will work with it, then my RMI applications, which are built on top of sockets and don't make any assumptions about the underlying network, should also be able to run on top of my new sockets.

Indeed, this turns out to be the case. RMI, through the definition of custom socket factories, contains a remarkably flexible way of letting you use whatever sockets you feel like using to handle the raw bits that need to get sent over the wire.

Why Use a Custom Socket Class?

By default, RMI uses the standard socket classes defined in the java.net package to send information over the wire. Servers use instances of ServerSocket to listen for connections, and clients initiate connections using instances of Socket.

These sockets send information as plain text, without any encryption or compression, and thus involve a trade-off. On the positive side, they involve the least CPU usage (information is not transformed in any way) and are the most straightforward to use. The latter is true because compression can get a little tricky. The semantics of flush( ), especially with GZIPOutputStream, are not entirely compatible with the idea of sending remote method invocations as discrete and self-contained units.

On the negative side, they use more bandwidth than needed, and information is very vulnerable while it's being sent over the network. This leads to two reasons for using custom sockets:

- If you're not on a secured network, and the information being sent across the wire is sensitive, you may want to use encrypting sockets, such as the SSL sockets we discussed in Chapter 2.
- If you're on a very congested network where bandwidth is an issue, you may want to compress information before sending it over the wire.

In both of these cases, an explicit trade is made: single-machine resources, such as CPU time, are used to transform data for better network characteristics.

In addition to these trade-offs, there are local (e.g., not involving how data is sent over the network) reasons to use a custom socket. One common reason is to monitor socket usage and track how much information is sent over the wire. This is an important part of performance profiling and may, in fact, lead to the use of compressing sockets.

Custom Socket Factories

Let's start by assuming that an appropriate custom socket and server socket class have already been written and are ready to be used. We can start with these assumptions for two reasons. First, we've already covered how to create custom sockets in Chapter 2. Second, the com.ora.rmibook.chapter18.sockets package includes a simple custom socket class called MonitoringSocket.

MonitoringSocket has an associated subclass of ServerSocket named Monitoring-ServerSocket. Together, they enable you to keep track of how many sockets are currently allocated and what RMI is doing with them. MonitoringSocket lets you track how many open connections exist at any given time and provides a simple and easy way for you to get a feel for your application's typical load and resource consumption. As such, it is useful for debugging, and a similar socket class could be useful if you wanted to implement a socket-level coordination strategy,* but it's not the sort of socket class that often makes it into production servers.

Given that we have a set of custom sockets, we need to do two things: create custom socket factories and modify our servers.

Creating Custom Socket Factories

The java.rmi.server package defines two socket factory interfaces: RMIClientSocket-Factory and RMIServerSocketFactory. In order to use custom sockets, you need to implement these interfaces. Fortunately, they're quite simple; each contains a single method. In the case of RMIClientSocketFactory, the method is:

```
public Socket createSocket(String host, int port)
```

In the case of RMIServerSocketFactory, the method is:

```
public ServerSocket createServerSocket(int port)
```

These methods are simply translations of the standard constructors for Socket and ServerSocket. That is, you can imagine writing an implementation of RMIClient-SocketFactory that simply called a constructor on the Socket class, as in the following code snippet:

```
public Socket createSocket(String host, int port)  {
    return new Socket( host, port);
}
```

It turns out that writing the complete socket factory is only a little bit more subtle than this. Here's the complete code for a client socket factory that uses our MonitoringSocket:

```
public class MonitoringSocket_RMIClientSocketFactory implements
    RMIClientSocketFactory, Serializable {
    private int _hashCode = "MonitoringSocket_RMIClientSocketFactory".hashCode( );
    public Socket createSocket(String host, int port) {
        try {
            return new MonitoringSocket(host, port);
        }
        catch (IOException e){}
        return null;
    }

    public boolean equals(Object object) {
        if (object instanceof MonitoringSocket_RMIClientSocketFactory) {
            return true;
        }
        return false;
    }
}
```

---

* For example, to limit the total bandwidth of your application at any given time.

```
        public int hashCode( ) {
            return _hashCode;
        }
    }
```

This class does three things: it creates instances of MonitoringSocket, it implements Serializable, and it overrides equals( ) and hashCode( ) correctly. It's clear why our socket factory needs to create instances of MonitoringSocket; but the other two tasks are just as important.

Implementing Serializable

An implementation of RMIClientSocketFactory needs to implement Serializable because the type of socket that a server uses is entirely a server-side property. In order for the client to even connect to the server, it must already be using the correct socket type. In order for the RMI runtime on the client to find out what type of socket to use, it must deserialize an instance of the appropriate socket factory. This happens automatically when the client deserializes the stub—the stub has a reference to an instance of an implementation of RMIClientSocketFactory. When the stub is bound into a naming service, serialization creates a copy of the correct socket factory. When the client obtains the stub from the naming service, it also obtains a copy of the socket factory, and can therefore connect to the server.

Implementing equals( ) and hashCode( )

The RMI runtime uses the socket factory instance in two ways: to create sockets and to index already existing sockets. In other words, the RMI runtime performs the following sequence of actions when a stub wants to send a message:

1. The runtime gets the stub's instance of RMIClientSocketFactory from the stub.

2. The runtime then uses the stub's instance of RMIClientSocketFactory as a key into a hashtable of open but currently unused sockets.

3. If this retrieval fails, the RMI runtime then uses the stub's instance of RMIClientSocketFactory to create a socket.

4. When the remote method invocation is finished, the client runtime returns the socket to the hashtable in step 2.

You may think that there's a better object to use as the hashtable key in step 2. For example, the stub itself may seem like an obvious choice. However, the stub doesn't work. Why? Two stubs to distinct servers, even if they're using the "same" socket factory, have to return different hashcodes and return false when equals( ) is called. Using the stubs to index sockets means that sockets can be reused across calls to a specific server but not across calls to distinct servers.

You can't use the stub's class object or the class of the stub's instance of RMIClientSocketFactory either. Using either of these as the key to the hashtable ignores the possibility that the client socket factory has state and may return differently configured sockets at different times. Consider, for example, the following, perfectly legal, client socket factory:

```
public class PropertyBasedMonitoringSocket_RMIClientSocketFactory implements
    RMIClientSocketFactory, Serializable {
    private static final String USE_MONITORING_SOCKETS_PROPERTY =
        "com.ora.rmibook.useMonitoringSockets";
    private static final String TRUE = "true";

    private int _hashCode = "PropertyBasedMonitoringSocket_RMIClientSocketFactory".
        hashCode( );
    private boolean _isMonitoringOn;

    public PropertyBasedMonitoringSocket_RMIClientSocketFactory( ) {
        String monitoringProperty = System.getProperty(
            USE_MONITORING_SOCKETS_PROPERTY);
         if ((null!=monitoringProperty) && (monitoringProperty.
            equalsIgnoreCase(TRUE)))   {
            _isMonitoringOn = true;
            _hashCode++;
        }
        else {
            _isMonitoringOn = false;
        }
         return;
    }

    public Socket createSocket(String host, int port) {
        try {
            if (_isMonitoringOn) {
                return new MonitoringSocket(host, port);
            }
            else {
                return new Socket(host, port);
            }
        }
        catch (IOException e){}
        return null;
    }

    public boolean equals(Object object) {
        if (object instanceof PropertyBasedMonitoringSocket_RMIClientSocketFactory)
        {
            return true;
        }
        return false;
    }

    public int hashCode( ) {
        return _hashCode;
    }
}
```

This does something a little unusual. As part of initialization, it checks a system property to see whether monitoring sockets should be used. Different servers may be running in different JVMs and have different settings for this value (especially since, as written, this depends on a parameter that can be set from the command line using a -D argument). Consequently, the following two command-line invocations will result in different types of sockets being used:

```
java -Dcom.ora.rmibook.useMonitoringSockets=false ...
java -Dcom.ora.rmibook.useMonitoringSockets=true ...
```

That a factory can have state has another interesting consequence. Serializing the socket factory can cause problems. If a server is launched and a stub is serialized, it would be very inconvenient for the socket factory to change the socket type afterwards. Any client that downloaded the old stub would wind up using the wrong type of socket when attempting to connect to the server. Practically speaking, this means that socket factories are configured very early in the server JVM's lifecycle, usually by system parameters, as we did in the code example.

However, if we use the stub's class object or the socket factory's class object as the key into the hashtable of available sockets, this distinction between the servers would be lost, and the wrong type of socket might be used.

Almost all of this discussion applies equally well to the implementation of an RMIServerSocketFactory. A factory that produces server sockets isn't sent over the wire to a client, so it need not be serializable.

On the other hand, the server's RMI runtime uses equals( ) and hashCode( ) internally. Because most servers in any given application use the same types of sockets, it makes sense to have servers share sockets. In order to handle this, RMI maintains a mapping from socket factories to open sockets. When a server needs a socket, RMI uses a map, which is keyed on the associated socket factory to see if there are any available sockets. In order for RMI to do this effectively, we must override equals( ) and hashCode( ).

Here's our implementation of a server socket factory using MonitoringSocket:

```
public class MonitoringSocket_RMIServerSocketFactory implements
    RMIServerSocketFactory, Serializable {
    private int _hashCode = "MonitoringSocket_RMIServerSocketFactory".hashCode( );
    public ServerSocket createServerSocket(int port) {
        try {
            return new MonitoringServerSocket(port);
        }
        catch (IOException e){}
        return null;
    }

    public boolean equals(Object object) {
        if (object instanceof MonitoringSocket_RMIServerSocketFactory) {
```

```
            return true;
        }
        return false;
    }

    public int hashCode( )  {
        return _hashCode;
    }
}
```

Deployment

I've mentioned previously that, in most cases, the stub classes need to be deployed with the clients. The reality is actually a little more complicated. The stub classes also need to be on the classpath of any naming services that are involved, and they need to be on the classpath of the activation daemon as well.

The same holds true for socket factories. The associated classes need to be available to the naming service and the activation daemon, as well as to the client.

In addition, there's a security issue. Code that uses nonstandard sockets needs special security exemptions, called socket permissions, in order to execute. And these permissions must also be set at the naming service and the activation daemon.

We'll discuss security permissions more thoroughly in Chapter 20.

Incorporating a Custom Socket into an Application

Now that we've got a custom socket factory, the next step is incorporating it into our application. There are two different ways to do this: we can either modify our server classes or we can set RMI's default socket factory. The first option, modifying individual server classes, gives us a very fine-grained level of control in which each server can use a different custom socket class. Setting RMI's default socket factory is a much coarser way to do things. Changing the default socket factory means that any servers that don't set their own socket factories will use the new default types.

Modifying Ordinary Servers

UnicastRemoteObject has three constructors:

```
protected UnicastRemoteObject( )
protected UnicastRemoteObject(int port)
protected UnicastRemoteObject(int port, RMIClientSocketFactory csf,
    RMIServerSocketFactory ssf)
```

Until this point, we've used only the first two of these in our servers. In fact, we've mostly used the first one, as in the following code snippet:

```
public class Account_Impl extends UnicastRemoteObject implements Account {
    private Money _balance;
    public Account_Impl(Money startingBalance) throws RemoteException {
        _balance = startingBalance;
    }
    //...
}
```

This is a perfectly reasonable thing to do; the zero-argument constructor gives the RMI runtime the ability to reuse an existing server socket, whereas the one-argument constructor forces the RMI runtime to create a server socket that listens on the specified port. However, in order to use custom socket factories, we need to use the third constructor. Consequently, the code change consists of modifying the previous code snippet to use the third constructor:

```
public class Account_Impl extends UnicastRemoteObject implements Account {
    private Money _balance;

    public Account_Impl(Money startingBalance) throws RemoteException {
        super(0, new PropertyBasedMonitoringSocket_RMIClientSocketFactory(),
                new PropertyBasedMonitoringSocket_RMIServerSocketFactory());
        _balance = startingBalance;
    }
    //...
}
```

 We still pass 0 in as the first argument. Using 0 as the value of port means that RMI is free to choose the port for the server socket, which in turn means that RMI is free to reuse an existing server socket, using the mapping described earlier.

Ordinary servers that aren't subclasses of UnicastRemoteObject are handled similarly. Recall that stubs for these types of servers are created using one of UnicastRemoteObject's static export( ) methods:

```
static RemoteStub exportObject(Remote obj)
static Remote exportObject(Remote obj, int port)
static Remote exportObject(Remote obj, int port, RMIClientSocketFactory csf,
    RMIServerSocketFactory ssf)
```

These methods are called from within the launch code, as in the following snippet from Chapter 9:

```
private static void launchServer(NameBalancePair serverDescription) {
    try {
        Account_Impl2 newAccount = new Account_Impl2(serverDescription.balance);
        RemoteStub stub = UnicastRemoteObject.exportObject(newAccount);
        Naming.rebind(serverDescription.name, stub);
        System.out.println("Account " + serverDescription.name + " successfully
            launched.");
```

```
        }
    catch(Exception e){}
}
```

The change to the launch code is exactly parallel to our changes of the subclasses of
UnicastRemoteObject. Instead of calling the one-argument version of export( ), we
call the four-argument version. The preceding code becomes the following:

```
private static void launchServer(NameBalancePair serverDescription) {
        try {
            Account_Impl2 newAccount = new Account_Impl2(serverDescription.balance);
            RemoteStub stub = UnicastRemoteObject.exportObject(newAccount, 0,
                    new PropertyBasedMonitoringSocket_RMIClientSocketFactory( ),
                    new PropertyBasedMonitoringSocket_RMIServerSocketFactory( ));
            Naming.rebind(serverDescription.name, stub);
            System.out.println("Account " + serverDescription.name + " successfully
                    launched.");
        }
        catch(Exception e){}
}
```

Modifying Activatable Servers

Recall that one of the major changes in making a server activatable is switching from
UnicastRemoteObject to Activatable. Servers that extended UnicastRemoteObject now
extend Activatable, and servers that used one of the static exportObject( ) methods
defined in the UnicastRemoteObject class now use one of the static exportObject( )
methods defined in the Activatable class.

This parallelism continues when you modify an activatable server to use a custom
socket factory. Here, for example, is the code for our activatable account server,
modified to use a custom socket factory:

```
public class Account_Impl extends Activatable implements Account {
    private Money _balance;
    public Account_Impl(ActivationID id, MarshalledObject data) throws
        RemoteException {
        super(id, 0, new PropertyBasedMonitoringSocket_RMIClientSocketFactory( ),
            new PropertyBasedMonitoringSocket_RMIServerSocketFactory( ));
        try {
            _balance = (Money) data.get( );
// ....
    }
```

That is, instead of calling the two-argument superclass constructor:

```
protected Activatable(ActivationID id, int port)
```

we need to call the four-argument superclass constructor:

```
protected Activatable(ActivationID id, int port, RMIClientSocketFactory csf,
    RMIServerSocketFactory ssf)
```

and pass in the socket factories we wish to use.

Similarly, `Activatable` defines four static export methods:

```
static Remote exportObject(Remote obj, ActivationID id, int port)
static Remote exportObject(Remote obj, ActivationID id, int port,
    RMIClientSocketFactory csf, RMIServerSocketFactory ssf)
static ActivationID exportObject(Remote obj, String location, MarshalledObject data,
    boolean restart, int port)
static ActivationID exportObject(Remote obj, String location, MarshalledObject data,
    boolean restart, int port, RMIClientSocketFactory csf, RMIServerSocketFactory
    ssf)
```

Making an activatable server that does not extend `Activatable` to use a custom socket factory is easy. Doing so consists entirely of switching the export method that is called to an export method that takes socket factories for arguments.

Modifying the Default Servers

RMI comes with an abstract class, `RMISocketFactory`, which implements both `RMIClientSocketFactory` and `RMIServerSocketFactory`. `RMISocketFactory` is defined in the `java.rmi.server` package and is the default socket factory used by RMI. That is, unless a server specifies that it is using a different socket factory, the server will wind up using an instance of `RMISocketFactory` for both its client socket factory and its server socket factory.

In addition to this, `RMISocketFactory` has five static methods used to customize the behavior of the RMI runtime with respect to socket factories. These methods are:

```
public static RMISocketFactory getDefaultSocketFactory()
public static RMISocketFactory getSocketFactory()
public static void setSocketFactory(RMISocketFactory fac)
public static RMIFailureHandler getFailureHandler()
public static void setFailureHandler(RMIFailureHandler fh)
```

The first three methods deal with getting and setting the socket factories that RMI will use (unless the choice is overridden for a particular class of server).

`getSocketFactory()` and `setSocketFactory()` are a pair of methods that enable you to find out, and set, the global socket factory that RMI will use by default. This global socket factory is a single subclass of `RMISocketFactory` used by RMI for all servers, unless the particular server is exported using `RMIServerSocketFactory` and `RMIClientSocketFactory`, as in previous sections.

`RMISocketFactory` is an abstract class that implements both `RMIClientSocketFactory` and `RMIServerSocketFactory`. Basically, writing a subclass of `RMISocketFactory` amounts to combining the two classes you would have written (the implementation of `RMIClientSocketFactory` and the implementation of `RMIServerSocketFactory`) into a single class.

`getDefaultSocketFactory()` returns the subclass of `RMISocketFactory` that RMI uses if neither the server classes nor the global socket factory have been set.

Here is a subclass of RMISocketFactory that uses our MonitoringSocket class:

```java
public class PropertyBasedMonitoringSocket_RMISocketFactory extends RMISocketFactory
    {
    private static final String USE_MONITORING_SOCKETS_PROPERTY =
        "com.ora.rmibook.useMonitoringSockets";
    private static final String TRUE = "true";

    private int _hashCode = "PropertyBasedMonitoringSocket_RMISocketFactory".
        hashCode( );
    private boolean _isMonitoringOn;

    public PropertyBasedMonitoringSocket_RMISocketFactory( ) {
        String monitoringProperty = System.getProperty(
            USE_MONITORING_SOCKETS_PROPERTY);
        if ((null!=monitoringProperty) && (monitoringProperty.
            equalsIgnoreCase(TRUE))) {
            _isMonitoringOn = true;
        }
        else  {
            _isMonitoringOn = false;
        }
        return;
    }

    public Socket createSocket(String host, int port) {
        try {
            if (_isMonitoringOn) {
                return new MonitoringSocket(host, port);
            }
            else {
                return new Socket(host, port);
            }
        }
        catch (IOException e){}
        return null;
    }

    public ServerSocket createServerSocket(int port) {
        try {
            if (_isMonitoringOn) {
                return new MonitoringServerSocket(port);
            }
            else {
                return new ServerSocket(port);
            }
        }
        catch (IOException e){}
        return null;
    }

    public boolean equals(Object object) {
        if (object instanceof PropertyBasedMonitoringSocket_RMIClientSocketFactory)
            {
```

```
            return true;
        }
        return false;
    }

    public int hashCode( ) {
        return _hashCode;
    }
}
```

Failure handlers

There are two additional static methods defined in RMISocketFactory: getFailure-
Handler( ) and setFailureHandler( ). These methods enable you to get and set the
RMIFailureHandler. The RMIFailureHandler is used by RMI when, for some reason, an
instance of ServerSocket is required, but cannot be created (e.g., when the socket factory that is supposed to create the ServerSocket throws an exception).

RMIFailureHandler is an interface with a single method:

```
    public boolean failure(Exception ex)
```

The boolean return value is used to tell RMI how to proceed. A return value of true
tells RMI to try to create the instance of ServerSocket again; a return value of false
tells RMI that the attempt to create a server socket has failed completely.

RMI's default implementation of RMIFailureHandler simply returns true. This is a
pretty reasonable default, and overriding it by calling setFailureHandler( ) is rarely
done. The typical reason for overriding this behavior is to log the failure.

Interaction with Parameters

In Chapter 16, we discussed a number of transport layer parameters. These are global properties of the JVM used to configure RMI's behavior with respect to sockets.
The transport layer parameters are sun.rmi.transport.connectionTimeout, sun.rmi.
transport.tcp.readTimeout, and sun.rmi.transport.proxy.connectTimeout. It's reasonable to wonder how these interact with the definition of custom socket factories.

The answer is that RMI uses the custom socket factories to create sockets, and then
calls methods on the sockets to configure them. The sequence RMI goes through to
obtain a server socket is:

1. Use the RMIServerSocketFactory associated with the server to see if a server
   socket has already been allocated. If so, use the existing server socket.

2. If not, call createServerSocket( ) on the RMIServerSocketFactory associated with
   the server and, after the socket has been created, configure the socket.

This means that, in practice, you set defaults for custom sockets and then override
the defaults using system properties. This is identical to what happens with ordinary
sockets.

RMI's Default Connection Strategy

`RMISocketFactory` is an abstract class that defines five static methods. The default implementation of `RMISocketFactory` used by Sun's implementation of RMI does not simply create instances of `Socket` and `ServerSocket`. Instead, it defines a three-tiered connection strategy.

The problem is this: corporate computing environments often have firewalls in place between the corporate intranet and the Internet. These firewalls block most socket-level communication, typically on the basis of the port involved. For example, a firewall policy may involve blocking all packets that aren't being sent to either a mail server or a web server. Ssuch a policy would block any RMI server listening on a randomly assigned socket.

In order to get around this, the default implementation of `RMISocketFactory` implements the following client-side connection strategy:

1. Attempt a direct socket connection using JRMP (the default RMI protocol).
2. If that fails, wrap up the remote method invocation inside an HTTP POST command, and attempt to post the remote method invocation to the server port.
3. If that fails, wrap up the remote method invocation inside an HTTP POST command, and attempt to post the remote method invocation to the server port, but with a predefined proxy machine.
4. If that fails, wrap up the remote method invocation inside an HTTP POST command, and attempt to post the remote method invocation to port 80 using the predefined proxy machine.

This strategy is both useful and dangerous. It's useful because it helps when users are outside a corporate firewall and need to connect to an RMI server. It's dangerous because, in essence, it breaches the firewall. To the extent that the firewall was necessary, RMI's default connection strategy is a security risk. We'll discuss this in greater detail in Chapter 22.

CHAPTER 19

Dynamic Classloading

Deploying a distributed application can be rather difficult. All of the computers that run parts of the application must have the relevant parts installed. For a local area network, this is usually a time-consuming, but not particularly difficult, process. However, when applications are deployed on a larger scale, and updated frequently, the deployment process becomes far more difficult.

Dynamic classloading is a technology, built into RMI, which attempts to make this deployment a little easier. At this point in the book, we've covered most of the basics of building a robust and scalable distributed application. We've gone through the rules for designing interfaces, we've spent a lot of time discussing threads, we've covered testing a distributed application, and we've even discussed how to optimize the distributed garbage collector. Now it's time to dig deep into the task of deploying (and redeploying) an application.

Deploying Can Be Difficult

Let's start by supposing that we're deploying the latest version of the banking application. We need to do the following:

- Configure the server machines.
- Add the stub classes to the naming service classpath, along with any other classes, such as socket factories and value objects, that might need to be instantiated inside the naming service.
- If this is a redeployment, as opposed to a first-time deployment, you'll probably have to restart the naming service and reregister all the objects to get rid of the existing class objects in the naming service's JVM.
- Install and configure the application on every client machine. This includes tracking machines that are currently unavailable (e.g., laptops out on loan or machines in for repair), so the application can be installed on them later.

Compare this to the deployment procedure for the typical applet, in which we must:

- Configure the server machines
- Write web pages that have an APPLET tag in them.

Put succinctly, deploying a web application doesn't involve changes to the client side or to a naming service. Instead, when a web browser downloads a web page containing an applet tag, it also downloads the Java class files necessary to run the applet. This way of deploying applications is much less time-consuming and much more likely to be done correctly.

 In addition to the time and effort spent in the intial deployment, you need to consider the inevitable deployment errors in the traditional scenario. A large part of the deployment hassle is the inevitable month or two of random bug reports and lost productivity that result from deployment errors.

How Often Do You Deploy?

Sometimes, when I mention how painful deployment can be, people respond by saying, "Yeah, but how often do you really redeploy an updated application? Once a year?"

This is a good question. Some applications don't get redeployed very often. However, the question has a slightly circular flavor to it; part of the reason why applications don't get updated and redeployed more often is that deployment is such a time-consuming and difficult process. When environments make it possible to easily deploy an updated applications, applications tend to get updated and redeployed much more frequently.

Web-based applications are the perfect example of this. You only need to reconfigure a few servers in order to redeploy a web-based application. And web-based applications are redeployed almost constantly.

However, every time you need to update or redeploy an application, this difference looms larger and larger.

Applets are, of course, limited in many ways. Because all of the bytecode is downloaded every time they're run, they have to be small, and because the browser may be using an older JVM, the developers who write an applet can't take advantage of a great deal of the latest Java features, such as the Swing GUI toolkit. In addition, because the browsers have a stringent security model, the applet's ability to open socket connections or files is severely limited.

These are all "even-if-the-browser-was-perfectly-implemented" objections to developing client-server applets. That is, they're valid and will always be valid objections, no matter how much the browsers improve. In addition to these, there's also the fact that the existing web browsers provide an incredibly slow and buggy JVM.

The good news is that RMI contains an interesting and useful technology, called *dynamic classloading*, that attempts to merge these two models. It lets you build standalone applications that, at least for some parts of your codebase, have an applet-like deployment model. That is, dynamic classloading allows an RMI application to dynamically load bytecode definitions of classes from an *http://* or *ftp://* URL at runtime, when the class definition is required.

Classloaders

You probably already know that Java source code compiles into *.class* files. Each *.class* file contains the bytecode (the compiled instructions for the JVM) for a single class. You probably also know that every Java class gets compiled separately, and the resulting bytecode goes into distinct *.class* files, which are then dynamically linked at runtime.

For ordinary application development, that's really all you need to know about how Java handles classes. However, we need to cover a little more in order to fully understand dynamic classloading.

How Classes Are Loaded

The Java virtual machine loads and validates individual classes through the use of objects known as *classloaders*. The classloading system works as follows:

1. When the JVM is first launched, a single classloader, often referred to as the *bootstrap classloader*, is created. This classloader is responsible for loading and creating most classes used within the JVM.

2. An application can programmatically create more classloaders. Every classloader, with the exception of the bootstrap classloader, has a parent classloader. The set of classloaders forms a tree with the bootstrap classloader at the root.

3. When a class object is needed, the JVM finds the appropriate classloader and asks it for the class object using one of the loadClass( ) methods. The classloader first asks its parent for the class and, if the parent returns null, it then creates the class itself.

The idea behind this is that classloaders are a way to partition the set of classes and isolate class definitions. Implicit in the last point, for example, is the fact that if two

Dynamic Linking

Most traditional programming languages use a static linking model. In order to generate an executable application, the source code must be compiled, and all references must be immediately resolved. In other words, the individual components of the application must be *linked* together.

Dynamic linking postpones the resolution process as long as possible. It is quite possible, with a running Java application, that some references are never actually resolved because, for example, the referenced method was never called.

This may seem a little strange at first; C++ programmers often have a hard time wrapping their minds around it. But if you think about it, some form of dynamic linking is absolutely necessary in order for Java to work. Consider the typical applet scenario:

- I write an applet on a Linux machine, using Sun's version of JDK 1.2.
- You download the web page on a Macintosh, and the applet executes inside MRJ, using Apple's version of JDK 1.1.6.

This sort of scenario is impossible with C++; linking has to be postponed until execution.

Unfortunately, dynamic linking can also cause problems when applications are only partially updated. If you change only a few *.class* files, you might inadvertently have two *.class* files that cannot be linked together (e.g., an old *.class* file calls a method that you've removed from one of the newer *.class* files).

Chapter 13 of *The Java Laguage Specification, Second Edition* edited by Bill Loy (Addison-Wesley) spells out in great detail the ways in which classes can change without breaking dynamic linking. It's well worth reading if you plan to use dynamic classloading as an integral part of your application.

---

sibling classloaders (have the same parent) are asked for the same class, the class object will be loaded and initialized twice.

Classloaders are useful in two distinct scenarios. The first is when you want to load class objects from a nonstandard source. The bootstrap classloader attempts to load classes from the file system using the CLASSPATH system variable. It expects that the package and name of a class will map cleanly to a *.class* file containing the bytecode for the class. If you want to load classes from a different source, for example from a URL, you need to install another classloader, such as java.net.URLClassLoader.

The second scenario involves having different versions of the same class running at the same time. Because classloaders only check their parents, not their siblings, to see if a class has already been loaded, it's possible to safely load different versions of the same class into a JVM. See Figure 19-1.

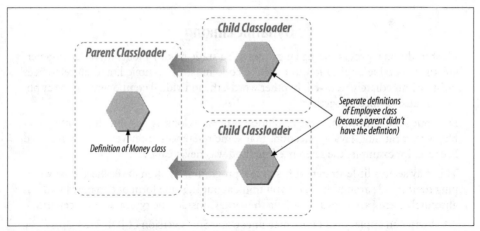

Figure 19-1. Classloaders define the scope of a class

How Dynamic Classloading Works

In Chapter 10, while discussing how RMI customizes the serialization algorithm, I said:

> ObjectOutputStream calls annotateClass( ) when it writes out class descriptions. Annotations are used to provide extra information about a class that comes from the serialization mechanism and not from the class itself. The basic serialization mechanism has no real need for annotations; most of the information about a given class is already stored in the stream...

> RMI, on the other hand, uses annotations to record *codebase information*. That is, RMI, in addition to recording the class descriptions, also records information about the location from which it loaded the class's bytecode.

These paragraphs, which may have seemed opaque before, should now make more sense. RMI's dynamic classloading is based on two ideas:

- If an object is serialized and sent over the wire, the required class definitions might not be available on the other side.
- Automatically including URLs from which classes can be downloaded inside serialized objects allows special-purpose classloaders, such as the URLClassLoader class, to automatically load classes from over the wire when they're needed to deserialize an object.

The basic algorithm, which is built into RMI's deserialization mechanism, works as follows:

1. An instance is sent over the wire. As part of the serialized information about the instance, all the related class definitions are also sent over the wire (including the definitions of interfaces). Each class is also accompanied by a string-delimited sequence of URLs called its *codebase annotation*.

The "related class definitions" include more than you might suspect. The class of which the object is an instance is included, as are all its superclasses and all the class objects for interfaces that it implements. But there's more: any class referred to in a method definition (either as an argument type or as a return value) is also included, as are the types of each field defined in any of these classes. All in all, it can be quite a list of class definitions.

2. The deserialization mechanism finds the appropriate classloader for the classes that have just been described. It can do this because the RMI runtime maintains an indexed collection of instances of URLClassLoader. This collection is indexed using the codebase annotations.

 In JDK 1.4, you can customize the classloader behavior by implementing the RMIClassLoaderSpi interface (RMIClassLoaderSpi is defined in the java.rmi.server package) and then setting the java.rmi.server. RMIClassLoaderSpi system property to the name of your new class. The behavior described in this chapter is the default behavior.

3. If the classes already exist, the instance of URLClassLoader simply returns them, and everything is fine. If the classes do not already exist, then the instance of URLClassLoader loads them.

   Because classloaders ask their parents for classes before attempting to load them, the first attempt to load the classes will be from the filesystem (e.g., the bootstrap classloader will first try to load the classes). The classes will be loaded using only the URLs inside the codebase annotation if the bootstrap classloader cannot load the class. See Figure 19-2.

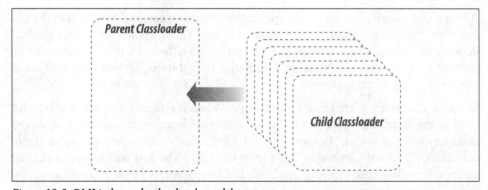

Figure 19-2. RMI indexes classloaders by codebase

Before we get into the actual mechanics of dynamic classloading, we will discuss two example scenarios to make the idea a little clearer.

A Redeployment Scenario

Suppose that you've implemented and deployed the bank example. Three months later, you must roll out a new version using the Account2 interface:

```
public interface Account2 extends Account { // has new reporting functionality
    public TransactionList getLastNTransaction(int numberOfTransactions) throws
        RemoteException;
    public TransactionList getTransactionsSince(Date since) throws RemoteException;
}
```

You have two options. The first is the traditional sweeping redeployment in which everything is shut down and you need to go to every client machine and reinstall the application in the next 24 hours (or however long it takes). The second option is a staged rollout. The key to the staged rollout is realizing that, since Account2 extends Account, the first client application will work perfectly well with the new server. The code that retrieved a stub from the naming service was:

```
private void getAccount( ) {
    try {
        _account = (Account)Naming.lookup(_accountNameField.getText( ));
    }
    catch (Exception e) {
        System.out.println("Couldn't find account. Error was \n " + e);
        e.printStackTrace( );
    }
    return;
}
```

This code will work fine if the stub implements Account2 because Account2 extends Account—the cast will succeed. The old client application won't be able to access the new functionality, but the old application is still a fine application and probably quite usable for most tasks.

If you could install the new server applications without needing to redeploy the client, then you could gradually phase in the new client application. This gradual deployment would be less stressful for IT and would allow for a much greater degree of testing for the new functionality. No matter how thoroughly you test an application, there's still a substantial risk when you roll it out to an enterprise.

Dynamic classloading lets you do exactly this. When you launch the new servers, and bind in the instances of Account2, the old client application will receive a serialized instance of the new stub. Because the old application doesn't have the appropriate classes locally, it will download them from the URL. The cast will succeed, and the server will be upgraded in a way that's totally transparent to the client application.

The same idea also applies for less drastic upgrades. For example, changing a supporting class, such as a socket factory, can be instantly accomplished if either the class name changes, or if the old class isn't actually deployed on the client's filesystem.

A Multiple-Deployment Scenario

The first scenario was about gradually rolling out an application change to the client side. Our second scenario is similar, but involves gradually rolling out updated server applications without causing problems for existing installations. In this scenario, we could wind up with two different versions of the same server bound into a single naming service. That is:

Server 1
> Uses a version of the server class that implements the Account interface as of 02/10

Server 2
> Uses a version of the server class that implements the Account interface as of 06/10

In this scenario, we cannot put the stub classes on the naming service's classpath. The bootstrap classloader will load only one class definition from the filesystem. Regardless of which is loaded, one of the servers won't be able to bind its stubs into the naming service.

The solution for this problem is simple: don't install any classes on the naming service's classpath, and give the two applications different codebase URLs. The RMI classloading algorithm will load both classes dynamically and use them correctly. This will happen automatically.

The Class Server

Implicit in the discussion so far is the idea that a class file can be downloaded from a URL. That is, from a codebase annotation for a class, which contains a string-delimited sequence of URLs, and a classname, the RMI deserialization algorithm can find and load a class. I've already mentioned that RMI uses instances of the URLClassLoader class to do this. In this section, we will discuss how URLClassloader works, and how you can create a server that responds to requests from a URLClassLoader.

In the discussion that follows, we will assume that all URLs are of the form *http://*. Instances of URLClassLoader can also handle URLs of the form *ftp://*. The decision to focus on *http://* URLs has two justifications. First, most applications use *http://* rather than *ftp://* URLs. Second, *ftp://* URLs are handled in pretty much the same way anyway. If you understand how the *http://* URLs are handled, you can figure out the *ftp://* URLs in under 10 minutes.

Requesting a Class

At this point, it's important for us to discuss how HTTP works in a little detail. The important points are these:

- HTTP works in request-response cycles. A client makes a request, typically through a GET or POST request, and a server sends back a response. After the

Marshalled Objects and Codebases

The idea that the server can download classes, as well as instances, leads to some interesting problems with serialization. Suppose, for example, that a client application needs to implement a simple persistence layer. One natural way to do this is via serialization: the client application can create an instance of `FileInputStream` and use serialization to make persistent copies of the objects.

This can break if the instances stored in the file are instances of classes that the client application downloaded (e.g., instances of classes not on the client application's classpath). When the client tries to deserialize the instances from the file, it needs the class definitions for the instances in the file. If the class definitions aren't on the client's classpath, deserialization will fail because the ordinary serialization and deserialization algorithms don't store a codebase property.

One solution to this is to use instances of `MarshalledObject`, which we previously discussed in Chapter 17. Recall that `MarshalledObject` is a class with instances that contain a single serialized instance of another class. In Chapter 17, I stated that `MarshalledObject` uses RMI's customized version of serialization to store data. This means that any instance serialized into an instance of `MarshalledObject` has a codebase, and when the instance is deserialized using get( ), the class is retrieved from the codebase location if necessary.

Thus, if you want to implement a simple client-side persistence layer using serialization for an RMI application, you should use the following three-step procedure:

1. Create an instance of `FileInputStream`.
2. Serialize the instances you want to store into instances of `MarshalledObject` by passing them as arguments to `MarshalledObject`'s constructor.
3. Serialize the instances of `MarshalledObject` to the instance of `FileInputStream`.

This is more complicated than directly serializing the instances to a file, but will help to guarantee that the serialized instances can be read back in later.

---

response is sent, the connection is over, and there are no obligations on either side.

- HTTP is an ASCII-based protocol. An HTTP message consists of a series of ASCII headers followed by a stringified version of any binary data that may need to be sent along with the message.

- The first line of an HTTP request consists of a method, a path, and a protocol. The path frequently corresponds to the physical path required to access a file on the server machine.

- The first line of an HTTP response consists of a status code and a description of the return value. After that, the response contains *content headers* (metadata that further describes the response) and then the *content body*.

HTTP messages are remarkably simple and easy to read. Even if you don't know much about HTTP, request-response cycles, or the World Wide Web, you can generally figure out what's going on. This simplicity is crucial to the success of HTTP and one of the big reasons why the Web is so important today.

Given this, an instance of URLClassLoader takes a URL of the form *http://machineName:port/path/* and a classname and does the following:

1. It creates a path from the classname by interpreting each package as a directory. For example, the class com.ora.rmibook.chapter9.valueobjects.Money becomes the path */com/ora/rmibook/chapter9/valueobjects/Money.class.*

2. It prepends the path from the URL to the path it just created in order to form a request path.

3. It then issues an HTTP GET to a web server running on *port* of *machineName*. This request has the following format:

        GET request-path HTTP/1.1

For example, if the URL is *http://localhost:80/*, and the classname is com.ora.rmibook. chapter9.valueobjects.Money, an instance of URLClassLoader will send the following request to port 80 of the localHost:

    GET /com/ora/rmibook/chapter9/valueobjects/Money.class HTTP/1.1

Receiving a Class

Once an instance of URLClassLoader sends a request, it needs to get back an HTTP response that contains the class. That is, it expects to receive a message with the following four characteristics:

- The response code must be HTTP 200 (indicating success).
- The Content-Length header must be set and must be accurate.
- The Content-Type header must be set and must be equal to application/java.
- After all the headers, the bytecodes for the class must be included.

This is fairly simple stuff. Almost any web server can be easily configured to send a correct response to a request coming from an instance of URLClassLoader.

Handling JAR files

What I've described works very well for individual class files. But it doesn't work for class files contained in a JAR file. The key to retrieving classes from a JAR is to remove the ending / from the URL. The retrieval algorithm used by URLClassLoader checks to see whether the URL ends in a /. If the URL ends with /, it follows the algorithm described earlier.

It's very easy to forget to end a codebase URL with a /. And, for some reason, if you do forget, you won't spot the error in your code. Instead, you'll probably spend half a day or so making sure that the filesystem is working.

On the other hand, if the URL doesn't end with a /, it is assumed to be complete and to describe the location of a JAR file. An instance of URLClassLoader will attempt to retrieve the JAR file, which must be returned the same way as an individual class, and then attempts to find the class from within the JAR file.

Thus, if the URL was *http://localhost:80/myclasses.jar*, and the class was com.ora. rmibook.chapter9.valueobjects.Money, an instance of URLClassLoader would do the following:

1. Send the following HTTP command to the web server listening on port 80 of localHost:

   GET /myClasses.jar HTTP/1.1.

2. Attempt to interpret the return value as a JAR and load com.ora.rmibook. chapter9.valueobjects.Money from the JAR file.

Sun's Class Server

Rather than force you to install and configure a web server, Sun Microsystems, Inc. has, at various times, provided a simple Java class that handles most of the details of serving class files in response to requests from an instance of URLClassLoader. Here's the entire class (with comments removed):

```
public abstract class ClassServer implements Runnable {
    private ServerSocket server = null;
    private int port;

    public abstract byte[] getBytes(String path) throws IOException,
        ClassNotFoundException;

    protected ClassServer(int port) throws IOException  {
        this.port = port;
        server = new ServerSocket(port);
        newListener();
    }

    public void run() {
        Socket socket;
        try {
            socket = server.accept();
        }
        catch (IOException e) {
            System.out.println("Class Server died: " + e.getMessage());
            e.printStackTrace();
```

```
            return;
        }
        newListener();

        try {
            DataOutputStream out = new DataOutputStream(socket.getOutputStream());
            try {
                BufferedReader in = new BufferedReader(new
                    InputStreamReader(socket.getInputStream()));
                String path = getPath(in);
                byte[] bytecodes = getBytes(path);
                try {
                    out.writeBytes("HTTP/1.0 200 OK\r\n");
                    out.writeBytes("Content-Length: " + bytecodes.length +
                        "\r\n");
                    out.writeBytes("Content-Type: application/java\r\n\r\n");
                    out.write(bytecodes);
                    out.flush();
                }
                catch (IOException ie) {
                    return;
                }
            }
            catch (Exception e) {
                out.writeBytes("HTTP/1.0 400 " + e.getMessage() + "\r\n");
                out.writeBytes("Content-Type: text/html\r\n\r\n");
                out.flush();
            }
        }
        catch (IOException ex) {
            System.out.println("error writing response: " + ex.getMessage());
            ex.printStackTrace();
        }
        finally {
            try {
                socket.close();
            }
            catch (IOException e) {}
        }
    }

    private void newListener() {
        (new Thread(this)).start();
    }

    private static String getPath(BufferedReader in) throws IOException {
        String line = in.readLine();
        String path = "";
        if (line.startsWith("GET /")) {
            line = line.substring(5, line.length()-1).trim();
            int index = line.indexOf(".class ");
            if (index != -1) {
                path = line.substring(0, index).replace('/', '.');
```

```
            }
        }
        do {
            line = in.readLine( );
        } while ((line.length( ) != 0) && (line.charAt(0) != '\r') && (line.charAt(0)
                != '\n'));
        if (path.length( ) != 0) {
            return path;
        }
        else {
            throw new IOException("Malformed Header");
        }
    }
}
```

How to Find ClassServer

For legal reasons, I can't include the source code for ClassServer with the source code
for this book; the code was written by Sun Microsystems, and they have fairly stringent
rules about who can ship their source code. Similarly, in Chapter 22, we discuss HTTP
tunneling and use examples written by Sun to illustrate the basic idea.

Fortunately, it's not that hard to find these, and other, examples on the Internet. The
two best places to look are:

Javasoft's web site (http://www.javasoft.com)
> This is the basic source of all things Java (and hence, of all things RMI). In partic-
> ular, there is a very nice RMI section.

The RMI mailing list (http://archives.java.sun.com/cgi-bin/wa?A0=rmi-users)
> The This is a high-quality mailing list. There are a lot of good developers who fre-
> quently post to the list (including many of the members of Sun's RMI develop-
> ment team). It is often the best place to look for answers to specific questions
> about RMI (the ability to search the archives is invaluable).

This may seem a little complicated. However, it's really a very simple class: it listens
on a port, parses HTTP requests that come in, and translates them into calls to the
abstract method getBytes( ). Moreover, as part of the parsing, it transforms the
request path into a classname. For example, it transforms:

```
GET /com/ora/rmibook/chapter9/valueobjects/Money.class HTTP/1.1
```

into a call on getBytes( ) using the argument com.ora.rmibook.chapter9.valueobjects.
Money. The return value from getBytes( ) is then packaged into an HTTP response with
a minimal set of headers and returned to the caller.

This is a very limited server. It doesn't handle either codebases that have paths or requests from JAR files very well. However, it's definitely good enough for development, quite possibly good enough for debugging, and occasionally good enough for deployment.

Of course, since `ClassServer` is an abstract class, it can't be used directly. Here's a concrete subclass that takes a root directory as a single command-line argument and serves class files based on that root:

```java
public class SimpleClassServer extends ClassServer {
    private static String _pathPrefix;
    public static void main(String[] args) throws IOException {
        _pathPrefix = args[0];
        new SimpleClassServer();
    }

    private SimpleClassServer() throws IOException  {
        super(80);
    }

    public byte[] getBytes(String path) throws IOException, ClassNotFoundException {
        path = path.replace('.', '\\');
        String actualPath = _pathPrefix + path +".class";
        FileInputStream fileInputStream = new FileInputStream(actualPath);
        ByteArrayOutputStream inMemoryCopy = new ByteArrayOutputStream();
        copy(fileInputStream,  inMemoryCopy);
        return inMemoryCopy.toByteArray();
    }

    private void copy(InputStream inputStream, OutputStream outputStream) throws
        IOException {
        int nextByte;
        while ((nextByte = inputStream.read()) != -1) {
            outputStream.write(nextByte);
        }
    }
}
```

To use `SimpleClassServer`, all you need to do is pass in a single command-line argument, which is the base directory where the class files are stored.

For example, I store my class files in the directories below *D:\classes* (i.e., the class com. ora.rmibook.chapter9.valueobjects.Money is contained in the directory *d:\classes\com\ ora\rmibook\chapter9\valueobjects*). On my system, the following invocation launches `SimpleClassServer` correctly:

```
start java examples.classserver.SimpleClassServer "D:\classes\\"
```

The \\ at the end is necessary because of how Sun parses command-line arguments.

It's worth repeating: the URL for SimpleClassServer cannot have a path. Path information will be treated as part of the package declaration for the class. If you need to have multiple class servers running (e.g., if you want to serve different versions of the same classes), you either need to write a version that understands paths a little better, or use different ports for different versions (e.g., "Port 1299 is for the classes from December of 1999").

Using Dynamic Classloading in an Application

Once you've set up a class server, either using a web server or a variant of the previous code, you still need to adapt your application. Adapting an application to use dynamic classloading doesn't require much work. However, the changes are pervasive (both the client and the server code changes), and it's easy to forget to make one. In what follows, we'll walk through the changes step by step, based on where the code is running. I should point out that most of the changes aren't code changes.

Instead, they're configuration changes and slight alterations in how the code is deployed.

Do We Really Need an HTTP Server?

It's reasonable to wonder why an HTTP server is necessary for dynamic classloading of stubs. You may think something like the following:

> The client got an instance of a stub class from the naming service. Why couldn't the client also have gotten the stub class directly from the naming service?

And, indeed, for the case of stub classes, this seems reasonable. Why should the client have to make a second request, from a second server?

As with most design decisions, there really isn't a decisive reason for why the RMI registry doesn't provide this functionality. But there are some points to keep in mind:

- The client needs to make a second request for the class files. The class files shouldn't simply be sent with the instances; automatically sending the class files would waste bandwidth.

- The client may actually require class files that the RMI registry doesn't know about. The RMI registry only knows about the stub class, the remote interfaces, and any classes mentioned in the remote interface. The server could easily wind up sending a subclass of a class mentioned in the interface (e.g., the server could send an instance of a subclass of Money as a return value for getBalance( )). This would involve class files the RMI registry doesn't know about and would naturally require another class server anyway.

Neither of these is a compelling argument, but they make the decision to require a separate class server seem more reasonable.

Server-Side Changes

The main change on the server side involves explicitly declaring the codebase. This is done by setting the java.rmi.server.codebase system parameter. java.rmi.server. codebase should be set to a string that contains a space-delimited sequence of URLs. For example, the following command-line invocation sets the codebase to http:// localHost:80/:

```
start java -Djava.security.manager -Djava.rmi.server.codebase="http://localhost:80/"
    -Djava.security.policy="d:\\java.policy" com.ora.rmibook.chapter9.applications.
    ImplLauncher Bob 10000 Alex 1223
```

RMI uses the value of java.rmi.server.codebase when trying to annotate class descriptions for serialized objects. RMI uses the following rules for determining which annotation is sent with a class description:

- If a class was loaded from the filesystem, and java.rmi.server.codebase is set, then the annotation for that class is equal to the value of java.rmi.server.codebase.

- If a class was loaded from the filesystem, and java.rmi.server.codebase has not been set, the class is not annotated at all.

- If a class wasn't loaded from the filesystem but was instead loaded via dynamic classloading, the original annotation, which was used to load the class in the first place, is retained and sent as the class annotation.

Ordinarily, it suffices to set the java.rmi.server.codebase property from the command line, as in the preceding example. In addition, setting java.rmi.server. codebase from the command line preserves flexibility. However, there is one code change that may be necessary if the servers in question are being launched by the activation framework.

Here's the code from Chapter 17 that created an activation group:

```
private static void createActivationGroup( ) throws ActivationException,
    RemoteException {
        ActivationGroupID oldID = ActivationGroup.currentGroupID( );
        Properties pList = new Properties( );
        pList.put("java.security.policy", "d:\\java.policy");
        pList.put("sun.rmi.transport.connectionTimeout", "30000");
        ActivationGroupDesc.CommandEnvironment configInfo = null;
        ActivationGroupDesc description = new ActivationGroupDesc(pList,
            configInfo);
        ActivationGroupID id = (ActivationGroup.getSystem( )).
            registerGroup(description);
        ActivationGroup.createGroup(id, description, 0);
        return;
}
```

In the middle of this code, pList is created and filled with the values of system properties for the JVM that will be launched by the Activation Framework. If the application is going to use dynamic classloading, then pList must also contain an entry for the java.rmi.server.codebase property.

The following code sets the value for java.rmi.server.codebase in pList to whatever the launching JVM's value for java.rmi.server.codebase is:

```
private static void createActivationGroup() throws ActivationException,
    RemoteException {
        ActivationGroupID oldID = ActivationGroup.currentGroupID();
        Properties pList = new Properties();
        pList.put("java.security.policy", "d:\\java.policy");
        pList.put("sun.rmi.transport.connectionTimeout", "30000");
        String codebase = System.getProperty();
        if ((null!=codebase) && (0!=codebase.length)) {
            pList.put("java.rmi.server.codebase", codebase);
        }
        ActivationGroupDesc.CommandEnvironment configInfo = null;
        ActivationGroupDesc description = new ActivationGroupDesc(pList,
            configInfo);
        ActivationGroupID id = (ActivationGroup.getSystem()).
            registerGroup(description);
        ActivationGroup.createGroup(id, description, 0);
        return;
}
```

You probably noticed when we started the servers that we also amended our security policy. This was necessary in order to prevent security exceptions from being thrown when the client attempts to make a connection to the registry or the server. We'll talk more about security policies in the next chapter. In the meantime (and only for the meantime), just use the following for the security policy file:

```
grant {
    permission java.security.AllPermission;
};
```

Naming-Service Changes

In most application architectures, the launch code binds stubs into a naming service, and clients retrieve stubs from the naming service. This means that the naming service, which has an instance of the stub, will need all the associated class definitions. In the banking application, for example, we bind stubs that implement the Account interface into the RMI registry:

```
public interface Account extends Remote {
    public Money getBalance() throws RemoteException;
    public void makeDeposit(Money amount) throws RemoteException,
        NegativeAmountException;
    public void makeWithdrawal(Money amount) throws RemoteException,
        OverdraftException, NegativeAmountException;
}
```

This means that the JVM containing the registry needs to load the following classes:

```
Account
AccountImpl_Stub
```

```
Money
NegativeAmountException
OverdraftException
```

The problem is this: if the registry had any of these classes on its local classpath, then it would load them from the filesystem instead of using the URLs contained in their annotation. However, if the naming service loads the class from the local filesystem, then, when the client requests the instance, the original annotation will be lost (the classes will either not have an annotation or will be annotated with the value of java. rmi.server.codebase that's set for the naming service's JVM). The only way we can guarantee to preserve codebase annotations is by paying attention to the third rule from earlier:

> If a class wasn't loaded from the filesystem but was instead loaded via dynamic class-loading, the original annotation, which was used to load the class in the first place, is retained and sent as the class annotation.

This means that no application-specific classes should be on the naming service's classpath.

Failing to clear the naming service's classpath is probably the single most common reason why dynamic classloading breaks down. It can be really annoying because the calls to bind( ) or rebind( ) will succeed. The failure will only become apparent when the client tries to retrieve the stub.

Client-Side Changes

On the client side, there are two things that need to be done. The first is that a SecurityManager must be installed. Without a SecurityManager, RMI will not dynamically load classes. Installing a SecurityManager usually amounts to adding a single line of code to the client, which will be executed very early in the application's lifecycle. For example, adding the following line to main( ) will do the trick:

```
public void main(String args[]) {
        System.setSecurityManager(new RMISecurityManager( ));
    ...
}
```

The second thing that must be done is that the classes that will be dynamically downloaded need to be removed from (or just not installed on) the client's classpath. That's it. With these changes, an RMI application can dynamically load classes from a server at runtime.

Once you install a security manager, you will also need to install a security policy. We'll discuss this in detail in Chapter 20. In the meantime, you can use the "wide-open" security policy that we defined for the server-side eariler and specify the -Djava.security.policy=file option on the command line for the client.

Disabling Dynamic Classloading Entirely

There are a number of situations when you may not want any form of dynamic class-loading to be enabled. For example, while it makes perfect sense to download classes to client applications, it's much dicier when clients upload classes to servers. Generally, that's a security risk a typical enterprise application might want to avoid.

There are two ways to do this. The first is to not install a security manager. We'll talk more about security managers in Chapter 20, but the basic point is that RMI won't dynamically load classes unless a security manager is installed. On the other hand, security managers are useful objects, and you probably want to use one.

The second way to disable dynamic classloading is to set a specific system property. If the java.rmi.server.useCodebaseOnly system property is set to true, then RMI will only load classes from the local filesystem, regardless of whether the class has a code-base annotation.

CHAPTER 20

Security Policies

Making a distributed system secure is a mindnumbingly difficult task. As a system acquires more users, it will naturally acquire more security holes. In this chapter, we'll discuss a general-purpose Java mechanism for safeguarding against a new type of security problem. By the end of this chapter, you will understand the security policy mechanism in Java 2, and know how to use it to safeguard some aspects of your RMI application.

RMI has been part of the Java platform for a long time. The first versions of RMI were "interim releases" that worked with JDK 1.2. With JDK 1.1, RMI became part of the Java specification. However, when Java 2 was released, something surprising happened. Working RMI applications suddenly failed. They compiled perfectly, they linked correctly, and they appeared to launch correctly. Yet whenever an application attempted to connect to an external process (e.g., the launch code tried to connect to the registry), a socket exception was thrown.

The reason for this: Java 2 contains a whole new security model. The net effect of the new security model is that a piece of code, unless explicitly granted permission, is not allowed to access anything that is not entirely contained within the JVM. This means that, for example, a legacy RMI application that doesn't have the appropriate permissions will no longer be able to open socket connections. Because all of RMI's messages travel across socket connections, the new security model quite effectively breaks legacy applications.

Technically speaking, this isn't quite true. Permissions are enforced by the security manager. Applications that don't have a security manager installed still behave as they used to behave. However, any program that installs a security manager (as RMI programs usually do) now requires a security policy. We'll discuss how SecurityManagers work in more detail later in this chapter.

A Different Kind of Security Problem

In Chapter 2, we discussed the three classical security problems that can arise in a distributed application.

Data confidentiality
> How do we prevent third parties from seeing confidential information?

Data integrity
> How do we make sure that the data received is identical to the data that was sent?

Authorization and validation
> How can we guarantee that a user or program is who or what it claims to be and, given this, how can we ensure that they are allowed to perform the operations they are attempting?

There's an interesting point about these three security problems: they all assume that the functional code will behave correctly, and that security problems arise as a result of failing to safeguard against devious or careless users. However, as veteran Java programmers know, applets introduced a whole new twist to security issues within an application. You can have a fully functioning encryption layer, and fully authenticated users, and still have a tremendous security problem: the code itself may not be trustworthy.

The archetypal applet scenario is a variation on the following:

1. The end user uses a web browser to view a web page.

2. The web page contains an applet. As part of displaying the page, the browser starts the applet running.

3. The applet begins to systematically remove files from the end user's hard drive (after, of course, first harvesting personal information from them and uploading it to a server).

The solution adopted inside of web browsers begins with a simple observation: if the applet can't access the hard drive, then the applet can't harvest information or delete files. This is a generalization of the following rule of thumb:

> If an applet can communicate only with the server that sent it, and cannot access any information outside of the web page in which it was downloaded, then the applet is a minimal security risk.

In such a scenario, the applet has access to only two types of information:

- Information that originally came from the server (the web page and anything the server sends the applet directly). Letting the applet access this information isn't a security risk. Since the applet came from the server and is part of a web-based client-server application, this really boils down to, "An application is allowed to have state, which can be passed around."

- Information that the user has explicitly given to the applet. While it's possible that this information is a security risk, the plain truth is that the user is in a much better position than our software to decide this.

This approach to security inside a web browser has become known as *putting the applet in a sandbox* or, more succinctly, *using a sandbox*.

The designers of Java 2 made an important observation: applets are simply mobile code. Conceptually, and from a security viewpoint, applets aren't all that different from our mobile-code scenarios outlined in Chapter 19. In fact, dynamic classloading can lead to massive security violations on a scale beyond the reach of applets. Suppose, for example, a malicious programmer somehow gains access to an application's source code and the RMI registry. She then does the following two things:

1. She creates new stubs that export the same interface as the old stub. These new stubs actually wrap an instance of the original stub and forward method calls to the old stub. However, they also do one other thing: they forward all information sent over the wire to a listening application located somewhere on the Internet.

2. She systematically replaces the stubs in your registry with her new stubs.

Now, suppose a user launches a client application and attempts to access a server:

1. The user gets an instance of a malicious stub from the registry. As part of doing so, the user automatically dynamically downloads the malicious stub class.

2. Because the malicious stub actually aggregates the real stub, and sends the messages to the server application, the client application appears to work perfectly.

3. The malicious hacker gets a copy of all the information sent over the wire.

This is actually a fairly plausible scenario, which we'll refer to as *client-side contamination*. The reason for referring to it as a "contamination" is, of course, that there is also the possibility of server-side contamination. Suppose, for instance, that a malicious hacker creates a new subclass of Money called SpyMoney, which tries to listen in on all the traffic on the server and forwards anything that sounds interesting. If a client application passes an instance of SpyMoney into a server operation, and the client has set the java.rmi.server.codebase property, then the server could wind up dynamically loading the SpyMoney class and then creating and using instances of SpyMoney.

 In the age of Internet appliances, it continues to get worse. We're rapidly heading into an age when your washing machine will download software patches from the Internet automatically. Lots of small, special-purpose programs will be flowing over the wires, and most of the traffic will occur without direct human supervision.

Permissions

The Java 2 solution to these sorts of problems is similar to the solution that the people who wrote web browsers introduced. Namely, Java 2 introduces the ability to define a custom sandbox.

More precisely, Java 2 introduces a list of *permissions* that must be *granted* to pieces of code. By default, an entire application runs inside the tightest and most restrictive sandbox possible. The sandbox can be selectively enlarged by granting portions of the codebase permission to perform certain actions, such as opening a socket connection on a certain port. Permissions are usually listed in a file, called a security policy. There are two main ways that security policies are created:

- Developers use them to list the permissions that their programs need in order to function correctly. They write a security policy that encapsulates this information and ship it with their application.

- Users* can have their own security policy, or alter ones that are shipped with applications, which defines what the program is allowed to do with respect to the external environment.

 Users rarely actually write their own security policies. But writing your own policies can be incredibly useful: if you download a Java application from the Internet, you may want to consider running it inside a fairly tight sandbox just to make sure that important files aren't put at risk.

There's a very subtle and interesting point here: permissions are not granted to an application as a whole, they're granted to classes within an application. This is because of dynamic classloading. Consider, for example, either of our contamination scenarios. The problem occurs because a bad class is loaded dynamically. If we granted permissions to the application globally, then instances of the contaminating class would also get those permissions.

The Types of Permissions

In Java 2, there are nine basic types of permissions:

AWT permissions
File permissions
Network permissions
Socket permissions

---

* Actually, this is more likely to be systems administrators.

Different Applications Need Different Sandboxes

You may wonder why Java 2 doesn't wholeheartedly adopt the web browser's solution: simply define a sandbox instead of introducing the ability to define custom sandboxes. The answer is that different applications can have very different security profiles.

For example, the client for the bank example will probably never need to write to the local drive. All the persistent state is stored on the servers. However, you could easily imagine that the client for the printer application may very well acquire the following store-and-forward functionality:

- If the selected printer is currently down, notify the user and offer her the option of sending the document to that printer anyway. If the user decides that the document should be printed using the currently unavailable printer, store the document on the client machine.

- Every now and then, in a background thread, check the local storage to see if there are any documents in it. For each document in local storage, check to see if the printer has come back up. If so, try to print the document, removing printed documents from the client-side store.

In this case, the client for the printer application will need to write to at least one directory on the local hard drive. Since we want to minimize the permissions our client application has, this means that the new printer client uses a different sandbox than the bank client.

Property permissions
Reflection permissions
Runtime permissions
Security permissions
Serializable permissions

Each of these permission types defines a specific way in which the sandbox can be breached. For a typical RMI application, the four most important types are AWT permissions, file permissions, socket permissions, and property permissions. In the following subsections, we will discuss each of these four permission types in more detail.

 In the discussion that follows, I will also give examples illustrating how each permission is assigned; the syntax of the examples and how the associated permissions are actually passed to the JVM will be explained later in "Setting Up a Security Policy."

AWT permissions

AWT permissions control access to resources associated with the screen. This type of permission was created in response to three possible security breaches:

Fooling the user

> A hostile piece of code could pretend to be a friendly piece of code. For example, it could pop up a "registration wizard" sequence of dialog boxes that, under the guise of helping the user with her software, captured personal information.

Capturing static information

> Alternatively, the hostile code could simply look at the clipboard, or capture what's on the screen. For example, hostile code downloaded into an email client could conceivably simply create GIF images of text windows and send them off for analysis.

Fooling the running application

> The third security breach involves mimicking the user. Java 2 includes a new mechanism, called the robot, which simulates user actions. While primarily intended for automated user-interface testing, the events generated via the robot mechanism are indistinguishable from actual user actions.

Because there are a variety of different security breaches involved, there are six subtypes of the AWT permission: accessClipBoard, accessEventQueue, listenToAllAwtEvents, readDisplayPixels, showWindowWithoutWarningBanner, and createRobot. They are all boolean values—a piece of code either has permission to perform the operation or it does not. Here's a permissions example granting all classes the ability to show windows without warning banners:

```
grant {
    permission java.awt.AWTPermission "showWindowWithoutWarningBanner";
};
```

Unless this permission is granted, an application window will be displayed with an applet warning banner across the bottom, as in Figure 20-1.

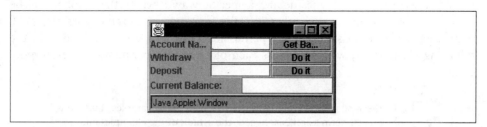

Figure 20-1. Applet window with warning banner

 These apply even if you aren't using AWT directly. For example, if you are using Swing components to build your GUI, the AWT permissions still apply since Swing is implemented as a layer on top of AWT.

File permissions

A file permission is simply the ability to perform an operation on a file. There are four basic file operations: reading, writing, executing, and deleting. Correspondingly, there are four types of file permissions: read, write, execute, and delete. Here is a permissions example granting all classes the ability to read, write, and delete— but not execute—all files in the *C:/temp/* directory and any of its subdirectories:

```
grant {
    permission java.io.FilePermission  "C:/temp/-" , "read, write, delete";
};
```

File permissions use a limited regular-expression syntax. A - is a recursive wildcard, and a * is a local wildcard. Thus:

```
permission java.io.FilePermission  "C:/temp/-" , "read, write, delete";
```

grants permission to modify any file in *C:/temp/* or in any of its subdirectories, while:

```
permission java.io.FilePermission  "C:/temp/*" , "read, write, delete";
```

grants permission to modify only files that are actually in *C:/temp/*.

Socket permissions

Socket permissions represent the operations on sockets. There are four basic socket-related operations:

Resolving an address
> This is the process by which a human-readable name is turned into an Internet address. For example, *www.oreilly.com* is translated into 209.204.146.22.

Connecting
> This is the actual process of creating a socket connection between two applications.

Listening for connections
> This is the process by which server sockets listen for connections.

Accepting a connection
> This is what happens after listening, when an instance of ServerSocket actually forms a connection with an instance of Socket.

Associated with these four operations are four socket permissions: resolve, accept, listen, and accept. The distinction between listen and accept is a little strange. It helps to think of accept as "accept from." That is, listen specifies on which ports a server socket is allowed to listen, while accept specifies from whom the server socket is allowed to accept connections.

These permissions are also somewhat strange in that while you can grant resolve or listen, you rarely do; resolve is implied by any of the other operations, and listen is implied by accept.

Socket permissions require you to specify a set of allowed computer addresses and a range of ports. Allowed addresses can be specified in any of the following forms:

Hostname
A single human-readable name, such as www.hipbone.com.

IP address
A single IP address, such as 209.220.141.161.

localHost
The actual string localHost, which specifies the local machine. Alternatively, if no computer is specified (or if " " is used), localHost will be assumed.

*.partial_domain_specification
You are allowed to use a * as a wildcard operator on the lefthand side of a human-readable name. Thus, for example, *.hipbone.com and *.com are both perfectly valid specifications.

 You cannot use an asterisk as a wildcard with an IP address. For example, 209.220.141.* is not a valid address specification.

Allowed ports can be specified as either a single number or a range. The allowed specifications are:

A single number
For example, 1024.

A minus sign followed by a number
This is used to specify "all port numbers less than or equal to the specified number." For example, -2048 specifies all port numbers less than or equal to 2048.

A number followed by a minus sign
This is used to specify "all port numbers greater than or equal to the specified number." For example, 2048- is used to specify all port numbers greater than or equal to 2048.

Two numbers, separated by a minus sign
This specifies a range of port numbers with both an upper and lower bound. For example, 2048-4096 specifies all port numbers greater than or equal to 2048 and less than or equal to 4096.

Here's an example of a permission that allows classes to accept connections from any machine in the domain *.oreilly.com, on any port greater than 1024:

```
grant {
    permission java.net.SocketPermission  "*.oreilly.com:1024-", "accept, connect";
};
```

Property permissions

The final type of permissions that we will discuss are property permissions. The System class, defined in the java.lang package, has a static reference to the singleton properties object, which you can obtain by calling System.getProperties( ).

This properties object is an instance of java.util.Properties. This object contains two things: a set of canonical name-value pairs that specify information about the JVM and all the command-line properties set by the -D flag. Many people like to think of the systems properties object as being analogous to the "environment variables" in a command shell.

Recall that our application in Chapter 18 was invoked using the command line:

```
java -Dcom.ora.rmibook.useMonitoringSockets=false ...
```

This created a property in the system properties object named com.ora.rmibook. useMonitoringSockets and set the value of the property to the string as false.

 Properties are usually named using a "dotted notation" consisting of a group name followed by a single period and then a descriptive name. For example, the canonical system properties contain properties named user.name, user.home, and user.dir.

By default, a class cannot read or set system properties. However, the read and write property permissions are used to remedy this. Properties are specified in one of three ways:

As a single asterisk
By itself, * is a wildcard that means all properties.

As an ordinary string
A property permission can be set for an individual property by giving the complete name of the property.

As a string followed by a dotted asterisk
Names of the form *groupname*.* match all properties that begin with *groupname*.

Here are some typical properties permissions, granting every class the ability to read but not change certain canonical properties:

```
grant {
        permission java.util.PropertyPermission "java.version", "read";
        permission java.util.PropertyPermission "java.vendor", "read";
        permission java.util.PropertyPermission "java.vendor.url", "read";
        permission java.util.PropertyPermission "java.class.version", "read";
}
```

Security Managers

Within a running JVM, permissions are enforced by an instance of the SecurityManager class. When a program attempts to do something that requires permission, the instance of SecurityManager is queried to see whether the operation succeeds. Thus, for example, attempting to read data from a file involves asking the security manager if the program is allowed to read data from the file.

To see this in action, let's look at the constructor from the FileInputStream class:

```
public FileInputStream(String name) throws FileNotFoundException {
        SecurityManager security = System.getSecurityManager();
        if (security != null) {
            security.checkRead(name);
        }
        fd = new FileDescriptor();
        open(name);
}
```

The first thing this constructor does is obtain the installed instance of SecurityManager and ask it whether the file can be read. If the application doesn't have permission to read the file, an exception is thrown. Similarly, the constructor for Socket begins with the following code snippet, which calls the installed security manager and checks to see if a connection is allowed:

```
private Socket(InetAddress address, int port, InetAddress localAddr,  int localPort,
    boolean stream) throws IOException {

    this();
    if (port < 0 || port > 0xFFFF) {
        throw new IllegalArgumentException("port out range:"+port);
    }
    if (localPort < 0 || localPort > 0xFFFF) {
        throw new IllegalArgumentException("port out range:"+localPort);
    }
    SecurityManager security = System.getSecurityManager();
    if (security != null) {
        security.checkConnect(address.getHostAddress(), port);
    }
    ....
}
```

It's important to note, however, that if there is no installed instance of SecurityManager, neither of these checks occurs. This is a general pattern: unless a security manager is installed, no permissions are checked, and applications have permission to perform any operation. This is necessary for backwards compatibility (retrofitting the Java 2 security model onto older applications is a time-consuming and difficult task) but makes the overall framework slightly more error prone.

Installing an Instance of SecurityManager

Only one instance of SecurityManager can be installed in a JVM, and it cannot be replaced. The simplest way to install a security manager is to set the java.security. manager system property when launching the JVM, as in the following example:

```
java -Djava.security.manager application
```

This will create an instance of the SecurityManager class and install it when the JVM is launched, before any application-specific code starts to run.

Using the system property to install a security manager is often very convenient. For example, when I download Java applications from the Internet, I always install a security manager from the command line. Doing this helps limit the damage a malicious or poorly written program can cause. You can also use the java.security.manager parameter to specify a particular security manager, as in the following example:

```
java -Djava.security.manager =java.rmi.RMISecurityManager application
```

Ordinarily, however, when you write an RMI application, you include a security manager by calling System.setSecurityManager( ), as in the following line of code:

```
System.setSecurityManager(new RMISecurityManager( ))
```

The reason for this is simple: RMI's dynamic classloading features won't work unless your application has an instance of SecurityManager installed. If you use dynamic classloading, relying on the user, or a batch file, to install an instance of SecurityManager is a bad idea.

RMI provides a simple security manager, named RMISecurityManager, in the java.rmi package. In Java 2, RMISecurityManager simply subclasses the standard security manager without adding any functionality at all. Most RMI applications use RMISecurityManager (or a custom subclass of it) for two very simple reasons. First, using RMISecurityManager instead of the standard security manager effectively documents why the security manager was installed (and thus makes it less likely that someone will modify the code to remove the security manager without thinking).

Second, it automatically allows code to evolve as RMI's security model gets more elaborate; if you use an instance of RMISecurityManager, then when the RMISecurityManager's implementation becomes more sophisticated, your code will automatically evolve.

How a Security Manager Works

As I've already indicated, a security manager works via a call-in policy. In other words, it relies on the Javasoft libraries to ask permission whenever a questionable operation is about to occur. The security sequence is:

1. A method that requires a security check is called.

2. As part of the implementation of that method, a call is made to the security manager. This call either throws an exception, indicating that a security violation has occurred, or returns silently, allowing the original method invocation to proceed.

The Javasoft implementations of SecurityManager actually do quite a bit of work in order to check whether an operation is allowed or not. They start by checking whether the object calling SecurityManager has the appropriate permission. Note that since the object calling SecurityManager is almost certainly part of the standard Java libraries, it has permission by default. All classes that are part of the standard Java libraries have permission to perform any operation. However, they need to check whether they can actually perform the requested operation or not.

After this, SecurityManager traverses the stack, checking to see whether each class in the stack trace has the appropriate permissions. If any of them do not, the check fails and SecurityManager throws an exception. Checking the stack is an important part of the security mechanism. Unless the entire stack is checked, there's really no way to prevent hostile code from initiating an action indirectly.

java.security.debug

You can watch SecurityManager at work by setting the java.security.debug system property. This property takes the following four basic values: all, access, policy, scl. Of these, access is the value that causes information about permissions checks to be printed to System.err.

access also has three advanced versions: stack, domain, and failure. access stack causes the calling stack to be printed out every time a permission is checked. access domain prints out the domains of all the objects in the stack trace. access failure, the most useful of all the flags, prints out the stack and the class domain for the class that failed the security check when a failure occurs. For example, invoking our banking application via the following command-line invocation gives us an overwhelming amount of information about which permissions are being checked and from where in our application:*

```
java -Djava.security.manager -Djava.security.debug="access daomin" com.ora.rmibook.
    chapter9.applications.BankClient
```

Setting Up a Security Policy

So far we've talked about the basic idea of permissions and how they're checked and enforced. The next logical step is to talk about how they're set. How does the JVM find out which permissions have been granted to particular classes?

---

* This can be very useful when trying to build a security policy. We'll discuss this in the next section.

The Three Policy Files

In most situations, two or three of the following security policies are used when running an application:

The global policy file
> This is a policy file that applies to all applications, run by any user. It's usually either the default policy that ships with the Java runtime environment or a policy file that's been defined by systems administrators (i.e., the people who configured a particular system). End users rarely alter this file. The global policy is installed, by default, in *${java.home}/jre/lib/security/java.policy*. On my machine, this resolves to *c:\program files\jdk1.3\jre\lib\security\java.policy*.

The user-specific policy file
> This is a policy file that applies to all applications started by a specific user. This usually either doesn't exist (there is no user-specific policy file that ships with the JRE) or is a policy file that's been defined by systems administrators. End users rarely alter this file either. The user-specific policy file has a default location of *${user.home}/.java.policy*. On my machine, this resolves to *c:\winnt\profiles\grosso\.java.policy*.

The application-specific policy file
> This is a policy file that ships with the application, defining the permissions that the application requires in order to run correctly. The application-specific policy file has no default location. Instead, the file location must be set with a system parameter when the application is launched.

Because each file lists permissions, it makes sense to take the union of all these files. That is, if any of these files says an operation is permissible, then the operation is permitted, even if the other two files are silent.

Setting the application-specific policy file

The application-specific policy file is defined using the `java.security.policy` system parameter. That is, to set the application-specific policy, you would use a command line such as:

```
java -Djava.security.policy="d:\java.policy"
```

Without a security manager, however, this doesn't have much meaning. If a JVM is invoked with a security policy, it's fairly common to install a security manager from the command line as well, as in the following example:

```
java -Djava.security.manager -Djava.security.policy="d:\java.policy"
```

There is one rather unexpected wrinkle in the java.security.policy system parameter. You can set it using == instead of =. That is, the following command line is perfectly valid:

```
java -Djava.security.manager -Djava.security.policy=="d:\java.policy"
```

This will instruct the JVM to use only the application-specific permissions file and ignore the other two permissions files. This has the effect of tightening the sandbox and can be useful during development, when you want to make sure you've figured out the correct security policy for your application, and when dealing with code you really don't trust, such as an application that you just downloaded from the Internet.

Inside a Policy File

A policy file consists of a sequence of grant statements. Each grant statement has the following format:

```
grant [signedBy Name] [codeBase URL] {
    // list of permissions
} ;
```

This translates to the following sentence:

> Any class that was loaded from the codebase specified by URL, and was digitally signed by Name, has the following permissions.

Square brackets indicate optional elements, and the words signedBy and codeBase are literals that must be used in front of their arguments. Thus, the following are all valid grant statements:

```
grant {
    // list of permissions
} ;

grant codeBase "http://www.oreilly.com/"{
    // list of permissions
} ;

grant signedBy WGrosso{
    // list of permissions
} ;

grant signedBy WGrosso codeBase "http://www.oreilly.com/"{
    // list of permissions
} ;
```

 We will skip over digitally signing code. It's complicated, and managing a keystore, while important, is outside the scope of this book. For more information on this and other advanced aspects of security, see *Applied Cryptography: Protocols, Algorithms, and Source Code in C, Second Edition* by Bruce Schnier (John Wiley & Sons).

The curly braces contain a comma-delimited list of permissions in the ASCII format I described earlier. Here, for example, is a grant statement that can run all the example programs in this book, provided the class files are installed in the correct location:

```
grant codeBase "file://d:/classes" {
    permission java.awt.AWTPermission "accessClipboard";
    permission java.awt.AWTPermission "accessEventQueue";
    permission java.awt.AWTPermission "listenToAllAWTEvents";
    permission java.awt.AWTPermission "showWindowWithoutWarningBanner";
    permission java.awt.AWTPermission "readDisplayPixels";
    permission java.net.SocketPermission ":1024-",
        "accept, connect, listen, resolve";
    permission java.io.FilePermission "<<ALL FILES>>", "read";
    permission java.io.FilePermission "<<ALL FILES>>", "write";
    permission java.io.FilePermission "<<ALL FILES>>", "delete";
    permission java.util.PropertyPermission "*", "read, write";
};
```

This allows any class located in a subdirectory of *D:\classes* to manipulate the GUI, create socket connections on nonsystem ports, manipulate files, and edit the system properties object. It does not, however, extend any permissions to dynamically loaded classes that come over the wire. As such, it's a perfectly good policy for both the server-side (where dynamically loaded classes are rarely used) and static clients. It would not, however, work in a scenario where the client dynamically downloads classes from the server.

Using Security Policies with RMI

You don't have to use a security manager with your RMI application. The only basic feature of RMI that won't work is dynamic classloading. However, both the RMI registry and the activation daemon do use security policies.

If you use either of these services, and don't give them a special security policy, your application can break in subtle ways. Consider, for example, binding a server that uses custom sockets into the RMI registry. The RMI registry will contain an instance of the stub class that refers to the original server. This deserialized stub will have an associated socket. Since the associated socket is an instance of a custom socket class, this means that the calling stack for the constructor for java.net.socket contained a non-Javasoft class. This means that the bind will fail unless the RMI registry has been given a more relaxed set of permissions.

 Recall that the -J flag is used to pass arguments to the underlying JVM for both the RMI registry and the activation daemon. For example, you need to use a command line invocation such as:

```
registry -J-Djava.security.policy= "d:\classes"
```

Because dynamic classloading is useful, and because using the activation daemon or the registry often forces you to write one anyway,* RMI applications usually wind up with a set of associated security policies: one for the servers, one for the naming service and activation daemon, and one for the clients.

Policy Tool

Java 2 comes with a simple GUI application, called `policytool`, that helps you edit policy files. You run it from the command line as follows:

```
policytool
```

The application allows you to open and edit a policy file, as shown in Figure 20-2.

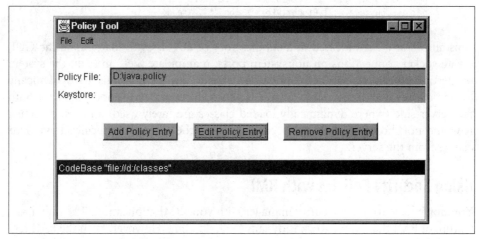

Figure 20-2. The policytool application

Each "policy entry" in the application corresponds to a single grant statement in the file. You can select an existing policy entry and then either edit it or remove it from the file, or you can create a new policy entry.

In the case of either creating or editing a policy entry, you wind up using the Policy Entry panel, shown in Figure 20-3. Choosing Add Entry or Edit Entry from this panel brings you to the Permissions panel (see Figure 20-4), which uses combo boxes to simplify the generation of individual permissions.

Some Final Words

We've only skimmed the surface of the permissions mechanism. After all, this is a book about RMI, and my goal is to explain how the permissions mechanism interacts with

---

* And because it's the right thing to do.

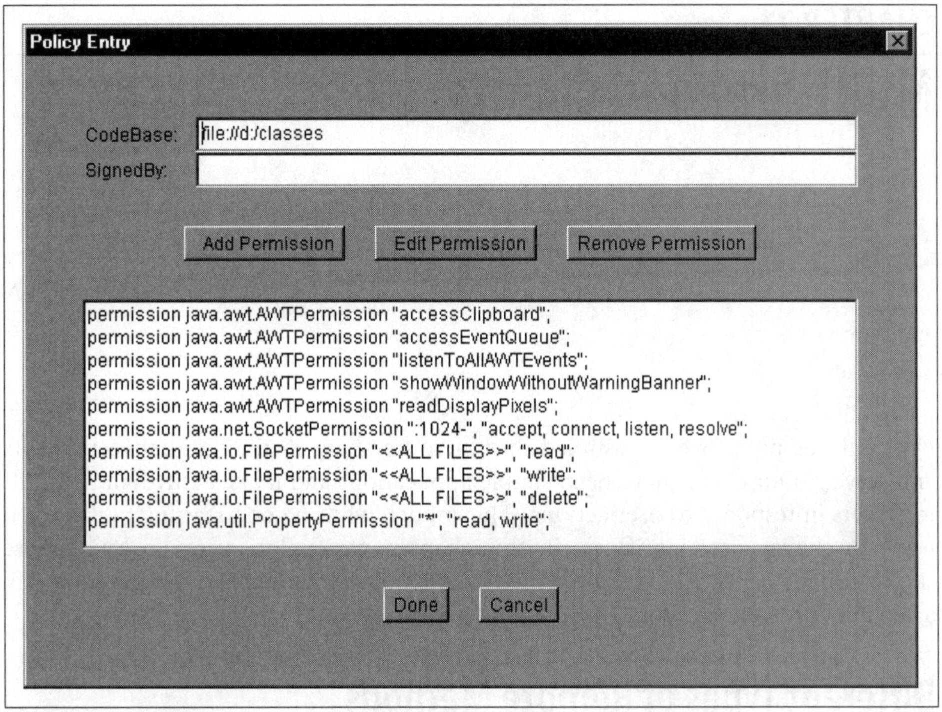

Figure 20-3. Policy entry panel

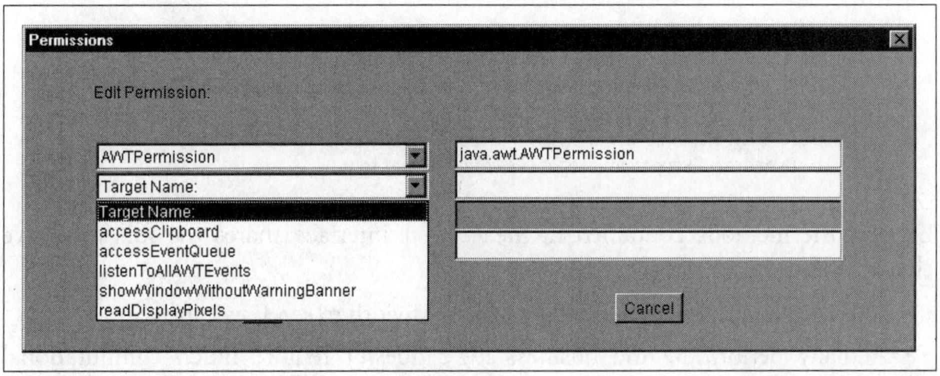

Figure 20-4. Permissions panel

RMI applications. If you need to know more, two great references are *Inside Java 2 Platform Security: Architecture, API Design, and Implementation* by Li Gong (Addison-Wesley) and *Java Security, Second Edition* by Scott Oaks (O'Reilly). If you even suspect you may need to know more about security, you should pick up one of those books. Security is serious (but interesting) stuff, and it's better to be safe than to be sorry.

CHAPTER 21

Multithreaded Clients

Up until this point, we've assumed that there's a sharp distinction between clients and servers. Our clients have been simple applications and make easily handled calls to servers in response to user actions. This model, while a good starting point, often leads to clumsy user interfaces. In this chapter, we explore ways to build more sophisticated clients. Along the way, we'll revisit our threading assumptions and talk again about remote iterators.

Different Types of Remote Methods

Consider, once again, the Account interface:

```
public interface Account extends Remote {
    public Money getBalance( ) throws RemoteException;
    public void makeDeposit(Money amount) throws RemoteException,
        NegativeAmountException;
    public void makeWithdrawal(Money amount) throws RemoteException,
        OverdraftException, NegativeAmountException;
}
```

Each of the methods contained in the Account interface shares the following five characteristics:

- Their arguments don't require a lot of bandwidth to send over the wire.

- Actually performing the business logic doesn't require much computational effort on the part of the server.

- All the methods require similar amounts of bandwidth and computational effort. Distinct calls, even ones from different clients accessing different accounts, have the same computational profile.

- They require a timely response.
- It's hard to say that one request is more important than another.[*]

When all five of these characteristics are present, requests are fairly small, and there's no clear benefit, in terms of server resources, to postponing or delaying some requests while immediately serving others. In this scenario, system architects usually opt for a limited model of client-server interaction known as *request-response cycles*.[†] In this model of client-server interaction, the client makes a request and the server responds immediately with the entire answer, and the transaction is over.

There is very little large-scale control over the sequence of remote method invocations (e.g., any sequence of remote method invocations is equally valid), and the server handles requests to a large degree on a first-come, first-served basis.

 Request-response is sometimes used to mean something a little stricter than the preceding definition. In particular, some authors also require that request-response systems be "memoryless." That is, the server and the client shouldn't have any knowledge about each other between cycles, and there is no shared state. The early web servers and browsers were request-response systems in this stronger sense. However, the advent of Java, Javascript, and cookies quickly pushed the Web into our weaker definition.

Printer-Type Methods

If all five characteristics aren't present, request-response cycles can break down. For example, consider our `Printer` interface again:

```
public interface Printer extends PrinterConstants, Remote {
    public boolean printerAvailable() throws RemoteException;
    public boolean printDocument(DocumentDescription document) throws
        RemoteException, PrinterException;
}
```

The first method, `printerAvailable()`, certainly has our five characteristics. `printDocument()`, however, does not. It can require substantial bandwidth to send the request, and it can take a long time to print a document. Moreover, while the client needs to be told whether the document was accepted in a timely manner, the really important piece of information the client wants is whether the document was

---

[*] This is partially because the requests are so computationally insignificant. You could conceive of ways to prioritize requests (based on the customer's total deposit, for example), but any implementation of a prioritization scheme would consume a significant percentage of the server's total processing time.

[†] And we'll call the associated methods *request-response methods*.

successfully printed. And that information cannot be returned immediately. We'll call methods like this *printer-type methods*.

Our solution to this problem was to simply return the answer to whether the print request had been accepted by the server and not tell the user if the request succeeded. However, that wasn't a very good solution; we'd like the application to track that information for the user automatically.

What's more, the natural extensions to the basic `Printer` interface don't have our characteristics either. For example, in Chapter 3, our list of future requirements included:

> Users will want to have different priorities for print jobs. Important documents should be moved to the top of a print queue; less urgent jobs should wait until the printer isn't busy.

This directly violates our fifth characteristic.

Report-Type Methods

Thinking about the bank example leads to another way these five characteristics can be violated. Suppose we wanted, in our banking application, to support certain types of reports. For example, our loans manager might think the following:

> I'd really like to look at all the checking accounts with a low balance and a large number of transactions. Accounts like that are really good sales prospects for overdraft protection.

This functionality, while important, is very different from what we've been implementing. It's computationally expensive, very low-priority in comparison to, say, people or businesses seeking to access their accounts, and it doesn't have a bound on the bandwidth consumed (e.g., it could conceivably return all the accounts).

In addition, unlike the printer, partial results are possible. A request to print a document takes a long time, and the outcome we want, while a simple boolean value, is completely unknown until the printer finishes. A partial answer to our accounts query, however, is quite reasonable: when the method is halfway finished, we ought to know half of the accounts that we will eventually return. I'll call methods like this *report-type methods*.

Handling Printer-Type Methods

Our implementation of `printDocument( )` in Chapter 4 was simple: we accepted the request. The return value of the `printDocument( )` method simply told the client whether the request had been successfully received. In essence, we treated `printDocument( )` as an ordinary remote method. As a result, our client application wasn't very user-friendly. The user doesn't simply want to know that the request was received by the printer. The user wants to know the status of the document as it prints, and when the document is finally done printing, the user wants to know about that as well.

The reason we wrote such a bad implementation was because it was in Chapter 4, and we were more concerned about introducing the basics of RMI than making fine distinctions between types of remote requests. Moreover, printer-type methods force the client to become a multithreaded application and therefore couldn't be handled before Chapters 11 and 12. Now that we know that RMI uses multiple threads, and now that we understand synchronization, we're ready to handle printer-type methods.

You may think that we can simply use the following strategy to implement printDocument( ):

- Accept all requests.
- Synchronize the methods in the implementation of Printer so that most requests block and wait for the printer to become available.
- The methods involved in the implementation of Printer can now return the result of the print job.

And, indeed, the code for this is simple; it boils down to adding the synchronized keyword in two places, one use for each method in the Printer interface. Here's part of an implementation of the Printer interface that simulates this behavior by sleeping for a random amount of time when the document should be printing:

```
public class SynchronizedPrinter {
    private PrintWriter _log;
    public SynchronizedPrinter(OutputStream log) throws RemoteException {
        _log = new PrintWriter(log);
    }

    public synchronized boolean printerAvailable( ) {
        return true;
    }

    public synchronized boolean printDocument(DocumentDescription
        documentDescription) throws PrinterException {
        if (null== _log) {
            throw new NoLogException( );
        }
        if (null==documentDescription) {
            throw new NoDocumentException( );
        }
        _log.println("Printed file");
        _log.flush( );
        if (_log.checkError( )) {
            throw new CantWriteToLogException( );
        }
        sleepForRandomAmountOfTime( );
        return true;
    }
    // ...
}
```

This solves part of our problem; the user gets to find out whether her request succeeded. However, it leads to a bad user-interface problem. Recall that our user interface consisted of the somewhat inelegant panel shown in Figure 21-1.

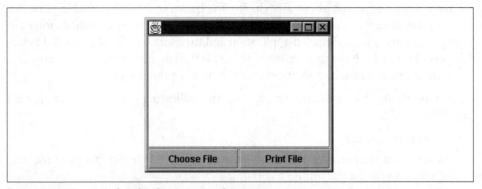

Figure 21-1. User interface for the printer application

The print request took place in an action listener for the Print File button. Here's the code we used:

```java
private class PrintFile implements ActionListener  {
        public void actionPerformed(ActionEvent event) {
            try {
                FileInputStream documentStream = new FileInputStream(_fileChooser.
                    getSelectedFile( ));
                DocumentDescription documentDescription = new
                    DocumentDescription(documentStream);
                Printer printer = (Printer) Naming.lookup(DEFAULT_PRINTER_NAME);
                printer.printDocument(documentDescription);
            }
            catch (PrinterException printerException)   {
                // exception handling omitted
            }
        }
    }
```

The problem is that actionPerformed( ) won't return until the remote method invocation finishes.

This causes a huge problem because Swing, the standard user-interface toolkit for Java applications, uses a single thread to handle all user-interface events. The same thread is also responsible for all repaints. This means that having the Swing thread block for several minutes is a user-interface disaster.

This is worse than it appears. If, on average, there are four print requests waiting, then the average time to complete a print request is four times the average time it takes to actually print a document because the clients have to wait for other print requests to finish. In other words, my GUI isn't just blocked while my print request is being handled, it's blocked while your print request is being handled as well. What would probably wind up happening is that the remote method invocation would time out. That is, the client application would freeze for a while, then report back that the request timed out. That's pretty awful.

A First Pass at a Solution

Working around this problem isn't too hard—the action listener can simply launch a new thread that makes the request and reports back. This is what the following code snippet does:

```
private class PrintFile implements ActionListener, Runnable {
        public void actionPerformed(ActionEvent event) {
            new Thread(this).start();
        }
```

```
    public void run( ) {
        try {
            FileInputStream documentStream = new FileInputStream(_fileChooser.
                getSelectedFile( ));
            DocumentDescription documentDescription = new
                DocumentDescription(documentStream);
            Printer printer = (Printer) Naming.lookup(DEFAULT_PRINTER_NAME);
            printer.printDocument(documentDescription);
        }
        catch (PrinterException printerException) {
            SwingUtilities.invokeLater(new
                PrinterExceptionMessage(printerException));
            return;
        }
        catch (Exception exception) {
            SwingUtilities.invokeLater(new ExceptionMessage(exception));
            return;
        }
        SwingUtilities.invokeLater(new SuccessMessage( ));
    }
}

private class PrinterExceptionMessage implements Runnable {
    private PrinterException _printerException;
    public PrinterExceptionMessage(PrinterException printerException) {
        _printerException = printerException;
    }

    public void run( ) {
        String errorMessage =  "Print failed after " +
            _printerException.getNumberOfPagesPrinted( ) + " pages.";
        JOptionPane.showMessageDialog(ClientFrameTwo.this, errorMessage,
            "Error in printing" , JOptionPane.INFORMATION_MESSAGE);
        _messageBox.setText("Exception attempting to print " + (_fileChooser.
            getSelectedFile()).getAbsolutePath() + "\n\t Error was: " +
             _printerException.getHumanReadableErrorDescription( ));
    }
}

private class ExceptionMessage implements Runnable {
    private Exception _exception;
    public ExceptionMessage(Exception exception) {
        _exception = exception;
    }

    public void run( )  {
        JOptionPane.showMessageDialog(ClientFrameTwo.this, "Print failed',
            "Error in printing" , JOptionPane.INFORMATION_MESSAGE);
        _messageBox.setText("Exception attempting to print " + (_fileChooser.
            getSelectedFile()).getAbsolutePath() + "\n\t Error was: " +
            _exception.toString( ));
        _exception.printStackTrace( );
    }
}
```

```
private class SuccessMessage implements Runnable {
    public void run( ) {
        JOptionPane.showMessageDialog(ClientFrameTwo.this, "Success!",
            "Document has been printed" , JOptionPane.INFORMATION_MESSAGE);
        _messageBox.setText("Print Request succeeded.");
    }
}
}
```

This code contains one interesting wrinkle: because Swing isn't threadsafe, we can't simply "report back" from another thread. Reporting back involves creating instances of JDialog (we will tell the user what happened inside a dialog box) and storing a permanent record of the results inside a JTextArea. Both of these operations can be done safely only from within the Swing thread.

Fortunately, Swing has one threadsafe object: the Swing event queue. You can drop off events, objects that implement the Runnable interface, into the Swing event queue. The Swing thread will, as it's processing button clicks and slider-drags, pick up the objects you drop off, and invoke their run( ) method *just as if they were ordinary events*. That is, the events generated by code and dropped off in the event queue eventually occur within the Swing thread. But, they block all user-interface events and repaints while they are executed Hence, it becomes crucially important that these code-generated events happen quickly and don't cause the GUI to "freeze."

 Keep in mind that even though the objects put into the Swing event queue implement Runnable, they are not assigned distinct threads. Instead they are processed serially by the Swing event thread. This takes a bit of getting used to (programmers used to dealing with Java threads are used to assuming that each Runnable gets a distinct thread).

In order to take advantage of the Swing event queue, we wrote two additional classes, PrinterExceptionMessage and ExceptionMessage, which encapsulate the code we use to alter the user interface. Our background thread simply drops instances of these classes off in Swing's event queue using the static method invokeLater( ) defined in the SwingUtilities class.

 This should look familiar, at least in outline. It's exactly what we discussed in Chapter 12 in the section "Use Containers to Mediate Interthread Communication." In addition, it's the same design pattern we used to handle print requests in BatchingPrinter in that same chapter.

This is now a decent solution from the client side. The button behaves correctly, and the Swing thread is free to refresh the screen and handle additional user events. Moreover, if the print request fails, the user will get a dialog box telling her about it.

Better Solutions

Unfortunately, this is still not a very good solution because it entails a significant commitment on the part of our server. The server is forced to keep a long-lived, and mostly unused, socket connection open with the client. Even worse, this is a socket that is in the middle of a method call at the time, and therefore isn't available for reuse.

 As a side note, this design would also almost certainly force us to increase RMI's connection timeout using the sun.rmi.transport.tcp.readTimeout parameter. Otherwise, when the printer's busy, all the clients will throw instances of RemoteException.

This discussion leads us to two better solutions, both of which are commonly used, depending on the circumstances.

The first solution is *client-side polling*. This solution is architecturally similar to our first solution. There's a background thread that reports back, but instead of making a single method call and holding the connection open, it makes a series of brief method calls. The first call drops off the print request. The subsequent remote method invocations check to see whether the printer has printed the document yet.

The second solution is *server-side callbacks*. In this solution, the client drops off the print request, as in the original application. The difference is that the client passes in another argument, which is itself a remote server. In other words, it's an object on the client side, but it implements Remote and is capable of receiving remote method invocations. When the server is done, it calls a remote method on this new server, and the new server is responsible for actually reporting the results back to the client application.

Client-side polling

There are two main reasons to use client-side polling. The first is that, architecturally, it's simpler. In this model, the client application calls the server application. The server doesn't have to track which clients called and which clients are waiting for responses, nor does it have to actually call them back. This makes for simpler code and makes it easier to have multiple types of clients, should that be necessary.

The second reason to use client-side polling is that sometimes clients can't accept socket connections from the server. One typical case for this is when the client is an applet. Most of the time, applets are forbidden from creating any instances of ServerSocket at all. This completely rules out the applet containing an RMI server.

Another typical case is when firewalls are involved. A firewall separates two parts of the network and restricts network traffic to certain sockets (or only allows data to flow in certain directions). The upshot is that sometimes, even if the client application is capable of creating instances of ServerSocket and thus, can actually contain an RMI server, the server application may not be able to connect to it.

Polling code in the printer application

The actual code we'll need for the printer application isn't too complex. The first change we'll need to make is to the Printer interface:

```
package com.ora.rmibook.chapter21.printer;
import java.rmi.*;

public interface PollingPrinter extends PrinterConstants, Remote {
    public boolean printerAvailable( ) throws RemoteException;
    public String printDocument(DocumentDescription document) throws RemoteException,
        PrinterException;
    public boolean isDocumentDone(String documentKey) throws RemoteException,
        PrinterException;
}
```

In redesigning this interface, we've broken our original printDocument( ) method into two methods: printDocument( ) and isDocumentDone( ). This is intended to work as follows:

1. The client calls printDocument( ) and receives back a string, which is a unique key.

2. The client can then call isDocumentDone( ) at any time to find out the status of the document.

After redesigning this interface, we need to alter the client to occasionally call isDocumentDone( ). Since we were already using a background thread to make the remote method invocation, this doesn't involve a lot of code changes. The only change is that, instead of waiting for an answer, we now repeatedly call isDocumentDone( ). Here's the new version:

```
private class PrintFile implements ActionListener, Runnable {
        private PollingPrinter _printer;
        private String _key;
        public void actionPerformed(ActionEvent event) {
            new Thread(this).start( );
        }

        public void run( ) {
            try {
                makeInitialRequest( );
                pollPrinter( );
            }
            catch (PrinterException printerException) {
                SwingUtilities.invokeLater(new
                    PrinterExceptionMessage(printerException));
                return;
            }
```

```
            catch (Exception exception) {
                SwingUtilities.invokeLater(new ExceptionMessage(exception));
                return;
            }
            SwingUtilities.invokeLater(new SuccessMessage());
    }

    private void makeInitialRequest() throws PrinterException, Exception {
        FileInputStream documentStream = new FileInputStream(_fileChooser.
            getSelectedFile());
        DocumentDescription documentDescription = new
            DocumentDescription(documentStream);
        _printer = (PollingPrinter) Naming.lookup(DEFAULT_PRINTER_NAME);
        _key = _printer.printDocument(documentDescription);
    }

    private void pollPrinter() throws PrinterException, Exception {
        while (false == _printer.isDocumentDone(_key)) {
        try {
            Thread.sleep(2000); // wait a bit and check again
        }
        catch (InterruptedException ignored) {}
        }
    }
}
```

Server-side callbacks

The second common solution for printer-type methods involves having an RMI server inside the client application. The server application receives a reference to this client-side server and uses it to call the client back when the server has finished the original request. That is, we have the following sequence of actions:

1. The client application makes a remote invocation on the server application. As part of this invocation, it passes in a reference to an RMI server inside the client application.

2. When the server application finishes handling the request, it makes a remote method invocation on the RMI server inside the client application.

Server-side callbacks have several advantages over client-side polling. The most important of these advantages are decreased bandwidth and decreased server-side processing. The longer it takes a document to print, the greater the advantage server-side callbacks have. If each client polls 20 times, and receives 20 nope-not-finished-yet return values for every print job, then switching to server-side callbacks can result in significant savings.

 Of course, how much of a gain this is depends on the frequency of polling versus the typical duration of a garbage collection lease. Because the server maintains a reference to the client, server-side callbacks still have the overhead of maintaining and renewing the distributed garbage collector's lease. This usually has a lot less traffic than polling, however.

The downside to server-side callbacks is that the code itself (and its deployment) becomes slightly more complex. To implement server-side callbacks, we need to perform the following three steps:

1. Define a client-side callback interface and change the `Printer` interface to accept instances of our callback interface, often referred to as the callback objects.

2. Implement the client-side interface, using the reporting code we've already written inside the callback objects, to report to the user.

3. Rewrite the server to track print requests, associate requests with the callback objects, and call the client back when requests are completed.

In the rest of this section, we'll walk through the first two steps in more detail.

Define a client-side callback interface

This is pretty simple. The only complication that arises is that the client may actually want to print more than one document. When a document is done printing, and the server wants to tell the client that the document is done, the server needs to also tell the client *which* document has finished printing. There are two basic approaches to this.

The first approach is to create multiple servers on the client side. That is, the client creates an instance of CallbackClient for each print request (e.g., if the client is printing three documents, it has three instances of CallbackClient, each waiting for a message from the server). In this case, the interfaces are:

```
public interface CallbackPrinter extends PrinterConstants, Remote {
    public void printDocument(CallbackClient clientMakingRequest, DocumentDescription
        document) throws RemoteException, PrinterException;
    public void printDocument( DocumentDescription document) throws RemoteException,
        PrinterException;
        //for when we don't need a callback
}

public interface CallbackClient extends Remote{
    public void documentIsDone( ) throws RemoteException;
    public void documentFailedToPrint(String reason) throws RemoteException;
}
```

The second approach is to use a single instance of CallbackClient on the client side, which receives all the documentIsDone( ) messages. In this case, an extra piece of information, which uniquely identifies the printRequest, also needs to be passed back and forth. One way to do this is via the following interfaces:

```
public interface CallbackPrinter extends PrinterConstants, Remote {
    public void printDocument(CallbackClient clientMakingRequest, DocumentDescription
        document, String documentKey) throws RemoteException, PrinterException;
    public void printDocument( DocumentDescription document) throws RemoteException,
        PrinterException;
        //for when we don't need a callback
}

public interface CallbackClient extends Remote{
    public void documentIsDone(String documentKey) throws RemoteException;
    public void documentFailedToPrint(String documentKey, String reason) throws
        RemoteException;
}
```

In this second set of interfaces, the client is responsible for generating a unique-to-the-client documentKey. In both of these approaches, the same general flow of control occurs:

1. The client sends a print request to the server and gets back an immediate response.

2. After the document is done printing, the server calls either documentIsDone( ) or documentFailedToPrint( ) on the client.

Implement the client-side interface

We will implement the first version of CallbackClient, the one without documentKey. We need to do two things: actually implement CallbackClient and then adapt our outside frame to use it correctly. Here's an implementation of CallbackClient. As in our previous examples, all it does is display a dialog box with the outcome of the print request:

```java
public class CallbackClient_DialogImpl extends UnicastRemoteObject implements
    CallbackClient {
    private static final String SUCCESS_WINDOW_TITLE = "Success!";
    private static final String FAILURE_WINDOW_TITLE = "Failure!";
    private String _documentName;
    public CallbackClient_DialogImpl(String documentName) throws RemoteException  {
        _documentName = documentName;
    }

    public void documentIsDone( ) throws RemoteException  {
        reportResultOfPrintRequest(SUCCESS_WINDOW_TITLE, _documentName +
            " is done printing.");
        ceaseBeingAServer( );
    }

    public void documentFailedToPrint(String reason) throws RemoteException {
        reportResultOfPrintRequest(FAILURE_WINDOW_TITLE, _documentName + " failed to
            print because " + reason);
    }

    private void reportResultOfPrintRequest(String windowTitle, String message) {
        SwingUtilities.invokeLater(new SendMessageToUser(windowTitle, message));
    }

    private void ceaseBeingAServer( ) {
        try {
            unexportObject(this, true);
        }
        catch (NoSuchObjectException e) {
            // Not much to do. The RMI runtime thinks we're not a server.
        }
    }

    private class SendMessageToUser implements Runnable {
        private String _windowTitle;
        private String _message;
        public SendMessageToUser(String windowTitle, String message) {
            _windowTitle = windowTitle;
            _message = message;
        }

        public void run( ) {
            JOptionPane.showMessageDialog(null, _windowTitle, _message,
                JOptionPane.INFORMATION_MESSAGE);
        }
    }
}
```

As you can see, this is a one-shot RMI server. CallbackClient_DialogImpl extends UnicastRemoteObject and, therefore, instances of CallbackClient_DialogImpl can receive remote method invocations. However, they never get registered in any naming service, and once an instance of CallbackClient_DialogImpl receives a remote method invocation, it immediately unexports itself.

There are three convenient aspects to this. First, the client application doesn't need to create any thread objects; the RMI runtime handles thread management issues for it. Second, most of the reported back code is encapsulated in a single class. We can easily change the method of reporting by simply using a different implementation of CallbackClient. Third, the rest of the client application doesn't need to keep a reference to instances of CallbackClient_DialogImpl at all. That is, an instance of CallbackClient_DialogImpl has the following lifecycle:

1. It is created.

2. It waits for a message. While it is waiting, it is exported, and the server has a reference to it. Therefore, the instance will not be garbage collected.

3. It receives a message. At this point, it unexports itself and is no longer a server. The RMI runtime no longer has any references to the instance of CallbackClient_ DialogImpl.

This means that, as long as we don't keep any references to the instance of CallbackClient_DialogImpl within the rest of the client application, it will automatically become eligible for garbage collection as soon as it receives a message from the server.

With that in mind, here's the new implementation of the Print File button's action listener:

```
private class PrintFile implements ActionListener  {
    private CallbackPrinter _printer;
    public void actionPerformed(ActionEvent event) {
        try {
            File fileToPrint = _fileChooser.getSelectedFile( );
            FileInputStream documentStream = new FileInputStream(fileToPrint);
            DocumentDescription documentDescription = new
                DocumentDescription(documentStream);
            _printer = (CallbackPrinter) Naming.lookup(DEFAULT_PRINTER_NAME);
            CallbackClient callbackClient = new
                CallbackClient_DialogImpl(fileToPrint.getName( ));
            _printer.printDocument(callbackClient, documentDescription);
        }
        catch (Exception exception) {
            SwingUtilities.invokeLater(new ExceptionMessage(exception));
            return;
        }
    }
}

private class ExceptionMessage implements Runnable {
    private Exception _exception;
    public ExceptionMessage(Exception exception) {
```

```
            _exception = exception;
    }

    public void run( ) {
        JOptionPane.showMessageDialog(CallbackClientFrame.this ,
            "Print failed" , "Error in printing" , JOptionPane.INFORMATION_
            MESSAGE);
        _messageBox.setText("Exception attempting to print "
                + (_fileChooser.getSelectedFile()).getAbsolutePath( ) + "\n\t
                Error was: " + _exception.toString( ));
        _exception.printStackTrace( );
    }

}
```

Handling Report-Type Methods

The next methods we identified were report-type methods. Recall my original description of report-type methods:

> [They're] computationally expensive, very low-priority in comparison to, say, people or businesses seeking to access their accounts, and it doesn't have a bound on the bandwidth consumed...In addition, unlike the printer, partial results are possible.

These method calls have three major problems:

- There's a potential for a long delay while the server fully computes an answer.
- They're very "bursty" in terms of bandwidth consumption. That is, they have long periods where no bandwidth is used at all, followed by a period of intense bandwidth consumption.
- There's a potential for a long delay while serialization and deserialization occur.

This third problem is one we haven't really discussed yet. Suppose, for example, we have a system with the following remote method:

```
public Account[] getAllAccountsWithBalanceOver(Money minimumOwed);
```

When a client calls this method, the following occurs:

1. The server figures out the list of people who owe money and returns it to the skeleton.
2. The RMI runtime serializes the instance of Account[] and sends it over the wire.
3. The RMI runtime deserializes the instance of Account[] and then returns it (to the stub).
4. The client code gets the instance of Account[] from the stub.

One of the helpful aspects of serialization, along with being stream-based, is that the second and third steps actually occur simultaneously. That is, as soon as serialization starts on the server side, the data starts being sent to the client. However, even with this in place, there's still a fundamental limitation: step 4 cannot occur until step 3 is completely finished. This means that the client code doesn't get to see the answer to the remote method invocation until the entire answer has been serialized, sent over the wire, and deserialized. More concretely: if the instance of Account[] has 2,300 entries, the client can't look at the first entry until entry 2,300 has made it over the wire.

Chapter 7 Revisited

I've already mentioned how to deal with these types of methods. In Chapter 7, during the discussion of interface design, one of the important questions was:

> Do individual method calls waste bandwidth?

And the discussion continued:

> The second bandwidth-related problem that can arise results from method calls that return multiple values. For example, we could imagine a MortgageSalesHelper server with an interface that contains methods such as:
>
> ```
> public interface SalesHelper extends Remote {
>     public ArrayList getAllAccountsWithBalanceOver(Money amount) throws
>         RemoteException;
>     // ...
> }
> ```
>
> This is a fairly typical remote method—it asks for all the accounts with a certain minimum balance. But there is no upper bound on the number of accounts that can be returned. If 50,000 accounts have a balance greater than amount, 50,000 accounts will be returned. Methods that can return an arbitrarily large number of distinct [and valid] return values, are usually bad design for a number of reasons...The solution to these problems is to use an iterator, which returns data in chunks. That is, use a pair of interfaces such as the following:
>
> ```
> public interface SalesHelper extends Remote {
>     public AccountIterator getAllAccountsWithBalanceOver(Money amount) throws
>         RemoteException;
>     .....
> }
> public interface AccountIterator extends Remote {
>     public int getNumberOfRemainingAccounts() throws RemoteException;
>     public AccountList getNext(int numberToFetch) throws RemoteException;
> }
> ```

Remote iterators are usually the correct solution for report-type methods. In general, they work as follows:

1. The client makes a request to the server.

2. The server returns two things to the client: a partial response (e.g., the first 50 records matching a query) and a reference to a second server, which implements a remote-iterator interface.

3. The client then requests data from the remote iterator as needed.

When you think about it, remote iterators, like the instances of `CallbackClient_DialogImpl` in the previous section, are one-shot servers. They encapsulate an answer to a single request and are rarely put into a naming service.

Server-evaluation models

If a server returns a result via a remote iterator, the implementers of the server need to make a policy decision: does the method use *full* evaluation, background evaluation, or lazy evaluation? In *full evaluation*, the server computes the entire answer to the client request as part of handling the original remote method invocation.

In *background evaluation*, the server computes the first group of responses and creates the remote iterator. It then sends a response to the client and continues figuring out the full answer.

In *lazy evaluation*, the server computes the first group of responses and creates the remote iterator. It then stops computing and waits for further client requests. When it receives requests for data it does not have, it then continues to compute until it has all the needed data.

In terms of coding difficulty, there's often not a substantial difference between these approaches. Generally speaking, background evaluation is the hardest to implement. However, once you have an implementation using full evaluation, the conversion to either a lazy or a background evaluation strategy is usually straightforward.

 This is, in fact, what's usually done. The first pass at implementation uses a full evaluation strategy. Later on, if there are performance problems, the code is changed to background evaluation. Lazy evaluation is rarely used in this context.

The reasons for doing so are also straightforward. Full evaluation can take a long time before returning the first responses; the server waits until it knows the entire answer before responding at all.

Background evaluation, in comparison, returns very quickly. It's also a more efficient use of resources: part of the answer is sent while the rest of the answer is computed. In addition, the client can do things with the partial answer, such as display the results in a `JTable`, while the server is processing.

Lazy evaluation returns from the initial request just as quickly as background evaluation does. However, it conserves server resources by postponing further processing until the client explicitly asks for the information. This slows the remote iterato since computation has to occur within each request for information.

Full and background evaluation have very similar semantics. They attempt to return the answer to a remote method invocation at the time the remote method invocation was made. Lazy evaluation is a little different. For example, suppose that the client makes a query of the form, "Show me all accounts with a balance under $1,000" and gets back a remote interator. The end user looks at some of the information and then realizes, "It's time for lunch. I'll look at the rest of this after lunch." What happens when the end user resumes work an hour later?

In the case of full and background evaluation, the server has already computed a response, which is presumably sitting inside a data structure. When the end user resumes looking at the data, she is looking at the answer to her query, as of the time the query was made. But in the case of lazy evaluation, the server needs to compute the response when the end user starts looking at the data again. If the answer changed in the interim, it's not clear what the iterator should do.

Iterators on the client side

If a server returns an answer via an interator, the client has to make repeated requests for the data. The usual way of doing this, called *background downloading*, uses a second thread whose sole responsibility is getting information from the server in small chunks. That is, the client pursues the following strategy:

1. The original request, which receives a partial answer, is initiated from an original thread (the Swing event thread). In many applications, this occurs in response to a user action (e.g., clicking a button).

2. After receiving the partial answer, the original thread creates a second thread, which continues to download information.

3. After creating the second thread, the original thread continues to process the partial answer. In many client applications, this amounts to displaying the partial answer in a GUI for an end user to look at.

4. Periodically, the second thread updates the original thread with more information. In many client applications, this boils down to creating instances of a class that implements Runnable and dropping them off in Swing's event queue.

This strategy is useful for two reasons. First, it minimizes the amount of time the client spends waiting. The first batch of data arrives quickly, and the rest follows in short order. The client spends almost no time waiting. Second, it minimizes the amount of server resources a client demands. If you've decided to pursue either a full or lazy evaluation strategy, then, once the answer is computed, there's no reason to store it on the server. It's static information to which no other client has access. Logically, it belongs with the client application.

Implementing Background Downloading on the Client Side

The architecture for implementing background downloading isn't all that different from the architecture for polling. In both cases, the same general thing happens: the background thread on the client side repeatedly makes the same request of a server until the return value from the request indicates a stop condition.

How Many Threads Is That?

It's worth stopping and counting just how many threads are involved in handling a remote iterator in a typical application. The client has two threads: the thread that makes the initial request and the thread that handles the background downloading.

The server, on the other hand, uses three threads. The first is the thread that listens on a server socket to establish the original connection. The second is the thread that listens on the original connection and handles the initial response to the request (including creating the remote iterator). Since sockets and their associated threads are reused, the thread that handles the initial request will probably also be the thread that handles the remote method invocations that the iterator receives. And, finally, the server has a thread that performs the background evaluation.

Of these five threads, four deal with devices. On the client side, one deals with the screen and one reads data off a socket. On the server side, two deal with sockets and one performs computations.

The nice thing about this arrangement is that all of these threads can be simultaneously active. Since most of them pursue individual tasks that can be impeded by external factors (for example, network congestion can cause some of the threads to slow down), the fact that the threads are mostly independent means we're taking full advantage of our available resources.

Viewed this way, iterators aren't just a convenient way to deliver partial responses to an impatient end user. They're also a way to write more efficient code. By breaking the response down to a set of small, individually handled chunks, we've come close to maximizing system throughput.

Assume our servers have the following two interfaces:

```
public interface SalesHelper extends Remote {
    public QueryResponse getAllAccountsWithBalanceOver(Money amount) throws
        RemoteException;
}
public interface AccountIterator extends Remote {
    public int getNumberOfRemainingAccounts() throws RemoteException;
    public AccountList getNext(int numberToFetch) throws RemoteException;
}
```

This requires two value objects: AccountList and QueryResponse. AccountList encapsulates a set of accounts; it is the basic unit of information sent from the server to the client:

```
public class AccountList implements Serializable {
    public int numberOfAccountsRequested;
    public int numberOfAccountsReturned;
    public boolean areThereMoreAccountsToFetch;
    public ArrayList accounts;
}
```

QueryResponse extends `AccountList` and adds a single attribute:

```
public class QueryResponse extends AccountList {
    public AccountIterator accountIterator;
}
```

Given all of this, the client's implementation of background downloading looks something like the following:

```
public abstract class AskServer implements Runnable {
    private AccountIterator _accountIterator;
    private String _salesHelperName;
    private Money _threshhold;
    private AccountList _currentAccounts;
    private int _fetchSize;

    protected abstract void handleResponseSet(ArrayList nextSetOfResponses);

    public AskServer(String salesHelperName, Money threshhold, int fetchSize) {
        _salesHelperName = salesHelperName;
        _threshhold = threshhold;
        _fetchSize = fetchSize;
    }

    public void performQuery( ) {
        try {
            makeInitialRequest( );
        }
        catch (Exception e) {
            System.out.println("Error in connecting to server");
            e.printStackTrace( );
            return;
        }
        new Thread(this).start( );
    }

    public void run( ) {
        while(_currentAccounts.areThereMoreAccountsToFetch) {
            try {
                _currentAccounts = _accountIterator.getNext(_fetchSize);
                handleResponseSet(_currentAccounts.accounts);
            }
            catch (RemoteException e) {
                // insert exception handling here
                // it's fairly customary to break the loop at this point
            }
        }
    }

    private void makeInitialRequest( ) throws Exception {
        SalesHelper salesHelper = (SalesHelper) Naming.lookup(_salesHelperName);
        QueryResponse queryResponse =
            salesHelper.getAllAccountsWithBalanceOver(_threshhold);
        _currentAccounts = queryResponse;
```

```
        _accountIterator = queryResponse.accountIterator;
        handleResponseSet(_currentAccounts.accounts);
    }
}
```

This does exactly what you'd expect: it establishes a connection in the main method and then delegates the background downloading to a secondary thread that it creates.

 In more complex systems, or for server-to-server communication, this secondary thread would probably be obtained from a pool of threads (see Chapter 12). However, for a typical client, creating threads on the fly doesn't lead to a lot of overhead.

There is an interesting point here, though. We didn't implement any exception handling inside the background-downloading loop. This code is rather tricky and application-specific. Ideally, we'd like to detect what causes the error (Was it a transient network failure? Did the server crash entirely? Was there a null pointer exception in that particular block of data?) and work around it. However, without knowing more about the server, it's hard to say what the correct behavior should be.

Generalizing from These Examples

The point of this chapter is simple: when your architecture goes beyond request-response cycles, you need to think carefully about what exactly your client is doing. Many times the boundary between clients and servers gets a little fuzzy, and the client starts responding to remote method invocations. More frequently, the client becomes a fairly complex application with a lot of threads performing secondary interactions with the server. The three basic techniques presented in this chapter—polling, callbacks, and interator-based data acquisition—go a long way towards solving a wide variety of client-server interaction design problems.

CHAPTER 22

HTTP Tunneling

One of the most pervasive problems in client-server computing is that servers are frequently inaccessible to clients. Sometimes this is because the server is down. More often, however, it's because a firewall has been erected between the computer running the client and the computer running the server. In this chapter, we'll cover one widely used method, known as HTTP tunneling, that an RMI application can use to circumvent firewalls and enable your application to function.

Before the Internet, corporate networks were isolated. Large companies frequently had multiple-computer networks, and computers on one network were often incapable of sending any information to computers on a different network. Now that the Internet has become a global network, the situation is quite different. Most computers are, at least occasionally, connected to the Internet.

This situation, while making things like the World Wide Web possible, makes life very difficult for systems administrators. They are called upon to build robust networks that are fully connected to the Internet so companies can take full advantage of what it has to offer while simultaneously preventing unauthorized users from accessing corporate information.

Firewalls

This dilemma is frequently solved by using a *firewall*. A firewall is a combination of software and hardware that separates two logically distinct networks. If the firewall is removed, the two networks are no longer connected to each other.

Because all traffic between the two networks must flow through the firewall, the firewall can screen all the packets sent between the two networks and throw away any packets that violate the firewall's security policy. For example, a company might place a firewall between its internal network and the Internet, and establish a policy such as:

- Personal computers behind the firewall may not access the Internet at all. No sockets between such computers and a computer outside the firewall are allowed.

- In order to allow the personal computers to access the World Wide Web, a small set of proxy servers behind the firewall are configured to handle Web-related traffic. Personal computers talk to the proxy servers, which talk to the Internet.

- The corporate web servers may only be accessed using HTTP and HTTPS, the protocols underlying the World Wide Web, on their well-known ports (80 and 443, respectively). No other corporate servers may be accessed from outside the firewall.

This policy is illustrated Figure 22-1.

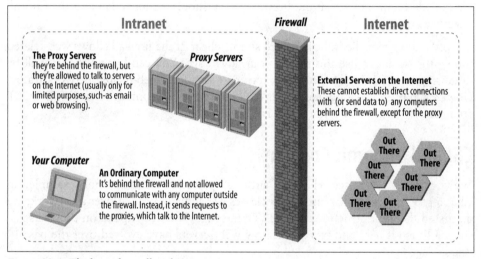

Figure 22-1. The basic firewall architecture

This policy may seem draconian, and it is. However, it has several nice aspects. Among them are:

- It doesn't prevent web browsing. The vast amount of information available on the Internet is also available to people using computers behind the firewall.

- The use of proxy servers also allows the company to monitor Internet usage and screen for inappropriate activity.*

---

* "Inappropriate activity" is frequently spelled "porn sites."

- Applications written to use a web browser as a client still work. Since many such applications use SSL, the information being sent might be secure even though it is travelling across the Internet.
- Limiting access to the corporate network limits security risks.

Unfortunately, it also has a severe side effect: if the client in an RMI application is on one side of the firewall, and the server is on the other side of the firewall, they won't be able to communicate via the standard RMI protocol JRMP, or any variation of it.

 To learn more about firewalls, see *Building Internet Firewalls, Second Edition* by Elizabeth D. Zwicky et al. (O'Reilly).

The right solution to this problem is to contact the people in charge of security and convince them that your application is important enough, and used by enough people outside the firewall, that the firewall policy should be amended and the firewall selectively breached.

It is often more expedient, however, to simply cheat. If the firewall allows web-related traffic, then you can use this fact to your advantage. You can bypass the firewall by disguising your RMI-related network traffic to look like Web-related network traffic. How? Encode each remote method invocation inside the content of an HTTP POST command. This practice is known as *HTTP tunneling*.

CGI and Dynamic Content

We've already discussed HTTP a little in previous chapters. For example, in Chapter 19, when we discussed how classes are actually vended over a network, we discussed the basic structure of an HTTP message. We will expand on those discussions a little bit here and talk about how web servers have evolved over the past 10 years.

HTTP is a communications protocol that was designed for the World Wide Web. It was designed to facilitate the retrieval of static pages of information. That is, the protocol assumed that the pages being sent already existed and were merely being retrieved from a server. A URL such as *http://www.salon.com/ent/tv/temptation/index.html* meant, "Go to the web server running on the machine named *www.salon.com* and fetch me the contents of the file to which */ent/tv/temptation/index.html* refers."

This is certainly what happens with our dynamic class server. When the RMI runtime requests the bytecode for a class, all our class server does is send the contents of a *.class* file back over the network.

The Common Gateway Interface

The next step in the evolution of the Web was the invention of dynamic pages. The invention of dynamic pages really boiled down to the realization that the client didn't care whether the information being returned already existed. All a web browser needs is a response; whether the web server read the response from a file (commonly referred to as *returning a static page*) or is somehow generating the page on the fly (*returning a dynamic page*) is irrelevant to a web browser. This means that a web server can run a program to generate an HTML page on the fly instead of simply returning the contents of a file without the browser ever noticing.

The first mechanism for creating dynamic pages was the Common Gateway Interface (CGI or CGI-BIN). In this system, and in all subsequent mechanisms for generating dynamic pages, requests are still specified to the web server using URLs. The difference is that, instead of mapping the path of the URL to a file, the web server is configured to forward the request to a second application. This second application returns an HTTP response to the web server, and this response is then relayed to the application that made the original request.

For example, Figure 22-2 shows a snapshot of the configuration applet for Sun's JavaWebServer.* In it, we see that a number of different URL patterns are mapped to various programs that will dynamically generate pages. For example:

- Any request with path ending of *.jhtml* will be forwarded to the pageCompile servlet.
- All requests with the path */cgi-bin/java-rmi.cgi* will be forwarded to the HTTP Tunneler servlet.

Servlets

The development of CGI, and the encoding of HTTP request information so that it can be passed to an external process, were major steps forward for dynamic web pages. However, the initial implementations of CGI performed badly. For example, in 1996, the most common CGI implementation was:

> Create a new process for every request. Set a special set of environment variables corresponding to the request parameters and then invoke the appropriate request-handling program as defined in the web server configuration. Whatever the request-handling program writes to standard-out is the response that should be sent back to the initiating browser.

This way of writing and installing programs to generate dynamic content is flexible and easy to implement. Moreover, it naturally lends itself to scripting languages such

---

* The use of JavaWebServer for examples in no way implies an endorsement of JWS for real-world applications. For these applications, the combination of the Apache web server and the Tomcat servlet engine is a much better choice.

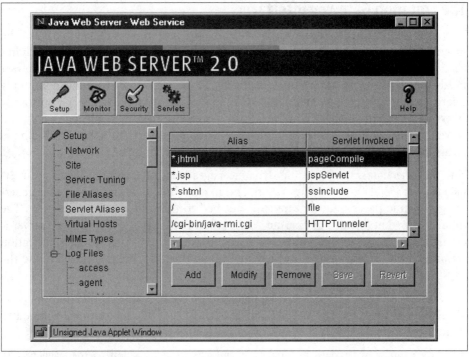

Figure 22-2. Sun's JavaWebServer

as Perl. However, naively using such an implementation of CGI leads to problems. Among them are:

Performance problems

Forking off a separate process, or even creating a new thread for every request, is expensive.

Language problems

There's a reason that programmers have gradually converted over to well-typed, object-oriented languages. Blithely ignoring the past 30 years of experience and reverting to "scripting languages" is, quite probably, a mistake.

Compatibility problems

Ideally, you'd like your dynamic page-generation programs to be part of the same codebase as, and reuse components and libraries from, your main enterprise applications.

Javasoft created the Servlet API to solve these problems.[*] As of this writing, the Servlet API is an impressive document; it is a mature specification that weighs in at over 300 pages. Fortunately, understanding the basic implementation of HTTP tunneling

---

[*] Javasoft probably had other reasons as well. But these are the important ones from a technical viewpoint.

in RMI doesn't require a thorough mastery of the specification. Instead, the following six paragraphs are sufficient.

The heart of the Servlet specification is the definition of the abstract class HttpServlet in the javax.servlet.http package. A servlet class extends HttpServlet and adds request-specific functionality. The servlet class corresponds, more or less, to a program in the CGI specification. That is, the HttpServlet class defines a way for the web server (or, more precisely, the *servlet runner*) to pass HTTP requests to an instance of the servlet class and then receive responses from the same instance.

Servlets are instantiated by a servlet runner. The servlet runner is responsible for managing the lifecycle of specific servlet instances and for maintaining connections with the web server. It usually exists in a separate process from the web server's.

The most important methods in the HttpServlet class are:

```
protected void doGet(HttpServletRequest req, HttpServletResponse resp)
protected void doPost(HttpServletRequest req, HttpServletResponse resp)
```

These two methods, which correspond to the HTTP GET and POST commands, have trivial implementations in HttpServlet. As written, they do nothing. However, almost every servlet class overrides both of these methods, and very few servlet classes override any other methods defined in HttpServlet.

The final point worth noticing is that the servlet specification defines a whole set of abstractions related to HTTP. The two most important data objects are HttpServletRequest, which encapsulates an incoming HTTP request, and HttpServletResponse, which encapsulates the response that will be sent to the HTTP client.

It's interesting to note the layers of abstraction. Network programming starts with UDP, and TCP/IP is layered on top. The next layer is comprised of the basic sockets library, as implemented by the operating system. Above that is the java.net package, which contains a set of classes that define an object-oriented interface for sockets.

The servlet specification then adds another layer of abstraction; from one instance of Socket, we get an instance of HttpServletRequest and an instance of HttpServletResponse. The instance of HttpServletRequest is a wrapper around the socket's input stream, and the instance of HttpServletResponse is a wrapper around the socket's output stream.

 If you want to learn more about servlets, *Java Servlet Programming, Second Edition* by Jason Hunter (O'Reilly) is a good place to start. I also highly recommend downloading and reading the latest version of the servlet specification from Javasoft's servlet pages (see *http://www. javasoft.com/products/servlet/index.html*).

HTTP Tunneling

The invention of CGI was an innovation on the server side; it involved changing a fundamental assumption about servers and allowing the response to be dynamically generated instead of simply read in from a file.

HTTP tunneling is a similar innovation, which builds upon the idea of dynamic pages. It involves relaxing the assumption that the web server receives or returns valid HTML. The reasoning is simple: if the web server simply forwards certain requests to an arbitrary application, and if the response from that application is simply rerouted to the client by the web server (without the web server doing anything to the data it is sending), then there's no particular requirement that the data be HTML. All of this infrastructure can be made to work with almost any data format.

In essence, HTTP tunneling involves using the Web as a communications protocol for non-Web applications. When you think about it, dynamic classloading was our first tunneling application. The request originated with an instance of URLClassLoader, not a web browser, and the response was the bytecode for a class, not an HTML page.

HTTP tunneling is widely used for two reasons, both very pragmatic. First, it allows application developers to reuse many of the components and infrastructure that already exist for web applications, and to easily define an application protocol using these components.

Moreover, doing so enables application developers to easily incorporate multiple languages. Since almost every modern language has a library that handles parsing and generating XML, using HTTP and XML to define an application protocol allows the client to be written in one language and the server in another.[*]

 XML-RPC is the most visible example of why to use HTTP tunneling. It is extensively discussed in *Java and XML* by Brett McLaughlin (O'Reilly). You can also look at the Simple Object Access Protocol (SOAP), which is largely based on XML-RPC.

The second reason for using HTTP tunneling is that it enables distributed applications to circumvent firewalls. To see why, consider a typical architecture that relies on HTTP tunneling, as illustrated in Figure 22-3.

The key point in this architecture is that the client uses a marshalling layer that encodes a request in the preferred protocol into a valid HTTP request. The server, on the other handle, has an extra layer of demarshalling code, which transforms an

---

[*] You have to write custom marshalling code, of course. But the existence of libraries that parse and generate XML makes this a lot easier than it would be otherwise.

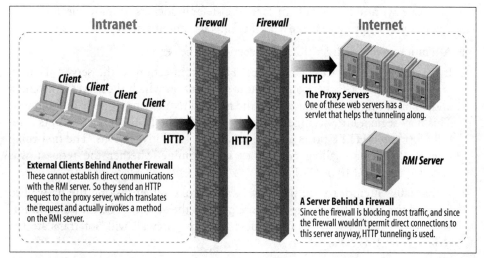

Figure 22-3. HTTP tunneling in action

HTTP request into the appropriate server-side request. Because of this, the firewall thinks the request is actually a Web-related request. This makes it more likely that the request will reach the server.

> In the general literature, tunneling refers to embedding one protocol inside another protocol. The outside world sees only the exterior protocol; programs and observers with extra knowledge can extract the tunneled protocol. HTTP tunneling is used to refer to the practice of embedding any protocol over HTTP. Because this book is about RMI, we use HTTP tunneling to refer to using HTTP to carry RMI messages (e.g., remote method invocations).

How RMI Tunnels Messages

At this point, it should be fairly clear what the goal of RMI's HTTP tunneling mechanism is: it will encode remote method invocations as HTTP POST requests, and then decode the returned "web pages" into the appropriate type of response.* RMI accomplishes this seamlessly by using an elaborate type of custom socket as the default socket type.

Recall that unless you install a different socket factory, RMI will use the default socket factory when creating connections. The sockets returned by RMI's default socket factory automatically attempt to use HTTP tunneling if ordinary attempts to

---

* And serialization will be used to generate both the HTTP request and response.

communicate with a server fail. In fact, the default sockets employ the following strategy when attempting to make a method invocation on a server:

1. Attempt to make a direct JRMP connection to the server.

2. If that fails, attempt to make a direct HTTP connection to the server. That is, attempt to make a socket connection to the port on which the server is listening and communicate by encapsulating the method request inside an HTTP request. This may seem a little strange at first. Essentially, the RMI runtime accepts carefully formatted HTTP posts as valid remote method invocations. The first thing that RMI's demarshalling code does is determine whether the request was encoded using JRMP or HTTP.

3. If that fails, attempt to use the firewall as a proxy server (asking the firewall to forward the request to the appropriate port on the server). The firewall will forward the request as an HTTP request (e.g., the firewall will not translate the request into RMI calls).

4. If that fails, attempt to connect on port 80 of the server machine and send the request to a URL beginning with /cgi-bin/java-rmi.cgi. The interpretation of this URL is that the request will be forwarded to a program that interprets the HTTP request and forwards it, as an HTTP request, to the appropriate port on the server machine.

5. If that fails, attempt to connect on port 80 of the firewalled machine and send the request to a URL beginning with /cgi-bin/java-rmi.cgi. The interpretation of this URL is that the request will be forwarded to a program that interprets the HTTP request and forwards it, as an HTTP request, to the appropriate port on the server machine.

This may seem like an overly complex way to handle communications. The key to understanding it is realizing that the options are ordered in terms of decreasing efficiency. That is, the first option is more efficient than the second option, the second option is more efficient than the third option, and so on. Moreover, the options are independent; it is possible to imagine deployment scenarios in which each of the five options is the only way to establish a communications link.

For example, suppose that a firewall has been installed that allows only HTTP connections to any server, and that an RMI server is behind the firewall. A client attempting to communicate with the server will need to use a different connection strategy depending on whether it is behind the firewall (e.g., located inside the intranet) or outside the firewall (e.g., located somewhere on the Internet). If the client is inside the firewall, then the first connection strategy (direct JRMP) is available and makes sense.

If the client is outside the firewall, however, there are two options, depending on the details of the firewall policy. If the firewall allows HTTP connections on any port and doesn't insist that HTTP traffic flow through port 80, then the second option of sending HTTP information directly to the port on which the server listens is most efficient. However, if the firewall insists that all HTTP traffic be sent to port 80, then the fourth option is the only one that will work.

Topological Assumptions

In most of this chapter, we're assuming that the server is behind a firewall and that the primary question is whether or not the client is behind the same firewall. That is:

- There's a firewall preventing "outside applications" from talking directly to the server.
- The client may or may not be an outside application.

However, sometimes the client is behind a firewall that prevents it from connecting to the server (because the client cannot connect to any outside server other than a proxy server for the Web).

HTTP tunneling also works in this second case. The fundamental fact is that JRMP connections won't work, and RMI will have to resort to tunneling. The owner of the firewall, and whether it's there to prevent the computer running the client application from calling out or to prevent unauthorized access to a server, is irrelevant when a client attempts to connect to a server.

Client-side firewalls are different from server-side firewalls in one important respect, however. Server-side firewalls often don't block callbacks; their goal is to prevent unauthorized access to a server, not to prevent the server from connecting to other machines.

Client-side firewalls, on the other hand, almost always block callbacks. Any machine that isn't allowed to make any connections without going through a proxy server is usually not allowed to accept connections either. This forces you to rewrite code that relies on server-side callbacks to instead use client-side polling.

Naming services and "the server machine"

Consider the previous five communications options.

An important and frequently overlooked point is that "the server machine" in the fifth option is an abstraction; it does not have to be the machine on which the actual server object runs. Instead, it's simply a machine name stored in the stub. This name is generated whenever a stub is created from a server. The algorithm is:

- If it is defined, use the value of the java.rmi.server.hostname property.
- Otherwise, use the IP address (in "dotted quad" format) of the machine on which the server runs.

This extra level of indirection allows HTTP tunneling to be implemented flexibly. For example, suppose a firewall restricted all incoming connections to be HTTP connections, on port 80, of a specific web server.

If we put our naming service outside the firewall, and set the value of java.rmi. server.hostname to be the name of the web server, then the fourth option will be used. That is, RMI will attempt to send messages to our servers by invoking a URL beginning with /cgi-bin/java-rmi.cgi.

Dealing with Network Address Translation

java.rmi.server.hostname can also be a very useful property when dealing with firewalls that perform Network Address Translation (NAT). When a server is behind such a firewall, it can have two symbolic names—the "internal" name (used by machines behind the firewall) and the "external" name (used by machines outside the firewall).

Stubs in RMI use symbolic names (not IP addresses). That is, when the stub is serialized and sent over the wire, names such as "ftp.oreilly.com" are sent instead of IP addresses such as 63.80.158.1.

In order for the client to be able to connect to the server, the correct name must be included with the stub. This can be easily accomplished by setting java.rmi.server. hostname to the correct value.

This does not force the RMI server to run on the same machine as the web server. It simply means that we need to write a servlet class[*] that can perform the final step in redirecting the RMI request and then configure the web server to send all requests with appropriate URLs to our servlet.

The resulting architecture resembles the diagram shown in Figure 22-4. The numbers show the flow of the messages, from 1 to 11.

A Servlet Implementation of HTTP Tunneling

For the fourth and fifth connection strategies to work, there has to be a way, hooked into a web server, to forward method invocations to the actual RMI server. The first implementation of this that Sun Microsystems, Inc. shipped was a compiled CGI script. Formally, it required the following:

- Each remote method invocation was sent as a HTTP POST request.
- The full URL being used was of the form /cgi-bin/java-rmi.cgi?forward=[port number].

---

[*] Or a CGI script. Servlets are usually a better idea, but there's nothing preventing you from writing this final redirection step in Perl.

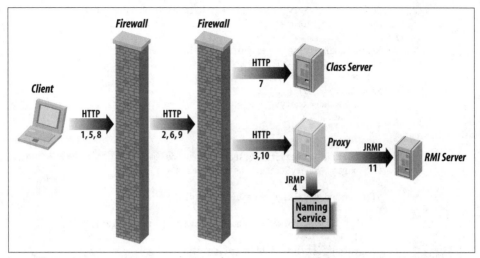

Figure 22-4. The entire flow

- The body of the POST contained all the data from the remote request as serialized objects that were then converted into an ASCII stream of characters.

After the servlet specification was defined, Sun shipped a servlet that provided the same functionality as the CGI script. In the discussion that follows, we will use a stripped-down version of the SUN class to demonstrate how HTTP tunneling works.

In the remainder of this section, we will examine the servlet code in detail.

The Servlet Code

The stripped-down servlet code consists of two main classes and a set of custom exception classes. The main classes are SimplifiedServletHandler and ServletForwardCommand. They have the following roles:

SimplifiedServletHandler
> This class extends HTTPServlet. It receives requests and performs preliminary validation (most of which centers around processing the URL).

ServletForwardCommand
> This is a set of static methods that know how to take an HTTP POST and resend it to an RMI server running on the same machine.

Here's the code for SimplifiedServletHandler:

```
public class SimplifiedServletHandler extends HttpServlet {

    public void init(ServletConfig config) throws ServletException {
        super.init(config);
        System.out.println("Simplified RMI Servlet Handler loaded successfully.");
    }
```

```java
public void doPost(HttpServletRequest req, HttpServletResponse res) throws
    ServletException, IOException {
    try {
        String queryString = req.getQueryString();
        String command, param;
        int delim = queryString.indexOf("=");
        if (delim == -1) {
            command = queryString;
            param = "";
        }
        else {
            command = queryString.substring(0, delim);
            param = queryString.substring(delim + 1);
        }
        if (command.equalsIgnoreCase("forward")) {
            try {
                ServletForwardCommand.execute(req, res, param);
            }
            catch (ServletClientException e) {
                returnClientError(res, "client error: " + e.getMessage());
                e.printStackTrace();
            }
            catch (ServletServerException e) {
                returnServerError(res, "internal server error: " + e.
                    getMessage());
                e.printStackTrace();
            }
        }
        else {
            returnClientError(res, "invalid command: " + command);
        }
    }
    catch (Exception e)  {
        returnServerError(res, "internal error: " + e.getMessage());
        e.printStackTrace();
    }
}

public void doGet(HttpServletRequest req, HttpServletResponse res) throws
    ServletException, IOException  {
    returnClientError(res, "GET Operation not supported: " +
        "Can only forward POST requests.");
}

public void doPut(HttpServletRequest req, HttpServletResponse res) throws
    ServletException, IOException {
    returnClientError(res, "PUT Operation not supported: " +
        "Can only forward POST requests.");
}

public String getServletInfo() {
    return "Simplified RMI Call Forwarding Servlet Servlet.<br>\n";
}
```

```
    private static void returnClientError(HttpServletResponse res, String message)
        throws IOException {
        res.sendError(HttpServletResponse.SC_BAD_REQUEST,
            "<HTML><HEAD><TITLE>Java RMI Client Error</TITLE></HEAD><BODY> " +
            "<H1>Java RMI Client Error</H1>" + message +  "</BODY></HTML>");
        System.err.println(HttpServletResponse.SC_BAD_REQUEST +
            "Java RMI Client Error" + message);
    }

    private static void returnServerError(HttpServletResponse res, String message)
        throws IOException  {
        res.sendError(HttpServletResponse.SC_INTERNAL_SERVER_ERROR, "<HTML><HEAD>
            <TITLE>Java RMI Server Error</TITLE></HEAD><BODY> " + "<H1>Java RMI
            Server Error</H1>" +  message + "</BODY></HTML>");
        System.err.println(HttpServletResponse.SC_INTERNAL_SERVER_ERROR + Java RMI
            Server Error: " + message);
    }
}
```

Almost all of the processing logic for SimplifiedServletHandler is contained inside the doPost( ) method. The doPost( ) method parses the URL to determine the port on which the server listens. If the URL is a valid URL and contains a port, the request is forwarded to the ServletForwardCommand's static execute( ) method.

ServletForwardCommand consists of the following static methods:

```
public static void execute(HttpServletRequest request, HttpServletResponse response,
    String stringifiedPort) throws ServletClientException, ServletServerException,
    IOException
    {
        int port = convertStringToPort(stringifiedPort);
        Socket connectionToLocalServer = null;
        try {
            connectionToLocalServer = connectToLocalServer(port);
            forwardRequest(request, connectionToLocalServer);
            forwardResponse(response, connectionToLocalServer);
        }
        finally  {
            if (null!=connectionToLocalServer) {
                connectionToLocalServer.close( );
            }
        }
    }

    private static int convertStringToPort(String stringfiedPort) throws
        ServletClientException {
        int returnValue;
         try {
            returnValue = Integer.parseInt(stringfiedPort);
        }
        catch (NumberFormatException e) {
            throw new ServletClientException("invalid port number: " +
                stringfiedPort);
        }
        if (returnValue <= 0 || returnValue > 0xFFFF) {
```

```
                throw new ServletClientException("invalid port: " + returnValue);
            }
            if (returnValue < 1024) {
                throw new ServletClientException("permission denied for port: " +
                    returnValue);
            }
            return returnValue;
        }

        private static Socket connectToLocalServer(int port) throws
            ServletServerException {
            Socket returnValue;
            try {
                returnValue = new Socket(InetAddress.getLocalHost( ), port);
            }
            catch (IOException e)  {
                throw new ServletServerException("could not connect to "
                    + "local port");
            }
            return returnValue;
        }

        private static void forwardResponse(HttpServletResponse response, Socket
            connectionToLocalServer) throws IOException, ServletClientException,
            ServletServerException
        {
            byte[] buffer;
            DataInputStream socketIn;
            try  {
                socketIn = new
                    DataInputStream(connectionToLocalServer.getInputStream( ));
            }
            catch (IOException e)  {
                throw new ServletServerException("error reading from " + "server");
            }
            String key = "Content-length:".toLowerCase( );
            boolean contentLengthFound = false;
            String line;
            int responseContentLength = -1;
            do {
                try {
                    line = socketIn.readLine( );
                }
                catch (IOException e) {
                    throw new ServletServerException("error reading from server");
                }
                if (line == null) {
                    throw new ServletServerException(
                        "unexpected EOF reading server response");
                }
                if (line.toLowerCase( ).startsWith(key))  {
                    responseContentLength =Integer.parseInt(line.substring(key.
                        length()).trim( ));
                    contentLengthFound = true;
```

```
            }
    }
    while ((line.length( ) != 0) &&  (line.charAt(0) != '\r') && (line.charAt(0)
        != '\n'));
    if (!contentLengthFound || responseContentLength < 0) throw new
        ServletServerException("missing or invalid content length in server
        response");
    buffer = new byte[responseContentLength];
    try {
        socketIn.readFully(buffer);
    }
    catch (EOFException e) {
        throw new ServletServerException("unexpected EOF reading server
            response");
    }
    catch (IOException e) {
        throw new ServletServerException("error reading from server");
    }
    response.setStatus(HttpServletResponse.SC_OK);
    response.setContentType("application/octet-stream");
    response.setContentLength(buffer.length);

    try {
        OutputStream out = response.getOutputStream( );
        out.write(buffer);
        out.flush( );
    }
    catch (IOException e) {
        throw new ServletServerException("error writing response");
    }
    }
}
```

There are three important points to notice about ServletForwarder. First, it uses sockets and streams to forward the body of the HTTP message to the RMI server and then simply pipes what the RMI server returns back into HttpServletResponse's output stream. There is no magical or mysterious code here, and HTTP tunneling involves nothing that you hadn't seen by the end of Chapter 2.

The second important point is that ServletForwarder forwards the message without demarshalling the data or understanding the message at all. Even though the body of the HTTP request contains serialized instances of classes, ServletForwarder doesn't need to have the classes on its classpath or treat the serialized instances as anything other than bytes to be copied from one stream to another. This means that HTTP tunneling is easy to deploy and doesn't need to be updated as the application evolves.

The final point is that, all tolled, this is really a simple piece of code that takes advantage of a lot of existing infrastructure. You can download the Apache web server (available at *http://www.apache.org*), install the Tomcat servlet engine (available at *http://jakarta.apache.org*), and, in the course of an afternoon, circumvent a firewall that took experienced systems administrators months to configure and install.

Modifying the Tunneling Mechanism

The default RMI socket factory will automatically attempt to tunnel over HTTP when more straightforward ways of connecting fail. You don't need to change the server or the client code. Instead, you simply need to make sure that a third server, which forwards the requests, has been installed and everything is configured correctly. Since all the code for this server is readily available, you may think that using HTTP tunneling boils down to an exercise in configuring your application. For the most part, this is true. In many cases, using HTTP tunneling boils down to installing the software and making sure all the servers are available. However, sometimes you will need to modify the tunneling mechanism. At this point, it is helpful to observe that the HTTP tunneling mechanism naturally divides into three parts:

The client
> Posts a request to the web server

The servlet
> Forwards the request to the RMI server's socket, preserving the HTTP structure of the client post

The server
> Automatically handles the HTTP post, in addition to ordinary JRMP commands

These three parts can change independently. The client will automatically post to the web server if it cannot reach the RMI server directly. This will happen regardless of whether the servlet performing the tunneling is Sun's implementation or a custom version you wrote. Similarly, the RMI server will accept either JRMP method invocations or HTTP posts, whether or not they came from a servlet doing HTTP tunneling on behalf of a client.

You can use this fact to your advantage. For example, one of the big limitations of the default implementation of HTTP tunneling is that it assumes the RMI server is running on the same machine as the web server. This assumption is so basic to HTTP tunneling that it even effects the URL being used; a URL of the form *http://cgi-bin/java-rmi.cgi?forward=[port number]* doesn't even include a destination server machine.

A custom servlet that implements HTTP tunneling is free to forward the request to other machines. The change is simple: the `connectToLocalServer( )` method simply needs to replace `InetAddress.getLocalHost( )` with a more appropriate server machine. Replacing one line of code can allow messages to be forwarded to different servers running on different machines.

The servlet can also look at the data it is forwarding. Instead of simply copying an instance of `InputStream` into an instance of `OutputStream`, it can examine the request and log which client requests which operations.

Unfortunately, while it's easy to change the forwarding mechanism, it's hard to change either the client or the server. It'd be nice to be able to use SSL when connecting to the web server. However, in order to do that, you need to use a different socket factory entirely—and implementing HTTP tunneling is a fair amount of work.

The Bank via HTTP Tunneling

HTTP tunneling is enabled by default in RMI. Using HTTP tunneling doesn't require any code changes on either the client or the server. Instead, all that is required is that a web server be installed and configured. The complete list of steps to accomplish this for the bank example are:

1. Install the web server. I chose to install JavaWebServer because, as far as I can tell, it is the easiest web server to install and configure.

2. Add the servlet to the web server. This boils down to somehow telling the web server that URLs beginning with */cgi-bin/java-rmi.cgi* are mapped to the servlet handling HTTP tunneling (in this case, SimplifiedServletHandler).

3. Test to make sure everything works.

Testing is sometimes a little tricky. Developers often don't have a firewall readily available in their development environment. To help get around this difficulty, Sun has provided a socket factory class, sun.rmi.transport.proxy.RMIHttpToCGISocket-Factory, which only uses HTTP tunneling when attempting to connect to a server. That is, of the five ways a default socket factory can connect to a server, instances of sun.rmi.transport.proxy.RMIHttpToCGISocketFactory will use only the final two. Namely:

1. It attempt to connect on port 80 of the server machine and send the request to a URL beginning with */cgi-bin/java-rmi.cgi*. The interpretation of this URL is that the request will be forwarded to a program that interprets the HTTP request and forwards it, as an HTTP request, to the appropriate port on the server machine.

2. If that fails, it attempts to connect on port 80 of the firewall machine and send the request to a URL beginning with */cgi-bin/java-rmi.cgi*. The interpretation of this URL is that the request will be forwarded to a program that interprets the HTTP request and forwards it, as an HTTP request, to the appropriate port on the server machine.

Hence, to run the bank example using HTTP tunneling, we simply add another line to the application that launches the client:

```
public class BankClient {
    public static void main(String[] args) {
        try {
            RMISocketFactory. setSocketFactory(new sun.rmi.transport.proxy.
                RMIHttpToCGISocketFactory( ));
        }
```

```
        catch (IOException ignored) {}
        (new BankClientFrame()).show();
    }
}
```

Of course, if you do this, all the remote method calls from a client, including those associated with the naming service and distributed garbage collection, go through the web server as well. This means that in order to use this socket factory, you need one machine running the web server, the naming service, and all of your servers. This is useful for functionality testing, but can skew results if you attempt to scale-test.

Drawbacks of HTTP Tunneling

HTTP tunneling is often considered a bad idea. There are five major reasons for this:

Security
> At its heart, HTTP tunneling involves deliberately circumventing a security mechanism that someone else thought was necessary and worked hard to install. It involves deliberately relaxing the security provisions on a trusted network.
>
> Ordinarily, this isn't such a big deal. You're a reasonable person and remote method calls aren't so big a risk (especially if you use a secure web server to handle the HTTP traffic). However, and this cannot be stressed enough, you should not enable dynamic classloading if your application will use HTTP tunneling. Downloading classes from outside a firewall and executing them inside a firewall constitutes gross negligence. I'd fire anyone who did it.

Bandwidth inefficiency
> RMI is already a verbose protocol; it encodes a lot of information in each message request. Taking an RMI message and wrapping it in an HTTP post by inputting the RMI message as the body of the post and then setting five or six message headers just adds insult to injury. Using HTTP tunneling could easily double bandwidth requirements for many remote interfaces. In particular, consider the output of LoggingServletForwardCommand, which simply prints out the HTTP headers from a request.

Connection inefficiency
> HTTP tunneling does not support keeping connections open and reusing them. Unlike JRMP, in which sockets may be reused for dozens of method calls, HTTP tunneling establishes a new socket connection for each request. While each socket connection is not necessarily expensive, the overhead can add up.

Application fragility
> HTTP tunneling introduces another way that your distributed application can fail. It makes your entire application vulnerable to changes in firewall configuration or network topology.

Even worse, when the application fails, you won't immediately think, "The firewall changed." Instead, you'll spend a day or two wondering just what happened, checking the server configuration, and trying to replicate the problem from other clients. Only after you've exhausted those possibilities will it occur to you that maybe it isn't your application.

Loss of protocol-specific features

HTTP tunneling uses HTTP and plain-text sockets. You can't change your application to use compressing sockets or RMI/IIOP (see Chapter 23 for details on RMI/IIOP). In addition, security is nonexistent—Sun's implementation of HTTP tunneling doesn't attempt to protect the data at all.

 This last point is easily overcome. You can sign a license, get the source code to RMI, and then use Sun's implementation of HTTP tunneling as a starting point for a secure implementation (or an implementation that uses RMI/IIOP). The first four points, however, are costs built into HTTP tunneling.

Tunneling Through Two Firewalls

Many, perhaps even most, corporate networks actually use two firewalls, dividing the world into three zones:

The Internet
This is not under corporate control at all and is viewed as being highly insecure.

The DMZ
This is behind the first firewall and in front of the second firewall. Proxy servers that interface to the outside world (such as HTTP and mail) servers are here. Contractors and software that is not fully under corporate control have frequent access to this part of the network.

The trusted network
This is the area behind the second firewall. Sensitive data, corporate applications, and most internal uses are inside the trusted network.

If you're developing for this type of network, you may have to tunnel through both firewalls. In order to do this, you will need to customize `ServletForwardCommand` for the outer web server (it should attempt to tunnel through the inner firewall instead of attempt to send a message to an RMI server).

That said, HTTP tunneling is also universally used. At the O'Reilly P2P Conference in February of 2001, I spent a good part of the first day asking attendees how they dealt with firewalls. I asked 13 people and received the following responses:

2 people said, "Firewalls are a problem."
11 people said, "Oh. We just tunnel through them."

I stopped asking when it sunk in that I'd just been told that 11 distinct protocols, for everything from distributed computation to performing a naming-service lookup, were all tunneling through HTTP.

Disabling HTTP Tunneling

Sun's implementation of HTTP tunneling is very nice and very convenient. However, there are situations when you just don't want to use it. For example, suppose there is no web server or servlet to forward the tunneled requests to the intended server. HTTP tunneling won't cause any functional problems in such a case. However, it doesn't help anything either, and could cause performance problems. When a server goes down, RMI will try four distinct ways to connect with it before deciding that the method call failed. If you know in advance that four of these ways will fail, you may as well save the bandwidth and processor cycles.

There are two ways to disable HTTP tunneling:

- Change the default socket factory. You can write a simple socket factory, one that returns plain-text sockets but does not do any sort of tunneling when requests fail. If you make this socket factory your default socket factory, then RMI will use it to get sockets for connections. Hence, HTTP tunneling will be disabled. Recall that serialized instances of socket factories are carried along with stubs. This means that the place to change the default socket factory is on the server.

- Set the java.rmi.server.disableHttp property to the string literal true. The sockets returned by the default socket factory check this property before attempting to tunnel. This property needs to be set on each client.

I prefer to use the first option. It involves a little more code and is less flexible—it forces all clients to obey the same policy—but it is a more thorough solution and is much harder to change. It requires a change to the server, which is presumably running in a controlled environment. Making such a change is much harder than changing a property in a client application.

I also like the first option because, morally speaking, the server should get to choose the protocol being used. But that's a rather idiosyncratic bias.

CHAPTER 23

RMI, CORBA, and RMI/IIOP

Since 1989, the Object Management Group (OMG) has been defining and refining a standard called the Common Object Request Broker Architecture (or CORBA). CORBA is a specification for distributed object-based computing that enables clients and servers to communicate. CORBA is explicitly platform- and language-independent and is quite heavily used in enterprise computing. In this chapter, I'll introduce CORBA, compare CORBA to RMI, and then discuss RMI/IIOP, which is a compromise that allows Java developers to take advantage of some of RMI's features while still writing CORBA applications. By the end of this chapter, you'll have an elementary understanding of CORBA and a clear understanding of when to use CORBA and when to use RMI.

At some point in the mid-1980s, a number of industry leaders began to realize that every large corporation has a fairly similar computing environment, consisting of the following five components:

A mixed set of hardware platforms

Many large and midsize companies have a incredibly diverse hardware base. Many servers are still on mainframes and likely will be for the foreseeable future, while many smaller applications are hosted on whatever hardware was handy at the time (and the applications are often too brittle to migrate to new platforms gracefully). Client machines are even more varied.

A mixed set of software environments

From operating systems to programming languages to libraries to network infrastructure choices such as database servers or email platforms, everything varies. It's not uncommon for three applications, performing fairly similar tasks, to be written in entirely different languages, and assume entirely different software environments.

Programmers with vastly different skill sets

Into this grand grab-bag of hardware and software comes the hired help. Programmers build new programs, maintain the old ones, and try to make sure that everything still works well enough as the corporation moves forward. Each programmer has their own set of special skills and tend to work best in a particular language, with a particular set of tools.

An overwhelming need to maintain and integrate legacy code and applications
Throwing away a useful program is just not an option in most computing environments. If it exists, and it works, it has to be maintained, supported, and extended.

A desire to avoid vendor lock-in
When you rely on a single vendor, you become vulnerable. If that vendor decides, for whatever reason, to stop supporting a product, you're left with very few options, and most of them are extremely painful. As people who depended on OS/2 or NeXTSTEP can attest, it's no fun to be left high and dry.

 Of course, this isn't true just in large corporations. Even within the author's relatively small startup (currently 45 people, less than two years old), we run five server operating systems, have code written in three different languages, and use two different servlet engines.

The question becomes: how do you build distributed systems in the face of all of these factors? Especially when many of the requirements are of the form, "Take those two existing systems and integrate them to provide this extra functionality."

CORBA is an attempt to solve this problem by defining a cross-platform, cross-language, vendor-independent specification for object-based distributed computing. OMG approved the first version of the CORBA specification in 1989; four years later, the specification was radically overhauled to define CORBA 2.0. And, eight years after that, things seem to be getting fairly stable. The current version of the specification is CORBA 2.3, and the much anticipated CORBA 3.0 doesn't change anything important.*

How CORBA Works

There are two basic ways to think about CORBA. One is to build out from RMI. CORBA is like RMI in that it defines a platform-distributed, object-based computing. However, because it is explicitly intended to handle corporate computing environments and help integrate legacy code, it can't make any assumptions about the programming languages being used, nor can it assume that a distributed application is written in a single programming language. Clients can be written in a different programming language than servers.

The other way to think about CORBA is to think about it in terms of the mission it's accomplishing. The basic CORBA task is to integrate two different programs, written

---

* From the point of view of an RMI programmer. There are many people out there who think that CORBA 3.0 does introduce important changes to the CORBA specification.

in different programming languages and running on different machines, into a single distributed application. To do this, CORBA needs to have a way to define how these programs communicate with each other, a way to define how values are passed between programs, and a well-defined (at the level of bits) wire protocol.

Fortunately, these are not incompatible ways of thinking about CORBA. Thinking of CORBA as a language-independent version of RMI leads you to suspect that the basic development cycle and architecture are much the same. That is, the CORBA development cycle will involve defining interfaces to servers and value objects, after which stubs and skeletons will be generated, and the client and server programs will be written. The architecture looks much like Figure 23-1.

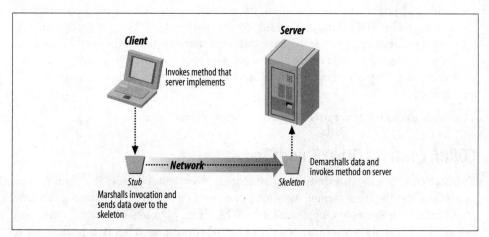

Figure 23-1. The CORBA architecture

Meanwhile, thinking about CORBA as a way to glue together two systems written in different languages on different platforms* leads you to realize that the interfaces have to be defined in a language-independent and easily understood way, and that there has to be mapping from the language-independent interfaces to various programming languages. Otherwise, we can't automatically use stubs and skeletons; if we can't do that, programmers will find other tools to use.

So that's the basic idea behind CORBA. At the heart of CORBA are the following three things:

An Interface Definition Language (IDL)
IDL is a language for defining interfaces. That is, it has a rich set of datatypes, ways to define value objects (known as structs) and exceptions, and ways to define methods. The only thing it doesn't have is a way to specify an implementation—IDL is only used to define how two programs communicate with each other, not what happens inside a method implementation.

 Of course, a little bit of language bias has crept into IDL. In particular, IDL files look a lot like C++ header files to me.

A wire protocol (IIOP)
Given IDL's rich set of datatypes, and the ability to define value objects, there needs to be a way to send these over the wire in much the same way that RMI uses serialization to define a wire format. IIOP is the formal mapping from IDL interfaces and datatypes to streams of bytes that can be sent over the wire.

A set of language mappings
The final important piece is a way to translate from IDL to programming languages. The IDL datatypes need to be mapped to programming-language datatypes. For example, IDL's long datatype maps to Java's int, and IDL's wchar maps to instances of Java's String class. Moreover, as part of the language mappings, the way to generate stubs and skeletons from IDL interfaces is fully defined.

This leads to the reference architecture shown in Figure 23-2.

CORBA Contains Other Things Too

The CORBA specification currently runs well over 1,000 pages. It contains a lot more than just the three items I mentioned earlier. For example, it defines an abstract layer, called the Portable Object Adapter (POA). The POA lies between the wire and the skeleton and plays a role analogous to the RMI runtime. That is, it pulls requests off the wire, demarshalls the data, and forwards the requests to the skeletons. The

---

* What the heck—add in "in different decades" as well.

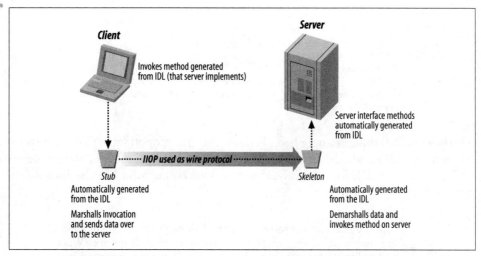

Figure 23-2. A more detailed architecture

POA is, however, vastly more flexible than the RMI runtime and allows programmers much more control over things like thread creation.

Another important aspect of the CORBA specification is the definition of standard services. The CORBA specification contains IDL interfaces, and fairly thorough discussions, of many of the common architectural components of a distributed application. For example, the CORBA specification contains a complete definition (in IDL) of a naming service, an event service, and a transactions-management service.

For more information on CORBA, see *Java Programming with CORBA* by Andrew Vogel and Keith Duddy (John Wiley & Sons) and *Advanced CORBA Programming with C++* by Michi Henning and Steve Vinosky (Addison-Wesley).

The Bank Example in CORBA

In order to make this more concrete, we will briefly walk through how to build the bank example using CORBA. However, since this is an RMI book, we will not dwell on the details—if you're interested, the complete code for this chapter is contained in the `com.ora.rmibook.chapter23.corbaaccounts` package.

Defining the Interface

The first step is to define the interface using IDL:

```
#pragma prefix "com.ora.rmibook.chapter23.corbaaccounts"

struct Money {
    long cents;
};
```

```
exception NegativeAmountException{};
exception OverdraftException{};

interface Account{
    Money getBalance( );
    void makeDeposit(in Money amount)  raises (NegativeAmountException);
    void makeWithdrawal(in Money amount) raises (NegativeAmountException,
        OverdraftException);
};
```

There are several things to note here. Perhaps the most important is that this is actually quite readable. We declare a struct, we declare some exceptions, and we define an interface. The IDL for our account servers looks quite a bit like the Java definitions we've used up until now.

 This shouldn't be a surprise. Chapters 5 through 7, which contained a fair number of design guidelines, weren't at all RMI-specific. When you add in the fact that both IDL and Java syntax are descended from C, it would be surprising if RMI programmers couldn't easily understand IDL interfaces.

Generating Stubs and Skeletons

The IDL contains all the information that defines how clients talk to servers. This means that, once we have the IDL, we can generate stubs and skeletons. In Java 2, this is accomplished through the use of the idlj program. For example, the command:

```
idlj -fall Account.idl
```

will compile our IDL file into a set of Java classes, including stubs, skeletons, and value objects. These classes can then be used to build our application.

There is an important difference between CORBA and RMI here. RMI, via rmic, requires the server classes to generate stubs and skeletons, not just the interfaces. CORBA requires only the IDL. Since the client and server can be written in different programming languages, it's hard to see how the details of the server implementation could be used by the IDL compiler.

The IDL compiler generates a lot of classes. Even the simple IDL file we used for our account server generates the following classes:

```
Account.java
AccountHelper.java
AccountHolder.java
AccountOperations.java
Account_Impl.java

Money.java
MoneyHelper.java
MoneyHolder.java
```

```
NegativeAmountException.java
NegativeAmountExceptionHelper.java
NegativeAmountExceptionHolder.java

OverdraftException.java
OverdraftExceptionHelper.java
OverdraftExceptionHolder.java

_AccountImplBase.java
_AccountStub.java
```

Among these classes are a stun, a skeleton, a value object (Money), and a lot of classes whose role is to help the CORBA runtime translate between Java datatypes and IDL datatypes.

The Server

Let's briefly look at the code for an account server. Here's a simple implementation:

```
package com.ora.rmibook.chapter23.corbaaccounts;
public class Account_Impl extends _AccountImplBase {
    private Money _balance;
    public Account_Impl(Money startingBalance) {
        _balance = startingBalance;
    }

    public Money getBalance( ) {
        return _balance;
    }

    public void makeDeposit(Money amount) throws NegativeAmountException {
        checkForNegativeAmount(amount);
        _balance.cents += amount.cents;
        return;
    }

    public void makeWithdrawal(Money amount) throws NegativeAmountException,
        OverdraftException {
        checkForNegativeAmount(amount);
        checkForOverdraft(amount);
        _balance.cents -= amount.cents;
        return;
    }

    private void checkForNegativeAmount(Money amount)  throws
        NegativeAmountException {
        int cents = amount.cents;
        if (0 > cents) {
            throw new NegativeAmountException( );
        }
    }
```

Accounts in C++

What happens when we compile `Account.idl` into other languages? Pretty much the same thing. Whereas the Java stub contains method definitions such as:

```java
public void makeWithdrawal (Money amount) throws NegativeAmountException,
    OverdraftException {
    org.omg.CORBA.portable.InputStream _in = null;
    try {
        org.omg.CORBA.portable.OutputStream _out = _request
            ("makeWithdrawal", true);
        MoneyHelper.write (_out, amount);
        _in = _invoke (_out);
    } catch (org.omg.CORBA.portable.ApplicationException _ex) {
        _in = _ex.getInputStream ();
        String _id = _ex.getId ();
        if (_id.equals ("IDL:com.ora.rmibook.chapter23.corbaaccounts/" +
            "NegativeAmountException:1.0")) throw
            NegativeAmountExceptionHelper.read (_in);
        else if (_id.equals ("IDL:com.ora.rmibook.chapter23.corbaaccounts/" +
            "OverdraftException:1.0")) throw OverdraftExceptionHelper.read
            (_in);
        else throw new org.omg.CORBA.MARSHAL (_id);
    } catch (org.omg.CORBA.portable.RemarshalException _rm) {
        makeWithdrawal (amount);
    } finally {
        _releaseReply (_in);
    }
} // makeWithdrawal
```

the C++ version of the stub contains:

```cpp
void Account::makeWithdrawal( const Money& _amount ) {
    CORBA_MarshalInBuffer_var _ibuf;
    CORBA::MarshalOutBuffer_var _obuf;
    while( 1 ) {
        _obuf = ___root->_create_request("makeWithdrawal", 1, 627418);
        VISostream& _ostrm = *(VISostream *)(CORBA::MarshalOutBuffer*)_obuf;
        _ostrm << _amount;
        try {
            _ibuf = ___root->_invoke(_obuf);
        } catch (const CORBA::TRANSIENT& ) {
        continue;
        }
        break;
    }
}
```

It's not really all that different.

```java
private void checkForOverdraft(Money amount) throws OverdraftException {
    if (amount.cents > _balance.cents) {
        throw new OverdraftException();
    }
```

```
            return;
        }
    }
```

This is a simple server, equivalent to the one we built for RMI back in Chapter 9, but it's worth looking at anyway. The main reason for doing so is that most of the server code is identical to the RMI version. CORBA involves writing interfaces in IDL, and it automatically generates value objects. However, once you get past the IDL, much of the code is the same. If you can build an RMI system, you can build a CORBA system.

The Launch and Client Code

The launch and client code should also feel familiar. Finding a CORBA naming service is a little harder than finding an RMI registry (but not harder than finding a JNDI naming context). However, the basic code and the overall structure of the application are the same.

Here, for example, is our launch code:

```
public class ImplLauncher {
    public static void main(String[] args) {
        Collection nameBalancePairs = getNameBalancePairs(args);
        Iterator i = nameBalancePairs.iterator();
        while(i.hasNext()) {
            NameBalancePair nextNameBalancePair = (NameBalancePair) i.next();
            launchServer(nextNameBalancePair);
        }
        (new JFrame("Dispatcher Server")).show();  // hack to keep JVM alive
                                                   // because JavaIDL uses Daemon
                                                   // threads

    }

    private static void launchServer(NameBalancePair serverDescription) {
        try {
            Account_Impl newAccount = new Account_Impl(serverDescription.balance);
            OrbSetup.bindAccountServer(serverDescription.name, newAccount);
            System.out.println("Account " + serverDescription.name + " successfully
                launched.");
        }
        catch(Exception e){ e.printStackTrace();}
    }
// ....
}
```

This is exactly parallel to the RMI launch code. The only difference is that we've added another class, OrbSetup, to handle the details of connecting to the CORBA naming service. Here's the entirety of that class:

```
public class OrbSetup {
    private static Properties _properties;
    private static Properties getProperties() {
        if (null==_properties) {
            _properties = new Properties();
            _properties.put("org.omg.CORBA.ORBInitialPort", "3500");
```

```
            _properties.put("org.omg.CORBA.ORBInitialHost", "localhost");
        }
        return _properties;
    }

    public static Account getAccount(String name) {
        try {
            Properties properties = OrbSetup.getProperties();
            ORB orb = ORB.init((String[]) null, properties);
            org.omg.CORBA.Object objRef = orb.
                resolve_initial_references("NameService");
            NamingContext nameServer = NamingContextHelper.narrow(objRef);
            NameComponent ourComponent = new NameComponent(name, "");
            NameComponent path[] = {ourComponent};
            org.omg.CORBA.Object accountRef = nameServer.resolve(path);
            return AccountHelper.narrow(accountRef);
        }
        catch (Exception e) {
            e.printStackTrace();
        }
        return null;
    }

    public static void bindAccountServer(String name, Account server) throws
        Exception {
        Properties properties = OrbSetup.getProperties();
        ORB orb = ORB.init((String[]) null, properties);
         orb.connect(server); // This is pretty much a JavaIDL hack
                              // JavaIDL doesn't really support servers well
        org.omg.CORBA.Object objRef = orb.resolve_initial_references("NameService");
        NamingContext nameServer = NamingContextHelper.narrow(objRef);
        NameComponent ourComponent = new NameComponent(name, "");
        NameComponent path[] = {ourComponent};
        nameServer.rebind(path, server);
    }
}
```

The client code changes in a similar way. By using the OrbSetup class, we've isolated the changes in the client application to a couple of lines in BankClientFrame's getAccount() method. It changes from:

```
private void getAccount() {
        try {
            _account = (Account)Naming.lookup(_accountNameField.getText());
        }
        catch (Exception e) {
            System.out.println("Couldn't find account. Error was \n " + e);
            e.printStackTrace();
        }
        return;
    }
```

to:

```
private void getAccount( ) {
        try {
            _account = OrbSetup.getAccount(_accountNameField.getText( ));
        }
        catch (Exception e) {
            System.out.println("Couldn't find account. Error was \n " + e);
            e.printStackTrace( );
        }
         return;
    }
```

A Quick Comparison of CORBA and RMI

At this point, we have two frameworks for building distributed systems. They're very similar; they involve the same design and architectural principles and they perform many of the same tasks.

But, as I've stressed, there are some significant differences. CORBA is designed to allow you to use multiple programming languages and easily adapt legacy code for distributed applications. In addition, there are large, and growing, bases of code built using CORBA. This includes a lot of standardized infrastructure, such as the services mentioned in the first section of this chapter.

> One very nice aspect of language independence is that the standard CORBA services are usually built in either C or C++ and optimized for the operating system/platform on which they run. There's something to be said for building infrastructure such as naming and event services this way.

On the other hand, using RMI to build complicated systems is much easier. Because RMI is Java-specific, the amount of code you need to write for a complex RMI application can be significantly smaller and simpler than the code you need to write for the equivalent CORBA application. Because RMI uses serialization, it's much easier to evolve and maintain an RMI application. And because CORBA is limited to what's available in all of its target languages, CORBA has nothing like RMI's distributed garbage collection mechanism. Most languages don't support garbage collection.

> RMI also contains a number of other nice features. For example, custom socket factories. There's no similar functionality in CORBA.

RMI on Top of CORBA

Deciding which framework to use really boils down to answering the following two questions:

- Will the application need to communicate with applications or pieces of code that aren't written in Java?
- Would the extra CORBA infrastructure be very useful?

If the answers to both of these are strongly positive, then the application ought to be built using CORBA. If the answers to both of these are strongly negative, then RMI is the natural choice for a distribution framework.

However, there are a great deal of intermediate cases. For example, suppose that most of the application will be written in Java. It'll have a few C++ components, either for speed or because that logic already exists, but the bulk of the code will be written in Java.

In this scenario, RMI is almost the right tool. RMI is easier to use than CORBA, has a much gentler learning curve, and is a much better fit than CORBA for most of the application. But you might wind up using CORBA anyway because you will need to integrate those C++ components somehow.[*]

 Two more reasons why you may want to use CORBA are programming language and vendor lock-in. Using RMI involves assuming that all future code that needs to communicate with your servers will also be written in Java. As much as I like Java, I find this assumption *really* implausible.

This scenario is one of the big motivating forces behind RMI/IIOP. The idea is this: keep as much of RMI as possible, which replaces JRMP, the RMI native protocol, with IIOP, the CORBA protocol.

RMI/IIOP applications are developed using the following sequence of steps:

1. Interfaces are defined just as they are with RMI. They use serializable value objects, they extend the Remote interface, and all the methods throw RemoteException.

2. The server is implemented differently than with RMI. In particular, instead of extending or using a static method defined in UnicastRemoteObject or Activatable, the server extends or uses a static method defined in PortableRemoteObject.

3. Stubs and skeletons are generated using rmic, as with RMI. However, the -iiop flag is used. This tells rmic to use IIOP as the communication protocol.

---

[*] And you really don't want to use JNDI unless you absolutely have to.

---

4. Any code that involves using a naming service (the launch code and the client code) must use the CORBA naming service instead of the RMI registry. This is usually done by JNDI.

5. IDL can be generated from an interface defined in step 1. This IDL enables non-Java programs to send and receive messages as part of the regular application flow. To the non-Java code, the whole application simply looks like a CORBA application.

While the second and fourth steps are slightly different than with RMI, this development sequence is reasonably natural and intuitive for Java developers.

EJB and RMI/IIOP

The Enterprise JavaBeans (EJB) specification was another big motivating force behind RMI/IIOP. The EJB specification defines two important concepts: the EJB container and the idea of an enterprise bean.

The EJB container is an incredibly flexible runtime environment that "holds" the enterprise beans and manages all client interactions with the beans. The beans can't do much (they're, in essence, event handlers), but the people writing the beans don't have to worry about many of the coding headaches traditionally associated with writing servers. In particular, the container is responsible for managing security, handling transaction management (as in our `transferMoney( )` example), and most threading issues.

The EJB specification is written using RMI, and it greatly simplifies developing a certain class of distributed applications. However, when the EJB specification was written, there were no EJB containers. The fastest way to get EJB containers on the market was to adapt similar programs already written using CORBA. RMI/IIOP was one of the technologies that made this possible.

The Fine Print

There are some drawbacks to using RMI/IIOP. I've already mentioned a few of them. For example, RMI/IIOP doesn't support distributed garbage collection. It also doesn't support the activation framework or custom socket factories.

In addition, there are several fairly straightforward things to watch out for:

- Constant definitions in remote interfaces must be either primitive types or instances of String that can be evaluated during compilation.
- Names of classes or exceptions can't differ only in their case. CORBA is not particularly case-sensitive.

- CORBA doesn't handle object identity very well. In particular, if you send the same object twice (e.g., as the first and second arguments to a method call), you may end up with two different objects after demarshalling. A similar warning applies with respect to equals( ). Two instances of equals( ) won't be == when they are demarshalled, and the definition of equals( ) (which is a method, not data) won't be transferred over the wire.

  In practice, this means that any code you have that depends on equals( ) or hashCode( ) must be well documented so that developers using another programming language can implement the tests correctly.

In addition to these problems, there is another, more subtle, issue that can arise. RMI/IIOP can depend heavily on a new and somewhat controversial part of the CORBA specification called Objects-By-Value (OBV). At this point, the OBV component of the CORBA specification is defined only for Java and C++. Moreover, very few vendors support OBV.

 How can you tell if a vendor supports OBV? OBV was defined as part of Version 2.3 of the CORBA specification. Check to see if the vendor is CORBA 2.3-compliant. If it isn't, it probably doesn't support OBV. If it does claim to be CORBA 2.3-compliant, ask anyway. It never hurts to make sure.

The rule of thumb is this: if an RMI interface doesn't involve passing any objects other than exceptions, the IDL that's generated won't need OBV. This leads to two benefits: there are more implementations of CORBA that can be used with the resulting IDL, and the full range of languages supported by CORBA can be used in the application.

If an RMI interface does use Java objects, either as arguments or return values, the generated IDL will use OBV. And therefore, only an up-to-date implementation of the CORBA specification can be used, and the only other language that can be used is C++.

Converting the Bank Example to RMI/IIOP

Rather than go through a complete implementation of the bank example using RMI/IIOP, we'll just focus on what changes (most of the code is the same).

The major change is that Account_Impl can no longer extend UnicastRemoteObject or Activatable. Instead, it must extend PortableRemoteObject (which is defined in the javax.rmi package). That is, the code changes from:

```
public class Account_Impl extends UnicastRemoteObject implements Account
```

to:

```
public class Account_Impl extends PortableRemoteObject implements Account
```

The next change is that the stubs and skeletons are generated using rmic with the -iiop flag:

```
rmic -keep -iiop -d d:\classes com.ora.rmibook.chapter23.rmiiiopaccounts.Account_Impl
```

The -keep flag is still valid and allows us to look at the stub code. As you might expect, the automatically generated stub code is completely different. Here, for example, is the stub implementation of getBalance( ):

```
public Money getBalance( ) throws RemoteException {
        if (!Util.isLocal(this)) {
            try {
                org.omg.CORBA_2_3.portable.InputStream in = null;
                try {
                    OutputStream out = _request("_get_balance", true);
                    in = (org.omg.CORBA_2_3.portable.InputStream)_invoke(out);
                    return (Money) in.read_value(Money.class);
                } catch (ApplicationException ex) {
                    in = (org.omg.CORBA_2_3.portable.InputStream) ex.
                        getInputStream( );
                    String id = in.read_string( );
                    throw new UnexpectedException(id);
                } catch (RemarshalException ex) {
                    return getBalance( );
                } finally {
                    _releaseReply(in);
                }
            } catch (SystemException ex) {
                throw Util.mapSystemException(ex);
            }
        } else {
            ServantObject so = _servant_preinvoke("_get_balance",Account.class);
            if (so == null) {
                return getBalance( );
            }
            try {
                Money result = ((Account)so.servant).getBalance( );
                return (Money)Util.copyObject(result,_orb( ));
            } catch (Throwable ex) {
                Throwable exCopy = (Throwable)Util.copyObject(ex,_orb( ));
                throw Util.wrapException(exCopy);
            } finally {
                _servant_postinvoke(so);
            }
        }
    }
}
```

Notice that even though the code is quite a bit different from the RMI stub we examined in Chapter 4, it accomplishes the same basic tasks. At a conceptual level, the stub is doing the same things it always did.

Finally, to convert the bank example to RMI/IIOP, we must use JNDI (with the CORBA naming service) instead of the RMI registry. Both the client code and the launch code need to change. We'll look at the launch code first:

```java
public static void main(String[] args) {
    try {
        namingContext = new InitialContext();
    }
    catch (Exception e) {
        System.out.println("Naming context unavailable");
        System.exit(0);
    }
    Collection nameBalancePairs = getNameBalancePairs(args);
    Iterator i = nameBalancePairs.iterator();
    while(i.hasNext()) {
        NameBalancePair nextNameBalancePair = (NameBalancePair) i.next();
        launchServer(nextNameBalancePair);
    }
}

private static void launchServer(NameBalancePair serverDescription) {
    try {
        Account_Impl newAccount = new Account_Impl(serverDescription.balance);
        namingContext.rebind(serverDescription.name, newAccount);
        system.out.println("Account " + serverDescription.name +
            " successfully launched.");
    }
    catch(Exception e) {
        E..printStackTrace();
    }
}
```

All this does is create a NamingContext when the program first starts running, and then bind the instances of Account_Impl into the instance of NamingContext instead of using the RMI registry as a naming service. However, because RMI/IIOP assumes that the NamingContext is actually the CORBA naming service, we need to set JNDI's system properties correctly. In this case, we simply set them as part of the command line. That is, we use the following command to launch our servers:

```
start java -Djava.naming.factory.initial=com.sun.jndi.cosnaming.CNCtxFactory -Djava.
naming.provider.url=iiop://127.0.0.1:3500 com.ora.rmibook.chapter23.rmiiiopaccounts.
applications.ImplLauncher Bob 10000 Alex 1223
```

The client code has one additional change: getAccount() used to cast the object returned by the RMI registry into an instance of Account, as in the following code snippet:

```java
private void getAccount() {
    try {
        _account = (Account)Naming.lookup(_accountNameField.getText());
    }
    catch (Exception e) { ...}
    return;
}
```

The correct way to do this when using RMI/IIOP involves calling `PortableRemote-Object`'s `narrow( )` method. The preceding code now becomes:

```
private void getAccount( ) {
        try {
               Context namingContext = new InitialContext( );
               Object account = namingContext.lookup(_accountNameField.getText( ));
               _account = (Account) PortableRemoteObject.narrow(account, Account.
                      class);
        }
        catch (Exception e) { }
        return;
}
```

Communicating via CORBA

The reason for using RMI/IIOP in the first place was to enable ordinary CORBA applications to communicate with our Java code. Unfortunately, the details of doing that are beyond the scope of this book.[*] However, before we drop the subject entirely, it's interesting to look at the IDL that rmic generates from the Account interface. Here's the IDL for Account:

```
/**
 * com/ora/rmibook/chapter23/rmiiiopaccounts/Account.idl
 * Generated by rmic -idl. Do not edit
 * Tuesday, December 26, 2000 12:33:18 AM PST
 */


#ifndef __com_ora_rmibook_chapter23_rmiiiopaccounts_valueobjects_Money__

module com {
    module ora {
    module rmibook {
    module chapter23 {
    module rmiiiopaccounts {
    module valueobjects {
        valuetype Money;
    }; }; }; }; }; // close all the interior module declarations
};

#endif

#include "com/ora/rmibook/chapter23/rmiiiopaccounts/NegativeAmountEx.idl"
#include "com/ora/rmibook/chapter23/rmiiiopaccounts/OverdraftEx.idl"
#include "orb.idl"

#ifndef __com_ora_rmibook_chapter23_rmiiiopaccounts_Account__
#define __com_ora_rmibook_chapter23_rmiiiopaccounts_Account__
```

---

[*] If you know CORBA, the hard part is either obtaining the IOR to the Java server (if you're using a non-Java client and a Java server) or setting up JNDI to recognize the naming service into which you've bound the server (if you're using a Java client and a non-Java server).

```
module com {
    module ora {
    module rmibook {
    module chapter23 {
    module rmiiiopaccounts {

    interface Account {
        readonly attribute ::com::ora::rmibook::chapter23::rmiiiopaccounts::
            valueobjects::Money balance;
        void makeDeposit( in ::com::ora::rmibook::chapter23::rmiiiopaccounts::
            valueobjects::Money arg0 ) raises (::com::ora::rmibook::chapter23::
            rmiiiopaccounts::NegativeAmountEx );
        void makeWithdrawal(in ::com::ora::rmibook::chapter23::rmiiiopaccounts::
            valueobjects::Money arg0 ) raises (::com::ora::rmibook::chapter23::
            rmiiiopaccounts::NegativeAmountEx, ::com::ora::rmibook::chapter23::
            rmiiiopaccounts::OverdraftEx );
    };

#pragma ID Account "RMI:com.ora.rmibook.chapter23.rmiiiopaccounts.Account:
    0000000000000000"

    };}; };}; // close all the interior module declarations
};

#include "com/ora/rmibook/chapter23/rmiiiopaccounts/valueobjects/Money.idl"
#endif
```

 This IDL was generated using the command `rmic -idl com.ora.rmibook.chapter23.rmiiiopaccounts.Account`. There is, however, one fairly annoying bug in `rmic` related to IDL generation—`rmic` does not keep track of classpaths accurately. As of JDK 1.3, you need to change directories to the base directory of your classpath in order to generate IDL. On my system, the *Account.class* file can be found in the directory *d:\classes\com\ora\rmibook\chapter23\rmiiiopaccounts*. So, to generate the IDL, I changed my directory to *d:\classes* (the base directory of my classpath) and then executed `rmic -idl com.ora.rmibook.chapter23.rmiiiopaccounts.Account`.

This is not as nice as our original version of `Account.idl`. In addition, since we used `Money`, which is a serializable object, in our `Remote` interface, the IDL generated by `rmic` uses the objects by value specification.

However, this IDL still isn't that bad: it's readable, it's not hard to understand (especially if you have access to the original Java interface), and it can be used to generate stubs and skeletons in C++, which will be able to communicate with the Java stubs and skeletons. This is really all that we could have hoped for.

Index

A

abstract classes
  Reader, 16–18
  ServerSocketFactory, 38–39
  SocketFactory, 38–39
  Transaction, 112
  Writer, 16–18
accept( ) method
  ServerNetworkWrapper and, 59–60
  ServerSocket class, 27–28
  Socket class and, 28
access, devices, synchronization
      and, 242–246
accessClipBoard, AWT permissions, 448
accessEventQueue, AWT permissions, 448
Account information
  metadata, 125
  UnicastRemoteObject, not
      extending, 135–137
Account interface
  designing, 111
  error handling, 127
  exceptions, 127
  getLock( ) method, 384
  iterators, 124
  method calls, bandwidth and, 121
  method objects, 113
  objects, return values, 119
  passing objects, 116–118
  primitive values, 116–118
  releaseLock( ) method, 384
  remote methods, 460–462
  UnicastRemoteObject class,
      subclassing, 134–135

Account option
  client interaction, 107–108
  code correctness, 109
  server failure, 109
  transferring money, 108
Account_Impl.java code listing, 135
AccountList object, 478
account-locking, 384–389
accounts option, 91
  scalability, 102–104
accounts, partitioning, 103
ActionListener, 23
  socket-based printer server, 61
actionPerformed( ) method, 202
Activatable class
  extending, 392
  static methods, 402
activatable objects, 392–395
  registering, 398
activatable servers
  modifying, 419–420
  shutting down, 401–403
activatable systems
  deploying, 398–399
activation, code changes, 392–398
activation daemon, 390
  client actions, 400
  registry, 399
  security, 457
Activation Framework, 390
  parameters, 405–407
  stubs, 391
ActivationDesc object, 400
ActivationGroup, 390
  object, 400

We'd like to hear your suggestions for improving our indexes. Send email to *index@oreilly.com*.

G

H

I

T

TCP (Transmission Control Protocol), 20–21
  buffering and, 21
  log, 363
temporary references, leasing (garbage collection), 358
terminating threads, 221–222
test applications, 147–148
test objects, 278
  building, 281–284
testing
  aggregate tests, 278, 284
  correctness, 277–278
  distributed applications, 276–277
    bank example, 277–287
  reporting mechanism, 287
  scalability, 277–278
  servers, 278–279
  thread containers and, 286–287
  threaded testers, 279, 284–286
  unit testing, 13, 278
Thread class, 219–224
  deserialization and, 169
  methods, defining, 223–224
thread container, testing and, 286–287
thread scheduler, deadlock and, 225
ThreadDeath exception, 221
threaded testers, 279, 284–286
ThreadedPool1, 265–267
threading, 65
  background threads, priority, 255–256
  code effectiveness, 230–231
  container classes and, 247–250
  containers and, 250–253
  data integrity, 231–239
  deadlocks, 231
    worker threads, 260–261
  guidelines for, 230–261
  implementation, 229–275
  locks, acquiring, 259–260
  naming services, 312–314
  objects, limiting interaction, 259
  pools, 261
    client threads, 261
    implementation, 262–263
    interfaces, 262
    overview, 261–262
    shrinking, 270–274
  reponse-time variance and, 258–259
  serialization and, 256–258
  SimplePool, creation thread, 265–267

stopping safely, 254–255
  synchronization and, 231
  using a batch thread, 246
threads, 198
  atomic operations, 210–211
  background, priority, 255–256
  batch threads, 246
  caches and, 212
  clients, multiple, 198–201
  creating, 219–221
  deactivating, 210–211
  dead, 210
  deadlock, 225–226
  green threads, 204
  individual, controlling, 209–210
  interference, 207
  Java support, 213
  lifecycles, 209
  local cache, synchronization and, 215–217
  locking, multiple times, 217–218
  major concepts, 206–209
  methods, Object, 218–219
  multithreaded code, 207
  native, 204
  notify methods, 219
  number of, 479
  overview, 204
  printer server and, 205–206
  prioritizing, 212–213
  purpose, 229–230
  return threads, 268–270
  RMI specifications, 227–228
  Runnable interface, 222
  running and active, 209
  running and inactive, 209
  stopping safely, 254–255
  suspended, 210
  Swing, 465
  synchronization, 213
  termination, 221–222
  threaded testers, 279
  treaded testers, 284–286
  unlocking, 215
  wait methods, 218–219
threadsafe, 207
  immutable objects, 253–254
  launch code, 229
  server, 229
thread-scheduler, 204
  prioritizing and, 212
threshold values, iterators, 123

write( ) method
  intermediate streams, 12
  OutputStream class, 8
write file permission, 449
write methods, serialization
        algorithm, 164–165
writeExternal( ) method, 192
writeFloat( ) method, 15
writeObject( ) method, 164, 181–182
  implementation, 79, 171–172
Writer abstract class, 16–18
writeToStream( ), DocumentDescription, 56
writing data, OutputStream class, 8–9
writing the simplified serialization
        algorithm, 181–182

X

Xms, 369
Xms parameter, Java, 369
Xmx parameter, Java, 369
XP (Extreme Programming), 278

Y

yellow pages, RMI registry
        directory, 300–301
yield( ), 223

About the Author

William Grosso is a relative newcomer to the computer revolution. After majoring in philosophy as an undergraduate, he decided to pursue a graduate degree in mathematics. At that time, he observed one of the early prototypes of the World Wide Web and thought, "Naaah. That'll never catch on." Since then, he's further demonstrated his almost total lack of vision by becoming fluent in Objective-C, mastering CORBA, and attempting to become wealthy by writing a book.

Java RMI, his first book, has been distilled from many years of experience building distributed systems, five years of experience using Java and RMI, and numerous questions asked while he was teaching a U.C. Berkeley Extension course on distributed programming.

His mother would like to thank you for buying the book.

Colophon

Our look is the result of reader comments, our own experimentation, and feedback from distribution channels. Distinctive covers complement our distinctive approach to technical topics, breathing personality and life into potentially dry subjects.

The animal on the cover of *Java RMI* is a European red squirrel (*Sciurus vulgaris*). The word squirrel comes from the Greek *skia*, meaning shadow, and *oura*, tail.

Squirrel species exist on every continent except Australia and Antarctica. The red squirrel is common throughout central Europe, but in Great Britain, where it was once also abundant, its numbers have been greatly reduced. The grey squirrel, a heartier species, has largely replaced it; there are now about 60 times as many grey squirrels as red in Great Britain.

The red squirrel is light-red to black in color on its head and back. All except those with black fur have white stomachs; the black ones are black all over. They have tufts of fur sticking up from their ears. They spend much of their time up in trees; their sharp claws make them good climbers, and they can survive falls of up to 100 feet. They eat mostly seeds, acorns, and nuts, but they'll also eat mushrooms, flowers, vegetables, and even eggs when their main food source is scarce.

Female red squirrels usually produce two litters of young each year, with five to seven babies in each. They're blind and hairless at birth and weigh only eight to twelve grams, but by eight weeks of age, they are weaned and fully independent— though they have a tendency to darken their mother's doorstep for a while longer, until they're ready to face the world on their own.

Matt Hutchinson was the production editor and copyeditor for *Java RMI*. Maureen Dempsey proofread the book. Claire Cloutier, Tatiana Apandi Diaz, Jane Ellin, and Sue Willing provided quality control. Sarah Sherman, Edie Shapiro, and Derek DiMatteo provided production assistance. Johnna VanHoose Dinse wrote the index.

Emma Colby designed the cover of this book, based on a series design by Edie Freedman. The cover image is a 19th-century engraving from the Dover Pictorial Archive. Emma Colby produced the cover layout with QuarkXPress 4.1 using Adobe's ITC Garamond font.

Melanie Wang designed the interior layout. Anne-Marie Vaduva reformatted the files in FrameMaker 5.5.6 using tools created by Mike Sierra. The text font is Linotype Birka; the heading font is Adobe Myriad Condensed; and the code font is Lucas-Font's Sans Mono Condensed. The illustrations that appear in the book were produced by Robert Romano and Jessamyn Read using Macromedia FreeHand 9 and Adobe Photoshop 6. The tip and warning icons were drawn by Christopher Bing. This colophon was written by Leanne Soylemez.

Whenever possible, our books use a durable and flexible lay-flat binding. If the page count exceeds this binding's limit, perfect binding is used.

Other Titles Available from O'Reilly

Java

Java Servlet Programming, 2nd Edition

By Jason Hunter with William Crawford
2nd Edition April 2001
780 pages, ISBN 0-596-00040-5

The second edition of this popular book has been completely updated to add the new features of the Java Servlet API Version 2.2, and new chapters on servlet security and advanced communication. In addition to complete coverage of the 2.2 specification, we have included bonus material on the new 2.3 version of the specification.

Java & XML, 2nd Edition

By Brett McLaughlin
2nd Edition September 2001
528 pages, ISBN 0-596-000197-5

New chapters on Advanced SAX, Advanced DOM, SOAP, and data binding, as well as new examples throughout, bring the second edition of *Java & XML* thoroughly up to date. Except for a concise introduction to XML basics, the book focuses entirely on using XML from Java applications. It's a worthy companion for Java developers working with XML or involved in messaging, web services, or the new peer-to-peer movement.

JavaServer Pages, 2nd Edition

By Hans Bergsten
2nd Edition August 2002
712 pages, ISBN 0-596-00317-X

Filled with useful examples and the depth, clarity, and attention to detail that made the first edition so popular with web developers, *JavaServer Pages*, 2nd Edition is completely revised and updated to cover the substantial changes in the 1.2 version of the JSP specifications, and includes coverage of the new JSTL Tag libraries—an eagerly anticipated standard set of JSP elements for the tasks needed in most JSP applications, as well as thorough coverage of Custom Tag Libraries.

Java and XSLT

By Eric M. Burke
1st Edition September 2001
528 pages, ISBN 0-596-00143-6

Learn how to use XSL transformations in Java programs ranging from stand-alone applications to servlets. *Java and XSLT* introduces XSLT and then shows you how to apply transformations in real-world situations, such as developing a discussion forum, transforming documents from one form to another, and generating content for wireless devices.

Enterprise JavaBeans, 3rd Edition

By Richard Monson-Haefel
3rd Edition September 2001
592 pages, ISBN 0-596-00226-2

Enterprise JavaBeans has been thoroughly updated for the new EJB Specification. Important changes in Version 2.0 include a completely new CMP (container-managed persistence) model that allows for much more complex business function modeling; local interfaces that will significantly improve performance of EJB applications; and the "message driven bean," an entirely new kind of Java bean based on asynchronous messaging and the Java Message Service.

Java Message Service

By Richard Monson-Haefel &
David Chappell
1st Edition December 2000
238 pages, ISBN 0-596-00068-5

This book is a thorough introduction to Java Message Service (JMS) from Sun Microsystems. It shows how to build applications using the point-to-point and publish-and-subscribe models; use features like transactions and durable subscriptions to make applications reliable; and use messaging within Enterprise JavaBeans. It also introduces a new EJB type, the MessageDrivenBean, that is part of EJB 2.0, and discusses integration of messaging into J2EE.

O'REILLY®

To order: *800-998-9938* • *order@oreilly.com* • *www.oreilly.com*
Online editions of most O'Reilly titles are available by subscription at *safari.oreilly.com*
Also available at most retail and online bookstores.

Java

Java Cookbook

By Ian Darwin
1st Edition June 2001
882 pages, ISBN 0-59600-170-3

This book offers Java developers short, focused pieces of code that are easy to incorporate into other programs. The idea is to focus on things that are useful, tricky, or both. The book's code segments cover all of the dominant APIs and many specialized APIs and should serve as a great "jumping-off place" for Java developers who want to get started in areas outside their specialization.

Java Performance Tuning

By Jack Shirazi
1st Edition September 2000
440 pages, ISBN 0-596-00015-4

Java Performance Tuning contains step-by-step instructions on all aspects of the performance tuning process, right from such early considerations as setting goals, measuring performance, and choosing a compiler. Extensive examples for tuning many parts of an application are described in detail, and any pitfalls are identified. The book also provides performance tuning checklists that enable developers to make their tuning as comprehensive as possible.

Learning Java, 2nd Edition

By Pat Niemeyer & Jonathan Knudsen
2nd Edition June 2002
832 pages, ISBN 0-596-00285-8

This new edition of *Learning Java* has been expanded and updated for Java 2 Standard Edition SDK 1.4. It comprehensively addresses important topics such as web applications, servlets, and XML that are increasingly driving enterprise applications. This edition provides full coverage of all Java 1.4 language features including assertions and exception chaining as well as new APIs such as regular expressions and NIO, the new I/O package. New Swing features and components are described along with updated coverage of the JavaBeans component architecture using the open source Net-Beans IDE the latest information about Applets and the Java Plug-in for all major web browsers.

Java Internationalization

By Andy Deitsch & David Czarnecki
1st Edition March 2001
451 pages, ISBN 0-596-00019-7

Java Internationalization shows how to write software that is truly multilingual, using Java's very sophisticated Unicode internationalization facilities. Java Internationalization brings Java developers up to speed for the new generation of software development: writing software that is no longer limited by language boundaries.

Java Management Extensions

By J. StevenPerry
1st Edition June 2002
312 pages, ISBN 0-596-00245-9

Java Management Extensions is a practical, hands-on guide to using the JMX APIs, Sun Microsystem's new Java-based tool for managing enterprise applications. This one-of-a kind book is a complete treatment of the JMX architecture (both the instrumentation level and the agent level), and it's loaded with real-world examples for implementing Management Extensions. It also contains useful information at the higher level about JMX (the "big picture") to help technical managers and architects who are evaluating various application management approaches and are considering JMX.

O'REILLY®

To order: *800-998-9938* • *order@oreilly.com* • *www.oreilly.com*
Online editions of most O'Reilly titles are available by subscription at *safari.oreilly.com*
Also available at most retail and online bookstores.

Java In a Nutshell Quick References

Java Enterprise in a Nutshell, 2nd Edition

By David Flanagan, Jim Farley &
William Crawford
2nd Edition April 2002
992 pages, ISBN 0-596-00152-5

Completely revised and updated to
cover the new 2.0 version of Sun
Microsystems Java Enterprise Edition
software, *Java Enterprise in a Nutshell*
2nd edition covers the RMI, Java IDL, JDBC, JNDI,
Java Servlet, and Enterprise JavaBeans APIs, with a fast-
paced tutorial and compact reference material on each
technology.

Java Foundation Classes in a Nutshell

By David Flanagan
1st Edition September 1999
748 pages, ISBN 1-56592-488-6

Java Foundation Classes in a Nutshell
provides an in-depth overview of the
important pieces of the (JFC), such as
the Swing components and Java 2D. It
also includes compact reference material
on all the GUI- and graphics-related classes in the numerous javax.swing and java.awt packages. Covers Java 2.

J2ME in a Nutshell

By Kim Topley
1st Edition, March 2002
462 pages, ISBN 0-596-00253-X

O'Reilly's *J2ME in a Nutshell* is as
definitive a reference to the heart of
the J2ME platform as the classic *Java
in a Nutshell* is for the Standard Java
platform. Its solid introduction to
J2ME covers the essential APIs for different types of
devices and deployments; the profiles (specifications of
the minimum sets of APIs useful for a set-top box, wireless phone, PDA, or other device); and the Java virtual
machine functions that support those APIs. The meat of
the book is its classic O'Reilly-style quick reference to all
the core Micro Edition classes.

Java in a Nutshell, 4th Edition

By David Flanagan
4th Edition March 2002
992 pages, ISBN 0-596-00283-1

This bestselling quick reference contains an accelerated introduction to
the Java programming language and
its key APIs, so seasoned programmers
can start writing Java code right away.
The fourth edition of *Java in a Nutshell* covers the new
Java 1.4 beta edition, which contains significant changes
from the 1.3 version.

Java Examples in a Nutshell, 2nd Edition

By David Flanagan
2nd Edition September 2000
584 pages, ISBN 0-596-00039-1

In *Java Examples in a Nutshell*, the
author of Java in a Nutshell has created an entire book of example programs that not only serve as great
learning tools, but can also be modi-
fied for individual use. The second edition of this bestselling book covers Java 1.3, and includes new chapters
on JSP and servlets, XML, Swing, and Java 2D. This is the
book for those who learn best "by example."

JXTA in a Nutshell

By Scott Oaks, Bernard Traversat &
Li Gong
1st Edition September 2002
400 pages, ISBN 0-596-00236-X

O'Reilly's pioneering reference is the
first and last word on this powerful
distributed computing technology.
JXTA in a Nutshell delivers all the
information you need to get started, including an
overview of P2P distributed computing, an explanation
of the JXTA Project's new platform, and ways that developers can become a part of the development effort. *JXTA
in a Nutshell* introduces major concepts in a hands-on
way by explaining them in context to the shell, and contains a complete reference to the JXTA application bindings. Also included is the full JXTA protocol specification.
The book covers important topics such as security, and
how the JXTA technology fits into the standard Java classes.

O'REILLY®

To order: 800-998-9938 • *order@oreilly.com* • *www.oreilly.com*
Online editions of most O'Reilly titles are available by subscription at *safari.oreilly.com*
Also available at most retail and online bookstores.

How to stay in touch with O'Reilly

1. Visit our award-winning web site

http://www.oreilly.com/

★ "Top 100 Sites on the Web"—PC Magazine
★ CIO Magazine's Web Business 50 Awards

Our web site contains a library of comprehensive product information (including book excerpts and tables of contents), downloadable software, background articles, interviews with technology leaders, links to relevant sites, book cover art, and more. File us in your bookmarks or favorites!

2. Join our email mailing lists

Sign up to get email announcements of new books and conferences, special offers, and O'Reilly Network technology newsletters at:

http://www.elists.oreilly.com

It's easy to customize your free elists subscription so you'll get exactly the O'Reilly news you want.

3. Get examples from our books

To find example files for a book, go to:

http://www.oreilly.com/catalog

select the book, and follow the "Examples" link.

4. Work with us

Check out our web site for current employment opportunities:

http://jobs.oreilly.com/

5. Register your book

Register your book at:
http://register.oreilly.com

6. Contact us

O'Reilly & Associates, Inc.
1005 Gravenstein Hwy North
Sebastopol, CA 95472 USA
TEL: 707-827-7000 or 800-998-9938
        (6am to 5pm PST)
FAX: 707-829-0104

order@oreilly.com
For answers to problems regarding your order or our products. To place a book order online visit:

http://www.oreilly.com/order_new/

catalog@oreilly.com
To request a copy of our latest catalog.

booktech@oreilly.com
For book content technical questions or corrections.

corporate@oreilly.com
For educational, library, and corporate sales.

proposals@oreilly.com
To submit new book proposals to our editors and product managers.

international@oreilly.com
For information about our international distributors or translation queries. For a list of our distributors outside of North America check out:

http://international.oreilly.com/distributors.html

O'REILLY®

To order: *800-998-9938* • *order@oreilly.com* • *www.oreilly.com*
Online editions of most O'Reilly titles are available by subscription at *safari.oreilly.com*
Also available at most retail and online bookstores.